Mozart in Vienna

Mozart's greatest works were written in Vienna in the decade before his death (1781–1791). This biography focuses on Mozart's dual roles as a performer and composer and reveals how his compositional processes were affected by performance-related concerns. It traces consistencies and changes in Mozart's professional persona and his *modus operandi*, and sheds light on other prominent musicians, audience expectations, publishing, and concert and dramatic practices and traditions. Giving particular prominence to primary sources, Simon P. Keefe offers new biographical and critical perspectives on the man and his music, highlighting his extraordinary ability to engage with the competing demands of singers and instrumentalists, publishing and public performance, and concerts and dramatic productions in the course of a hectic, diverse and financially uncertain freelance career. This comprehensive and accessible volume is essential for Mozart lovers and scholars alike, exploring his Viennese masterpieces and the people and environments that shaped them.

SIMON P. KEEFE is James Rossiter Hoyle Chair of Music at the University of Sheffield. He is the author of three books on Mozart, including *Mozart's Requiem: Reception, Work, Completion* (Cambridge, 2012), which won the 2013 Marjorie Weston Emerson Award. He is also the editor of six volumes for Cambridge University Press, including *Mozart Studies* and *Mozart Studies 2*, and is general editor of the Royal Musical Association monographs series. In 2005 he was elected a life member of the Academy for Mozart Research at the International Mozart Foundation in Salzburg.

Mozart in Vienna

The Final Decade

SIMON P. KEEFE

University of Sheffield

CAMBRIDGE UNIVERSITY PRESS

CAMBRIDGE
UNIVERSITY PRESS

University Printing House, Cambridge CB2 8BS, United Kingdom

One Liberty Plaza, 20th Floor, New York, NY 10006, USA

477 Williamstown Road, Port Melbourne, VIC 3207, Australia

314–321, 3rd Floor, Plot 3, Splendor Forum, Jasola District Centre,
New Delhi – 110025, India

79 Anson Road, #06–04/06, Singapore 079906

Cambridge University Press is part of the University of Cambridge.

It furthers the University's mission by disseminating knowledge in the pursuit of
education, learning, and research at the highest international levels of excellence.

www.cambridge.org
Information on this title: www.cambridge.org/9781107116719
DOI: 10.1017/9781316337752

© Simon P. Keefe 2017

First published 2017
3rd printing 2019

Printed in the United Kingdom by TJ International Ltd. Padstow Cornwall

A catalogue record for this publication is available from the British Library.

Library of Congress Cataloging-in-Publication Data
Names: Keefe, Simon P., 1968– author.
Title: Mozart in Vienna : the final decade / Simon Keefe.
Description: Cambridge, United Kingdom ; New York, NY : Cambridge University Press,
2018. | Includes bibliographical references and index.
Identifiers: LCCN 2017026226 | ISBN 9781107116719 (alk. paper)
Subjects: LCSH: Mozart, Wolfgang Amadeus, 1756-1791 – Criticism and interpretation. |
Composers – Austria – Vienna.
Classification: LCC ML410.M9 K24 2018 | DDC 780.92–dc23
LC record available at https://lccn.loc.gov/2017026226

ISBN 978-1-107-11671-9 Hardback

For Celia, Abraham and Madeleine

Contents

Illustrations

Tables

Musical Examples

Acknowledgements

A biographical study of this length and scope invariably incurs debts to institutions and individuals. It is a pleasure to record thanks to colleagues at the University of Sheffield, my place of work since April 2008, especially for granting me extended periods of sabbatical leave in 2011–2012 and 2015–2016. I am also grateful to All Souls College Oxford for a visiting fellowship in autumn 2016, which provided an ideal, collegial environment for completing the volume, and to Vicki Cooper and Kate Brett, commissioning editors at Cambridge University Press, for their warm support of my project throughout its extended genesis. Audiences in recent years at papers and seminars at the universities of Leeds, Sheffield, Huddersfield, Manchester and Oxford, at the Akademie für Mozartforschung of the Internationale Stiftung Mozarteum in Salzburg, and at the Mozart Colloquia at Harvard University offered advice and encouragement, regularly pointing out potential new lines of enquiry. And a very memorable week in early February 2014 filming 'Mozart in Prague: Rolando Villazón on *Don Giovanni*' in the Czech capital for the BBC provided inspiration for Chapter 8; I extend special thanks to Villazón and to the director, Guy Evans. At the University of Sheffield Library, the British Library in London, the Knight Library of the University of Oregon and the Bodleian Library in Oxford, staff responded courteously and efficiently to my numerous requests for books, articles, facsimiles and editions.

I am grateful to late eighteenth-century scholars and friends for acts of generosity, including David Wyn Jones, Cliff Eisen, Ian Woodfield and Paul Corneilson for sending me unpublished materials, and to the three anonymous readers at Cambridge University Press for their comments and constructive criticism. I am indebted to Cliff Eisen and John Rice for taking time away from their own work in order to help me with mine: Cliff read the volume in its entirety, and John read drafts of Chapters 2, 6, 7, 8, 9 and 12. Their trenchant observations, born of deep knowledge of Mozart and his repertory, working methods and Viennese environments, were much appreciated.

My families in the US and UK have provided unconditional love and support. My in-laws, Robert and Virginia Hurwitz, Rachel Hurwitz, Martha Westland, Alison Hurwitz and Charlie Holst have offered encouragement from near and far; and my parents, Terry and Sheila Keefe, and sister and brother-in-law Rosanna Keefe and Dominic Gregory, are always on hand in Sheffield for drinks, meals and chats, providing most welcome distractions from the rigours of scholarly work. Fittingly, my earliest thoughts for this book, scribbled on a Continental Airlines napkin in summer 2009, date from a family trip between the UK and US, with my wife and children around me. Each has helped immeasurably in their own way. My daughter Madeleine enquired more than once whether I was still working on *The Magic of Figaro*. Happily accompanying me to a recent production of *Don Giovanni* at the Lyceum in Sheffield, and eagerly anticipating the entry of the Commendatore in the Act 2 finale, she somehow contrived to sleep through this most dramatic of operatic moments. My son Abraham, no great lover of opera (Mozartian or otherwise), has developed his own individual appreciation of classical music performance and composition, seemingly uninfluenced by the interests of his parents. And my wife, Celia Hurwitz-Keefe, offers a wonderful example to the three of us of dedicated and committed instrumental teaching and music making, day after day. I dedicate my book to them, as a small token of my love and appreciation.

Parts of Chapters 4 and 5 rework material from my following article and chapters: '"We hardly knew what we should pay attention to first": Mozart the Performer-Composer at Work on the Viennese Piano Concertos', *Journal of the Royal Musical Association*, 134 (2009), pp. 185–242; 'Composing, Performing and Publishing: Mozart's "Haydn" Quartets', in Keefe (ed.), *Mozart Studies 2* (Cambridge: Cambridge University Press, 2015), pp. 140–167; 'On Instrumental Sounds, Roles, Genres and Performances: Mozart's Piano Quartets K. 478 and K. 493', in Martin Harlow (ed.), *Mozart's Chamber Music with Keyboard* (Cambridge: Cambridge University Press, 2012), pp. 154–181.

Notes on Musical Examples

Wherever possible, musical examples in this book are prepared in consultation with Mozart autographs and first editions. Editorial standardization is kept to a minimum (for example, text underlay, instrument names, standard SATB clefs not C clefs for vocal parts, and – unless important to an argument – simplified dynamic markings such as *p* and *f* rather than *pia:* and *for:*). Mozart's presentational order for an orchestral score is retained, with violins and violas at the top, cellos and basses at the bottom, wind and brass in the middle, and voices and instrumental soloists (as appropriate) above the bass line. (Where instruments are added by Mozart above or below the score brace to produce an unconventional layout, and an autograph has been consulted, I follow Mozart's layout in my example.) Empty staves are excluded for reasons of space unless relevant to a point being made, and first and second parts for the same wind instrument are often brought together on the same stave when Mozart included them on separate staves.

Where musical examples are not provided in the main text, the reader is encouraged to consult the *Neue Mozart-Ausgabe* (NMA), freely available online via the Digital Mozart Edition from the Stiftung Mozarteum Salzburg: http://dme.mozarteum.at/DME/main/index.php.

Abbreviations

LMF   Emily Anderson (trans. and ed.), *The Letters of Mozart and his Family*. 3rd edn. London: Macmillan, 1985.

MBA   Wilhelm A. Bauer, Otto Erich Deutsch and Joseph Heinz Eibl (eds.), *Mozart: Briefe und Aufzeichnungen, Gesamtausgabe*. 8 vols. Kassel: Bärenreiter, 1962–2005.

MDB   Otto Erich Deutsch, *Mozart: A Documentary Biography*. Translated by Eric Blom, Peter Branscombe and Jeremy Noble. 3rd edn. London: Simon & Schuster, 1990.

MDL   Otto Erich Deutsch, *Mozart: Die Dokumente seines Lebens*. Kassel: Bärenreiter, 1961.

NMA   Wolfgang Amadeus Mozart, *Neuer Ausgabe sämtlicher Werke*. Kassel: Bärenreiter, 1955–2007.

NMD   Cliff Eisen (ed.), *New Mozart Documents: A Supplement to O. E. Deutsch's Documentary Biography*. London and Palo Alto, CA: Stanford University Press, 1991.

Introduction: Mozart the Performer-Composer in Vienna

Biographers from Otto Jahn (*Life of Mozart*, 1856) onwards have continually made connections between Mozart's life and music which are shaped by individual orientations, predilections and interpretations of available evidence. The proliferation of stimulating biographies over more than two centuries attests to a collective need to re-tell the story – in whole or in part – of Mozart's life and music. With a remarkable body of family correspondence, a large quantity of reception-related documents from the late eighteenth century, and some of the most revered music in Western culture, Mozart represents fertile biographical territory.[1]

Vienna, seat of the combined Holy Roman Emperor and Austro-Hungarian monarchy as well as Mozart's place of residence for the last ten years of his life, also provides a rich backdrop for a biographical study of a late-eighteenth-century musician.[2] Cosmopolitan to its core, in spite of a considerably smaller population than London and Paris at around 250,000,

---

[1] Mozart's correspondence, together with other family letters, is published in MBA and LMF, and reception documents compiled in MDL, MDB and NMD. All translations from MBA and MDL are my own unless otherwise indicated. LMF and MDB references – in different translations – are also given. For selections of letters in English translation, see in particular Robert Spaethling (ed. and trans.), *Mozart's Letters, Mozart's Life* (London: Faber, 2000), and Cliff Eisen (ed.), *Mozart: A Life in Letters*, trans. Stewart Spencer (London: Penguin, 2006).

[2] For solid, informative introductions to musical life in Vienna in the second half of the eighteenth century, see Daniel Heartz, *Haydn, Mozart and the Viennese School, 1740–1780* (New York: Norton, 1995), pp. 3–78; Dorothea Link, 'Mozart in Vienna', in Simon P. Keefe (ed.), *The Cambridge Companion to Mozart* (Cambridge: Cambridge University Press, 2003), pp. 22–34; Mary Sue Morrow, *Concert Life in Haydn's Vienna: Aspects of a Developing Social Institution* (Stuyvesant, NY: Pendragon Press, 1989), pp. 1–236; Morrow, 'Vienna', in Cliff Eisen and Simon P. Keefe (eds.), *The Cambridge Mozart Encyclopedia* (Cambridge: Cambridge University Press, 2006), pp. 517–526; Andrew Steptoe, *The Mozart-Da Ponte Operas: The Cultural and Musical Background to 'Le nozze di Figaro', 'Don Giovanni', and 'Così fan tutte'* (Oxford: Clarendon Press, 1990), pp. 13–76; John A. Rice, 'Vienna under Joseph II and Leopold II', in Neal Zaslaw (ed.), *The Classical Era: From the 1740s to the End of the 18th Century* (London: Macmillan, 1989), pp. 126–165; Rice, *Music in the Eighteenth Century* (New York: Norton, 2013), pp. 200–221. For an engaging account of Viennese music in historical and social context from c. 1790 to c. 1815, see David Wyn Jones, *Music in Vienna: 1700, 1800, 1900* (Woodbridge and Rochester, NY: The Boydell Press, 2016), pp. 72–149. General introductions to eighteenth-century Austria without an explicitly musical focus are found in Charles W. Ingrao, *The Habsburg Monarchy 1618–1815* (2nd edition, Cambridge: Cambridge University Press, 2000); and Ernst Wangermann, *The Austrian Achievement 1700–1800* (London: Thames and Hudson, 1973).

it offered an environment appealing to artists. For Baron Karl Philipp von Reitzenstein, visiting the city in 1789–1790, nowhere in the world outside Italy had more refined musical taste among amateurs and connoisseurs alike; music, he said, was a 'dominant passion' (*herrschende Leidenschaft*) embraced in every family home.[3] The ruler from 1780 to 1790, Emperor Joseph II, was described by Michael Kelly, the first Don Basilio and Don Curzio in *Le nozze di Figaro*, as 'passionately fond of music, and a most excellent and accurate judge of it' at 'perhaps the most brilliant [Court] in Europe'. Moreover, Kelly explained: 'All ranks of society [in Vienna] were doatingly fond of music . . . and most of them perfectly understood the science.'[4] According to Viennese chronicler and Mozart contemporary Johann Pezzl, a musician 'possesses a certain cachet in society, where he is respected and welcomed, especially in the great houses'. The staging of a new opera, often a significant event, generated activity in town: 'The stampings of the horses and the barkings of the coachmen as they cross the Graben and the Kohlmarkt' on the way to the theatre 'combine to produce a hellish concert.' In addition, Pezzl explained; 'one can never enter any fashionable house or society without hearing a duet, a trio, a finale' from one of Vienna's popular opera buffe sung or played at the keyboard.[5] For another writer,

[3] Baron Karl Philipp von Reitzenstein, *Reise nach Wien* (Hof, 1795), pp. 244–246. Von Reitzenstein's trip to Vienna took place in 1789–1790 (a large part of it in winter, p. 333). His account – a combination of undated recollections and reflections on places and activities, including music – was written at that time, as indicated by references in the present to a number of events: he first meets Emperor Joseph II (who died on 20 February 1790) when Joseph fell ill soon after returning from the battlefield; he subsequently documents further meetings with Joseph as well as the Emperor's recurring health problems and eventual death; he mentions celebrations for the recent taking of Belgrade in the Turkish war (the siege concluding successfully on 8 October 1789); he refers to the Theater auf der Landstrasse (which opened in 1790) as being under construction but not yet complete; he states that the Kärntnertortheater had not staged operas 'for several months' (when it stopped doing so in spring 1788 and recommenced in autumn 1791); and he mentions Italian and German actors giving alternate performances, a practice that continued in one way or another at the Burgtheater until 1791. See *Reise nach Wien*, pp. 69, 91, 133–156, 179–181, 294–299, 342, 392–393, 398–400. On the alternating performances see Dorothea Link, *The National Court Theatre in Mozart's Vienna: Sources and Documents, 1783–1792* (Oxford: Clarendon Press, 1998), p. 14.

[4] Michael Kelly, *Reminiscences of Michael Kelly, of the King's Theatre, and Theatre Royal Drury Lane* (1826) (Cambridge: Cambridge University Press, 2011), 2 vols., vol. 1, p. 197. For a magisterial study of Joseph II's reign, which almost exactly coincided with Mozart's decade in Vienna, see Derek Beales, *Joseph II: Against the World, 1780–1790* (Cambridge: Cambridge University Press, 2009). Joseph II's earlier life, including the period of co-regency with his mother (1765–1780), is discussed in Beales, *Joseph II: In the Shadow of Maria Theresa, 1741–1780* (Cambridge: Cambridge University Press, 1987).

[5] See Johann Pezzl, 'Sketch of Vienna' (1786–1790), translated in H. C. Robbins Landon, *Mozart and Vienna* (New York: Schirmer, 1991), pp. 186, 84, 137. Pezzl's account as a whole (pp. 54–191) includes information on Vienna's size, cosmopolitan nature and strengths in the arts.

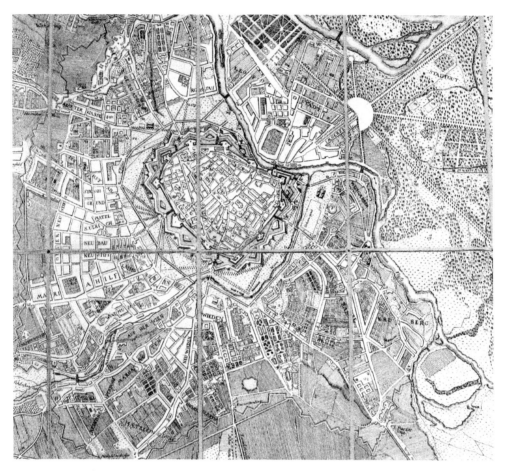

Figure 1 Map of Vienna, drawn and engraved by Maximilian Grimm (1783).

Johann Kaspar Riesbeck, reporting back to his Paris-based brother from Vienna (c. 1780), music received 'excellent attention', including from the supportive nobility, and orchestral performances were of an exceedingly high standard.[6] And for Friedrich Schulz a few years later, music was the favourite Viennese pastime after the theatre, with probably more

[6] Johann Kaspar Riesbeck, *Briefe eines Reisenden Franzosen über Deutschland an seine Bruden zu Paris* (2nd edition, Zurich, 1784), vol. 1, pp. 275–276. Like Pezzl's 'Sketch of Vienna' and von Reitzenstein's *Reise nach Wien*, Riesbeck's nineteen lengthy letters from Vienna (pp. 181–395) contain wide-ranging observations and insights on Viennese life at the time of Mozart's residency, including on the theatre (for example, pp. 257–271, 277–280). They were written around 1780. (See the reference on p. 301 to Maria Theresia's death, which occurred on 29 November 1780.) Riesbeck wanted to speak to the 'famous [Joseph] Haydn' when Haydn was in Vienna for a concert, but was unable to do so (p. 357).

music lovers and true virtuosos than any other city and opportunities to attend public or domestic concerts every day.[7] Von Reitzenstein also identified the very high quality of amateur instrumental playing in Vienna, especially among female pianists; such skilled performers could do justice to 'the most difficult piece of a Mozart, a Paisiello', he explained.[8] Musical accompaniment to eating, drinking and card-playing in Vienna did not impress everyone,[9] but bears witness to the important social role music fulfilled.

The jewel in the city's crown was the emperor's own National Court Theatre (Burgtheater), a venue for operas, plays and concerts frequented by the established aristocracy, the 'new' nobility (appointed barons, baronesses, etc.) and the high bourgeoisie, with a capacity of around 1,000–1,350.[10] The Kärntnertortheater, also owned and operated by the court and with room for between 1,000 and 1,800,[11] together with smaller spaces suitable for concerts in residential buildings, restaurants and at the homes of aristocrats, provided further opportunities for musicians to develop profiles and generate income. The nascent music publishing industry in Vienna, including distribution in manuscript copies and the chance to take on affluent individual pupils, offered additional revenue streams. Vienna was known to Mozart before 1781, from several earlier visits: in 1762, when he played twice for Empress Maria Theresia; in 1767–1768, when he wrote his first opera buffa *La finta semplice* and first Singspiel *Bastien und Bastienne* and had a mass, a (lost) offertory and (lost) trumpet concerto performed; and in 1773, when he composed the string quartets K. 168–173 and the orchestral serenade in D, K. 185.[12] Three years before finally settling in Vienna, Mozart was encouraged to move there by family friend Joseph Mesmer, cousin of the eponymous instigator of the

---

[7] Friedrich Schulz, *Reise eines Liefländers von Riga nach Warschau* (Berlin, 1796), vol. 6, p. 217.

[8] Von Reitzenstein, *Reise nach Wien*, pp. 247–248, 251.

[9] See Friedrich Nicolai, writing around 1780, as reported in Morrow, *Concert Life in Vienna*, p. 54.

[10] On the Burgtheater, and the higher numbers quoted for the capacities of both court theatres (p. 14), see Link, *National Court Theatre*. For useful descriptions of the Burgtheater itself (which was demolished in 1888), see Mary Hunter, *Mozart's Operas: A Companion* (New York: Oxford University Press, 2008), p. 177, and Dexter Edge, 'Mozart's Reception in Vienna, 1787–1791', in Stanley Sadie (ed.), *Wolfgang Amadè Mozart: Essays on His Life and His Music* (Oxford: Clarendon Press, 1996), pp. 66–117, at 73.

[11] On the size and dimensions of the Kärntnertortheater, see Malcolm S. Cole, 'Mozart and the Two Theaters in Josephinian Vienna', in Mark A. Radice (ed.), *Opera in Context: Essays on Historical Staging from the Late Renaissance to the Time of Puccini* (Portland, OR: Amadeus Press, 1998), pp. 111–145, at 132. Von Reitzenstein (*Reise nach Wien*, p. 342) reports the Kärntnertortheater as larger than the Burgtheater.

[12] On Mozart's early trips to Vienna, see in particular Landon, *Mozart and Vienna*, pp. 9–44. For Leopold's account of machinations and envy surrounding Mozart in Vienna in 1768, see MBA, vol. 1, pp. 254–258; LMF, pp. 80–83 (30 January–3 February 1768).

dubious hypnotic practice of Mesmerism parodied by 'doctor' Despina in the Act 1 finale of *Così fan tutte*. Promising free boarding and lodging in the city for as long as was needed, Mesmer wrote to Mozart's father Leopold: 'There is always decent room here for a great talent, only it sometimes does not happen straight away. But through the support of good friends one duly gets to one's goal – and, all said and done, it is still best to live in Vienna.'[13]

Biographies like mine, orientated above all towards Mozart's music, have a venerable history. As early as 1801, Johann Karl Friedrich Triest called for a 'musical biographer ... to dissect [Mozart's] works and weigh their relative merits'; while Ignaz Arnold duly obliged in a short book published two years later, landmark nineteenth-century biographies such as those by Jahn and Alexandre Oulibicheff did not slant discussion primarily towards Mozart's music.[14] In the twentieth century, substantial tomes by Georges de Saint-Foix and Théodore de Wyzewa (5 vols., 1912–1946), Hermann Abert (1919–1921), Alfred Einstein (1945), Jean and Brigitte Massin (1959) and Konrad Küster (1996) entered the canon of musical biographies.[15] In spite of innumerable, enduring critical insights, the first four are now (unsurprisingly) outdated in many respects. And Küster's chronological survey of isolated works and groups of works is selective in coverage, compressing Mozart's entire career into fewer than 400 pages.

More important, no biography – including Abert's, probably the greatest of the twentieth century – has accounted substantively for a fundamental feature of Mozart's musical career: his dual role as performer and composer. To take a single example, biographers implicitly or explicitly recognize (quite rightly) that the Viennese piano concertos owe their existence to

---

[13] MBA, vol. 2, p. 243; LMF, p. 454 (as quoted in a letter from Leopold to Mozart on 29 January 1778). See also MDL, p. 154; MDB, p. 172.

[14] See Triest, 'Remarks on the Development of the Art of Music in Germany in the Eighteenth Century', trans. Susan Gillespie, in Elaine Sisman (ed.), *Haydn and His World* (Princeton: Princeton University Press, 1997), pp. 321–394, at 364; Arnold, *Mozarts Geist: seine kurze Biographie und ästetische Darstellung seiner Werke* (Erfurt: Henningschen Buchhandlung, 1803); Otto Jahn, *Life of Mozart* (1856), trans. Pauline D. Townsend (London: Novello, Ewer & Co., 1891), 3 vols; Oulibicheff, *Nouvelle Biographie de Mozart* (Moscow: Auguste Semen, 1843), 3 vols.

[15] Saint-Foix and Wyzewa, *W. A. Mozart: sa vie musicale et son oeuvre* (Paris: Desclée de Brouwer, 1912–1946); Hermann Abert, *W. A. Mozart* (1919–1921), trans. Stewart Spencer, ed. Cliff Eisen (New Haven: Yale University Press, 2007); Einstein, *Mozart: His Character, His Work*, trans. Nathan Broder and Arthur Mendel (London: Cassell, 1945); Massin and Massin, *Wolfgang Amadeus Mozart* (Paris: Fayard, 1959); Küster, *Mozart: A Musical Biography*, trans. Mary Whittall (Oxford: Clarendon Press, 1996).

Mozart's status as a performer-composer, but have not yet adequately investigated the musical potential for his interwoven roles to transmit understandings and fuel interpretations of the works. Mozart often separated composition and performance in evaluating the music of others: he 'found little and missed much' in Herr Freyhold's performance on the flute, Freyhold's 'whole bravura [consisting] of double tonguing', but stated that Freyhold 'would not be a bad composer' if he 'learned composition properly'; and the oboist J. C. Fischer 'plays like a wretched student' with an 'entirely nasal' tone, writing concertos where 'each ritornello lasts a quarter of an hour – then our hero appears, lifts up one leaden foot after the other and stamps on the floor with each alternately'.[16] He also implicitly separated performance from compositional activity when stating in 1778 that he would rather '*so to speak* neglect the clavier than composition, because the clavier is only my secondary thing, though thank God, a very strong secondary thing'.[17] But vibrant continuities between the two were also a practical reality for Mozart from his formative years onwards: in his keyboard improvisations; in Leopold's promotion of him on the Grand Tour of 1763–1766 as a performer-composer; in his accommodation of specific singers' needs in his earliest arias; and in traces of performance activities and experiences left in his earliest published works, including exuberant virtuosity and ornamentation, and compositional impetuosity probably attributable to memories of early renditions.[18] After leaving court service for the first time in late 1777 to seek fame and fortune in musical centres north of Salzburg, Mozart had a taste of life as an independent performer and composer responsible for promoting his own career in both areas. In the darkest period of his life so far, the six-month stay in Paris (24 March–26 September 1778) during which he experienced the death of his mother, came to detest the French capital and much of what it represented, fell out spectacularly with his host and advisor Melchior Grimm, failed to secure an acceptable appointment, earned insufficient income and was unsuccessful at procuring an operatic commission, Mozart continued to engage passionately with combined performing and composing activities, thereby inviting us to situate these combined activities at the heart

---

[16] MBA, vol. 3, p. 301, vol. 4, pp. 40–41; LMF, pp. 867, 907 (letters of 20 February 1784 and 4 April 1787).

[17] MBA, p. 264; LMF, p. 468 (7 February 1778).

[18] See Simon P. Keefe, 'Mozart the Child Performer-Composer: New Musical-Biographical Perspectives on the Early Years to 1766', in Gary MacPherson (ed.), *Musical Prodigies: Interpretations from Psychology, Music Education, Musicology and Ethnomusicology* (New York: Oxford University Press, 2016), pp. 550–575.

of the biographical enterprise.[19] Writing to Leopold just hours after his mother's death and immediately after relaying news of her grave illness (while withholding news of her actual death), Mozart energetically expressed his desire to jump into the orchestra to snatch the violin from concertmaster Pierre Lahoussaye and lead the premiere of the 'Paris' Symphony K. 297 himself had it been poorly played, enforcing the role of performer-composer. (For Mozart, relating news of a good live musical experience – he was ultimately delighted by the orchestra's rendition of K. 297 and the audience reaction – was apparently the best substitute for an actual live experience, even at such a troubled moment in his life.) Less than a month later, with Maria Anna's death still raw for father and son, he wrote to Leopold: 'You know that I am, so to speak, stuck in music [*sie wissen dass ich so zu sagen in der Musique stecke*], that I am involved with it the whole day and that I like to plan, study, think [it] over.'[20]

Mozart's Viennese decade, which provides the subject matter for my book, was the most significant period of his career as a performer-composer; with one or two notable exceptions, including *Idomeneo* staged in Munich (January 1781) immediately before the move to Vienna, Mozart wrote his finest music between 16 March 1781 and his death on 5 December 1791. Starting out in the city with no secure income, and without anyone to bankroll him (as Leopold had done on the 1777–1779 trip), Mozart's livelihood depended unambiguously on artistic and financial success as a performer and composer achieved through activities in both areas and including publishing (as well as a limited amount of teaching). *Mozart in Vienna: The Final Decade* therefore focuses on intersections between performance and composition in his Viennese oeuvre and general musical activities, looking in particular at ways in which issues around performance affected compositional processes. Since performance was an ever-present concern for Mozart – in operas, in informal, formal, public and private concert settings, and in music for publication – all of his Viennese works should bear its imprint in one way or another.

The wide range of performing contexts for Mozart's Viennese works encompasses his own participation and the involvement of others either known or unknown to him. At one end of the spectrum are works and

[19] On this topic in the context of the Parisian stay, see Simon P. Keefe, 'Mozart "Stuck in Music" in Paris (1778): Towards a New Biographical Paradigm', in Keefe (ed.), *Mozart Studies 2* (Cambridge: Cambridge University Press, 2015), pp. 23–54.

[20] MBA, vol. 2, p. 427; LMF, p. 587 (31 July 1778). For discussion of Mozart's musical mindset in Paris 1778, see Keefe, 'Mozart "Stuck in Music" in Paris'.

musical experiences such as the piano concertos and keyboard improvisations in which Mozart's composition and performance is thoroughly
intertwined: here 'the ideal of the composer-performer as a dual
entity ... ubiquitous in almost all eighteenth-century treatises on performance', and evident (for example) in Mozart's expectation that Georg
Vogler would sight-read one of Mozart's pieces in such a way as to appear
to have composed it himself, is especially apparent.[21] Numerous critics
witnessing Mozart in action found mutually reinforcing *what* he performed and *how* he performed it. Improvisations occupied a special place
in this respect, demonstrating in equal measure fertility of compositional
imagination and supreme performance dexterity and expression. The early
Mozart biographer Franz Xaver Niemetschek (1798) reported his performance in Prague on 19 January 1787: 'Mozart at the end of the academy
improvised alone at the pianoforte for more than half an hour and
enhanced delight to the highest degree. And actually this improvising
exceeded everything that we could imagine from piano playing, the highest
degree of compositional art united with the most perfect skill in playing.'[22]
During Mozart's life and after it, writers related time and again the all-
consuming nature of the improvisatory experience: 'What a richness of
ideas! What variety! What changes in passionate tones! We swim away
with him unresistingly on the stream of his emotions' (1785); 'This small
man and great master [on 24 August 1788] twice *extemporized* on a *pedal
piano*, so wonderfully! so wonderfully! that I didn't know where I was.
The most difficult passages and the loveliest *themes* interwoven' (1789);
'inexhaustible ideas' rendered Mozart 'author and performer simultaneously' (1808); and the 'bold flight of his fantasy, to the highest regions
and to the depths of the abyss, could not be adequately admired or
wondered by even the most experienced musical master. Even now, an

---

[21] For the quoted material, see Tom Beghin, '"Delivery, Delivery, Delivery!" Crowning the
Rhetorical Process of Haydn's Keyboard Sonatas', in Beghin and Sander M. Goldberg (eds.),
Haydn and the Performance of Rhetoric (University of Chicago Press, 2007), pp. 131–171, at
152, and Beghin, *The Virtual Haydn: Paradox of a Twenty-First Century Keyboardist* (Chicago:
University of Chicago Press, 2015), p. 60. For Mozart's statement, see MBA, vol. 2, p. 228; LMF,
p. 449 (17 January 1778).

[22] Niemetschek, *Leben des K. K. Kapellmeisters Wolfgang Gottlieb Mozart* (1798), ed. E. Rychnovsky
(Munich: Bibliothek zeitgenössicher Literatur, 1987), p. 27 (my translation). 'Aber dieser Zustand
lösete sich dann, als Mozart zu Ende der Akademie allein auf dem Pianoforte mehr als eine halbe
Stunde phantasirte und unser Entzücken auf den höchsten Grad gespannt hatte, in laute
überströmende Beyfallsäusserung auf. Und in der That übertraf dieses Phantasiren alles, was man
sich vom Klavierspiele vorstellen konnte, da der höchste Grad der Kompositionskunst, mit der
vollkommensten Fertigkeit im Spiele vereiniget ward.' For a different translation, see Niemetschek,
Life of Mozart, trans. Helen Mautner (London: Hyman, 1956), p. 36.

old man, I hear those heavenly and unforgettable harmonies resound in me' (1826).[23] Friend and associate Maximilian Stadler also claimed (pre-1830) that 'Mozart had no equal in the art of free fantasy. He improvised in such an orderly fashion, as if he had had them lying in front of him'.[24] Strong reactions are also witnessed away from improvisation specifically. For Niemetschek at the Prague academy in 1787: 'We did not know what we should admire most, whether the extraordinary compositions [probably including a piano concerto], or the extraordinary playing; both together made a complete impression on our souls similar to a sweet bewitchment!'[25] And for Leopold Mozart, experiencing a 'marvellous concerto' (*herrliches Konzert*) by his son at a concert in Vienna on 13 February 1785 and conveying the impact to his daughter Nannerl: 'I was only two boxes away from the really beautiful Princess of Wurtemberg and had the pleasure of hearing so splendidly all the interplay of the instruments that tears filled my eyes from sheer delight. When your brother left, the Emperor passed down a compliment hat-in-hand and shouted out "Bravo, Mozart!" When he came back to play, he was applauded.'[26]

Mozart was fully cognizant of the mutually reinforcing impact of performance and composition, desiring and appreciating the kind of close attention to both activities that facilitated the impact. An announcement for the Burgtheater academy on 10 March 1785, presumably written by

---

[23] MDL, pp. 206 (Johann Schink), 285 (Joachim Daniel Preisler), 440 (Placidus Scharl), 480 (Ambros Rieder); MDB, pp. 233, 325, 512, 566. Karl Ditters von Dittersdorf also records Mozart's skills as an improviser – contrasting them with the lesser skills of his imitators – and universal admiration for Mozart's playing among musicians in general. See Karl Ditters von Dittersdorf, *Lebensbeschreibung. Seinem Sohne in der Feder diktirt*, ed. Carl Spazier (Leipzig, 1801), trans. by A. D. Coleridge as *The Autobiography of Karl von Dittersdorf* (London: Richard Bentley and Son, 1896), pp. 44–45, 251. (In an interview with the emperor, relayed in the autobiography, Dittersdorf acknowledges having heard Mozart play three times by 1786–1787. See *Autobiography*, p. 251.)

[24] See MDL, p. 465; MDB, p. 543. Stadler went on to describe composer and organist Johann Georg Albrechtsberger's delight at an hour-long Mozart improvisation, which convinced Albrechtsberger that Mozart's improvisations were not pre-prepared. This anecdote also appears in Nerina Medici and Rosemary Hughes (eds.), *A Mozart Pilgrimage: Being the Travel Diaries of Vincent and Mary Novello in the Year 1829* (London: Novello, 1955), p. 168.

[25] Niemetschek, *Leben*, p. 27 (my translation). 'Er ließ sich dann auf allgemeines Verlangen in einer großen musikalischen Akademie im Operntheater auf dem Pianoforte hören. Nie sah man noch das Theater so voll Menschen, als bey dieser Gelegenheit; nie ein stärkeres, einstimmiges Entzücken, als sein göttliches Spiel erweckte. Wir wußten in der That nicht, was wir mehr bewundern sollten, ob die ausserordentliche Komposition, oder das ausserordentliche Spiel; beydes zusammen bewirkte einen Totaleindruck auf unsere Seelen, welcher einer süßen Bezauberung glich!' For a different (considerably looser) translation see *Life of Mozart*, p. 36.

[26] MBA, vol. 3, p. 373; LMF, p. 886 (16 February 1785).

Mozart himself, promoted a cocktail of new work, distinctive sound and improvisation: 'He will play not only a *new*, just *finished Fortepiano Concerto* [K. 467], but will also use a particularly *large pedalled Fortepiano* [a keyboard played with the feet to reinforce low notes] in his *Fantasy*.'[27] As he explained to his father from Paris (1 May 1778): 'Give me the best clavier in Europe but an audience who understand nothing, or do not want to understand and who do not feel with me what I play, and I will lose all pleasure.'[28] Never immune to positive press or to an enthralled audience, he took particular pleasure in the rapt attention of listeners to his keyboard performances: the Mannheim elector who 'sat down [. . .] beside me and remained motionless'; the French duke who 'listened with all his attention'; and the Viennese audience's 'astonishing silence' (with some 'Bravos' thrown in for good measure) at the Kärntnertortheater concert on 3 April 1781.[29]

He was just as alert to performing matters when writing for others. As is well known, he tailored operatic and concert arias to the needs of individual singers.[30] And, according to Leopold, he adapted operas to the needs of orchestras as well as vocalists.[31] Mozart wrote a number of Viennese instrumental works with specific performers in mind, highlighting their strengths, capabilities and predilections. It was undeniably in the interests of both Mozart and his singers and players to nurture mutually reinforcing appreciation of composition and performance wherever possible. As the critic Johann Friedrich Schink remarked in commending the composition and performance of *Die Entführung aus dem Serail* at the original production at the Burgtheater in Vienna (1782): 'The singers of the national stage here deserve praise: they have felt what they sang; they convey with their whole soul what Mozart wrote; their song also came from the heart; they did not just gurgle, but spoke . . . When composer and singers thus work with combined energy to fulfill the true purpose of music, so our hearts become interested as a result; and where art interests our hearts, there its impression is also constant and lasting.'[32] Equally, Mozart would have

---

[27] MDL, pp. 212; MDB, p. 239. A few weeks later Leopold also reported to Nannerl the large and heavy pedal for the fortepiano: see MBA, vol. 3, p. 379; LMF, p. 889 (12 March 1785).

[28] MBA, vol. 2, p. 344; LMF, pp. 531–532.

[29] MBA, vol. 2, pp. 110, 344, and vol. 3, p. 103; LMF, pp. 363, 532, 722 (letters of 8 November 1777, 1 May 1778, 8 April 1781).

[30] We need also to bear in mind that sometimes Mozart may not have exploited an individual voice to the full, opting (for artistic and/or practical reasons) to write for a voice type instead. See Julian Rushton, 'Buffo Roles in Mozart's Vienna: Tessitura and Tonality as Signs of Characterization', in Mary Hunter and James Webster (eds.), *Opera Buffa in Mozart's Vienna* (Cambridge: Cambridge University Press, 1997), pp. 406–425.

[31] See MBA, vol. 1, p. 440; LMF, pp. 199–200 (28 September 1771).

[32] MDL, p. 186; MDB, pp. 210–211.

wanted in published works to foster the kind of enduring relationships with performers and listeners that ultimately could have had positive financial and artistic ramifications for him. Mozart's acute sensitivity to the sound of music in performance, emerging in correspondence and from contemporaries, therefore would have had an effect on the music he produced, irrespective of his own direct involvement in renditions of it. Reflecting on fortepiano-maker Johann Andreas Stein's concern for musical sound rather than financial profit, Mozart describes the rarely experienced escapement action that always provides an even tone however hard a note is struck and prevents 'jangling and echo'.[33] Nannerl, relating her memories of Mozart in childhood, explained that 'as long as the piece of music lasted, he was all music himself', noticing 'the slightest mistake even in fully orchestrated music' and being 'incensed [*aufgebracht*] by the slightest noise during a piece of music'.[34] Niemetschek followed suit, his own experiences of Mozart's playing and Mozart's music in mind, as well as, perhaps, the observations of Constanze, his principal source: 'His hearing was so sensitive, he understood the differences in sounds so certainly and correctly, that he noticed the slightest mistake or discord even in the largest orchestra and could indicate exactly which character or instrument made it. Nothing incensed him more than restlessness, a racket or chattering during music.'[35] And Michael Kelly, the original Don Basilio and Don Curzio in *Le nozze di Figaro*, remembered Mozart as 'so very particular, when he played, that if the slightest noise were made, he instantly left off'.[36] 'Noise' may not have been uncommon at musical events, but Viennese audiences were also capable of rapt attention: during arias in general; and at Salieri's *Axur* in particular (1789 or 1790), when they listened and watched in the 'holiest silence' (*heiligste Stille*), waiting to show enthusiastic approval until the end of numbers.[37]

Primary sources, especially autograph scores and first editions published during the composer's lifetime, offer a musical complement to accounts of Mozart's intense and creative engagement with performance, and are central to my attempt to bring philological and critical interpretations

---

[33] MBA, vol. 2, p. 68; LMF, pp. 327–328 (17 October 1777).   [34] MDL, p. 404; MDB, p. 462.

[35] Niemetschek, *Leben*, p. 57 (my translation): 'Sein Gehör war so fein, faßte die Verschiedenheit der Töne so gewiß und richtig auf, daß er den geringsten Fehler oder Mißton selbst bey dem stärksten Orchester bemerkte, und dasjenige Subjekt oder Instrument, welches ihn begieng genau anzugeben wußte. Nichts brachte ihn so sehr auf, als Unruhe, Getöse oder Geschwätz bey der Musik. [. . .] Alles was er vortrug, empfand er selbst auf das stärkste – sein ganzes Wesen war dann Gefühl und Aufmerksamkeit'. See also *Life of Mozart*, p. 65.

[36] See Kelly, *Reminiscences*, p. 223.   [37] Von Reitzenstein, *Reise nach Wien*, pp. 344, 250–251.

into closer and deeper alignment than in previous biographies.[38] Of course, neither our knowledge of Mozart's *modus operandi* nor the sources themselves suggest that composition- and performance-based thinking were always separate, clearly defined cognitive exercises for Mozart. Indeed, the idea that a 'composer functions not only as a composer but also as a performer and listener during the course of composition, reacting to what he plays and hears and altering and developing the composition accordingly'[39] implies an entwinement of activities that complicates identification of specific performing motivations on Mozart's part. But primary sources can point to instances where players, singers and issues around performance assumed prominence for him. His standard compositional process, at least in its principal notational stages after a 'pre-written' stage,[40] often sharpens our focus. Mozart first compiled a continuous draft of melodic content and bass line for a piece with additional annotations here and there (*particella*) and then finished the remaining parts in a later phase, or phases, of work (collectively to be termed the completion). (Different ink colours in the autographs frequently distinguish material notated in the *particella* from material notated in the subsequent completion of a piece.) Writing operatic and concert arias, for example, regularly involved run-throughs in *particella* with the intended singer; the arias were then completed after experiencing a rendition and receiving feedback from the singer, therefore potentially telling a story about the impact of both on the compositional process. Surface details in autographs such as dynamics and articulation can orientate us to performing concerns irrespective of when they are notated, as they engage with players and singers in domains where performance choices, decisions and interpretations have notable impact; when added late in the compositional process they apparently coincide with Mozart envisioning the piece as a performable whole. And alterations, adjustments and interpolations to autograph materials (when

---

[38] For a useful summary of the different types of Mozart manuscript – the autographs, draft scores, sketches – as well as styles of writing, ink colours in the manuscripts and the correction of errors, see Ulrich Konrad, *Mozarts Schaffensweise: Studien zu den Werkautographen, Skizzen und Entwürfen* (Göttingen: Vandenhoeck & Ruprecht, 1992), pp. 341–366. Performance copies and performing scores of Mozart's operas that carry annotations by Mozart also will be mentioned, following the work of Dexter Edge in particular. See Edge, 'Mozart's Viennese Copyists' (PhD thesis, University of Southern California, 2001). Performing parts for Mozart's Viennese instrumental and other vocal works unambiguously associated with the composer are few in number. See Edge, 'Mozart's Viennese Copyists', pp. 1278–1289.

[39] See John Butt, *Playing with History: The Historical Approach to Musical Performance* (Cambridge: Cambridge University Press, 2002), p. 87.

[40] For a summary of Mozart's typical process, see Ulrich Konrad, 'Compositional Method' (trans. Ruth Halliwell), in Eisen and Keefe (eds.), *Cambridge Mozart Encyclopedia*, pp. 100–108.

straightforward notational or grammatical errors are not at issue), and unusual notational practices and materials, may also expose performance-based thinking. Examples here include instruments appended to an autograph in connection with a specific performance, which thus represented the *raison d'être* for the new material; the rescoring of a work, or the re-envisaging of instrumentation at the completion stage, indicating attention to instrumental timbres and effects in performance; autographs unfinished at a premiere and completed soon after it, with the original rendition no doubt ringing in the composer's ear as he wrote; and an instrumental part conceived some way through the genesis of a piece – as demonstrated (for instance) by its unconventional location in an autograph – indicating consideration of the effect of the piece in performance. In works written for Mozart to play himself while also promoting his compositional talents, and with the aforementioned attention to sonic detail factored into the equation, changes to autographs can illuminate the composition-performance nexus, Mozart wanting to impress in both areas. And when Mozart engaged with one of his own chamber works between submitting it to a publisher and seeing it in print, he sometimes revised or added to performance markings (dynamics, articulation etc.) through annotations to copies produced in advance of the engraving procedure. In all these respects, performances – either contemplated or experienced for real – and performers have a tangible impact on Mozart's compositional process.

In short, the vivid, 'live' nature of Mozart's musical experiences in 1781–1791, so easy to sideline in biographical contemplation of a magnificent oeuvre but essential to recapture in holistically representing his Viennese achievements, is well represented in primary sources. An autograph score can bring to life Mozart's compositional practices in straightforward ways: he changes a quill; momentarily forgets he is writing for a transposing instrument; overlooks the established alignment of instruments and staves when moving on to a new page; and uses signs (including human faces) to alert copyists to add material.[41] But autographs – and primary sources in general – can help to generate interpretations of his music as well. In essence, the late-eighteenth-century player and singer was expected to carry on a composer's creative work through (*inter alia*) embellishments, elaborations, and interpretation of dynamics and articulation, continuity between performing and writing music thus representing

---

[41] For these particular examples, see the high-quality facsimile of the Piano Concerto in C minor, K. 491: Mozart, *Klavierkonzert C-moll, KV 491: Bärenreiter Facsimile* (Kassel: Bärenreiter, 2014).

a practical reality in Mozart's time.[42] The spirit of such continuities has led late-eighteenth-century texts and sources to be interpreted as musical events, encapsulations of written-down performances, and confluences of creative compositional and performance acts rather than as totemic 'works'.[43] Mozart's musical texts leave much to the discretion of player and singer, thereby accentuating the roles of performers in communicating Mozart's music to – and producing its meanings for – audiences. According to Johann Friedrich Reichardt (1808), Mozart as 'a performing artist himself … entrusted far more [than Joseph Haydn] to the players'.[44] The notion of *Werktreue* (fidelity to the work), which 'arises from the belief that a musical text can circumscribe and contain a performance … [acting] as a constraint on musical performers, leading them to try to play only the notated para-meters and suppress the others',[45] is therefore of little relevance to Mozart's music. Mozart's combination of detailed performance markings in some passages of his autographs and first editions and sparsely notated markings

[42] For a rhetorical context for this continuity, where delivery intersects with invention, disposition, elocution and memory in an oration, see Beghin, 'Crowning the Rhetorical Process', p. 132. On changing attitudes to the performer-composer-work dynamic at the end of eighteenth and beginning of the nineteenth centuries, see Mary Hunter, '"To Play as if from the Soul of the Composer": The Idea of the Performer in Early Romantic Aesthetics', *Journal of the American Musicological Society*, 58/2 (2005), pp. 357–398. For more on the performer continuing the composer's work, see Edward Klorman, *Mozart's Music of Friends: Social Interplay in the Chamber Works* (Cambridge: Cambridge University Press, 2016), pp. 104–108. See also Butt, *Playing with History*, pp. 96–122.

[43] See Butt, *Playing with History*, pp. 53–73, especially p. 69; Lydia Goehr, *The Imaginary Museum of Musical Works* (Oxford: Clarendon Press, 1992); Cliff Eisen, 'The Primacy of Performance: Text, Act and Continuo in Mozart's Piano Concertos', in Dorothea Link and Judith Nagley (eds.), *Words About Mozart: Essays in Honour of Stanley Sadie* (Woodbridge: Boydell & Brewer, 2005), pp. 107–119; John Irving, *Understanding Mozart's Piano Sonatas* (Aldershot: Ashgate Publishing, 2010), especially pp. 5–8; Mary Hunter, 'Haydn's London Piano Trios and His Salomon String Quartets: Private vs. Public?' in Sisman (ed.), *Haydn and His World*, pp. 103–130.

[44] As given in H. C. Robbins Landon, *Haydn, Chronicle and Works: Volume 5, Haydn: The Late Years, 1801–1809* (London: Thames & Hudson, 1977), p. 409. For one example of where Haydn – in contrast to Mozart – asserts 'visible and audible control over the physical intimacies of performance' while also 'allowing room for … performative "delivery" of the music', see Mary Hunter, 'Haydn's String Quartet Fingerings: Communications to Performer and Audience', in Hunter and Richard Will (eds.), *Engaging Haydn: Culture, Context, and Criticism* (Cambridge: Cambridge University Press, 2012), pp. 281–301, quoted material at pp. 297, 298.

[45] See Bruce Haynes, *The End of Early Music: A Period Performer's History of Music for the Twenty-First Century* (New York: Oxford University Press, 2007), p. 90. For a negative appraisal of *Werktreue* in the context of Mozart's piano concertos, nonetheless identifying positive features of recordings adhering to its philosophy, see Richard Taruskin, *Text and Act: Essays on Music and Performance* (New York: Oxford University Press, 1995), pp. 273–291. On the problematic nature of *Werktreue* for many in the nineteenth century, see Nicholas Cook, *Beyond the Score: Music as Performance* (Oxford and New York: Oxford University Press, 2013), pp. 21, 95.

in others in the same piece or movement, for example, points to his view of the roles and responsibilities of performers relative to his music: he would have wanted to guide interpreters of texts, but also to nurture the kinds of decision-making expected of late-eighteenth-century singers and players – the 'invention and imagination' to be cultivated not confined, according to Anselm Bayly (1771).[46] A performer's mindset along these lines, promoting spontaneity and creativity, is as relevant and important to interpreting Mozart today as it was in the late eighteenth century.[47] Influenced by historical predilections, considerations and concerns, and more than 225 years after Mozart's death, our relationship to Mozart's music in performance is naturally different from the relationship he had with his own performers. Where our interpretations – both as writers and practitioners – move beyond those likely to have been made in the late eighteenth century, they can still remain true to the imaginative spirit of interaction in Mozart's time between composer and performer, composition and performance.

Mozart's primary sources thus capture energetic engagement with experiences, perceptions, practicalities and interpretations related to performers and performance rather than the pursuit of perfectly chiselled, definitively finished works in a so-called *Fassung letzter Hand*. For one scholarly expert on Mozart sources: 'Mozart was in most cases not striving to produce a "work", but rather to produce a successful performance.'[48] For another: 'Autographs represent not only the "substance" of his works but also – in a very real sense – actual performances.'[49] And for a third, also a high-profile pianist well known for eschewing fidelity to notated

---

[46] For the quotation, see Anselm Bayly, *Practical Treatise on Singing and Playing with Just Expression and Real Elegance* (London, 1771), pp. 47–48. On decision-making by performers about un-notated dynamics, see Daniel Gottlob Türk, *School of Clavier Playing* (1789), trans. Raymond H. Haagh (Lincoln: University of Nebraska Press, 1982), p. 340.

[47] In a similar spirit, see Klorman, *Mozart's Music of Friends* and (for Haydn) Beghin, *The Virtual Haydn*. Referencing Mozart among others, see Taruskin, *Text and Act*; Fred Maus, 'Musical Performance as Analytical Communication', in Salim Kemal and Ivan Gaskell (eds.), *Performance and Authenticity in the Arts* (Cambridge: Cambridge University Press, 1999), pp. 129–153 (at 148; 'one could think of a performer . . . as a kind of composer, a partner in an act of collaborative composition'); Irving, *Understanding Mozart's Piano Sonatas*, p. 11 ('texts that release rather than confine, the imagination of the reader'); Lewis Lockwood, 'Performance and Authenticity', *Early Music*, 19 (1991), pp. 501–508 (at 506; '[creating] the illusion that [the conductor] and the orchestra were composing [the end of the 'Jupiter' Symphony Andante] as they produce it'). For a wide-ranging study of music as performance rather than 'music as writing', emphasizing the creative act of performance over representations of works in notated form, see Cook, *Beyond the Score*.

[48] Edge, 'Mozart's Viennese Copyists', p. 2117. See also Eisen, 'The Primacy of Performance'.

[49] Cliff Eisen, 'Preface', in Mozart, *Symphonie D-dur (Prager) KV504* (Wiesbaden: Breitkopf, 2002), pp. vi–vii.

material in Mozart's scores by embellishing and improvising: 'It is almost impossible to imagine a *Fassung letzter Hand* for Mozart. He lived in an age of spontaneous performance, improvisation, embellishment, and the inescapable demands that economics imposed on musical activities.'[50]

Faced with a wide variety of primary sources in the context of a biographical study of a decade of music in Vienna, it is difficult nonetheless to theorize a connection between Mozart, his sources and his performers that is applicable across all genres and can account for differences both among the sources themselves and the players and singers – known and unknown alike – for whom the pieces were intended. To be sure, all sources are incomplete in the sense that Mozart would not have considered his notation cast in stone in any individual one. The degree of incompletion varies considerably, though, as we shall see (for example) in autographs of piano concertos, operatic numbers, and chamber works for publication with Vienna-based Artaria and Anton Hoffmeister. Diverging amounts of performing detail in the sources finds a parallel in contrasting positions from Mozart on the performance of his musical texts: at one moment he expects that 'all the notes, appoggiaturas etc.', will be played 'as written' or commends 'accuracy in … piano and forte' or is concerned about adjustments to one of his early operas, but at another that he will perform 'always what comes to mind' or 'something missing' from a solo part in a concerto, or that a singer is expected to embellish one of his notated texts.[51] Relationships between text and act – which rarely yield 'unequivocal answers' for late-eighteenth-century repertories[52] – and information conveyed by primary sources, are therefore evaluated empirically in my study rather than according to a firmly theorized position,

---

[50] 'Speaking Mozart's Lingo: Robert Levin on Mozart and Improvisation', in Bernard Sherman (ed.), *Inside Early Music: Conversations with Performers* (Oxford: Oxford University Press, 1997), pp. 315–338, at 318. Levin succinctly summarizes his credo in 'Improvising Mozart', in Gabriel Solis and Bruno Nettl (eds.), *Musical Improvisation: Art, Education, and Society* (Urbana and Chicago: University of Illinois Press, 2009), pp. 143–149. For further arguments against the concept of a *Fassung letzter Hand* in the late eighteenth century, see Mary Hunter, *The Culture of Opera Buffa in Mozart's Vienna: a Poetics of Entertainment* (Princeton: Princeton University Press, 1999), p. 16; and Edge, 'Mozart's Viennese Copyists', pp. 69–70.

[51] See MBA, vol. 2, pp. 228, 327, vol. 1, pp. 516–517 and vol. 3, pp. 251, 318; LMF, pp. 449 (17 January 1778), 517 (24 March 1778), 259 (14 January 1775), 837 (22 January 1783), 880 (9 June 1784). Mozart wrote embellishments for his own aria 'Ah, se a morir' from *Lucia Silla*, which are extant in Nannerl's hand.

[52] Clive Brown, *Classical and Romantic Performing Practice, 1750–1900* (Oxford: Clarendon Press, 1999), p. 5.

guided biographically by the purpose and function of the piece under consideration.[53]

Since Mozart sought appreciation in the present not the future, often writing music for which only a single concert performance or opera production was envisaged (even if more were naturally always desired),[54] the initial impact a work made on audiences and performers was paramount. It is not surprising in this respect that beginnings and ends of pieces (as will be shown) receive more than their fair share of special timbral, textural, dynamic, melodic and harmonic effects – often prominent in one way or another in primary sources – in an attempt to capture attention immediately or to sign off distinctively in a manner encouraging approbation. In fact, timbral and textural effects of all kinds in Mozart's Viennese works reflect the vitality of engagement with players, singers and audiences.[55] Of course Mozart's decisions about timbres and textures affect compositional aspects of form, structure and instrumental interaction (for example), as has often been recognized.[56] But, as we shall see, these decisions are also informed pragmatically by the predilections, strengths and limitations of individual players and singers and the needs and

[53] As Tom Beghin has pointed out (*The Virtual Haydn*, pp. 14–16) relationships between the text and performance of Haydn's keyboard sonatas can vary according to the purpose for which they were written. His book includes imaginative descriptions of how several works were composed specifically with their dedicatees in mind. See in particular, Chapter 4 ('"Your Most Humble and Obedient Servant"'), Chapter 5 ('An Opus for the Insightful World'), and Chapter 6 ('A Contract with Posterity'), pp. 127–254.

[54] As Lydia Goehr points out (*Imaginary Museum of Musical Works*, p. 186): 'Rarely did musicians [pre-1800] think of their music as surviving past their lifetime in the form of completed and fixed works.'

[55] For an introduction to orchestral effects in the eighteenth century, see John Spitzer and Neal Zaslaw, *The Birth of the Orchestra: History of an Institution, 1650–1815* (New York: Oxford University Press, 2004), pp. 436–506. On Mozart specifically, in aesthetic and historical context, see Simon P. Keefe, '"Greatest Effects with the Least Effort": Strategies of Wind Writing in Mozart's Piano Concertos', in Keefe (ed.), *Mozart Studies* (Cambridge: Cambridge University Press, 2006), pp. 25–46; Keefe, 'The Aesthetics of Wind Writing in Mozart's "Paris" Symphony in D, K. 297', *Mozart-Jahrbuch 2006*, pp. 329–344; Keefe, '"Die Ochsen am Berge": Franz Xaver Süssmayr and the Orchestration of Mozart's Requiem, K. 626', *Journal of the American Musicological Society*, 60 (2008), pp. 1–65; and Keefe, '"Die trefflich gewählte Instrumente": Orchestrating Don Giovanni's Defeat', in Kathryn Libin (ed.), *Mozart in Prague: Essays on Performance, Patronage, Sources, and Reception* (Prague: Czech Academy of Sciences, 2016), pp. 343–369.

[56] For representative discussion, see Janet M. Levy, 'Texture as a Sign in Classic and Early Romantic Music', *Journal of the American Musicological Society*, 35 (1982), pp. 482–531 (looking at Mozart among others); Jonathan P. J. Stock, 'Orchestration as Structural Determinant: Mozart's Deployment of Woodwind Timbre in the Slow Movement of the C Minor Piano Concerto K. 491', *Music & Letters*, 78 (1997), pp. 210–219; and Simon P. Keefe, *Mozart's Piano Concertos: Dramatic Dialogue in the Age of Enlightenment* (Woodbridge and Rochester, NY: The Boydell Press, 2001).

expectations of intended performers more generally; timbre and texture are therefore situated at the composition-performance nexus and will receive attention in my study. Father-son discussion of orchestral and vocal textures and effects in *Idomeneo*, a few months before Mozart's move to Vienna, features practical performance matters alongside compositional and dramatic considerations. In addition to contemplating dramatic effects – such as the scene with the subterranean voice to which they repeatedly return – Leopold stresses that his son needs 'the greatest friendship and enthusiasm of the whole orchestra' in order for the full effect of the opera to be experienced in the theatre; that he must keep the orchestra in good humour and well disposed towards him on account of his music requiring 'constant, astonishing attention from the players of all instruments'; and that his compositions, written 'so judiciously' for all instruments, preclude a less-than-excellent orchestra from doing them justice.[57] A decade earlier, Leopold penned about Mozart's *Ascanio in Alba*: 'I know what he [Wolfgang] has written and what an effect it would have, because it is more than certain that it is as really well written for the singers as for the orchestra.' Moreover, the famous castrato Giovanni Manzuoli and other singers were not only extremely happy with their own material in their arias but also eagerly anticipated hearing the arias fully orchestrated.[58] The mutual support of vocal and instrumental writing thereby implied in the effect of the whole can also be situated against the backdrop of perceived sonic associations in the late eighteenth century between instruments and the human voice and a belief that wind players in particular should model their execution, timbre and tone on the practices of good singers.[59] (Mozart himself recognized that instrumentalists often imitated the natural 'trembling' of the voice.[60]) The Viennese Burgtheater orchestra

[57] MBA, vol. 3, p. 70, LMF, p. 697 (25 December 1780); MBA, vol. 3, p. 70, LMF, p. 696 (25 December 1780); MBA, vol. 3, p. 45, LMF, p. 681 (4 December 1780). For vocal, wind and brass effects discussed by Leopold and Mozart in their correspondence on *Idomeneo* (including for the subterranean voice and instrumental accompaniment, and the march in Act 2), see MBA, vol. 3, pp. 23, 48, 74–75, 79; LMF, pp. 666, 682, 700, 703 (18 November 1780, 5 December 1780, 29 December 1780, 3 January 1781).

[58] MBA, vol. 1, p. 440; LMF, pp. 199–200 (28 September 1771).

[59] On the links between the sounds of wind instruments and voices see, for example, Othon-Joseph Vandenbroek, *Traité général de tous les instrumens à vent à l'usage des compositeurs* (Paris: Boyer, 1793), p. 63; Johann von Schönfeld, *Jahrbuch der Tonkunst von Wien und Prag* (Vienna, 1796), pp. 191–194; W. [Berhard Wessely], 'Über den Gebrauch der Blasinstrumente, für angehende Komponisten', *Musikalisches Wochenblatt*, 10 (1791), p. 78. On wind instrumentalists modeling themselves on singers, see Johann Georg Tromlitz, *The Virtuoso Flute Player* (1791), trans. and ed. Ardal Powell (Cambridge: Cambridge University Press, 1991), pp. 152, 112.

[60] MBA, vol. 2, p. 378; LMF, p. 552 (12 June 1778).

was described as the best in Europe in 1789–1790, taking instrumental performance to a new level, and praised for its excellent ensemble and responsiveness to the singers in Salieri's *Axur*: 'When the agony of strained passion gradually subsided to exhaustion, and the intense surges of softening sentiments took its place, the orchestra gradually relaxed the beat and rendered the melodies slower and slower, in the most exact concordance with the singers.'[61] The quality of orchestral accompanying was so high, von Reitzenstein explained, that singers were inspired to sing better than ever before; instruments responded superbly to changing affects and emotions. The much-travelled castrato Luigi Marchesi (Marchesini) also told von Reitzenstein that he had not considered such lovely orchestral accompaniment for voices possible until experiencing it for himself in Vienna in 1785.[62] Mozart, in consequence, would have had reason to expect combined instrumental-vocal timbres, textures and effects to be successfully realized in Viennese performances. (After commenting on the orchestra, in fact, von Reitzenstein said that it was a 'true delight' [*wahre Wonne*] to hear a Mozart, Salieri or Paisiello opera at the Burgtheater in Vienna.)[63] Thus, when looking at how Mozart tailored vocal music to the needs of individual singers in the last ten years of his life, I shall widen the investigative remit beyond the usual concern for vocal writing by itself to orchestral effects produced in combination with bespoke vocal material.

Foregrounding performance in a biographical account of Mozart's Viennese decade cannot be accomplished solely by scrutinizing primary sources, which are sometimes unavailable, not readily accessible, missing substantial segments, or are no longer extant; it also requires research elsewhere. I focus on individual concerts and dramatic productions, for example, and on reasons for composing works, in an attempt to determine how music was shaped by experiences of and sensitivities to players and singers. And I investigate Mozart's attention both to the needs of known performers and to his perceived expectations of unknown ones and of

---

[61] See von Reitzenstein, *Reise nach Wien*, pp. 253, 255–256, 256–257: 'Wenn das Toben gespannter Leidenschaft nach und nach zur Erschöpfung herunter sank, und die heftigen Wallungen mildern Gefühlen Platz machten, so liess auch das Orchester, im genauesten Einverständnisse mit den Sängern, den Takt nach und nach sinken, und die Melodieen langsamer und immer langsamer fortwallen'. In 1789 and 1790, Salieri's *Axur* was performed on 23 January; 6, 9, 18 February; 23, 25 September; 7, 13 October; 7, 17, 25 November; 7, 29 December (1789); and 3 February; 26 August; 1, 20, 29 September; 13, 16, 22 October; and 3 December (1790); see Link, *National Court Theatre*, pp. 134–162.

[62] Von Reitzenstein, *Reise nach Wien*, pp. 256, 258–259. On Marchesi's acclaimed performances in Vienna in 1785, see Link, *National Court Theatre*, pp. 220, 250–252.

[63] Von Reitzenstein, *Reise nach Wien*, p. 259.

varied audiences (including purchasers of manuscript copies and publications, private and public audiences at formal and informal concerts, and attendees at opera productions). Focal points here include accommodation in piano-based solo and chamber works of Mozart's own predilections as a player and the apparent needs of purchasers of editions; visual aspects of instrumental performance processed by audiences and players; combined sensitivity to the strengths and weaknesses of individual singers and to demonstrations of orchestral prowess in vocal works; attention to the limits and potential of particular instruments in the hands of master practitioners; integration of performance aspirations and distinctive instrumental sounds and effects in orchestral works; and juggling of performing-, composing- and publishing-related priorities in chamber music. I pay attention to music in notated form that highlights the act of performance, through decorative variation, embellishments and improvisatory qualities – the type of music 'as if . . . merely invented on the spur of the moment' even when actually written down according to theorist and pianist Daniel Türk (1789).[64] I also focus on dynamics and articulation, which depend more than other musical parameters for the communication of meaning on the execution and interpretation of players and singers. And the specific instruments and voices for which Mozart wrote, brings to the fore issues of pitch and melody. A one-volume account of Mozart's decade in Vienna cannot address more than a fraction of performing issues in all repertories, but it can orientate biographical discussion towards fundamental features of Mozart's professional persona by tracing consistencies and changes in his *modus operandi* over time and by shining a light where appropriate on other prominent musicians, audience expectations, publishing practices, and concert and dramatic practices and traditions. It thereby offers new biographical and critical perspectives on Mozart and his music.

In keeping with mainstream biographical traditions and expectations, I proceed broadly chronologically through Mozart's Viennese decade. Temporal overlaps between chapters are the inevitable result of organizing material primarily by activity and genre – as befits orientation towards

---

[64] For the quoted material, see Türk, *School of Clavier Playing*, p. 301. For two essays consonant with this approach, see Hunter, 'Haydn's London Piano Trios and His Salomon String Quartets', in Sisman (ed.), *Haydn and His World*, pp. 103–130; and James Webster, 'The Rhetoric of Improvisation in Haydn's Keyboard Music', in Beghin and Goldberg (eds.), *Haydn and the Performance of Rhetoric*, pp. 172–212. On Mozart as 'an important figure in the move towards notated ornamentation', see Corey Jamason, 'The Performer and the Composer', in Colin Lawson and Robin Stowell (eds.), *The Cambridge History of Musical Performance* (Cambridge: Cambridge University Press, 2012), pp. 105–134, at 122.

performance – rather than by strict order of composition. For example, Parts III and IV, on the Da Ponte operas *Le nozze di Figaro, Don Giovanni* and *Così fan tutte* and on instrumental music from the second half of the decade, cover the same time period, as do the two chapters in Part I (1781–1782) and several in Part II (1782–1786). (Appendix 1 provides a list of Mozart's principal activities and works from 1781 to 1791 in chronological order.) Structuring a biography in this way embraces Mozart's final decade as a series of different, if related, musical stories and journeys, rather than as a single, straightforward career trajectory (such as the now discredited trope of Mozart's popularity peaking in the mid-1780s and declining thereafter, the composer being passed over in Vienna until dying in poverty).[65] In fact, Mozart's ability (near) simultaneously to engage with singers and instrumentalists, publishing and public performance, and concerts and dramatic productions, while coping with the demands of a hectic, diverse and financially uncertain freelance career as a performer-composer who continually needed to exploit revenue-raising opportunities, deserves to be properly promoted biographically alongside the quality of the music produced.[66]

For the first time in a half-century or so every major work or group of works from Mozart's decade in Vienna is covered in a biographical study.[67] A number of pieces traditionally marginalized in biographical literature on account of perceived quality or position in Mozart's oeuvre are given proper exposure, including instrumental music from 1781 to 1782, vocal music between *Die Entführung* and *Figaro* (mid-1782 to mid-1786), and *La clemenza di Tito* (which often loses out to its contemporary *Die Zauberflöte*).[68] Mozart's perennially popular Viennese works on which

---

[65] For a composite, traditional narrative along these lines (on p. 66) and a thorough rebuttal, see Edge, 'Mozart's Reception in Vienna, 1787–1791'.

[66] Mozart's hectic career as an independent, freelance musician in Vienna is ably captured in Leopold's letters to his daughter Nannerl when visiting Mozart in spring 1785. See MBA, vol. 3, pp. 372–388; LMF, pp. 885–889 (extracts only).

[67] Volkmar Braunbehrens' volume *Mozart in Vienna, 1781–1791*, trans. Timothy Bell (New York: Grove Weidenfeld, 1989) and H. C. Robbins Landon's *Mozart: The Golden Years, 1781–1791* (London: Thames & Hudson, 1989) are weighted towards Mozart's life. And Landon's *Mozart and Vienna* is dedicated above all to the publication of Pezzl's 'Sketch of Vienna'.

[68] On *La clemenza di Tito* in this respect, see most recently Christoph Wolff, *Mozart at the Gateway to His Fortune: Serving the Emperor, 1788–1791* (New York: Norton, 2012). It is surprising that Wolff's volume contains no significant discussion of *Tito*, an opera for Emperor Leopold II's coronation in Prague, given Wolff's belief that Mozart was proud of his imperial appointment and serious about the ambassadorial responsibilities that came with it. While Otto Jahn's three-volume *Life of Mozart* (1856) and Abert's *W. A. Mozart* – probably the longest biographies of the nineteenth and twentieth centuries respectively – devote

critical attention has been lavished also receive extended treatment. Fragments – works left incomplete in score that Mozart probably planned to return to at some stage – are not generally examined in detail, for reasons of space and on account of a lack of evidence for most of them about both the intended performers and the uses to which the works would have been put in a finished state.[69] But many of the lengthy ones are considered, including the Fantasia K. 397, *L'oca del Cairo, Lo sposo deluso*, the Mass in C minor, the Basset-Horn Concerto K. 584b, and the Requiem, and others are discussed from time to time.[70] My hope is that this book will appeal not only to Mozart aficionados, musicologists, and general music lovers, but also to performers interested in recapturing the vibrant performance-composition dynamic of an earlier era.[71]

considerable space to *Tito*, their chapters on *Die Zauberflöte* are four times longer. Sweepingly negative remarks on *Tito* are still encountered in biographically orientated volumes, including that 'in his heart of hearts, Mozart considered [the opera] a failure'. See Jane Glover, *Mozart's Women: His Family, His Friends, His Music* (London: Macmillan, 2006), p. 294. Piero Melograni (*Mozart: a Biography*, p. 235) is also equivocal: '*Tito* does indeed display a number of limitations, due in part to its hasty composition, but . . . portions of the work are very beautiful . . . Still, anyone who hopes to find in *La clemenza di Tito* the freshness, vivacity, and modernity of *Figaro, Don Giovanni, Così fan tutte*, or *The Magic Flute* would be disappointed.' For an overview of critical negativity towards *Tito*, including the 'roots of [its] misfortune', see Sergio Durante, 'Mozart and the Idea of "Vera" Opera: A Study of *La clemenza di Tito*' (PhD thesis, Harvard University, 1993), pp. 10–52.

[69] Intended performers of fragmentary works from Mozart's Viennese decade – had they been completed – include Constanze Mozart and Josepha Hofer (for the arias 'In te spero, o sposo amato', K. 440, and 'Schon lacht der holde Frühling', K. 580, respectively).

[70] Many of Mozart's fragments are given in facsimile in NMA, X/30/4. For useful discussion in a biographical context of fragments and sketches left at Mozart's death, see Wolff, *Mozart at the Gateway to His Fortune*, pp. 159–194.

[71] In this vein, John Butt remarks (*Playing with History*, p. 94): 'Recognition of a performing persona in the notation greatly informs our own interpretative role as "external spectators" or music critics, but the same persona may also enliven our musical experiences as performers and listeners.'

PART I

Beginnings, 1781–1782

1 | Settling in Vienna
Exploiting Opportunities for Instrumental Performance and Composition, 1781–1782

Arriving in Vienna from Munich on 16 March 1781, Mozart immediately began to exploit opportunities as a performer-composer. He expressed disgruntlement on 24 March at initially being prevented by Archbishop Colloredo from playing at a Kärntnertortheater concert of the Tonkünstler-Societät (a society of musicians benefiting the widows and orphans of musicians) on account of the perceived impact he thought he would have:

I am sorry only on account of the following. I should not have played a concerto, but (because the Emperor sits in the proscenium box) I should have extemporized alone (Countess Thun would have given me her beautiful Stein pianoforte into the bargain) and played a fugue and then the variations on 'Je suis Lindor' [K. 354]. Whenever I have played this programme in public, I have received the greatest applause – because each [item] stands out so well against the others, and because everyone has something to suit them. But pazienza![1]

Once Colloredo relented and allowed Mozart to play, a programme issued by the theatre on 2 April, a day before the concert, stressed Mozart's combined credentials as a composer and performer, highlighting his expertise 'partly in the matter of composition and also in regard to art in general, and special skill and delicacy of touch'.[2] Writing to Leopold on 4 April, Mozart drew attention both to the musical success of the concert and to the possibilities for big remuneration in the future:

I can truly say that I was really pleased with the Viennese public yesterday. . . . I had to begin all over again, because there was no end to the applause. What do you think I would make if I were to give an academy of my own now that the public knows me? Only our arch-oaf [Colloredo] does not allow it. He does not want his people to make a profit but a loss.[3]

Four days later Mozart added: 'What most pleased me, and astonished me was the amazing silence – and also the cries of Bravo in the middle of my playing.' He then went on to describe another concert earlier on 8 April at the residence of Colloredo's father in Vienna for which he wrote three new

---

[1] MBA, vol. 3, p. 99; LMF, p. 718 (24 March 1781).   [2] MDL, p. 173; MDB, p. 195.
[3] MBA, vol. 3, pp. 101–102; p. LMF, p. 720 (4 April 1781).

works, the Rondo in C for violin and orchestra (K. 373), an accompanied sonata for piano and violin (K. 379 in G), and probably the concert aria 'A questo seno deh vieni', K. 374, for the castrato Francesco Ceccarelli, 'which he had to repeat'.[4] Unfortunately, Mozart explained, this (unpaid) concert clashed with one at Countess Thun's residence, at which the singers Johann Valentin Adamberger and Madame Weigl each received 50 ducats.[5]

After his account of the 8 April concert Mozart seriously broached for the first time with Leopold the possibility of remaining in Vienna. He had mentioned the topic in his previous letter (4 April), but more in connection with delaying his departure for Salzburg – an option Colloredo's chamberlain and councillor Count Arco apparently left open to musicians – than of not returning at all. On 8 April, he went considerably further, raising the idea of leaving Colloredo's service, which he would do without hesitation were it were not for Leopold: he could make at least 1,000 thalers each year in Vienna by giving a grand concert and taking on four pupils, and he would not be squandering his talents in such a 'rubbish place' as Salzburg. He needed Leopold's advice, he explained, in order to state his intentions to Colloredo.[6]

In the next two momentous months, which included the infamously testy exchanges with Count Arco and Colloredo and dismissal from Salzburg service, Mozart returned twice in his letters to what he called the 'Archbishop's academy': 'to be badly paid and on top of everything mocked, despised and bullied – that is really too much', he explained, before reviewing events of two months earlier on 13 June.[7] No doubt the initial mention of the concert *immediately* before a first substantive pitch for independence was part tactical ploy, an attempt to convince Leopold that artistic and financial success was guaranteed if he remained in Vienna. But the biographical significance of the concert must not be overlooked; here, Mozart performed and composed new works *in* Vienna and *for* Vienna for probably the first time (at least as an adult). A key Mozart grievance relating to the 8 April academy and a later Colloredo-sponsored one too (perhaps the concert on 27 April) is that he played with such zeal and to such general audience acclaim, including in an extended improvisation, that 'if the Archbishop had only a little humanity, he would surely have felt delighted.

---

[4] MBA, vol. 3, p. 103; LMF, p. 722 (8 April 1781). Doubts expressed about the performance of K. 374 on 8 April are discussed below.

[5] MBA, vol. 3, p. 105; LMF, p. 723 (11 April 1781).

[6] MBA, vol. 3, pp. 102, 104; LMF, pp. 720–711, 722 (4 April, 8 April 1781).

[7] MBA, vol. 3, p. 128; LMF, p. 742 (13 June 1781). See also MBA, vol. 3, p. 105; LMF, p. 725 (11 April 1781).

Instead of at least showing me . . . his pleasure and satisfaction, he treats me like a street urchin and tells me to my face that I should clear out, that he could get hundreds to serve him better than I'.[8] For Mozart, complete musical commitment and indubitable artistic achievement represented appropriate service, trumping words and (non-musical) deeds.

Ultimately, Mozart, his antagonists Colloredo and Arco and his interlocutor Leopold did not cover themselves in glory in their words and deeds of late spring 1781. True to form, Colloredo appears haughty and unpleasant in his audiences with Mozart, but was probably justified in finding Mozart 'arrogant' (*hofärtig*), even based only on information gleaned from Mozart's letters: Mozart refused point blank to take an important package from the Archbishop to Salzburg on his projected return trip; he asked sarcastically whether Colloredo was satisfied with him and left angrily with a parting shot that he would have no more to do with him; he was furious at not receiving a fee for composing works for the 8 April concert, 'refusing to see the matter in the light of his failure over the past months to provide the court with anything in return for his salary';[9] and he expressed a desire one day to return Count Arco's 'kick on my behind'.[10] The content of Leopold's lost letters to Mozart can only be surmised from Mozart's responses, but contained some ungenerous accusations, such as that Mozart had never loved him. Equally, Leopold's reactions were at least partially grounded in not unreasonable perceptions of Mozart's practical and financial miscalculations on the extended trip to Munich, Mannheim and Paris (1777–1779) that Leopold himself had effectively bankrolled. If we have sympathy for Mozart and his plight it is as much, perhaps more, because he had to fight simultaneously on two fronts – with Colloredo in Vienna and Leopold in Salzburg – than because working conditions under Colloredo had become intolerable for him. Colloredo, self-evidently, was not a perfect employer, but Mozart and Leopold were not good employees either.[11]

Once the dust had settled and Mozart was finally an independent musician in Vienna, the hard work had to start. It no longer mattered whether he completely believed what he wrote about prospects in Vienna in letters to Leopold in spring 1781 or intended statements for rhetorical emphasis – for example that he could make substantial amounts of money

---

[8] MBA, vol. 3, p. 128; LMF, p. 742 (13 June 1781).

[9] Robert Gutman, *Mozart: A Cultural Biography* (New York: Harcourt Brace, 1999), p. 535.

[10] See MBA, vol. 3, pp. 110–111, 124, 129; LMF, pp. 728 (9 May 1781), 739 (2 June 1781), 743 (13 June 1781).

[11] For more on this last point, see Cliff Eisen, 'Mozart and Salzburg', in Keefe (ed.), *The Cambridge Companion to Mozart*, pp. 7–21.

in the 'land of the clavier'.[12] It was only important now that musical activities brought artistic and financial success. In addition to obtaining an operatic commission (*Die Entführung aus dem Serail* is discussed in Chapter 2), trying to procure a position at Joseph II's court, and teaching a few pupils, Mozart needed performances, compositions and publications of new instrumental works to help ensure a secure existence in Vienna.

On the whole, Mozart's instrumental works from spring 1781 to summer 1782 have received little scholarly attention and not the best critical press. With the notable exception of the Sonata for two pianos in D, K. 448 (November 1781), routinely praised by twentieth- and twenty-first-century writers,[13] these works as we shall see often pass more or less unnoticed in the general biographical and scholarly literature (the Rondo for violin and orchestra K. 373; the accompanied sonatas K. 376, 377, 379, 380; and the concert arias K. 374, 383), get mixed reports (the keyboard works K. 394, 397) or suffer persistent criticism (the Rondo in D for piano and orchestra K. 382). Sandwiched between *Idomeneo* (January 1781) and *Die Entführung* (July 1782) and written during a period of personal upheaval, they have been squeezed out biographically; some critics probably also concur with Maynard Solomon's view that 'the quality of his output as a whole in the eighteen months after his arrival [in Vienna] did not represent an advance over his achievements in Paris in 1778, in Salzburg in 1779–80, or in Munich in 1780–81'.[14] But from a musical-biographical perspective Mozart's early Viennese instrumental works are too significant in effect to overlook, offering insight into how he navigated his musical way in Vienna at an uncertain and self-evidently crucial stage of his career.

Orchestral Music

The 8 April 1781 concert at the Colloredo residence, presumably for a select audience, provided an early Viennese opportunity for Mozart to demonstrate skills as a composer of orchestral music and as a performer-composer

---

[12] MBA, vol. 3, p. 125; LMF, p. 739 (2 June 1781).

[13] Abert, *W. A. Mozart*, p. 642; Einstein, *Mozart: His Character, His Work*, p. 285; Georg Knepler, *Wolfgang Amadé Mozart*, trans. J. Bradford Robinson (Cambridge: Cambridge University Press, 1994), p. 226; Julian Rushton, *Mozart* (New York: Oxford University Press, 2006), p. 110; Daniel Heartz, *Mozart, Haydn and Early Beethoven, 1781–1803* (New York: Norton, 2009), p. 42.

[14] Maynard Solomon, *Mozart: A Life* (New York: HarperCollins, 1995), p. 287.

of instrumental music. The Rondo in C for violin and orchestra K. 373 was written for Colloredo's leading violinist, Antonio Brunetti. Mozart and Leopold wrote repeatedly and disparagingly of Brunetti's personal conduct, regarding him as 'a coarse fellow' (*grober Kerl*) of loose morals; unsurprisingly, then, Mozart welcomed Brunetti's departure for Salzburg soon after the concert.[15] But there was mutual musical respect as well, with Brunetti complimenting Mozart's skills as a violinist and Mozart earlier writing at Brunetti's request a new Adagio to the Violin Concerto in A K. 219 (K. 261, 1776).[16] Naturally, Mozart would have wanted to write for violin and orchestra in ways that promoted Brunetti's performing talents and his own compositional talents. Indeed, a number of violin-playing qualities prized by Mozart would have been immediately apparent in an appropriately skilled realization of K. 373: assuming the André edition from 1800 as a faithful reflection of Mozart's intentions in the absence of an extant autograph, strokes written throughout facilitate the clarity of playing and 'beautiful staccato' that Mozart admired; and the absence of figuration-laden passagework confirms Mozart as 'no great lover of difficulties'.[17]

With information about Brunetti's individual skills and predilections as a violinist unavailable and no autograph or first edition of the Rondo from the composer's lifetime to consult, it is not possible to determine how the performer – and Mozart's knowledge of his playing – had an impact on the compositional process. But Mozart's material for soloist and orchestra in his ABA'CA" movement still points to simultaneous promotion of the principal performer and the elegant composition. Brilliant writing for the soloist, for example, is carefully calculated for effect.[18] The solo writing in the second half of A is slightly more intricate than in the first half and more intricate again in B, with unaccompanied elaborations in triplet semiquavers and demisemiquavers and increased athleticism (bars 38, 40, 51–52, 62–53).

---

[15] See, for example, MBA, vol. 2, pp. 290, 303, vol. 3, p. 104; LMF, pp. 487 (22 February 1778), 496 (25/26 February 1778), 563 (9 July 1778), 722 (11 April 1781).

[16] MBA, vol. 2, pp. 41–42; LMF, pp. 301, 302 (9 October 1777).

[17] For both quotations see MBA, vol. 2, p. 137; LMF, p. 384 (22 November 1777). Strokes in Mozart's autograph scores either denote short light articulation, accents with heavier articulation, or a phrase ending where an earlier articulation is counteracted; the performer must decide which is appropriate when considering the moment in its musical context. See Cliff Eisen, 'Performance Practice' in Eisen and Keefe (eds.), *The Cambridge Mozart Encyclopedia*, p. 395. For useful, broad-ranging discussion of dots and strokes in the late eighteenth and nineteenth centuries see Brown, *Classical and Romantic Performing Practice*, pp. 200–227.

[18] Throughout this study I use 'brilliant' and 'brilliance' to denote technically virtuosic writing, not as a marker of quality.

Example 1.1 Mozart, Rondo in C for violin and orchestra, K. 373, bars 45–49.

The demisemiquavers in bars 47–48 (Example 1.1) bring together, for the movement thus far, the registral peak (g''') and the moments of most pronounced brilliance and most extended unaccompanied playing; violin turn figures in the run-up to the A' rondo return (again unaccompanied) then provide a highpoint of ornamental intricacy. While the C section is more an opportunity for expressive than for brilliant playing, with gentle melodic elaborations on the repeat, the final A'' brings the virtuosic climax of the piece (Example 1.2): the soloist traverses three octaves in demisemiquavers, from its bottom note g to g''', is agile and athletic in the approach to the cadence, and receives only its second bar-long trill. Brunetti, then, was given every opportunity modestly to shine in technical and expressive ways.

As well as facilitating a skilled performance by his soloist, Mozart writes for the orchestra in ways that promote compositional prowess. Participation in A, comprising accompanimental string support and full-orchestra thematic statements, is broadened in B to include wind phrase links, wind-only sustained-note support, and strings and wind semiquaver segments that generate solo violin semiquavers (bars 65–73). The role of the orchestra is expanded further in the C-minor passage in section C (bars 124ff.), featuring a new pizzicato effect and the most sustained passage of orchestral-solo dialogue witnessed hitherto (bars 131–139). In the final A'', the passage yielding the soloist's virtuosic climax is also significant for the orchestra: after progressively prominent participation, the wind and strings engage for the first time in dialogue exclusively with each other (see Example 1.2, bars 165–168).

Example 1.2 Mozart, Rondo in C for violin and orchestra, K. 373, bars 164–171.

Example 1.3 Mozart, Rondo in C for violin and orchestra, K. 373, bars 175–182.

Given increasingly rich roles assumed independently and interactively by the soloist and the orchestra over the course of the piece, Mozart's ending is a fittingly expressive and virtuosic *tour de force* (Example 1.3). He writes the first strings-winds-violin three-way dialogue, reflecting the importance orchestral writing has acquired; he expands wind timbral support for the soloist (when unsupported by strings) to quaver chords right at the end; and he reserves the soloist's highest note of the piece until the very end (c''''), a gesture of exquisite virtuosity that Brunetti would have had an opportunity to exploit in order to encourage audience approbation. The effect of this concluding passage resonates with the spirit of the piece as a whole by simultaneously capturing modest virtuosity, increased orchestral prominence, and wind timbral support. Assuming Brunetti played well, performer and composer would have had every chance to unite solo panache and orchestral elegance and concision in pursuit of artistic success.

Mozart's other orchestral work for 8 April was a concert aria for the castrato Francesco Ceccarelli, who had been employed at the Salzburg court since 1777. Although the aria is traditionally thought to be K. 374 to a text from Giovanni de Gamerra's *Sismano nel Mogol*, 'A questo seno deh vieni – Or che il cielo', it is not impossible that K. 374 was composed in early 1781 for Josepha Duschek instead and that Ceccarelli performed another work at the Archbishop's concert.[19] In spite of initial reservations about Ceccarelli's voice, Leopold warmed to him over time. So too did Mozart, who enjoyed his company. Ceccarelli was popular in Vienna in 1781: he sang for Count Pálffy and twice for Prince Galitzin in March and returned to the city late in the year, performing at court on 21 December.[20] Mozart told Leopold that Ceccarelli was 'not so well known as I am' in Vienna, but later admitted that the castrato had made more money than he had in the spring.[21] As a concertizer, Ceccarelli was perhaps of a similar entrepreneurial mindset to Mozart; he would want to share a concert, Mozart explained, once in Vienna again in late 1781.[22] If Michael Haydn's Perseus is a guide, a role created for Ceccarelli in *Andromeda und Perseus* (1787), the versatile singer could be called upon to perform dramatic music with agility and brilliance ('Tod, ja war deine Losung', 'Beglucken die Menschen') and suave, expansive lyricism ('Du hast mir, o König').

Mozart simultaneously focuses attention on the soloist's performance and on orchestral timbres at the climax of K. 374, as at the corresponding moment of the Rondo K. 373. The extension of vocal closing gestures in the exit passage is conventional. But its eighteen bars of continuous singing gave Ceccarelli – assuming K. 374 was indeed written for him and performed on 8 April – ample opportunity to demonstrate that his breath did not 'give out' like Vincenzo Dal Prato's (the *Idomeneo* castrato compared unfavourably to Ceccarelli by Mozart).[23] The aria ends for the soloist with a final, demisemiquaver flourish peaking on b-flat" for the only time and coinciding with a new effect in the winds, namely falling crotchets in thirds (Example 1.4). The winds have a limited role in the aria, but provide soothing sighs and sustained notes in the introduction and later thematic dialogue and sustained notes in support of the soloist. A new wind link (two oboes, two horns) in bars 162–163 also heralds the extended exit

---

[19] See Ian Woodfield's careful argument, which leaves open the possibility of either Ceccarelli or Duschek as the original recipient of K. 374, in *Performing Operas for Mozart: Impresarios, Singers and Troupes* (Cambridge: Cambridge University Press, 2012), pp. 136–147.

[20] MBA, vol. 3, pp. 94, 98, 188; LMF, pp. 714 (17 March 1781), 717 (24 March 1781), 790 (22 December 1781).

[21] MBA, vol. 3, p. 102, 155; LMF, p. 721 (4 April 1781), 763 (5 September 1781).

[22] MBA, vol. 3, p. 177; LMF, p. 780 (24 November 1781). Mozart goes on to explain that he would not entertain such an arrangement, but that he and Ceccarelli could perform at each other's concerts.

[23] MBA, vol. 3, p. 13; LMF, p. 660 (8 November 1780).

Example 1.4 Mozart, 'A questo seno deh vieni – Or che il cielo a me te rende', K. 374, bars 177–182 (original version).

passage; the corresponding junctures in A and A' are greeted only by silence and a held vocal note (bars 52–53, 105–106). Double sustained notes in oboes and horns (bars 173–175), heard for the first time since the aria's instrumental introduction, add to the wind timbre at an important formal juncture and also prepare for the return to introductory material after the vocal exit. Thus, Mozart's modest orchestral effects at the climax of the aria, drawing attention to compositional attributes, simultaneously support the star performer's special opportunity to prove his (or possibly her) mettle.

Mozart revised and extended the final bars of the vocal exit, originally 177–180, for a later performance (see Example 1.5), marking a large cross 'X' on the autograph score to link to the new eight-bar passage written on a separate page.[24] He asked Leopold to return Ceccarelli's aria to him on 5 September 1781, repeating the request on 12 April 1783, and duly acknowledged receipt of it a few weeks later from Franz Wenzel Gilowsky, a Salzburg

[24] For the autograph of the Aria K. 374 see Staatsbibliothek zu Berlin, Mus. ms. autogr. W. A. Mozart 374. A set of orchestral performing parts were included in material Constanze Mozart sold to the publisher Johann André in 1800; they contain no annotations by Mozart. He may have used these parts for a performance in the 1780s. See Edge, 'Mozart's Viennese Copyists', pp. 641, 1140, 1281.

Example 1.5 Mozart, 'A questo seno deh vieni – Or che il cielo a me te rende', K. 374, variant to replace bars 177–180.

friend visiting Vienna.[25] Whether a performance of K. 374 subsequently took place in Vienna is uncertain, although opportunities presented themselves at Ceccarelli's academy on 10 March 1782 and Duschek's Viennese appearances in spring 1786.[26] The aria was certainly heard at Duschek's academy in Leipzig on 22 April 1788, where the text is given on the concert programme, and possibly also at Mozart's academy in Frankfurt on 15 October 1790, at which Ceccarelli participated.[27] A similarity between the variant and Donna Elvira's 'Mi tradì' may indicate temporal proximity to the Viennese *Don Giovanni* in 1788.[28] Come what may, the new segment – eight bars to replace the original four – provides more semiquaver brilliance for the singer than in the original as well as a one-bar fragment of oboe brilliance in imitation of the voice, the only occasion the oboe plays in this way. The new highpoint for both singer and winds thus serves the apparent needs of both soloist and composer, providing an additional opportunity for the singer to display 'grace and . . . perfect method' and admirable 'passages, ornaments and trills' and for Mozart further to demonstrate the 'beautiful' qualities of his piece.[29]

On 3 March 1782, eleven months after the Colloredo concert, Mozart staged his first public academy, possibly at the Burgtheater. On 23 January 1782 he was irritated that a mooted extension to the theatre season could jeopardize his event scheduled for the third Sunday in Lent, although the extension did not ultimately come to pass.[30] Opportunities for academies were few and far between, once time restrictions and the demands of foreign musicians, prominent singers, and organizations such as the Tonkünstlergesellschaft were accommodated. Mozart needed fully to exploit his single academy, moreover, as finances were tight.[31] Still a relative newcomer to Vienna, he wisely sought counsel:

---

[25] See MBA, vol. 3, pp. 156, 264, 269; LMF, p. 764 (5 September 1781), 845 (12 April 1783), 849 (21 May 1783).

[26] Woodfield, *Performing Operas for Mozart*, pp. 146–147.

[27] See Woodfield, *Performing Operas for Mozart*, pp. 139–140 (for a reproduction of the concert programme) and MDL, p. 330; MDB, pp. 375 (for Ceccarelli's contribution to Mozart's Frankfurt academy).

[28] Woodfield, *Performing Operas for Mozart*, pp. 144–146.

[29] In the words of Count Ludwig von Bentheim-Steinfurt in his report of Mozart's 'scena and rondeau' (assumed to be K. 374) performed in Frankfurt on 15 October 1790. See MDL, pp. 329–330; MDB, p. 375.

[30] MBA, vol. 3, pp. 193–194; LMF, p. 794 (23 January 1782). Any residual doubt that Mozart's academy actually took place (see Dexter Edge, 'Review Article: Mary Sue Morrow, *Concert Life in Haydn's Vienna: Aspects of a Developing Musical and Social Institution*', *Haydn Yearbook* 17 [1992], pp. 108–166, at 143) is put to rest by its listing in the *Indice de' teatrali spettacoli*; see Woodfield, *Performing Operas for Mozart*, p. 146.

[31] For general information on Burgtheater academies see Link, *National Court Theatre*, pp. 17–22.

Countess Thun, Adamberger and other good friends advise me to extract the best things from my Munich opera [*Idomeneo*] and then perform them in the theatre; and [play] nothing other than one concerto and improvise at the end. I had also already thought of this [. . .][32]

The advice was sensible: *Idomeneo*, a success in Munich one year earlier, would serve as a useful advertisement for operatic skills soon to be demonstrated in *Die Entführung*; keyboard improvisation was Mozart's virtuosic stock and trade; and a piano concerto would situate Mozart the performer-composer of orchestral music centre stage, beginning to demonstrate (Mozart hoped) that 'my [specific] field is too popular for me not to be able to support myself [in Vienna]'.[33] Attempting to maximize success at this vital moment of public exposure in Vienna, Mozart shrewdly returned to a piano concerto that had served him well in the past, K. 175 in D (1773): he had previously taken it to Munich in 1774 and also played it in Mannheim in 1778, revising oboe and horn parts in 1777–1778.[34]

A revision of a much more substantial kind was carried out in spring 1782 when Mozart replaced the original finale with the Rondo in D, K. 382. K. 175/iii builds on established musical procedures from the first and second movements, *inter alia* increasing slightly the volume of colouristic wind writing, matching the grandeur and brilliance of the first movement, and adding drama to solo-orchestra interaction, including in an exchange between the bold, unison main theme and the solo quaver figurations in the transition. Mozart may have sensed that the finale did not adequately complement or contrast with the previous movements, even though he apparently did not think this way in the mid- to late 1770s. Or perhaps he felt that K. 175/iii showed its age more than the earlier movements: he never again wrote a sonata-form finale for a piano concerto; and the contrapuntal writing could have reminded him too strongly of earlier contrapuntal contemplations from 1773 (including the fugal finales to the string quartets K. 168 and K. 173) rather than studies conceivably now in progress with Baron van Swieten.[35] But it is reasonable to suppose that promoting himself effectively as a performer-composer

[32] MBA, vol. 3, p. 194; LMF, p. 794 (23 January 1782).

[33] MBA, vol. 3, p. 124–125; LMF, p. 739 (2 June 1781).

[34] See Klaus Hortschansky, 'Autographe Stimmen zu Mozarts Klavierkonzerten KV 175 im Archiv André zu Offenbach', *Mozart-Jahrbuch 1989–90*, pp. 37–54 and Cliff Eisen, 'The Mozarts' Salzburg Copyists: Aspects of Attribution, Chronology, Text, Style and Performance Practice', in Eisen (ed.), *Mozart Studies* (Oxford: Oxford University Press, 1991), pp. 253–307.

[35] Mozart first refers to the weekly Sunday afternoon sessions with Baron van Swieten on 10 April 1782, but does not say when they started.

trumped other considerations and therefore directly influenced his decision to write a replacement movement. Ultimately, K. 382's stylistic appropriateness as a conclusion to K. 175 relative to the original finale[36] would have mattered less to Mozart than that the new movement scored an unambiguous hit with the Viennese.

Mozart pulled out all the stops in an attempt to make K. 382 as appealing as possible. For a start he drew on a popular vocal theme with which his audiences were probably familiar, later known as 'Fleuve du Tage'.[37] Explicitly promoting the brilliant and expressive sides of his virtuoso persona, he wrote a piece notable for both simplicity and complexity, thereby attending to uninformed listeners and cognoscenti alike. The theme, simplicity personified with in-built repetition and a tonic-dominant fixation, reappears in unadulterated form in bars 33ff. and 73ff.; several variations depart only slightly from the theme as well. But the expressive and formal implications and functions of several variations are less straightforward and would have challenged educated listeners. Variation 5 (bars 97–120) could be heard more as a thematic return than as a variation: it follows the *minore*, no. 4, and confines elaborative activities to trills in the piano. It could also be experienced as a conclusion to the first, Allegretto section of the movement, ending with a pause and preceding an Adagio (variation 6). The 3/8 Allegro, a third section, again plays with expectations of return and conclusion: the elements of return (bars 137–152, 185–200) book-end figuratively rich iterations of the first and second halves of the theme, and precede a still clearer return at the Tempo primo in bar 218; and the new Allegro tempo, perhaps expected as a last decisive act, ultimately gives way to the original Allegretto grazioso.

In certain respects K. 382 is a concerto within a concerto; three different tempi (plus a return to the Allegretto to end), coinciding with changes in affect and character, suggest an independently performable work as well as a finale for K. 175. Indeed, the Viennese music dealer Lorenz Lausch offered K. 382 for sale by itself in April 1785.[38] Criticism of it as 'a shamelessly popular display piece', 'tiresome', and 'a series of insipid variations' of 'distressing banality'[39] may derive from insufficient sensitivity to

---

[36] This has been debated in the scholarly literature. For preferences for the original finale, see Einstein, *Mozart*, p. 305 and Cuthbert Girdlestone, *Mozart and His Piano Concertos* (London: Cassell, 1948; reprint New York: Dover, 1964), pp. 81, 127–128.

[37] See Manfred Hermann Schmid, 'Variation oder Rondo? Zu Mozarts Wiener Finale KV 382 des Klavierkonzerts KV 175', in *Mozart Studien*, 2 (1992), pp. 59–80.

[38] MDL, p. 214; MDB, p. 242.

[39] Joseph Kerman, 'Mozart's Piano Concertos and Their Audience', in James M. Morris (ed.), *On Mozart* (Cambridge: Cambridge University Press, 1994), p. 166; Heartz, *Mozart, Haydn,*

biographical issues and undue attention to purportedly superficial stylistic qualities. It was the first piece for piano and orchestra by one of Europe's most distinguished pianists at his first public concert in the 'land of the clavier'. But success, a *sine qua non* for Mozart, was not of course guaranteed. K. 382 is best understood biographically and musically as a blueprint for Mozart's Viennese piano concertos: situating his combined talents as performer and composer at the heart of the audience experience, Mozart targeted connoisseurs and amateurs alike. In the process, moreover, he took minimal musical risks, demonstrating the kind of astute thinking that would be essential to a productive freelance career. He used accessible thematic material and wrote in a form (variations) close to the world of improvisatory performance in which he had already received considerable acclaim.[40] A concerto of proven popularity (K. 175), a new, popularly orientated finale, and a link to the safe haven of keyboard improvisation provided every chance of success. And, sure enough, K. 382 was a triumph, as Mozart reported to his father three weeks after the concert: 'I am sending you . . . *the last rondo* which I wrote for my concerto in D major and which is making such a big noise in Vienna. Please guard it like a *jewel* – and not give it to anyone to play, not even to Marchand and his sister [who were living with, and receiving tuition from, Leopold]. I wrote it *specially* for myself – and no-one else but my dear sister may play it.'[41] Mozart had immediately recognized the special cachet of combining virtuoso piano performance with virtuoso composition.

Keyboard Music

Between the Colloredo concerts in April 1781 and the academy on 2 March 1782, Mozart's major new keyboard work in addition to the accompanied sonatas (discussed below) was the sonata for two pianos in D, K. 448. It was written for Mozart and his student Josepha Auernhammer to perform together at a private concert at the Auernhammer residence on

---

Early Beethoven, pp. 44, 94; Girdlestone, *Mozart and His Piano Concertos*, pp. 81, 127. Elaine Sisman, a rare proponent of K. 382, argues similarly to me that 'perhaps our traditional modes of understanding and valuation have not been fully adequate to deal with this piece, and have taken insufficient account of its design'. See Sisman, *Haydn and the Classical Variation* (Cambridge, MA: Harvard University Press, 1993), p. 40.

[40] On relationships between Mozart variation sets and improvisation, see Katalin Komlós, '"Ich praeludirte und spielte Variazionen": Mozart the Fortepianist', in R. Larry Todd and Peter Williams (eds.), *Perspectives on Mozart Performance* (Cambridge: Cambridge University Press, 1991), pp. 27–54.

[41] MBA, vol. 3, p. 199; LMF, p. 798 (23 March 1782).

23 November 1781. Mozart disliked Josepha's physical appearance and even more her infatuation with him, but was positive about her practical skills: she 'plays delightfully; she only lacks the true delicate singing style in Cantabile [playing]. She clips everything.'[42] In early summer 1781 Mozart went to the Auernhammer's 'almost daily after lunch';[43] her tutelage was an important source of income in his early months in Vienna. He also liked Josepha's father, Johann Michael, whose death he related solemnly and sympathetically to Leopold in March 1782.[44] Reports on Josepha's playing in the two decades after Mozart's death were mixed, but almost always acknowledged her distinguished status in Vienna. Johann Ferdinand Ritter von Schönfeld (1796) explained that 'She has . . . become a great pianist, has taste and feeling, and it is now up to her to make her art truly distinguished'; Joseph Rohrer (1804) identified her as one of the finest living composers of piano music, alongside the likes of Beethoven, Ferrari, Förster and Vanhal; and Ernst Ludwig Gerber drew attention to her dexterity (*Fertigkeit*) and artistic knowledge (*Kunstkenntnisse*).[45] The Leipzig-based *Zeitung für die elegante Welt* and *Allgemeine musikalische Zeitung* were not enamoured with her playing, citing a lack of power, certainty, precision, expression and clarity, but remarked upon her skill at overcoming technical difficulties (at least at the Burgtheater in 1799).[46]

While Mozart had given four-hand keyboard performances with sister Nannerl before moving to Vienna, the Sonata K. 448 represented a unique compositional and performance venture for him at this stage of his career: he wrote a piece to play exclusively with a student at a concert sponsored by her family. The participation of Mozart and Auernhammer together – the concerto for two pianos K. 365 (1779) also featured on the programme –

---

[42] MBA, vol. 3, p. 135; LMF, p. 748 (27 June 1781); see also MBA, vol. 3, pp. 150–152; LMF, pp. 759–761 (22 August 1781).

[43] MBA, vol. 3, p. 135; LMF, p. 748 (27 June 1781).

[44] MBA, vol. 3, pp. 151, 199; LMF, pp. 760 (22 August 1781), 798 (23 March 1782).

[45] Schönfeld, 'A Yearbook of the Music of Vienna and Prague, 1796', trans. Kathrine Talbot in Sisman (ed.), *Haydn and His World*, pp. 289–320, at 294 (a partial translation of Schönfeld, *Jahrbuch der Tonkunst von Wien und Prag*); Rohrer, *Bemerkungen auf einer Reise von der Türkischen Gränze über die Bukowina durch Ost und Westgalizien Schlesien und Mähren nach Wien* (Vienna, 1804), p. 286; Gerber, *Neues historisch-biographisches Lexicon der Tonkünstler* (Leipzig, 1812–1814), 4 vols., vol. 1, col. 449.

[46] See *Zeitung für die elegante Welt*, 3 (1803), p. 363; *Allgemeine musikalische Zeitung*, 1 (1798–1799), cols. 523–524, 6 (1803–1804), col. 472, 7 (1804–1805), col. 469. See also Morrow, *Concert Life in Haydn's Vienna*, pp. 209–210, 216. For more on Auernhammer, including her family background, see Michael Lorenz, 'New and Old Documents Concerning Mozart's Pupils Barbara Ployer and Josepha Auernhammer', *Eighteenth-Century Music*, 3/2 (2006), pp. 311–322, at 319–322.

was no doubt the crucial ingredient in the evening's entertainment, for Auernhammer herself and also her parents. Mozart's relationship with Auernhammer, the masterful pianist instructing the gifted pupil, was thus on show to the audience. On 24 November Mozart recounted to his father the presence of Countess Thun (whom Mozart had invited), Baron van Swieten, Baron Godenus, Baron Karl Abraham Wetzlar von Plankenstern, Count Firmian, and Herr von Daubrawaick and his son.[47] The invitation to Countess Thun was shrewd business on Mozart's part, probably with two related aims: as a friend and patron she would again experience his talents first hand; as a musician lauded by Charles Burney for possessing 'as great skill . . . as any person of distinction I ever knew', she would also witness firsthand the accomplishments of someone under Mozart's tutelage performing with him, perhaps planting an idea for future musical activities of her own.[48]

Since Mozart's musical relationship with Auernhammer was the *raison d'être* for the Sonata K. 448 and for the November concert, it is reasonable to suppose that composer, performers and audience would have paid special attention to the interaction between the two players in the work itself. K. 448 is to all intents and purposes a sonata of equals; the parts are similarly taxing. J. A. P. Schulz, a late-eighteenth-century aesthetician, acknowledged that a composer of a sonata 'might want to depict a passionate conversation between similar or complementary characters'.[49] And K. 448 contains energetic dialogue between the two pianists, especially in the outer movements where it supports *concertante*-like exchanges of brilliant material. But the variety of interaction, including dialogue, is often most noticeable of all. In the development section of the first movement, for example, Mozart progresses swiftly through a series of events: a *p* – *f* exchange of a descending theme; an *ff* statement from both players together supporting a shift to the minor (d); dialogue and elaboration of the descending material again, now marked *dolce* (implying a 'dynamic intensity greater than

---

[47] MBA, vol. 3, p. 176; LMF, pp. 779–780 (24 November 1781).

[48] Charles Burney, *The Present State of Music in Germany, the Netherlands and United Provinces* (1775) (New York: Broude, 1969), p. 221. Countess Thun had soirées at her home where music making was common; see Peter Clive, *Mozart and His Circle: A Biographical Dictionary* (New Haven: Yale University Press, 1993), pp. 156–157.

[49] Johann Georg Sulzer (ed.), *Allgemeine Theorie der schöne Künste* (Leipzig, 1771–1774); translation from Nancy Kovaleff Baker and Thomas Christensen (eds.), *Aesthetics and the Art of Musical Composition in the German Enlightenment: Selected Writings of Johann Georg Sulzer and Heinrich Christoph Koch* (Cambridge: Cambridge University Press, 1995), p. 103. Heinrich Christoph Koch later cited Mozart's as well as Haydn's sonatas as 'new' representatives of Schulz's aesthetic. See Koch, *Musikalisches Lexikon* (Frankfurt, 1802), col. 1417.

Example 1.6 Mozart, Sonata in D for two pianos, K. 448/i, bars 102–106.

piano');[50] and finally the *coup de grace* of a single melodic line – which grows from the preceding elaboration – split between the two pianists (bars 103[4]–105, Example 1.6). Interaction is dynamic and changeable, in a word dramatic, as between piano and orchestra in Mozart's later Viennese piano concertos.[51] Needless to say, the melodic line in bars 103[4]–105 does not have to be split between the players in order for the music to move smoothly to the A7 harmony (bar 106) that prepares for the recapitulation a few bars later. But the equal relationship and dynamic interaction between the players in effect makes it desirable. Elsewhere, too, exchanges are so quick that material would sit perhaps more comfortably with a single player (for example the semiquaver passages in the finale, bars 100–116, 293–303); for Mozart the aural and visual effect of hearing and seeing antiphonal playing supersedes

[50] See Robert D. Levin's definition of *dolce* in 'The Devil's in the Details: Neglected Aspects of Mozart's Piano Concertos', in Neal Zaslaw (ed.), *Mozart's Piano Concertos: Text, Context, Interpretation* (Ann Arbor, MI: University of Michigan Press, 1996), p. 34.

[51] See Keefe, *Mozart's Piano Concertos*.

other considerations.[52] Here and there attention would have turned to Mozart's interaction with Auernhammer when other aspects of the music were downplayed: the relative lack of harmonic movement in passages from the slow-movement exposition (bars 13–20, 29–32) shifts eyes and ears to the exchange and elaboration of material between the two players. Even when thematic events take an unexpected, ostentatious turn in the slow-movement reprise – the codetta theme from the exposition is replaced by *sf* accents, a grand gesture and diminished harmony – Mozart includes a poignant exchange of melody and accompaniment immediately afterwards that captures the spirit of the movement as a whole (see Example 1.7). Throughout the sonata, then, the interactive musical relationship between Mozart and Auernhammer, bold, subtle and dramatic in turn, surely would have been prominent in the musical consciousness of the original listeners.

Exchanges between pianists in K. 448, watched as well as heard by the first audience for mutually reinforcing biographical and musical reasons, provided a special illustration of Mozart and Auernhammer's collaboration. Auernhammer's parents no doubt took pride in seeing and hearing their daughter play alongside Mozart (on the first keyboard part as well)[53] in a work written for her and the performer-composer to convey shared expressive and brilliant virtuosity. When in December 1777 Rosa Cannabich played the piano sonata that Mozart had written for her, probably K. 309, several of those present (including Mozart) were moved to tears by the confluence of biographical circumstance, musical association and serious rendition.[54] (Mozart's departure from Mannheim, and from his close friends, was by then inevitable as he had been unable to secure a post with the Elector.) The success of the K. 448 performance – communicated to Leopold – probably related partially at least to a confluence and reinforcement of events and music. Mozart performed the sonata with another talented student, Barbara Ployer, on 13 June 1784 in a similar context – a concert featuring several of Mozart's works

---

[52] On at least one occasion in Mozart's youth the combined aural and visual impact of a four-hand keyboard performance was equally essential. Nannerl recalls Mozart sitting on the stool with J. C. Bach in London (1765) and performing an 'entire sonata', which only those watching would have been able to tell was played by two musicians rather than one. See MDL, p. 400; MDB, p. 456. On the visual dimension in a 'performance-orientated reading' of Chopin's Mazurka in B minor Op. 33 no. 4, see Lawrence Kramer, *Interpreting Music* (Berkeley, CA: University of California Press, 2011), pp. 264–270. For a study promoting the 'experience of Liszt in performance [being] as much about watching as about listening … [returning] repeatedly to the visual dimension of his virtuosity', see Dana Gooley, *The Virtuoso Liszt* (Cambridge: Cambridge University Press, 2004), quotation at p. 11.

[53] MBA, vol. 3, p. 190; LMF, p. 791 (9 January 1782).

[54] MBA, vol. 2, p. 178; LMF, pp. 413–414 (10 December 1777).

Example 1.7 Mozart, Sonata in D for two pianos, K. 448/ii, bars 106–113.

sponsored by the student's father to promote his daughter at his own residence (in Döbling, a few miles north of Vienna). Explaining that he would take Paisiello 'to let him hear my compositions and my pupil',[55]

---

[55] MBA, vol. 3, p. 318; LMF p. 880 (9 June 1784).

Mozart would have recognized the added value of showing off both simultaneously in K. 448.

A collaborative keyboard endeavour gave way to a competitive one on 24 December 1781 when Mozart and Clementi had an informal duel at court in the presence of Emperor Joseph II. It came at another troubled time in the relationship between Mozart and his father. He had revealed to Leopold his love for Constanze on 15 December, emphasizing his high moral standards and her moral virtues, only vehemently to have to defend himself and his future wife seven days later against gossip spread by the composer Peter Winter. What is more, Mozart now had to explain to his father the marriage contract into which he had entered at the insistence of Constanze's guardian, Johann von Thorwart, undertaking to marry her within three years or else pay her 300 gulden annually thereafter. The writing of this long letter begun on 22 December lasted at least until 26 December: towards the end Mozart first mentioned Emperor Joseph's high praise for his playing at the duel and the much-needed 50 ducats the emperor had gifted him.[56] Three weeks later (16 January 1782) a more detailed account of events was forthcoming: Clementi went first, improvising and then performing a sonata; Mozart subsequently improvised, and played variations; movements of Paisiello sonatas were then split between the two of them; finally, both men improvised on a Paisiello theme from the sonatas.[57] The contest clearly made an impression on Emperor Joseph; he was still talking about it (to Zinzendorf) almost a year later.[58]

The duel tested Mozart's keyboard skills and simultaneous performance and composition (through improvisation), areas in which he was well equipped to prosper. No further information is forthcoming on how exactly Mozart carried out his tasks on this occasion, but light is perhaps shed on his activities as a solo performer-composer in keyboard variations from early in the Viennese decade.[59] These variations exist for Mozart at the nexus of performance and composition, many sets beginning life as improvised performances and (in published form) building on his high

---

[56] MBA, vol. 3, pp. 184–188; LMF, pp. 787–790 (22 December 1781).

[57] MBA, vol. 3, pp. 192–193; LMF, p. 793 (16 January 1782).   [58] MDL, p. 184; MDB, p. 207.

[59] Exact dates have yet to be determined for several of Mozart's early Viennese sets of keyboard variations, including K. 353 ('La Belle Françoise'), K. 352 ('Dieu d'amour'), K. 264 ('Lison dormait'), and K. 265 ('Ah, vous dirai-je, maman'), although K. 265 is now thought to come from 1781–1782, based on autograph studies by Alan Tyson and Wolfgang Plath. See Rupert Ridgewell, 'Mozart's Publishing Plans with Artaria in 1787: New Archival Evidence', *Music & Letters*, 83 (2002), p. 53.

stock as a keyboard player.[60] For example, the ebb and flow of 'Ah, vous dirai-je, Maman', K. 265, maybe one of three sets Mozart wrote for his student Countess Rumbeke, no doubt partially mirrors his own spontaneous improvisations, embellishments and ornamentations, modelling in the musical text – at least to the extent Mozart would have considered possible in a publication intended for amateur players – his creativity as a performer-composer:[61] running semiquavers and triplet figures are passed from right to left hand from variation to variation (nos. 1–2, 3–4), the former being picked up later in the piece as well; exchanges between right and left hands in no. 5 resurface in modest imitative activity in nos. 8 and 9; and energetic figuration, including protracted semiquavers simultaneously in right and left hands for the first time and a 12-bar flourish after the variation proper, bring K. 265 to a rousing close after a relatively subdued series of variations (nos. 8, 9, and 11 comprising the *minore*, a simple near-reprise of the theme, and an Adagio).

A few months after the duel with Clementi, Mozart wrote the Prelude and Fugue in C, K. 394 (April 1782). Sending it to Nannerl, Mozart explained Constanze's role in its genesis. She had regularly heard him play fugues 'off the top of [his] head' (*aus dem Kopf*) and did not rest until he had written one down for her.[62] The K. 394 fugue, like the incomplete suite for keyboard, K. 399 (1782), is also associated with Mozart's contemplation of Bachian and Handelian practices nurtured by Baron van Swieten.[63] K. 394 contains standard fugal procedures from the *Well-Tempered Clavier* including stretto, a pedal point towards the end, and an entry in augmentation, as well as less obviously Bachian features such as imbalance between numbers of fugal entries in outer and inner parts and absence of goal directedness.[64] Similarly, K. 399 is marked both by adherence to Handelian keyboard-suite traditions and by exploration of key changes and chromaticism that reveal Mozart's own stylistic

[60] On origins in improvised performances, see Komlós, 'Mozart the Fortepianist', p. 40.

[61] For ornamentation in Mozart's keyboard publications reflecting a 'stylized version … of his own performance', see also Brown, *Classical and Romantic Performing Practice*, p. 400 (citing the Sonata K. 332 in F and the Rondo in A minor, K. 511). On K. 265 as one of three sets for Rumbeke, see Ridgewell, 'Mozart's Publishing Plans with Artaria', p. 53.

[62] MBA, vol. 3, pp. 202–203; LMF, p. 801 (20 April 1782).

[63] The encounter with van Swieten in Vienna may not represent the 'Bach epiphany' usually described in biographies, as Mozart had been exposed to the music of the Bach family in Salzburg. See Viktor Yün-Liang Töpelmann, 'The Mozart Family and *Empfindsamkeit*: Enlightenment and Sensibility in Salzburg 1750–1790' (PhD thesis, King's College London, 2016), pp. 18–19, 249–266. For a useful biographical sketch of van Swieten and an account of his musical interests and activities see Jones, *Music in Vienna*, pp. 83–86.

[64] See Küster, *Mozart: A Musical Biography*, pp. 136–137.

fingerprint.[65] K. 394, at least, has not generally been well received by twentieth- and twenty-first-century writers, who criticize its uncertain, opaque and meandering qualities.[66]

The prelude preceding the fugue is Mozart's earliest fantasia-like piece passed down to us from the Viennese years. Standard fantasia features such as rhythmic and structural freedom, strangeness of effect, and figuration[67] contribute to a sense of improvisation, thereby accentuating links between performance and composition. The prelude followed the fugue in the work's genesis: Mozart devised it (*ausdenken*) while writing down the fugue that he had already composed (*die Fuge schon gemacht*),[68] testifying to the workings of a remarkable musical mind able simultaneously to juggle different musical activities. Did the unusual genesis have an effect on the finished (that is, written) prelude? The fugue's quick-fire imitation infiltrates the beginning of the Adagio (Example 1.8): right-hand to left-hand imitation at a crotchet's distance at bar 3 redistributes the weight of the original downbeat rather than replicating the original effect. The increase in musical activity at bar 3 compared to bar 1 also foreshadows a more intense increase at the onset of the Andante a few bars later (Example 1.8). The diminished harmony heard at both the climax of the contrapuntal portion of the fugue and the onset of the concluding, homophonic Adagio (see bar $66^{1\text{-}2}$) looms large in a prelude that also alternates the fugue's Andante and Adagio tempi: it appears in a descending arpeggio with strokes (bar 6 in Example 1.8, in effect generating the ascending arpeggio with strokes at the opening of the Andante) and in a similarly articulated brilliant sequence (bars 15–18); and it dominates the Più Adagio, including the free-floating demisemiquavers of the cadenza-like passage. Capturing the improvisatory dreaminess of the fantasia, diminished harmony also nurtures a link between prelude and fugue.

The intended destination for K. 394 was a private one, like the motivation for composing it. Once he had had chance to write five more fugues,

[65] Abert, *W. A. Mozart*, p. 843; and John Irving, 'Shorter Piano Pieces', in Eisen and Keefe (eds.), *Cambridge Mozart Encyclopedia*, p. 458. K. 399 contains an Ouverture (Grave – Allegro), an Allemande, and a Courante, but only six bars of a Sarabande, and no Gigue.

[66] See, for example, Abert, *W. A. Mozart*, pp. 836–837; Einstein, *Mozart*, p. 259; Arthur Hutchings, 'The Keyboard Music', in H. C. Robbins Landon and Donald Mitchell (eds.), *The Mozart Companion* (New York: Norton, 1956), p. 59; Leonard Ratner, *Classic Music: Expression, Form, and Style* (New York: Schirmer, 1980), p. 264; Heartz, *Mozart, Haydn and Early Beethoven*, pp. 63–64. Einstein is also critical of the fugal writing in K. 399; see *Mozart*, p. 164.

[67] Ratner, *Classic Music*, p. 308.

[68] MBA, vol. 3, pp. 202–203; LMF, pp. 800–801 (20 April 1782).

Example 1.8 Mozart, Prelude (Fantasia) and Fugue in C, K. 394, bars 1–9.

Mozart explained to Nannerl, he would present them to Baron van Swieten to add to van Swieten's small, high-quality collection. 'Because of that', he continued, 'I ask you to keep your promise, and not let anyone see it'.[69] Since Mozart made a similar request to Leopold about the Rondo K. 382 less than one month earlier (see above), we can reasonably infer a similar desire to exploit the prelude and fugue as its performer-composer. Had he completed his self-appointed task and written other pieces, Mozart no doubt would have played K. 394 for van Swieten at a Sunday event. In committing to paper a prelude and a fugue normally existing only in unnotated improvisation, he would illuminate the continuity between performance and composition in writing and deed. Mozart realistically could have expected his mutually reinforcing text and act as performer-composer to confirm K. 394's place in van Swieten's pantheon.

Since fantasias 'enjoy the option of giving the impression that they are free of all deliberation',[70] keyboardists playing them from notated texts fulfil especially creative roles in the performance process. Much is at stake in the sum of endless small interpretative decisions that need to be taken, for example, in the Fantasia K. 397 (which perhaps dates from 1782). While

---

[69] MBA, vol. 3, p. 203; LMF, p. 801 (20 April 1782).

[70] Mark Evan Bonds, *Wordless Rhetoric: Musical Form and the Metaphor of the Oration* (Cambridge, MA: Harvard University Press, 1991), pp. 114–118, at 117.

Mozart did not publish it during his lifetime and, indeed, left it unfinished, the act of notating it on paper obviously implies an intention for someone to perform from the musical text. Would Mozart (or another contemporary keyboard player) have smoothed out contrasts between adjacent sections, or accentuated contrasts, or done both at different times? The legato in the opening Andante subsides in the final bars, perhaps to prepare for the ensuing non-legato Adagio (just as the neighbour notes in bar 10 prepare thematically for the Adagio). With its own 'changes of mood', the sensibility-style Adagio invites 'subtle variations of tempo' at the performer's behest.[71] The return to the Adagio (bar 29) is both expected and unexpected: harmonically prepared, following previous iterations of A minor in bars 26 and 27, it is nonetheless preceded by a surprising bar's rest with accompanying pause. The beginnings of the brilliant prestos grow directly from the ends of the Adagios (see the a" – c"' – b" in bars 33 and 34, and the registral preparation for bar 44 in bar 43), but frame an uneven transition to the Adagio's chordal segment at bar 35. In Mozart's hands, would the short cadenza-like Presto segment (bar 44) in the middle of the Tempo primo have supported cadential confirmation of D minor (bar 45), or evidenced either or both a reconciliation of contrasting material and an affirmation of the importance of contrast? Was the D-major Allegretto, a segment criticized as 'rather incongruous' and 'celestially childlike … far too short really to complete the work',[72] a product of the reconciliation of contrasting segments, or a continuation of striking contrasts?

Such fundamental interpretative questions lie at the heart of the Fantasia K. 397 as well as the Prelude K. 394: they need to be addressed by all performers, with Mozart providing no direct answers.[73] Self-evidently, Mozart would not have required interpretative clues on the scores for his own performances. By writing the pieces down, and moving slightly towards composition on the performance-composition continuum (at least relative to the position occupied by unwritten improvisations), Mozart perhaps risked K. 394 falling into the wrong hands, as he acknowledged. But the written works offer genuine opportunities for later

---

[71] Ratner, *Classic Music*, p. 22.

[72] Komlos, 'Mozart the Fortepianist', p. 47; Einstein, *Mozart*, p. 259.

[73] These questions probably would have remained unanswered even had the K. 394 (prelude) and K. 397 autographs not been lost. It is thought that the last 10 bars of K. 397 in the Bureau d'Arts et d'Industrie edition (Vienna, 1804) used for the NMA are by A. E. Muller. Neal Zaslaw has suggested that either the last page of the original score was lost, or an improvised cadenza expected for the end of the piece. See Solomon, *Mozart: A Life*, p. 561, footnote 1.

performers. Encouraging proactive interpretation, Mozart invites his player to move towards a creative role that inhabits 'composition' as well as performance.[74]

Wind Serenades

Mozart left a detailed description of the genesis (and initial performances) of the Wind Serenade in E-flat K. 375 in October 1781:

> At twelve o'clock I drove to Baroness Waldstädten at Leopoldstadt, where I spent my name-day [31 October]. At eleven o'clock at night I got [a performance of] a serenade [*Nachtmusik*] with two clarinets, two horns and two bassoons – and in fact of my own composition. I wrote this music for St. Theresa's Day [15 October] – for Frau von Hickel's sister, or the sister-in-law of Herr von Hickel, Court Painter, where it was performed [*producirt*] for the first time. The six men who executed it are poor devils who nevertheless play quite nicely together, in particular the first clarinet and the two horns. But the main reason I wrote it was in order to let Herr von Strack, who comes there daily, hear something from me. And because of that I also wrote it rather carefully [*vernünftig*]. It has won applause from everyone as well. It was played in three different places on St. Theresa's Night. For as soon as they were finished with it somewhere, they were led off somewhere else and paid for it.[75]

Johann Kilian Strack was Joseph II's chamberlain and a keen musician who frequently organized chamber music performances with the emperor; Mozart continued to cultivate Strack's friendship in 1782 on account of his perceived influence.[76] Joseph favoured the wind timbre, forming a *Harmonie* in spring 1782 that comprised Burgtheater musicians Georg Triebensee, Johann Nepomuk Went (oboes), Anton Stadler, Johann Stadler (clarinets), Jakob Eisen, Martin Rupp (horns), Wenzel Kauzner and Ignaz Drobney (bassoons).[77] Whether Mozart initially envisaged

---

[74] This resonates with Robert D. Levin's view: ' If modern performers tried to adopt the posture of performer *as composer*, Mozart's music would be played more profoundly, more expressively and above all more spontaneously – for spontaneity is an essential element of his art.' See Levin, 'Improvisation and Embellishment in Mozart's Piano Concertos', *Musical Newsletter* 5/2 (1975), pp. 3–14, at p. 3. Levin repeats this statement in 'Mozart's Working Methods in the Keyboard Concertos', in Sean Gallagher and Thomas Forrest Kelly (eds.), *The Century of Bach and Mozart: Perspectives on Historiography, Composition, Theory and Performance in Honor of Christoph Wolff* (Cambridge, MA: Harvard University Press [Isham Library Papers 7], 2008), pp. 379–406, at p. 406.

[75] MBA, vol. 3, pp. 171–172; LMF, p. 776 (3 November 1781).

[76] MBA, vol. 3, pp. 194, 201; LMF, p. 794 (23 January 1782), 799 (10 April 1782).

[77] For detailed information on the Imperial *Harmoniemusik*, including its formation and the salaries of its members, see Link, *National Court Theatre*, p. 209 (footnote 15).

a court performance of the E-flat serenade is unknown, but his revision of 1782 for an octet with two oboes implies the prospect at least of such a performance. At any rate, Joseph preferred opera arrangements, most of which were carried out by the oboist Went, to new *Harmonie* compositions. Mozart was sensitive to the possibilities and demands of transcribing operas for *Harmonie*, explaining that he had hastily to complete an arrangement of *Die Entführung* in July 1782 or else be beaten to the task, and the profits, by someone else: 'You cannot believe how difficult it is to arrange something like that for Harmonie – so that it is suitable for wind instruments and yet in the process does not lose any of the effect.'[78]

Mozart's appeal to a self-evident connoisseur (Strack) by writing 'carefully' therefore would have involved exploiting the ensemble's distinctive timbres and textures.[79] While detailed aesthetic consideration of wind effects was not widespread in the late eighteenth century, the earliest relevant treatises, all of which were French, could have become familiar to Mozart during his six-month stay in Paris in 1778.[80] Indeed, the 'Paris' Symphony K. 297 (1778), the first Mozart had scored for a full contingent of double woodwind plus horns, trumpets and timpani, displays the kind of nuanced effects described by Valentin Roesner, Jean-Laurent de Béthizy, Louis Joseph Francoeur and others, as well as the more popular effects mentioned in his letters.[81]

The exposition of the first movement of K. 375 amounts to a mini manifesto of wind timbres and sounds judged in relation to late-eighteenth-century aesthetics. Francoeur's 'agreeable and harmonious effect that results from a chord of two clarinets, two horns, and often two bassoons' no doubt reflects the popularity of this instrument combination in late-eighteenth-century France;[82] and Ancelet (1757) lauded

---

[78] MBA, vol. 3, p. 212; LMF, p. 808 (20 July 1782). For further discussion, and identification of Went as the probable competitor for transcribing the opera, see Roger Hellyer, 'The Transcriptions for *Harmonie* of *Die Entführung aus dem Serail*', *Proceedings of the Royal Musical Association*, 102 (1975–1976), pp. 53–66.

[79] 'Vernünftig' could also be translated as 'neatly' or 'sensibly' (see Landon, *Mozart: The Golden Years*, p. 75), although 'carefully' seems the most appropriate translation when read in context.

[80] Three treatises were published in the decade and a half before his trip: Valentin Roesner, *Essai d'instruction à l'usage de ceux qui composent pour la clarinette et cor* (Paris, 1764); Jean-Laurent de Béthizy, *Exposition de la théorie et de la pratique de la musique* (Paris, 1764); Louis Joseph Francoeur, *Diapason général de tous les instrumens à vent avec des observations sur chacun d'eux* (Paris, 1772).

[81] See Keefe, 'The Aesthetics of Wind Writing in Mozart's "Paris" Symphony'.

[82] See Francoeur, *Diapason général*, p. 35 ('On connoit assez l'effet agréable et harmonieux qui résulte de l'accord de deux Clarinettes, deux Cors, et souvent deux Bassons'). The popularity of private French wind bands comprising clarinets, horns and bassoons is cited in Steven Zohn, 'The Overture-Suite, Concerto Grosso, Ripieno Concerto and *Harmoniemusik* in the

Example 1.9 Mozart, Wind Serenade in E-flat, K. 375/i (1781), bars 1–6.

the combination of horns and clarinets, the latter having 'on our hearts and on our ears rights which were unknown to us [in France]'.[83] In the first five bars (Example 1.9) Mozart exploits the clarinets-horns-bassoons sextet effect, carefully notating dynamics on each of the five staves in the autograph score.[84] With no melodic content or change of chord, the elongated and harmonious timbre occupies our attention: the *sf*, *sfp* and *fp* dynamic indications in the first six beats require nuanced delivery.[85] (Although not necessarily related to the dynamics performed, Mozart mentioned being surprised at Leopoldstadt 'in the most pleasant way with the first chord in E-flat'.[86]) The return of the sound at formal junctures (the beginnings of the development, recapitulation and coda) is aesthetically as well as structurally significant, reminding us of the full sextet's warmth; dynamic annotations in the autograph are again precise.[87] After the opening bars, Mozart explores sounds and effects commended by contemporary commentators. Praised by Béthizy, as well as by the *Musikalischer Almanach* in 1782, the graceful, tender timbre of

Eighteenth Century', in Simon P. Keefe (ed.), *The Cambridge History of Eighteenth-Century Music* (Cambridge: Cambridge University Press, 2009), p. 571.

[83] As given in Albert R. Rice, *The Baroque Clarinet* (Oxford: Oxford University Press, 1992), p. 133.

[84] For the autograph score, see Staatsbibliothek zu Berlin Mus. ms. autogr. W. A. Mozart 375.

[85] Mozart's 16-bar fragment for two oboes, clarinets, bassoons and horns, K. Anh. 96 (1781–1783) also contains a conspicuous array of *fp*, *sf* and *sfp* dynamics. For a facsimile, see NMA, X/30/4, p. 73.

[86] MBA, vol. 3, p. 172; LMF, p. 776 (3 November 1781).

[87] Mozart does not notate the beginning of the recapitulation of the first movement in the autograph score, including a 'Da capo 35 Täckt' indication instead.

the bassoon especially in its high register is evident throughout the first-theme section in interplay with the clarinets (bars 6–24).[88] Sustained notes, again recommended for wind instruments,[89] appear frequently, for example as accompaniment to the B-flat minor theme (see bars 48–53) and as a poignant accessory to the changing harmonies of the second theme (bars 54–57). Each instrument 'shines in turn' in the words of French critic Jean-François de Chastellux on concerto-like wind involvement in German symphonies (1765),[90] including in the horn statement in bars 26–31 and the *concertante* exchanges of semiquaver material between clarinets and bassoons after the second theme. The horns show both sides of the musical personality identified for them by Nicolas Etienne Framery (1791): loud playing associated with the hunt in the thematic statement from the transition (bars 26–31); and mellifluous playing, briefly, in the run-up to the reconfirmation of B-flat in the secondary theme (bars 63–67).[91] Both are also explored later. The new horn theme in the recapitulation (bars 151–159) takes a lead from the hint of warm horn melody in the exposition, while a later cadential gesture marks a return to the world of the hunt (bars 193–194); a lyrical horn phrase link in the first minuet and trio (bar 16) foreshadows the gentle thematic prominence of both horns together in the trio; the horn promotes tender melodic content in the third-movement Adagio, presenting thematic material in first- and second-theme sections and in the lead-in to the recapitulation; and the hunting character returns in the second minuet and trio.

When Mozart revised K. 375 in 1782 as an octet with two oboes to match the instrumentation of the emperor's *Harmonie*, he continued to promote sounds and effects that resonated with musical connoisseurs. In the hands of leading practitioners like Triebensee and Went the 'distinctive *empfindsam* gentleness of character and tone' of the classical oboe would have supported the splitting of thematic materials with the clarinets, as well as adding colour to the sustained notes and doublings of

---

[88] Béthizy, *Exposition de la théorie et de la pratique de la musique*, p. 306; *Musikalischer Almanach auf das Jahr 1782* (Alethinopel, 1782), pp. 93–94.

[89] See Béthizy, *Exposition de la théorie et de la pratique de la musique*, p. 306; Francoeur, *Diapason général*, p. 22; Augustus Frederick Christopher Kollmann, *An Essay on Practical Musical Composition* (London, 1799), p. 18.

[90] Given in Neal Zaslaw, *Mozart's Symphonies: Context, Performance Practice, Reception* (Oxford: Clarendon, 1989), p. 157.

[91] Framery, 'Cor', in Framery and Pierre-Louis Ginguené (eds.), *Encyclopédie méthodique: musique* (Paris, 1791; reprint New York: Da Capo, 1971), vol. 1, p. 379.

Example 1.10 Mozart, Wind Serenade in E-flat, K. 375/i (revised 1782), bars 39–48.

other instruments.[92] Mozart invariably introduces clarinet-oboe dialogue in first-movement passages in which the two clarinets exchanged material in the original version. Such dialogue often follows passages in which Mozart preserves intact the original clarinets-horns-bassoons scoring (see bars 39ff. [Example 1.10], 54ff. and – with the exception of bars 71–72 – 67ff.). Not surprisingly, Mozart wanted simultaneously to exploit virtues of the original scoring and possibilities for further textural and timbral diversity.

Like its counterpart in the E-flat serenade, the first movement of the Wind Serenade in C minor, K. 388 (1782) foregrounds changing wind

---

[92] Quote from Bruce Haynes, 'Mozart and the Classical Oboe', *Early Music*, 20 (1992), p. 58.

timbres and textures, in this case promoting musical contrasts. *Forte* and *piano* (for example) do not signify absolute dynamic levels in the performance of Mozart's works, nor do they necessarily denote sharp differentiation between adjacent passages.[93] In the near-contemporary wind Adagio in B-flat, K. 411 (probably 1782–1783), for example, *forte* and *piano* require nuances rather than stark contrasts: refined dynamic gradations thus work in tandem with the understated ebb and flow of imitative and homophonic textures.[94] But events at the opening of the C-minor serenade – a strident unison gesture followed by an *empfindsam piano*, with sigh figures in the oboes (Example 1.11) – demand dynamic contrast from performers.[95] The same applies to the *forte* onset of the transition (bar 22) after the conclusion of the first-theme section and to the *forte* / *piano* oscillations a few bars later. Mozart intensifies contrasts in the development section: in bars 106–108 (Example 1.12), an octave b-flat'' – b-flat', ending *p* after a *sfp*, is followed by a bar's rest for the whole ensemble and a *forte* diminished seventh chord; and in bar 115 a *Sturm und Drang* passage beginning in G minor and proceeding sequentially, immediately follows a lightly scored homophonic *piano* segment (Example 1.12). The *Sturm und Drang* subsides to a *piano* dynamic at the end of the development (bar 128) – a *piano* perhaps best reached gradually not suddenly on this occasion – and is followed by a bar's rest that sets up the onset of the main theme at the beginning of the recapitulation as another moment of dynamic contrast.[96] The lead-in to the secondary theme, where the end of

---

[93] The execution of dynamics in Mozart's piano works is discussed at length in Eva and Paul Badura-Skoda, *Interpreting Mozart: The Performance of His Piano Pieces and Other Compositions* (2nd edition, New York and London: Routledge, 2008), pp. 43–69. On gradual rather than sudden changes between *piano* and *forte* passages at certain junctures see Wolfgang Amadeus Mozart, *Violin Sonatas*, ed. Cliff Eisen (London: Peters, 2003), p. iv and Mozart, *Konzert für Klavier und Orchester ('Jeunehomme') Es-dur KV 271*, ed. Eisen and Robert D. Levin (Wiesbaden: Breitkopf, 2001), 'Preface'.

[94] On the dating of K. 411 to 1782–83 based on the paper type of the autograph, see Alan Tyson, *Mozart: Studies of the Autograph Scores* (Harvard, MA: Harvard University Press, 1987), p. 145. Roger Hellyer has suggested that K. 411, and the short Adagio in B-flat for two basset-horns and bassoon, K. 410, could have been written for processional (possibly Masonic) purposes. See Hellyer, 'Wind Music', in Eisen and Keefe (eds.), *Cambridge Mozart Encyclopedia*, p. 536. K. 410 may also date from 1782–1783; see Tyson, *Studies of the Autograph Scores*, p. 277.

[95] No *forte* is written in the autograph at the opening of the serenade; the NMA (vii/17/2) includes an editorial *forte* marking. For the autograph see Staatsbibliothek zu Berlin – Preußischer Kulturbesitz, Musikabteilung mit Mendelssohn-Archiv, Signatur Mus. ms. autogr. W. A. Mozart 388.

[96] As in the first movement of the wind serenade K. 375, Mozart does not notate the beginning of the recapitulation in the autograph, on this occasion writing 'Da capo 24 Täckt'.

Example 1.11 Mozart, Wind Serenade in C minor, K. 388/i, bars 1–8.

a *forte* phrase is echoed as a *piano* link to the new material, marks a more nuanced contrast (see bars 38–42); the expansion of the passage in the recapitulation (bars 169–177), rather than fulfilling a harmonic or tonal function, reveals subtler collaborative interaction between the instruments than elsewhere in the movement, providing a refined effect to complement the powerful effects of the development.

While dynamic contrasts have a less noticeable impact in later movements of K. 388, the changes of timbre with which they are associated continue to focus the listening experience. In the Andante's transition, for example, Mozart builds towards the full-wind texture of the bucolic, popularly orientated second theme through two-instrument then three-instrument sonorities. Similarly, the development and recapitulation both begin with full-wind statements and explore smaller instrumental groupings in between. The articulation of a full-wind timbre plays a structural and aesthetic role in the theme and variations finale: variations 1 and 4 promote sonorous full-wind textures after smaller groups had ruled the roost in the theme and then the second and third variations; and variation 8, another scored for full wind, enacts the movement's decisive modal shift (C minor to C major), also representing a climax to the three preceding variations that build towards – and offer glimpses of – full-wind textures.

Example 1.12 Mozart, Wind Serenade in C minor, K. 388/i, bars 103–116.

Whether or not Mozart deliberately '[cocked] a snoop at convention' in K. 375 and K. 388 '[conveying] a mood of dramatic intensity totally alien to the informal background music normally associated with the serenade type',[97] he

[97] Roger Hellyer, 'Wind Music', in Eisen and Keefe (eds.), *Cambridge Mozart Encyclopedia*, p. 535.

focused on timbral contrasts and complementarities elicited by a wind band, thus exploiting the textural qualities of this serenade sub-genre.[98] By providing an array of effects, engaging with popular and aesthetically valued sonorities in restrained and powerful ways, Mozart pitched his works pragmatically at both connoisseurs and general listeners.

Accompanied Sonatas

The story of Mozart's six accompanied sonatas, four of which were composed in 1781, occupies much of his first year in Vienna. He performed one new sonata, K. 379 in G, with Brunetti at the 8 April concert at the Colloredo residence, wrote K. 376 in F, K. 377 in F and K. 380 in E-flat in summer 1781, and published all four with Artaria, alongside K. 296 in C (1778) and K. 378 in B-flat (1779–80), as his 'Op. 2' (November 1781).[99] He hoped that the sonatas would bring financial rewards, referring repeatedly to their engraving and publication in the spring and summer.[100] They were duly advertised in the *Wiener Zeitung* on 4 December 1781 as 'six sonatas for the clavier with accompaniment for a violin',[101] the conventional description for sonatas scored for keyboard and violin.

On 4 April 1783, the sonatas were reviewed very favourably in Cramer's *Magazin der Musik*:

These sonatas are quite unique. Rich in new ideas and traces of their author's great musical genius. Very brilliant and suited to the instrument. At the same time the violin accompaniment is so craftily combined with the clavier part that both instruments will constantly remain prominent; so that these sonatas demand as accomplished a violinist as clavier player. But it is not possible to give a full description of

---

98 Similarly, Mozart responded to the two clarinets and three basset-horns for K. 411 (1782–1783) – a more homogeneous, less varied sound than that of the wind serenades – by writing a less texturally adventurous work.

99 Mozart's recent 'Op. 1' (as well as 'Op. 1' from his childhood, K. 6–7) was also a set of accompanied sonatas: K. 301–306, published in Paris (1778) and dedicated to Elizabeth Auguste, Electress of the Pfalz. On the K. 301–306 Op. 1 designation '[proclaiming] Mozart's arrival as a serious composer', see Peter Walls, 'Opus 1, take 2: Mozart's Mannheim and Paris Sonatas for Keyboard and Violin', in Martin Harlow (ed.), *Mozart's Chamber Music with Keyboard* (Cambridge: Cambridge University Press, 2012), pp. 45–68.

100 See MBA, vol. 3, pp. 118, 120, 138, 141–142, 177; LMF, pp. 734 (19 May 1781), 736 (26 May 1781), 741 (4 July 1781), 753–754 (25 July 1781), 780 (24 November 1781).

101 MDL, p. 175; MDB, p. 198. By 1785 they were on sale in Paris with Boyer; MDL, p. 223; MDB, p. 254. Publication soon followed in Amsterdam (1790) and London (1790); see NMA, viii/23/1–2, Kritischer Bericht, p. 72.

this original work. Amateurs and connoisseurs must play them through themselves, and then they will find out that we have exaggerated nothing.[102]

A similarly minded review also appeared fifteen months later in the *Magazin der Musik* (9 July 1784):

Mozart's sonatas with obbligato violin please me very much. They are very difficult to play. Although the melodies are not entirely new, the accompaniment for the violin is masterly; it is well-fitted to the harmony and frequently introduces imitations at the proper times. The sonatas must be heard often.[103]

The 1783 reviewer brought comprehension of stylistic qualities of the sonatas – brilliance, instrumental interaction, rich ideas – into the realm of performance, stating that musicians of all abilities would fully appreciate them only by playing them. (One year later the recognized difficulty of the works perhaps encouraged the reviewer to suggest that they were 'heard often' rather than played often.) Understanding Mozart's sonatas involved understanding them in performance: text and act were mutually reinforcing, then, for purchaser and player. And Mozart's own situation mirrored this critical position. With one eye on playing the works himself and the other on writing them for others, he would have actively negotiated performance and compositional priorities and concerns. For one sonata, K. 379, the relationship came into especially sharp relief, as he performed it for the first time before it was fully written down. Mozart explained to Leopold that it was 'composed yesterday night [7 April 1781] between eleven and twelve – but in order to finish it, I wrote out only the accompaniment part for Brunetti and remembered my own part'.[104] The autograph at least partially supports Mozart's assertion: he notated only a violin line for the fifth variation and coda of the finale in the main portion of the autograph, subsequently appending a page with the requisite keyboard material; and he wrote bits of the first two movements very quickly, including notational abbreviations.[105] The often cramped notation and dark ink for the piano, in contrast to the more spaciously notated lighter ink for the violin, also suggests pen put to paper at a later stage for the piano part than for the violin.

Mozart's sonatas as represented by the finished autographs and first edition capture in a variety of ways his interests in the issues and opportunities associated with performing the works and the decisions to be taken by

---

[102] MDL, p. 190; MDB, p. 214.   [103] As given in Cliff Eisen's translation in NMD, pp. 97–98.

[104] MBA, vol. 3, p. 102; LMF, p. 722 (8 April 1781).

[105] See Robert Riggs, 'Mozart's Sonata for Piano and Violin, K. 379: Perspectives on the "One-Hour" Sonata', *Mozart-Jahrbuch 1991*, pp. 708–715. The autograph is now located at the Library of Congress in Washington, DC (ML30.8b.M8 K.379).

players. The opening 16 bars of K. 377/i, true to the spirit of the *Magazin der Musik* review, come alive in performance, even though on paper they represent a straightforward exchange of the main theme from piano to violin (Example 1.13). The violin is rigidly motor-like in its repeated-note accompanimental triplets at the beginning – a quality conveyed to a lesser or greater degree in performance but invariably apparent at an Allegro tempo. Light keyboard writing, including no left-hand contribution in bar 2, also exposes the violin triplets. But the repeat of the theme from bar 9, where melody and accompaniment change instruments, opens like a flower. Visually and technically, the violinist will probably be – or appear to be – more at ease with the theme than with the repeated-note triplets; the piano right-hand arpeggiated triplets certainly provide a smoother accompaniment than the violin's earlier material. The piano left hand also fills in its earlier octaves with full chords, including a warm vi6 harmonization in bar 10 for the previously unharmonized bar 2. This is a passage not only to be played and heard, Mozart tells us, but also actively interpreted. We can accentuate, even play down if so inclined, the differences between the dialogued phrases by varying the tautness, breadth, dynamic levels and warmth of our renditions. But we need to take a musical stand of some kind. For the continuity and contrast inherent in the initial 16-bar statement – consistent triplets in the accompaniment to different effect in the first and second halves – surfaces in articulation later in the movement as well. The octave leap passed between the piano left hand and the violin in the transition features strokes on the low notes in the violin, but not the piano; and strokes on violin crotchets in the final bar of the transition (36) appear neither in the piano left-hand crotchets nor in the right-hand quaver triplets that had received them in preceding bars.[106] The original contrast in accompaniment across dialogued phrases at the opening does not reappear at the beginning of the recapitulation. Instead, Mozart places the longest single slur in the movement (violin, bars 84–85, Example 1.14) against strokes in the piano right hand and an unarticulated left hand in imitation of the right, thus reimagining the original diversity and contrast of articulation. In short, Mozart's differentiation of articulation among the violin and the piano right and left hands in K. 377/i necessitates an engaged interpretation to address *inter alia* the coexistent smooth rhythmic exterior, comprising quaver triplets from beginning to end, and less smoothly articulated interior.

Performers of the K. 377 finale have equally important decisions to make in communicating with their audiences. Comprising a minuet

---

[106] See the autograph of K. 377 housed at the British Library (Zweig MS 53).

Example 1.13 Mozart, Sonata for piano and violin in F, K. 377/i, bars 1–16.

Example 1.14 Mozart, Sonata for piano and violin in F, K. 377/i, bars 83–87.

and, in effect, two trios – without the traditional minuet repeat between trios – the finale juxtaposes nobleness (minuet) and demonstrative brilliance (trios). Mozart leaves it to the imagination of his players to determine the degree to which this basic contrast is conveyed. The pianist will need to decide, for example, whether to accentuate the onset of brilliance dynamically and gesturally at the beginning of trio 1 in bar 48^2 (Example 1.15) thus reinforcing the contrast between minuet and trio, or to treat the notated embellishments in the final bars of the minuet – plus any others they choose to add – as a foreshadowing of things to come, thus lessening the contrast.[107] How one interprets the significance (or otherwise) of the transition back to the minuet, which starts with thick chords in the piano and violin together (bars 101–104) and could perhaps denote a return to the more overtly collaborative environment of the minuet after the piano-dominated trios, will also affect how the passage is played. The same applies to the imitative dialogues in the last 29 bars, after little exchange of this kind in the movement.[108] If they are regarded as evidence of participatory parity between violin and piano, perhaps the violinist will be encouraged to introduce semiquaver embellishments to the dotted minims in bars 165–168 to match the semiquavers in the piano?

Elsewhere in his set, Mozart at times presents acts of performance as 'seamlessly co-extensive' with compositional features of his works – exploiting decorative variation, improvisatory qualities, and dynamics and articulation

---

[107] Dynamics included in the first edition but not in the autograph may strengthen the case for contrast. (Whether Mozart himself was responsible for communicating these markings to Artaria is not known.) The first-edition f at bar 48^3 to coincide with the onset of the pianistic brilliance for the first trio moves away from the prevailing p dynamic level, but does not necessarily presume an accentuated dynamic contrast. The transition back to the minuet after the second trio also provides *rinf* markings for the violin in the first edition (bars 101, 103) and f and p indications for the piano (bars 100^3 and 104^3).

[108] The final 29 bars follow 46 un-notated bars in Mozart's autograph, which are covered by his annotation 'Thema da capo 46 täckt'.

Example 1.15 Mozart, Sonata for piano and violin in F, K. 377/iii, bars 41–52 (with dynamics from Artaria first edition in bold italics).

that 'by virtue of their auxiliary relation to the notes themselves, could be considered part of the *performer's* domain' – and at other times as 'something separate from the act of composition' whereby 'performers re-create music in such a way as to communicate a composer's concepts as faithfully as possible, regardless of whether the composer is physically present or not'.[109] K. 379/i opens in declamatory, improvisatory style (Example 1.16), thus suggestive of the former scenario: after the spread chords and ornaments of bars 1–4, the piano takes its ornamentation further in the second phrase (especially bar 7). The violin continues the process of elaboration (see bar 10 in relation to bar 2), subsequently melting into bar 12 alongside the piano at the reconfirmation of the tonic, G. The demisemiquavers in the piano in bar 12 are foreshadowed, as rhythmic diminutions, in the elaborations of bar 7; the move from thematically ornate to thematically straightforward material at a cadence point (bars 10–12) is also prefigured in bars 7–8. But bar 12 is experienced as a moment of change as well as a moment of arrival: the declamatory and improvisatory cede precedence to the 'regularity' of a melody and accompaniment texture. In effect, Mozart moves from an opening in which performance and composition are seamlessly joined to

---

[109] See Mary Hunter's distinctions along these lines between Haydn's Op. 71/74 string quartets and his London piano trios: 'Haydn's London Piano Trios and His Salomon String Quartets', pp. 103–130; quotations at pp. 110, 118–119, 125.

Example 1.16 Mozart, Sonata for piano and violin in G, K. 379/i, bars 1–13.

a continuation where the performers are apparently required to engage more in re-creative than 'compositionally' creative acts. And he reverses the process at the end of the movement (bar 45, Example 1.17).[110] The piano accelerates towards the confirmation of V/G with the movement's only hemidemisemiquavers (bar 44), whereupon the violin re-enters after a seven-bar absence on its melodic highpoint of the movement (d''') to coincide with the sudden end of the piano's quick notes. The violin thus builds on previous decelerations at cadential junctures (bars 7–8, 28–31) in a gesture of dramatic declamation.

---

[110] K. 379/i is best understood as a sonata-form movement lacking a recapitulation. The V/G chord in the final bar (with a pause) suggests a return to G for the recapitulation; instead, Mozart moves directly on to an Allegro movement in G minor. I follow the *Neue Mozart-Ausgabe* in continuing the bar numbers from the Adagio into the Allegro.

Example 1.17 Mozart, Sonata for piano and violin in G, K. 379/i, bars 44–49.

Example 1.18 Mozart, Sonata for piano and violin in G, K. 379/ii, bars 130–145.

The creative, performance-orientated activities of K. 379/i continue in the later movements. In addition to foregrounding ornamentation and grace notes in the main theme of the Allegro, Mozart gives interpretative latitude to performers in the recapitulation (see bars 136–145, Example 1.18, in comparison to the exposition's 67–73).[111] Mozart does not extend this secondary development passage for harmonic or tonal reasons: it ends in bar 145 on the same V/g harmony with which the main theme section of the exposition had come to a close (bar 73). He

---

[111] Viewed in late-eighteenth-century context, fermatas imply freedom in performance irrespective of whether embellishments are to be added and accepting that the sign itself has several different meanings. See Brown, *Classical and Romantic Performing Practice*, pp. 588–596; Badura-Skoda and Badura-Skoda, *Interpreting Mozart*, pp. 285–288.

encourages a relatively free rendition instead, introducing a lengthy ral-
lentando and pauses. The fifth variation of the finale casts a backward
glance to the opening of the first movement: it is marked 'Adagio' in
contrast with the prevailing 'Andantino'; and its second half is improvisatory in character. Like the beginning of the first movement, it also introduces a distinctive effect, namely the violin's only pizzicato in the entire
sonata.[112] As Mozart had not written down the piano part for the fifth
variation before the first performance, it is quite possible that the published
text of the variation was inspired by Mozart's memories of its first realization in a formal concert setting.

K. 380 in E-flat and K. 376 in F draw attention to fluid boundaries
between performance and composition, while putting piano and violin on
the kind of equal footing recognized in the *Magazin der Musik*. K. 380/i
begins with the piano in elaborative and decorative mode in the main
theme section (bars 1–12, Example 1.19): individual semiquaver figures are
twice repeated up an octave; bar 10 elaborates bar 8 with a semiquaver
scale; and bars 3–4 prolong the dominant with brilliant material, situating
unaccompanied piano virtuosity centre stage. By including only tonic and
dominant harmony as well – with the exception of subdominant in bar 6 –
Mozart offers little to distract from the piano's musings. If solo brilliance is
a point of interest in the first twelve bars then so, by implication, is the
limited role assigned to the violin, which is to change in the remainder of
the exposition and the development: the violin attains new thematic
autonomy through dialogue with the piano in the transition and especially
the initial presentation of the full second theme; it offers glimpses of
semiquaver brilliance towards the end of the exposition; and it operates
as the piano's bona fide equal in the development.[113] The second movement takes up where the first leaves off, continuing to promote the equal

---

[112] Mozart's near-contemporary twelve variations for keyboard and violin in G on 'La Bergère
Célimène', K. 359 (June 1781), follow a similar pattern. The penultimate variation, 'Adagio'
against the prevailing 'Allegretto', brings the violin's only pizzicato of the piece; the piano can
also render freely the pause, trill and unaccompanied bar towards the end. This Adagio, in
turn, recollects the freedom performers acquire in the two-bar Adagio, with pauses, in the
middle of variation 8. The variations for keyboard in F on 'Dieu d'amour' from Grétry's *Les
mariages samnites*, K. 352 (probably mid-1781), also include a penultimate variation at an
Adagio tempo.

[113] A similar process is evident in the accompanied sonata fragment, K. 372 (24 March 1781), for
which almost the complete exposition – 65 bars – survives in Mozart's hand. While the violin is
a relatively subdued participant in the first-theme section, it attains greater thematic and
virtuosic prominence in the transition and second theme. For the fragment in facsimile, which
was subsequently completed by Mozart and Constanze's friend and associate Maximilian
Stadler, see NMA, X/30/4, pp. 70–71.

Example 1.19 Mozart, Sonata for piano and violin in E-flat, K. 380/i, bars 1–12.

participation of violin and piano through the exchange of nearly all material. As in the first movement, unremarkable harmonies encourage players to highlight concomitant performance effects: four consecutive bars of V7/B-flat (15–18) in preparation for the confirmation of the secondary key area heighten contemplation of the new, rich repeated chords and the coordinated registral high and low points of the movement (FF – e-flat''', bar 17);[114] and repeated I-V-I chords in the development (bars 34–35, 40–41) direct attention to the piano and violin's precisely articulated and coordinated decorative motif. The rondo finale follows a similar trajectory to the first movement, highlighting piano brilliance as well as a progressively prominent violin. The repetition of the semiquaver

---

[114] FF is typically the lowest note on a 1780s fortepiano. On ranges of late-eighteenth-century fortepianos, see David Rowland, *Early Keyboard Instruments: A Practical Guide* (Cambridge: Cambridge University Press, 2001), pp. 36–39.

Example 1.20 Mozart, Sonata for piano and violin in F, K. 376/i, bars 1–18.

continuation to the main theme at the beginning (bars 17–24, 29–36) fulfils no thematic function, being designed instead to establish piano brilliance as a core component of the finale. The violin, not particularly active in the A section, rules the roost in the presentation of thematic material in the B section just as the piano dominates semiquaver brilliance. Section C balances thematic and brilliant writing more equally in the two instruments, culminating in fast and furious semiquavers simultaneously in piano and violin to mark the virtuosic climax of both movement and work.

A self-perpetuating process of thematic decoration lends an air of quasi-improvisation to K. 376/i (see Example 1.20): a phrase link in bar 6 leads to further decoration in bars 8–9, which in turn generates the semiquaver accompaniment from bar 10 onwards; the cadential extension in bar 14, elaborated in bar 15, is consolidated in the semiquaver rush to the half close in both piano and violin, bona fide brilliance thus emerging from a sequence of elaborations and embellishments; and additional elaborative activity in bars 23–27 leads to a short exchange in which the piano generates an ornamental turn from the violin's preceding quavers (bars 28–29). As in K. 380/i the violin begins the exposition as de facto subsidiary, with long notes heard as unambiguous accompaniment, and gradually becomes the piano's equal, participating in exchanges of both scalar semiquavers and the second theme (bars 30–43). Fittingly, in the final four bars of the exposition, the violin and piano have equal, if different, roles: the piano, in brilliant mode, presents its most demonstrative material of the section, while the violin is in charge of the thematic element of the cadence making.

Prominent writing for violin as well as piano, including the 'craftily combined' melodies and accompaniments mentioned in the *Magazin der Musik*, is characteristic of Mozart's entire sonata set. In addition to movements discussed above, the K. 376 Andante combines near-perpetual exchange of material between piano and violin, redolent of participatory parity, with intricately evolving accompaniment figurations. At the opening, for example (Example 1.21), piano melody and violin accompaniment exhibiting little similarities in bars 1–4 (turn-like figures, neighbour notes, and two beats together a tenth apart at the end) come together in bars 7–8^2. The piano's accompaniment to the ensuing violin statement (bar 9ff.) initially combines the violin's neighbour notes of bars 1–4 with the less conjunct accompaniment to bars 5–8, morphing into arpeggios in a new semiquaver triplet rhythm (bars 13–14). Seamless ebb and flow of melody and accompaniment is also a feature of the middle-movement theme and variations of K. 377. Ignaz Arnold captured the effect of these kinds of accompaniments in one of the earliest book-length critical studies of Mozart's music (1803): figures are exchanged so inconspicuously that a new one always seems a natural consequence of the preceding one; an instrumental accompaniment 'breathes every time the spirit of feeling that dominates the whole'; and melody and accompaniment are made 'into an inseparable and beautiful whole, so exactly interwoven that one cannot happily be imagined without the other'.[115]

---

[115] Arnold, *Mozarts Geist*, p. 191 ('Sie athmet jedesmal den Geist der Empfindung, der über das Ganze herrscht'); p. 188 ('Er machte Melodie und Begleitung zu einem unzertrennlichen schönen Ganzen, zu einer so genauen Verwebung, dass sich eines ohne das andere nicht wohl denken lässt').

Example 1.21 Mozart, Sonata for piano and violin in F, K. 376/ii, bars 1–8.

The two pre-Vienna works in the set, K. 296 in C and K. 378 in B-flat, as well as the aborted K. 372 sonata movement from Mozart's earliest days in Vienna, share the later sonatas' predilections for equal participation between piano and violin and for carefully crafted accompaniments.[116] On the whole, though, the earlier sonatas do not contain as pronounced continuities between composition and performance as the later Viennese ones. For example, there is little evidence in K. 296 and 378 of improvisatory and declamatory material (K. 379/i, K. 379/iii), of elaborations and decorations as important generators of musical discourse (K. 376/i and K. 380/i), and of different effects accruing either to exchanged melodies and accompaniments or to differently articulated materials (K. 377/i). Perhaps Mozart was particularly attentive to the composition – performance dynamic in the sonatas written in and for Vienna because the intertwining of his own needs as performer-composer and the perceived needs of players purchasing the edition could have had an impact on his early artistic and financial success as an independent musician. Attempting simultaneously to please himself, the Viennese public and other potential performers of the works would have been a fine balancing act, one captured in composition – performance continuities – including at the outset of each of the four new sonatas – and also implicit in the claim from the *Magazin der Musik* that the sonatas must be played in order to be fully appreciated.

---

[116] The first movement of K. 296 is an exception where participation is concerned, featuring for the most part a more prominent piano than violin part.

Hearing Mozart himself in action as the performer-composer of the sonatas retained its cachet, irrespective of internal negotiations provoked by circumstances of production. As Maximilian Stadler explained: 'Artaria brought the first print with him, Auernhammer played the F.P. [fortepiano] – Mozart accompanied on a second fortepiano that was nearby, instead of on the violin, and I was completely delighted by the playing of the master and the pupil and never again in my life heard it performed so incomparably.'[117]

*****

Within 15 months or so of arriving in Vienna, Mozart had experienced a wide range of activities related to instrumental music-making in the city: private concerts; public concerts; outdoor concerts; teaching; publishing; weekly soirées; and even a keyboard duel. Taking advice – including on the timing of subscriptions and the programme for his academy[118] – he made wise choices: performing the Piano Concerto K. 175 at his academy on account of earlier successes with it; inviting Countess Thun to the Auernhammer concert; and befriending Strack, including through his music. He was probably unlucky on occasion too, for example writing urbane, new wind serenades when Joseph II preferred opera arrangements for his *Harmonie*. The instrumental music from 1781 to 1782 reflects tactical astuteness: the Rondo K. 382 in its populist leanings and inner sophistication; the Sonata K. 448 in accommodating both the Auernhammers' desire to promote Josepha collaborating with her teacher and Mozart's own desire to exploit the added value of a master-pupil venture; the wind serenades in their diverse timbres, textures and themes in deference to both connoisseurs and amateurs; and accompanied sonatas in accommodating the expectations of their exceptional performer-composer as well as their less talented player-purchasers. Mozart's juggling of teaching, composition, publication and performance activities in 1781–1782 involved him adapting to the needs – or perceived needs, at least – of all interested parties. He no doubt hoped that musical ventures initiated for private reasons would ultimately lead to financial and artistic benefits in more public settings. (Impressing van Swieten in K. 394, for example, could never be an altruistic matter exclusively.) Private and public activities and orientations routinely overlapped in any case: in the Sonata K. 448, written for a private event but in ways suiting performances in larger venues (through stereophonic sound, virtuosity, thick textures); and in the wind serenade K. 375, written

---

[117] MDL, p. 465; MDB, p. 543.
[118] See MBA, vol. 3, pp. 141, 194; LMF, p. 753 (25 July 1781), 794 (23 Jan 1782).

for Hickel and to impress Strack, but performed repeatedly in a variety of venues for general audiences. Mozart's grumbling and obstinacy in spring 1781 may have shown him to be 'out of tune and touch with the realities of the Salzburg court',[119] but it quickly gave way to a pragmatic, practical attitude to producing music as an independent Viennese performer-composer.

It is misleadingly simplistic, then, to suggest that in his first eighteen months in Vienna Mozart 'seemed to be responding to compositional opportunities rather than creating them', perhaps 'not quite certain how to proceed'.[120] Ultimately, opportunities of various kinds at this early stage opened Mozart's mind to possibilities for future successes in Vienna achievable by exploiting situations simultaneously in different ways: as a performer and composer of works for himself; as a performer and composer of printed works for himself and others; and as a teacher drawing on the artistic and financial benefits of instructing students and also performing with them. Count Arco warned Mozart in their relatively civilized encounter in May 1781: 'Believe me, you let yourself be far too dazzled here [in Vienna]. A man's reputation here lasts a short time. At first, you are eulogized and make a great deal [of money] – but for how long? After a few months the Viennese again want something new.'[121] Mozart's combined willingness to move away from Vienna if necessary and to exploit his prodigious keyboard skills in the 'land of the clavier' would, he believed, help beat the odds.[122] More important, the breadth of his early Viennese musical experiences – across instrumental genres (not just those related to the keyboard) and among many different people – in effect maximized the potential for success and minimized the risks associated with his chosen career path.

It is noticeable, of course, that Mozart's sophisticated music produced in spring 1781 when severance from the Salzburg court was still in doubt (the Rondo K. 373, Aria K. 374, and Sonata K. 379) is not matched by a correspondingly nuanced attitude to personal circumstances and relationships. On two occasions, Mozart told Leopold that Leopold's strong objections to him remaining in Vienna were rendering him 'inactive' (*unthätig*) and of an insufficiently 'cheerful mind and calm disposition' for composition.[123] Even if such comments were designed to get Leopold off his back, it would be entirely reasonable for Mozart to have felt less

---

[119] Gutman, *Mozart*, p. 533.   [120] Solomon, *Mozart: A Life*, p. 287.
[121] MBA, vol. 3, p. 124; LMF, p. 739 (2 June 1781).   [122] Ibid.
[123] MBA, vol. 3, pp. 116, 127; LMF, p. 733 (16 May 1781), 742 (9 June 1781).

productive than normal in spring 1781 on account of the momentous personal upheaval he was experiencing (and irrespective of the ongoing disputes with Leopold that the upheaval had caused). Equally the arrogance, impatience and lack of realism during the same period and manifest in (for example) an assumption about a prominent place in the order of succession at court, a jibe about not performing in Linz on the projected trip to Salzburg on account of its small size, and a desire to return Count Arco's kick,[124] can be at least partially attributed to the stress under which Mozart was operating. In any case, by the turn of the year and into spring 1782 he had become decidedly more realistic, circumspect and strategically minded, in spite of inevitable anxieties brought about by tight finances. 'What use is a dreadful fuss – and quick luck?' he asked Leopold rhetorically in his letter of 22–26 December. 'It never lasts. *Chì và piano và sano* [Slowly but surely]. One must live within one's means.'[125] Mozart explained that the emperor was very complimentary about him at the duel with Clementi, but that he (Mozart) remained sanguine about the employment prospects at court, asking 'Who knows?'[126] Even when a position at court was strongly rumoured, he told Leopold simply that he had 'had no word'; he went to see Strack from time to time, but not too often to arouse suspicions of an ulterior motive, and talked only about music.[127] Leopold's famous complaint in a letter to Baroness Waldstätten that Mozart by nature was unable appropriately to balance patience and impatience no doubt still had some truth to it in August 1782.[128] But Mozart's careful, calculated thoughts and attitudes had also begun to bring his behavioural strategies into closer alignment with subtle strategies implicit in his music than had been the case in spring 1781. And this would bode well for the future.

---

[124] MBA, vol. 3, pp. 106, 107, 133–134; LMF, p. 724 (11 April 1781), 725 (18 April 1781), 746 (20 June 1781).

[125] MBA, vol. 3, p. 188; LMF, p. 790 (22 December 1781).

[126] MBA, vol. 3, p. 193; LMF, p. 793 (16 January 1782).

[127] MBA, vol. 3, p. 201; LMF, p. 799 (10 April 1782).

[128] MBA, vol. 3, pp. 222–223; LMF, pp. 815–816 (23 August 1782).

2 | Singers and Effects
Seeking Operatic Success in Die Entführung aus dem Serail

Mozart's steep learning curve in the instrumental music of 1781–1782 was paralleled in *Die Entführung aus dem Serail*. Occupying ten months, on and off, from 30 July 1781 to 30 May 1782, the genesis of *Die Entführung* is the longest of any of Mozart's Viennese operas.[1] The libretto was by Johann Gottlieb Stephanie, a distinguished playwright, actor and leading light at Joseph II's nascent (and short-lived) National Singspiel in Vienna. Stephanie adapted a text by Christoph Friedrich Bretzner, *Belmont und Constanze, oder Die Entführung aus dem Serail*, published in Leipzig in 1781 and set by Johann André for a premiere at the Döbbelin Theatre in Berlin on 25 May 1781. Mozart originally hoped that the opera would be staged in conjunction with a state visit to Vienna of the Grand Duke Paul Petrovich of Russia and his wife in mid-September 1781, but it was delayed initially by a postponement to the visit and then by a court decision to stage Gluck's *Iphigénie en Tauride* and *Alceste* instead. The hold-ups allowed *Die Entführung* to ferment in Mozart's musical and dramatic imagination for an extended period, leading to significantly more departures from Bretzner's plan in the second and third acts than in the first act (most of which was composed on the assumption of a tight compositional timeframe).[2]

Mozart documents the genesis of *Die Entführung* in letters to his father, and in considerable detail for the first act. On 1 August 1781 he explained

[1] These outer dates for the composition of *Die Entführung* derive from Mozart's correspondence. On the genesis of the work see Ulrich Konrad, 'Musicological Introduction', trans. J. Bradford Robinson, in W. A. Mozart, *'Die Entführung aus dem Serail', K. 384: Facsimile of the Autograph Score* (Los Altos, CA: The Packard Humanities Institute, 2008), vol. 2, pp. 12–19; Thomas Bauman, *W. A. Mozart: 'Die Entführung aus dem Serail'* (Cambridge: Cambridge University Press, 1987), pp. 12–26; and Daniel R. Melamed, 'Evidence on the Genesis of *Die Entführung aus dem Serail* from Mozart's Autograph Score', *Mozart-Jahrbuch 2003–2004*, pp. 25–42.

[2] For useful summaries of the similarities and differences between the musical items and plots of Bretzner's *Belmont und Constanze* and Stephanie's revisions for Mozart, see Bauman, *Die Entführung*, pp. 14–15, 36–61. On Blonde specifically in Bretzner/André and Stephanie/Mozart settings, see Berta Joncus, '"Ich bin eine Engländerin, zur Freyheit geboren": Blonde and the Enlightened Female in Mozart's *Die Entführung aus dem Serail*', *Opera Quarterly*, 26 (2010), pp. 552–587.

that Stephanie had found him a libretto; that the principal singers were in place, namely Johann Valentin Adamberger (Belmonte), Caterina Cavalieri (Konstanze), Johann Ernst Dauer (Pedrillo), Therese Teyber (Blonde) and Johann Ignaz Ludwig Fischer (Osmin); and that he had already written the first arias for Cavalieri and Adamberger and the concluding trio to Act 1.[3] A week later he had also composed Osmin's 'Solche hergelauf'ne Laffen', mentioning that Cavalieri, Adamberger and Fischer were all very happy with their arias, and by 22 August had completed the entire first act.[4] He reported the delay in the Russian state visit on 29 August and his happiness at having more time to write the work, and confirmed the performing personnel to include Dominik Jautz in the speaking role of Pascha Selim in mid- to late September. He then explained that major changes to Bretzner's libretto were in the offing as of 26 September ('and actually at my desire'), including alterations to the plot and a shifting of the ensemble at the beginning of Act 3 to the end of Act 2.[5] Mozart also reported the completion of two numbers from Act 2 on 26 September: the drinking duet for Osmin and Pedrillo, 'Vivat Bacchus', and an unidentified aria (probably Blonde's 'Durch Zärtlichkeit').[6] Frustrated at Stephanie's slow progress on the libretto on 6 October, but aware that his opera would still have been behind Gluck's *Iphigenie* and *Alceste* in the queue were it complete,[7] Mozart went quiet on *Die Entführung*, focussing instead on musical matters such as the performance of the wind serenade K. 375 at Baroness Waldstätten's, the concert with Josepha Auernhammer that included the Two-Keyboard Sonata K. 448 and the duel with Clementi at court (see Chapter 1). He reminded Leopold on 30 January 1782 that the requisite changes to the libretto and the staging of Gluck's operas had caused the delays in completion and production, and

---

[3] MBA, vol. 3, pp. 143–144; LMF, pp. 754–755. We subsequently learn that these three numbers were written in *particella* (voice(s), bass line and occasional instrumental additions) in one day, and completed in a further day and a half. See MBA, vol. 3, p. 165; LMF, p. 771 (9 October 1781). On the players in the Burgtheater orchestra between 1781 and 1784, including their yearly salaries, see Theodore Albrecht, 'The Soloists in "Martern aller Arten", Mozart's Sinfonia Concertante Movement for Flute, Oboe, Violin, Violoncello, and One-Eyed Soprano', *Mozart Society of America Newsletter*, 17/1 (January 2013), pp. 6–11.

[4] MBA, vol. 3, pp. 145, 152; LMF, pp. 756 (8 August 1781), 761 (22 August 1781).

[5] MBA, vol. 3, pp. 153, 161, 163; LMF, pp. 762 (29 August 1781), 768 (between 19 and 26 September 1781), 770 (26 September 1781).

[6] MBA, vol. 3, p. 163; LMF, p. 770 (26 September 1781). Both Melamed and Konrad identify 'Durch Zärtlichkeit' as the second-act aria written by 26 September 1781, based on the paper's watermark in the autograph score. See Melamed, 'Evidence on the Genesis of *Die Entführung*', p. 29; Konrad, 'Musicological Introduction', p. 16.

[7] MBA, vol. 3, p. 165; LMF, p. 771 (6 October 1781).

envisioned a first performance straight after Easter.[8] (The opera ultimately premiered at the Burgtheater on 16 July 1782.) After a further three-month silence on *Die Entführung*, he wrote of playing Acts 2 and 3 for Countess Thun (8 May, 29 May); rehearsals would start, he explained, on 3 June.[9] In the absence of documentation in Mozart's letters, it is more difficult to determine exactly when numbers were composed in Acts 2 and 3 than in Act 1. But paper types in the autograph score suggest that Blonde and Osmin's duet No. 9 'Ich gehe, doch rate ich dir', Konstanze's arias No. 10 'Traurigkeit' and No. 11 'Martern aller Arten', and Belmonte's aria No. 15 'Wenn die Freude Tränen fliessen' were written during a brief second phase of work in November to early December 1781, before the remainder of the opera in early 1782.[10]

More remarkable than the information Mozart provides on *Die Entführung*'s genesis is his musical and aesthetic commentary and consequent delineation of musical priorities and strategies. Much is conveyed in a single, oft-quoted letter (26 September 1781), one that comments on every number in Act 1 and summarizes the state of play in Acts 2 and 3 as well.[11] Mozart's observations underscore several priorities: a need to take advantage of the prowess of the singers, including Fischer's 'excellent bass voice', Cavalieri's 'supple throat' and Adamberger's specific vocal qualities, and (for Fischer at least) to exploit established popularity with the Viennese musical public; a desire actively to respond to implications in the text (Konstanze's 'Ach ich liebte' and Belmonte's 'O wie ängstlich'), but to promote musical moderation and propriety in certain circumstances (such as depicting Osmin's anger in 'Solche hergelauf'ne Laffen' and its Allegro assai coda); a wish to employ instrumental effects to enhance expression ('O wie ängstlich' and, implicitly, the 'Turkish Music' of the Overture, Osmin's rage and the Janissary Chorus); and a need to retain control over the content and shape of the libretto in the interests of maximizing musical and dramatic potential (the opening 'arietta' and duet in Act 1, the text of Konstanze's 'Ach ich liebte', and modifications to Act 2 and Act 3), with Stephanie revising the libretto in all cases exactly as Mozart requested. These were not individually self-contained and circumscribed priorities, of course.

---

[8] MBA, vol. 3, p. 196; LMF, p. 796. Melamed suspects that the alterations Mozart required 'were concentrated in Act III, in which every one of Bretzner's original numbers was replaced'. See 'Evidence on the Genesis of *Die Entführung*', p. 31.

[9] MBA, vol. 3, pp. 208, 211; LMF, pp. 804, 807.

[10] See Melamed, 'Evidence on the Genesis of *Die Entführung*', p. 30; Konrad, 'Musicological Introduction', pp. 16–17.

[11] MBA, vol. 3, pp. 161–164; LMF, pp. 768–770.

Rather, they would have overlapped for Mozart in pursuit of an overarching aim, namely communicating as effectively as possible with the audience in order to maximize the work's success. Mozart specifically mentioned several times in his letter engaging the audience (exploiting Fischer's popularity; including the Janissary Chorus to please them; writing a quick, noisy trio to bring the first act to a spirited close and to encourage applause), but it ultimately lay behind every point he made.

If the aforementioned network of musical and dramatic priorities informed Mozart's early work on *Die Entführung*, it can reasonably be assumed to have informed the later work as well. Of particular interest in this respect are the cuts Mozart made to the autograph score once the opera was complete and just before it generated the performing score.[12] As Mozart explained when mailing the autograph to his father in Salzburg on 20 July 1782, four days after the premiere: 'I send you here the original [score] and two libretti. You will find in it lots of crossings out; that is because I knew that here the score is copied immediately. Consequently I gave free rein to my ideas – and before I sent it to be copied I first made my alterations and cuts here and there. And as you have it, so it was performed.'[13] Mozart's final 'alterations and cuts' would have involved him considering their impact on the individual singers, on text expression and orchestral material, and on the shape of the music and drama, all in relation to the essential prerequisite of impressing the Viennese musical public.

Critics have pointed enthusiastically to parallels between Mozart's life in 1781–1782 and characters and situations in *Die Entführung*: Mozart and Pedrillo's 'uprootedness and distance from home'; Mozart's descriptions of Colloredo and Osmin; the rescuing of Konstanze (from the harem) and Constanze (from her domineering mother); and Konstanze's defiance (in 'Martern aller Arten') and Mozart's defiance (towards his father and the Salzburg authorities).[14] Even Edward Dent, sceptical of links between

---

[12] This performing score is extant at the Austrian National Library and catalogued as OA 322. It contains a number of markings in Mozart's hand, including a triangle part for the overture, a few new dynamics, and corrections to the copyist's work (such as accidentals and missing dynamics). For a listing of Mozart's annotations to the performing score, see NMA, II/5/12, Kritische Berichte, pp. 60–62. While the original performing parts have not survived, a set for the Burgtheater revival in 1801 is extant and described in Edge, 'Mozart's Viennese Copyists', pp. 1380–1383. For Edge (pp. 1382–1383) the existence of these parts 'suggests that the original parts from the production of 1782 must already have been unavailable – for if they had been available, the theater would not have needed to go to the expense of having them recopied'.

[13] MBA, vol. 3, p. 212; LMF, p. 808.

[14] Knepler, *Wolfgang Amadé Mozart*, pp. 200, 201–202; Glover, *Mozart's Women*, pp. 115, 230; Michael Levey, *The Life and Death of Mozart* (London: Penguin, 1971), pp. 156–157. For further connections along these lines identified in the critical literature, see Matthew Head,

Konstanze and Constanze and no great fan of the opera, inclined towards a biographical reading: 'If Mozart had not been so much distracted by the painful circumstances of his engagement, he might very possibly have produced a work that was better planned and more consistent in style.'[15] Those citing connections between Mozart's heroine and his future wife could even lay claim to a venerable historical precedent, Nissen's biography, to which Constanze contributed: Mozart's friends dubbed the opera 'die *Entführung aus dem Auge Gottes*' (the Abduction from the Auge Gottes), we are told, referencing the name of the Weber house in which Constanze resided with her mother before her marriage to Mozart on 4 August 1782.[16]

Such suggestive parallels perhaps gave rise to a wry smile or two from Mozart himself, but bear little relation to the central biographical feature of *Die Entführung*: it was Mozart's first (mature) opera for the city he hoped would provide 'honour, fame and money',[17] written at a time of considerable professional uncertainty when his ability to sustain a career in Vienna remained unproven. Similar to the Rondo for piano and orchestra K. 382, performed at Mozart's first academy on 3 March 1782, success was a *sine qua non* where *Die Entführung* was concerned – in order for Mozart to cement his reputation in Vienna, secure further operatic commissions and, ultimately, obtain the much-desired position at court. Based on feedback received by 19 September 1781, Mozart considered the success of his opera highly probable: if so, 'then I shall also be popular here [in Vienna] in composition as on the clavier'.[18] While associating *Die Entführung* with admiration for his 'composition', then, Mozart's performance concerns also leave an indelible impression on the autograph score, *inter alia* in the arias tailored to individual singers, the effects aimed at – and perhaps making concessions to – the Viennese audience, and the cuts made before the premiere. (In addition, he participated at the keyboard on several

---

Orientalism, Masquerade and Mozart's Turkish Music (London: Royal Musical Association, 2000), p. 107.

[15] Dent, *Mozart's Operas: A Critical Study* (2nd edition, 1947) (Oxford: Clarendon Press, 1991), p. 70.

[16] Georg Nikolaus von Nissen, *Biographie W. A. Mozarts* (1828) (Hildesheim: Georg Olms, 1991), p. 465.

[17] MBA, vol. 3, p. 116 ('Ehre, Ruhm und Geld'); LMF, p. 733 (16 May 1781). *Bastien und Bastienne*, K. 50, was written in Vienna in 1768. Whether it was performed at F. A. Mesmer's garden theatre in Vienna, as stated by Nissen, cannot be established for certain in the absence of corroborating evidence. See Linda Tyler, '*Bastien und Bastienne*', in Eisen and Keefe (eds.), *Cambridge Mozart Encyclopedia*, pp. 44–46.

[18] MBA, vol. 3, p. 158 ('dann bin ich auch in der komposition wie im clavier hier beliebt'); LMF, p. 766.

occasions, as mentioned below.) Above all, Mozart recognized that the composition of *Die Entführung* would complement his piano-orientated achievements (as a performer-composer), enlarging and enhancing his musical profile at a self-evidently crucial stage of his Viennese career.

The essential requirement of a successful reception for *Die Entführung* is indirectly corroborated by Mozart's concert aria, 'Nehmt meinen Dank', K. 383, probably written for Aloysia Lange. It was Mozart's first self-standing aria in German for a soloist and orchestra – only four more followed, three of which remained unfinished[19] – and was completed on 10 April 1782 three months before the premiere of *Die Entführung*. Assuming Aloysia as the intended performer, it is considerably less grand and vocally brilliant than her two previous arias from Mozart, 'Alcandro lo confesso – Non sò d'onde viene', K. 294 (1778) and 'Popoli di Tessaglia – lo non chiedo', K. 316 (1779). 'Alcandro lo confesso', with semiquaver passagework, leaps to high notes, and melodic peaks on d''' and e-flat''' at the end, was written 'exactly for Mlle Weber', fitting her 'like a dress on the body';[20] it promotes her talent (as identified by Mozart) for singing bravura arias and for providing excellent cantabile and portamento.[21] 'Popili di Tessaglia' is more brilliant still: a long, multi-sectional recitative and aria on a grand scale, complete with large quantities of passagework and obbligato winds, it is not far from the world of 'Martern aller Arten'. 'Nehmt meinen Dank', then, is of a different ilk, short (at around three minutes) and lacking brilliant virtuoso display. To be sure, Aloysia would have been able effectively to communicate her 'lovely, pure' vocal sound[22] and skilled cantabile and portamento. But instrumental effects, such as in

---

[19] 'Ich möchte wohl der Kaiser sein', K. 539 (5 March 1788), a short and straightforward aria for the bass F. Baumann, was completed on 5 March 1788. The unfinished 'Schon lacht der holde Frühling', K. 580 (17 September 1789), was written for Josepha Hofer – the first Queen of the Night in *Die Zauberflöte* – to insert into a German version of Paisiello's *Il barbiere di Siviglia*. Two aria fragments from 1783, 'Müßt ich auch durch tausend Drachen', K. 435, and 'Männer suchen stets zu naschen', K. 433, may have been written in connection with Mozart's proposed setting of a translated version of Goldoni's *Il servitore di due padroni*. See MBA, vol. 3, p. 255; LMF, p. 839 (5 February 1783).

[20] MBA, vol. 2, pp. 304–305 ('accurat für die weberin zu machen'), 517 ('wie ein kleid auf den leib'); LMF, pp. 497, 638 (letters of 28 February 1778 and 3 December 1778).

[21] MBA, vol. 2, pp. 227, 287, 318; LMF, pp. 448, 486, 506 (letters of 17 January 1778, 19 February 1778, 7 March 1778). Further evidence of her skill at portamento can be found in Christian Friedrich Daniel Schubart, *Ideen zu einer Aesthetik der Tonkunst* (Vienna, 1806), pp. 135–136, as given in Paul Corneilson, 'Vogler's Method of Singing', *Journal of Musicology*, 16 (1998), pp. 91–109, at 106. For contemporary discussion of portamento singing, see Suzanne J. Beicken (ed. and trans.) *Treatise on Vocal Performance and Ornamentation by Johann Adam Hiller* (1780) (Cambridge: Cambridge University Press, 2001), pp. 56–57, 64.

[22] MBA, vol. 2, p. 227; LMF, p. 447 (17 January 1778).

bars 15–23 (Example 2.1, repeated in bars 50–58), receive perhaps more attention from Mozart than vocal ones. Against a prevailing accompanimental pizzicato, *arco* strings are reserved for bars 15–23 (and 50–58), their sustained notes combined with drifting wind arpeggios to create a swathe of orchestral sound that envelops the voice. As if provoked or inspired by the orchestral accompaniment at this juncture, the soprano produces her one modestly demonstrative gesture, a leap of a sixth to a'', her registral peak (bars 22, 56). A delicate orchestral effect is also heard at the end of the aria (Example 2.2): once the soprano has exited, the wind both retain their octave figure (bassoon) and continue·the vocal melody (flute and oboe); the oboe then plays the delicate arpeggiated string accompaniment for the one and only time.

The language of the aria's text, the date of composition and the melodic context of the main theme offer clues as to why Mozart paid attention to orchestral effects. With the premiere of *Die Entführung* looming, it would have been reasonable for Mozart to regard it – an aria in German – as an advertisement for his upcoming Singspiel; eleven months later, on 12 March 1783, he considered his performance of Piano Concerto K. 175 + 382 at Aloysia's academy a 'good announcement' of his own academy on 23 March.[23] A demonstration of orchestral acumen in a vocal work would have served his audience with a tasty hors d'oeuvre to the orchestral effects of the main course (*Die Entführung*). Mozart's principal theme also gave advance notice of Pedrillo's melody at the opening of the allegretto of the Act 2 quartet (bars 208–212).[24]

In the ensuing discussion I evaluate *Die Entführung*, and Mozart's pursuit of an all-important first operatic hit in Vienna, in light of the priorities articulated in his famous letter of 26 September 1781, paying particular attention to the writing for individual singers, orchestral effects, text expression, and the shaping of the music and drama, and making special reference to the late cuts in the autograph score.[25] Concurring with an established

---

[23] MBA, vol. 3, p. 259; LMF, p. 841 (12 March 1783). Aloysia was not in the original production of *Die Entführung*, although she subsequently became the renowned Konstanze of her day (see Chapter 6).

[24] On this thematic parallel, see Abert, *W.A. Mozart*, p. 642 and Ellwood Derr, 'Some Thoughts on the Design of Mozart's Opus 4, the "Subscription Concertos" (K. 414, 413, and 415)', in Zaslaw (ed.), *Mozart's Piano Concertos*, pp. 187–210, at p. 189.

[25] For detailed consideration of the five principal singers in *Die Entführung*, emphasizing biographical and contextual information in particular, including other roles sung, see Christiane Schumann, *Mozart und seine Sänger: Am Beispiel der 'Entführung aus dem Serail'* (Frankfurt: Peter Lang, 2005). On Adamberger, see Helmut Barak, 'Valentin Adamberger: Mozarts Belmonte und Freund', in Ingrid Fuchs (ed.), *Internationaler Musikwissenschaftlicher Kongress zum Mozartjahr 1991, Baden-Wien* (Tutzing, 1993), pp. 463–474.

Example 2.1 Mozart, 'Nehmt meinen Dank', K. 383, bars 15–23.

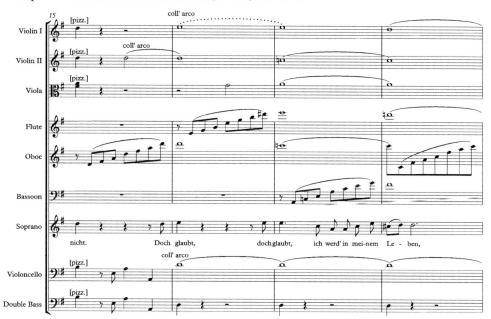

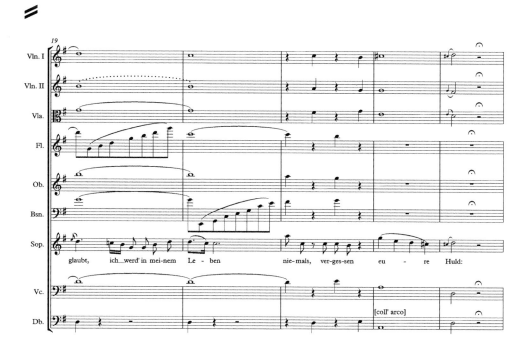

Example 2.2 Mozart, 'Nehmt meinen Dank', K. 383, bars 70–75.

critical view of *Die Entführung* as 'more a drama of character than one of situation',[26] I shall not proceed diachronically through the score, but shall focus instead on the ways in which selected arias and ensembles as represented in the autograph underscore Mozart's pragmatic and aesthetic priorities relating to both the composition and the performance of the work.

Singers and Effects

As is often pointed out, Osmin is Mozart's great musical and dramatic creation in *Die Entführung*.[27] Bretzner's libretto, Mozart remarked to his father, had Osmin sing only in the opening Lied, the Act 1 trio and the

[26] See Thomas Bauman, 'Coming of Age in Vienna: *Die Entführung aus dem Serail*', in Daniel Heartz, *Mozart's Operas*, ed. Bauman (Berkeley: University of California Press, 1990), pp. 64–87 at p. 73. For similar comments that foreground the delineation of character in *Die Entführung*, see Janos Liebner, *Mozart on the Stage* (London: Calder & Boyars, 1972), p. 82; Küster, *Musical Biography*, p. 151; Paolo Gallarati, 'Mozart and Eighteenth-Century Comedy', in Mary Hunter and James Webster (eds.), *Opera Buffa in Mozart's Vienna* (Cambridge: Cambridge University Press, 1997), pp. 98–111, at p. 99.

[27] See, for example, Einstein, *Mozart: His Character, His Work*, p. 474; Bauman, *Die Entführung*, p. 66; Heartz, *Mozart, Haydn, Early Beethoven*, p. 10.

finale, and would thus be revised to include arias for him in Acts 1 and 2.[28] The expansion in Osmin's role, it would appear, was both dramatically motivated and designed to exploit Fischer's talents.[29] Fischer was especially renowned for his low register; Mozart explained that he let Fischer's 'beautiful deep notes glow' in the Act 1 aria 'Solche hergelauf'ne laffen', and Ignaz Holzbauer, Antonio Salieri and Johann Friedrich Reichardt did likewise in 1777, 1781 and 1789.[30] Others remarked on this aspect of Fischer's technique too, the late-eighteenth-century Viennese dramatist Tobias von Gebler citing his ability to sing 'the lowest notes with a fullness, ease and pleasantness that one normally encounters only in the case of good tenors'.[31] Johann Friedrich Reichardt's more detailed account (1792) praised Fischer's low register and other vocal qualities. Fischer was

an admirable bass singer whose voice has almost the depth of a cello and the natural height of a tenor [its range was C-a'], yet his low notes never grate and his high notes are never thin; his voice is flexible, secure and agreeable. In praise of his style of singing, it is sufficient to note that he is an excellent pupil of the great tenor Raaff, who was regarded – and is still regarded – as the leading tenor in the whole of the European singing world. He has more skill and ease in his throat than perhaps any other bass singer, and in terms of his acting he can hold his own on both the serious and the comic stage.[32]

Mozart exploited Fischer's low register before 'Solche hergelauf'ne Laffen', in the Lied and duet preceding it in the finished score (if not in the opera's genesis). Both dynamics and changing orchestral textures would have allowed Fischer's low notes (B-flat – A – G) in each of the three verses of his Lied to 'glow' in slightly different ways: the instruments are marked *pp*

---

[28] MBA, vol. 3, p. 162; LMF, p. 768 (26 September 1781). The intended Act 2 aria for Osmin did not materialize, but he received 'O, wie will ich triumphieren' in Act 3.

[29] Bauman, *Die Entführung*, p. 66.

[30] MBA, vol. 3, p. 162; LMF, p. 769 (26 September 1781). For editions of the arias for Fischer by Holzbauer, Salieri and Reichardt see Paul Corneilson (ed. and trans.), *The Autobiography of Ludwig Fischer: Mozart's First Osmin* (Malden, MA: Mozart Society of America, 2011), pp. 81–98, 110–121.

[31] As quoted in Stewart Spencer's English translation in Abert, *W. A. Mozart*, p. 661. For more on Fischer, as conveyed primarily through his autobiography from 1790 (which does not mention his role as Osmin), see Paul Corneilson, 'The Mannheim Years of Ludwig Fischer (1745–1825)', in Ludwig Finscher, Baerbel Pelker and Ruediger Thomsen-Fuerst (eds.), *Mannheim: Ein 'Paradies der Tonkünstler'? Kongressbericht Mannheim 1999* (Frankfurt: Peter Lang, 2002), pp. 375–386. For further extended discussion of Fischer, including operatic roles sung, arias written for him, and the translated text of his autobiography, see Corneilson (ed. and trans.), *The Autobiography of Ludwig Fischer*.

[32] Johann Friedrich Reichardt, *Musikalische Monatsschrift* (1792), pp. 67–68. Given in Corneilson, 'The Mannheim Years of Ludwig Fischer', p. 375. Translation from Spencer in Abert, *W. A. Mozart*, p. 661.

Example 2.3 Mozart, *Die Entführung aus dem Serail*, 'Solche hergelauf'ne Laffen', bars 120–126.

thus accentuating the cadential echo and not detracting from the vocal effect; and the accompaniment first from oboes and strings then oboes, bassoons, horns and strings becomes a warm, wind-dominated sonority third time around.[33] Osmin's responses to Belmonte's insistent questioning in the duet again luxuriate in low notes ('Das ist des Bassa Selim Haus', 'Ich bin in seinen Diensten, Freund', E-flat and F); as in the Lied, light and quiet instrumental participation (marked *p*) accompanies cadential confirmation. The responses are also preceded by pauses that perhaps would have encouraged Fischer to play up his gestures in performance. By 'Solche hergelauf'ne Laffen', then, the audience is prepared for the delicately scored cadential gesture (Example 2.3), greeted with a 'glowing' low note, heard immediately before the aria's (first) coda at 'Drum, beim Barte des Propheten'. After preparing the low registral ground in preceding iterations of 'ich hab' auch Verstand' ('I've got some sense too'), Mozart has the orchestra drop from *f* to *p*, and the oboes enter with sympathetic sustained notes, to coincide with the onset of Osmin's cadential gesture that culminates in an F, the vocal low point of the aria (bars 121–124, Example 2.3).[34] From the autograph score, it is clear that Mozart had envisaged the essence of the effect at the early stage of composition,

---

[33] Only the cellos from the string section are included on the third iteration of the figure in bars 48–49. The absence of a *pp* here either indicates an assumption from Mozart that the dynamic would match earlier iterations or permits the wind instrumentalists a slightly louder dynamic in order to enrich the wind-dominated effect.

[34] Bauman (*Die Entführung*, p. 68) also identifies the '[rapid] rising scales from the depths' in the aria as '[capitalizing] on one of Fischer's great assets'.

when writing his *particella* (voice, instrumental bass and occasional other instrumental indications): with the exception of the oboes, and the violas, which are in the faded ink colour of the second phase when Mozart completed the orchestration, all of the material – including the *p* – was written down at the early stage.

The autograph score, viewed alongside the letter of 26 September 1781, sheds light on Mozart's conception of 'Solche hergelauf'ne Laffen' beyond his sensitivity to Fischer's specific vocal qualities. At the initial *particella* stage of the raging Allegro assai coda, Mozart wrote the vocal part, instrumental bass, first violin line and a brief segment for second violin, as well as all of the dynamic markings for the first violins and instrumental bass (*f, p, sfp, sf, crescendo*): in short, the coda's effect was set in his mind from the start of the notational process. But in the preceding Allegro con brio much of the dynamic and performance detail contributing to the aria's dramatic effect was not in place at the earlier stage. Osmin twice explains 'doch mich trügt kein solch Gesicht' ('But I'm not fooled by that sort of face'), in the context of the cavatina's twofold iteration of the text, on both occasions stating the text twice (bars 27–31, 80–84, Example 2.4). While the second and third pauses and the 'Adagio' were written in to the initial *particella*, the 'ad libitum' and its accompanying pause followed only at the completion stage (revealed by the faded ink). So, Mozart's two pauses and 'Adagio' early in the compositional process gave latitude to Fischer to perform freely, and the later 'ad libitum' and additional pause further increased his freedom. Osmin gets an opportunity to exaggerate his resolute statement about not being fooled by those he perceives – in paranoid fashion – to be ogling his women, and thus to enhance a comedic effect to complement those Mozart had written for him in the early stages of the genesis of the Allegro assai coda.[35] Many dynamic inflections and intensifications were also added at the completion stage of the Allegro con brio:[36] *fp*s early in both statements of the text (bars 11–14, 66–9); *fp*s in bars 73 and 92 (which have no equivalent in the first statement); and *p*s at bars 107–109, perhaps to encourage performers to emphasize the *f* at the upcoming pause. Alternating *sf* and *p* markings accrue to the 'Drum, beim Barte des Propheten' at bars 134–138 (accepting that the *particella* included *f* and

---

[35] Mozart explained that in the Allegro assai 'Osmin's rage is made comical, because Turkish music is brought in there'. See MBA, vol. 3, p. 162; LMF, p. 769 (26 September 1781).

[36] Where Mozart's dynamic markings are assigned to instruments written in the *particella*, these markings are taken as fixed for other instruments receiving them in the completion stage at the same juncture.

Example 2.4 Mozart, *Die Entführung aus dem Serail*, 'Solche hergelauf'ne Laffen', bars 80–84 (all other staves empty).

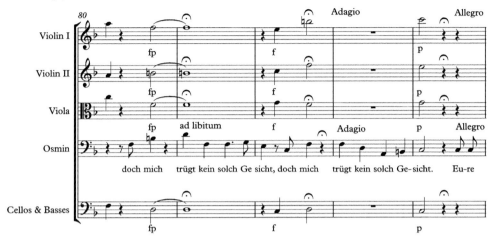

p indications for strings at the opening of the section, in bars 125–126); Osmin's first descent into rage, with a more remarkable one to follow in the Allegro assai, is thus accentuated at the completion stage.

Mozart wrote of maintaining a tonal link between the two sections of the aria in order to avoid unduly offending the ear at the explosive onset of the Allegro assai.[37] If Mozart was stimulated by his own Allegro assai to characterize Osmin more sharply in the Allegro con brio than originally envisaged in the *particella*, he was perhaps guided again by a desire to moderate or contextualize Osmin's Allegro assai outburst by revealing slightly more of the character's extreme musical personality in the Allegro con brio than (maybe) initially planned.

Osmin's numbers from Acts 2 and 3 continue to prioritize combined musical-dramatic and singer-orientated effects. In the Act 3 aria 'O, wie will ich triumphieren' Osmin's obsession with revenge is captured in an internally repetitive main theme heard across four statements of the short ABA'CA"B'A''' rondo, as well as in numerous cadential iterations at the end. The musical energy increasingly generated across the aria is complemented by the progressive exploitation of Fischer's low register. Mozart gives the audience a tantalizing glimpse of Fischer's low D (bar 62) in the first B section, draws him repeatedly downwards in C, introduces new low notes into A" following melismatic brilliance, and saves

---

[37] MBA, vol. 3, p. 162; LMF, p. 769 (26 September 1781).

the *pièce de résistance*, an eight-bar sustained D, until B' (bars 183–190, Example 2.5).[38] In the drinking duet with Pedrillo, 'Vivat Bacchus', Osmin's self-contained Adagio segment descends chromatically from C to G and is delineated by pauses to coincide with his declaration of bravery at having consumed the wine ('das heiss ich gewagt!', bars 35–38, Example 2.6): had Fischer taken (surely entitled) liberties in performing this segment, he could have simultaneously savoured deep, resonant tones and milked the dramatic situation (incipient drunkenness), exploiting renowned acting and musical skills together. Osmin's low register is contested by Blonde in the duet 'Ich gehe, doch rate ich dir': refusing to leave the garden until Blonde promises to obey him, Osmin descends mostly chromatically from B-flat to E-flat, a drop in the volume of the orchestral accompaniment to *p* again directing audience attention to Fischer's resonant low register. But Blonde is having none of it. Upping the ante dynamically, with *fp*s in her response (bar 35ff.), she mimics his descent, now offsetting it performatively with a pause at the beginning as well as the end: 'Her comic defiance of Osmin's authority transgresses into the masculine register; she marks the (vocal) limit of Osmin's authority by alluding, at the bottom of her descent, to a point beyond which no voice, not even Osmin's, can pass.'[39] Osmin is undone by a feisty musical challenge to his effect-laden safe haven.[40]

Other singers and characters receive comparable attention from Mozart to that lavished on Fischer as Osmin. Critical discussion of Belmonte's music tends to focus on the Act 1 aria 'O wie ängstlich', which Mozart said he 'wrote exactly for Adamberger's voice', depicting Belmonte's throbbing heart, swelling breast and whispering and sighing with various

---

[38] Abert memorably describes B' as follows (*W. A. Mozart*, p. 683): 'The third episode is remarkable for its use of coloratura to depict Osmin's "little song of joy", lumbering, blustering its way down to a low E, then skipping back up again through a staccato scale to a trill – the perfect picture of a brutal sensualist who remains uncultured even when enjoying himself.' Salieri and Reichardt also wrote extended vocal sustained notes (five-bar F-sharps) in their arias for Fischer; see Corneilson (ed. and trans.) *The Autobiography of Ludwig Fischer*, pp. 95–96, 116–117.

[39] Head, *Mozart's Turkish Music*, p. 93. Head's line of argument goes back as far as Otto Jahn, who remarks: 'Although [Osmin] endeavours to overawe her with the deepest notes of his deep bass voice, her persiflage drives her unwieldy antagonist quite out of the field.' See Jahn, *Life of Mozart*, vol. 2, p. 240. Abert explains (*W. A. Mozart*, p. 676): 'When [Osmin] thinks that he has trumped [Blonde] with his portentous descent into the lowest reaches of the bass register, she humiliates him with her merciless mimicry.'

[40] For more on this duet, in the course of a sensitive reading of contextual and musical aspects of Blonde's music, see Joncus, 'Blonde and the Enlightened Female in Mozart's *Die Entführung aus dem Serail*', pp. 574–575.

Example 2.5 Mozart, *Die Entführung aus dem Serail*, 'O, wie will ich triumphieren', bars 181–190.

Example 2.6 Mozart, *Die Entführung aus dem Serail*, 'Vivat Bacchus', bars 34–39.

instrumental effects described in his letter.[41] Ignaz Arnold (1803), one of the earliest writers to comment in detail on a large proportion of the composer's output, praised the portrayal of Belmonte's anxious heart in the violins and the 'fitting' (*passend*) use of the flute at 'War das ihr Lispeln?' both identified by Mozart himself.[42] Since Arnold almost certainly did not have access to Mozart's letter he would have made text-painting associations without a written lead from the composer, probably indicating other early listeners did likewise.[43] At any rate, effects beget

[41] MBA, vol. 3, pp. 162–63; LMF, p. 769 (26 September 1781). For a focus on 'O wie ängstlich' among Belmonte's arias, see Bauman, *Die Entführung*, pp. 85–88. Adamberger's career and musical attributes are discussed in detail in Thomas Bauman, 'Mozart Belmonte', *Early Music*, 19 (1991), pp. 556–563, where 'O wie ängstlich' is again at the centre of attention because the 'two other substantial arias for Adamberger in [Acts 2 and 3 of] *Die Entführung* do little more than embroider the personality created in "O wie ängstlich", and one or the other is usually cut in modern performances'. (p. 561)

[42] Arnold, *Mozart Geist*, pp. 371–372.

[43] Mozart's letters assume a prominent position in the biographical tradition only with Georg Nissen's *Biographie W. A. Mozarts* of 1828. (Nissen collaborated on it with his wife and Mozart's widow Constanze; she completed it with Johann Heinrich Feuerstein following her second husband's death in 1826.)

effects in the orchestral accompaniment to the aria, right up until the end, where demisemiquavers in all three principal winds are heard alongside pizzicato strings (as at 'War das ihr Lispeln?'), which *decrescendo* to *pp* at the close. This may represent either or both a final endorsement of Belmonte's emotional sensitivity and an indication of the momentum orchestral effects acquire during the aria such that they continue beyond the end of the vocal contribution. They begin, moreover, in the recitative preceding the aria: Mozart's attention to performance detail here includes *sotto voce* markings for the strings and a *dolce* for the oboe,[44] culminating in a *rinf* inflection on the final word ('dich', namely Konstanze) that encapsulates Belmonte's tender love and anxiety.[45] Mozart distinguished Konstanze's 'Ach ich liebte' from Belmonte's preceding 'O wie ängstlich' – both drafted on the same day and completed in a further one and a half days – by virtue of having 'sacrificed a little to Miss Cavalieri's supple throat' in a bravura context.[46] But he also forged a connection between the respective recitatives through the instrumental effects employed. Like Belmonte's recitative, Konstanze's includes sustained notes in the winds, a *dolce* indication for the oboe, and an accent on a pause preceding the aria (now *sf* and the first of two pauses rather than one). The swells in her recitative, *p – mf – p*, *p – cresc – p*, and *cresc – sf – p*, invoke the innumerable swells in Belmonte's Andante.[47] Mozart integrates the material from Konstanze's recitative into the aria proper at an Allegro tempo (see bars 54–75), the resulting *crescendi*, swells, wind sustained notes and pauses (with *sf*) again bringing to mind Belmonte's recitative and aria.

Instrumental effects and responses to Adamberger and Cavalieri's needs are mutually reinforcing elsewhere in *Die Entführung*. Belmonte's opening arietta 'Hier soll ich dich denn sehen', rarely discussed in the secondary literature, marked an important musical and biographical moment in Mozart's engagement with his audience, namely the first exposure of Adamberger, indeed of any singer, in his first mature Viennese opera. Adamberger was praised two years after the premiere for his refined singing and portamento, defined by Johann Adam Hiller in the *Treatise on*

---

[44] This oboe contribution is admired by Arnold, in *Mozarts Geist*, p. 372.

[45] *Rinforzando* can designate a crescendo – perhaps more intense than a regular crescendo – or a single-note accent, or a forceful type of performance in a given passage; see Brown, *Classical and Romantic Performing Practice*, pp. 62, 87–88.

[46] MBA, vol. 3, p. 163; LMF, p. 769 (26 September 1781).

[47] One of the *crescendi* in Belmonte's 'O wie ängstlich' – plus a subsequent *f* and *p* (see bars 96–99) – appears in Mozart's hand not in the autograph but in the instrumental bass part of the performing score (OA 322). See NMA, II/5/12, Kritische Berichte, p. 60.

Vocal Performance and Ornamentation (1780) as the skill of 'connecting the voice from one note to the next with perfect proportion and unity in ascending and descending motion alike' avoiding an 'unpleasant slur or [a] pull through smaller intervals'.[48] He had ample opportunity to demonstrate good portamento here, especially when given latitude to perform relatively freely at (and between) various fermatas, including by probably introducing embellishments to some of them. Bars 47–53 'und bringe mich ans Ziel' ('and bring me to my goal', that is to say Konstanze, Example 2.7), direct listeners towards both the intricate clarinet demisemiquavers and the vocal approach to the final exit: the static C-major harmony[49] does not compete for their attention. The consecutive pauses immediately before the last cadence for the voice (bars 53–54, Example 2.7) include decrescendo hairpins in the clarinets and horns: as at the other vocal pauses in the arietta, all greeted by orchestral *piano*s, Mozart ensured that the limelight fell on Adamberger. In a similar vein, the *forte* from bar 3 of the orchestral introduction is recast as an *mf* for strings at the corresponding point in Belmonte's statement, perhaps to ensure that Adamberger, and his word 'Konstanze', was not dynamically comprised by instrumental participation. Cavalieri's cavatina 'Traurigkeit', like Adamberger's 'O wie ängstlich', is a study in self-perpetuating instrumental effects, Arnold lauding the orchestral depictions of 'Gleich der Wurm . . . Leben hin' and 'Selbst der Luft . . . mein armes Herz' towards the end (bars 85–131).[50] Instruments and voice ebb and flow in sympathy with each other throughout. The winds set the sombre, reflective mood by themselves at the start (heightened by basset-horns employed for the only time in the work and played by the virtuoso brothers, Anton and Johann Stadler), as if illustrative of Arnold's claim that the instrumental music of *Die Entführung* 'speaks on its own', that is without the text.[51] The approach to the musical reprise, where Mozart moves from B-flat back to G minor, overlaps with the start of the textual reprise (see bars 62–67, Example 2.8): Konstanze's

---

[48] For the praise for Adamberger see Friedrich Nicolai, *Beschreibung einer Reise durch Deutschland und die Schweiz im Jahre 1781* (Berlin, 1784), p. 591. Hiller's quotations are taken from *Treatise on Vocal Performance and Ornamentation*, p. 56. For more on portamento, including evolving views from 1750 to 1900, see Brown, *Classical and Romantic Performing Practice*, pp. 558–574. Further late-eighteenth-century commentary on Adamberger is given in Bauman, 'Mozart's Belmonte'.

[49] Excepting a single quaver of dominant harmony in bar 49.

[50] Arnold, *Mozarts Geist*, p. 370.

[51] See Arnold, *Mozarts Geist*, p. 378 ('Wahrlich! Die Musik spricht allein'). This comment refers to the Allegro assai coda to Osmin's 'Solche hergelauf'ne Laffen', but also captures Arnold's general belief in the expressive power of instrumental writing in Mozart's operas.

Example 2.7 Mozart, *Die Entführung aus dem Serail,* 'Hier soll ich dich denn sehen', bars 48–56.

Example 2.8 Mozart, *Die Entführung aus dem Serail*, 'Traurigkeit', bars 62–70.

'Traurigkeit' motif thus prefigures the wind motif heard at the onset of the musical reprise, which in turn foreshadows Konstanze and the strings two bars later. In addition, the winds build progressively to the full flutes/oboes/basset-horns/bassoons sonority heard at the reprise, including an inversion of the chromatically falling wind minims from the setting of 'Schmerz' (see bars 41–43) as chromatically ascending oboe minims. Thus, Mozart's reprise is as meticulously prepared as the opening of the aria is timbrally unanticipated, and both are equally evocative. Konstanze's 'Martern aller Arten', which immediately follows 'Traurigkeit' and a brief spoken exchange and is the only instance in Mozart's Viennese operatic repertory of back-to-back, full-length arias for the same character,[52] extends further the elaborate combination of vocal and instrumental effects: placing a long coloratura aria for Cavalieri at the centre of his drama, just as Ignaz Umlauf had done in *Die Bergknappen* for the opening

---

[52] Don Giovanni's 'Deh vieni' and 'Metà di voi' are separated only by a recitative, but the former is a short canzonetta (44 bars) rather than a full-length aria.

of the National Singspiel at the Burgtheater (1778),[53] Mozart partially prepared for its stylistic ostentation with the give and take between Cavalieri and her accompanying orchestra in 'Traurigkeit'. ('Martern aller Arten' is discussed in detail below.)

Conversing with Anton Raaff about *Idomeneo*, Mozart explained that he would always write arias to suit individual singers, but that he had to be allowed a free hand to compose what he himself deemed appropriate in trios and quartets.[54] While he may not have been able to accommodate the specific vocal predilections of Adamberger, Cavalieri, Dauer and Teyber in the multi-sectional Act 2 quartet of *Die Entführung*, then, he did not pass up opportunities offered by four of his five principals appearing on stage together for the first time. Each occasion that the four sing together is rendered musically distinctive in one way or another. At the end of the opening Allegro, when describing their collective rapture, joy and bliss at impending freedom ('Voll Entzücken, Freud und Wonne'), Mozart carefully marks each voice *sotto voce* – implying either a dynamic above *p* with expressive intensification, or one between *p* and *pp* with an emotional quality[55] – and has them accompanied initially only by trumpets and timpani at *piano*. Sustained oboes are added on the second occasion and *sotto voce* markings repeated for all voices (Example 2.9). Distinctive instrumental and vocal effects therefore reinforce each other in representing the magical emotion. At the crisis point in the Adagio (bars 187–192), where Belmonte and Pedrillo express their conviction about Konstanze and Blonde's fidelity but the women are incredulous at the men's earlier doubts, the strings are instructed to decrescendo from a semibreve *p* on an augmented 6th of A to the V/A harmony that precedes the Andantino. In so doing they not only produce a smooth transition to the tranquil Andantino opened by the orchestra alone, but also provide a functional resolution to an augmented 6th for the first time in the quartet, after several

---

[53] See Heartz, *Mozart, Haydn and Early Beethoven*, p. 15. Another precedent for 'Martern', in the pronounced participation of winds, is Maximilian Ulbrich's *Frühling und Liebe* (1778), where Cavalieri sang the primary role of Giannina. The Act 2 aria 'Singt mir dein Lied an die Nachtigallen' 'features concertante woodwinds – solo flute, oboe, and bassoon which provide miniature ritornelli and counterpoint against the voice'. See Patricia Lewy Gidwitz, 'Vocal Portraits of Four Mozart Sopranos' (PhD thesis, University of California at Berkeley, 1991), p. 53. 'Wen den Adler' from Salieri *Der Rauchfangkehrer* (1781), written for Cavalieri, also has similarities with 'Martern' (Gidwitz, 'Vocal Portraits of Four Mozart Sopranos', p. 58).

[54] See MBA, vol. 3, p. 73; LMF, p. 699 (27 December 1780).

[55] See Frederick Neumann, *Performance Practices of the Seventeenth and Eighteenth Centuries* (New York: Schirmer, 1993), p. 17, and Badura-Skoda and Badura-Skoda, *Interpreting Mozart*, p. 48.

Example 2.9 Mozart, *Die Entführung aus dem Serail*, 'Ach, Belmonte!', bars 78–81.

earlier unresolved ones.[56] The Andantino itself is the quartet's beautiful centrepiece, the orchestra perhaps revealing the reconciliation between male and female characters before the women verbalize it, in line with the kind of prominent expressive role assigned to the opera orchestra by the likes of Gluck, Grétry, Adam Smith and Pierre-Louis Ginguené in the late eighteenth century.[57] It opens with the wind and strings *p*, followed by the strings *pp* and the entering voices *p*: the discrepancy in the dynamic level of simultaneous strings and voices invites the voices to distinguish themselves slightly in volume from their instrumental accompanists and to create a bond with the introductory orchestral statement of the theme, which is also marked *p*. Finally, in the rousing Allegro conclusion, an ode to love following jealousies now forgiven, the singers end with their first unaccompanied four-voice sonorities, peaking on a dramatic, decisively resolved augmented 6th pause ('nichts', bar 348) that recalls this chord's role in the quartet as a whole. A harmonic and timbral effect reinforces the dramatic impact of the moment, then, capturing the combined assertiveness and subtlety characteristic of Mozart's writing for his four singers together in the quartet as a whole.

The Vaudeville at the end of *Die Entführung*, bringing together all five principal singers (now including Osmin), links to earlier instrumental and vocal effects and thus represents an apposite conclusion to the (musical) drama. While Pedrillo's spoken interjection in 'Solche hergelauf'ne Laffen' sets off Osmin's furious response, Blonde's criticism now ignites Osmin's abridged reprise of his original Allegro assai material. Osmin does not descend immediately into rage, but rather approaches the Allegro assai in a staged acceleration from *più Andante* to *Allegretto* to *stringendo il tempo* (Example 2.10). Ink colours in the autograph apparently show Mozart accentuating this acceleration late in the notational process: several of the *Allegretto* and *stringendo il tempo* indications for individual parts were written in to the *particella*, but all the *più Andante* markings followed only at the completion stage. Thus, Mozart's view about moderating Osmin's rage in the Act 1 aria so that it remains 'music' may also be represented in his compositional process in the run up to the Vaudeville's Allegro assai by a more incremental tempo increase than originally envisaged.

But there is more at stake in Osmin's participation here than a gradual approach to the rage and an eventual reprise of the earlier Allegro assai. For

---

[56] For Mozart's evolving augmented 6th progressions in the Act 2 quartet, see Keefe, *Mozart's Piano Concertos*, pp. 122–126.

[57] See Keefe, *Mozart's Piano Concertos*, pp. 19–20, 124.

Example 2.10 Mozart, *Die Entführung aus dem Serail*, Act 3 Vaudeville, bars 64–73.

the climax to Osmin's preparation for the Allegro assai, three bars of augmented 6th of A minor emphasized by *stringendo* and repeated *fp* markings (Example 2.10), returns to the dramatic augmented 6ths of the Act 2 quartet perpetrated by the four characters who are now the recipients of Osmin's anger. Once Osmin has said his piece and hurried off, Belmonte, Konstanze, Pedrillo and Blonde first acknowledge his angry outburst in their music as well as their text: the Andante sostenuto (Example 2.11) begins in A minor, referencing Osmin's key and (implicitly) the powerful augmented 6th through which it was confirmed, and initially continues the *f – p* inflections that characterize the run-up to Osmin's rage (as *fp*s) and the rage itself. But the lovers also invoke their own Act 2 quartet: the *sotto voce* indication on the first occasion they participate together without Osmin in the Vaudeville brings to mind the *sotto voce* at 'Voll Entzücken' the first time they sing together in the quartet; and the tranquil, *p* homophony (at 'Hingegen menschlich . . . grossen Seelen Sache'), lightly accompanied, summons up the quartet's Andantino. In fact, the brief Andante sostenuto from the Vaudeville captures the Act 2 quartet in microcosm: slight anxiety, joy and forgiveness (albeit the latter only implicit in the quartet's Andantino) are coordinated in text and music. And recognizing such a connection involves attributing it primarily to Mozart's concentration on matters of performance and effect, acknowledging both his attention to performance and dramatic detail and his uncanny understanding (to quote Niemetschek and Arnold at the turn of the nineteenth century) of 'the economy of conjuring up his greatest effect with the least effort, often through the single note of an instrument, through a chord, a trumpet blast, a drum roll'.[58]

Mozart's Cuts

As Ulrich Konrad has explained, the customary practice at the Burgtheater of producing the performing score (what he calls the *Direktionsexemplar*) from the autograph score in advance of the premiere 'triggered a creative process in Mozart that is found nowhere else in his operas'. The principal aim of the substantive cuts Mozart made to the autograph before it was

---

[58] Niemetschek, *Leben*, p. 49, *Life of Mozart*, pp. 57–58 (translation amended); repeated in Arnold, *Mozarts Geist*, pp. 209–210. For more on both the Act 2 quartet and Act 3 vaudeville, in the context of Germanic traditions of morality and didacticism, see Martin Nedbal, *Morality and Viennese Opera in the Age of Mozart and Beethoven* (London: Routledge, 2017), Chapter 2, pp. 48–83.

Example 2.11 Mozart, *Die Entführung aus dem Serail*, Act 3 Vaudeville, bars 95–109 (voices only).

copied, according to Konrad, 'was not to save time in performance or to simplify the vocal parts, but to fine-tune the dramatic structure of his composition'.[59] My contention is that Mozart's 'alterations and cuts' (*veränderungen und abkürzungen*), all of which occur in Acts 2 and 3, are more significant still, shedding light on the interaction and balance of individual singers' needs, instrumental effects and dramatic shaping.

Broadly speaking, Mozart's substantive alterations and cuts fall into two categories: those that delete musical material replicated (with or without slight modifications) before and/or after the cut in question; and those that delete a sizeable amount of material that is unheard elsewhere in the number. The former category includes bars 72–78 of Blonde's aria 'Durch Zärtlichkeit', bars 116–127 of Konstanze's 'Traurigkeit', and bars 275–289 of Konstanze's 'Martern aller Arten'.[60] Mozart probably would have kept in mind Teyber's and Cavalieri's reactions, or even involved his singers directly in the abridgement process. At any rate, not a great deal appears to have been at stake musically, dramatically, or performatively in these particular cuts.

The other type of cut, where a chunk of music not present elsewhere is excised, shines a brighter light on Mozart's concerns and priorities. In the Adagio of Belmonte's two-tempo aria 'Wenn die Freude Tränen fliessen', for example, Mozart deleted an entire musical iteration of the eight lines of text assigned to this section (bars 37–62), thus providing two statements in total rather than the originally planned three. (In the facsimile of the autograph score, we can see that pp. 304–305 were originally stuck together, that the remaining twelve bars of the statement were crossed out on pp. 306–307, and that Mozart denoted the beginning and end of the cut on p. 303 and p. 307 with one of his standard indicators, a circle with a line through it.) While the first eleven bars of the deleted material slightly embellish and expand the opening of the original statement (bars 1–9), the second half departs much more noticeably from the corresponding portion of the first statement. Arpeggios are required of Adamberger

---

[59] Konrad, 'Musicological Introduction', p. 19. He advances his argument at greater length in '"mithin liess ich meinen gedanken freyen Lauf": Erste Ueberlegungen und Thesen zu den "Fassungen" von W. A. Mozarts *Die Entführung aus dem Serail* KV384', in Werner Breig (ed.), *Opernkomposition als Prozess* (Kassel: Bärenreiter, 1996), pp. 47–64. Only one number is discussed in detail, Blonde's 'Durch Zärtlichkeit' (pp. 55–57, with a facsimile of the relevant segments of Mozart's autograph on pp. 61–64).

[60] See Mozart, *'Die Entführung aus dem Serail': Facsimile of the Autograph Score*, vol. 1, p. 155; vol. 2, pp. 81–82; vol. 1, pp. 238–240. My bar numbers in the discussion below reference the full uncut versions of each piece, following the NMA (which publishes full pieces, noting where cuts were made).

towards the end, from his upper to his lower and back to his upper registers; orchestral dynamics are also intensified, with *sf – p* indications and a *cresc* for the first time in the aria. Furthermore, the deleted statement departs from the harmonic and tonal scheme of its predecessor: the I – V outline of the first statement is replaced by a I – IV – iii outline for the second, ending with a Neapolitan 6 – i6/4 – V7 – i progression in D minor that partly coincides with one of Adamberger's arpeggios.

Mozart may have come to consider the effect of intensified harmonies and dynamics in the second statement as more than was necessary for a repeat of Belmonte's text.[61] The retained third statement contains modest dynamic amplification similar to its deleted predecessor, but begins and ends in the tonic (B-flat), casting the Adagio as a whole as a simple and familiar I – V, I – I slow cavatina rather than the more harmonically adventurous structure originally envisaged. So, perhaps this Adagio illustrates Mozart first giving 'free rein to [his] ideas' and subsequently reining himself in, as explained to Leopold (20 July 1782). Equally, Adamberger could have proposed the specific cut, or just a cut of some kind, in order to save his voice. Or maybe Mozart's compositional imagination was jointly stimulated by views on text setting *and* a request from Adamberger.

Singer and composer together could also have set in motion the cut to the Allegretto of Belmonte's aria. On this occasion Mozart deletes not an entire musical statement of the section's text, but rather sustained melismas on, and repeated iterations of, the final line only ('Welchen Schmerz die Trennung macht' – 'What pain separation creates'; partially given in Example 2.12). Without doubt, Mozart excises the most technically demanding material written for Adamberger in the Allegretto, including the *tour de force* of strident arpeggios across nearly two octaves in bars 142–144 (Example 2.12). The cut also amounts to approximately one third of the total length originally envisaged (33/90 bars) like the cut in the Adagio (26/85 bars). Only four bars of sustained notes are excised from the winds in the extended deletion: all of the obbligato wind writing in the Allegretto survives. Indeed, with the cut enforced, listeners can more readily than in the uncut version make aural connections between the wind sonorities in the orchestral introduction, midway through the vocal

---

[61] A comparable situation may apply to the cuts in Blonde's 'Welche Wonne, welche Lust' (bars 120–133, 142–151). In addition to streamlining the B' and A" sections of this ABA'B'A" single-tempo rondo, Mozart deletes the only segments that feature *sf – p* and *sf* and *sfp* markings. Perhaps these markings were redolent of an increase in the intensity of Blonde's emotions over the course of the aria that Mozart came to consider unnecessary or adequately captured in other material (such as Blonde's strident octaves towards the end).

Example 2.12 Mozart, *Die Entführung aus dem Serail*, 'Wenn die Freude Tränen fliesen', bars 135–162 (including cut material to bar 157 inclusive).

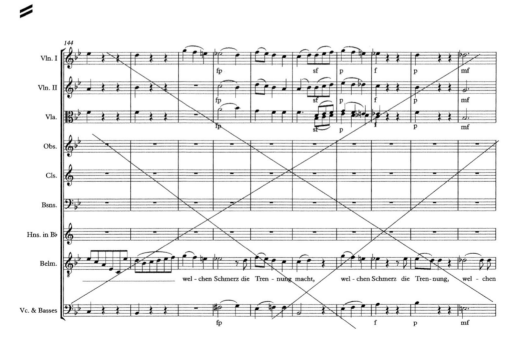

Example 2.12 (cont.)

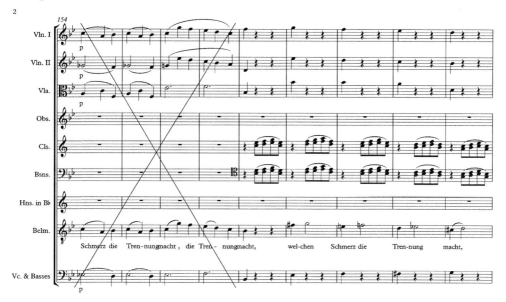

statement and immediately after the cut, especially the distinctive writing in thirds for clarinets and bassoons (given at the end of Example 2.12). In sum, whether Mozart was originally motivated to make cuts in the Adagio and Allegretto by Adamberger, by his own perception of dramatic structure and text expression, or by a combination of the two, he simultaneously cuts proportionally in the two sections, excises Adamberger's most difficult material, and protects, even promotes, wind effects. And, in so doing, he engages actively with the priorities set out in his letter of 26 September 1781 pertaining to compositional and dramatic shape, the needs of a singer, and the virtues of orchestral effects.

Mozart's cut to the secondary theme section of the solo exposition of 'Martern aller Arten' (bars 109–119) again points to concurrent engagement with different priorities.[62] (The beginning and end of the cut material is given in Examples 2.13 and 2.14.) The solo flute, oboe, violin and cello operate as a unit for the eight-bar presentation of the secondary theme (bars 93–100), subsequently pairing off *inter alia* to reinforce the vocal line, to provide harmonic support and to offer end-of-phrase semiquaver

---

[62] For 'Martern aller Arten' I follow Martha Feldman's formal designations in 'Staging the Virtuoso: Ritornello Procedure in Mozart, from Aria to Concerto', in Zaslaw (ed.), *Mozart's Piano Concertos*, pp. 149–186, at 172. For biographical information on the four instrumental soloists in the aria as well as Cavalieri, see Albrecht, 'The Soloists in "Martern aller Arten"'.

Example 2.13 Mozart, *Die Entführung aus dem Serail*, 'Martern aller Arten', bars 107–109 (including the deleted bar 109).

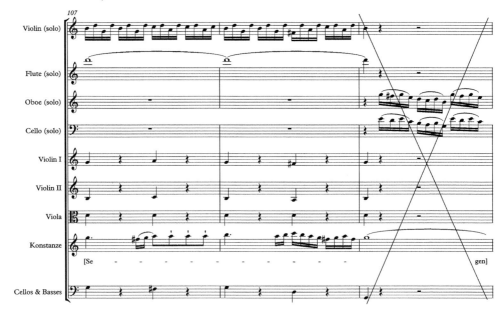

Example 2.14 Mozart, *Die Entführung aus dem Serail*, 'Martern aller Arten', bars 118–121 (including three deleted bars, 118–120a).

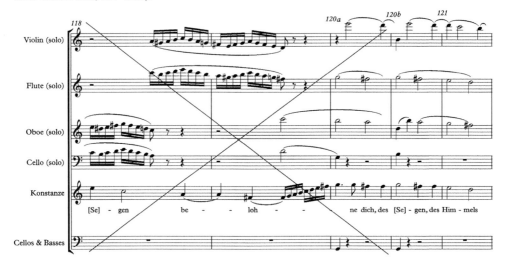

segments. They go considerably further in the deleted passage, diversifying their support with semiquaver writing in imitation of the voice, in effect taking a lead from their own frilly semiquavers preceding the excision. With the cut observed, Mozart moves straight from the sustained notes of the horns, solo oboe and flute (bars 100–108, partially in Example 2.13) to rich syncopated wind minims (bars 120–123, partially in Example 2.14); the ensuing semiquaver scales passed among the winds are no longer predicted by either the vocal scale or the semiquaver imitative material contained in the cut. Thus, in making his excision, Mozart puts sonorous support of the voice from his orchestra ahead of thematic and dialogic elaboration of material.

In attempting to explain Mozart's deletion in the secondary theme section, we must also turn to the corresponding segment of its reprise in the tonic. When 'Des Himmel segen' is heard after the presentation of the secondary theme, Konstanze receives the first sustained note (g", bars 209–212) and solo instruments the thematic material, reversing events of the solo exposition. As a result, Konstanze sets the scene for her own extraordinary c'" that extends across four bars at the end of the section (bars 234–237, Example 2.15). And at this climactic juncture of the aria Mozart coordinates several effects: the ascending semiquaver scales in the solo instruments now include Konstanze, allowing a virtuosic sweep from low to high registers in two bars (b – c'"; 230–232); and a three-beat rest in bar 233, enabling Cavalieri to catch her breath before the c'" in bars 234–237, is filled with a final, emphatic orchestral rendition of the ascending semiquaver scale (Example 2.15). When reviewing 'Martern' in its entirety, then, before sending off the autograph to generate the performing score, Mozart possibly decided through his cut both to give slightly more attention to the wind sustained notes in the solo exposition secondary theme section (the net effect of the cut) and less to semiquaver scalar wind writing (contained in the deleted material). In so doing, the cut does double duty: Cavalieri's climactic sustained c'" gains import from its relationship to activity in the solo exposition as well as the reprise; and the power of the semiquaver scales, no longer 'compromised' by the scalar semiquavers contained in the deleted passage, are fully and freshly experienced in the reprise.

Like 'Wenn die Freude Tränen fliessen', Belmonte's Act 3 aria 'Ich baue ganz auf deine Stärke' was significantly revised in the autograph score. In this case, Mozart glued two new pages over two he no longer needed midway through the aria and then a single page over another one that had become surplus to requirements at the end.[63] The type of paper used for the inserted material points to the adjustments taking place late in the compositional process.[64] In both of these major revisions, Mozart promoted wind effects to

---

[63] See 'Die Entführung aus dem Serail': Facsimile of the Autograph Score, pp. 388–393, 402–405.
[64] Melamed, 'Evidence on the Genesis of Die Entführung aus dem Serail', pp. 31–32.

Example 2.15 Mozart, *Die Entführung aus dem Serail*, 'Martern aller Arten', bars 232–236.

a greater extent than originally planned. The first (bars 79–94), coinciding with the repetition of the penultimate and last lines of the aria text in the dominant, sees the flutes, clarinets, horns and bassoons answer the voice in an antecedent-consequent dialogue (with a new triplet-quaver accompaniment, Example 2.16) and play phrase links as well; in the original, in contrast, they support the voice at two isolated moments[65] and are otherwise absent. The full-wind timbre of flutes, clarinets, bassoons and horns, heard immediately before the second revision, continues for five bars into the revision itself as the exclusive accompaniment for the voice (partially given in Example 2.17). In addition, Adamberger acquires a new virtuosic four-bar flourish adapted from the immediately preceding triplet-quavers in the

---

[65] *'Die Entführung aus dem Serail': Facsimile of the Autograph Score*, p. 388.

Example 2.16 Mozart, *Die Entführung aus dem Serail*, 'Ich baue', bars 83–86 (late-stage revision, winds only).

Example 2.17 Mozart, *Die Entführung aus dem Serail*, 'Ich baue', bars 144–149 (including two bars of the revision, 148–149).

clarinets and ultimately owing its rhythmic origin to the triplet-quaver wind accompaniment incorporated into the first big revision to the aria (bars 83–86, Example 2.16). Again, then, Mozart in carrying out modifications may have accommodated both Adamberger's virtuosic predilections and his own conception of the aria's instrumental sound world.

After the Premiere: Success Achieved

As in the Rondo K. 382 for his first Viennese academy on 3 March 1782 (see Chapter 1), Mozart left no stone unturned in eliciting audience

appreciation of *Die Entführung.* Attention to the needs of singers, to
instrumental and vocal performance effects and to musico-dramatic concerns all homed in on pleasing a Viennese theatrical public naturally
disposed to Turkish themes.[66] Demonstrably virtuosic music written for
instruments as well as voices probably accommodated listener predilections similar to those that Mozart had already accommodated in Vienna as
a keyboard performer-composer: his stated desire to end the trio 'Marsch,
marsch, marsch!' in a manner appropriate for the conclusion of an act, that
is with 'lots of noise' to encourage applause, is supported by instrumental
roulades that close numbers such as 'Martern aller Arten', 'Frisch zum
Kampfe', the Act 2 quartet, and 'O, wie will ich triumphieren'. Mozart's
belief that the compositional popularity of *Die Entführung* would complement the popularity of his keyboard playing is not confined to a rhetorical
flourish in a letter to Nannerl (see above), then, but is also supported by the
music written. And he reaped the rewards of focusing so closely on the
desires of his audience, explaining to Leopold on 27 July 1782: 'People are,
can I say, really mad [*recht Närrisch*] about this opera. It makes one happy
when one receives such approval.'[67] The compositional virtuosity of *Die
Entführung,* recognized by Ignaz Arnold (1803) in the richness of musical
ideas and instrumentation and the stylistic flowering of a youthful spirit
experiencing true strength for the first time,[68] is best understood as a no-
holds-barred pitch for popularity. *Die Entführung* is indeed quite different
stylistically from Mozart's later operas, as Arnold and later Carl Maria von
Weber claimed,[69] a fact attributable at least in part to Mozart's fragile
professional position in Vienna in 1781–1782 and his resulting need to
actively seek out unqualified and enthusiastic audience approbation.

Parallels between Mozart's instrumental music of 1781–1782 and *Die
Entführung* extend further than general interests in compositional and
performance-orientated virtuosity. Public and private performances of
Die Entführung both took place, as for the instrumental works of
1781–1782 (see Chapter 1), Mozart using private renditions for the likes

---

[66] On 'Turcomania' in late-eighteenth-century Vienna, see Bruce Alan Brown, 'Gluck's *Rencontre
Imprévue* and Its Revisions', *Journal of the American Musicological Society*, 36 (1983),
pp. 498–518, especially 501–502. See also Nicholas Till, *Mozart and the Enlightenment: Truth,
Virtue and Beauty in His Operas* (London: Faber, 1992), pp. 102–105.

[67] MBA, vol. 3, p. 215; LMF, p. 810.   [68] Arnold, *Mozarts Geist*, p. 388.

[69] Arnold, *Mozarts Geist*, p. 388; for Weber's view (in translation), see Bauman, *Die Entführung*,
p. 2 and Konrad, 'Musicological Introduction', p. 20. Niemetschek had earlier identified a 'full
stream of youthful imagination' on display in both *Idomeneo* and *Die Entführung*. See *Leben*,
p. 67, *Life of Mozart*, p. 76 (translation amended).

of Countess Thun and his singers to drum up support in advance of public exposure and to bring influential individuals onside. Activities of this kind had long been part of Mozart's operatic *modus operandi*, needless to say, but assumed greater significance than ever when his livelihood depended on the successful reception of compositions and performances carried out in a freelance capacity. Mozart also tried to maximize the impact of *Die Entführung* for artistic and financial gain, just as he exploited the special cachet of concurrent performance and composition to maximum advantage in the contemporary instrumental works: he wrote the concert aria K. 383 as an advertisement for *Die Entführung* (as argued above); he intended to complete his own arrangement of the opera for winds soon after the premiere;[70] and, in late September 1782, he asked Leopold to have the opera copied in Salzburg in order to accommodate a projected performance in Berlin.[71] Above all, Mozart's enthusiasm for composing *Die Entführung*, abundantly clear in his letters,[72] and resolute commitment to following it through to a triumphant conclusion bring to mind his passion for keyboard performance in 1781–1782 and firm belief that audience acclaim demonstrated (among other things) appropriate service to erstwhile employer Colloredo (see Chapter 1).

Mozart's devotion to *Die Entführung*, no doubt attributable to the important place it occupied in a compositional portfolio representing a fledgling Viennese career, helps to explain some of his reactions after its premiere. He proudly reported its continued, stupendous success in a number of letters to Leopold and rebuked his father unusually sternly (at least over a musical matter) on learning that Leopold had not had time to look at the score by the end of July 1782.[73] He was also intensely irritated at

---

[70] Whether Mozart ultimately completed this arrangement is not known; P. J. Martin advertised a performance of *Die Entführung* for winds at one of his summer concerts, on 18 August 1782. See MDL, p. 182; MDB, p. 206.

[71] MBA, vol. 3, pp. 231–232; LMF, p. 822 (25 September 1782). In the event, the Berlin premiere of *Die Entführung* (at the National Theatre) did not take place until 16 October 1788.

[72] See, for example, MBA, vol. 3, pp. 143–144, 163, 165; LMF, pp. 755 (1 August 1781), 770 (26 September 1781), 771 (6 October 1781).

[73] See MBA, vol. 3, pp. 215, 216, 219, 224, 231, 244, 254; LMF, pp. 810, 811, 813, 817, 822, 832, 839 (letters of 27 July, 31 July, 7 August, 24 August, 25 September, 21 December 1782, 5 February 1783). There is ample independent verification of *Die Entführung*'s success in Vienna, even in Mozart's lifetime; see, for example, MDL, pp. 186, 189, 196; MDB, pp. 210, 214, 221 (1782, 1783, 1784) and Ernst Ludwig Gerber, *Historisch-Biographisches Lexicon der Tonkünstler* (1790), in MDL, p. 337; MDB, p. 383. In an obituary for Mozart (4 January 1792), the *Musikalische Korrespondenz* identified *Die Entführung* as the pedestal on which Mozart built his reputation; NMD, p. 74. For the rebuke to Leopold for failing to look at the opera, see MBA, vol. 3, p. 216; LMF, p. 811 (31 July 1782).

the breakdown of the Act 1 trio in the second performance, demanding a rehearsal for the singers before the opera was given again.[74] The 'free rein to … ideas' that Mozart allowed himself and subsequently self-censored implicitly recognize passion for the work: his alleged response to Emperor Joseph's supposed reaction to the opera '[…] an extraordinary number of notes, dear Mozart', 'Just as many, Your Majesty, as are necessary'[75] perhaps testifies simultaneously to one highly influential auditor's view of Mozart's overabundant compositional enthusiasm and to Mozart's own steadfast commitment to the integrity of the work and the processes that lead to its completion. (Did carrying out the late-stage cuts – Mozart's own reflection on overabundant ideas – condition his putative response to the emperor?)

The strong impact of writing and successfully staging *Die Entführung* is illustrated by Mozart's ruminations on the experience in the final months of 1782. He was frustrated at having received only a flat fee (100 ducats) when box-office takings from performances were so high, encouraging an ultimately unrealized plan of an independent production in order to maximize personal profits.[76] And he expressed no disappointment at missing out on a yearly salary of 400 gulden associated with teaching Princess Elisabeth von Würtemberg; he explained that the teaching would have taken attention away from pursuing money through composition, among other things, and no doubt had *Die Entführung*'s success in mind.[77] He may have been frustrated at not receiving a court appointment in the aftermath of *Die Entführung*'s triumph,[78] and perhaps (in years to come) at not benefiting financially from the opera's widespread success. Although it was staged across northern and central Europe during his lifetime and was repeatedly published in whole or in part in vocal scores and other arrangements, Mozart would have derived no direct financial benefit himself.[79] We detect Mozart's mental wheels in motion in late 1782

---

[74] MBA, vol. 3, p. 212; LMF, pp. 807–808 (20 July 1782).

[75] Originally given in Niemetschek, *Leben*, p. 23; *Life of Mozart*, p. 32.

[76] MBA, vol. 3, p. 236; LMF, p. 826 (5 October 1782).

[77] MBA, vol. 3, p. 238; LMF, p. 828 (12 October 1782).

[78] Halliwell, *The Mozart Family*, p. 386.

[79] For a useful list of around 40 different towns and cities in which *Die Entführung* was staged during Mozart's lifetime, including dates of premieres, see Bauman, *Die Entführung*, pp. 103–104. Further information on performances of *Die Entführung* outside Vienna from 1783 onwards is given in Dexter Edge and David Black (eds.), *Mozart: New Documents*, http://dx.doi.org/10.7302/Z20P0WXJ For advertisements for copies of the published score in Mozart's lifetime, see MDL, pp. 203–204, 219, 306; MDB, pp. 229–230, 249, 348–349, and NMD, pp. 40, 104–105. There are also advertisements for manuscript copies from Lorenz Lausch and Wenzel Sukowaty, both based in Vienna: see MDL, pp. 201, 214, 215, 216, 221;

in determining how best to capitalize on compositional success in an uncertain world for a freelance musician, one yet to benefit from musical and social structures to support established career routes. Given his obvious affection for *Die Entführung* and need for it to boost his profile, it is no surprise that Mozart decided to participate himself in a performance for Russian dignitaries in mid-October 1782: 'My opera was given for them recently, for which I deemed it good to play on the clavier again and to conduct, partly to awake the slumbering, sinking orchestra again, and partly – because I am just here – in order to show myself to the ladies and gentlemen present as the father of my child.'[80] Performance, at the heart of the work's genesis where singers and the orchestra were concerned, now encouraged the enterprising Mozart to demonstrate compositional authority.

MDB, pp. 226, 242, 243, 244, 251. By 1789, Johann Georg Meusel could remark that 'the frequently published score . . . has become well known' (NMD, p. 117) and Preisler said he knew the work almost by heart (MDL, p. 285; MDB, p. 325). A previously unnoticed advertisement for the Overture alone was published in *Beylage zu der Neuen Leipziger Gelehrten Zeitung* (Leipzig, May 1785), p. 78.

[80] MBA, vol. 3, p. 239; LMF, p. 828 (letter of 19 October 1782). Mozart also conducted a performance at Aloysia's benefit at the Kärtnerthortheater on 25 January 1784. See MDL, p. 196; MDB, p. 221.

PART II

Instrumental and Vocal Music, 1782–1786

3 | Consolidating Experiences and Expanding Horizons
The Instrumental Music, 1782–1783

Mozart's personal life underwent twists and turns between the premiere of *Die Entführung* on 16 July 1782 and the end of 1783. Pleading with Leopold in two letters at the end of July for consent to marry Constanze, Mozart went ahead without it at St Stephen's Cathedral on 4 August 1782, enjoyed a wedding banquet laid on by Baroness von Waldstätten and received his father's blessing only after the event.[1] Constanze's subsequent pregnancy, as well as weather conditions and Viennese commitments, delayed the planned bridal visit to Salzburg, which ultimately took place between 28 July and 27 October 1783 after she had given birth to Raimund Leopold on 17 June.[2] On the return trip to Vienna, the Mozarts spent a month in Linz as guests of Count Johann Joseph Anton Thun (1711–1788), father-in-law of Viennese supporter Countess Thun: 'I cannot say enough to you how much we are being showered with courtesy in this house', Mozart wrote to his father.[3] Baby Raimund did not travel to Salzburg with his parents, remaining in Vienna with a carer, and died of intestinal cramp on 19 August.

Rich and varied instrumental activities between mid-1782 and the end of 1783 included a considerable number of appearances at Viennese public concerts. In late spring and summer 1782 Mozart began an association with the impresario Philipp Jakob Martin, who planned twelve Sunday concerts at the Augarten, a park frequented year round by 'posh people' on account of 'pleasant passages, hedges and amusing little woods'.[4] As Mozart explained to his father: 'The subscription for the whole summer is two ducats. Well, you can easily imagine that we will get enough subscribers. All the more so as I am taking it on and am associated with it.'[5] Mozart certainly participated in

---

[1] MBA, vol. 3, pp. 215, 216–217, 218–219; LMF, pp. 810, 811, 813 (27 July, 31 July, 7 August 1782).

[2] See the explanations for delays to the Salzburg trip in MBA, vol. 3, pp. 241, 242; LMF, pp. 830, 831 (13 and 20 November 1782).

[3] MBA, vol. 3, p. 291; LMF, p. 859 (31 October 1783).

[4] Johann Georg Keyßler, *Neueste Reisen durch Deutschland, Böhmen, Ungarn, die Schweiz, Italien und Lothringen* (Hannover, 1751), p. 1227: 'Der Au-Garten steht zu aller Jahreszeit offen, und ist wegen seiner angenehmen Gänge, Hecken und lustigen Wäldlein niemals vornehme Leute'. For another positive assessment of the Augarten from the late eighteenth century, see Reitzenstein, *Reise nach Wien*, pp. 323–324.

[5] MBA, vol. 3, p. 208; LMF, p. 805 (8 May 1782).

the first concert on 26 May, attended by Baron van Swieten, Archduke Maximilian and Countess Thun among others, contributing a symphony (possibly K. 338) and the Two-Piano Concerto K. 365 with Auernhammer.[6] It is not known, though, what Mozart provided (if anything) for a subsequent Martin concert on 9 June, attended by the emperor, or related events at the Neumarkt on 11 and 18 August.[7] His involvement was praised by Viennese musician Benedikt Schwarz: 'Herr Kapellmeister Mozart, one of the greatest European virtuosos, obliged the society no less, since several times at his unrivaled pianoforte he produced the sweetest enchantment and the appropriate admiration through his brilliant performance.'[8] Autumn, winter and spring of 1782–1783 saw public appearances gain a head of steam, in addition to private renditions at the residences of Countess Thun, Councillor Anton von Spielmann and Count Esterházy (14 December, 4 January, 12 March): on 3 November he played a concerto at Auernhammer's concert at the Kärntnertortheater; on 11 January he contributed the rondò 'Mia speranza', K. 416, sung by Aloysia Lange, to a concert at the Mehlgrube; and on 11 and 30 March he performed the piano concertos K. 175 + 382 and K. 415 at Lange's and Therese Teyber's academies respectively, both at the Burgtheater. At Teyber's event, he held the audience in the palm of his hand:

I had to repeat the rondo – so I sat down again – but instead of repeating the rondo I had the rostrum taken away in order to play alone. You should have heard how this little surprise delighted the audience. They not only clapped, but shouted 'bravo' and 'bravissimo'. The emperor also fully heard me out – and as I left the piano he left the box – so, he was still there only to hear me.[9]

And on 23 March, Mozart gave his own academy at the Burgtheater (discussed in detail at the end of this chapter), including several old and new orchestral and vocal works, and obligatory improvisations. Soon after returning from the trip to Salzburg, he played a piano concerto and provided a vocal rondò for Adamberger at a Tonkünstler-Societät concert on 22 December 1783, again at the Burgtheater.[10]

[6] MBA, vol. 3, p. 209; LMF, p. 805 (25 May 1782).

[7] On the Martin concerts, see Morrow, *Concert Life in Haydn's Vienna*, pp. 55–57, 251, with corrections in Dexter Edge, 'Review Article: Mary Sue Morrow, *Concert Life in Haydn's Vienna*', p. 144. A wind-band arrangement of *Die Entführung* was performed at the concert on 18 August. While the arranger is unknown, Mozart's involvement cannot be ruled out. See the advertisement from Martin in the *Wiener Zeitung*, 7 August 1782, in MDL, p. 182; MDB, p. 206.

[8] MDL, p. 184; MDB, p. 208.   [9] MBA, vol. 3, p. 265; LMF, pp. 845–846 (12 April 1783).

[10] On this Tonkünstler-Societät concert, see David Black, 'Mozart's Association with the Tonkünstler-Societät', in Keefe (ed.), *Mozart Studies 2*, pp. 55–75, at 60–61.

By 1782–1783, Mozart's life as a performer-composer of instrumental music had several well-developed strands: writing works for himself to perform; responding to *ad hoc* commissions; writing for an ever-expanding network of friends and professional contacts; and composing music intended for public sale. All instrumental works from 1782 to 1783 fit into one or more of these categories. Mozart may have been upset not to procure a court appointment after the success of *Die Entführung* in summer 1782; buoyed by the support of the Viennese nobility but disappointed that the emperor had not tried harder to keep him in Vienna, he actively considered a move to Paris.[11] Once the decision to stay in Vienna was made, all sources of income – pupils, performances at private concerts and salons, opera commissions, academies, and publishing[12] – had to be pursued, especially with Constanze now to support. Publishing assumed particular significance for Mozart between mid-1782 and the end of 1783 (and in later years too, as we shall see): after the six accompanied sonatas K. 296, 376–380 with Artaria in November 1781 (Chapter 1), Mozart directed increasing attention to the dissemination of his music. In 1783, Artaria published two old four-hand piano sonatas, K. 381 in D (1772) and K. 358 in B-flat (1773–1774). New works were written with public sales in mind: the three piano concertos K. 413 in F, K. 414 in A and K. 415 in C; and the piano sonatas K. 330 in C, K. 331 in A, K. 332 in F and K. 333 in B-flat. He also began a set of six string quartets in 1782 that would eventually be published by Artaria in 1785 (see Chapter 5). Mozart's activities as an instrumental performer-composer were increasingly bound up with writing music for others as well as himself to perform, a fact reflected not only in biographical events and circumstances but also, as will be shown, in the music produced. I shall turn first to the piano concertos, performable either by a chamber group or a full orchestra (according to Mozart), and then to a horn concerto and horn quintet composed sensitively and cheekily for Joseph Leutgeb, one of the best horn players of his generation. Discussion of four piano sonatas follows, including differences between Mozart's autographs and first editions. Finally the symphonies and string duos with Salzburg and Linz connections are considered. By way of conclusion I look at Mozart's academy at the Burgtheater on 23 March 1783, probably the most important single musical event for him between mid-July 1782 and the end of 1783.

---

[11] See Ruth Halliwell, *The Mozart Family: Four Lives in a Social Context* (Oxford: Clarendon, 1998), p. 386 and MBA, vol. 3, pp. 220–221; LMF, pp. 814–815 (17 August 1782).

[12] For useful summaries of income streams, see Julia Moore, 'Mozart in the Market Place', *Journal of the Royal Musical Association*, 114 (1989), pp. 18–42, reprinted in Simon P. Keefe (ed.), *Mozart* (Farnham: Ashgate, 2015), pp. 65–89; and Halliwell, *The Mozart Family*, pp. 390–395.

The Piano Concertos

In order to understand Mozart's three Viennese piano concertos K. 413, 414 and 415, written in 1782–1783, we need to begin with the circumstances surrounding their composition.[13] The concertos were intended both for Mozart himself and for musicians who purchased manuscript copies through the kind of subscription scheme that was not uncommon among composers, music copyists and publishers in 1780s Vienna.[14] Announcing their sale in the *Wiener Zeitung* on 15 January 1783, Mozart explained that they 'can be performed with a large orchestra with wind instruments, as well as *a quattro*, namely with 2 violins, 1 viola and violoncello . . . and will be issued (finely copied and looked over by himself) only to those who have subscribed to them'.[15] Just over two weeks earlier, he wrote famously to his father: 'The concertos are a happy medium between too easy and too difficult, are very brilliant, pleasing to the ear, and natural, without falling into emptiness. Here and there connoisseurs alone can derive satisfaction, but in a way that the general listener cannot fail to be pleased either, although without knowing why.'[16] Mozart's newspaper announcement may represent an attempt to broaden the market for the concertos, but it is also an implicit invitation to evaluate them in the context of two different types of performance. The passage from the letter to Leopold, one of the most frequently cited in the family correspondence, can be interpreted in many ways, but above all directs attention to Mozart's engagement with, and expectations of, his listeners and performers.[17]

---

[13] In spite of the complicated genesis of the concertos, it is generally thought that K. 414 was completed first. See John Arthur, 'Some Chronological Problems in Mozart: The Contribution of Ink Studies', in Sadie (ed.), *Mozart: Essays on His Life and His Music*, pp. 35–52; John Irving, *Mozart's Piano Concertos* (Aldershot: Ashgate, 2003), pp. 192–194.

[14] On sales through subscription ('Pränumeration'), including by the composers Anton Eberl and Emanuel Aloys Förster, see Edge, 'Mozart's Viennese Copyists', pp. 142–144.

[15] MDL, pp. 187–188; MDB, p. 212. Mozart also drew attention to the potential for *a quattro* performance as well as by a full orchestra when offering the concertos to the Parisian publisher Jean Georges Sieber. See MBA, vol. 3, p. 266; LMF, p. 846 (26 April 1783).

[16] MBA, vol. 3, pp. 245–246; LMF, p. 833 (28 December 1782).

[17] On interpretations of Mozart's quoted material from his letter, see Simon P. Keefe, 'The Concertos in Aesthetic and Stylistic Context', in Keefe (ed.), *The Cambridge Companion to Mozart*, pp. 78–91, at 78–79. Ellwood Derr's argument that K. 413–415 'evidence a string of connections and progressions in various dimensions that serve to coalesce the three concertos into one splendidly integrated larger work, in which operations set forth in K. 414 are expanded upon in K. 413 and finally culminated in K. 415' is designed to show 'something of what Mozart meant when he wrote "here and there only connoisseurs can derive satisfaction"'. See Derr, 'Some Thoughts on the Design of Mozart's Opus 4, the "Subscription Concertos" (K. 414, 413, and 415)', in Zaslaw (ed.), *Mozart's Piano Concertos*, pp. 187–210 (quotations at pp. 190, 207).

On occasion, absent winds in a strings-only performance of K. 413–415 are noticeable for reasons aside from timbre, or on account of a pronounced wind effect at a given moment in a full orchestral rendition: echoes in the opening bars of K. 413/ii are not duplicated in the strings (see Example 3.1); the A' reprise in K. 413/iii (bars 91–105) and three bars from the development section of K. 414/ii (67–69) are unaccompanied when winds are absent; momentary silences occur in K. 415/iii without the sustained wind notes in bars 28–30; and the beautiful effect of the sustained winds and brass at the end of K. 415/iii – the horns and trumpets quietening from *p* to *pp* to coincide with entering oboes, bassoons and timpani – is lost in a strings-only performance.[18] But the relative rarity of such moments suggests that K. 413, 414 and 415 can indeed be performed *a quattro* without significant impoverishment: in other words, as a reasonable alternative to employing a full orchestra with winds, in line with Mozart's claim.[19] In the refined introduction to K. 413/ii, for example (bars 1–8, Example 3.1), some instrumental effects will be lost or reduced in a chamber performance, such as the aforementioned wind echoes in bars 2 and 3, and the swells in bar 8. Potentially, though, other effects will be more not less audible in reduced scoring, notably the succession of *sf* – *p* – *sf* – *p* dynamics in the first violins in bars 6–7 and the move from pizzicato to coll'arco in the cellos and basses in bars 7–8. Arguably, then, gains balance losses where instrumental effects are concerned in strings-only and orchestral renditions.

It is unclear whether *a quattro* in Mozart's formulation designates one player on each string part, or four string parts with more than one player on each.[20] But the former does not appear to be ruled out either by Mozart in his advertisement or by contextual information from the late eighteenth century: both iconographical evidence and surviving parts for a wide range of concertos from 1750–1780 suggest that one-to-a-part renditions took place.[21] A basic difference between instrumental interaction in Mozart's Viennese chamber works, as represented (for example) by the 'Haydn' string quartets, and in his later 'grand' piano concertos – which he tells us

---

[18] The NMA standardizes all winds and brass to *pp* in bar 259 of K. 415/iii, even though Mozart gives a *pia:* (i.e. *p*) to the oboes, bassoons and timpani. For autographs of the three piano concertos held in the Biblioteka Jagiellońska in Kraków, see Mus. ms. autogr. W. A. Mozart 382/413/414/415.

[19] Critics for whom impoverishment in wind-less performances of K. 413–415 is nonetheless tangible include Marius Flothuis, *Mozart's Piano Concertos* (Amsterdam: Rodolpi, 2001), p. 24; and Heartz, *Mozart, Haydn, Early Beethoven*, p. 51.

[20] Neal Zaslaw, 'Contexts for Mozart's Piano Concertos', in Zaslaw (ed.), *Mozart's Piano Concertos*, pp. 10–12.

[21] See Zaslaw, 'Contexts for Mozart's Piano Concertos', p. 10; Richard Maunder, *The Scoring of Early Classical Concertos, 1750–1780* (Woodbridge and Rochester, NY: The Boydell Press, 2014).

Example 3.1 Mozart, Piano Concerto in F, K. 413/ii, bars 1–9.

cannot be performed by a small orchestra without wind[22] – can offer a vantage point from which to evaluate small- and larger-scale performances of K. 413, K. 414 and K. 415. In the piano concertos, relationships between the soloist and the orchestra evolve through dialogue in individual passages and across movements and entire works. Interwoven cooperation and confrontation has defined the dialogue as dramatic to critics and aestheticians ever since the late eighteenth century – dramatic both as an energized process of negotiating relationships and, from time to time, as an intensified moment of exchange.[23] In contrast, dialogue in Mozart's 'Haydn' string quartets is less about the four instruments negotiating their respective positions in the ensemble than it is about the act of conversing itself. The latter lies at the heart of widespread analogies between the string quartet and conversation in the late eighteenth and early nineteenth centuries, where the social aspect of spoken discourse is reflected in the quartet (most famously Goethe's 'four intelligent people conversing among themselves').[24] Late-eighteenth- and early-nineteenth-century conversationalists address general relations among participants, but more from the perspective of a prized equality of contribution than an active negotiation and renegotiation of internal relationships.[25] Needless to say, Mozart's two violins, viola and cello, often do not participate in any sense 'equally' in passages, sections or whole movements of his 'Haydn' quartets. But through mutual musical support they invariably speak as a single unit in which explicit internal contradiction is rarely evident. The same cannot always be said of the piano concertos from 1784 to 1786: confrontations between piano and orchestra, virtuosic brilliance for the soloist, and different levels of orchestral participation in the context of evolving solo-orchestra relationships across movements suggest multiple units speaking with sometimes similar, sometimes different voices.

Where do K. 413, 414 and 415 sit in relation to the expectations for interaction in Mozart's string quartets and later piano concertos,

---

[22] MBA, vol. 3, pp. 314, 315; LMF, pp. 877 (15 May 1784), 877 (26 May 1784).

[23] Keefe, *Mozart's Piano Concertos*.

[24] For a recent interpretation of Mozart's chamber music using conversation and sociability as its point of departure see Klorman, *Mozart's Music of Friends*.

[25] For discussions of relations among participants in conversation, see, for example, William Traugott Krug, *Allgemeines Handwörterbuch der philosophischen Wissenschaften, nebst ihrer Literatur und Geschichte* (Leipzig: Brockhaus, 1827), p. 532; and Johann Georg Walch, *Philosophisches Lexikon* (Leipzig, 1775; reprint, Hildesheim, 1968), 2 vols., vol. 1, p. 638. On 'Privilege of Turn', implying equality of contribution, see Anthony Ashley Cooper, 3rd Earl of Shaftesbury, *Characteristics of Men, Manners, Opinions, Times* (London, 1711; reprint, Hildesheim, 1978), 3 vols., vol. 1, p. 76.

accepting that both chamber and orchestral performing models may apply to these three concertos? Needless to say, passages of brilliant writing in the outer movements distinguish participants. Elsewhere in the first movements in particular, though, attention is drawn to *both* similarities and differences between piano and orchestral material and their respective roles as soloist and accompanists, illuminating a connection between chamber and orchestral-concerto interaction. The dynamic between similarity and difference is exposed soon after the soloist enters in K. 414/i. The second part of the theme is embellished in the piano (bars 76–82, Example 3.2), an act that distinguishes soloist from orchestra and is perhaps illustrative in notated form of the kind of unnotated embellishments Mozart himself would have carried out in performance. But the piano's scalar elaborations also morph into ritornello material duly picked up by the strings; a connection between piano and orchestra coexists with an accentuation of their different roles. Similarity and difference is also insinuated in the tiny variation to the orchestra's articulation from the end of the ritornello at the beginning of the transition in the piano (bars 84–86, Example 3.2). Mutual dependence and independence surface in the second half of the development and in the recapitulation: a close exchange between piano and first violins – including modest quaver embellishments for both on the repeat – leads to *sfp* accents that distinguish the strings from the piano (see bars 172–186); and an A-major cadential figure in the piano (bars 251–252, Example 3.3) is taken up immediately by the first violin but in less elaborate form (bars 252–253) to begin the reprise of a theme from the orchestral exposition. While Mozart's adjustments to piano figurations in the autograph of the solo exposition transition could have been carried out for a number of reasons (bars 99, 103; see Examples 3.4 and 3.5), they do bring the piano in the revision into close alignment with the preceding orchestral link by recreating the orchestral stress on b' and b. In sum, Mozart directs attention to both the codependence and independence of solo and orchestral material and roles, as in later piano concertos, but places less emphasis than in the later concertos on the dramatic evolution of relations between the two parties over extended periods and more on the momentary, small-scale and harmonious refinements in interaction characteristic of his 'Haydn' quartets.

In K. 415/i, Mozart provides players with special opportunities to shape instrumental interaction. Varied (and equally viable) interpretations of the piano's dynamic levels early in the solo exposition can affect how the relationship between piano and orchestra is processed: in short, whether

Example 3.2 Mozart, Piano Concerto in A, K. 414/i, bars 74–87.

Example 3.3 Mozart, Piano Concerto in A, K. 414/i, bars 250–253.

Example 3.4 Mozart, Piano Concerto in A, K. 414/i, bars 96–102 (final version).

Example 3.5 Mozart, Piano Concerto in A, K. 414/i, bars 99, 103 (original piano material).

they work cooperatively or are on somewhat different wavelengths. At its initial solo entry (Example 3.6), the pianist has to determine whether to emulate the loud, exiting orchestra or to contrast with it, and, similarly, whether to finish *piano* at the end of the segment in bar 67 in order to match the dynamic of the entering first violins, or to distinguish itself by sustaining a *forte* (or a dynamic in between *p* and *f*) through to the end. The subsequent passage from the octave leaps in bar 70 until the imperfect cadence in bar 77 invites similar decisions from the pianist relative to the orchestra's prevailing *piano* then *forte* dynamics. The secondary theme, to which the first violin provides a refined, *piano* link, appears to be a more unambiguously collaborative solo-orchestra environment. Mozart's semiquaver runs in the approach to the cadential trill (see bars 142–145), the product of an autograph revision, also prepare more thoroughly for the orchestral scalar writing in the middle ritornello than the original angular semiquavers would have done, perhaps again accentuating piano-orchestra collaboration.

In the development and recapitulation of K. 415/i, as in the exposition, performance decisions have an effect on the perceived relationship between the piano and the orchestra. The orchestra clearly ends the middle ritornello *forte*. But at what dynamic levels should the piano begin and end their matching passages in bars 160–166 (Example 3.7) and 168–176 in the first half of the development, and should the passages themselves be similarly or differently orientated? Options for the piano at bars 160–168 include *f – p* to match the dynamics of the exiting then entering orchestra; *f – f* or *p – p* to complement and contrast; or *p – f* to contrast with the orchestra's exiting and entering levels, but to pre-empt the orchestral crescendo from *p* to *f* in bars 166–168. Dynamic gradations between *f* and *p* are entirely possible too, of course; decisions by performers will contribute to understandings of piano-orchestra relations irrespective of the specific dynamic levels chosen. A pianist must also decide whether to duplicate or to alter dynamic levels from the solo exposition in the recapitulation. Performing K. 415 *a quattro*, or with a full orchestra, may shape

Example 3.6 Mozart, Piano Concerto in C, K. 415/i, bars 57–67.

Example 3.7 Mozart, Piano Concerto in C, K. 415/i, bars 158–167.

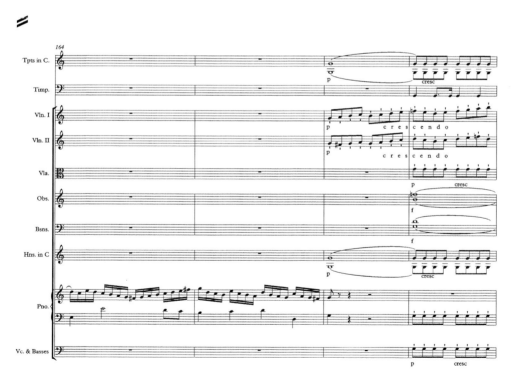

a pianist's interpretations of the first movement from moment to moment and over an extended period. A fundamental feature of the concerto's identity is at stake here – its status as a dramatic work in the manner of Mozart's later concertos, as a conversational work in a chamber-like idiom, or as something in between. Full-orchestra performance may orientate players towards drama and *a quattro* performance towards conversation, but other interpretations are possible.

While the first movements of K. 414 and K. 415 capture a dynamic relationship between *a quattro* and orchestral versions of the concertos in the spirit of the *Wiener Zeitung* announcement, the slow movements model the roles of creative performer and performer-composer to the purchasers of the concertos. Mozart's innumerable written embellishments of piano material in the three middle movements, primarily melodic and rhythmic, do not represent 'repetition mania' redolent of uninspired composition,[26] but they demonstrate imaginative performance to prospective soloists. (No doubt Mozart would have added further, unnotated elaborations in his own performances.) Orchestral instruments are also involved in the embellishment process. The orchestral introduction to K. 415/ii, for example, initiates it with two eight-bar iterations of the main theme where the second is a melodic, rhythmic and instrumental elaboration of the first. Thereafter the piano receives written embellishments at every available opportunity, including ornaments, rhythmic modifications and melodic decorations, and in progressively shorter units over the course of the exposition and reprise. The piano's decorative *tour de force* at the beginning of the recapitulation inspires the orchestra to embellish its own bars 11–12 in 61–62, which in turn catalyzes further elaborative activity in the piano's continuation of the orchestral statement. Bars 74–77 (Example 3.8) are a climactic moment for the solo piano, with free-floating elaborations, and for the orchestra, which combines *pf, f – p*, and *p – decrescendo* dynamic effects,[27] thus bringing together highpoints

---

[26] See Girdlestone, *Mozart and His Piano Concertos*, p. 154. Others critical of K. 415 include Flothuis, *Mozart's Piano Concertos*, p. 28 and Arthur Hutchings, *A Companion to Mozart's Piano Concertos* (London: Oxford University Press, 1948), p. 76. In contrast, Abert admires ornamental embellishment in K. 413–415, singling out K. 415 for special praise. See *W. A. Mozart*, pp. 874–875.

[27] The NMA (V/15/3) heavily edits the orchestral dynamics written by Mozart into his autograph at bars 74–77. The *fp* given by the NMA for the oboes in bar 74 was written as *pf* by Mozart – standing for 'poco forte' and '[indicating] a dynamic level between *f* and *mf* (Brown, *Classical and Romantic Performing Practice*, p. 61) – and the NMA's *f – p* in the basses in bars 74 and 75 by Mozart as *pf – p*. The violin and viola parts in bar 75 are clearly annotated by Mozart on separate notes as *f – p*, but are rendered *fp* in the NMA.

Example 3.8 Mozart, Piano Concerto in C, K. 415/ii, bars 74–78.

for the soloist *qua* soloist and the orchestra as purveyor of refined sound. The orchestra also contributes to decorative activities in K. 414/ii and K. 413/ii: the thrice-repeated cadential gestures early in the development section of the former activate different piano embellishments on each occasion; and products of piano elaborations in the recapitulation of the latter (semiquaver neighbour-note figures) are imitated in the first violins (bar 46), the act of embellishment thereby stimulating piano-orchestra dialogue.

Perhaps the rarefied decorations for soloist and orchestra (or *a quattro* players) witnessed in the concerto slow movements begin to offer an explanation for both the artistic success *and* commercial failure of K. 413–415, at least in 1783.[28] To be sure, Mozart's high price for his manuscript copies – a popular way of distributing music in early 1780s Vienna – would have affected sales, and the price was progressively lowered in 1783.[29] But one wonders whether the nature of the works themselves affected audiences and prospective performers. Mozart certainly had considerable success as the performer-composer of K. 415, playing it a number of times in 1783 in Vienna, including at Therese Teyber's academy on 30 March, where an encore of the finale was requested, and once in Salzburg; the exalted reception of the 23 March Burgtheater academy was also partially attributed by contemporary critics to his performance of K. 415 (see below).[30] It is possible nevertheless that the very qualities audiences would have found so remarkable on those occasions, including the finely executed embellishments for both soloist and accompanists, came to be considered to all intents and purposes inimitable by audiences and potential performers. To be sure, there is no evidence that purchasers were put off Mozart's published keyboard variation sets by his exemplary (and probably significantly longer) improvised performances on their themes at concerts. But those purchasing the concertos – and Mozart's subscription scheme principally targeted amateurs – would have had to face the reality of neither emulating Mozart's performing achievements

---

[28] Sales of the works were higher after publication by Artaria in 1785; at least 500 copies were sold between 1785 and 1801. The greater success of K. 413–415 after 1785 could be attributed to the distribution of the concertos individually, rather than as a set of three, or to Artaria's marketing skills. See Irving, *Mozart's Piano Concertos*, p. 195; Landon, *Golden Years*, p. 88. The remarkable increase in Mozart's posthumous reputation in the 1790s also may have boosted sales.

[29] See Halliwell, *Mozart Family*, pp. 395–396.

[30] On the Teyber academy, see MBA, vol. 3, p. 265; LMF, p. 845 (12 April 1783). For the Salzburg performance, see Halliwell, *The Mozart Family*, p. 416. On performance parts used at the Salzburg performance, but originating with Joseph Arthofer in Vienna, see Dexter Edge, 'Recent Discoveries in Viennese Copies of Mozart's Concertos', in Zaslaw (ed.), *Mozart's Piano Concertos*, pp. 51–65. K. 415 may have been the piano concerto Mozart performed at the Tonkünstler-Societät concert on 22 December 1783; see H. C. Robbins Landon, *Haydn, Chronicle and Works: Volume 2, Haydn at Eszterháza, 1766–1790* (London: Thames & Hudson, 1978), p. 16.

nor doing justice to their sophisticated and elaborate orchestral writing. Playing experiences might have proved less than fulfilling as a result, especially if one of Mozart's own renditions were simultaneously ringing in their ears.

Mozart thought carefully about the effects of K. 415 in performance, but probably more about how he and his own orchestra would benefit in concert than the purchasers of the manuscript copies and their co-players. The needs of these two intended groups were not mutually exclusive, of course. Nevertheless, the presence of a large orchestra in the outer movements (including bassoons, trumpets and timpani as well as oboes and horns) and the pianistic brilliance of the finale would have been more obvious to his advantage than to the advantage of his subscribers. Perhaps Mozart's needs trumped those of the subscribers in other respects too. If he rejected the original C-minor version of his slow movement because he did not want to undermine the C-minor Adagio in the finale, and if he cancelled a German augmented 6th chord in the original run-up to the finale Adagio because he did not want to steal the thunder of the chord's appearance four bars before the end of the Adagio (bar 60), he was probably considering more proactively the expressive effects of his own performance than those of his potential manuscript purchasers.[31] Even the aforementioned delicateness of the finale's conclusion – a special instrumental effect reserved for the end as in the Rondo for violin and orchestra K. 373 – would have benefited a Mozart performance primarily. Mozart's claim to have written brilliant and pleasing concertos that occupy the middle ground between the easy and the difficult is reasonable based on empirical musical evidence alone. But piano concertos were a highly personal medium for Mozart, more closely linked to his own combination of performing and compositional talents than works in any other genre. Even though K. 413–415 were intended for sale right from the start, then, Mozart's own performance needs remained paramount for practical (and maybe psychological) reasons. As a result, the popularity for which he strove was always going to be more achievable in relation to the expectations of his concert audiences than the expectations and needs of his (mainly amateur) subscribers.

---

[31] The connection between the aborted C-minor second movement and the C-minor passages in the finale has been noted in the secondary literature. See NMA, V/15/3, p. x; Derr, 'Some Thoughts on the Design of Mozart's Opus 4', in Zaslaw (ed.), *Mozart's Piano Concertos*, p. 205; Heartz, *Mozart, Haydn and Early Beethoven*, p. 51. As revealed in the autograph score, Mozart originally envisaged that the tutti chords preceding the Adagio in the K. 415 finale would begin in bar 44 and including a German augmented 6th – V progression (subsequently revised to diminished 7th – V).

Mozart made two contributions to the piano concerto genre in 1782–1783 in addition to K. 413, 414 and 415. He began K. 449 in E-flat alongside K. 413–415, composing as far as the middle ritornello in the first movement, then set the work aside and completed it in spring 1784 for the subscription concerts at which K. 450 in B-flat, K. 451 in D and K. 453 in G were also premiered.[32] The protracted genesis of K. 449 results in a hybrid of K. 413–415 and K. 450, 451 and 453, 'a concerto of an entirely special manner, composed rather for a small orchestra than for a large one' according to Mozart himself, in which explicit dramatic confrontation between piano and orchestra enters the stylistic equation.[33] No such interruptions affected the composition of the Rondo in A for piano and orchestra, K. 386 (19 October 1782). Long thought to be either an original or replacement finale for the A-major concerto K. 414, it was just as likely intended as an independent work, one perhaps building on the success of the Rondo K. 382 earlier in 1782.[34] Whatever the case may be, the ending of K. 386, newly discovered by Alan Tyson in 1980,[35] incorporates multi-tiered effects like K. 413–415 and gives Mozart a special opportunity to shine as performer-composer. The statement of the main theme in the piano towards the end gives way to a brisk antecedent-consequent dialogue between piano and orchestra (the strings are marked *forte*), and an eventual brief elaboration of the quaver-quaver-crotchet consequent with semiquavers and semi-quaver triplets in the piano (see Example 3.9). The oscillation of C-sharp and A in a new, four-quaver piano figure delicately imitated in the orchestra generates the arpeggiated piano demisemiquavers and string semiquavers that bring the work to a close (Example 3.9). Mozart apparently intended a staged crescendo to the *forte* marked for all orchestral instruments four bars from the end: an *f* is given in the strings in the middle of the sixth last bar and a crescendo across the sixth and fifth last

---

[32] See Chapter 4 for discussion of K. 449 and the piano concertos from 1784–86. Critics have speculated that Mozart set aside K. 449 midway through the first movement because it had grown 'too big for what he wanted', had a more difficult piano part than K. 413–415, and duplicated the triple meter of K. 413. See Küster, *Musical Biography*, p. 177; Flothuis, *Mozart's Piano Concertos*, p. 30; Elaine Sisman, 'Observations on the First Phase of Mozart's "Haydn" Quartets', in Dorothea Link and Judy Nagley (eds.), *Words About Mozart: Essays in Honour of Stanley Sadie* (Woodbridge and Rochester, NY: The Boydell Press, 2005), pp. 33–58, at 49–50.

[33] See Simon P. Keefe, '"An Entirely Special Manner": Mozart's Piano Concerto No. 14 in E-flat, K. 449, and the Stylistic Implications of Confrontation', *Music & Letters*, 82 (2001), pp. 559–581 and *Mozart's Viennese Instrumental Music: A Study of Stylistic Re-Invention* (Woodbridge and Rochester, NY: Boydell Press, 2007), pp. 19–42. For Mozart's comment, in a letter to his father, see MBA, vol. 3, p. 315; LMF, p. 877 (26 May 1784).

[34] See Tyson, *Autograph Scores*, pp. 281, 289.   [35] Tyson, *Autograph Scores*, pp. 262–289.

Example 3.9 Mozart, Rondo for piano and orchestra, K. 386, conclusion.

bars in the oboes (also implied for the horns); the soloist must decide whether to start its demisemiquavers at a *forte* dynamic, before the strings' *forte*, or to align itself dynamically with either the strings or the winds.[36] Thus, the combination in K. 386's last 25 bars of forceful and

---

[36] Mozart's *for:* indication to the strings midway through the sixth last bar may imply a crescendo to *forte* in the first half of the bar, but it surely denotes the moment this dynamic level arrives rather than the beginning of a crescendo. For the same *for:* indication is given to the strings six beats later in the coordinated *forte* arrival for the full band.

refined dialogue, gentle solo elaboration and virtuosic brilliance, and a staggered increase in volume to the coordinated climax, promotes both Mozart's expressive and dexterous virtuosity and his compositional ingenuity.

The Horn Concerto and Horn Quintet

Mozart wrote both the Horn Quintet K. 407 (late 1782) and the Horn Concerto K. 417 (27 May 1783) for his friend Joseph Leutgeb. The two men had known each other in Salzburg, where Leutgeb played in the court orchestra from 1762/1763 onwards, and then reconvened in Vienna; Leutgeb had opened a cheese shop in the city some time before Mozart's arrival in 1781. Identified by Karl Ditters von Dittersdorf as one of the era's great horn virtuosos,[37] Leutgeb was best known for his expressive playing. The *Mercure de France* reported him performing two concertos at the Concert Spirituel in May 1770 'as artistically as is possible. He gets intonations from this instrument that connoisseurs do not stop hearing with surprise. His merit above all is to sing the Adagio as perfectly as the most mellow, interesting and true voice could do'.[38] *L'Avantcoureur feuille hebdomadaire* wrote of the same performance that 'the music and amazing playing were applauded equally'.[39]

Mozart exploited Leutgeb's cantabile playing in the Andante of the concerto K. 417, remaining simultaneously attentive to the capabilities and limitations of the natural horn. Both of the principal themes in the horn (bars 11–14 and 29–36) feature open notes almost exclusively, facilitating consistency of tone. Hand-stopped notes in conjunction with open ones, moreover, often support other musical implications: the half-stopped b-natural' (sounding d') at the end of bar 14 follows two open notes, creating a natural falling away at the end of the phrase (Example 3.10); the open g", e" and d" in bars 22–23 (Example 3.10) directly follow a tricky note for the natural horn, f-sharp", bringing forth

---

[37] Ditters von Dittersdorf, *Lebenbeschreibung*, p. 50.

[38] See *Mercure de France* (May 1770), p. 164. 'M. Seikgeb . . . a donné deux concertos avec tout l'art possible. Il tire de cet instrument des intonations que les connoisseurs ne cessent d'entendre avec surprise. Son mérite est sur-tout de chanter l'adagio aussi parfaitement, que la voix la plus moëlleuse, la plus intéressante & la plus juste, pourroit faire.'

[39] *L'Avantcoureur feuille hebdomadaire* (Paris, 1770), p. 250: 'la musique & l'étonnante exécution ont été également applaudies'.

Example 3.10 Mozart, Horn Concerto in E-flat, K. 417/ii, bars 11–28.

a spontaneous crescendo into the ensuing orchestral phrase (an imitation of the horn's preceding phrase) that contains its own notated crescendo to *forte*; and segments with a concentration of problematic horn f-sharps" (bars 38–9, 62–3, including difficult a"s as well) are buttressed by string

Example 3.11 Mozart, Horn Concerto in E-flat, K. 417/ii, bars 80–85.

semiquavers.[40] The last six bars of the movement (Example 3.11) combine expressive virtuosity for the soloist with refined effects for soloist and orchestra together. The horn descends two octaves from its registral highpoint to low-point for the movement (written g", sounding b-flat' to g, sounding B-flat), and simultaneously from the top to the bottom of the orchestral texture; the horn and orchestral winds are heard together for the only time, the *f* dynamic climax three bars from the end coinciding with a horn open note (written d") to facilitate *forte* playing; and the full group produce a collective, coordinated drop to the softest dynamic level of the movement, *pp*, reached in the penultimate bar. As in works such as the Rondo for violin and orchestra K. 373 and the Piano Concerto K. 415, Mozart introduces special effects for both soloist and orchestra right at the end, exploiting one final opportunity (at least in this movement) to demonstrate combined performance and compositional acumen.

---

[40] For a succinct summary of open and hand-stopped notes on the natural horn, see John Humphries, *The Early Horn: A Practical Guide* (Cambridge: Cambridge University Press, 2000), pp. 58–62.

Example 3.12 Mozart, Horn Concerto in E-flat, K. 417/i, bars 114–118.

While no autograph materials survive for the Andante, the autograph of the first movement of K. 417 shows Mozart attuned to timbral and textural resonances in combined solo and orchestral parts.[41] The only dynamic marking given to the solo horn is an *sf* for the b' semibreve (sounding d') in the bar before the recapitulation (Example 3.12). Since the b' is a half-stopped note, and a crescendo also assigned to the strings in this bar, the *sf* in part ensures the soloist's audibility. Mozart carefully delineates the end of the strings' crescendo, aligning all four colons (*cresc:*) with the end of the bar and thus accentuating the drop to *p* at the moment of recapitulation. The *sf*, designating more than a momentary dynamic inflection,[42] is probably to remain in force until the bar-line as well, a distinctive horn sound and a swelling string sound thus contributing equally to the surge in intensity and subsequent dynamic drop.

The rondo finale of K. 417, which again exploits Leutgeb's expressive playing in a poignant theme in the D section (bars 112–120), is above all a humorous musical complement to Mozart's jocular scrawl on the autograph taking pity on Leutgeb, 'donkey, ox and fool' (*Esel, Ochs und Narrn*). The stuttering main theme at the final return, followed immediately by the quicker 'Più Allegro', is a case in point (Example 3.13). The autograph suggests that the stuttering was an afterthought:[43] he

---

[41] The autograph of K. 417 breaks off after bar 176 of the first movement, 14 bars before the end, and resumes at the beginning of the finale (which is extant in complete form). For a facsimile, see Hans Pizka (ed.), *Das Horn bei Mozart: Facsimile Collection* (Munich: Schöttner, 1980).

[42] See Levin, 'The Devil's in the Details', in Zaslaw (ed.), *Mozart's Piano Concertos*, p. 32.

[43] An alternative interpretation is that Mozart intended it from the start, but momentarily forgot to include it when he reached the requisite phrase.

Example 3.13 Mozart, Horn Concerto in E-flat, K. 417/iii, bars 145–158.

smudged out the original horn material in bar 148 (where the stuttering
starts), but an e-flat" and c" are still visible as the original second and
third quavers of the bar and are the notes the horn would have received
had it progressed straightforwardly through the theme. Unexpected
events at the end of this standard rondo movement – a fragmented
theme followed by the 'Più Allegro' – parallels Haydn's finale to Op. 33,
No. 2 ('Joke'), another uncomplicated rondo until the famous final
return, and a work exerting an influence on Mozart at the time of the
horn concerto's composition, notably as he carried out a first phase of
work on the set of string quartets eventually dedicated to Haydn.

Mozart's humour in K. 417/iii also surfaces in the semiquaver-
semiquaver-quaver rhythm that activates the horn's stuttering in bars
147^2–148^1 and appears throughout the movement. Heard as a repeated-
note figure, it is one of few pieces of material resistant to dialogue
between soloist and orchestra: the orchestra does not pick it up from
the horn either in the B section, or at the opening of C. Indeed, in C, its
place is taken by a mocking, acciaccatura violin figure (bars 73–89). It is
perhaps surprising, then, that the strings subsequently adopt it, *forte*, as

Example 3.14 Mozart, Horn Quintet in E-flat, K. 407/iii, bars 1–9.

a link to the A" return (see bars 95–96), and that the full orchestra, plus the solo horn, employ it as a comically overused backdrop to the 'Più Allegro' (see Example 3.13). Mozart thus engages Leutgeb, orchestral performers and his audience with the predictability, unpredictability and humorous implications of his thematic material.

The Horn Quintet K. 407 (late 1782), often likened to the horn concertos, shares K. 417's sense of humour and sensitivity to instrumental limitations.[44] The main theme of the rondo finale, for example, is intrinsically comical (Example 3.14). Mozart plays with metrical implications and expectations, his upbeat conveyed as a downbeat especially once the tonic is reached in the middle of bar 2. The two violas and cello, entering on the notated downbeat in the first phrase but on the notated upbeat in the second, also confuse matters. Internally repetitive – bars 5–8 are a near replica of bars 1–4 – the theme is self-consciously unpromising. What is more, Mozart in effect 'overuses' his limited theme by including it in the dominant (bars 39–46) shortly before the first rondo return.

[44] On connections between the Horn Quintet K. 407 and the horn concertos see Abert, *W. A. Mozart*, p. 866; Gutman, *Mozart*, p. 637; Cliff Eisen, 'Mozart's Chamber Music', in Keefe (ed.), *Cambridge Companion to Mozart*, p. 116; Sarah Adams, 'Chamber Music: Mixed Ensembles', in Eisen and Keefe (eds.), *Cambridge Mozart Encyclopedia*, p. 86; Nicole Schwindt, 'Die Kammermusik', in Silke Leopold (ed.), *Mozart Handbuch* (Kassel: Bärenreiter, 2005), p. 429. Julian Rushton identifies K. 407 as 'delightfully witty' and details Mozart's knowledge and skill at writing for the horn when reshaping material from the first-movement exposition in the recapitulation in order to promote melodic variety and to accommodate the technical limitations of the instrument. See Rushton, *Mozart: Master Musicians*, p. 169 and 'Play or Compulsion? Variation in Recapitulations in Mozart's Music for Wind Instruments', in Simon P. Keefe (ed.), *Mozart Studies* (Cambridge: Cambridge University Press, 2006), pp. 47–73, at 57–59.

Example 3.15 Mozart, Horn Quintet in E-flat, K. 407/iii, bars 115–127.

In addition to promoting a theme of dubious distinction, Mozart jokes with Leutgeb and the string ensemble. In the run-up to the final Rondo return (bar 108ff., Example 3.15) the horn begins a pattern of scalar ascents taken up first by the violin and then by each of the strings in turn. Once they have imitated the figure, in ascending order and at one-bar intervals, it is reasonable to expect the horn to continue the process. Instead, the horn repeatedly presents a simple neighbour-note figure around G (sounding B-flat), up and down octaves; it is as if Mozart ribs Leutgeb about his ability. More of the same is to follow towards the end of the work, when the horn gets stuck on c′ for six consecutive bars (157–162). But now there is a twist: as if frustrated at going nowhere, the horn explodes into an archetypally virtuosic flourish (arpeggiated triplet quavers over two and a half octaves) that takes it to a concerto-like cadential trill. The boot is then on the other foot, as the strings rigidly imitate the main theme, leaving the horn to come to the rescue with an entry that brings unproductive imitative matters to a close. As in the concerto K. 417/iii, then, Mozart plays games with his horn-playing friend.

The Piano Sonatas

The four piano sonatas K. 330 in C, K. 331 in A, K. 332 in F and K. 333 in B-flat cannot be dated as securely as the other works discussed in this chapter to the eighteen months from July 1782 to December 1783. Nevertheless, the prevailing critical opinion is that they were in fact written during this period; Alan Tyson proposed late 1783 specifically, on account of the ten-stave paper on which the autograph scores were written, and that Mozart used for compositions originating in Salzburg.[45] Tyson's suggestion that the sonatas 'would then take their place as teaching works prepared for the busy season that awaited Mozart on his return to Vienna' is also reasonable.[46] The lengthy two-part writing and regularity of phrasing in K. 330, the model embellishment of a repeated harmonic pattern in the first-movement variations in K. 331 and the topical variety of K. 332/i have been offered as further evidence of didactic orientation.[47] But fully factoring into the equation performance-related features associated with composition and publication will necessitate an important refinement to ideas about probable function. Such discussion takes us beyond the strict temporal remit of this chapter and into 1784.

The first edition of K. 330, K. 331 and K. 332 was published by Artaria in summer 1784 and incorporated substantive changes presumably made by Mozart himself.[48] As we shall see in Chapters 5 and 10, a period of at least a few months generally separated submission of an autograph to Artaria and publication of the edition, in some instances providing an opportunity for the composer to introduce additions or changes by annotating a performance copy generated from the autograph.[49] Mozart's decision to append a four-bar

---

[45] Tyson, *Autograph Scores*, pp. 30, 231–232. For the autographs, see Biblioteka Jagiellońska Kraków Mus. ms. autogr. W. A. Mozart 330 (for K. 330); Biblioteca Mozartiana der Internationalen Stiftung Mozarteum Salzburg, Signatur: KV 300i (for K. 331); Scheide Music Library, Princeton, New Jersey, MS 134 (for K. 332); Staatsbibliothek zu Berlin – Preußischer Kulturbesitz, Musikabteilung mit Mendelssohn-Archiv, Signatur: Mus. ms. autogr. W. A. Mozart 333 (for K. 333). Part of the incomplete autograph of K. 331 was recently rediscovered in Budapest: see Balázs Mikusi, '"Possible, Probable or Certain Errors in the First Edition"? Evaluation of a Newly Found Autograph Fragment of the Sonata in A major, K. 331', *Mozart-Jahrbuch 2014*, pp. 335–346.

[46] Tyson, *Autograph Scores*, p. 231.

[47] Irving, *Mozart's Piano Sonatas: Contexts, Sources, Style* (Cambridge: Cambridge University Press, 1997), p. 67.

[48] For Artaria announcements of the publication of K. 330, K. 331 and K. 332 in 1784 see MDL, p. 202 and MDB, p, 227 (25 August); MDL, p. 202 and MDB, p. 228 (18 September). For the edition see *Trois sonates pour le clavecin ou pianoforte composée par W. A. Mozart* (Vienna: Artaria [1784]): https://iiif.lib.harvard.edu/manifests/view/drs:14495231$1i.

[49] On one occasion Haydn asked Artaria to delay publication of a lieder collection until he had had an opportunity to try out the lieder in performance. See Beghin, *The Virtual Haydn*, p. 52.

Example 3.16 Mozart, Piano Sonata in C, K. 330/ii, bars 31–40.

coda to the Andante cantabile of K. 330 is enlightened first of all by the autograph: his initial impulse was to end the B section of his ABA' movement without the four-bar codetta passage (bars 37–40, Example 3.16) that would later correspond with the interpolated coda at the end. Mozart first wrote 'Da Capo maggiore' after bar 36, then scrubbed it out, composed the four-bar codetta and added 'Da Capo maggiore senza Repliche'.[50] By writing the new codetta he more or less replicates the beginning of the B section (with a twist in the last two bars). He also reproduces the effect created at the nexus of A and B: an implied diminuendo from *f* to *p* at the end of A continuing to the *pp* at the beginning of B is matched by an implied diminuendo from *f* to *pp* into the codetta of B (Example 3.16).[51] The onset of B is perceived as a musical beginning as well as a continuation of the diminuendo at the end of A, introducing the minor mode and a new dynamic level. But the codetta to B is an end in itself, bringing the section thematically and dynamically full circle.

Mozart already plays with the idea of beginnings, endings and continuations, then, when working on the autograph and before handing over the score to Artaria to begin the publication process. The new four-bar coda to end the movement in the Artaria edition (see Example 3.17) does more than just balance the codetta to B. Continuing the diminuendo effects from the A-B join and into the B codetta it provides, first and foremost, a version of this material in the tonic major suitable for concluding the Andante

---

[50] See the facsimile in the Preface to the NMA and the Kritische Berichte in NMA, IX/25/1–2, p. 83.

[51] A *p* added to bar 35 beat 2 in the edition that does not appear in the autograph, perhaps indicates Mozart's intention to bring out the correspondence.

Example 3.17 Mozart, Piano Sonata in C, K. 330/ii, bars 56–64 (with dynamics accruing to the Artaria edition given in bold italics and bars 60 [second half]–64 appearing only in the Artaria edition).

cantabile. It also anchors the expressive discourse, presented three times over the movement as a whole and as a definitive closing gesture on the last occasion.[52] In a movement with numerous notated dynamic nuances (in the first edition especially), this four-bar phrase is the only one set at a single, unchanging dynamic level, and the softest level of the Andante cantabile as well. Expressive and dynamic uniformity, in short, appear to be as significant here as dynamic and expressive variety is elsewhere.

Above all, judging by the autograph and the first edition of K. 330/ii, Mozart's putative pedagogical intentions for the piano sonatas are not limited *either* to composition *or* to performance. Published keyboard music in the late eighteenth century may have been aimed primarily at players who did not want to compose.[53] But by bringing together expression, formal design, dynamic nuance, and cues for beginnings and endings, Mozart models engagement between compositional and performance activities that a performer-composer will want ideally to foster.

A dynamics-related discourse characterizes the finale of K. 330 as well as the slow movement. While there are no dynamic markings in the autograph, a number appear in the first edition and presumably can be attributed to Mozart himself, given his involvement in the preparation of the second movement for publication. They include those added to the reprise of the main theme (bars 96–123), which is left unnotated and

---

[52] William Kinderman argues that connections between iterations of this material 'need to be felt and conveyed in performance, so that the listener perceives how the theme is drawn into the darker sphere of the minor and subsequently reclaimed in the major mode'. See Kinderman, *Mozart's Piano Music* (New York: Oxford University Press, 2006), p. 48.

[53] See Beghin, *The Virtual Haydn*, p. 74.

Example 3.18 Mozart, Piano Sonata in C, K. 330/iii, bars 77–101 (with markings accruing to the Artaria edition given in bold italics).

indicated by a 'Da Capo' in the autograph. Given its rarity as a marking in Mozart's piano sonatas, the *sotto voce* at the moment of recapitulation (bar 96, Example 3.18) is of interest, requiring an emotional quality to the playing.[54] Mozart's request for different interpretations of the main theme at the beginnings of the reprise and the exposition may be explained by the events of the development section. The second eight bars of the development (bar 77ff., Example 3.18) embellish the first eight bars with a left-hand semiquaver accompaniment, an *fp* inflection, and a two-bar sequenced pattern with further *f* – *p* markings. Subsequent harmonic colouring (C minor, bars 87–92, Example 3.18) is accompanied by notated thematic embellishment and followed by dynamic 'embellishment': the final two bars of the section (94–95), prolonging the rhythm and dominant harmony of the preceding bars, are reduced to *pp*, the only such dynamic in the movement. (The performer needs to pay attention to the reduction in

---

[54] Badura-Skoda and Badura-Skoda, *Interpreting Mozart*, p. 48. According to the authors, *sotto voce* appears on only one other occasion in Mozart's piano sonatas, in the Adagio of K. 457 (p. 48).

volume to *pp* in light of the simultaneous thickening of the left-hand chords in bar 94–95.) Thus, the *sotto voce* reprise of the main theme continues a process started in the development section; just as Mozart writes embellishments in the development, now he asks the performer to 'elaborate' the main theme at the beginning of the recapitulation by interpreting it differently from earlier on, perhaps at a different dynamic level and certainly with more emotion. Executing dynamics and character indications always involves taste, judgement and interpretation from performers, of course, but here it requires close engagement with the written text over a protracted musical span. How exactly will a *sotto voce* rendition differ from the earlier *p* rendition, and how might the character of the theme evolve or change as a result? By inviting his performer to ponder these issues, after providing a model of thematic, dynamic and harmonic embellishment in the preceding section, Mozart encourages the performer playing from the edition to adopt the mindset of a performer-composer.[55]

The Adagio of K. 332, like the finale of K. 330, contains a passage at the beginning of the reprise that is covered only by a 'Da Capo' in the autograph but is notated in full (with important adjustments) in the first edition, where Mozart provides an embellished version of seven and a half bars (see Example 3.19). Evaluating these embellishments – which continue until the end of the reprise – as well as dynamic interpolations, informs our understanding of the movement as a whole.[56] In the exposition, the first theme and transition (bars 1–8) are distinguished from the thematic material in the secondary key area (bars 9–20) in several ways: the former has an alberti bass accompaniment, generally smooth phrasing and a declamatory climax (bar 7), while the latter is marked by crisp articulation (with numerous strokes) and a repeated-note accompaniment pattern, at least up to bar 14. Both, though, share a penchant for modest embellishment. In the autograph, *sfp* markings are included in the secondary theme but not the first, offering another point of contrast. On the one hand, the first-edition *sfp*s appearing in the first theme bring it slightly more into alignment with the secondary theme; on the other hand, the *sf – p* in bar 7 of the first edition actually accentuates the climax in bar 7, which was one

---

[55] For more on the implications for performers and performances of differences between the autograph and first editions of K. 330, see Irving, *Understanding Mozart's Piano Sonatas*, pp. 59–62. The interaction of dynamics and thematic material in performing the first movement of K. 330 is also discussed (pp. 84–88).

[56] Irving suggests that Mozart may have revised the reprise in order to demonstrate 'his tasteful command of the subtle art of embellishment', or out of consideration for musical events in K. 330 and K. 331, or to extend his pedagogical influence to those purchasing his works. See Irving, *Understanding Mozart's Piano Sonatas*, p. 55.

Example 3.19 Mozart, Piano Sonata in F, K. 332/ii, bars 21–28 (from Artaria first edition).

of the original points of contrast between primary and secondary thematic material.

The written embellishment at the reprise of the first edition (Example 3.19) not only provides an elaboration of a 'plain' text, but also contributes to perceptions of thematic similarity and difference. For embellishments involve articulation as well as melody: the strokes in bars 23 and 24 (first theme) invoke the secondary theme from the exposition; several protracted slurs in bars 35 and 38 (second theme) correspondingly invoke the first theme from the exposition.[57] By making the first theme more demonstrative than earlier on, especially with the hemidemisemiquaver flourish (bar 26), does Mozart contradict the message apparently conveyed by his articulation that distinct themes converge somewhat in the reprise, or does his quick-fire syncopation in the second theme (bars 34–35) provide a counterbalance to the earlier flourish? Ultimately it is left to the performer to decide how to characterize thematic similarities and differences throughout the movement. The embellishments and dynamic interpolations in the first-edition reprise are not only a model for the performer, then, but also a stimulus to interpret, encouraging the performer to assume an imaginative posture. Thus, Mozart's published movement does not cater exclusively to the performer, aiming at the aspiring performer-composer as well.

Torricella published Mozart's Piano Sonata K. 333, also in 1784, alongside the Piano Sonata K. 284 (1775) and the new violin sonata for Regina Strinasacchi, K. 454 in B-flat.[58] It seems Mozart was responsible for dynamic interpolations in the first edition, as in the K. 330–332 Artaria edition.[59] Like K. 330/ii, the Andante cantabile of K. 333 includes written embellishments to the exposition in the reprise, and on this occasion in the autograph as well as the first edition. The only dynamic indication in the autograph is a *pp* in the penultimate bar. The rising quaver figure to which it is attached marks a moment of harmonic stability, namely a resolution to E-flat to end the movement, rather than (as in earlier iterations) a link to the harmonic audacity of the development section at the end of the exposition and at the recapitulation's first-time bar.[60] The association in the autograph between

---

[57] While a single stroke appears in the first theme of the exposition (bar 2, beat 4), strokes are a distinctive feature of the second theme. Phrase markings in the first theme from the exposition extend over more than one beat on several occasions, but do not do so in the second theme.

[58] For an advertisement, see MDL, p. 200; MDB, p. 225–226 (7 July 1784).

[59] Irving, *Understanding Mozart's Piano Sonatas*, p. 62.

[60] Striking harmonic passages in the development of K. 333/ii include the first four bars, where the short step to F minor is made in an unconventional way. Also, an implied C minor in bar 39 is unrealized; a G in the left hand subsequently moves to A-flat to create (in effect) a staggered

Example 3.20 Mozart, Piano Sonata in B-flat, K. 333/ii, bars 43–49 (with dynamics accruing to the Torricella edition given in bold italics).

a distinctive harmonic moment and a distinctive dynamic marking is strengthened in the development section of the first edition at the point of furthest remove from the tonic, the modulation to D-flat minor in bars 46–47 (Example 3.20). In the previous two bars *sf* and *p* indications are positioned a beat (and in the right hand, beat-and-a-half) apart, but are adjusted to simultaneous *sfp*s for the V-i in D-flat minor. The performer, then, is asked to introduce different dynamic inflections into this segment of the development and by extension to ponder associations between harmonies and dynamic nuances in the movement as a whole.

Orchestral and Chamber Music for Salzburg, Linz and Vienna

Mozart's musical life from mid-1782 to late 1783 involved backward glances to Salzburg days as well as a three-month visit to the town itself. Naturally he did not relish returning to a place he detested, even proposing to Leopold a meeting in Munich instead, ostensibly fearing arrest after having received no formal discharge from court service in spring 1781.[61] To those unaffected by past professional circumstances, though, Salzburg was an enticing destination in the 1780s. Travel writer Johann Riesbeck

interrupted cadence even though C minor is never established. Such harmonic progressions perhaps gave rise to Kinderman's interpretation of a development section '[harbouring] passages of probing and even disturbing import'. See Kinderman, *Mozart's Piano Music*, p. 55.

[61] See MBA, vol. 3, p. 270; LMF, p. 849 (21 May 1783).

had a longer than anticipated stay on account of the town's offerings, considering it a 'wonderful play of nature and art' (*bewundernswürdiges Spiel der Natur und Kunst*), with a pretty town centre, excellent buildings and statues, and beautiful places to visit in the surrounding area, including the Untersberg, Hallein and Hellbrunn.[62] In addition: 'Everyone here [in Salzburg] breathes the spirit of enjoyment and fun. One feasts, dances, makes music, loves and plays on the grass, and I have never seen a place where one can have so much sensual enjoyment with so little money.'[63] Once back in residence, Mozart no doubt enjoyed visits with old friends, eating ices and drinking punch, shooting, bathing, taking walks and making music with Nannerl, Leopold and friends.[64] Linz, furthermore, would have been a pleasant place for Mozart and Constanze's one-month layover on their return trip to Vienna. Friedrich Nicolai described it in 1783 as a nicely built, not overly crowded town of about 16,500 inhabitants; Friedrich Schulz a few years later praised its conviviality, excellent views, fine churches and other buildings, and attractive people who benefited from the famous 'Linz blood' (*Linzer Blut*), identifying it as 'lively enough' (*lebhaft genug*), in contrast to Salzburg, which was 'more quiet than lively' (*mehr still, als lebhaft*).[65] Riesbeck cooed over magnificent views of mountains and the Danube, describing it as a pretty town built almost entirely in stone, and an enchanting blend of the rural and urban.[66]

As well as probable work on the piano sonatas and on *L'oca del Cairo* and the Mass in C minor K. 427 (see Chapter 6), Mozart's three months in Salzburg saw the composition of the string duos K. 423 in G and K. 424 in B-flat, which helped Michael Haydn finish a set of six duos for Archbishop Colloredo unable to be completed through illness.[67] Whether Mozart was complicit in

---

[62] Riesbeck, *Briefe eines Reisenden Franzosen*, vol. 1, pp. 118–121, 139.

[63] Riesbeck, *Briefe eines Reisenden Franzosen*, vol. 1, p. 159. 'Alles athmet hier den Geist des Vergnügens und der Lust. Man schmaußt, tanzt, macht Musiken, liebt und spielt zum Rasen, und ich habe noch keinen Ort gesehen, wo man mit so wenig Geld so viel Sinnliches geniessen kann.'

[64] Nannerl records the activities of Mozart and others (from which my list derives) in her diary; see MBA, vol. 3, pp. 282–291, and in tabular form Halliwell, *Mozart Family*, pp. 408–423.

[65] Nicolai, *Beschreibung einer Reise*, vol. 2, p. 522; Schulz, *Reise eines Liefländers von Riga nach Warschau*, vol. 6, pp. 125–127, 129, 80.

[66] Riesbeck, *Briefe eines Reisenden Franzosen*, vol. 1, pp. 176–177.

[67] This story, related by Nissen in his Mozart biography (1828), originates in an early biography of Michael Haydn: F. J. Otter and G. J. Schinn, *Biographie Skizze von J. M. Haydn* (Salzburg, 1808). For a translation of Nissen's statement, and a facsimile of Mozart's autograph score of the duos, see Wolfgang Amadeus Mozart, *Zwei Duos für Violone und Viola: Faksimile der autographen Partitur von 1783 und Stimmen-Ausgabe nach dem Urtext, und Berücksichtigung der Varianten des Artaria-Erstdrucks von 1792*, ed. Ulrich Drüner (Winterthur, Switzerland: Amadeus Verlag, 1980), p. ii. In spite of Otter and Schinn's claim that Haydn kept the K. 423 and 424 autograph

Example 3.21 Mozart, Duo for violin and viola in G, K. 423/i, bars 1–12.

any initial attempt to conceal his own authorship is not known. Even if so, the works quickly circulated under Mozart's name; he also requested Leopold send them to Vienna in December 1783, soon after he had returned, presumably with informal performances in mind.[68] The duos, then, are more than just friendly gestures towards Haydn, more than the 'charming pastiches' identified by H. C. Robbins Landon 'in Michael Haydn's style, since [Mozart] did not want to compromise Haydn by possible detection'.[69]

As in the piano sonatas K. 330–332 and K. 333, Mozart encouraged players to adopt a creative mindset. The opening of the first movement of K. 423 is a case in point (bars 1–12; Example 3.21),[70] with players needing to negotiate similarities and differences between musical materials by interpreting articulation and dynamic markings. The violin semiquavers in bar 3, evolving from the preceding ornaments, feed a process of organic growth that extends to both violin and viola in the taut imitation of bar 5.

'like a sacred relic, in undying remembrance of Mozart' (p. ii), there is no evidence that Haydn owned it at any stage (NMD, p. 31).

[68] For advertisements from mid-1788 in the *Wiener Zeitung*, explaining that four duos were by Haydn and two by Mozart, see MDL, pp. 280, 281; MDB, pp. 319, 321. See also NMD, pp. 30–31. For the letters to Leopold (6 December and 24 December 1783), see MBA, vol. 3, pp. 295, 299; LMF, pp. 862, 865.

[69] Landon, *Golden Years*, p. 90. The duos have been likened in general ways to Mozart's string quartets and quintets: see Abert, *W. A. Mozart*, p. 858; Schwindt, 'Die Kammermusik', in Leopold (ed.), *Mozart Handbuch*, p. 434; Keller, 'The Chamber Music', in Landon and Mitchell (eds.), *Mozart Companion*, p. 135.

[70] For the autograph, see Mozart, *Zwei Duos für Violine und Viola*.

But a slight elaboration of the bar 5 material in bar 9 alters the relationship between violin and viola; the rhythm and articulation in bar 9 produces a melody-accompaniment texture rather than imitation. We witness, in part, the magical mutability of melody and accompaniment identified by Charles Rosen as a feature of the classical style in Haydn's Op. 33 no. 1.[71] But performers are responsible for literally and metaphorically articulating changes in their relationship as well. They have to decide (for example) how to convey the different implications of bars 5 and 9, and the subsequent return to imitative exchange in bars 10 and 12. Mozart throws down the interpretative gauntlet at the beginning of K. 423/i, then, encouraging contemplation of the violin-viola relationship. In the remainder of the movement, differences in the articulation of corresponding material for the two instruments invite continued appraisal and reappraisal of that relationship: in the quaver figures passed between instruments (bars 75–78); in the arpeggiated V7 harmony split between violin and viola in the bar before the recapitulation (81), where a five-note slur is followed by a two-note slur and three strokes; and in the run-up to the reprise of the secondary theme (bars 104–105).[72] Both 'dolce' and bar-long slurs are absent from the viola part at the second-theme reprise in the autograph, raising the question of whether the corresponding articulation from the exposition should be adopted (as editorially in the NMA) or Mozart's literal notation followed. And this is no small interpretative matter: the chosen approach potentially affects how relationships between instruments and themes are communicated over extended periods and, therefore, how the work is understood.

The 'Haffner' and 'Linz' symphonies, K. 385 in D (1782) and K. 425 in C (1783), neatly book-end Mozart's instrumental output from the premiere of *Die Entführung* until his return to Vienna at the end of 1783.[73] Neither was written for first performance in Vienna – rather for Salzburg and Linz – but both were subsequently played at Viennese concerts. K. 425 was also heard on 15 September 1784 in Salzburg, at the residence of the Barisani family, friends of the Mozarts.[74]

---

[71] Rosen, *The Classical Style: Haydn, Mozart, Beethoven* (London: Faber, 1971), pp. 116–117.

[72] Variations in articulation patterns also occur in corresponding segments for each instrument in the exposition (the violin semiquavers at bars 24–25 and 34–36 and the viola quavers at bars 45 and 47, for example).

[73] The orchestral minuet and trio K. 409 (May 1782) predates the 'Haffner' by two months. It was probably intended as an independent concert piece, rather than (as long thought) an addition to the symphony K. 338. See Zaslaw, *Mozart's Symphonies*, p. 364.

[74] K. 385 and 425 were played at Mozart's Burgtheater academies in Vienna on 23 March 1783 and 1 April 1784. Leopold mentioned to Nannerl the performance of Mozart's 'new, excellent

The commission for the 'Haffner' Symphony, from Leopold in mid-July 1782 to celebrate the ennoblement of Siegmund Haffner the younger in Salzburg, came at an especially busy time for Mozart. Writing to his father on 20 July, four days after the *Entführung* premiere, Mozart explained that he had quickly to arrange his opera for wind instruments or risk leaving the task (and the profits from it) to someone else. But he promised to deliver the symphony in regular instalments, working as efficiently and effectively as he could. Although it took slightly longer than anticipated, it had reached Leopold by late August and clearly met with Leopold's approval; the date of the premiere, and whether it actually coincided with the party for Haffner's ennoblement, is not known.[75] Mozart referred to K. 385 as his 'Sinphonie', but it functioned as a serenade in Salzburg, complete with a march and two minuets.[76]

After several requests to Leopold to return the work to him in Vienna, beginning with a letter on 4 December 1782 that was lost in transit, Mozart finally received it in early February 1783, remarking that 'the new Haffner Symphony completely amazed me – for I did not remember a note of it. It must certainly produce a good effect'.[77] Mozart's claim to forgetfulness perhaps should be taken with a pinch of salt, given his obvious eagerness to perform K. 385 at the Burgtheater concert on 23 March 1783, not to mention his prodigious powers of musical memory.[78] But it is possible that looking through the 'Haffner' Symphony seven months or so after its rapid composition was a genuinely surprising experience for Mozart, sparking his putative exaggeration. The 'effect' of the work, and instrumental effects in general, was prominent in his mind at the time of composition. One of the obstacles to a quick completion of K. 385, transcribing *Die Entführung* for *Harmonie*, focussed Mozart's mind on

---

symphony' (*neue excellente Synfonie*) in Salzburg; see MBA, vol. 3, p. 333 and LMF, p. 883 (17 September 1784).

[75] For Mozart's letters on the genesis of K. 385, see MBA, vol. 3, pp. 213–219; LMF, pp. 808–813 (letters of 20 July, 27 July, 31 July, 7 August 1782). Mozart recorded his father's approval on 24 August 1782; see MBA, vol. 3, p. 225 and LMF, p. 817.

[76] For Mozart's 'Sinphonie' references see MBA, vol. 3, p. 213 (20 July) and p. 216 (31 July). With support from early sets of parts originating in Salzburg and Vienna, Neal Zaslaw (*Mozart's Symphonies*, p. 381) has argued that 'minuets' (plural) may mean 'one minuet and its trio … rather than two sets of a minuet and trio each'.

[77] MBA, vol. 3, p. 257; LMF, p. 840 (15 February 1783).

[78] Zaslaw suggests the comment might have been intended ironically (*Mozart's Symphonies*, p. 379). Others, however, accept it at face value. See Küster, *Musical Biography*, p. 55; Jens Peter Larsen, 'The Symphonies', in *Mozart Companion*, p. 184; Wolfgang Hildesheimer, *Mozart*, trans. Marion Faber (New York: Vintage, 1983), p. 203.

wind-instrument sounds, timbres and textures.[79] As he explained to Leopold: 'You cannot believe how difficult it is to arrange something like that for Harmonie – so that it is suitable for wind instruments, and yet in the process does not lose any of the effect [*Wirkung*].'[80] And when imagining the intended effect of his symphony in performance, he later explained: 'The first Allegro must go really fierily; the last, as fast as possible.'[81] Once he started to plan his Burgtheater concert for March 1783, wind roles and effects would have again come to the fore, as he added two clarinets and two flutes, writing them onto the top and bottom lines of his autograph.[82] A reviewer of a Frankfurt performance in 1786 (presumably the version for the Viennese academy, which had been published a year earlier) was struck by the work's effect, at individual moments and as a whole, identifying 'so much fire and solidity . . . Everything hung together from one beat to the next: tempo, execution, *forte, piano*, and crescendo were in every respect perfect, and I had nothing more to wish for'.[83]

The musical-biographical position of the 'Haffner' Symphony in Mozart's oeuvre – written in Vienna for first performance in Salzburg and revised for subsequent performance in Vienna – illuminates connections between Mozart's musical past and present. As implied in the fieriness and speed mentioned to Leopold, K. 385 is a brilliantly virtuosic work, extending to musical gestures and effects such as at the openings of the Allegro con spirito and minuet, as well as to frenetic semiquaver and quaver passages in the first and last movements respectively. A number of Mozart's serenades and symphonies for Salzburg in the 1770s begin (like K. 385) with forceful unisons, a standard indicator of 'authoritative control',[84] and implicitly strong, rather than weak, contrasts between alternating *forte* and *piano* writing. K. 161, 184, 182, 183 and 200 are somewhat similar to K. 385, but not as brilliant or demonstrative; K. 318 and K. 338 come closer, but again are not as gesturally ostentatious as K. 385 or as varied and brilliant in the orchestral effects they engender. The opening of several of Mozart's earlier

---

[79] Wind effects also play a prominent role in the trio section of the orchestral minuet and trio K. 409 from May 1782, where flutes, oboes, bassoons and horns rule the roost.

[80] MBA, vol. 3, p. 213; LMF, p. 808 (20 July 1782).

[81] MBA, vol. 3, p. 219; LMF, p. 813 (7 August 1782).

[82] For a facsimile of the autograph see Mozart, *Symphony No. 35 in D, K. 385. 'Haffner' Symphony. Facsimile of the Original Manuscript Owned by the Orchestral Association, New York*, ed. Sydney Beck (New York: Oxford University Press, 1968). For the autograph itself, see Mozart, *Symphonies, K. 385, D major*. Autograph manuscript. The Morgan Library and Museum. Cary 483.

[83] Translation from NMD, p. 103. For an advertisement for the sale of K. 385 from Traeg, see MDL, p. 210; MDB, p. 237.

[84] Levy, 'Texture as a Sign in Classic and Early Romantic Music', p. 507.

minuets foreshadow K. 385/iii, including K. 133/iii, K. 183/iii and K. 319/iii, but ultimately lack the powerful presence and grandiose sweep of its *f* arpeggios over two octaves and triple-stop chords in the initial four bars. In fact, K. 385's kindred spirit among Mozart's earlier orchestral works is a symphony not for Salzburg, but for France, namely the 'Paris' Symphony, K. 297 (1778).[85] Mozart was sensitive in K. 297 not only to effects required to satisfy the layman, famously related to his father in July 1778, but also to refined instrumental scorings and textures appealing to connoisseurs.[86] As in K. 385/i, effects of power and nuance both take centre stage in K. 297/i, reaping the benefits of a large orchestra. (K. 297 and K. 385 – at least the revised version for performance in Vienna – are Mozart's only two symphonies scored for the so-called high classical orchestra of double flutes, oboes, clarinets, bassoons, horns and trumpets, plus timpani and strings.) The beginnings of both finales are also similar, accepting that the distinctive *piano* to *forte* effect occurs in earlier Mozart symphonies as well.[87]

What might Mozart have thought realistically could be gained by writing a symphony for Salzburg, aside perhaps from the kind of self-validation brought about by impressing despised former employers? Whether or not he considered its potential benefits to him in Vienna when originally writing it, Mozart included arresting musical material and effects appropriate for engaging a public Viennese audience perhaps unfamiliar at that time with his symphonic repertory.[88] Like the near contemporary wind serenades K. 375 in E-flat (in its revised version with two oboes) and K. 388 in C minor, the 'Haffner' contains a feast of effects: in the first-movement exposition alone, gestural flamboyance, semiquaver brilliance, tutti-accented brilliance, tutti staccati, repeated drum calls, and solo, slowing-moving winds.[89] In addition to setting aside the original march that presumably opened the Salzburg performance and writing flute and

---

[85] Julian Rushton also makes a general connection between Mozart's 'Paris' and 'Haffner' symphonies, explaining that the 'instrumental and rhetorical lessons of the "Paris" inform much of his later work [including the 'Haffner' and 'Prague' symphonies]' (*Mozart*, p. 98).

[86] See Keefe, 'Aesthetics of Wind Writing in the "Paris" Symphony, K. 297'.

[87] See, for example, K. 133/iv, K. 134/iv, K. 184/iv, K. 199/iii, K. 183/iv.

[88] K. 385 was one of just three Mozart symphonies to appear in print during his lifetime, and the only one from his Viennese years; see Cliff Eisen, 'Sources for Mozart's Life and Works', in Eisen and Keefe (eds.), *Cambridge Mozart Encyclopedia*, p. 487. For the Traeg advertisement for K. 385 on 16 February 1785, see MDL, p. 210; MDB, p. 237. K. 385 was available in London by the middle of December 1787 (NMD, p. 143) and was performed there in 1788 (MDL, p. 290; MDB, p. 331).

[89] On the drum calls in the 'Haffner' first movement that 'imply preparation, generate energy, and heighten our sense of impending arrival by suggesting the march's inexorable forward motion'

clarinet parts for the Allegro con spirito and Presto (which are discussed below), one of Mozart's only adjustments to the K. 385 score for Vienna was deleting the exposition repeat in the first movement. Its exclusion has an impact on the discourse of orchestral effects. Since Mozart concludes the exposition *forte*, the onset of a repeated exposition (*forte*) would not have made as powerful an impression as the original opening of the work. (The progressions from exposition to development and from development to recapitulation preserve *forte – piano* and *piano – forte* contrasts respectively.) Perhaps when he returned to the 'Haffner' and thought about rescoring it, Mozart paid still more attention to sequences of orchestral effects than he had at the original composition stage, conscious of it opening his Burgtheater academy on 23 March 1783. At any rate, with brilliance on the keyboard and brilliant writing in *Die Entführung* having already reaped benefits for Mozart in Vienna (see Chapters 1 and 2), it is not surprising that he chose to perform K. 385 at this important concert.

The added flutes and clarinets for the Burgtheater performance of the first and last movements of the 'Haffner', visible in a lighter ink colour in the autograph,[90] illuminate Mozart's compositional priorities. The flutes make their presence felt in bars 35–40 of the first movement, with tied notes an octave higher than the second violins and independent semibreves as well. In bar 58, coinciding with the long-awaited confirmation of the secondary key area, the *sciolto* semiquaver run in the violins (the second of the movement) is duplicated, *forte*, by the clarinets then the flutes, each for two beats.[91] In terms of combined wind–strings participation, the effect is new and texturally distinctive; Mozart envisaged it only for the Burgtheater concert, too, as no other winds are present. The ensuing wind solo, the most thematically and timbrally prominent of the movement so far (bars 67–73), is also enhanced through the participation of flutes and clarinets. In the development section, a sustained c-sharp''' in the flutes (bars 115–116), imitating the clarinets' c-sharp' from the preceding two bars, floats an octave above the coordinated quavers in the strings to accentuate the point of furthest harmonic remove from the tonic (V/iii); in the recapitulation, semiquaver scales in the flutes and clarinets, doubling the first violins, provide a more equal imitative balance to the preceding scale in the bassoons, violas and cellos than the first violins alone had

---

see Melanie Lowe, *Pleasure and Meaning in the Classical Symphony* (Indianapolis: Indiana University Press, 2007), p. 39.

[90] See Mozart, 'Haffner' Symphony: Facsimile.

[91] The *sciolto* marking, in this particular instance, 'may . . . be intended to prevent slurring but avoid staccato'. See Brown, *Classical and Romantic Performing Practice*, p. 189.

done in the original version of the work. In the sonata-rondo finale, new, independent minims, semibreves and tied notes are added to the B section/ secondary theme (flutes, bars 46–53) and to the C section/development (flutes and clarinets, bars 92–103). Thus, Mozart's flutes and clarinets are not simply a mechanical addition to the first and last movements, even though they do in fact double other instruments a lot of the time. Building on an already prominent wind profile, they knit together brilliant virtuosity and the expressive *virtù* of varied timbres and effects, thereby demonstrating the importance of orchestration and orchestral effects in Mozart's compositional aesthetic.[92]

Mozart may have composed, or at least started to compose, several short orchestral works during his Salzburg stay, including the two minuets and contredanses, K. 463, the contredanse K. 610 (with a *Verzeichnüß* date of 6 March 1791) and the three minuets K. 363.[93] The first minuet from K. 363 in particular resonates with the demonstrative opening of the corresponding 'Haffner' movement, featuring emphatic march rhythms for two horns, two trumpets and timpani. But the Symphony in C, K. 425, written in the space of five or six days for a concert at Linz's theatre,[94] was Mozart's most important orchestral work away from Vienna in 1783. The venue for the premiere points to Linz's strong theatrical tradition, no doubt of interest to Mozart, who bemoaned the absence of one in Salzburg.[95] Operas, for example, had been regularly staged in Linz since the 1760s.[96] Nicolai wrote of a theatre company under Heinrich Bulla's direction that gave two or three weekly performances; he also attended Herr Schmalögger's three-act ballet *Der junge Werther* set to music by Kapellmeister Deller (31 May 1781).[97] A number of plays were published in Linz around the

---

[92] On *virtù* as expressive virtuosity in the concerto see Joseph Kerman, *Concerto Conversations* (Harvard, MA: Harvard University Press, 1999), pp. 61–82, and Cliff Eisen, 'The Rise (and Fall) of the Concerto Virtuoso in the Late Eighteenth and Nineteenth Centuries', in Simon P. Keefe (ed.), *The Cambridge Companion to the Concerto* (Cambridge: Cambridge University Press, 2005), pp. 177–191. On the aesthetics of orchestration in Mozart music see Keefe, 'Süssmayr and the Orchestration of Mozart's Requiem'; and Keefe, *Mozart's Requiem: Reception, Work, Completion* (Cambridge: Cambridge University Press, 2012), Chapters 4 and 5.

[93] See Tyson, *Mozart. Studies of the Autograph Scores*, pp. 30, 229, 231 (K. 363), p. 228 (K. 463), and pp. 227–228 (K. 610).

[94] See Mozart's letter to Leopold of 31 October 1782 in MBA, vol. 3, pp. 291–292, and LMF, pp. 859–860.

[95] For Mozart's catalogue of objections to Salzburg, including the absence of theatre and opera, see MBA, vol. 2, pp. 437–441, at 439; LMF, pp. 592–597, at 594 (7 August 1778). In fact he would have been able to attend the theatre when in Salzburg in late 1783, as Kühne's theatrical troupe were resident from 12 September until Advent. See Halliwell, *Mozart Family*, p. 403.

[96] 'Linz', *Grove Music Online*, accessed 24 January 2012.

[97] Nicolai, *Beschreibung einer Reise*, pp. 528–529 and p. 530.

time of Mozart's visit, including three by Anton Cremeri: *Alles in Schuh und Strümpfen* (1782); *Andromeda und Perseus* (1783); and *Losenstain und Hohenberg, ein Schauspiel aus der Oberösterreichischen Geschichte* (1783).[98] Cremeri, in fact, was an important and influential Enlightenment figure, in Linz and beyond, as the town's censor, as a renowned dramatist, and as a strong supporter of Emperor Joseph II's reforms, theatrical and otherwise.[99] Shortly after his arrival, Mozart stated that 'almost all Linz' was to assemble at Ebelsberg (six miles southeast of the town) for an opera performance at Prefect Steurer's house, perhaps also attesting to a well-developed theatrical culture.[100]

Given theatrical traditions in Linz as well as Mozart's own predilection for opera and spoken drama, it is not surprising that the 'Linz' Symphony comes across as a dramatic work. Characteristic of the outer movements of the 'Haffner' Symphony, drama is more noticeable still in K. 425, especially when understood to represent moments of intensity captured in extended musical processes.[101] It is not known why Mozart chose to begin the work with a slow introduction; he had started serenades this way, including K. 203 in D (1774) and K. 320 in D (1779), but not a symphony.[102] Whatever the reason, he infused it with drama right from the start, with the lunge to B-flat in bar 3 (Example 3.22).[103] While Mozart could have

---

[98] See *Theater Kalender auf das Schalt-Jahr 1784*, ed. Heinrich August Otto Reichard (Gotha, 1784), p. 183; *Intelligenz-Blätter der Reichstadt Lindau, Zweyter Jahrgang* (Lindau, 1784), n.p.

[99] For Cremeri's book extolling Joseph II's virtues as a reformer see *Sympathien mit Joseph den II* (Linz, 1784). For more on Cremeri, see Edmund J. Goehring, 'Of Libertines and Theologians: an Apology for the Theatre from the Austrian Enlightenment', in Libin (ed.), *Mozart in Prague*, pp. 313–341.

[100] MBA, vol. 3, p. 291; LMF, p. 859 (31 October 1783).

[101] For explanations of drama along these historical lines in Mozart's Viennese instrumental works see Keefe, *Mozart's Piano Concertos* and Keefe, *Mozart's Viennese Instrumental Music*. On operatic elements in K. 385, see Lowe, *Pleasure and Meaning in the Classical Symphony*, p. 45; and Elaine Sisman, 'Genre, Gesture and Meaning in Mozart's "Prague" Symphony', in Cliff Eisen (ed.), *Mozart Studies 2* (Oxford: Clarendon Press, 1997), pp. 81–82. The general dramatic qualities of K. 425 are recognized in Abert, *W. A. Mozart*, p. 867; Landon, *Mozart: the Golden Years*, p. 96; Gutman, *Mozart*, p. 661; Lowe, *Pleasure and Meaning in the Classical Symphony*, p. 58.

[102] Küster (*Musical Biography*, p. 165) speculates that Mozart heard a serenade in Linz that stimulated composition of a slow introduction, or that he reacted to something encountered in Count Thun's library. Slow introductions were infrequent in symphonies at that time (including those of Joseph Haydn). It should be noted that one of Mozart's works immediately preceding K. 425, the string duo written in Salzburg, K. 424, also features a slow introduction.

[103] The autograph of the 'Linz' Symphony is lost. Musical examples for this work are compiled in consultation with an edition drawing on a set of parts held at the Mozarteum in Salzburg that were copied from the autograph and are now considered closest to the musical text performed in Linz in 1783 and in Salzburg in 1784: see Mozart, *Symphony in C Major, No. 36, K. 425 'Linz'*, ed. Cliff Eisen (London: Edition Peters, 1992).

Example 3.22 Mozart, Symphony in C ('Linz'), K. 425/i, bars 1–10.

treated bars 1–2 as an antecedent to which (theoretically at least) a 'regular' two-bar consequent could have been added, the B-flat negates this possibility, affecting the course of the introduction. The chromatic cell c' – b-natural – b-flat outlined in the opening three bars is exploited in a succession of seventh chords supporting the f-sharp' – f-natural' – e' descent in the first violins (bars 8–10, Example 3.22) and in the melodically decorative chromatic lines that coincide with the confirmation of V/C in preparation for the Allegro. A subsequent gesture at the end of the slow introduction (Example 3.23) matches bar 3 for raw effect. Mozart could simply have retained the prevailing *p* dynamic for the final chord to produce a seamless join between Adagio and Allegro spirituoso, but decided on a *forte*, tutti chord instead. As a result, the last two bars of the introduction intensify existing features of Mozart's exordium: the earlier *fp* and *f* – *p* swells reappear in the strings on all three beats of bar 18; and the *pp* to *f* in the winds provides the starkest dynamic contrast so far.[104]

It is fully expected that a Mozart slow introduction would have an impact on melodic, thematic, harmonic, rhythmic, and textural aspects of the remainder of the movement; indeed, majestic, lyric and ombra affects from the K. 425 introduction could be seen to foreshadow in a general way the events of the Allegro.[105] More noteworthy, though, Mozart's gestures of unmissable dramatic import in bars 3 and 19 provoke equally dramatic gestures in the Allegro, navigating a path for listeners through the movement.[106] In the introduction, the big B-flat orientates the music towards the subdominant – heard in major and minor modes in bars 4 and 11–12 – and the chordal explosion at the end intensifies dynamic contrast. These harmonic and dynamic elements then act together to influence events later in the movement. Following a move to E minor (vi/G) in the secondary key area, for example, Mozart introduces an unaccompanied, homophonic wind-band timbre, a new effect in the

---

[104] The *pp* is also the winds' softest dynamic level in the first movement. As Cliff Eisen has pointed out in his evaluation of authentic Donaueschingen and Salzburg parts for this work, there are in fact only three *pp* indications in the entire work. See Eisen, 'New Light on Mozart's "Linz" Symphony', *Journal of the Royal Musical Association*, 113 (1988), pp. 81–96, at 90.

[105] A. Peter Brown, *The Symphonic Repertoire, Volume II. The First Golden Age of the Viennese Symphony: Haydn, Mozart, Beethoven, and Schubert* (Indianapolis, IN: Indiana University Press, 2002), p. 401.

[106] Volker Scherliess recognizes changing musical gestures as crucial to both contrast and variation in the first movement of K. 425. See 'Instrumentale Szenerien: Wien 1783 und 1786', in Leopold (ed.), *Mozart Handbuch*, p. 306. For a rare inference of slight disappointment with the Allegro after the Adagio, the Adagio's 'note of pathos . . . [presaging] something more profound than that which actually follows', see Jens Peter Larsen, 'The Symphonies', in Landon and Mitchell (eds.), *Mozart Companion*, p. 186.

Example 3.23 Mozart, Symphony in C ('Linz'), K. 425/i, bars 17–23.

movement, temporarily tonicizing the local subdominant (C major); the material then acquires harmonic and textural force on its repeat, presented *forte* in the full orchestra (see bars 75–77 and 83–85). The harmony accompanying the timbral and dynamic surprises (coupled with the E-minor *forte* a few bars earlier at a juncture where lyricism not force is expected[107]) of course provides a straightforward pivot back to the secondary key G, bringing together the kind of unexpectedness and inevitability that often characterizes Mozart's instrumental music.[108] But these complementary qualities do not seem applicable to events in the development section, where B-flat and the subdominant rear their heads in a different way. First appearing at the melodic peak of a sequenced pattern, supporting diminished seventh harmony that activates the modulation to D minor (bar 130), b-flat" surfaces ten bars later as the highpoint of a *forte*, full-orchestra iteration of V7/F harmony that leads to the confirmation of

---

[107] As Küster explains (*Musical Biography*, p. 166), this moment 'is absolutely out of the ordinary symphonic run of things'.

[108] On the piano concertos in this respect, see David Rosen, '"Unexpectedness" and "Inevitability" in Mozart's Piano Concertos', in Zaslaw (ed.), *Mozart's Piano Concertos*, pp. 261–284.

F. It is as if the premature return to the tonic, C (the arrival point of the preceding sequence in bar 137), sparks an emphatic return to the B-flat's original role as generator of harmonic momentum. There are only two *forte* explosions in the development, including the V7/F that begins in bar 140, both intensifying earlier material.[109] Mozart impels his listeners to sit up and take note of the harmonic and dynamic power of his dramatic material.

Up until now, the B-flat gesture (and resulting subdominant orientation) has issued mixed messages, supporting both harmonic defiance and harmonic affirmation. But it moves decisively towards the latter in the recapitulation. Standard recapitulatory procedures support the process, needless to say: B-flat and the subdominant are emphasized in the secondary development; and the wind-band segment in the secondary theme, repeated *forte* in the full orchestra, now has F as its subdominant rather than C. The beginning of the coda also invokes both the end of the exposition and the middle segment of the development. The initial violin line peaks on b-flat" whereupon the unfolding sequence (as in the development) again moves to D minor then C major. But C is now affirmed (bar 274), rather than angrily rebuked.

The drama of Mozart's introductory gestures and subsequent transformations in the first movement is also characteristic of the finale, especially in the memorable *Sturm und Drang* passage from the development section (bars 180–200) with sudden *forte* in the full orchestra, intense accompaniment, and final climax on b-flat" to modulate to F. As in the Allegro spirituoso, this passage's import derives in part from correspondences with material earlier in the movement, in this case the unison *forte* from the transition (bars 28–32). Its dramatic potential is suppressed in the *piano* statements at the opening of the development (bars 164–179), where the first four bars are straightforwardly repeated, but is then fully realized in the *Sturm und Drang* passage. As well as invoking events from the first movement, the *Sturm und Drang* passage builds on swathes of wind sound from the Andante that exploit a notably unconventional retention of the full-wind and brass contingent from the first movement.[110] The Andante promotes orchestral effects throughout (albeit not in powerful orchestral gestures representative of the first and last movements), signalling the unusual full-wind and brass sonority to the audience as

---

[109] The second (bars 152–158) features a rhythmic intensification of the exposition's march-like material, especially though the repeated semiquavers in the second violins and violas.

[110] Landon, *Golden Years*, p. 96; Brown, *First Golden Age of the Viennese Symphony*, p. 403.

early as bar 5 (Example 3.24). Its rich array of timbral nuances comple-ments the orchestral force of the first movement, building *inter alia* on the kind of refined wind writing already witnessed in the wind serenades K. 375 and 388, and the 'Haffner' Symphony. The first-theme section alone (bars 1–12, Example 3.24) includes a *piano* phrase link in the two horns (bar 4); a pizzicato in the lower strings in bars 5–8 combined with coordinated cello-horn arpeggios and *piano* quavers in the timpani; and a light wind accompaniment for a poignant return to coll'arco in the cellos (bar 9) that yields additional impact for the wind re-entry in bar 10 and their first *forte* in bar 11.[111]

Perhaps Mozart, working on the 'Linz' Symphony in a theatrically cultured city and promoting dramatic musical materials, had something similar in mind to the classical French aesthetician Bernard Germain, Comte de Lacépède, who explained in 1785 that a symphonic composer should consider his work as

just three great acts in a play, to be thinking that he was working on a tragedy, or a comedy or a pastoral . . .

The first piece, the one that we call the *allegro* of the symphony would present so to speak the overture and the first scenes; in the *andante* or second piece, the musician would place the depiction of the tremendous events, the fearful passions, or the agreeable objects which were to constitute the basic content of the piece; and the last piece, which we usually call the *presto*, would offer the last effects of these frightful or touching passions; the *dénouement* would also show itself there, and we would see following it the pain, terror and consternation that a fateful catastrophe inspires, or the joy, happiness and frenzy to which pleasant and happy events give rise.[112]

---

[111] For a classical view of brief instrumental absences in Mozart's works enhancing the impact of their subsequent reappearance, in the context of the 'wise economy' (*weise Oekonomie*) of his orchestration, see Arnold, *Mozarts Geist*, 'Die Oekonomie der Instrumente', pp. 209–231, especially pp. 229–231. Arnold's discussion of Mozart's orchestration has been used to support the analysis of Mozart's work on the Requiem and its subsequent completion by Franz Xaver Süssmayr in Keefe, 'Süssmayr and the Orchestration of Mozart's Requiem'; and Keefe, *Mozart's Requiem*, Chapters 4 and 5.

[112] Lacépède, *La poëtique de la musique* (Paris, 1785), 2 vols., vol. 2, pp. 331–332. 'Mais ensuite il faudroit qu'il ne les considérat que comme trois grands actes d'une pièce de théâtre, qu'il crût travailler à une tragédie, à une comédie, ou à une pastorale . . . Le premier morceau, celui que l'on appelle l'*allegro* de la symphonie, en présenteroit pour ainsi dire l'ouverture & les premières scenes; dans l'*andante* ou le second morceau, le musicien placeroit la peinture des évenemens terribles, des passions redoubtables, ou des objets agréables qui devroient faire le fonds de la pièce; & le dernier morceau, auquel on donne communément le nom de *presto*, offriroit les derniers efforts de ces passions affreuses ou touchantes; le dénouement s'y montreroit aussi, & l'on verroit à sa suite la douleur, l'effroi & la consternation qu'inspire une catastrophe funeste, ou la joie, le bonheur & le délire que seroient naître des événémens agréables & heureux'.

Example 3.24 Mozart, Symphony in C ('Linz'), K. 425/ii, bars 1–12.

At any rate, Mozart's slow introduction to Michael Haydn's Symphony in G, Perger 16 (K. 444, probably early 1784), demonstrates a similar propensity for drama as the near-contemporary 'Linz'.[113] Mozart was apparently stimulated by events in Haydn's work when writing his twenty-bar opening to it: bars 7–8 match the shift to the tonic minor (c), angular gestures and thematic-rhythmic continuity of the onset of the middle section of Haydn's Andante; and the climactic augmented 6th four bars from the end of the slow introduction invokes distinctive occurrences of ♭VI harmony in both the exposition and recapitulation of Haydn's finale (reached *p – f* and delineated by a half-bar rest in the full orchestra; see bars 36, 135).

Conclusion: The Burgtheater Academy, 23 March 1783

Probably the single most important musical event for Mozart between the premiere of *Die Entführung* on 16 July 1782 and the end of 1783 was his academy at the Burgtheater on 23 March 1783. In a letter to Leopold six days later, Mozart gave the complete programme in the order in which items were performed: (1) the 'Haffner' Symphony (probably just the first three movements); (2) the aria 'Se il padre perdei' from *Idomeneo*, featuring Aloysia Lange; (3) the Piano Concerto K. 415; (4) the scena 'Misera! dove son' K. 369 with Adamberger; (5) the 'little concertante symphony' (*kleine Concertant-Simphonie*) from the 'Posthorn' Serenade, K. 320 (movements 3 and 4); (6) the piano concerto in D, K. 175 with the replacement finale K. 382; (7) the scena 'Parto m'affretto' from *Lucio Silla*, with Therese Teyber; (8) a short fugue (in deference to the emperor, who was present) and variations on Paisiello's 'Salve tu, Domine' and Gluck's 'Unser dummer Pöbel meint'; (9) the rondò 'Mia speranza' K. 416 with Lange; and (10) the last movement of the 'Haffner' Symphony.[114]

The amount of work required for a concert on this scale was considerable, including writing some of the music, engaging the orchestral players for rehearsal(s) and performance, and having parts copied.[115] Indeed,

---

[113] For a dating of early 1784 for K. 444 based on the autograph's paper type, see Alan Tyson, 'Proposed New Dates for Many Works and Fragments Written by Mozart from March 1781 to December 1791', in Cliff Eisen (ed.), *Mozart Studies* (Oxford: Clarendon Press, 1991), pp. 213–226, at 219–220. For Zaslaw's discussion of K. 444, in the context of symphonies Mozart may have performed at his Viennese academies, see *Mozart's Symphonies*, pp. 391–396.

[114] MBA, vol. 3, pp. 261–262; LMF, p. 843 (29 March 1783). Variation sets on Paisiello's and Gluck's themes were subsequently published as K. 398 and K. 455 respectively.

[115] Halliwell, *The Mozart Family*, pp. 398–399.

Mozart appears to have been actively planning the event at least three and a half months prior.[116] Above all, the overall shape of the programme and the selection of items demonstrate careful thought on Mozart's part, adhering to local tradition as well.[117] After the initial symphony, arias alternated with concertante pieces up to item 5, the 'Posthorn' Serenade, the end of which represented the approximate midpoint of about two and a half hours of music;[118] a concerto and solo pieces then alternated with arias until item 9, 'Mia speranza', before Mozart rounded off the concert with the 'Haffner' finale. The most substantive items on the programme, aside from the 'Haffner' Symphony at the opening, understandably placed Mozart the performer-composer at the centre of activities. But other pieces were also integrated circumspectly into the whole. 'Se il padre perdei' and the serenade, for example, would have exploited the talented wind players that Mozart's Viennese works on the programme required. Lange's arias were strategically positioned after the symphonic movements at the beginning and before the symphonic finale at the end. If the audience admired her rendition of the first aria, moreover, they would have had every opportunity to be more impressed still by her performance of the second, since 'Mia speranza' is considerably more demanding vocally than 'Se il padre perdei', at almost twice the length and with frequent peaks on e-flat''' and f'''. The pinnacle of Mozart's solo activities, his improvisations at the keyboard, was complemented by the climax to vocal activities, Lange's 'Mia speranza', items 8 and 9 thus working together to create a rousing climax to the evening's entertainment.[119]

Given the enthusiastic reactions to his Viennese public appearances prior to March 1783, Mozart was no doubt confident of success in this

---

[116] On 21 December 1782, Mozart wrote to Leopold requesting the return of the 'Haffner' Symphony to Vienna for intended performance at the Burgtheater academy; Mozart summarized here a request he had first made to Leopold on 4 December 1782 in a letter Leopold did not receive. See MBA, vol. 3, p. 244; LMF, p. 832.

[117] For example, alternation of vocal and instrumental pieces – partly evident in his programme – was a standard feature of late-eighteenth-century Viennese academies; see Morrow, *Concert Life*, p. 144.

[118] This calculation assigns thirty minutes to Mozart's fugal and variation improvisations in item 8. Although it is generally assumed that the first three movements of K. 385 were played at the beginning of the concert and in the finale at the end, it is not impossible that the whole of the symphony was heard initially and the finale reprised at the end. See James Webster, *Haydn's 'Farewell' Symphony and the Idea of Classical Style: Through-Composition and Cyclic Integration in His Instrumental Music* (Cambridge: Cambridge University Press, 1991), p. 175.

[119] Teyber's scena on the academy programme, 'Parto m'affretto' from *Lucio Silla*, is also brilliantly virtuosic. But it is shorter than 'Mia speranza' and features a smaller accompanying orchestra (strings only, in comparison to two oboes, two bassoons, two horns and strings).

academy. But as with the replacement finale K. 382 written in 1782 for a concerto that had previously received acclaim in its original version (see Chapter 1), he left nothing to chance. Instead of promoting new works exclusively, Mozart combined the (acclaimed) old and the (untested) new. He played K. 175 + 382 again, when either K. 413 or K. 414 could have been offered as a second piano concerto, having performed it to rapturous applause at Aloysia Lange's academy on 11 March;[120] he programmed arias from successful pre-Viennese operas as well as the freshly composed 'Mia speranza'; and he exploited the virtuosic safe haven (for him) of keyboard improvisation.

Mozart's astuteness harnessed to extraordinary performing skills paid dividends and the academy was a triumph. Writing to Leopold on 29 March, Mozart suspected that news of it would already have reached Salzburg: 'Suffice to say, the theatre could not possibly have been more full and all the boxes were taken. But the best thing for me was that His Majesty the Emperor was also present, and how pleased he was, and what loud applause he gave me. It is just normal for him to send money to the box office before he goes to the theatre, otherwise I would have been fully entitled to expect more as his delight was boundless. He sent 25 ducats.'[121] Mozart's enthusiasm was justified, judging by two near-identical reports in the *Müncher Zeitung* (April 1783) and Cramer's *Magazin der Musik* (Hamburg, 9 May 1783):

(Vienna, 22 March 1783 [*sic*]) . . . Today, the famous Herr Chevalier Mozart gave an academy at the National Theatre, at which pieces of his already very popular composition were performed. The academy was honoured with extraordinarily forceful acclaim, and the two new concertos and other fantasies that Herr M. played at the fortepiano received the loudest applause. Our monarch, who, contrary to habit, honoured us with his presence for the whole academy, and the entire audience granted him such unanimous applause of which we know of no other instance here. The takings are estimated to total 1,600 gulden.[122]

By now, Mozart had perfected his rapport with the Viennese concert audience, both influential individuals in it and the collective body. His fugue and improvised variations 'Unser dummer Pöbel meint' on

---

[120] MBA, vol. 3, p. 259; LMF, p. 841 (12 March 1783)

[121] MBA, vol. 3, p. 261; LMF, p. 843 (29 March 1783).

[122] The quotation is taken from Cramer. See MDL, pp. 190–191; MDB, p. 215. See also *Müncher Zeitung*, 59 (April 1783), pp. 234–235. It is difficult to determine whether the 1,600 gulden represents a gross or a net receipt and how much of it Mozart himself received. See Halliwell, *The Mozart Family*, p. 394; Edge, 'Review Article: Morrow, *Concert Life*', p. 125.

23 March nodded unambiguously in the direction of the emperor and of Gluck, both of whom were present. A week later, at Teyber's concert, he played K. 415 again and had the finale encored, but improvised by himself instead to the audience's delight.[123] Through his own brand of calculated spontaneity, Mozart the performer-composer ebbed and flowed harmoniously with the desires and expectations of his concert audience, putting into practice his belief that complete musical commitment and achievement in the act of performance trumped all other considerations (see Chapter 1).

The channels of communication between Mozart and potential performers of his works in manuscript copies and printed editions mirror the close engagement he achieved with his concert audiences. In the case of Leutgeb, a personal friendship yielded humorous and poignantly expressive musical results. When other works passed from his direct control Mozart imbued them with the spirit of the performer-composer. Mozart, the creative and imaginative performer in concert, was not only paralleled in the works he sold, but also in the mindset of the performer-composer he tried to engender. He may have been too personally and intimately connected to the production and performance of his own piano concertos to do so entirely successfully for the intended amateur purchasers of K. 413–415. But the piano sonatas K. 330–332 and K. 333 were a different matter, affording him opportunities through publications to nurture comparable creativity in his players to that he exhibited himself in performance. And when Mozart had neither an immediately apparent intention to publish nor a starring role in performance, as in the 'Haffner' and 'Linz' symphonies, he ensured that dramatic musical qualities – allied with the expressivity, charm, intensity and surprise characteristic of his keyboard playing – provided chances to enthral the audience. In spring 1784 he would find, in the 'grand' piano concerto, the ideal medium in which to unite the dramatic with the intensely personal.

---

[123] MBA, vol. 3, p. 265; LMF, p. 845 (12 April 1783). (Quoted above.)

4 | 'You Can Easily Imagine That I Must Inevitably Play Some New Things'
Mozart's Piano Concertos and Other Instrumental Works for Concerts, 1784–1786

Following his achievements of 1781–1783, Mozart entered the most productive and successful period of his life as a keyboard performer-composer. He listed in a letter to Leopold a remarkable twenty-two concert engagements for the five weeks between 26 February and 3 April 1784, including two at the Burgtheater (one of which was ultimately cancelled); three to comprise his own March subscription series at the private hall of the Trattnerhof, where he was then living and which attracted 174 subscribers; several at the salons of the influential Prince Galitzin and Count Esterházy; and three at concerts staged by the pianist Georg Friedrich Richter (b. 1749).[1] The relatively small size of the Trattnerhof hall, at around 87 square meters, meant that Mozart's subscribers probably had to stand during his performances.[2] In addition, Mozart played at the houses of Count Leopold Pálffy and Prince Kaunitz on 9 and 10 April and performed the Accompanied Sonata K. 454 in B-flat with the visiting Italian violinist Regina Strinasacchi at her academy at the Kärntnertortheater on 29 April.[3] Six subscription concerts with audiences of more than 150 followed at the Mehlgrube Casino on consecutive Fridays in February and March 1785, beginning on the day that Leopold arrived for his ten-week Viennese visit (11 February).[4] The Mehlgrube, used for concerts since the 1740s, was described by late-eighteenth-century travel writer Carl Gottlob Küttner as 'a large building on the Neuer Markt . . . where the greatest number of those present are well and stylishly dressed . . . It is the particular place of

---

[1] See MBA, vol. 3, pp. 303–304; LMF, pp. 869–870 (3 March 1784). The subscribers to the Trattnerhof concerts are listed in MBA, vol. 3, pp. 305–307; LMF, pp. 870–872. On Richter, including new biographical information, see Rita Steblin, 'A Problem Solved: The Identity of Georg Friedrich Richter, Virtuoso "Claviermeister" from Holland, Mozart's Friend and Partner in the Trattnerhof Subscription Concerts of 1784', *Mozart Society of America Newsletter*, 13/2 (2009), pp. 5–9.

[2] For an account of the Trattnerhof, including the sizes of Mozart's apartment and the hall at which his subscription concerts took place, see Michael Lorenz, http://michaelorenz.blogspot .co.at/2013/09/mozart-in-trattnerhof.html (accessed 3 May 2016).

[3] MDL, p. 199; MDB, p. 224.

[4] The number of subscribers is given by Leopold in MBA, vol. 3, p. 378; LMF, p. 888 (12 March 1785).

amusement for the good bourgeois class, the well-to-do shopkeeper, some artists, government workers, rich artisans and the like'.[5] Mozart also gave his annual academies on 10 March 1785 and 7 April 1786, performed at numerous other events in spring 1785, at a Tonkünstler-Societät concert as an entr'acte to Dittersdorf's oratorio *Esther* on 23 December and at a New Crowned Hope concert on 15 December where his piano concerto and keyboard improvisation were the central and final events; and he apparently gave three more subscription concerts at the end of 1785.[6] At the heart of almost all these activities were the eleven piano concertos written between early 1784 and early 1786: K. 449 in E-flat, K. 450 in B-flat, K. 451 in D, K. 453 in G for 1784; K. 456 in B-flat, K. 459 in F, K. 466 in D minor, K. 467 in C for spring 1785; and K. 482 in E-flat, K. 488 in A, K. 491 in C minor for winter to spring 1785–1786.[7]

Mozart's piano concertos extended the remit of the performer-composer beyond what was possible in solo improvisations, accepting of course that improvisation featured in Mozart's concerto performances, including in *Eingänge*, cadenzas and embellishments.[8] For a composer with a razor-

---

[5] As given in Morrow, *Concert Life in Haydn's Vienna*, p. 100.

[6] Evidence that Mozart held subscription concerts in late 1785 comprises a letter from Leopold to Nannerl communicating the contents of a (now lost) letter from Mozart dated 28 December 1785. Mozart had explained to Leopold that the concerts were hastily organized, that he wrote K. 482 in E-flat specifically for these events and had to repeat the Andante, and that 120 people subscribed. See MBA, vol. 3, p. 484; LMF, p. 895 (13 January 1786). For the programme for the New Crowned Hope concert on 15 December 1785, listing Mozart's piano concerto as the fourth of seven items and his improvisation as the last, see MDL, p. 226; MDB, p. 257.

[7] Two of Mozart's Viennese piano concertos were written for his virtuoso student Barbara Ployer (K. 449, 453) and one in all likelihood for another leading Viennese pianist, Maria Theresia von Paradies (K. 456). All three were performed by Mozart soon after being entered into the thematic catalogue (9 February, 12 April, 30 September 1784); they represent works for Mozart the performer-composer, then, like the other Viennese piano concertos from 1784 to 1786. On the protracted genesis of K. 449, begun in 1782–1783 and left for a year or more as a fragment (a *particella* up to bar 170 of the first movement), see Tyson, *Autograph Scores*, p. 19. For a stylistic reading of K. 449 that takes Tyson's findings as its point of departure, see Keefe, *Mozart's Viennese Instrumental Music*, pp. 19–42.

[8] Mozart commented famously to his father (22 January 1783) that *Eingänge* for the Rondo K. 382 would comprise 'always what comes to mind'; see MBA, vol. 3, p. 251 and LMF, p. 837. The extent to which Mozart's improvisations in the piano concertos were spontaneous or preplanned is a contentious matter. For differing viewpoints see Eva and Paul Badura-Skoda, *Interpreting Mozart on the Keyboard*, and Eva Badura-Skoda, 'On Improvised Embellishments and Cadenzas in Mozart's Piano Concertos', in Zaslaw (ed.), *Mozart's Piano Concertos*, pp. 365–371, at 367; Robert D. Levin, 'Instrumental Ornamentation, Improvisation and Cadenzas', in Howard Mayer Brown and Stanley Sadie (eds.), *Performance Practice After 1600* (London: Macmillan, 1990), pp. 267–291; Frederick Neumann, *Ornamentation and Improvisation in Mozart* (Princeton, NJ: Princeton University Press, 1986), especially pp. 240–256 (Chapter 16: 'The Special Case of the Piano Concertos'). See also Richard Taruskin, 'A Mozart Wholly Ours', in *Text and Act*, pp. 273–291.

sharp ear, highly attentive to the nuances of orchestral effects,[9] and a keyboard performer with abilities famed across Europe, the piano concerto offered a unique medium for simultaneously promoting keyboard performance and orchestral compositional skills.[10] Mozart's experience of writing several early piano concertos to premiere himself (probably K. 175 in D, K. 238 in B-flat and K. 365 in E-flat for two pianos, with Nannerl) as well as concertos initially for others and then as his own solo vehicles (K. 242 in F, K. 246 in C, K. 271 in E-flat) would have alerted him to the prospect of protracted success in the genre; and in Vienna he had already come to understand the cachet of performing his own concertos (see Chapters 1 and 3). But in 1784–1786 he moved beyond his earlier achievements in mounting subscription events at which numerous new concertos were the principal points of focus. He explained the Trattnerhof concerts to Leopold on 3 March 1784:

> Now you can easily imagine that inevitably I must play some new things – therefore one must write. [. . .] I must tell you quickly how it is that in an instant I am giving private academies [at the Trattnerhof]. The clavier master *Richter* is giving six Saturday concerts in the said hall. The nobility subscribed, but said they would have had no pleasure had I not played. Herr Richter asked me to do so. I promised him I would play three times. And I arranged three subscription concerts for myself, to which they all subscribed.[11]

Centre stage in every respect (*his* works, *his* performances, *his* taking the plaudits), Mozart had laid the foundations for an exclusive audience experience distinguished by his own involvement as both virtuoso performer and virtuoso composer.

While Mozart's self-promotion as both performer and composer is the undeniable catalyst for the Viennese piano concertos from K. 449 in E-flat onwards, it has yet to exert a serious influence on our perception either of the works themselves or of the mindset that produced them. Situating the performer-composer experience centre stage in a way not hitherto witnessed in the secondary literature requires us to account for the effects of the special circumstances of production on Mozart as he worked. His acute attention to

---

[9] See Keefe, 'Strategies of Wind Writing in Mozart's Viennese Piano Concertos'; and Keefe, 'The Aesthetics of Wind Writing in the "Paris" Symphony'.

[10] The fact that the orchestra remained outside Mozart's physical control – in contrast to the keyboard at which he performed himself – provided a source of frustration in one symphonic context at least, that is the 'Paris' Symphony K. 297 (1778). Mozart wrote to his father that he would have been prepared to snatch the violin from lead violinist Pierre Lahoussaye in order to direct the premiere himself had it been poorly played. See MBA, vol. 2, p. 388; LMF, pp. 557–558 (3 July 1778).

[11] MBA, vol. 3, p. 303; LMF, p. 869 (3 March 1784).

detail, intense personal involvement and commitment, and desire and ability to enthral his audience – all described in my introduction – point to a performer-composer intent on harnessing specific musical events (sounds, timbres, instrumental and solo effects) to more general ends that ultimately encourage listeners to perceive performance and composition as mutually reinforcing features of a complete musical experience. A critical picture of this kind was painted on 28 October 1777, in a review of Mozart's Augsburg performance of his Concerto for Three Pianos in F, K. 242, with the organist Johann Michael Demmler and distinguished piano-maker Johann Andreas Stein on the other two solo parts:

The work [K. 242] is thorough, fiery, varied [*mannigfaltig*] and simple; the harmony so full, so powerful, so unexpected, so elevating; the melody so agreeable, so playful, and everything so new; the performance on the fortepiano so nice, so clear, so full of expression and yet at the same time extraordinarily fast, that we hardly knew what we should pay attention to first, and all the listeners were enraptured with delight [*alle Zuhörer zum Entzücken hingerissen wurden*]. We saw here mastery in the thoughts, mastery in the performance, mastery in the instruments, all combined together. One thing always elevated another so that the numerous assembly was displeased with nothing but that their pleasure did not last still longer. The patriotically minded had the special pleasure of seeing from the stillness and the general applause of the listeners that we know here how to appreciate true beauty – to hear a virtuoso who may place himself alongside the great masters of our nation, and yet is at least half our own – and to hear instruments [namely Stein pianos] which according to the judgment of foreigners surpass by far all others of this kind.[12]

This practical and theoretical perspective yields vantage points from which we can survey specific issues that Mozart himself must have implicitly or explicitly surveyed in negotiating performing and compositional priorities. For example, what would be the implications for the appreciation of his piano part of adopting a particular combination of instruments at a given juncture, or, turned around, the implications for the appreciation of orchestral writing of including a particular type of piano writing? How are solo effects conveyed by him as soloist complemented, contradicted or reinforced by effects in the orchestra (and vice versa)? Is the 'completeness' of experiencing Mozart in action as a performer-composer recognized by the Augsburg reviewer and implicitly by Leopold in his account of the 'marvellous concerto' in February 1785[13] ultimately matched by interacting performance- and composition-orientated activities from Mozart?

---

[12] MDL, p. 150; MDB, p. 168.   [13] MBA, vol. 3, p. 373; LMF, p. 886 (16 February 1785).

Almost all of Mozart's musings on such issues are lost forever, consigned to the irrecoverable past along with his performances. Manuscript sources, however, provide material for a partial recovery operation. Little is known about the performing parts Mozart used for his Viennese concerto performances; in addition, there are very few extant authenticated Viennese copies of the piano concertos K. 449–491 potentially to illuminate Mozart's thought processes as performer-composer.[14] So, it is the autograph scores of the Viennese piano concertos written for academies and subscription events between 1784 and 1786 that provide the most promising source for enquiring into Mozart's intertwining compositional and performance-related priorities characteristic of the production and execution of the works. As we shall see, adjustments, modifications and revisions in particular catch Mozart in the act of negotiating performing needs as soloist and compositional needs as author.[15] Naturally, some alterations can be straightforwardly attributed to compositional concerns, such as harmonic details, structure or simple notational errors.[16] But revisions in which solo and orchestral profiles are at issue – as a result of interleaving material, individual solo and orchestral sounds, orchestration choices, and virtuosic effects, for example – are germane to understanding and appreciating Mozart's frame of mind as performer-composer.

Mozart the keyboard player was lauded above all for technical dexterity and expressive presence. Likewise, solo virtuosity in a Mozart concerto comprises both the brilliance of figuration and passagework, and the

---

[14] On authentic copies for the Salzburg and Viennese piano concertos – those prepared in consultation with Mozart and probably used by him for performance purposes – see Christoph Wolff, 'The Many Faces of Authenticity: Problems of a Critical Edition of Mozart's Piano Concertos', in Zaslaw (ed.), *Mozart's Piano Concertos*, pp. 19–28; and Cliff Eisen, 'The Scoring of the Orchestral Bass Part in Mozart's Salzburg Keyboard Concertos: The Evidence of the Authentic Copies', in Zaslaw (ed.), *Mozart's Piano Concertos*, pp. 411–425.

[15] In a similar spirit – albeit not rooted in evidence from primary sources – Roman Ivanovitch states: 'If we look in the right ways, we shall frequently find that there is an element of *compositional* bravura in the display episodes [of Mozart's piano concertos], a counterpart to the performative fireworks.' See Ivanovitch, 'Variation in the Display Episodes of Mozart's Piano Concertos', *Journal of Music Theory*, 52 (2008) pp. 181–218, at 189.

[16] The change to the horn part in bar 14 of K. 453/iii, for example, is probably harmonically motivated. Mozart originally gives a full semibreve, continuing the tied semibreves of bars 12–13. The revision replaces the semibreve with one crotchet and three crotchets rest and likely accounts for the fact that the continuation of the horn D would not have fitted the harmony on beat 3. (The same applies to the horn part in the second half of Variation 3, bar 86.) In K. 482/ii, Mozart initially forgot bar 121, adding it in by manually extending by a few centimetres the staves on the left-hand side of the manuscript paper. At the beginning of the Andante cantabile section of K. 482/iii the first two bars in the flute are crossed out, but were never intended for the flute as they are notated at transposed clarinet pitch. On 'types of errors' (*Fehlertypen*) in general in Mozart's autographs, see Konrad, *Mozarts Schaffensweise*, pp. 356–366.

expressiveness of thematic and melodic playing,[17] collective attributes that lie at the heart of the late-eighteenth-century concerto soloist's experience *qua* soloist. I shall consider separately alterations to autograph scores in passages of solo brilliance (including alterations to orchestral parts) and passages with less demonstrative technical virtuosity likely designed for expressive effect.[18] My attention will focus for the most part on small-scale alterations to Mozart's fundamentally clear and 'orderly' Viennese autographs, where the musical thoughts and negotiations of performer-composer will emerge with greatest clarity.[19]

Mozart's piano concertos may have dominated his output for Viennese public and private events in 1784–1786, but other works also appeared at concerts. Following my investigation of the concertos, I turn to the Quintet for Piano and Winds, K. 452, written for Mozart's Burgtheater academy on 1 April 1784, the Wind Serenade K. 361 performed at clarinet virtuoso Anton Stadler's academy on 23 March 1784, and Masonic Funeral Music, K. 477, probably heard on several occasions in 1785 in semi-private rather than public settings. (I discuss in Chapter 5 the Accompanied Sonata K. 454, premiered by Mozart and visiting violin virtuoso Regina Strinasacchi at her academy on 29 April 1784, in the context of its publication by Torricella later in 1784.) As we shall see, timbral and textural sensitivities in all three are similar to those in the piano concertos. In the piano and wind quintet Mozart created a role for himself different to concerto soloist and solo improviser on display elsewhere in the 1784 academy, challenging performers and listeners alike to get to grips

---

[17] On the *virtù* of concerto virtuosity – in which expressiveness plays an important role – see Kerman, *Concerto Conversations*, pp. 61–82; and Eisen, 'The Rise (and Fall) of the Concerto Virtuoso in the Late Eighteenth and Nineteenth Centuries', pp. 177–191. See also Elisabeth Le Guin, *Boccherini's Body: An Essay in Carnal Musicology* (Berkeley, CA: University of California Press, 2006), Chapter 4, 'Virtuosity, Virtuality, Virtue', pp. 105–159.

[18] This is not to suggest that technical brilliance is in any way inexpressive – as late-eighteenth-century writers implicitly or explicitly do in deriding concertos for overly ostentatious brilliance – but simply to recognize that a soloist's figurative passagework and thematic-melodic presentation are demonstrably different in virtuosic effect.

[19] The autograph score of the C-minor concerto, K. 491, is an example of a more 'disorderly' manuscript, at least where the notation of the solo part is concerned. For a consideration of this autograph, and the textual problems arising from it, see Levin, 'The Devil's in the Details', in Zaslaw (ed.), *Mozart's Piano Concertos*, pp. 29–50, especially 35–50. (He refers to it as 'one of the most disorderly in the *oeuvre*', on p. 44.) As Levin explains, 'The solo staves were at first sketched in a hurried and barely legible script, often limited to schematic outlines' (p. 44); on occasion (as in the second variation in the finale) revisions are so extensive that 'no final form can be said to exist' (p. 40). Furthermore, 'The exact reading of certain scale passages in the last movement of K. 491 [in Mozart's shorthand] cannot be surmised' (p. 42). See also Levin's critical notes in Mozart, *Klavierkonzert C-moll, KV491: Facsimile*, pp. 5–19. Ulrich Konrad attempts to decipher layers of revision to the piano part in variation 2 of K. 491/iii (bars 40–48 and 56–64), giving a facsimile and his own transcriptions, in *Mozarts Schaffensweise*, pp. 485–487.

with a new type of work. The wind serenade, written either for Stadler's academy or at some stage between 1781 and 1784, would have met Stadler's needs in again promoting performing talents around timbre different from those associated with other items on the programme. The orchestration of Masonic Funeral Music was revised late in the compositional process to include three basset-horns and contrabassoon, apparently to exploit timbres and effects possible in the hands of masterly practitioners.

The Piano Concertos: Brilliant Virtuosity and Orchestral Participation

A glance at the autograph scores of Mozart's Viennese piano concertos from K. 449 in E-flat onwards reveals certain types of adjustment as more common than others: for example, changes to solo piano figurations are more frequent either than changes to presentations of more ostensibly thematic material (piano and orchestra), or than adjustments to orchestral parts in general.[20] Mozart's normal procedure in writing down his piano concertos perhaps offers a partial explanation. For he usually began the notational phase of compositional activity by compiling a *particella* that comprised the piano part, the bass part and some passages for orchestral instruments usually thematic-melodic in orientation (especially when the piano is not present in a solo role, such as in first-movement ritornello sections).[21] The act of putting pen to

[20] The following autographs and facsimiles of piano concertos were consulted for the ensuing two subsections of this chapter: Biblioteka Jagiellońska Kraków, Mus. ms. autogr. W. A. Mozart 449 (for K. 449); Herzogin Anna Amalia Bibliothek Weimar: Mus V: 125 (for K. 450); Biblioteka Jagiellońska Kraków, Mus. ms. autogr. W. A. Mozart 451 (for K. 451); Biblioteka Jagiellońska Kraków, Mus. ms. autogr. W. A. Mozart 453 (for K. 453); Staatsbibliothek zu Berlin: Mus. ms. autogr. W. A. Mozart KV 456 (for K. 456); Gesellschaft der Musikfreude Wien: VII 3405 (K. 466); Mozart, *Piano Concerto No. 21 in C major, K. 467: The Autograph Score* (New York: Dover, 1985); Staatsbibliothek Preußischer Kulturbesitz Mus. ms. autogr. W. A. Mozart 482 (for K. 482); Mozart, *Klavierkonzert A-dur, KV 488: Faksimile nach dem Autograph Ms. 226 im Besitz der Musikabteilung der Bibliothèque nationale de France, Paris* (Munich: Henle, 2005).

[21] We witness the *particella* compositional layer especially in Mozart's piano concertos that remained incomplete fragments for a period of time (including K. 449, 488, 503; see Tyson, *Autograph Scores*) and where different ink colours underscore the temporal separation of the *particella* from the completed composition. See, for example, the recent high-quality facsimile of K. 488 where oboe parts written in the opening ritornello of the first movement during the first phase of composition in 1784 are discernibly different in ink colour from the clarinet parts finally conceived in 1786 and written on the same staves; Mozart, *Klavierkonzert A-dur KV488: Faksimile.* For further discussion of Mozart's compositional methods, see Konrad, *Mozarts Schaffensweise*; and for a succinct summary, Konrad, 'Compositional Method' in Eisen and Keefe (eds.), *Cambridge Mozart Encyclopedia*, pp. 100–108. Recently, in a concerto context, see Levin, 'Mozart's Working Methods in the Keyboard Concertos'.

paper to produce an initial continuous draft designed to fix details in his mind would have provided an opportunity for Mozart to refine earlier (likely unnotated) ideas for the work.

Prime position for the piano in Mozart's compositional process does not in itself imply that he prioritizes his own solo performance of the concertos over their orchestral component. Of course, Mozart could have made some changes to brilliant figurations in order better to match his predilections as a performer. Examples may include K. 466/iii, bars 135–137 (arpeggios and leaps in preference to chromatic writing in the run-up to the B theme) and bars 161–167 (an altered arpeggiated approach to the A' in the sonata-rondo exposition); and K. 482/i, bar 284 (scalar rising semiquavers in favour of rising semiquavers in thirds).[22] But there is no reason to assume that revisions were intended simply to promote a more ostentatious technical dexterity than witnessed in the discarded versions and thus to act as a conduit only for self-serving pianistic brilliance. In fact, several piano revisions are, if anything, less showy than their rejected versions: in K. 482/i, bar 325, Mozart initially intended semiquaver scales in the left hand as well as the right, but subsequently crossed them out. Mozart, by his own admission, was not a fan of brilliant virtuosity for its own sake: he claimed to be 'no great lover of difficulties' *per se* in assessing Ignaz Fränzl's considerable performance skills in a violin concerto; and he intended to strike 'a happy medium between too easy and too difficult' in his first Viennese piano concertos, K. 413, 414 and 415.[23]

It cannot be assumed, then, that Mozart *necessarily* made changes to piano figuration with his own piano part (and projection of his own solo persona) either exclusively or primarily in mind. Even when adjustments are made at the early, piano-centred phase of the compositional process and in a section in which the piano ostensibly dominates with brilliant figuration (such as between the end of the secondary theme and the cadential trill in a first-movement solo exposition or recapitulation), issues outside the piano's immediate remit were probably on Mozart's mind as well as solo-orientated communication with the audience. K. 488/i illustrates the difficulties of assigning a specific motivation to Mozart for a specific change even during a piano-dominated passage and, by implication, the intertwined nature of

---

[22] It is difficult to determine when *exactly* Mozart carried out these changes, and most of the other changes discussed below. It would seem reasonable to assume variability in practice: some changes made immediately; some after further material had been written; and some after a performance.

[23] MBA, vol. 2, p. 137, vol. 3, pp. 245–246; LMF, pp. 384, 833 (22 November 1777, 28 December 1782).

Example 4.1 Mozart, Piano Concerto in A, K. 488/i: rejected material for piano between bars 113 and 114 (all other staves blank).

Example 4.2a Mozart, Piano Concerto in A, K. 488/i: rejected material for piano between bars 125 and 126 (all other staves blank).

performance and compositional concerns. The passage in the solo exposition from the end of the secondary theme to the cadential trill gave Mozart pause for thought. There are two extended deletions to the piano part – six bars between the finalized bars 113 and 114, immediately after the secondary theme (Example 4.1) and seven bars and one beat between the finalized 125 and 126, in the run-up to the cadential trill (Examples 4.2a and 4.2b). We do not know for certain whether Mozart rejected the first passage before going on to write the music from bar 114 onwards or *after* writing it, and, if the latter, whether he rejected the six bars at the *particella* stage in or around 1784, or at the later 1786 stage when the work was being completed. (The resolution to bar 114 is musically effective whether preceded by the deleted bars or not.) In contrast, it is clear that Mozart crossed out the later passage (between bars 125 and 126) before continuing on, since the orchestral parts are aligned with the first beat of bar 126 proper (rather than the final beat of the original passage) and 126 has five beats in the piano including the deleted

Example 4.2b Mozart, Piano Concerto in A, K. 488/i, bars 125–137 (final version).

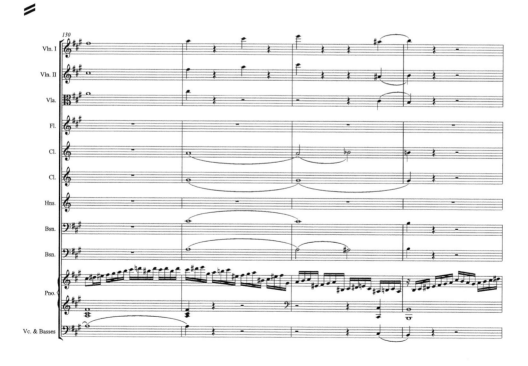

Example 4.2b (cont.)

beat.[24] In addition, it seems Mozart envisaged his revision as an extension of the original passage between bar 125 and the end of the solo exposition: the original culminates with a section-ending cadential trill after six bars and the revision after eleven.

The original piano passages in the K. 488/i solo exposition could have been deleted for a number of reasons that relate to the piano part and Mozart's performance of it, and/or to wider compositional concerns (harmony, structure, orchestration). Mozart may have been unhappy (for whatever reason) with the originally conceived figurations for the six bars between 113 and 114, perhaps becoming uncomfortable with the first protracted figurative semiquavers simultaneously in left and right hands appearing at this juncture. He might have disliked harmonic implications of the six bars between 113 and 114, such as the inflection to F-sharp minor stealing the thunder of the subsequent turn to A minor, or the end-orientated flavour of the sequential component. Or, on reflection, he may have decided to stick closely to the pattern of thematic presentation

---

[24] See Ernst-Günther Heinemann, 'Einleitung/Introduction', in Mozart, *KV488 Faksimile*, pp. xi, xv.

from the orchestral ritornello, deleting the semiquaver figuration in order directly to align the succession of secondary and A-minor themes with the earlier section (see bars 46–47).

Equally, given the complementary nature of original and revised materials, the two deletions in the solo exposition could have been carried out in tandem. Both, for example, engage with the issue of figurative continuity (or otherwise): the first deleted passage is immediately followed by a thematic interruption to figuration and the second revised version begins (on the third and fourth beats of the finalized bar 126) with a momentary pause in figuration. The deletion of the first passage also could have compensated for the extension of the second passage (or vice versa), a result of Mozart keeping in mind the balance between pianistic virtuosity and thematic presentation. More specifically, the extension of the ii6 (F-sharp minor harmony) from one bar to three in the original and revised second passages may have led Mozart to cut the original first passage with its inflection to F-sharp minor. At any rate, the second revision broadens the virtuosic sweep to the cadential trill in relation to the rejected passage: the range from g-sharp' – e''' in the original expands to g-sharp – e''' in the revision and is especially noticeable in the flourish accompanying the revised cadential I6/4 (bars 133–135). Mozart's intentions for the orchestration of the original six- and seven-bar passages are unlikely to have provoked the revisions – most of the orchestration was carried out in the later compositional phase in 1786 – but are not impossible as a contributing factor, as the deletion of the first passage cannot be assigned with absolute certainty to 1784 rather than 1786. Mozart exploits for orchestration purposes the implications and potential of the piano's revised materials, alongside the new timbral opportunities (in 1786) offered by clarinets. The second revised passage retains the echo effect from bar 114ff., now between strings and flutes/clarinets/bassoons (bars 127–128), and is demarcated more clearly than would have been possible in the original end-of-section passage, since a registral shift down an octave in the revised piano part does not appear in the original piano part. In addition, Mozart establishes a rapport between clarinets and bassoons in the final three bars of the secondary theme (111–113, where the clarinet takes over from the flute), and twice exploits the sonority later in the solo exposition: in the tied semibreves representing the winds' only contribution to a piano-strings dialogue (see bars 120–123); and as the winds' only participation in the concluding bars of the section (see bars 131–133).

Whether Mozart was actively contemplating either or both his performed piano part and harmonic, structural and textural issues when

Example 4.3a Mozart, Piano Concerto in C, K. 467/i, bar 183 (original version for piano).

Example 4.3b Mozart, Piano Concerto in C, K. 467/i, bars 188–189 (original version for piano).

Example 4.3c Mozart, Piano Concerto in C, K. 467/i, bar 192 (original version for cellos and basses).

deleting and revising material in the solo exposition of his A-major concerto, his revisions had implications for all areas. At some level of musical consciousness, then, Mozart juggled multifarious performing and compositional concerns in producing his own piano part.

Smaller scale changes to the autograph scores – including to both piano and orchestral parts in quick succession – bring performance- and composition-related negotiation into sharp focus. The run-up to the cadential trill in the solo exposition of K. 467/i features three alterations (see Example 4.3a–c for the original material and Example 4.3d for the final version of the passage): the dotted quaver rhythms in the right hand of the piano in bar 183 are changed to quavers and the left-hand semiquavers adjusted as well; the semiquaver sweep in octaves in bars 188–189 is modified to include an ascent in thirds; and the complete bar of repeated quavers in the string basses one bar before the cadential trill is cancelled in favour of a single crotchet. All three follow sequential semiquaver patterns of the kind so common at this juncture of Mozart's first movements. The first two revisions merge more seamlessly into a continuous musical fabric than their originals: bar 183 cancels the distinctive right-hand dotted rhythm, and bars 188–189 maintain

Example 4.3d Mozart, Piano Concerto in C, K. 467/i, bars 180–193 (final version).

semiquaver movement in thirds rather than offering new neighbour-note figures. In contrast, the third alteration, thinning out string participation by eliminating three beats in the basses, creates space for the piano's new triplet quaver rhythm to be accentuated. Collectively, the three alterations suggest a vision for the figurative climax of this section, namely figurative fluidity enhanced rhythmically (and thematically) in bars 183 and 188–189 so as not

Example 4.3d (cont.)

to detract from the rhythmic novelty of bar 192, which is itself emphasized by a lighter accompanying orchestral texture than originally envisaged. Even if pianistic brilliance – projected in his own performance – is Mozart's primary concern here, it is a brilliance far removed from the empty ostentation often

Example 4.4a Mozart, Piano Concerto in B-flat, K. 450/i, bars 126–128 (original material for piano).

Example 4.4b Mozart, Piano Concerto in B-flat, K. 450/i, bars 126–128 (final version; all other staves blank)

criticized in the concertos of other late-eighteenth-century composers, being calculated for maximum effect at the precise moment that the more ostensibly brilliant semiquavers give way to triplet quavers, and being concerned with the effects of timbre and rhythm as well as of technical dexterity.

Combined attention to precise effects of solo brilliance and instrumental participation also underscores a series of changes to the piano part in the final twelve bars of the solo exposition of K. 450/i (see the finalized and original versions in Examples 4.4a–b, 4.5a–b and 4.6a–b).[25] First, in bars 126–128 (Examples 4.4a and 4.4b), three bars of semiquavers are crossed out. The revised version, written on the two staves above, omits the original left-hand semiquavers on beats 2 and 4 in favour of a quaver and quaver rest, thus more clearly supporting (rather than potentially obscuring) the *f* – *p* oscillations in the strings. (In addition, the right-hand semiquavers on beats 2 and 4 are modified in the revision.) Irrespective of whether the

[25] For a brief discussion of these changes, intended to 'challenge a philological creed that has governed musicology since its outset [. . . that] the object of the scholar is to approach a musical work of art as part of a definitive legacy and establish a text that reflects the composer's ultimate, final version', see Levin, 'Mozart's Working Methods', pp. 403–405.

Example 4.5a Mozart Piano Concerto in B-flat, K. 450/i, bars 130–132 (rejected material for piano).

Example 4.5b Mozart Piano Concerto in B-flat, K. 450/i, bars 130–132 (final version; all other staves blank).

revision to the piano left hand was conceived and carried out before or after the string *f – p* material was written, the two operate in tandem, with Mozart remaining simultaneously attentive to orchestral and pianistic effects. Second, in bars 130–132 (Examples 4.5a and 4.5b), Mozart changes left-hand semiquavers to triplet quavers and right-hand minims to a crotchet – minim – crotchet syncopated effect; both these revised rhythms are new to the piano part in the solo exposition. Finally, in bar 135 (Examples 4.6a and 4.6b), Mozart substitutes upward-rising quaver triplets with a descent from on high. Sensitivity to surrounding material is evident here, piano and orchestral alike: the f″ in the right hand and the triplet rhythm revisit the registral highpoint and (revised) left-hand rhythm from three bars earlier (given in Example 4.5b); and the piano's descent from the upper reaches provides crystal-clear registral differentiation from the string parts (in contrast to the original version). Thus, the mutually complementary nature of Mozart's changes – affecting the piano alone in projecting brilliant virtuosity, and the piano and orchestra together in highlighting timbre – shows performance and compositional concerns at one.

Example 4.6a Mozart Piano Concerto in B-flat, K. 450/i, bars 134–135 (original material for piano).

Example 4.6b Mozart Piano Concerto in B-flat, K. 450/i, bars 134–135 (final version; all other staves blank).

Interlinked issues of virtuosity and timbre are also a feature of the autographs of the E-flat concertos K. 482 and K. 449. In the recapitulation of K. 482/i, when a theme is heard for the first time since the opening orchestral ritornello (bars 314–328), Mozart makes adjustments to both piano and clarinet parts (see Example 4.7 for bars 322–326). He initially envisaged the clarinet doubling the first violin, flute, first horn and first bassoon in bar 324 (and presumably not therefore adopting the flute's decorative descent from bar 323 in bar 325) and the piano performing semiquavers in both right and left hands (bar 325). The decisions to give the decorative descent to the clarinet and to delete the piano's left-hand

Example 4.7 Mozart, Piano Concerto in E-flat, K. 482/i, bars 322–326 (final version, including deletions marked in autograph score).

Example 4.8a Mozart, Piano Concerto in E-flat, K. 449/i, bars 190–192 (rejected material for piano).

Example 4.8b Mozart, Piano Concerto in E-flat, K. 449/i, bars 188–192 (final version).

doubling of the right hand were probably made together, as the left-hand semiquavers in the second half of bar 325 would have exactly duplicated (at pitch) the semiquavers in the clarinet; attention to timbre thus leads to marginal sacrificing of pianistic brilliance (one hand rather than two). And deletion of the next bar – where the piano would have repeated bar 325 with right and left hands again an octave apart – creates another slight diminishment of pianistic brilliance.

Timbral clarity and brilliant writing for the piano are also aligned in the development section of K. 449/i. Each of the piano's two-bar contributions to the extended sequence in the first half of the section (see bars 190–191, Examples 4.8a and 4.8b, and 194–195, 198–199, 202–203) originally comprised dotted minims in octaves in the first bar (left hand) and ascending arpeggiated semiquavers and stepwise descending semiquavers in the two bars together (right hand).[26] Whether motivated to involve the left hand in the figurative play, to cancel the resounding octave dotted minims, to furnish registral peaks at the beginning rather than halfway through a beat (see the original versions of bars 191 and 199), or to provide closer sequential repetitions from segment to segment, Mozart's revision affects the piano's interaction with the orchestra as well as the virtuosity profile of his own instrument. The participation of the left hand in the revised ascending semiquavers allows for more dramatic virtuoso sweeps than the earlier version; the cancellation of the resonant left-hand octaves also lends greater textural clarity to the semiquaver solo figuration. Piano and orchestral material are more sharply differentiated in the sequential passage as a result of the adjustments: the waves of ascending semiquavers contrast more markedly than their figurative predecessors with the orchestra's conjunct descents; and the arrival point of the orchestra's octave descents (B-flat, C, F, G), previously affirmed by left-hand dotted-minim octaves, is now de-emphasized, accentuating the opposition of orchestral and piano material. The stylistic significance of this sequential passage – Mozart's first outright confrontation between soloist and orchestra in his piano concerto repertory[27] – perhaps explains why he stiffened contrast between adjacent segments. In any case, with attention tuned to solo figurations, solo textures and piano-orchestra interaction, his revision again satisfies performance and compositional needs simultaneously.

K. 450/i and K. 449/i show Mozart alert to orchestral effects at moments of maximum exposure as brilliant-orientated virtuoso (in the run-up to a solo exposition cadential trill, for example), even when changes were not made to the orchestral parts. Adjustments to the horn parts in the final bars of the solo exposition of K. 459/i (see Example 4.9) provide further evidence of Mozart's timbral attentiveness. He initially notates tied semibreves for the horns in bars 173–180 inclusive (sounding c, c'), subsequently deleting two-and-three-quarter bars at the end to exclude them from the three bars in which the upper winds play the grace-note figure (bars 178–180). Mozart perhaps imagined the continuation of the tied notes in the horns obscuring the piano figuration, both occupying the same register at least in bars 178–179. But the horns' presence as sole wind representatives in bars 183–185, beat 1, and exactly in the piano's register, renders exclusion from bars 178–180 unlikely merely for occupying pianistic registral territory. Given the horns'

---

[26] Mozart's original version of bars 188–203 appears in two pages inserted into Nannerl's Salzburg copy of K. 449, annotated by Nannerl as 'extra manieren in das erste Allegro'. See *Kritischer Bericht*, NMA V/15/4, p. 7.

[27] See Keefe, *Mozart's Viennese Instrumental Music*, pp. 19–42.

Example 4.9 Mozart, Piano Concerto in F, K. 459/i, bars 173–190 (final version).

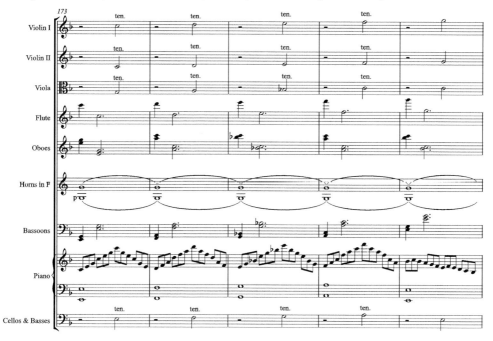

Example 4.9 (cont.)

2

exclusion in bars 178–80 when the flute, first oboe and first bassoon are present, and their *inclusion* in bars 183–185 when the rest of the winds are absent, the deletion of the semibreves in bars 178–180 could in fact pertain to the specific wind sonorities and effects desired rather than (or as well as) the link-up between piano and winds. The horns' participation in the solo exposition so far – limited to a few bars before, during and after the secondary theme – to all intents and purposes sets them apart from the rest of the wind section; their sustained notes (an effect new to the movement), first simultaneously with octave figures in the other winds and then by themselves (bars 173–180; 183–185), accentuate the separation. Mozart's original idea, crossed out in the autograph, of having the horns play the main theme's head motif in the cadential trill bar (188), alongside the violas and basses but with no other wind, confirms the distinctive role intended for them; retaining the horns in bar 188 would have preserved alteration between flute/oboes/bassoons and horns across the last eleven bars of the solo exposition.[28] Mozart's deletion of the horns in bar 188 reveals active negotiation of wind orchestration and effect, wind-strings-piano timbre, and pianistic brilliance.

An adjustment to the horns in K. 451/i again sheds light on Mozart's sensitivity to orchestral effects at an important moment of exposure as brilliant virtuoso (Example 4.10). Initially, the horns are given tied semibreve As in octaves in the bar before and bar of the final cadential trill (305–306), matching the octave As in the bassoons, but are revised to (untied) D-F sharp and A-E semibreves. The alteration is not made for harmonic reasons: the I6/4 – V7 progression takes effect whichever horn notes are employed. Perhaps Mozart felt that he would have had a surfeit of As had the original octave As been retained in the horns as well as the bassoons; or perhaps he felt greater presence was needed for the D-F sharp in I6/4 and the E in V7. At any rate, instrumental effects may have factored into the equation. There is nothing 'wrong' (in harmonic or timbral respects) with the horns and the bassoons both retaining octave As; indeed they (and the flute and oboes) receive four and a half consecutive bars of octave As in bars 299–303. The latter occupies a distinctive position in the movement as a whole – a timbral highpoint for the winds as supportive sonic reinforcement for the piano hot on the heels of a thematic highpoint as elaborators of dialogue (bars 286–268).[29] It is entirely possible, then, that Mozart altered the horns in bars 305–306 in order to avoid partial replication of the preceding instrumental effect.

---

[28] The crossed-out bar for horn cannot be a simple notational error on Mozart's part, as it is written at the correct transposed pitch for a horn in F (d', sounding g) that doubles the violas/basses and is similarly marked *forte*.

[29] See Keefe, "'Greatest Effects with the Least Effort'", pp. 35–37.

Example 4.10 Mozart, Piano Concerto in D, K. 451/i, bars 302–307 (final version, including horn deletions marked in the autograph score).

In 1806 a writer for the *Allgemeine musikalische Zeitung* contrasted a certain Mr. Stein's fiery performance of the D-minor Piano Concerto K. 466 with Mozart's own performance of it: 'Mozart himself delivered this concerto with more seriousness and imposing dignity. With him the profound, rich spirit of the composition was more noticeable; with Stein, more the brilliant execution of the virtuoso.'[30] Thus, Stein privileged the technical virtuosity of the performer, while Mozart privileged the holistic virtuosity of the performer-composer. Mozart, as 'author', may have known better than Stein how to give a convincingly integrated account of the work, complete with distinguished *gravitas*, explaining his greater success than Stein at the mutual reinforcement of performance and composition. Alterations to the autographs by the performer-composer reveal comparable depth: instrumental effects, combined instrumental and piano timbres, and intricate piano-orchestra interaction all contribute (alongside pianistic showiness) to the listening experience.

The Piano Concertos: Expressive Virtuosity and Orchestral Participation

Compositional and performance aspects of Mozart's musical personality interact in expressive, undemonstrative solo displays as well as in brilliant virtuosity. The end of the Andante middle section of K. 482/iii is a case in point. The piano's right-hand offbeat semiquavers in bars 253–259 (see Example 4.11) were apparently notated after some or all of the orchestral parts: the notation is cramped and the piano's bar-line in bar 254 extends into the territory of bar 255. Presumably Mozart planned at first not to include the piano at this juncture or to include it with material that would have required less space to notate. The bars in question coincide with the harmonic transition from the minuet (A-flat major) back to the rondo (E-flat major): Mozart moves from the re-confirmation of A-flat in bar 253 to a confirmation of E-flat in bars 260–265[31] via dim7 (bar 256), F minor (257), dim7 (258), and i (259) harmonies. The transitional role of bars 253–259 extends to piano and orchestral participation as well, in the context of the Andante and the ensuing Primo tempo. For bars 253–259

---

[30] *Allgemeine musikalische Zeitung*, 8 (1805–1806), col. 729. 'Mozart selbst dies Konzert mit mehr Ernst und imponirender Würde vortrug. Bey ihm wurde mehr der tiefe, reiche Geist der Komposition, bei Stein mehr der glänzende Vortrag des Virtuosen bemerkbar'.

[31] The progression re-establishing E-flat is as follows: German Augmented 6th (bar 260) – V / i6/4 (261–63) – V (264) – I (265).

Example 4.11 Mozart, Piano Concerto in E-flat, K. 482/iii, bars 253–260 (where, in the autograph, the right-hand piano notation is cramped and the bar-line for the right-hand part at 254 is extended).

bridge the gap between participatory parity earlier in the Andante (eight-bar statements alternating between winds and piano/strings in 218–249),[32] and brilliant-orientated pianistic prominence (with active orchestral participation) in the Primo tempo. Parity is evident in several ways: the lack of discernible melody; the textural distinctiveness of each of the piano, wind and string groupings; and the partial mirroring of the strings in the piano right hand. But the right hand also comes modestly to the fore in gesture and texture: the ascending-descending arpeggiated motion is more pronounced than for the strings, increasing by a half step each time (a-flat' – e-flat'''; a-flat' – e-natural'''; a-flat' – f'''), and 'mediates' between the wind and strings by remaining in rhythmic and thematic sympathy with the strings while matching and surpassing the registral highpoints in the wind.

Irrespective of when the decision to include it was made, the right hand of the piano is seemingly motivated (at least in part) by timbral considerations; Mozart's piano line adds a distinctive strand to an already distinctive texture (strings marked *pizzicato* for the only time in K. 482, and a full wind contingent – minus trumpets – given sustained notes together for the first time in the movement, a pristine effect re-visited in the final bars). Assuming the cramped score confirms Mozart's notation of the piano right hand later than the orchestral parts, it also accentuates his negotiation of performance and composition in garnering audience appreciation as both performer and composer. The right hand fulfils a timbral role, reinforces the transitional function of the passage, and allows Mozart a chance to shine as a soloist who reveals himself – delicately on this occasion – as *primus inter pares*. The same might be said (without the transitional implications) of other piano right-hand segments squashed in by Mozart apparently after orchestral parts were written, including the semiquaver/demisemiquaver flourishes in the continuation of the main theme towards the end of K. 482/iii (see bars 404, 406, 408).[33] Orchestral lines are gently embellished, not ostentatiously usurped.

Simultaneous attention to performance and composition may also explain Mozart's adjustments to the left hand of the piano part in variation 4 (the *minore*) of K. 453/iii: he originally wanted minims on the first and third beats of bars 105–107, 109–111 (Examples 4.12a and 4.12b) and

---

[32] The wind statements in the Andante are informed by the Viennese tradition of *Harmoniemusik*. The sextet employed by Mozart – two clarinets, two bassoons, two horns – is also the wind combination praised by French aesthetician Louis Francoeur in a landmark early treatise on orchestration (*Diapason général de tous les instrumens à vent* (1772), pp. 35, 51, 54–55; see Chapter 1 in this volume). This treatise would have been circulating in Paris during Mozart's visit in 1778.

[33] From outside the 1784–1786 period, see also the piano's semiquaver elaboration of the first violin's chromatically falling quavers at the close of K. 537/ii (bars 102, 104).

Example 4.12a Mozart, Piano Concerto in G, K. 453/iii, bars 105–112 (original version of the piano part).

Example 4.12b Mozart, Piano Concerto in G, K. 453/iii, bars 105–112 (final version of piano part; all other staves are blank).

121–125 (Examples 4.13a and 4.13b), replacing them with minims beginning on weak beats and tied across bar-lines notated on the stave below.[34] These changes occur in the run-up to the most powerful instrumental effect of the movement so far – the onset of variation 5 *fortissimo* in the full orchestra – where texture, dynamics and tonality (the return to G major) create a show of raw orchestral strength that is itself foreshadowed by the *forte* wind outbursts at the end of variation 4 (bars 122–123, 124–125). It is entirely possible, of course, that Mozart carried out his adjustments to the

---

[34] In addition, Mozart altered the upper line of the revised left-hand part of bars 106–107 (notated on the stave below) before coming up with his finalized version. Mozart's dense crossing out here makes it difficult to determine for certain what he first envisaged for the revision, although it would appear that he intended the revised syncopated rhythm either on c' and e-flat' together or on e-flat' only. The rejected left-hand part in bar 106 also contains a crossed out minim (or crotchet) c', for which Mozart substitutes the semibreve c'.

Example 4.13a Mozart, Piano Concerto in G, K. 453/iii, bars 121–125 (original version; piano part only).

Example 4.13b Mozart, Piano Concerto in G, K. 453/iii, bars 121–125 (final version; all other staves blank).

piano left hand in variation 4 for reasons associated with the piano part alone. But the precise point that the crossing out ends – bar 125, coinciding with the end of the wind outbursts – suggests intertwining visions for orchestra and piano. Mozart's revisions provide rhythmic motion in the piano at every quaver, in contrast to the orchestral segments and combined right and left hand of the the original piano version, which move respectively in crotchets and both crotchets and quavers. Thus, the revised second halves of the two parts of the variation (for piano) rhythmically intensify the first halves (for orchestra) in a more pronounced way than the original versions. Moreover, forward momentum generated by the revised piano part is enhanced by the wind outbursts, a kind of double intensification lending rhythmic and gestural urgency to the concluding bars of variation 4, which ultimately drive on to the big orchestral effect at the onset of variation 5.

Whatever motivated Mozart to revise the piano left hand in variation 4 – the piano right-hand part, the wind *forte* support for the right-hand gestures, or just a preference for the new rhythm itself – his revision affects piano performance and orchestral effects alike. It brings greater fluidity to the piano line and perhaps greater potential for melodic expressiveness as a result; it also acts with the wind outbursts to project the music forwards to the dramatic onset of variation 5. Mozart's inclusion of flowing piano writing (the perpetual motion in quavers) and the rhythmic and gestural intensification of the final bars of the variation render the orchestral onset of variation 5 more a moment of arrival than of surprise.

Mozart's simultaneous sensitivity to expressive orchestral and pianistic effects is also evident in smaller-scale changes to his autographs. In the recapitulation of K. 467/i a theme from the orchestral ritornello absent in the solo exposition returns in dialogue between the wind (first statement, bars 351–355) and the piano (second statement, bars 355–359). (See the finalized version in Example 4.14.) Mozart originally intended the piano left hand to double the two oboes/two bassoons accompaniment figure in bars 357–358, but then changed his mind, giving the left hand the theme an octave below the right instead. The revision brings the piano statement exactly into line with the preceding flute, oboe and bassoons statement, both presented in octaves; by implication, Mozart the performer demonstrates awareness of the orchestral instruments playing around him. Equally, the revision gives the piano and oboe/bassoon greater sonic clarity than in the original, neither now doubling the other: the wind (albeit in an ostensibly subsidiary role) continue to make an independent contribution to the texture, just as in both the harmonious full-wind echo one bar earlier (356) and the preceding thematic statement; and the piano distinguishes itself as the exclusive carrier of the melody. Thus, several goals resonate as one: solo prominence in performance; textural clarity; and mutual piano/orchestral sensitivity to surrounding material.

Similar attention to detail is apparent at the end of K. 456/ii (see Example 4.15 for the final version of bars 185–196). After crossing out

Example 4.14 Mozart, Piano Concerto in C, K. 467/i, bars 351–359 (final version).

Example 4.15 Mozart, Piano Concerto in B-flat, K. 456/ii, bars 185–196 (final version).

the initial version of bar 185 (where the oboe carries a minim c") in favour of c" and c-sharp" oboe crotchets, Mozart deletes tied c-sharp' and d'" crotchets in the bassoon and flute (bars 185–186; 186–187) in order to delineate more clearly than in the original the re-entries of the oboe, bassoon and flute, assembling the sounds one by one an octave apart ready for a presentation of the main theme in octaves (bars 188–192). The piano's subsequent continuation of the theme (bars 192–196) matches the preceding wind contributions by playing in octaves. Although the piano octaves disappear in the ensuing give and take, the deletion of the chordal reinforcements of the piano right hand's final points of imitation (bars 205–206, 207–208) illustrates continued attention to orchestral timbre: the simultaneous d' d' horn quavers (marked *pianissimo*) are more audible than they would have been had right-hand chordal reinforcement remained; and the horn and piano quavers two octaves apart now parallel the preceding and succeeding imitative points in the wind one octave apart.

The Piano and Wind Quintet K. 452 and Mozart's Academy, 1 April 1784

On 1 April 1784 the *Wienerblättchen* published an advertisement for Mozart's academy at the Burgtheater:

Today, Thursday 1 April, Herr Kapellmeister Mozart will have the honour to hold a great musical concert for his benefit at the I. & R. National Court Theatre. The pieces for it are as follows: 1) A grand symphony with trumpets and drums. 2) An aria sung by Herr Adamberger. 3) Herr Kapellmeister Mozart will play a completely new concerto on the fortepiano. 4) A fairly new grand symphony. 5) An aria sung by Mlle Cavalieri. 6) Herr Kapellmeister Mozart will play a completely new grand quintet. 7) An aria sung by Herr Marchesi, senior. 8) Herr Kapellmeister Mozart will improvise entirely alone on the fortepiano. 9) To end, a symphony. Except for the three arias, everything is a composition of Herr Kapellmeister Mozart.[35]

As for the academy on 23 March 1783 discussed in Chapter 3, Mozart framed his event with symphonic movements, included his *tour de force* of improvisation as the penultimate item and followed Viennese convention in alternating arias and instrumental pieces.[36] He then reported to his father on 10 April 1784:

Through my three subscription concerts I have covered myself in glory. Also my academy in the theatre turned out very well. I wrote two grand concertos and then a quintet, which received extraordinary applause; I think of it myself as the best [work] I have yet written in my life. It consists of one oboe, one clarinet, one horn, one bassoon and the pianoforte. I wish you could have heard it! And how beautifully it was performed! To tell the truth, incidentally, I was really tired out by the end – from nothing but playing. And it does me no small honour that my listeners *never* were.[37]

Mozart's letter implies either that he performed both K. 450 and K. 451 at the academy (contrary to the text of the advertisement) or that he wrote his two grand concertos for a combination of the Trattnerhof and Burgtheater concerts. Irrespective, it is the piano and wind quintet K. 452 that induces

---

[35] MDL, p. 198; MDB, p. 223. Deutsch suggests that the first symphony was K. 385 (both items 1 and 9) and item 4 the 'Linz' Symphony K. 425. He also proposes either K. 450 or K. 451 as the piano concerto. Item 6 was the piano and wind quintet, K. 452. For a facsimile of the concert notice, see Martin Harlow, 'Action, Reaction and Interaction, and the Play of Style and Genre in Mozart's Piano and Wind Quintet, K. 452', in Harlow (ed.), *Mozart's Chamber Music with Keyboard*, pp. 198–219, at 201.

[36] On the latter point see Morrow, *Concert Life*, p. 144.

[37] MBA, vol. 3, p. 309; LMF, p. 873 (10 April 1784). (The emphasis is Mozart's own.)

special memories and warrants a special assessment. Explicitly comparing it to other works after the event suggests Mozart may have had comparisons in mind when writing it as well, which would be unsurprising given his lack of experience (at that time) of chamber music for piano and multiple instruments, and his rare public performance of a chamber work when larger-scale works were the norm. The primary reference point for him and for those in the academy audience would have been his piano concertos composed shortly before K. 452: even listeners unfamiliar with them ahead of 1 April 1784 would have heard either K. 450 or K. 451 (possibly both) thirty minutes or so earlier, witnessing Mozart first at the keyboard in front of an orchestra and then at the keyboard alongside four wind players.[38] Applauding himself for maintaining listener attention throughout the academy also implies prior consideration of the complementary and distinguishing nature of his own contributions that evening. As K. 452 does not make the performer 'sweat' (*schwitzen*) – Mozart's own description of K. 450 and 451 – and is scored for solo winds rather than a large ensemble, the obvious context of the piano concerto for the academy audience would have meshed with expectations for chamber works, including *Harmoniemusik*.[39] Since Mozart's playing in K. 452 and by extension that of his wind instrumentalists would have been compared to playing earlier in the evening, it is necessary to explore factors relating to the performance of K. 452 in order to understand its significance in the academy programme.

---

[38] It is possible that the other performers of K. 452 were from the emperor's *Harmonie*, namely Anton Stadler (clarinet), Georg Triebensee (oboe), Wenzel Kauzner (bassoon) and Jakob Eisen (horn); see Harlow, 'Style and Genre', p. 205.

[39] For Mozart's reference to K. 450 and K. 451, see MBA, vol. 3, p. 315; LMF, p. 877 (15 May 1784). Critical opinion of K. 452 has focused on its hybrid status relative to the piano concertos and other chamber music; for summaries of reception see Keefe, *Mozart's Viennese Instrumental Music*, pp. 169–170 and Harlow, 'Style and Genre', pp. 202–204. Harlow himself proposes a corrective to the focus on genre: 'Surely more important to the contemporary listener than subtle intertextual and intergeneric references was the rubbing up, the gradual unfolding of the essentials of that music, of its localized actions, reactions and interactions, of *il filo*, its thread.' ('Genre and Style', p. 206) But several of Harlow's interpretations are questionable, in my view, in light of broad (rather than subtle) parallels with events and activities in Mozart's music: the completion of the second theme by the wind does not come across as a 'rude . . . interruption' (p. 210) when compared to the piano concertos; the opening *forte-tenuto* chords do not have a 'straitjacketing effect' (p. 207) when set in the context of the opening of the wind serenade K. 375 (see below); the purple patches in the slow movement are not 'voids' in any meaningful way (pp. 214–215); and the statement that K. 452's 'expressive effect . . . was dependent upon it being neither public nor private' (p. 219) does not factor in the reality that it was (in effect) a private work performed in public.

Example 4.16 Mozart, Quintet for piano and wind, K. 452/i, bars 1–10.

The instruments of Mozart's ensemble move between modest individuality and unambiguous collective endeavour in the first movement,
especially in the slow introduction where meticulous performance markings in the autograph contribute to this process.[40] (See Example 4.16 for
bars 1–10.) The tutti tenutos in bars 1–3, requiring the crotchets to occupy
their full notated value, rejoice in the glorious sound of the complete
ensemble like the opening chords of the wind serenade K. 375 from 1781
(see Chapter 1), as do uniform *forte* chords at the end of the introduction.
The *dolce* indications in bars 5–9, necessitating intensified expression and
(possibly) a dynamic level above the average *p*,[41] direct attention to the
wind imitation by distinguishing each entry. The *dolce* marking for the
horn at bar 9, when it would have been expected at bar 8 alongside the *dolce*
clarinet, encourages smooth progression from the brief imitations to the
horn's lyrical line. Judging by the cramped piano notation in bars 10–11 of
the autograph, Mozart may not have originally intended to introduce
demisemiquavers into the piano – or at least had not determined what
was required when first notating the winds' imitative lines and drawing bar
lines according to the amount of space occupied by the imitations. The
rhythmic nuance of the accompaniment is matched by Mozart's instruction to himself to shade the dynamics of his demisemiquavers (threefold *f* –
p indications in bars 10–11). The expressive flexibility Mozart the composer asks of Mozart the pianist is further in evidence from bar 12 onwards,
where the slurred semiquavers offered by the wind are finally passed to the
right hand of the piano, but then immediately transformed in the left hand
(supported by the bassoon) to a robust *forte*, unslurred descent: in one
change of dynamic and articulation, then, lyricism gives way to martial
assertiveness, the same musical material in essence generating both.

Timbral considerations in the slow introduction to the piano and wind
quintet and in the piano concertos are not dissimilar, requiring close engagement from all players (Mozart included) at all times, but the wind preparation
for brilliant pianistic virtuosity elsewhere in the first movement is a less
common feature of the concertos. For the pianist in the exposition, for
example, scalar demisemiquavers grow from immediately preceding semiquavers in the oboe and clarinet (bar 34), and arpeggiated demisemiquavers
from the elaboration of an end-of-phrase gesture in the oboe (bars 38 and 40–
42). Another relationship between material is forged in the secondary

---

[40] For a facsimile of K. 452, see Mozart, *Quintette pour piano, hautbois, clarinette, cor et basson, K.*
452: manuscript autographe 1784, ed. Michel Giboureau (Courlay: Editions J. M. Fuzeau, 1999).

[41] Badura-Skoda and Badura-Skoda, *Interpreting Mozart*, p. 49.

Example 4.17 Mozart, Quintet for piano and wind, K. 452/i, bars 53–58.

development: quaver and semiquaver arpeggios in the wind generate demi-semiquaver arpeggiated flourishes in the piano (bars 93–94). Even when the piano unilaterally initiates figuration, such as after the secondary theme, it is subsequently picked up in the bassoon's triplet semiquavers and transformed into a succession of imitative points in ascending demisemiquavers among winds and piano (bars 50–60; for an excerpt see Example 4.17). Similar to the piano in bar 12 of the slow introduction, moreover, the syncopated writing in the wind is expressively transformed by a change from *f* to *p* and a reduction in the texture (bars 54–57, Example 4.17). Brilliant and expressive virtuosity, often discrete activities in the piano concertos, thus become more difficult to distinguish in the first movement of K. 452.

As in the first movement, Mozart exploits the sound of the full ensemble in the Larghetto. In the seven-bar run-up to the recapitulation (bars 67–73), for example, this sonority is supported by alternations of *p* and *f* dynamics and diminished and 6/4 harmonies; texture, harmony and dynamics are at one. Bars 100–108 of the remarkable secondary development (partially given in Example 4.18), again for the full ensemble, initially

Example 4.18 Mozart, Quintet for piano and wind, K. 452/ii, bars 104–109.

promote a two-bar sequence with diminished sevenths on alternate quavers. Three exclusively diminished bars then derail the third iteration of the
sequence, each bar presenting all three possible diminished chords (bars
106–108). In addition, harmonic contortions are reinforced by *forte* surges
that coincide with several of the initial diminished sounds and by a two-bar
crescendo that ratchets up the tension of the upward-moving progression.
Mozart and his fellow performers dramatize the adventurous compositional materials: flanked by tonic and dominant harmonies in bars 99 and
109, this passage is functionally 'unnecessary' to the tonal and structural
design of the movement, thus situating centre stage the expressive powers
of Mozart and his fellow performers.[42]

---

[42] K. 452/ii concludes with a refined 're-transitional' fall to the tonic (bars 109–113) – pre-echoing
several of his piano concertos – and an imitative, archetypically string-quartet-like *tour de force*

In spite of concertos remaining a reference point for the audience, Mozart repeatedly reminds them that his piano and wind quintet is public chamber music not a piano concerto. While the sonata-rondo finale contains more free-flowing pianistic brilliance than the first movement, it also brings the wind to prominence in the development section and especially the 'Cadenza in tempo' (bars 88–129, 159–205). The 6/4 pause in bar 158 and lengthy cadential trill in bars 200–205 would have been unmissable moments of cadenza rhetoric for the Burgtheater crowd, who witnessed a muted piano and buoyant winds in between, seeing and hearing conspicuous winds at this most soloistic of concerto-related moments. As in the piano concertos discussed above, small modifications to the autograph score of K. 452 may catch Mozart negotiating performance and composition. For example, the replacement of the original left-hand quaver arpeggios in bars 34–35 of the first movement with crotchet octaves and crotchet rests allows a clearer transference of brilliant virtuosity from oboe and clarinet to piano than a fuller left-hand part would have done, and avoids slightly obscuring arpeggiated material in the winds. Mozart ultimately required a different type of participation from himself and his co-performers in K. 452 than in the piano concertos: expressive flexibility, wind-generated brilliance and equality for piano and winds in effect brings about continuity between expressive and brilliant virtuosity. Mozart thus offered his audience for K. 452 something aurally (and visually) different to a piano concerto and a solo improvisation, the mainstays of his Burgtheater academies to date. He thereby challenged himself (as performer-composer), his fellow players and his listeners to create practical and imaginative space for the performance and meaning of this new type of work. In the dynamic of safety and risk characterizing Mozart's programmes for the 1782 and 1783 academies (see Chapters 1 and 3), the performance of K. 452 leaned more towards the latter than the former given the unfamiliar medium, even if the risk was mitigated by Mozart's rapidly growing reputation as a performer-composer and the audience's probable receptivity to any piano music he offered them at that time. Players and listeners were obviously up to the task: it was indeed to Mozart's credit as performer-composer that the novel K. 452 was so well

that considerably extends the motivic dialogue from the corresponding juncture of the exposition (see bars 113–121 in comparison to 36–40). For similar kinds of passages falling into reprises in piano-concerto slow movements, with winds in prominent roles, see K. 466/ii, bars 115–119; K. 491/ii, bars 61–63 (wind only); K. 503/ii, bars 69–76. For comparable first-movement passages, including brilliant piano writing, see K. 467/i, bars 270–274; K. 482/i, bars 259–264; K. 491/i, bars 358–362.

received and that his varied piano participation in the academy kept the attention of listeners throughout.

The Wind Serenade K. 361 and Anton Stadler's Academy, 23 March 1784

On 23 March 1784, nine days before Mozart's rendition of the piano and wind quintet, the virtuoso clarinettist Anton Stadler (1753–1812) held an academy at the Burgtheater, including on the programme the only known performance during Mozart's lifetime of the Serenade in B-flat, K. 361, scored for twelve wind instruments and double bass.[43] Stadler and his brother Johann (1755–1804), also a clarinettist, had been employed by Joseph II since 1779, acquiring posts in the court orchestra and the newly formed *Harmonie* in 1781 and 1782.[44] It was common for distinguished performers, including those with imperial posts, to be granted academies at a time of year (Lent) when plays and operas were not staged: in the 1784 season alone recipients included singers Stefano and Maria Mandini, Nancy Storace and Ludwig Fischer, pianists Anton Eberl and Mozart, and the visiting Italian violinist Regina Strinasacchi (at whose concert the Accompanied Sonata K. 454 in B-flat was premiered).[45]

It is not known whether Mozart wrote the wind serenade K. 361 specifically for Stadler's academy or at some other stage between moving to Vienna in spring 1781 and March 1784; scholarly consensus usually now favours 1783–1784.[46] Even if not composed in the run-up to 23 March

---

[43] The suggestion that Mozart may not have been present at Stadler's academy on account of a competing concert at Ployer's residence is wrong. MDL (p. 198) documents the Ployer concert via an entry in Zinzendorf's diary, mistaking the date 23 March 1785 for 23 March 1784. The error in MDL is corrected tacitly in MDB (p. 241). For Zinzendorf's diary entry in 1785, see Link, *National Court Theatre*, p. 242.

[44] For biographical information on Anton Stadler, see in particular Pamela Poulin, 'A Little-Known Letter of Anton Stadler', *Music & Letters*, 69 (1988), pp. 49–56; and Poulin, 'A View of Eighteenth-Century Musical Life and Training: Anton Stadler's Music Plan', *Music & Letters*, 71 (1990), pp. 215–224.

[45] See the Burgtheater performance listings in Link, *National Court Theatre*, pp. 38–39.

[46] On the dating to 1783–1784 see in particular Daniel N. Leeson and David Whitwell, 'Concerning Mozart's Serenade in B-flat for Thirteen Instruments, K. 361 (370a)', *Mozart Jahrbuch 1976–77*, pp. 97–130; and Leeson, 'A Revisit: Mozart's Serenade for Thirteen Instruments, K. 361 (370a), the "Gran Partitta"', *Mozart Jahrbuch 1997*, pp. 181–223. On 1781 as the *terminus ante quem*, based on the types of paper appearing in the autograph score, see Roger Hellyer, 'Wind Music', in *Cambridge Mozart Encyclopedia*, p. 534. Hellyer also speculates on links to 1781 in 'Mozart's "Gran partita" and the Summer of 1781', *Eighteenth-Century Music*, 8 (2011), pp. 93–104.

1784, it is likely that Mozart had the Stadlers in mind as performers. He probably met Anton at Countess Thun's in 1781; Anton and Johann may also have been two of the 'poor devils' who played his wind serenade K. 375 at Baroness Waldstätten's residence at Leopoldstadt on 31 October 1781 (see Chapter 1).[47] In a letter from 6 November 1781 requesting employment at the Wallerstein court, Stadler stressed his and Johann's ability to play both the clarinet and the basset-horn in a variety of chamber and orchestral contexts.[48] Given the presence in Vienna from 1783 to December 1785 of virtuoso Bohemian basset-horn players Anton David and Vincent Springer, the Stadlers probably took the clarinet parts in the performance of K. 361.[49] The availability of David and Springer, as well as the Stadler brothers, in all likelihood explains the revised scoring in late 1785 of Masonic Funeral Music, K. 477 (discussed below), and may account for the existence of several other works such as a fragment for piano, oboe, clarinet, basset-horn and bassoon quintet K. 452a (1783), the Adagio for two clarinets and three basset-horns K. 411 (probably 1782/1783) and the Adagio for two basset-horns and bassoon K. 410 (c. 1784/1785). But it may not explain a number of works and fragments for which connections to David and Springer are sometimes mooted.[50]

Clearly Stadler's inclusion of the wind serenade K. 361, whether or not commissioned specifically for the concert, indicates that a performance of it was considered personally advantageous at such a high-profile event. The remainder of the concert programme is not known, but it is likely that Stadler found ways to highlight his own brilliant and expressive virtuosity while also adhering to the Viennese academy convention of combining vocal and instrumental works: at subsequent academies on 17 March 1785 and 20 February 1788, he included the oratorio *Der Tod Jesu* and

---

[47] On both points see Poulin, 'Letter of Anton Stadler', pp. 55–56. For the letter identifying the 'poor devils' who performed K. 375, see MBA, vol. 3, pp. 171–172; LMF, p. 776 (3 November 1781). The 'Notschibi' of Mozart's affectionate nickname for Anton, 'Notschibinitschibi', means poor booby or miser (see Colin Lawson, *Mozart: Clarinet Concerto* [Cambridge: Cambridge University Press, 1996], pp. 18–19), perhaps also hinting at Stadler's participation in the K. 375 performance.

[48] Poulin, 'Letter of Anton Stadler', p. 53.

[49] David and Springer were unable to procure permanent posts in Vienna. Two benefit concerts to raise money for their return journey to Bohemia took place at Viennese Masonic lodges on 20 October and 15 December 1785. See MDL, pp. 223–224, 226; MDB, pp. 254–255, 256–257.

[50] Lawson (*Clarinet Concerto*, p. 19) connects 13 Mozart works featuring basset-horns to 1783–1785. But several are now thought to date from 1786 onwards: for example the part songs K. 346 (1786/7), K. 436–439 (1787 or later); and the beginning of an Allegro for two clarinets and three basset-horns, K. 484b (1786 or later). All the dates in the text and footnote are taken from Ulrich Konrad, *Mozart: Catalogue of His Works* (Kassel: Bärenreiter, 2006). For Tyson's intimation of a date of 1782–1783 for K. 410, see *Autograph Scores*, p. 277.

Reichardt's cantata *Ariadne auf Naxos*.[51] Perhaps he performed one or two of his own works; he was recognized as a composer, as well as a virtuoso, during his lifetime.[52] Stadler could have regarded the wind serenade performance as an opportunity to bathe in reflected Mozartian glory, but (even if so) will certainly have expected his playing to be scrutinized at his own concert. Assuming the clarinet and basset-horn parts in K. 361 were closest to Stadler's heart, in the context either of a commission or of evaluating a previously completed work, he surely would have been enthused by what he saw and heard. For it is difficult to regard K. 361 as anything other than 'the single most important milestone in Mozart's development as a composer for the clarinet and basset horn', featuring an 'ever-increasing appreciation of the vocal qualities' of these instruments and a remarkable array of textures for them.[53]

In 1785, Johann Friedrich Schink published an account of Stadler's concert, which he attended on a visit from Graz:

Musical Academy by Stadler, Clarinet Virtuoso

Have my thanks, brave virtuoso! What you do with your instrument I have never heard. Never would I have thought that a clarinet would be able to imitate the human voice as remarkably as you imitate it. Your instrument has so soft and so lovely a tone that nobody who has a heart can resist it, and I have one, dear Virtuoso; let me thank you!

I also heard today music for wind instruments by Herr Mozart, in four movements – marvellous and sublime! It consisted of thirteen instruments, namely four horns, two oboes, two bassoons, two clarinets, two basset-horns, a double bass, and at each instrument sat a master – oh, it made an effect – marvellous and grand, excellent and sublime![54]

The vocal quality of Stadler's playing was also implicitly recognized in an account of Joseph II's *Harmonie* in the *Magazin der Musik* (1783): in their frequently performed arrangements of operas, the clarinet together with the oboe '[took] the place of the voice'.[55] After referring first to the work

---

[51] Link, *National Court Theatre*, pp. 58, 121.

[52] See, for example, Ernst Ludwig Gerber, *Historisch-biographisches Lexicon der Tonkünstler*, 2 vols. (Leipzig, 1790–1792), vol. 2, p. 556; Johann Georg Meusel, *Teutsches Künstlerlexikon oder Verzeichniss der jetztlebenden teutschen Künstler* (Lemgo, 1809), vol. 2, pp. 384–385. Stadler's *18 Terzetten* for basset-horns are listed in Johann Traeg's catalogue of 1799 and advertised four years earlier in the *Wiener Zeitung*; see Albert R. Rice, *From Clarinet d'Amour to the Contra Bass: A History of Large Size Clarinets, 1740–1800* (New York: Oxford University Press, 2009), pp. 221–222.

[53] Lawson, *Clarinet Concerto*, p. 23.   [54] MDL, p. 206; MDB, pp. 232–233.

[55] *Magazin der Musik* (Hamburg, 1783), pp. 1400–1401, as given in Poulin, 'Letter from Anton Stadler', p. 54.

Example 4.19 Mozart, Serenade in B-flat, K. 361/ii, bars 31–37.

itself ('marvellous and sublime') Schink's recollection of the rendition by distinguished players led to an intensified judgement ('marvellous and grand, excellent and sublime'). At least for this audience member, then, work and performance had a mutually reinforcing impact.

Which material for clarinets and basset-horns would have caught Stadler's attention in contemplating and performing the wind serenade? For a start he would have found clarinet and basset-horn sonorities to his liking in the first and second movements. At the opening of the Largo, for example, a lyrical solo clarinet emerges, *dolce*, from the resonant sound of the full ensemble, beginning in bars 2 and 3 on the exact pitch at the top of the texture vacated by the first oboe. The opposite happens at the end of the Largo, the clarinet now joined by the basset-horns to build towards the *forte* full-ensemble sonority at the concluding pause. The clarinets and basset-horns then become increasingly prominent during the Molto allegro, taking separate leads in the presentation of the first and second themes in the exposition, and appearing together as an unaccompanied sonority for four bars in the development and for extended periods in the secondary theme of the recapitulation (see bars 164–190). The first trio of the second movement, scored exclusively for two clarinets and two basset-horns, is a logical outgrowth of attention to this sonority in the Allegro. And for three bars in its reprise (35–37, Example 4.19), initiated by a uniform *sfp*, the four instruments play together in dotted minims, abandoning the prevailing crotchet pulse and providing an opportunity for performers to exploit, and listeners to admire, a special timbral quality.

In the remainder of the work, Mozart continues to promote timbres, textures and effects involving the clarinets and basset-horns, including in collaboration with other members of the ensemble. In the famous Adagio, the first clarinet and basset-horn comprise two of the three solo melodists and the second clarinet and basset-horn two of the four

Example 4.20 Mozart, Serenade in B-flat, K. 361/iii, bars 43–46.

semiquaver accompanists, performers being given an opportunity to negotiate the broad lyricism and uniformly articulated accompaniment of the interlocking textures. At the end (Example 4.20), contrasting groupings are alternated repeatedly for two bars, a microcosm of musical activity in the Adagio as a whole that culminates in a *pp* – the only one in the movement – in support of a delicate effect. As in the Largo of the first movement, the clarinets and basset-horns help facilitate build-ups to full-ensemble textures in the Romance and the clarinet is given individual opportunities to shine, including by emerging out of a full-ensemble sonority. Pauses on three occasions may also encourage the clarinettist to take small interpretative liberties (see bars 16, 87, 103). Several effects for clarinets and basset-horns new to the work appear in the Theme and Variations: a *dolce* sustained clarinet floating above a *dolce* thematic basset-horn in the second variation; a virtuosic demisemiquaver second-clarinet accompaniment to a melodically leading clarinet in the third variation; and a shimmering, coordinated *pp* accompaniment in both clarinets and basset-horns in the fifth variation.

Assuming Schink's account of the academy on 23 March 1784 is accurate, Stadler and fellow musicians played only four of the seven movements of the wind serenade, which is unsurprising when the complete work lasts over fifty minutes. Irrespective of the movements chosen, Stadler had every reason to think that the wind serenade would meet his needs. Like the piano and wind quintet in Mozart's academy, K. 361 sheds light on a kind of playing from the concert protagonist that is distinct from the brilliant and expressive virtuosity no doubt on display at other times in the evening. With prominent and varied writing for clarinets and basset-horns, including a rich array of timbres, textures and effects, the wind serenade offered Stadler an opportunity to promote himself as a chamber musician *par excellence*, at one moment *primus inter pares*, at another delicate accompanist. Much remains – and perhaps will always remain – uncertain about the genesis of K. 361. But the perspectives offered by the Stadler performance begin to explain the wind serenade's significance as a work written in and for Vienna. Since 'a master' played each instrument, success for Stadler – and by implication for Mozart too – was more or less guaranteed.

Masonic Funeral Music, K. 477

Like the wind serenade K. 361, the genesis of Masonic Funeral Music, K. 477, is somewhat difficult to determine; the scoring of the final version of the work for clarinet and three basset-horns probably (again) accommodated the participation of the Stadler brothers, as well as David and Springer. Mozart may have composed the work in July 1785, the date given in the *Verzeichnüß*, but must have entered it into his catalogue considerably later because it is recorded as 'Masonic Funeral Music on the deaths of the Brothers Meklenburg (*sic*) and Esterhazy', both of whom died in early November 1785.[56] It has been suggested that K. 477 was performed three times at Masonic events in late 1785: on 12 August with vocal parts (no longer extant); on 17 November at the ceremony for Mecklenburg and Esterházy in the orchestra-only scoring listed in the *Verzeichnüß* (two violins, two violas, one clarinet, one basset-horn, two oboes, two horns and basses); and on 7 December at another ceremony for Mecklenburg, now including two further basset-horns and a contrabassoon.[57]

---

[56] See Philippe A. Autexier, 'Wann würde die Maurerische Trauermusik uraufgeführt?' *Mozart-Jahrbuch 1984–85*, pp. 6–8; and Küster, *Musical Biography*, p. 201. Duke Georg August zu Mecklenburg-Strelitz was an Austrian major-general and Franz, Count Esterházy von Galantha, an Austrian court councillor.

[57] See Auxetier, 'Maurerische Trauermusik', pp. 6–8; and Küster, *Musical Biography*, pp. 200–204. On the possible 12 August 1785 performance, see also Heinz Schuler, 'Mozarts *Maurerische*

Example 4.21 Mozart, Masonic Funeral Music, K. 477, bars 1–8 (all other staves blank).

Irrespective of when the two basset-horns and contrabassoon were added – most likely in late November or early December 1785, after the original instrumentation had been entered into the *Verzeichnüß* – they provide timbral interest rather than supplementary melodic and thematic interest.[58] Almost everything for them doubles existing material in the score, either at the unison or at the octave. Thus, the three added parts primarily offer a window into Mozart's world of timbre and effect, exploiting the skills in all probability of Theodor Lotz (contrabassoon), David and Springer.[59] The distinctive swells – semibreves marked with consecutive crescendi and descrescendi, and quick successions of *fortes* and *pianos* – would have been accentuated with a larger wind cohort: for example, the

    Trauermusik KV 477/4/9a: Eine Dokumentation', *Mitteilungen der Internationalen Stiftung Mozarteum*, 40 (1992), pp. 46–70.

[58]   The first and second basset-horns are notated separately from the rest of the autograph on folio 5 recto and the contrabassoon line written on the bottom stave of the main body of the autograph on folios 1–4. For the autograph, see Staatsbibliothek zu Berlin – Preußischer Kulturbesitz, Musikabteiliung mit Mendelssohn-Archiv: Mus. ms. autogr. W. A. Mozart, 477. See also facsimiles in NMA, IV/11/10, Preface, pp. 12–13 and Kritischer Bericht, NMA, IV/11/10, pp. 8–10.

[59]   Lawson identifies Lotz, David and Springer as the likely performers (*Clarinet Concerto*, p. 20), but does not distinguish between possible performances of K. 477 on 17 November and 7 December 1785.

wind-only bars 3–4 (Example 4.21) double in size to six participants in the re-orchestration, three basset-horns perhaps lending an 'otherworldly' quality to the revised opening of the work.[60] In addition, the Gregorian chant Lamentations of Jeremiah quoted in the wind parts in bars 25–44 receives more emphasis in the revision than in the original: heftier wind unisons introduce its first and second halves (*sf* and *f*, bars 22–23 and 34); and the second half for oboes, clarinet, three basset-horns, contrabassoon and two horns (*f*) contrasts more markedly with the first half for oboes and clarinet (*p*) than in the earlier version on account of the larger scoring. Mozart's attention to the special timbral quality of the basset-horn is further apparent from his introduction of a second one at the lead-in to the modified reprise (bar 50) in unison with the basset-horn already *in situ*. A second might be assumed to make little difference in a reduced unison texture, but, as ever, Mozart's ear was precisely attuned to timbral resonance. In short, and similar to the 'Haffner' Symphony K. 385 for his academy in spring 1783 (see Chapter 3), Mozart built opportunistically on an already prominent wind profile in his revised orchestration of the work. In so doing orchestral sounds and timbres come to the fore and confidence is by implication expressed that specific players will perform them effectively on a specific occasion. As in the piano concertos, if not now with Mozart participating as a soloist, textures and timbres in Masonic Funeral Music are central to both compositional and performance endeavours.

Conclusion: The Performer-Composer Then and Now

Neither late-eighteenth-century reports lauding Mozart's skills as a performer-composer nor Mozart's negotiation of performance and compositional needs (evident in the autograph scores) imply that his own renditions of the piano concertos and the piano and wind quintet were inherently unsurpassable; it would have been entirely reasonable, of course, for an audience member who heard Mozart and later another pianist play the same work to prefer the latter to the former. But it is difficult to envisage a more 'complete' performance than the one given by Mozart himself – complete in embracing the reciprocity of creation and execution so essential to the production of these works. Stadler's performance of the wind serenade K. 361 acquires a similar status, not only because he superbly played music

---

[60] For the 'otherworldly' sound of basset-horns, see Colin Lawson, *The Early Clarinet: A Practical Guide* (Cambridge: Cambridge University Press, 2000), p. 103.

(perhaps) written specifically for him, but also because he no doubt had discussed aspects of the work with Mozart in advance.

The total musical experience afforded to the Augsburg reviewer in October 1777 and implicitly to Leopold for Mozart's concertos, to Johann Friedrich Schink for the wind serenade K. 361, and to Niemetschek and others for Mozart's improvisations (see the introduction to my book), is paralleled in Mozart's own immersion in performance activities as recorded by contemporaries. It is also matched by a correspondingly complete commitment in the process of creation and execution to negotiating performance and compositional activities and motivations. Mozart wrote first and foremost for the present, not the future: adjustments to piano and orchestral parts in the concertos and attention to dynamic placement and other performance markings in the piano and wind quintet reflect a desire not for posthumous appreciation of a perfectly chiselled composition, but for immediate appreciation (with both artistic and financial rewards, Mozart hoped) in the here and now as both performer and composer.[61] At least for the piano concertos and K. 452, then, Mozart's acute sensitivity to individual instrumental sounds, related by Nannerl and Niemetschek and apparent in the autograph scores, illuminates the performance-composition nexus, enhancing appreciation of both his expressive and brilliant virtuosity and attention to surrounding instrumental material as a performer, and his understanding of texture, timbre and instrumental effects as a composer. Recognizing that piano passages may have been motivated by instrumental concerns, and instrumental passages by piano-related concerns, captures the spirit of Mozart's piano concertos and piano and wind quintet as organisms existentially dependent on Mozart's dual status as performing composer and composing performer. And it is not farfetched to regard Stadler as Mozart's proxy for the performance of K. 361, the clarinet–basset-horn parts and oboe–horn–bassoon–string-bass parts as analogous to the piano and the other instrumental parts in the concertos and quintet.

Intertwining performance and composition are also captured in similarities between performing qualities acknowledged by Mozart and musical qualities demonstrated (for example) by revisions to the piano concerto autographs. We know that Mozart valued precision, clarity and expression in keyboard playing and those who heard him in action praised his grace and elegance.[62] And these particular qualities emerge as priorities in the

---

[61] For an article arguing a related point – 'that a source is as representative of performance as it is representative of a "work"' (p. 116) – see Eisen, 'The Primacy of Performance'.

[62] From Mozart himself – often criticizing others for lacking such qualities – see MBA, vol. 2, pp. 146–147, 228 and LMF, p. 391, 448–449 (26 November 1777, 17 January 1778) on the clear and

autograph revisions discussed: small adjustments to an instrumental or keyboard part signal a desire for sonic precision and clarity; modifications small and large uncover additional expressive layers (for example the piano line at the end of the K. 482/iii Andante and the adjusted left-hand part in variation 4 of K. 453/iii); and adjustments to thematic presentations add elegance (as in the recapitulation of K. 467/i). Naturally, aesthetic qualities along these lines are general enough to apply to a wide range of late-eighteenth-century musical activities. But specific commitment to them in simultaneous performing and compositional contexts represented a way for Mozart to integrate different musical activities and responsibilities in the piano concertos, and thus to lay a foundation for appreciation as a performer-composer.

Ultimately, evaluation of Mozart's concert works from 1784 to 1786 in light of the prevailing performer-composer dynamic encourages us to rethink strategies for playing them today. Reflecting on the dynamic in the context of improvisation in the concertos, Robert D. Levin explains that 'Mozart presented himself to the public in the guise of composer *as performer*; if modern performers tried to adopt the posture of performer *as composer*, Mozart's music would be played more profoundly, more expressively and above all more spontaneously – for spontaneity is an essential element of his art'.[63] But this represents only one part of the equation. For Mozart's concert works underscore precise calculation of instrumental effect and solo virtuosic effect (brilliant and expressive alike); no doubt Mozart would have wanted such effects to convey a kind of calculated 'spontaneity' in live performance. His fascination with individual sounds and textures, whether in advance of or as a result of a specific performance experience, often accentuates links between passages. A single effect in a concerto movement or the Larghetto of the piano and wind quintet, say, feeds into a sequence of effects through which networks of interrelated, interposed and juxtaposed sounds and timbres come to the fore. Many of Mozart's adjustments to the piano concerto autographs appear at defining structural, functional and expressive moments: just before the exit of the soloist at the end of a solo exposition, recapitulation

---

precise keyboard playing; and MBA, vol. 3, p. 192, 312 and LMF, pp. 793, 875 (16 January 1782, 28 April 1784) on expressive playing. Grace and elegance are recorded by Clementi (see Leon Plantinga, *Clementi: His Music and Life* [London: Oxford University Press, 1977], p. 65), by Georg Friedrich Richter (quoted by Mozart himself in MBA, vol. 3, p. 312 and LMF, p. 875 (28 April 1784)), and by Niemetschek, as given in the introduction to this book.

[63] Levin, 'Improvisation and Embellishment in Mozart's Piano Concertos', *Musical Newsletter*, 5/2 (1975), pp. 3–14, at 3. He re-quotes this passage in 'Mozart's Working Methods', p. 406.

or entire movement (K. 450/i, K. 451/i, K. 456/ii, K. 459/i, K. 467/i); at a stylistically innovative moment in a development section (K. 449/i); as part of a transition between two contrasting sections (K. 482/iii); during a *minore* variation that precedes a big tutti orchestral effect (K. 453/iii). They therefore assume significance in establishing and maintaining lines of communication between Mozart and his audiences, and can do the same for today's performers and their audiences. We cannot know for sure what motivated Mozart either to make the adjustments discussed in the piano concerto autographs or to engage closely with performance issues at certain moments in the quintet, wind serenade and Masonic Funeral Music. But as creatively inclined players we may even benefit from not knowing when using adjustments and markings to stimulate our own performances of the works.[64] By foregrounding those blends of sounds and relationships between individual sounds and effects that Mozart himself emphasized (even if often inadvertently), we will retain something of the musical spirit that produced the works in the first place.

But situating the concerns of Mozart the performer-composer at the heart of our own performing experience of the concert works from 1784 to 1786 should not be confined to moments where Mozart himself made revisions. While Mozart the performer-composer was lost to us after his death, enough of his thought processes survive in the autograph scores to encourage reconsideration, even realignment, of performance priorities in general. For Mozart's preoccupation with individual sounds and textures, as they blend into his musical landscapes, can inspire performances where *every* performer – conductor (if deployed), soloist and orchestral member alike – pays close attention to the context in which every note is played; for example, Mozart's fascination with precise horn effects, witnessed in K. 451/i and K. 459/i and elsewhere,[65] can motivate today's musicians to nurture like-minded sonic interests of their own. Sounds and textures – even ostensibly straightforward accompaniment figures, including blends of sustained notes – can help guide listeners through a work alongside the

---

[64] David Grayson makes a similar remark in the context of pursuing 'authentic' performance: 'We can strive for an "authentic" Mozart as long as we do not know precisely what it is but can convince ourselves that we are close to it. If we actually had an authentic Mozart on compact disc . . . then we would surely lose the desire to imitate it, because our performances could then never be authentic, but would be, at best, accurate copies.' See Grayson, 'Whose Authenticity? Ornaments by Hummel and Cramer for Mozart's Piano Concertos', in Zaslaw (ed.), *Mozart's Piano Concertos*, p. 386.

[65] Another example is K. 453/ii, bar 18, where the horn octave Gs in quavers are apparently a late addition. Mozart originally gives the horns tied-octave Cs in bars 19–20 and 22–23, replacing the Cs with Gs when adding to bar 18.

acknowledged discourses of tonality and theme, encouraging listeners to make sonic associations, draw sonic parallels, and perceive changing roles for individual instruments and groups of instruments.[66] And it is the obligation of performers – whether on historical or modern instruments – to make this possible by situating sounds and textures centre stage in their interpretations. Solipsism and complacency, rarely attractive musical attributes, are particularly injurious even in modest form to a performance of a Mozart instrumental work – to the soloist or instrumental player who pays insufficiently close attention to surrounding sounds and textures or to the potential resonance of a theme, phrase or individual note. Asking soloists in full-fledged brilliant mode in the run-up to a cadential trill to 'interact' (in whatever way deemed interpretatively appropriate) with a significant if straightforward orchestral effect will likely require a change of mindset for many pianists, but the process will bring them closer to the performer-composer mindset that produced the work.

---

[66] In like-minded fashion in a study of continuo performance, Eisen remarks ('Primacy of Performance', p. 119): 'Multiplicity of function, and multiplicity of voices, suggests that texture, which can include the interplay of voices and functions all at the same time [. . .] is as important for understanding Mozart's concertos as questions of form that have traditionally dominated the study of these works.'

5 | Composing, Performing and Publishing
The 'Haydn' String Quartets and Other Chamber Music for Publication, 1784–1786

The successes Mozart enjoyed as a performer-composer on the public stage in his first five years in Vienna were complemented by his well-developed profile as a composer of published instrumental music. A number of his works had appeared in print before 1781, of course, but he made a concerted effort to publish only after moving to Vienna and while establishing himself as a freelance musician. After the sonatas for piano and violin K. 376, 377, 379 and 380, and the three piano concertos K. 413–415 written for publication and distribution in manuscript copies, as well as for his own performances, in 1781 and 1782–1783 respectively,[1] Mozart gained a considerable head of steam, bringing into the public domain old and new works alike. (See Table 5.1.) Artaria published the four-hand piano sonatas K. 381 (written 1772) and K. 358 (1773–1774) in 1783,[2] and the solo piano sonatas K. 330–332 in 1784; Torricella also issued the piano sonatas K. 333 and K. 284 (written 1775) and the Accompanied Sonata K. 454 in 1784. A flurry of publications followed in 1785: from Artaria, the symphonies K. 385 and K. 319 (1779), the set of six string quartets dedicated to Haydn, the piano concertos K. 413–415, the 'Maurerfreude' Cantata K. 471 (discussed in Chapter 6) and the Fantasia and Piano Sonata K. 475 and K. 457; from Torricella, the piano variations K. 455 and K. 265; from Le Duc in Paris the piano variations K. 264; and from Johann Traeg and Lorenz Lausch, manuscript copies of a number of works.[3] Hoffmeister's subscription series, for which he 'made agreements with our best local composers ... as well as foreign masters ... to receive new products,[4] also began in 1785, bringing out the Piano Quartet K. 478 and the Piano and Violin Sonata K. 481 in the first few months. Leopold, who saw announcements for Mozart's works during his Viennese sojourn from 11 February to 25 April 1785, reported to Nannerl later in 1785 the words

---

[1] See Chapters 1 and 3. [2] MDL, p. 191; MDB, p. 215.

[3] For advertisements, see MDL, pp. 208–228; MDB, pp. 234–260 (*passim*). B. Schott in Mainz also published a keyboard arrangement of *Die Entführung aus dem Serail* in 1785, carried out by Abbé Stark and unsanctioned by Mozart, who at one stage worked on his own arrangement. See MBA, vol. 3, p. 471; LMF, p. 895 (Leopold to Nannerl, 16 December 1785); MDL, pp. 219–220; MDB, pp. 249–250; NMD, pp. 40–42.

[4] NMD, p. 36.

Table 5.1 First publications of Mozart's instrumental works composed between 1781 and 1785 (in order of publication, 1781 to early 1786)

Works	Dates of Composition (from the *Verzeichnüß* from February 1784)	First Publication
Sonatas for piano and violin, K. 376 in F, K. 377 in F, K. 379 in G, K. 380 in E-flat	Spring–summer 1781	Artaria, November 1781 (as 'Op. 2', alongside K. 296 in C [11 March 1778] and K. 378 in B-flat [1779–80])
Piano concertos K. 413 in F, K. 414 in A, K. 415 in C	Late 1782–early 1783	Distribution in manuscript copies through subscription, 1783. [Subsequent publication Artaria, January 1785, as 'Op. 4']
Piano sonata in B-flat, K. 333	1783	Torricella, August 1784 (as 'Op. 7', alongside K. 284 in D [early 1775] and K. 454)
Sonata for piano and violin in B-flat, K. 454	21 April 1784	Torricella, August 1784 (as 'Op. 7', alongside K. 284 in D [early 1775] and K. 333)
Piano sonatas K. 330 in C, K. 331 in A, K. 332 in F	1783 (K. 330, 331); early 1780s (K. 332)	Artaria, August 1784 (as 'Op. 6')
Symphony in D ('Haffner'), K. 385	July 1782; revised early 1783	Artaria, 1785 (in parts as 'Op. 7')
'Maurerfreude' Cantata, K. 471	20 April 1785	Artaria, August 1785
String quartets K. 387 in G, K. 421 in D minor, K. 428 in E-flat, K. 458 in B-flat, K. 464 in A, K. 465 in C ('Dissonance')	31 December 1782 (K. 387); June 1783 (K. 421); June–July 1783 (K. 428); 9 November 1784 (K. 458); 10 January 1785 (K. 464); 14 January 1785 (K. 465)	Artaria, September 1785 (as 'Op. 10')
Fantasia and piano sonata in C minor, K. 475 and K. 457	14 October 1784 (K. 457); 20 May 1785 (K. 475)	Artaria, December 1785 (as 'Op. 11')
Piano variations in C, K. 265 ('Ah, vous dirai-je Maman')	c. 1781	Torricella, 1785
Piano variations in C, K. 264 ('Lison dormait')	c. 1781	Paris: Le Duc, 1785 (later Artaria, 1786)
Piano variations in G, K. 455 (on Gluck, 'Unser dummer Pöbel meint')	25 August 1784	Artaria, 1786 (also Torricella 1785? See MDB, p. 246)
Piano variations in F, K. 398 (on Paisiello, 'Salve, tu, Domine')	c. March 1783	Artaria, 1786 (also Torricella 1785? See MDB, p. 246)
Piano quartet in G minor, K. 478	16 October 1785	Hoffmeister, November/ December 1785
Sonata for piano and violin in E-flat, K. 481	12 December 1785	Hoffmeister, January 1786

of the Salzburg journalist Lorenz Hübner: 'It is quite astounding what quantity of things your son is publishing. In all music advertisements I always see nothing but Mozart. The Berlin advertisements, when announcing the [string] quartets, state only the following: "It is unnecessary to recommend these quartets to the public. It is sufficient to say that they are by Herr Mozart."'[5] It is tempting to dismiss as publisher's hyperbole Torricella's mention of the 'eagerness with which the works of this famous master are particularly yearned for by people on all sides'.[6] But Mozart's presence in the musical marketplace suggests that such 'eagerness' was perhaps a reality.

As a thoroughly practical musician, Mozart naturally would have brought to the table multifarious views as a performer and a performer-composer when writing works primarily for publication rather than for his own personal use. After all, markings in such works represented his only way of exerting influence on the interpretation of his music by players beyond his immediate control. As already witnessed in the accompanied sonatas K. 376, 377, 379, 380, the piano concertos K. 413–415 and the piano sonatas K. 330–332 and K. 333, which were written with public dissemination in mind, Mozart actively negotiated performance and compositional concerns, encouraging imaginative interpretation from his players. In addition (as we have seen), Mozart included material in the first edition of the piano sonatas that does not appear in the autographs. Thus, it is important to determine how Mozart's creative processes were affected by the composing-performing-publishing dynamic in the 'Haydn' string quartets, the accompanied sonatas K. 454 and 481, the Fantasia and Sonata K. 475 and K. 457 and the Piano Quartet K. 478, all of which were published between 1784 and early 1786. Informal performances of the 'Haydn' quartets by Mozart and others in advance of publication, and a concert performance of K. 454 in the Kärntnertortheater with violinist Regina Strinasacchi, apparently influenced materials Mozart provided to Artaria and Torricella for publication. Issues around performance and publication will consequently inform our under-standings of Mozart's chamber works.

Composing the 'Haydn' Quartets

The protracted genesis of the 'Haydn' quartets K. 387 in G, K. 421 in D minor, K. 428 in E-flat, K. 458 in B-flat, K. 464 in A and K. 465 in C includes two main phases of compositional activity from late 1782 to

---

[5] MBA, vol. 3, p. 439; LMF, p. 893 (3 November 1785).   [6] MDL, p. 522; MDB, p. 246.

summer 1783 and November 1784 to January 1785. It is complicated by K. 458's appearance in both phases, by aborted sketches for several movements, and by near-simultaneous work on non-adjacent movements (for example K. 428/ii and K. 421/i, and K. 421/iv and an insert for K. 387/iv).[7] Mozart planned a set of six published string quartets at least as early as spring 1783. Writing to the Parisian publisher J. G. Sieber on 26 April he offered his piano concertos K. 413–415 and also six string quartets (of which only one was complete at that stage), presumably feigning displeasure at Artaria's printing of the accompanied sonatas in 1781 in order to strengthen his pitch:

I have already now been in Vienna for two years. You will probably know about my sonatas for piano with accompaniment for one violin that I have had engraved here by Artaria and Co. But I am not all that much pleased with the local engraving, and, even if I were, would like once again to give something to my fellow countrymen in Paris, so hereby let you know that I have finished three piano concertos . . . Further, I am now writing six quartets for two violins, viola and cello. If you would also like to engrave them, I will also give them to you. But these cannot be so cheap [as the piano concertos, for which 30 louis d'or was requested] – I cannot give you these six quartets for under 50 louis d'or. Consequently, if you can and will make a deal with me, you can just reply to me and I shall give you an address in Paris where you will receive my work in exchange for your payment.[8]

While Mozart's proposed fee was high, with 50 louis d'or equating to approximately 550 florins,[9] it did not turn out to be wholly unrealistic. When he eventually sold them to Artaria in 1785, Sieber having apparently declined, he received 100 ducats (450 florins) (Figure 2). The high financial value Mozart placed on the quartets transmogrified into the artistic value Artaria cited as justification for producing a lavish edition and charging a high price for it:

Mozart's works need no praise, so giving some would be completely unnecessary; one can only affirm that here is a masterpiece. One can affirm this all the more since the author dedicated this work to his friend Joseph Haydn, Kapellmeister to Prince

---

[7] See Tyson, *Autograph Scores*, pp. 83–93, 94–105. On the fragments, see also Christoph Wolff, 'Creative Exuberance vs. Critical Choice: Thoughts on Mozart's Quartet Fragments', in Wolff (ed.), *The String Quartets of Haydn, Mozart, and Beethoven: Studies of the Autograph Manuscripts* (Cambridge, MA: Harvard University Press, 1980), pp. 191–210. Stages of work on each quartet, as determined by different ink colours in the autograph, are discussed by Ludwig Finscher and Wolf-Dieter Seiffert in the NMA, viii/20/1–2, Kritischer Bericht, pp. 20, 47–48, 73, 92, 107–108, 133.

[8] MBA, vol. 3, p. 266; LMF, p. 846.   [9] Heartz, *Mozart, Haydn, Early Beethoven*, p. 74.

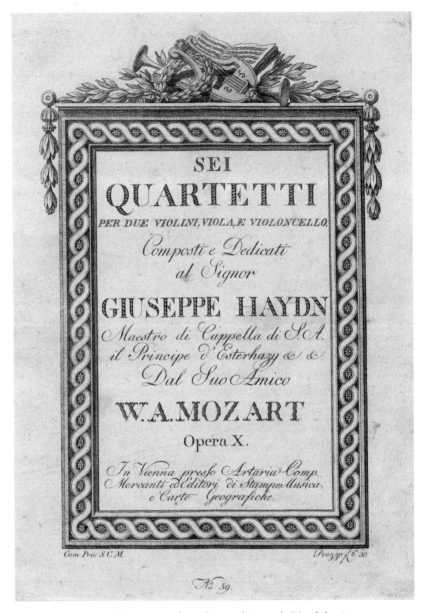

Figure 2 Title page of the Artaria first edition of Mozart's 'Haydn' string quartets (Vienna: Artaria, 1785).

Esterházy, who has honoured it with all of the approval of which only a man of great genius is worthy. In view of this, the publishers have also spared no costs to put this work in the hands of amateurs and connoisseurs beautifully and clearly engraved both in paper and in print, confident that the fixed price will not be considered too high when the quartets come to 150 pages and could not have been written out for less than 12fl.[10]

Clearly Haydn's approval and association with the quartets carried weight; but Mozart's own reputation also justified the price of purchase. By the time Artaria had printed the requisite copies of its 1785 edition and re-issues from 1787 and 1789, the original plates had worn out, and were re-engraved in 1791.[11] The quartets thus appear to have sold well during Mozart's lifetime.

After his death, Mozart's quartets secured a reputation as compositions for connoisseurs, Haydn pre-eminent among them. As Niemetschek explained (1798):

Mozart certainly could not have honoured Haydn with a better work than with these quartets, which are a treasure trove of precious thoughts and are models of composition. In the eyes of the connoisseur this work has just as much value as any of Mozart's operatic compositions. Everything in it is thought through and perfected. One sees in these quartets that he took the trouble to earn Haydn's praise.[12]

Arnold (1803) considered the quartets to be the very best of Mozart's work in the genre, their beauties only coming properly to light after diligent listening and study.[13] He also claimed later (1810) that these 'excellent quartets show unmistakeable evidence of the trouble that he gave to their composition'.[14] According to Ernst Ludwig Gerber (1813), the chromaticism and dissonance in the finale of K. 464 required intricately skilled players, explaining 'why the honorable composer wrote ... [it] not for public performance by a full orchestra, but rather for the private music making of a quartet for musicians and educated friends of art'.[15] And Nissen (1828), reiterating Niemetschek's views, thought Mozart worked specifically to elicit Haydn's approval.[16] Twentieth-century critics and

---

[10] MDL, pp. 221–222; MDB, p. 252 (17 September 1785). The announcement goes on to distance Mozart's new string quartets from K. 168–173, which had been advertised by Torricella one week earlier in the same publication, the *Wiener Zeitung*. See MDL, p. 220; MDB, p. 251 (10 September 1785).

[11] See Kritische Berichte, NMA, VIII/20/1–2, pp. 6–7.

[12] Niemetschek, *Leben*, p. 24, *Life of Mozart*, p. 34 (translation amended).

[13] Arnold, *Mozarts Geist*, p. 449. Other late-eighteenth-century musicians such as Thomas Attwood and Gaetano Latilla also recommended – and benefited from – repeated performances and repeated study of the 'Haydn' quartets: see Landon, *Haydn Chronicle and Works, 1766–1790*, p. 511.

[14] Ignaz Arnold, *Joseph Haydn: seine kurze Biographie und ästhetische Darstellung seiner Werke: Bildungsbuch für junge Tonkünstler* (Erfurt, 1810), p. 53.

[15] Given in Gretchen Wheelock, *Haydn's Ingenious Jesting with Art: Contexts of Musical Wit and Humor* (New York: Schirmer, 1992), pp. 114–115.

[16] Nissen, *Biographie W. A. Mozarts*, pp. 489–490.

biographers largely endorsed and built upon the view of the 'Haydn' quartets as connoisseur-orientated above all: the works reflect 'a special effort in view of his expert dedicatee'; they are '"music made of music", "filtered" art'; their creative energy is 'harnessed so effectively that it carries the quartets into an unearthly region of pure musicality'; they were 'meant for those who could play their way into them at home'; and they were primarily for private consumption, 'for the connoisseur, the denizen of the chamber', manifesting a wide array of sophisticated musical processes.[17] For writers old and new Mozart's own reference to the quartets as the 'fruit of a long and laborious study' in the dedication to Haydn for the Artaria edition perhaps offers clinching proof of orientation towards connoisseurs, as does Haydn's praise of Mozart's compositional abilities after performances of K. 458, K. 464 and K. 465, first quoted by Schlichtegroll in his Mozart obituary (1793) and originating in a letter from Leopold to Nannerl: 'I say to you before God and as an honest man that your son is the greatest composer I know in person or by name. He has taste and more than that the greatest compositional knowledge.'[18]

Few will disagree with the prevailing view that Mozart's 'Haydn' quartets are precisely and elegantly constructed works. In addition to collective perceptions of intrinsic musical quality, Mozart's revisions to the autograph score attest in many instances to the chiselling of exquisitely crafted compositions, as well as (perhaps) to general difficulties encountered in writing string quartets later in life.[19] Deletions, alterations and corrections, large and small alike, assume rhythmic, harmonic, melodic and structural significance. Among countless examples, Mozart deleted one bar between 33 and 34 of K. 428/i (Example 5.1), which, in emphasizing the dominant of the dominant, would have probably precluded further play on the A-natural/A-flat conflict that characterizes both the main theme and subsequent discourse in the transition (see bars 24–29), symbolizing the

---

[17] See Keller, 'The Chamber Music', in *The Mozart Companion*, eds. Landon and Mitchell, p. 102; Einstein, *Mozart*, p. 192; Levey, *Mozart*, p. 180; John Rosselli, *The Life of Mozart* (Cambridge: Cambridge University Press, 1998), p. 56; Wye Jamison Allanbrook, '"To Serve the Private Pleasure": Expression and Form in the String Quartets', in Sadie (ed.), *Mozart: Essays on his Life and Music*, pp. 132–160, at p. 156.

[18] MBA, vol. 3, p. 373; LMF, p. 886 (16 February 1785). See also Friedrich Schlichtegroll, *Johannes Chrysostomus Wolfgang Gottlieb Mozart* (1793), ed. Erich Hermann Müller von Asow (Leipzig, 1942), p. 15. For the complete dedication as published (in Italian) in the Artaria edition, see MDL, p. 220 and MDB, p. 250; MBA, vol. 3, p. 404 and LMF, pp. 891–892.

[19] On the latter point see Tyson, *Mozart: Studies of the Autograph Scores*, pp. 46–47. The autograph is housed at the British Library in London. For a facsimile see Wolfgang Amadeus Mozart, *The Six 'Haydn' Quartets: Facsimile of the Autograph Manuscripts in the British Library, Add. MS 37763* (London: The British Library, 1985).

Example 5.1 Mozart, String Quartet in E-flat, K. 428/i, bars 33–40 (including Mozart's deletion).

respective pulls of dominant and tonic. The cancellation of the original
bar allows A-flats a temporary foothold once again (35–36) before a firm
German Augmented 6th – I6/4 – V7 – I confirmation of the dominant
B-flat (37–40). Five quavers of a 6/8 bar are also excised early in the second
half of the theme section of K. 421/iv (Example 5.2) presumably because
their inflection to the relative major would have detracted from the perfect
cadence in F at the midpoint of the section. In K. 428/ii, a four-and-a-half
bar deletion (Example 5.3) provides not only material re-barred immediately after it in the autograph, but also a harmonic progression in its last six
quavers (I6 – IV/II6 – I6/4 – V) that is prolonged in the finalized bars
26–30. A crotchet – quaver – quaver – crotchet – crotchet rhythm new to
the finale of K. 387 is squeezed in to the second violin, viola and cello parts
in bars 221–224 (Example 5.4), Mozart presumably realizing after first
writing the fugue subject in the top line that the impact of the side-step
to ♭VI could be dramatically enhanced by the accompaniment. And the
original order of the K. 464/iii variations – 1, 2, 3, 6, 5, Coda, with the

Example 5.2 Mozart, String Quartet in D minor, K. 421/iv, bars 9–11 (including Mozart's deletion).

minore variation 4 notated at the end – may have been revised to group the 'regular' and 'irregular' variations together, or to change the position of the 'luminous fifth variation ... to create a convincing, even if more conventional, close'.[20] It is surely indisputable that 'Mozart was still shaping and reshaping [the 'Haydn' quartets] while writing [them] down', envisaging compositional improvements in the process.[21]

That said, our perception of Mozart's achievements in the 'Haydn' quartets is unnecessarily limited by consideration only of compositional connoisseurship and of a purported appeal exclusively to connoisseurs. The resulting impression is of a compositional endeavour carried out semi abstractly, where fastidious work to perfect the quartets in order to impress the dedicatee Haydn and other musical connoisseurs took precedence over the reality of writing music for publication and for performance. In fact, Mozart may have decided to dedicate his quartets to Haydn only on seeing Ignaz Pleyel dedicate his Op. 2 to Haydn for publication by the Vienna-based Graeffer in mid-December 1784.[22] More important, Mozart could not have ignored the need to sell his quartets to a publisher and for that publisher then

[20] Marius Flothuis, 'A Close Reading of the Autographs of Mozart's Ten Late Quartets', in Wolff (ed.), *The String Quartets of Haydn, Mozart and Beethoven*, pp. 154–173, at 158; Sisman, *Haydn and the Classical Variation*, pp. 210–214, at 214.

[21] See Ludwig Finscher, 'Aspects of Mozart's Compositional Process in the Quartet Autographs: I. The Early Quartets, II. The Genesis of K. 387', in Wolff (ed.), *The String Quartets of Haydn, Mozart and Beethoven*, pp. 121–153, at 132. For more on Mozart's autograph revisions, see Flothuis, 'A Close Reading of the Autographs of Mozart's Ten Late Quartets'.

[22] See Mark Evan Bonds, 'Replacing Haydn: Mozart's "Pleyel: Quartets', *Music & Letters*, 88/2 (2007), pp. 201–225, at 218. Needless to say, this is not to deny the influence of Haydn – the pre-eminent composer of string quartets at that time – on the four earlier quartets in the 'Haydn' set that were already complete by December 1784, namely K. 387, 421, 428 and 458. On Haydn's influence, see in particular Bonds, 'The Sincerest Form of Flattery? Mozart's "Haydn" Quartets and the Question of Influence', *Studi musicali*, 22 (1993), pp. 365–409.

Example 5.3 Mozart, String Quartet in E-flat, K. 428/ii, bars 22–30 (including Mozart's deletion).

to sell copies to the musical public; Mozart's remit consequently extended beyond refined and talented connoisseurs.[23] It has recently been argued that

[23] The sale of the quartets to Artaria took place late in their gestation period. On 22 January 1785, Leopold reported to Nannerl receiving a short letter that very day from Mozart, which stated *inter alia* that he had sold his quartets to Artaria for 100 ducats. See MBA, vol. 3, p. 368; LMF, p. 885. (K. 464 and K. 465 were entered into the *Verzeichnüß* on 10 January and 14 January respectively.)

Example 5.4 Mozart, String Quartet in G, K. 387/iv, bars 221–226 (where the notation for v2, va and vc in bars 221–224 inclusive is compressed).

Mozart accommodated a broad audience of listeners in the 'Haydn' quartets. Evidence comprises Mozart's famous letter about striking a happy medium in his piano concertos, where the 'default mode of writing ... is to appeal first and foremost to the non-connoisseurs and to create moments from which connoisseurs alone will obtain satisfaction', as well as individual movements from K. 387, 428 and 465, which try 'to balance ... contrasting modes of writing that will appeal to connoisseurs and amateurs alike' and to juxtapose 'the difficult and the clear ... inscribing both *Kenner* and *Liebhaber* into these works, just not necessarily at the same time'.[24]

Concern for prospective performers of the 'Haydn' quartets perhaps weighed more heavily on Mozart's mind than concern for prospective listeners, both because the published works were intended not for public concerts with large audiences but for private renditions in small, intimate gatherings, and because players naturally would have been expected to purchase more copies than listeners. The documented difficulties of playing and listening to the quartets in the fifteen years or so post publication,[25] often cited in the secondary literature, have probably influenced our

---

[24] See Mark Evan Bonds, 'Listening to Listeners', in Danuta Mirka and Kofi Agawu (eds.), *Communication in Eighteenth-Century Music* (Cambridge: Cambridge University Press, 2008), pp. 34–52, at 41–43. Elaine Sisman argues in a similar vein that the reference to the 'happy medium' in Mozart's letter about K. 413–415 (28 December 1782) is more applicable to the 'Haydn' quartets than the piano concertos, to Mozart's 'challenge of *demonstrating art* for the Kenner demanding satisfaction, while also *concealing art* for the Nichtkenner seeking more passive pleasures'. Thus, the string quartets from 1782–1783 'represented Mozart's attempt to forge a new path between the Viennese Kenner scene, mediated by Baron Gottfried van Swieten's quartet sessions in fugal repertory, and the broader social world promised by Haydn's newly published op. 33 quartets'. See Sisman, 'Observations on the First Phase of Mozart's "Haydn" Quartets', in Link and Nagley (eds.), *Words About Mozart*, pp. 33–58, at 41 and 42.

[25] For comments from the classical era, see Keefe, *Mozart's Viennese Instrumental Music*, pp. 89–90.

understanding of the works more than they should, since the corollary is that difficulties experienced even by connoisseurs at the end of the eighteenth century were difficulties Mozart deliberately intended, without finding it necessary to appeal to a broad spectrum of listeners and players. As will be shown, attention to performers and performances of the quartets significantly affected Mozart's path to publication and the publication itself.[26]

Composing, Performing and Publishing the 'Haydn' Quartets

As is well known, a lot of discrepancies exist between the musical text of Mozart's autograph of the 'Haydn' quartets and the parts published by Artaria for the first edition in September 1785, many of which can be attributed with near certainty to Mozart himself.[27] In one case in particular, the first eighteen bars of the development section of the K. 387 finale (125–142), Mozart made several revisions in his autograph, subsequently arriving at his final version only in the first edition.[28] Here, and elsewhere, Mozart would have notated changes intended for the published edition on performance copies generated from the autograph. In accordance with normal practice, Artaria would then have used marked-up copies rather than the autograph in preparing the musical text for the edition.[29]

In comparing the autograph and the first edition, the largest number of additions and alterations for the printed text involve dynamics.[30] Since Mozart probably made the adjustments either during or after one of the

---

[26] For a recent performer-centred interpretation of Mozart's chamber music informed by the idea of 'multiple agency', which is defined as 'multiple personas engaged in discourse that are understood to act autonomously and to possess the consciousness and volition necessary to determine their own statements and actions ... [capturing] the notion that a chamber music score is, above all, something to be *played*, an encoded musical exchange in which each player assumes an individual character, similar in many respects to a theatrical script', see Klorman, *Mozart's Music for Friends* (quotation at pp. 122–123).

[27] See Wolf-Dieter Seiffert, 'Mozart's "Haydn" Quartets: An Evaluation of the Autographs and First Edition, with Particular Attention to mm. 125–42 of the Finale of K. 387', in Eisen (ed.), *Mozart Studies 2*, pp. 175–200. For the first edition see *Sei Quartetti per due violini, viola, e violoncello composti e dedicati al Signor Giuseppe Haydn... .dal suo amico W.A Mozart* (Vienna: Artaria, 1785). The publication is given on the title page as Artaria's plate number 59 and as Mozart's 'Op. 10'.

[28] Seiffert, 'Evaluation of the Autographs and First Edition', pp. 176–190.

[29] Seiffert, 'Evaluation of the Autographs and First Edition', pp. 194–195.

[30] There are also a lot of cautionary accidentals in the first edition that do not appear in the autograph: 'In all likelihood ... [they] derive from the experience of specific performances before the engraving was begun.' Seiffert, 'Evaluation of the Autographs and First Edition', p. 194.

play-throughs of the quartets before publication, the practical effects of his works in performance presumably affected him above all when interpolating or changing markings. As has been pointed out: 'Mozart's lingering indecision on [dynamic signs and tempo indications] demonstrated in the autographs, was finally overcome in trial performances, in which he decided on the "final" text.'[31] Even though performance copies of the 'Haydn' quartets originating before the first edition are no longer extant, we know of their erstwhile existence from performances documented in Mozart's correspondence. Several took place in early 1785 (15 January, 12 February, 2 April), but also in 1784 before the set was complete, judging by Mozart's reference to the violinist Zeno Franz Menzel sight-reading them better than anyone else in Vienna.[32] Leopold had also received K. 387, 421 and 428 before his trip to Vienna in early 1785, and doubtless played them in Salzburg.[33]

The Artaria first edition has various limitations, probably related for the most part to the mechanics of the engraving process. As is often the case in late-eighteenth-century editions, slurs and phrase-marks are imprecise: they are sometimes divided seemingly to accommodate changes in stem direction and only occasionally snake between segments with both upward- and downward-pointing stems; and their duration is frequently either unclear, or self-evidently too long or too short.[34] The positioning of dynamic marks is affected by the typesetting process: they are often moved to the left of their ideal location, for example, if a note on a leger line gets in the way. The standard indication for a crescendo, '*cresc:*', is only rarely elongated (such as by a broken line, _ _ _ _), its end thus being more open to question than at the corresponding points of Mozart's autograph. Since '*cresc:*' occupies a uniform amount of typeset space on every occasion, no doubt on account of the same

---

[31] Seiffert, 'Evaluation of the Autographs and First Edition', p. 195.

[32] See MBA, vol. 3, p. 368 and LMF, p. 885 (letter of 22 January 1785 from Leopold to Nannerl); MBA, vol. 3, p. 373 and LMF, p. 886 (letter of 16 February 1785 from Leopold to Nannerl); MBA, vol. 3, p. 384 (letter of 2 April 1785; not in LMF); MBA, 3, p. 310; LMF, p. 874 (letter of 10 April 1784). Seiffert explains ('Evaluation of the Autograph and First Edition', p. 192): 'We can conclude from various documentary references that at least two complete manuscripts existed before the first edition appeared.' Performance copies of the string quintet in C, K. 515, annotated by Mozart, have recently been discovered and are examined in Chapter 10.

[33] MBA, vol. 3, p. 373 and LMF, p. 886 (16 February 1785).

[34] On the latter point, see for example K. 458/i (cello), bar 180; K. 458/iv (viola), bars 42–43 and 109; K. 428/i (second violin), bars 19–20; K. 428/i (first violin), bars 65–67; K. 464/i (viola), bars 12–14, 145. For a rare instance of a slur snaking between eight semiquavers, four with the stems pointing upwards and four with stems downwards, see K. 428/i (second violin), bar 122. On the unreliability of phrasing in general in late-eighteenth-century editions, see Christina Georgiou, 'The Historical Editing of Mozart's Keyboard Sonatas: History, Context and Practice', PhD thesis, City University London, 2011, p. 67.

Example 5.5 Mozart, String Quartet in E-flat, K. 428/iii, bars 48–54 (with no staccati in bars 50–52 inclusive, in either the autograph or the Artaria edition).

steel punch being used for each engraving, the extent of the musical material covered by it depends on how compact or spread out the instrumental notation is at the moment in question.[35] There are also a number of errors in the edition, involving dynamics, slurs and absent accidentals.[36]

Nevertheless, close similarities between the autograph and the first edition in a number of revealing passages underscore Artaria's serious intention accurately to reproduce Mozart's text throughout the publication process (that is, from performance copies generated, in turn, from the autograph) and not to add material themselves. For example, in K. 428/iii (bars 48–54, Example 5.5), K. 428/iv (bars 82–87), K. 464/i (bars 33–35), and K. 464/iii (bars 126[4]–134), only the exact staccati given in Mozart's autograph appear in the edition, even though the clear implication is that the staccati should continue when unnotated: reproducing Mozart's text is more important to Artaria, then, than standardizing it editorially. Also in K. 428/iv, only a single *p* is given in the second violin in bar 27, as in the autograph, when an altered

---

[35] Places where '*cresc.*' indications are *not* extended across a protracted passage in the edition and where the autograph indicates they should be extended, include: K. 464/i, bars 134–137, 191–193; K. 464/iii, bars 157–159; K. 465/i, bars 114–115 (second violin, viola, cello); K. 465/ii, bars 20–22, 40–42, 63–65; K. 465/iv, bars 382–386. Extended crescendi are given in (for example): K. 465/i, bars 100–102 (viola, but not in first violin and second violin); K. 465/ii, bars 69–71 (viola); K. 465/iv, bars 389–390 and 396–399 (both cello). On the steel punches used in the engraving process in late-eighteenth-century Viennese publications, see Rupert Ridgewell, 'Biographical Myth and the Publication of Mozart's Piano Quartets', *Journal of the Royal Musical Association*, 135 (2010), pp. 41–114, at 87–88.

[36] See, for example, the following: K. 421/i (cello), bar 83, beat 3, *p*; K. 421/i (cello), bar 98, beat 3, *f* (which appears two bars early); K. 421/iv (cello), bar 31, *p* (which appears one bar late); K. 458/iv (first violin), bar 129 (a minim rather than a crotchet); K. 458/iv (second violin), bar 259 (absent slur, when the first violin receives one and the second violin is unnotated and marked 'in 8tava' in the autograph); K. 465/iii (cello), bar 59, *p* (against *f* in all the other instruments and given as *f* in the autograph); K. 464/iv (cello), bars 97, 120 (respectively lacking a g-sharp altogether and a sharp sign); K. 465/iii (viola), bar 24 (lacking a flat sign).

version of the first eight bars to round off the rondo theme section implies a standardization to simultaneous *ps* for all four instruments. In the development section of K. 465/i (bars 107–155), the first edition adheres absolutely precisely to the staccati and strokes notated by Mozart,[37] even when continuations unnotated in the autograph are certainly implied. The fact that the first edition (and seemingly the performance copies as well) did not take even a small editorial liberty in these passages, indicates the seriousness with which copying and engraving were approached *vis-à-vis* the material provided by Mozart.

Thus, all things considered, it is unlikely that the Artaria edition deliberately incorporated material not sanctioned by Mozart via annotations to the performance copies. Put another way, dynamic indications in short and long passages of the first edition for which no dynamic markings exist in the autograph are likely to derive from Mozart himself, from his continued thoughts about the quartets arrived at when playing through performance copies that would ultimately generate the published edition.[38]

Ink colours in Mozart's autograph show that he revised and added to his musical texts on at least two passes through the autograph before handing it over for copying.[39] In a number of movements, dynamics were inserted into the score at these later stages of work. Thus, where dynamics are concerned, continuity can be posited between work on the autograph and annotations to the performance copies that made their way into the edition: in some cases Mozart revisited a movement to add dynamics before surrendering the autograph for copying purposes; in other cases he waited until he was working with performance copies to include them. Similarly, no hard-and-fast distinction can be made between 'compositional' and 'performance-orientated' phases in Mozart's creative process: plainly, he will not have started thinking about performance issues and stopped thinking about compositional aspects of his works when working with the performance copies, just as he will not have excluded thoughts about performance when working with the autograph.

Mozart added dynamics to both K. 421/ii (Andante) and K. 458/ii (minuet and trio) in one of his passes through the autograph after writing

---

[37] With one exception, the viola in bar 137.

[38] For applicable segments and passages in the first three quartets in the published set, see, for example, K. 387/i, bars 17–19, 125–127, 150–152; K. 387/iii, bars 43–46, 98–99; K. 387/iv, bars 268–278; K. 421/iv, bars 49–52, 57–61, 65–71, 113–134; K. 458/i, bars 125–126, 137–138; K. 458/iii, bar 49; K. 458/iv, bars 30–36, 102–106, 115–120, 228–233, 297–300, 308–312. The NMA (VIII/20/1–2) records them in footnotes to the printed musical texts of all six quartets.

[39] Seiffert, 'Evaluation of the Autographs and First Edition', p. 191.

Example 5.6 Mozart, String Quartet in D minor, K. 421/ii, bars 1–12.

Example 5.7 Mozart, String Quartet in D minor, K. 421/ii, bars 21–26.

the music.[40] Dynamics in K. 421/ii ultimately support expression in timbral, textural and especially harmonic-tonal domains. Over the course of the A section (bars 1–26; see Examples 5.6 and 5.7) Mozart adds gently to the effects requested of performers, inviting them progressively to intensify musical expression. For example, the *mf*s in bars 2–3, slightly increasing the initial volume, lead in turn to the crescendo to *f* at the reappearance of the same figure in bars 6–7. After the double bar, and perhaps responding

[40] Seiffert, 'Evaluation of the Autographs and First Edition', p. 191.

to an expansion of the harmonic palette to include Cm and V/g, Mozart moves more quickly than in bars 1–8 between *p* and *f*, echoing bar 10 twice in *p* and *pp* increments (bars 11, 12). A thematic extension (bars 21–26, Example 5.7) appended to the return of the opening material that brings the A section to a close coincides with a kind of dynamic synopsis of the movement thus far in its alternation of *f*, *p* and *mf* dynamics (minus notated crescendos). In the B section, perhaps again to reinforce the (expected) expansion of the movement's harmonic profile, Mozart asks for the longest *forte* passages so far (two full bars, 31–32 and 47–48) and three crescendi in quick succession (bars 36–41, in the A-flat major passage). The consecutive crescendi at the end of the movement in A' take a procedural lead from the B section, then, while extending dynamics-related activities from A. Judging by ink colours in the minuet of K. 458/ii, four *p*s (bar 11, early in the B section) and four *f*s (bar 21, at the beginning of the reprise) were written into the autograph alongside the notes. (See Example 5.8 for bars 9–28.) At a later stage, indicated by the darker ink, Mozart deleted the four *p*s and two of the *f*s (first violin and cello) and added all of the minuet's other dynamic markings (including the *sf*s and *crescendi*). While the *p*s are simply displaced by two bars from their original location in bar 11 to bar 13, adjustments to the *f*s apparently capture an important re-evaluation of the B section's link to the reprise. Initially, Mozart envisaged the first violin carrying a one-bar *crescendo* by itself into the reprise (bar 20). The revision, though, sees the original *crescendo* crossed out and a new one written for the first violin, second violin and viola in bars 18–19; an *f* is therefore reached at the beginning of bar 20. Moreover, this juncture of the minuet – with its multi-instrument *crescendo* – is now aligned with the corresponding run-up to the reprise in the trio. The late-stage *sf*s in the minuet (bars 3–5, 23–25) also bring it into line with the *sf*s and *sfp*s in the trio, including several placed distinctively on the weak beats of both minuet and trio.[41]

It is clear from K. 421/ii and K. 458/ii that Mozart contemplated expressive contributions by performers while still working on the autographs and that (in the case of K. 458/ii at least) his views evolved over time. Mozart naturally could not have expected absolute sound levels from his performers when writing *p*, *mf*, *f*, etc. But his dynamic refinements, linked to harmonic-tonal and formal procedures, need to be actively

---

[41] Small differences between the autograph and first edition of K. 458/ii might be attributable to Mozart, including the clarification in the edition that the second violin and viola reach *f* by the end of their crescendo at the end of the minuet B section, and the *f* – *p* / *fp* markings for second violin, viola and cello in place of *sf* – *p* / *sfp* in the trio (cello, bar 8).

Example 5.8 Mozart, String Quartet in E-flat, K. 458/ii, bars 9–28 (including Mozart's deleted dynamics).

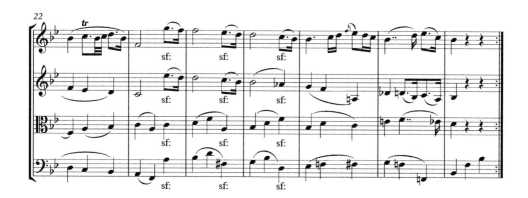

interpreted by players in response to synergies he promotes between dynamic effects and harmonic-tonal effects.

Many dynamics not present in the autograph but included in the first edition also appear to support notable textural, harmonic and tonal procedures. In the concluding Più Allegro of K. 421/iv (Example 5.9), Mozart added a number of markings to the single marking in the autograph (an *f* in bar 139 accompanying the *tierce de picardie* shift to D major three bars before the end). *Piano*s and *forte*s coincide with distinctive harmonic moments, as if to support the mutually reinforcing harmonic and dynamic effects for bar 139 conceived at the autograph stage: a *forte* coincides with chromatic intensification, *piano*s with consecutive and different diminished harmonies, a *forte* with a rescoring of the diminished passage, and a *piano* with the final D-minor cadences of the work (bars 120–124, 124–128, 129–133, 134–138 respectively; Example 5.9). Similarly, the textural intensification of variation 2 (bars 49–72), each instrument receiving its own discrete musical strand at the opening of A, B and A' sections, is enhanced in the Artaria edition with *fp*s and *f*s for viola and cello. It is not surprising that Mozart almost certainly notated dynamic intensifications to the performance copies of this variation – and indeed the Più Allegro at the end of the movement – after hearing it played, for the textural ebb and flow conveys a special energy in performance that is augmented by additional dynamics. Pre-publication renditions of K. 421/iv and K. 428/i could have motivated other additions as well. An *f* accruing to the end of bar 38 of K. 421/iv in the edition creates a 4 (*f*) + 2 (*p*) + 2 (*f*) profile for the first eight bars of the second section of the first variation, rather than the 4 (*f*) + 4 (*p*) profile of the autograph; one can imagine Mozart hearing the variation and desiring not only an increased emphasis on the modulation to F (*p* in the theme section and originally *p* in the first variation at bars 39–40) but also a quicker alternation of dynamics than initially envisaged, as a precursor to the change of dynamics almost every bar in the second half of the section. Considerable energy also accrues to the development section of K. 428/i between the autograph and the first edition: *f*, *fp* and *p* dynamics added to the edition in bars 77–91 (Example 5.10) augment the *f* – *p* contrasts given in the autograph at the beginning and the end of the development. Each type of material in bars 77–91 receives its own discrete marking: the triplet arpeggios are *f*; sustained notes are *fp*; and semiquaver/quaver figures are *p*. All three types are then combined in bars 85–91, the back and forth of different dynamics encouraging a vigorous performance not implied in the autograph.

Example 5.9 Mozart, String Quartet in D minor, K. 421/iv, bars 120–142 (with Artaria dynamic additions in bold italics).

Example 5.10 Mozart, String Quartet in E-flat, K. 428/i, bars 77–91 (with Artaria dynamic additions in bold italics).

Example 5.11 Mozart, String Quartet in E-flat, K. 428/iii, bars 60–66 (with Artaria dynamic additions in bold italics).

Elsewhere in the 'Haydn' set, dynamics accruing to the first edition accentuate existing musical drama. The passage from bar 60–66 in K. 428/iii (Example 5.11), already a climactic juncture of the minuet in the autograph with an *ff*, quick-fire imitation in the first violin, second violin and viola and *sfs* in the cello, becomes more climactic still: additional *sfs* in the upper three parts create a ripple of accented sounds (bars 60–63). The run-up to the recapitulation of K. 464/i is similar (Example 5.12). In the autograph Mozart includes two *sfps* for the cello on the second beats of bars 158 and 159 to coincide with diminished harmonies that interrupt the E-pedal preparing for the reprise; in the edition *fps* accrue to the upper parts (*f* – *ps* in the viola), now emphasizing both dominant and diminished harmonies. The climactic moment in the B section of the minuet K. 464/ii, a *forte* half-diminished chord presented by a united quartet, acquires notes in the edition's cello part (octave g/Gs rather than single gs, bars 42–3), lending further weight to the gesture.[42]

Dynamics notated only in the first edition of the entire trio of K. 464/ii also reinforce a prevailing compositional strategy. Unusually for Mozart, A' comprises a modest decorative elaboration of A rather than a straightforward reprise, a process complemented by a dynamic adjustment to A in A': the *p* – *cresc* (A, Example 5.13) is replaced by the *forte* in bar 29 (A', Example 5.14). The combined *forte* and textural intensification in the last four bars of the trio thus support a moment of mild climax.

While the reinforcement of musical processes through dynamics is clearly a feature of the 'Haydn' string quartets it by no means tells the

---

[42] The NMA does not follow the first-edition cello part in bars 42–43, sticking with the autograph text instead.

Example 5.12 Mozart, String Quartet in A, K. 464/i, bars 157–162 (with Artaria dynamic additions in bold italics).

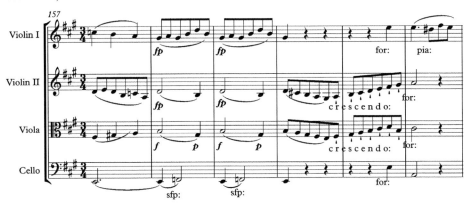

Example 5.13 Mozart, String Quartet in A, K. 464/ii, bars 1–8 (all dynamics from Artaria edition).

full story. For on a number of occasions discrepancies between dynamics in the autograph and the first edition point to Mozart's views about performance evolving over time. Of course, in the absence of the actual performance copies Mozart used, it cannot be established absolutely for certain that specific differences between autograph and first edition originated with Mozart rather than creeping inadvertently into the first edition as a result of copying errors. But Mozart's potential involvement gains credibility where patterns of differences emerge, and especially once the seriousness with which Artaria went about the task of reproducing Mozart's text for the first edition is taken into account (see above).

The Andante cantabile K. 387/iii contains numerous discrepancies between dynamics written in the autograph and printed in the first

Example 5.14 Mozart, String Quartet in A, K. 464/ii, bars 25–32 (all dynamics from Artaria edition).

edition. In bars 43–46 and 98–99, dynamics accrue to the edition (see Examples 5.15 and 5.16). Both segments contain markings that are unaligned among instruments playing imitated material: an *sfp* and *f – p* for first and second violins in bar 46;[43] and an *fp* for viola, *sfp* for second violin and cello and nothing for first violin in bars 98–99. In bar 47, too, a uniform *forte* for all four instruments in the autograph becomes *fps* for first and second violin and *fs* for viola and cello in the edition. Such dynamic non-alignment becomes potentially significant once dynamics elsewhere in the movement are factored into the equation, including the cultivation of a degree of dynamic autonomy for individual instruments in both autograph and edition. For example, instruments are set apart dynamically, even if only slightly, in both the first-theme and transition sections

---

[43] Even if the second violin *f – p* in the first edition is an incorrect rendering of an intended *fp*, dynamics between the first and second violins remain unaligned.

Example 5.15 Mozart, String Quartet in G, K. 387/iii, bars 43–48 (with Artaria dynamics in bold italics and autograph dynamics above each stave).

Example 5.16 Mozart, String Quartet in G, K. 387/iii, bars 98–101 (with Artaria dynamic additions in bold italics).

of the autograph. In the continuation of the first theme (bar 7ff., Example 5.17, and 58ff. in the reprise), the cello is asked to crescendo from *pp* to *p*, the first violin that imitates the cello presumably to play *p* (given in bar 4) and the second violin and viola presumably to retain the

Example 5.17 Mozart, String Quartet in G, K. 387/iii, bars 1–9 (from the autograph).

pp notated in bar 6,[44] Mozart indicating a little more prominence for the cello – first violin imitation than for the inner parts. Similarly, the cello triplet-semiquavers in bars 15–18 of the transition are *forte*, while the first violin and viola receive differently lengthened *f – ps* with corresponding material[45] and the second violin *fps*; in the second theme, the first violin has an *sf* accent (with a subsequent descrescendo) and the second violin, viola and cello *fps* (bar 36).

On account of the autograph of K. 387/iii, we need to give serious consideration as composer-endorsed readings to alterations in the edition that foreground non-alignments and realignments of dynamics among the four instruments. The beginning of the first theme (bars 1–4, Example 5.18) is a case in point. Dynamic independence in line with the 1 + 2 + 1 texture is already evident in the autograph (see Example 5.17): an *f* is reached in the first

---

[44] The NMA gives an editorial *p* for the second violin and viola in bar 8. But there is no reason to assume a standard *p* dynamic level for all four instruments at this moment.

[45] The viola's *ps* in the NMA are given on the fourth quavers in bars 15–16 to match the *ps* in the first violin, even though the markings clearly occur in the autograph on the third quavers.

Example 5.18 Mozart, String Quartet in G, K. 387/iii, bars 1–4 (from the first edition).

violin in bar 3 via a crescendo in bars 1–2, when the second violin, viola and cello reach *f* only in bar 4; and the cello has no crescendo in bar 2, when both the second violin and viola receive one. The first violin in the edition has no crescendo at all, either as a result of a copying error or of Mozart crossing it out on a performance copy.[46] Potentially at least, the difference is no small matter in performance, affecting musical relationships among members of the group. With a crescendo in bars 1–2, the first violin aligns itself with the accompaniment in the second violin and viola, preparing for its *f* at the beginning of bar 3, but without one comes closer to the cello quavers, permitting (should a performer be so inclined) a more sudden arrival of a *forte* dynamic at bar 3.[47] Discrepancies between autograph and first-edition markings at corresponding junctures of the transition and secondary development (bars 15ff. and 70ff.) perhaps also demonstrate revised intentions on Mozart's part. The *f*s (first violin, second violin, viola) and *p*s (second violin, viola, cello) not in the autograph and added to the first edition in bars 17 and 19 result in an *f* dynamic for the first violin's demisemiquavers in bar 19ff. against a *p* in the lower parts in the edition, rather than a uniform *p* for all four in the autograph. The corresponding passage in the recapitulation (Example 5.19) has the first violin demisemiquavers *p* in bar 74, following on from the *p* in bar 73. However, the placement of the *p*s in the first violin, second violin and viola in bars 72 and 73 is now different in the

---

[46] An instruction Mozart wrote at the beginning of the autograph score of K. 387/iii indicates that the first violin had already been copied ('schon geschrieben') by the time the second violin, viola and cello were to be copied.

[47] The presence of a first-violin crescendo in the edition at the corresponding point in the recapitulation of K. 387/iii (bar 52) does not necessarily imply that the original absence of the crescendo was an error. Mozart may have envisaged a slightly different performance effect at these two junctures of the movement.

Example 5.19 Mozart, String Quartet in G, K. 387/iii, bars 70–74 (with Artaria adjustments to the autograph in bold italics above each stave).

autograph and first edition, namely synchronized in the first edition in bar 72, but not 73, and in the autograph in bar 73 but not 72.

In both autograph and first edition of the 'Haydn' set, dynamic non-alignments point to Mozart's concern for variety rather than regularity of sound.[48] The autograph of the first two movements of K. 387 foreshadows the Andante cantabile in this respect. In bars 21–24 of K. 387/i (Example 5.20), the first violin figure is initially set *p* against *f*s in the other strings, the four instrumentalists then coming together with coordinated *fp*s and a *p*. We therefore hear the first violin as separate from the group dynamically as well as texturally at the outset and then aligned with

---

[48] For an article making a similar point about Mozart's dynamic annotations to a manuscript copy of Haydn's string quartet Op. 17 No. 6, see Cliff Eisen, 'Mozart Plays Haydn', *Mozart-Jahrbuch 2006*, pp. 409–421, at 413.

Example 5.20 Mozart, String Quartet in G, K. 387/i, bars 19–24 (including Mozart's deletion in the autograph and Artaria markings in bold italics above the stave).

it. Mozart originally thought to align them all dynamically from the start, demonstrated by the first violin *for:* crossed out at bar 21 in the autograph and replaced with a *pia:*; his ultimate desire for contrast at this juncture is confirmed by the alteration. The *fps* for first violin throughout the corresponding segment of the recapitulation in the first edition (bars 129–132) support a different effect rather than justifying editorial intervention in the transition.[49] The edition's crescendo for first violin by itself in bar 19 (see Example 5.20) rather than alongside the second violin, viola and cello in bar 20 (as in the autograph) also supports the temporary non-alignment of the first violin and the rest of the ensemble. In the minuet and trio K. 387/ii, Mozart makes a particular feature of unsynchronized dynamics: the distinctive beat-by-beat alternation of *p* and *f* in the main theme, when heard simultaneously in second violin and viola, sets the two dynamics directly against each other on every crotchet of bars 14 and 16.

[49] The NMA issues a cautionary *fp* for the first violin in bar 21^1 and 22^1, lacking support from autograph and first edition.

Example 5.21 Mozart, String Quartet in G, K. 387/i, bars 27–32 (with the articulation change for the cello in the Artaria edition in square brackets).

Elsewhere, too, discrepancies between the autograph and the edition point tentatively to Mozart seeking alignments of instrumental sounds and textures different from those originally envisaged, after experiencing the works firsthand in performance. In the autograph of the trio of K. 458/ii, the first violin passes an *sfp* octave figure to the cello (bars 7–8) with uninflected *p*s in the second violin and viola accompaniment, whereas in the first edition *f* – *p*s are given to the second violin, viola and cello in bar 8 and no *sfp* to the cello. K. 428/ii opens *p* – *sf* – *p* in all four instruments in the autograph (bars 1–2), but *p* – *f* – *p* in the edition. (The *sf* markings are clear in the autograph, so are unlikely to have been misinterpreted in the copying process.) And the end of both sections of the third variation of K. 464/iii finishes with *fp*s in the violins and viola and *sfp*s in the cello in the autograph but *fp*s for all four instruments in the edition. Differences in articulation in the autograph and edition also suggest changed instrumental alignments. In the second theme of K. 387/i, the cello half-step oscillation (bar 30, see Example 5.21) is slurred in the autograph and aligned with the immediately preceding slurred semiquavers, but demarcated by strokes in the first edition that now foreshadow the semiquaver oscillations with strokes in the first violin and viola at the start of the restatement. Ultimately, neither articulation is 'better' than the other. Presumably after hearing the work played, Mozart came to prefer a presentiment of upcoming articulation (strokes) to an imitative rounding off of a previous one (slurs). The resulting impression is that the cello in the edition stands slightly apart from the second violin and viola at the moment of delivery; the 1 + 3 texture that saw the first violin separated dynamically from the other instruments 9 bars earlier in the transition (see above, Example 5.20) now morphs into a 2 + 1 texture in which the cello is momentarily distinguished by its different articulation. At the corresponding juncture of the recapitulation (bar 138) the autograph slur is retained in the edition,

Mozart looking for a different alignment of instruments than in the exposition as he had done in the secondary development passage (bars 129–132) relative to the transition passage.

Practical decisions taken by performers today about the primacy of the autograph or first edition must be informed by the reality that the 'Haydn' quartets continued to evolve in their composer's mind after he had ceased working on the autograph. Responding to prepublication performances by marking up performance copies, Mozart sometimes reinforced compositional processes by interpolating dynamics but sometimes changed his mind about renditions as evidenced by dynamic alterations. Such reactions would have been conditioned not only by Mozart's experiences of the quartets in performance but also (perhaps) by his perception of the needs and expectations of the customers purchasing the edition. Much more is at stake in Mozart's additions and alterations for the first edition than philological supremacy. Dynamics alone – their placement by Mozart and their interpretation by performers – create and refine relationships among quartet participants, shedding light on issues of interaction and individual and collective identity, on how (in short) the 'conversation' between individual participants is heard at a particular moment and over an extended period. Mozart's experiences of performance in the run-up to publication, the traces of which are communicated in the first edition, are therefore intrinsic to the identity, meaning and expression of the quartets.

Thus, the dominant historical view of the 'Haydn' quartets as beautifully crafted compositions meticulously written and revised in order to please only a small, rarefied group of musicians, offers too narrow a critical perspective on their ontological significance. Mozart's opinions on performance evolved over time, affecting the published product, and perhaps continued to evolve beyond publication as well; they were 'live' works for Mozart, reinforced and altered after being contemplated in sound. And modern-day performers can capture this vibrancy. Ultimately, specific decisions about adopting autograph or first-edition markings on a case by case basis matter less than following Mozart's lead in thoughtfully and energetically interpreting the music in performance. The lively relationship between autograph and edition, mediated through performances Mozart experienced, can be reflected in our own animated renditions of the works, which might even take dynamic differences in the two principal sources as hermeneutic points of departure.

While Mozart's 'Haydn' quartets do not owe their existence to his dual status as performing composer and composing performer, their texts are as influenced by performance experiences and concerns as the piano concertos from 1782 to 1786 and the piano sonatas from c. 1783 (see Chapters 4 and 3). The spur to creative interpretation engendered by the concertos and sonatas, where the performer is encouraged to assume the imaginative mantle of the composer, again characterizes the 'Haydn' set; Mozart's mindset as a performer is ever present even when he is writing instrumental music primarily for others rather than for himself.

The Piano Sonata and Fantasia, K. 457 and K. 475

The continuation of Mozart's creative process in the 'Haydn' quartets between handing over the autograph to be copied and the publication of the first edition finds a parallel in the Fantasia in C minor, K. 475, and Piano Sonata in C minor, K. 457, published together by Artaria in 1785.[50] Mozart first generated a *Widmungs-Kopie* (dedication copy) of the sonata from the autograph accompanied by a handwritten dedication dated 14 October 1784 to Therese von Trattner, one of his students and the wife of his landlord at the Trattnerhof. The dedication copy as well as the main body of the autograph for the second movement, a five-part rondo which comes after the finale in the autograph and was seemingly written down at a different time from the outer movements,[51] contains unnotated 'Da Capo' repeats for the two returns, has only two dynamic markings (the *sf* in bar 16 and *p* in bar 53), and lacks ornaments and runs subsequently included in the first edition.[52] Since we know little about Therese von Trattner's keyboard skills, it is unclear whether the dedication copy was designed to accommodate limited skill on her part (the rondo returns being performed unembellished, for example) or conversely to reflect

---

[50] For the autograph of both see the CD-ROM Wolfgang Amadeus Mozart, *Fantasie und Sonate C-moll: Die Originalhandschrift an Mozarts Clavier Interaktiv zum Klingen gebracht* (Salzburg: Internationale Stiftung Mozarteum, 2006). Whether K. 475 and K. 457 belong together in performance is a matter of debate. For a summary of the arguments, see Kinderman, *Mozart's Piano Music*, pp. 57–58. Christoph Wolff considers connections between K. 457 and 475 and between K. 533 and 494 so strong that 'for reasons both practical and philosophical it would make good sense to drop the second Köchel number in listings of the two cyclical works'; see Wolff, 'Two Köchel Numbers, One Work', in Melania Bucciarelli and Berta Joncus (eds.), *Music as Social and Cultural Practice: Essays in Honour of Reinhard Strohm* (Woodbridge and Rochester, NY: Boydell Press, 2007), pp. 81–99, at 99.

[51] See Eugene K. Wolf, 'The Rediscovered Autograph of Mozart's Fantasy and Sonata in C Minor, K. 475/457', The *Journal of Musicology*, 10/1 (1992), pp. 3–47, at 22. Wolf suggests that the slow movement could have been intended as a teaching piece for Trattner.

[52] See the NMA text of the second movement (IX/25/2, pp. 86–90) – compiled before the rediscovery of the autograph – which footnotes differences between dedication copy and edition.

an aptitude for playing that rendered a fully marked-up text – including embellishments and dynamics – surplus to requirements. Or, perhaps Mozart was in a hurry to produce a dedication copy for her, thus sending the sonata away to be printed before all of the final performance details were fixed. It is quite possible that Mozart used the dedication copy in his lessons with Trattner;[53] his small number of handwritten additions to the dedication copy supports this hypothesis. In the finale, in particular, a number of dynamics in Mozart's hand appear in the dedication copy that do not appear in the autograph, such as the *p* in the left hand in bar 1, the *f*s for the right and left hands in bar 96 and 98 and the *f* and *p* in bars 211 and 213. The 'agitato' Mozart appended to the 'Allegro assai' tempo indication at the beginning of the finale is also found only in the dedication copy.

Whatever Trattner's keyboard predilections and skills, it is clear from the autograph score as a whole and from markings in the first edition not appearing in the autograph and probably originating from Mozart himself, that private and public contexts demanded different musical materials. In other words, a work for public consumption was a quite different proposition from a dedication copy intended for a single player. On the page after the main part of the autograph of the second movement Mozart wrote embellished variants of the main theme for A' and A". On a loose leaf later bound into the autograph another set of three variants for the two reprises and bars 49–53 (the coda) were provided. The first set, which lacks dynamics, appears to be sketches for the second set for A' and A".[54] In similar fashion to the 'Haydn' quartets, Mozart's creative process then seemingly continued beyond the autograph and on a (lost) *Stichvorlage* generated from the autograph, on which Mozart, we may surmise, annotated dynamics that subsequently found their way into the first edition.[55]

Evaluating together the autograph variants for K. 457/ii and the markings in the first edition suggests that Mozart wanted players to broaden the expressive profile of the movement as it progressed. The considerable dynamic detail in the initial A section, appearing only in the edition, indicates surges and fall-backs (repeated *f* – *p*s), the opening *sotto voce* implying an emotional quality as well.[56] The end of the B section in the edition goes noticeably

[53] Preface to NMA, IX/25/2, p. xiv.

[54] Wolf, 'Rediscovered Autograph', p. 40. No variant for bars 49–53 appears in the first set.

[55] Preface to NMA, IX/25/2, p. xiv. For a succinct tabular summary of the relationship between the principal sources for K. 457, see Wolfgang Plath and Wolfgang Rehm's Kritische Berichte, NMA IX/25/1–2, p. 129.

[56] Badura-Skoda and Badura-Skoda, *Interpreting Mozart*, p. 48.

Example 5.22 Mozart, Piano Sonata in C minor, K. 457/ii, bars 15–17 (with performance marking additions from Artaria in bold italics).

further (Example 5.22), first with the instruction to die away to *pp* (*mancando*, bar 15), a quieter dynamic level than requested in A, and then with the *sf* – *p* surge and release (bar 16) to coincide with the harmonic move back to E-flat for A'.[57] The ebb and flow of dynamics reaches a new level of nuance in the second variant for A' in the autograph, where Mozart asks for an *f* – *p* – *f* – *p* – *f* – *p* alternation every demisemiquaver (bar 21, Example 5.23). The embellishments in A' also enable the keyboard player to enhance their profile as an expressive virtuoso. In C, the autograph's sketched notation for a virtuosic flourish (bar 29) is fleshed out in the first edition to become a moment of full-fledged brilliance, offering an opportunity for the demonstration of technical virtuosity to complement the expressive virtuosity in A' (and before the harmonic and tonal scope of the movement is expanded: G-flat – B-flat-minor – C minor, bars 32–37).[58] Fittingly, the concluding A'' and coda expand both virtuoso and dynamic profiles: the brilliant four-octave flourish in bar 52 included only in the first edition is more demonstrative than the flourishes in A'; and the *pp* at the final pause in bar 52, immediately preceded and followed by *p*s, and the twofold *f* – *p* – *pp* in the final bars (Example 5.24) suggest refinement to the dynamic effects from A.

The rondo variants for the autograph and apparent annotations to a *Stichvorlage* for the first edition thus emerge as a coherent body of alterations

---

[57] As mentioned, the *sf* is one of only two dynamic indications to appear in the main body of the autograph draft. (More are given in the second set of variants for A' and A''.)

[58] See Kritische Berichte, NMA IX/25/2, p. 152 for transcriptions of the notation in light ink in both the autograph and the dedication copy.

Example 5.23 Mozart, Piano Sonata in C minor, K. 457/ii, bars 21–22.

Example 5.24 Mozart, Piano Sonata in C minor, K. 457/ii, bars 56–57 (with performance marking additions from Artaria in bold italics).

and additions in spite of happening at different stages in the compositional process. As with the 'Haydn' quartets, some activities are not confined to a single stage: dynamics, for example, are added both to A' and A" variants in the autograph and presumably to a *Stichvorlage* for sections A, B and C. In his additions and adjustments, Mozart nurtures the kind of creative engagement with the music that he demonstrated himself as performer-composer. As in the piano sonatas K. 330–332 and K. 333 published in 1784 (see Chapter 3), K. 457/ii invites a discourse on dynamics, provides variants probably not part of the original conception of the movement, and encourages the player to cultivate links between harmonic, gestural, and virtuoso effects.

Mozart's sensitivity to nuances of keyboard sound at the post-autograph stage in K. 457/ii may help to explain important notational discrepancies between the autograph and the first edition of the finale (an ABA'CB'A" sonata-rondo). In the autograph, hand-crossings in bars 93–97 and 290–308 (partially given in Example 5.25) require inter-hand stretches of almost four octaves; the adjustments for the first edition reduce these stretches to a maximum of two and a half octaves. The NMA preface (focusing on the dedication copy in the absence of the then-lost autograph) refers to a 'difficult' version and an 'easier' version; the latter, suggest the NMA, could have been carried out at Artaria's request but almost certainly with Mozart's agreement, presumably because Artaria thought the original

Example 5.25 Mozart, Piano Sonata in C minor, K. 457/iii, bars 304–310 (first edition and autograph).

too tricky.[59] In truth, though, the autograph versions are not especially difficult to play on a standard five-octave late-eighteenth-century forte-piano. So, motivation for the changes probably resides elsewhere. And the most distinctive feature of the relevant passages in the autograph, namely the repeated exposure of the lowest notes on the fortepiano, perhaps offers a clue.[60] Originally in the autograph Mozart took the right hand down to the bottom of the keyboard, emphasizing the G_1 in the first passage, with a handwritten *f* inserted into the dedication copy (bar 96); in bars 304–308 (Example 5.25), Mozart first conceived the F-sharp$_1$, G_1, A_1, F-natural$_1$, G_1 dotted minims an octave higher, subsequently crossing out the original notes and putting them down an octave. (The first edition in fact restores Mozart's original idea.) So the sound of these notes, growling for five bars shortly before the end of the work and heard *f* in bar 98, was certainly on Mozart's mind. It is possible that the effect of two other forays into the fortepiano's nether regions had an impact on Mozart's decision to revise the autograph passages. In the B section from the exposition and B' that opens the sonata-rondo reprise, Mozart takes the music down to the bottom and then jumps up demonstratively almost to the top of the keyboard register on both occasions (bars 68–69, 189–191, see Example 5.26).[61] If Mozart did indeed rethink effects when contemplating the *Stichvorlage* in advance of publication, he could have concluded that the low notes in the hand-crossing passages detracted from the special effect created at the other

[59] Preface to NMA IX/25/2, p. xiv.

[60] On standard ranges of keyboard instruments in the late eighteenth century, see Rowland, *Early Keyboard Instruments: A Practical Guide*, pp. 36–39.

[61] In bars 189–190 of K. 457/iii, strokes appear in the first edition for the expansive arpeggio from the bottom of the keyboard to the top, but are not present in the autograph or dedication copy.

Example 5.26 Mozart, Piano Sonata in C minor, K. 457/iii, bars 185–192.

junctures in B/B': the low-note-to-high-note effects in B/B' are unique to the movement in the first edition, but not in the autograph and dedication copy (for example bars 303–304 in the right hand). With Mozart's known sensitivity to timbres and textures, it is unlikely he would have overlooked the local and more wide-ranging effects of the registral modifications to the right hand in the first edition as he readied his score for publication.

The first edition of the Fantasy in C minor, dated 20 May 1785 in the *Verzeichnüß*, is similar to the first edition of K. 457/ii in incorporating a large number of dynamic indications that did not appear in the autograph. As Eugene Wolf pointed out soon after the rediscovery of the fantasy and the sonata autographs in Pennsylvania in 1990, only *f*s and *p*s are found in Mozart's score except for one *fp* (bar 22) and one crescendo (bars 173–174). The more expressive markings in the edition, considered by Wolf to be its most notable feature relative to the autograph, thus 'represent Mozart's last-minute thoughts on the performance of the Fantasy – a kind of second level of instructions going beyond the more structural dynamic contrasts of the autograph to the subtler realm of nuance.'[62]

Even if Wolf's assessment is basically correct, the autograph dynamic markings are actually more nuanced than he implies: the variable speed of *f* and *p* alternations in the first and last sections on the one hand, and the early part of the second and third sections on the other, encourages a performer using only the autograph to contemplate differences and correspondences between dynamics across the piece. More important, the first-edition dynamics are as revealing for what is *not* included as for

---

[62] Wolf, 'Rediscovered Autograph', p. 31.

Example 5.27 Mozart, Fantasy in C minor, K. 475, bars 120–126.

what is included. To be sure, the first edition expands the expressive profile of the piece with *pp*s, *sf* – *p*s, crescendi, descrescendi, etc., and introduces other subtleties as well, most notably in the second halves of the first, second and fourth sections (Adagio; Allegro; Più Allegro). Equally, though, after additions to the *p*s and *f*s from the first eleven bars of the third section (Andantino), the first edition accrues no further markings until the second half of the Più Allegro: the *f* at the onset of the Più Allegro (bar 125, in the autograph; Example 5.27) is therefore the only dynamic indication of any kind for almost 50 bars (bar 96–140). Perhaps Mozart felt that the performer would introduce dynamic nuances of his or her own in the run-up to the Più Allegro (although that did not stop him adding in a significant number elsewhere). Or perhaps he intended a relatively uninflected second half to the Andantino (*piano*), allowing the performer to maximize the impact of the *forte*, G-minor onset to the Più Allegro, one of the most dramatic effects in Mozart's entire solo piano repertory. Irrespective, fundamental differences in the approach to dynamic additions for the first edition resonate beyond the markings (or absence of markings) themselves. For they direct the attention of performers both to dynamic inflections at individual moments and to the dynamic narrative of the piece as a whole. The swift *sf* – *p*s accruing to the first edition in the run-up to the Primo tempo (bars 153–156), pave the way for the alternation of *f*s and *p*s in the returning main theme; and the *pp*s in the final two bars of the Più Allegro section (159–160) predict the *pp* fade-away effect of the second bar of the Primo tempo (162) while also encouraging genuine dynamic and expressive contrast between the end of the penultimate section and the beginning of the last, with resulting emphasis on the *forte* moment of reprise. At this juncture of the piece, as at the end of the Adagio, which accrues *sf* – *p*s as well as a crescendo to *f* and a further *p* in advance of the *f* at the onset of the Allegro (see bars 32–36), first-edition dynamics actively encourage performers to shape transitions between contrasting sections.[63] Much is left to interpretation in the aforementioned move from the Andantino to the Più Allegro (Example 5.27) – for example, whether the repeated three-note dotted figures convey a nervousness (*inter alia* through dynamic nuance) that partially prepares for the dramatic onset of the demi-semiquavers, or whether an uninflected rendition of the concluding bars maximizes the contrast between the two sections. As in the fantasies from 1781–1782, then, pronounced interpretative licence in K. 475 sets the stage for the 'complicity between creator and executant' demanded by a written-down fantasy whereby the music 'must give the illusion that it has never been written, just as the performer must enact the role of spontaneous creator'.[64] Thus Mozart, even if not using the work primarily to demonstrate his own prodigious skills as a performer-composer, nurtures through his musical text the kind of creativity required of a performer-composer.

Accompanied Sonata, K. 454

The accompanied sonatas K. 454 in B-flat (1784) and possibly K. 481 in E-flat (1785) occupy a middle ground between works written primarily for concert performance in the mid-1780s (discussed in Chapter 4) and those written for publication. K. 454 owes its origins to a Viennese visit from the distinguished Italian virtuoso Regina Strinasacchi, who played it with Mozart at her academy at the Kärntnertortheater on 29 April 1784. Like the Accompanied Sonata K. 379 at Archbishop Colloredo's concert in April 1781, K. 454 was apparently premiered with only the violin part written down in full; indeed, very little of the keyboard part may have been in the score at the time of the concert. Ink colours and cramped piano notation in the autograph indicate that the violin and keyboard parts originated at different times, the latter once the space between bar-lines had already been set by the violin notation.[65] Mozart initially included

---

[63] For further discussion of how 'connections between the sections [of K. 475] are carefully signalled, with a variety of meticulously contrived transformations', see Cliff Eisen and Christopher Wintle, 'Mozart's C minor Fantasy, K. 475: An Editorial "Problem" and Its Analytical Consequences', *Journal of the Royal Musical Association*, 124 (1999), pp. 26–52, at 48.

[64] Eisen and Wintle, 'Mozart's C minor Fantasy, K. 475', p. 48.

[65] See the facsimile of K. 454, *Sonat för cembalo och violin av W. A. Mozart Köchel nr 454* (Stockholm: Stiftelsen Musikkulturens Främjande, 1982). See also the preface to NMA, VIII/23/2, p. xiv.

some of the piano part in sketch notation on the autograph as well, before writing the finalized version over it.[66] Thus, the story from Rochlitz (1799, 1825) reported in Nissen (1828) that the violin part was sent to Strinasacchi only on the day before the concert and that no time remained for Mozart to notate his own music before performing it is at least partially vindicated by the autograph.[67] In contrast to the circumstances surrounding K. 454, it is not known whether Mozart performed K. 481 in Vienna. Published as part of the Hoffmeister subscription series in January 1786, the 'multitude of questionable additions' probably not attributable to Mozart in the edition[68] make it less reliable as a source of Mozart's intentions for performance than the Artaria first editions of the 'Haydn' string quartets and the Fantasy and Sonata K. 475 and K. 457. In addition, the short period between the completion of K. 481 on 12 December 1785 and the publication by Hoffmeister renders involvement from Mozart unlikely between auto-graph and edition, a situation similar to the Piano Quartet in G minor K. 478 (discussed below).

The Strinasacchi concert not only motivated the composition of K. 454, but also helped to shape the musical text for concert and publication and the sales pitch for the edition. Mozart composed K. 454 with Regina Strinasacchi in mind. He had heard her play before the academy, remark-ing to Leopold: 'We now have here the famous Mantuan Strinasacchi, a very good violinist. She has a great deal of taste and feeling in her playing. I am writing just now a sonata that we are going to play together on Thursday at her academy in the theatre.'[69] Leopold shared his son's high opinion of her, explaining eighteen months or so later to Nannerl: 'She plays not a note without feeling, even in the symphony [that is ritornello] she played everything with expression, and no one can play the Adagio

---

[66] See Konrad, *Mozarts Schaffensweise*, pp. 47–49 and Nicole Schwindt, 'Die Kammermusik', in Leopold (ed.), *Mozart Handbuch*, p. 427.

[67] See *Allgemeine musikalische Zeitung*, 1 (1798–1799), col. 290; 'Mozarts Gedächtniß', *Journal für Literatur, Kunst, Luxus und Mode*, 40, no. 29 (7 April 1825), pp. 226–228; Nissen, *Biographie*, pp. 482–483. Nissen's source is the 1825 article, not the earlier version of the anecdote; I thank Anja Morgenstern (Internationale Stiftung Mozarteum) for this information. Emperor Joseph is reported to have gone up to Mozart after the performance and signalled astonishment at the fact that there were only bar-lines and empty, unnotated bars on Mozart's part. The (partial) veracity of the story based on philological evidence is highlighted by a number of scholars. See, for example: Derek Carew, *The Mechanical Muse: the Piano, Pianism and Piano Music, c. 1760–1850* (Aldershot: Ashgate Publishing, 2007), p. 465; Landon, *Golden Years*, p. 120; Nicole Schwindt, 'Kammermusik', in Leopold (ed.), *Mozart Handbuch*, p. 427; Eduard Reeser, Preface, NMA viii/23/2, p. xiv.

[68] See 'Comments' in Mozart, *Werke für Klavier und Violine: Urtext*, ed. Wolf-Dieter Seiffert and Ernst Fritz Schmid (Munich: Henle, 2000), p. 388.

[69] MBA, vol. 3, p. 311; LMF, p. 875 (24 April 1784).

with more feeling and more touchingly than she. Her whole heart and soul are in the melody that she performs. And her tone is just as beautiful and powerful.'[70] Father and son were not alone in their admiration. A brief biographical sketch of Strinasacchi a year before her death cites the wonderment with which her playing was received in the 1780s.[71] Certain features of K. 454, including the broad lyricism of the slow movement first labelled Adagio and then changed to Andante, may have been designed to accommodate Strinasacchi specifically.[72]

Torricella's advertisements on 7 July and 28 August described K. 454 as the work 'recently played at the theatre by the famous Mlle Strinasachy and Herr Mozart to universal applause, and therefore needs no further recommendation'.[73] The positive reception of a Mozart performance thus becomes an enticement to purchase an edition of the work, even a full four months after the event.[74] Perhaps it is indicative of Mozart's blossoming Viennese reputation as a performer, composer and performer-composer in mid-1784 that no attempt is made by Torricella to assuage potential concerns of amateur musicians about the difficulty of K. 454; Mozart's esteem as a performer-composer carries the requisite weight in marketing terms. Nissen's biography, paraphrasing Rochlitz, also recorded 'the greatest delight of the public for the composition and the performance'.[75] And a description of Strinasacchi in *The Musical World* (1839) described an ideal spontaneity to her collaboration with Mozart in K. 454 (admittedly at a concert the author is unlikely to have experienced first hand over fifty years earlier): 'Had Mozart, I will not say studied, but merely played over, this music once with the lady, it would not have been so wonderful.'[76]

---

[70] MBA, vol. 3, p. 467 (8 December 1785). (Not in LMF.)

[71] Gustav Schilling, *Encyclopädie der gesammten musikalischen Wissenschaften, oder Universal-Lexicon der Tonkunst* (Leipzig, 1825), vol. 6, pp. 209–210. See also Johann Georg Meusel, *Teutsches Künstlerlexikon oder Verzeichniss der jetztlebenden Teutschen Künstler* (Lemgo, 1809), vol. 2, p. 278.

[72] Küster, *Musical Biography*, p. 186. For the crossing out of the Adagio tempo indication for the second movement and its replacement with Andante, see the facsimile *Sonat för cembalo och violin*. And for further discussion of K. 454 in the context of gender issues and subjective matters of performance, see Samuel Breene, 'Mozart's Violin Sonatas and the Gestures of Embodiment: The Subjectivities of Performance Practice' (PhD thesis, Due University, 2007), pp. 222–254.

[73] MDL, p. 200; MDB, pp. 226, 227–228.

[74] Mozart's performance of K. 454 is no longer mentioned in an advertisement for the work on 18 March 1786. See MDL, p. 234; MDB, pp. 267–68. For a 1786 advertisement in London's *Daily Universal Register*, see NMD, p. 142.

[75] Nissen, *Biographie*, p. 482. ('Bey der Production spielte er die Sonate mit ihr, zum höchsten Entzücken des Publicums über Composition und Vortrag.')

[76] 'Female Performers on the Violin', *The Musical World*, 22 (16 May 1839), pp. 34–37, at 36.

The completion of the skeletal score for submission to Torricella probably happened soon after the April premiere, as K. 454 appeared in print at the end of August 1784 and the publication process, including engraving, proofreading and printing, often took time.[77] It appears either that the autograph of K. 454 was used directly to generate the print or that any *Stichvorlage* produced by Torricella for Mozart to examine was used to communicate very few additional markings to the publisher.[78] Several dynamics accrue to the edition, and several are omitted from it.[79] On the whole, though, dynamics in the two sources correspond closely, unlike the autograph and edition of the 'Haydn' quartets and the fantasy and sonata, K. 475 and K. 457. Torricella printed together the three sonatas K. 333, K. 284 and the piano part of K. 454, labelling them Sonata I, Sonata II and Sonata III, and alerting purchasers on the title page to the violin part in the third (which was printed separately).

No doubt Mozart completed the keyboard part of K. 454 with the original Strinasacchi concert experience in mind. Similar to K. 379 and the accompanied sonatas K. 376, 377, 380 (all 1781), co-extensive performance and compositional qualities capture K. 454's dual identity as a work for Mozart himself and for others (see Chapter 1). The opening slow introduction (see Example 5.28), which Rochlitz considered 'ceremonial' (*ein feierlich Adagio* [*sic*]),[80] comes alive in performance much like passages already discussed in the earlier accompanied sonatas. After a four-bar antecedent-consequent in

---

[77] At least according to the Artaria model; see Rupert Ridgewell, 'Mozart's Publishing Plans with Artaria in 1787: New Archival Evidence', *Music & Letters*, 83/1 (2002), pp. 30–74, at 48. Hoffmeister turned around publications more quickly. K. 481, for example, was dated 12 December 1785 in Mozart's *Verzeichnüß* and appeared in print the next month.

[78] The publication process for the Piano Sonata in B-flat, K. 333, one of K. 454's companion works in Torricella's edition, apparently worked differently, perhaps on account of a lengthier period between the completion of the autograph and publication: dynamics in the edition but not the autograph of the middle movement indicate Mozart's involvement. (See Chapter 3.)

[79] Examples of added markings for the piano in the K. 454 edition include: cautionary *p*s at the beginning of the development of the first movement after a quick page turn and for the left hand in bar 104 of the Andante in advance of the *p* two beats later that Mozart clearly intended for both hands; *sf – p*s, a crescendo and a *p* at the opening of the Andante (bars 4, 8–9, 12); and *sfp*s in bars 92, 93 bringing the first rondo return in the finale into line with the original statement. (In the latter, Mozart notates the return in the autograph, rather than using his familiar shorthand 'Da capo [xx] täckt'.) Dynamics appearing in the piano part of the autograph but not the edition include: an *f* in bar 111 of the first movement; *p*s in bars 2 and 79 of the Andante; and two crescendi in the Andante (bars 60–61, 65–66). Eduard Reeser's short Kritische Berichte for K. 454 in NMA, VIII/23/1–2, pp. 86–90 lists only departures from the autograph for its edition, attributing NMA text-related decisions to the Torricella edition on just two occasions. For the edition see *Trois sonates pour le clavecin ou pianoforte. La troisième est accomp. d'un Violon oblg: composées par Mr W. A. Mozart* (Vienna: Torricella, 1784), Oeuvre VII.

[80] Friedrich Rochlitz, *Für Freunde der Tonkunst* (Leipzig: Carl Knobloch, 1825), vol. 2, p. 286.

Example 5.28 Mozart, Sonata for piano and violin, K. 454/i, bars 1–13.

which the violin's answer matches the piano's question, an instinctive, improvisatory elaboration comes to the fore. In bars 7–9, the piano goes into decorative mode, including an initial demisemiquaver flourish followed by appoggiaturas and turns heard less ornately in the violin in the two previous bars. Further elaboration follows in the final segment of the introduction, the violin getting in on the act by imitating the piano's elaboration of the cadential gesture from bar 11 in bar 12. The seamless interweaving and interaction of two renowned virtuosos, which came to be so effectively realized in the notated text of the slow introduction, was surely one of the main draws of the academy performance and a partial explanation for the positive reactions to both work and first rendition. In the exposition, Mozart plays with the independent and dependent identities of the violin and the piano: the *f* and *sf* phrase-joins in the piano, and the distinctive arpeggios in the violin, suggest the former, but imitative exchanges and material in thirds and octaves the latter. At the repeat of the closing theme, violin and piano separately elaborate their material from the initial statement, coming together in cadence making (bars 58–65, Example 5.29) that restores the spirit of self-perpetuating elaboration from the slow introduction. This same spirit pervades the quasi-improvisatory second theme of the Andante: following the piano's decorative writing the violin produces still more ornate hemidemisemiquavers (bar 32).[81]

By providing opportunities for performers to foreground their creative roles, the finale of K. 454 – an ABA'CA"B"A'" sonata rondo – also highlights continuities between performance and composition. As a *tour de force* of player-centred activity, the concluding rondo statement (bars 240–269, Example 5.30) is a case in point. After a stop-start opening that encourages a relatively free rendition (bars 240–249), the violin produces a stream of brilliant triplet-quavers (bars 251–258); the piano then embellishes this material in semiquavers simultaneously with a violin figure that is itself duly elaborated (bars 259–266). Effects to be exploited by performers are strategically placed to coincide with rondo returns: *mfps* provide an opportunity for slight surges in bars 89 and 238 (Example 5.30) immediately before returns of the main theme; and repeated *sfps*, prefiguring the rondo statement, accompany a descent to the bottom of the keyboard register in the run-up to the recapitulation, culminating in an unaccompanied rendition of the neighbour-note figure – including the *sfp* – on F_1 and $G\flat_1$ (see bars 143–150; Example 5.31). Mozart's piano from Viennese maker Anton Walter

---

[81] Earlier in the Andante, after statements of the main theme, the violin and piano elaborate in tandem (see bars 15–19).

Example 5.29 Mozart, Sonata for piano and violin, K. 454/i, bars 58–65.

resonates beautifully in its extreme low register; he no doubt hoped other fortepianos would do likewise.[82]

Piano Quartet in G Minor, K. 478

Six weeks or so after Mozart completed his Piano Quartet K. 478 in G minor (16 October 1785), Hoffmeister published it in his nascent monthly subscription series.[83] (K. 493 in E-flat, unconnected to Hoffmeister contrary to prevailing scholarly opinion, was published by Artaria in December 1786.[84])

---

[82] Mozart's Walter piano is housed, and occasionally performed, at the Tanzmeistersaal of the Mozart-Wohnhaus in Salzburg. It can be heard – resonant lower register included – in Florian Birsak's recording of the fantasy and sonata, K. 475 and K. 457: Mozart, *Die Originalhandschrift an Mozarts Clavier Interaktiv zum Klingen gebracht.*

[83] According to Rupert Ridgewell, K. 478 was published in late November/December 1785 in Hoffmeister's first 'cahier' of piano music, alongside works by Albrechtsberger, Vanhal and Hoffmeister himself. See Ridgewell, 'Biographical Myth and the Publication of Mozart's Piano Quartets', pp. 61–62. For the edition, see *Quatuor pour le clavecin ou forte piano, violon, tallie et basses composé par Mr Wolfg. Amad. Mozart* (Vienna: Hoffmeister [1785]): https://iiif.lib .harvard.edu/manifests/view/drs:14728776$3i.

[84] On the association of K. 493 solely with Artaria rather than a combination of Hoffmeister and Artaria, see Ridgewell, 'Publication of Mozart's Piano Quartets'. No autograph survives for this work.

Example 5.30 Mozart, Sonata for piano and violin, K. 454/iii, bars 235–264.

Example 5.31 Mozart, Sonata for piano and violin, K. 454/iii, bars 143–153.

Such a short period of time between completion and publication renders unlikely the kind of post-autograph and pre-publication work from Mozart that characterizes the 'Haydn' quartets and the Fantasy and Sonata K. 475 and K. 457. Therefore, differences between the autograph and edition texts – most of which involve staccati, slurs and accents – probably do not derive from the composer himself.[85] The small dynamic discrepancies between autograph and edition do not point convincingly to Mozart's involvement either.[86]

Several biographical factors – the position of the piano quartets in Mozart's *oeuvre*, their publication, and the challenge of working in an ostensibly new genre[87] – suggest that Mozart would have negotiated his

[85] See Mozart, *Klavierquartette: Urtext*, ed. Ernst Herttrich (Munich: Henle, 1998), p. 3. In the Kritische Berichte, NMA, VIII/22/1, p. 6, Hellmut Federhofer describes the first edition as 'quite faulty' (*ziemlich fehlerhafter*).

[86] For example, and uncharacteristically for Mozart chamber music, the violin and cello are often marked at a higher dynamic level than the other two instruments in statements of the main theme in the edition where all four play in unison or in octaves. See bars 1 (violin and piano), 5 (violin), 145 (violin), 224 (violin and piano) and 239 (violin, although in octaves only with the viola and cello).

[87] Although Mozart had previously written a piano trio, K. 254, and the Piano and Wind Quintet, K. 452, the piano quartet was new to him in 1785 and had few eighteenth-century precursors. On the history of the piano quartet, and piano chamber music more generally, in the eighteenth

own needs as a performer-composer and the perceived needs of other musicians and listeners when writing K. 478 and 493. In addition to writing the piano quartets for publication we know that he played one of them (probably K. 493) on 12 January 1787 at Thun's Palace in Prague, shortly after arriving in the city for performances of *Le nozze di Figaro*.[88]

K. 478 is poised chronologically between piano concertos and strings quartets to which outward resemblance is closest among Mozart's Viennese instrumental works: it was completed just a few weeks after the publication of the 'Haydn' quartets and in the middle of Mozart's run of twelve piano concertos from spring 1784 to December 1786 (K. 449–K. 503). As has long been implicitly or explicitly acknowledged, the public piano concerto and the private string quartet both exerted a stylistic influence on the piano quartets.[89] But it cannot necessarily be assumed that influences operated straightforwardly or coexisted comfortably; indeed, a review in the *Journal des Luxus* (1788) highlighting a problematic collision of public and private performing worlds in one of Mozart's piano quartets (probably K. 493) indicates that they did not.[90] As explained in Chapter 3 for the piano concertos K. 413–415, instrumental dialogue helps to gauge the position of a work on the orchestral concerto–string quartet continuum, in the context of relation-defining activity in the former and acts of conversation in the latter. Based on discussion of Mozart's published chamber music above, dynamics may also shed light on performance expectations. And, as demonstrated in Chapter 4, the manipulation of instrumental sounds, roles and effects is representative of Mozart's *modus operandi* in the piano concertos. Thus, I shall attempt to illustrate that the concerto–quartet continuum, a feature of how K. 478 is heard and processed, is enlivened and energized by the performance-composition dynamic.

The vibrant relationship between K. 478 and Mozart's concertos and string quartets is signalled right at the outset, in the first theme section and first half of the transition, which combine characteristics of concerto style with

century, see Basil Smallman, *The Piano Quartet and Quintet: Style, Structure, and Scoring* (Oxford: Clarendon, 1994), pp. 1–24.

[88] See MDL, p. 25 and MDB, p. 284; Rudolph Angermüller, *Mozart, 1485 bis 2003. Band 1: 1485/86 – 1809* (Tutzing: Hans Schneider, 2004), p. 271. See also MBA, vol. 4, p. 10; LMF, p. 903 (letter to Baron Gottfried von Jacquin, 15 January 1787).

[89] On the dual stylistic heritage, see, for example, Abert, *W. A. Mozart*, pp. 862–263; Einstein, *Mozart: His Character, His Work*, p. 264; Massin and Massin, *Wolfgang Amadeus Mozart*, p. 1001; Keller, 'The Chamber Music', in Landon and Mitchell (eds.), *The Mozart Companion*, p. 136; Küster, *Musical Biography*, p. 253.

[90] See MDL, pp. 279–280; MDB, pp. 317–318.

Example 5.32 Mozart, Piano Quartet in G minor, K. 478/i, bars 1–4.

fragments of chamber-like discourse. Grand, brilliant and intimate qualities woven into Mozart's concertos appear in the first four bars: a bold two-bar tutti opening is followed by a solo semiquaver descent and *piano* conclusion (see Example 5.32).[91] Mozart's *pia:* on the autograph in bar 4 may indicate either or both a diminuendo through part of bar 3 into bar 4 and a continued diminuendo from *pia:* to a lower dynamic level by the end of bar 4.[92] Irrespective of player interpretation, these opening bars establish a pattern of quick-fire stylistic change that continues in the bars ahead. Following an answer to bars 1–4 with the same material in bars 5–8, the piano's octave leap that initially activated the brilliant descent appears first in an intimate *piano* dialogue with the strings and then in a grand, unison *forte* gesture (see bars 9–16). It is unclear whether the subsequent dialoguing of the harmonized head motif between strings (*p*) and piano (*f*) signifies a unity of purpose among all four instruments, or the piano's dominance over – and independence from – the soft strings. (Performers have to decide how much to differentiate Mozart's *p* and *f* markings at this point, accepting that they do not denote specific, absolute volume levels.) But independence, for individual string parts as well as the piano, certainly comes to the fore in the passage ahead (bars 23–29; Example 5.33), which features uncoordinated *sf* –

[91] For a facsimile of the autograph see Mozart, *Quartett in g für Klavier, Violine, Viola und Violoncello KV 478. Faksimile nach dem Autograph im Museum der Chopin-Gesellschaft Warschau mit einer Einführung von Faye Ferguson* (Salzburg: Internationale Stiftung Mozarteum, 1991). The autograph is a little worn and discoloured and contains some c. 3 cm^2 blank spots – holes filled in during the restoration of the manuscript in the 1950s – on each of the first few pages.

[92] For the realization of Mozart's dynamics along these lines see Mozart, *Violin Sonatas*, ed. Eisen, p. iv and Mozart, *Konzert für Klavier und Orchester KV 271*, ed. Eisen and Levin, 'Preface'.

Example 5.33 Mozart, Piano Quartet in G minor, K. 478/i, bars 23–30.

p, *f* – *p* and *sfp* accents. Since Mozart's *sforzato* 'is employed . . . as a dynamic marking and normally remains valid until countermanded by a subsequent indication' and must preserve 'an audible intensity of sound . . . beyond the initial attack',[93] surges in volume will last not just momentarily but for up to two beats in several cases.

Mozart thus mixes a colourful stylistic cocktail in the first 29 bars of K. 478/i. The piano and strings sometimes speak in a single voice and elsewhere more independently (as archetypically in the string quartet and the piano concerto respectively) with individuality asserted through sonic prominence or brief virtuosity.

Stylistic delineation in the remainder of the exposition is more clear-cut. Dialogue among ensemble members and brilliant piano passagework

[93] Levin, 'The Devil's in the Details', in Zaslaw (ed.), *Mozart's Piano Concertos*, p. 32.

appear without fail in first-movement transition sections of Mozart's 'Haydn' quartets and concertos respectively. Both materialize unambiguously in bars 30–57 of the piano quartet: dialogue first in the strings then simultaneously between the piano left and right hands and among violin, viola and cello; and brilliance in the piano's protracted semiquavers. Gradual change from one type of piano brilliance to another is also put into effect, a crescendo in bar 36 connecting the taut 3rds and 4ths in three-note semiquaver units (*p*) to more fluent, ostentatiously sweeping semiquavers (*f*). Mozart may or may not have intended the beginning of the second theme section to invoke the unaligned accents from early in the transition: the autograph and Hoffmeister edition disagree on the placement of the *sforzandi* in bars 58 and 62, the autograph attaching them to the last beats of both bars in the piano, violin and viola and the third beat in the cello (bar 62) and the edition placing all of them on the third beats of bars. In any case, piano and strings are balanced in the remainder of the section, indicating a string-quartet-like ideal of equal participation for material not out of place in a Mozart piano concerto: both the melody and accompanying semiquavers from the strings' theme (bars 65–74) are passed to the piano (bars 74–80), and the piano imitated by the violin; and subsequent dialogued semiquaver scales culminate in a concerto-like cadential trill realized by the violin and viola as well as the piano.

The codetta (bars 88–99; see Example 5.34) continues the prevailing style of dialogue, with both melody and accompaniment being passed from strings to piano. The autograph reveals Mozart's initial intention to give accompanying quavers to the viola (bars 92–93) and different, no-longer-readable material to the piano left hand.[94] Mozart's adjustment to the autograph preserves the second-theme section's dialoguing of accompaniment and melody and allows surrounding sounds to assume greater prominence than would have been possible had the viola and piano left hand played as originally intended: the lighter scoring for the piano statement in the revision than in the original promotes the G-flat appoggiatura figure in the violin, the semibreve tied note passed from cello to violin, and the onset of the viola's doubling of the piano in bar 96 (after nearly four bars rest in the final version). In similar fashion to the piano concerto autographs, an ostensibly straightforward adjustment to the autograph of the piano quartet catches Mozart accommodating instrumental sounds and roles. At the

---

[94] Ferguson, 'The Work and the Manuscript', in *KV478 Faksimile*, p. 13. We cannot be absolutely certain that Mozart wrote 'pia:' rather than 'p:' for the violin on the autograph at bar 88³ as the exact indication is obscured by an autograph disfiguration (a small blank spot, formerly a hole in the manuscript).

Example 5.34　Mozart, Piano Quartet in G minor, K. 478/i, bars 88–96.

end of his exposition, then, Mozart highlights both the equal participation and the distinctive timbral contribution of individual members of his ensemble.

The development section of K. 478/i, characterized at first by chamber-like expressive intimacy, moves via snippets of semiquaver scalar brilliance in the strings (bars 126–132) towards unadulterated, concerto-like grandeur at the end (Example 5.35). The scalar semiquavers are finally taken up by the piano in bar 133 and pitched against the main theme's head motif in the strings in the kind of overlapping, equal-length segments characterizing piano-orchestra confrontation in Mozart's concerto development sections (bars 133–138, Example 5.35).[95] (The *f* surges at the lead-in to

---

[95] On historically based definitions of dialogic confrontation applied to Mozart's piano concertos, see Keefe, *Mozart's Piano Concertos*, pp. 32–34, and Keefe, *Mozart's Viennese Instrumental Music*, p. 30.

Example 5.35 Mozart, Piano Quartet in G minor, K. 478/i, bars 131–142.

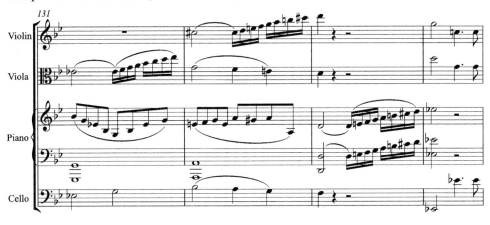

imitative entries in the first half of the development – bars 110–111, 115–116 and 119–120 – may also be heard as grand utterances, depending on how the contrasts between *f* and *p* are interpreted in performance.) This dialogic confrontation is atypical of Mozart's string quartets, but is quickly resolved in a manner invoking ideals of participatory equality and equanimity; the piano takes up the strings' head motif and the cello plays the piano's semiquaver scale (bars 138–140).

The remainder of the movement continues to promote dynamic engagement between styles, especially in the coda. New dialogue from early in the recapitulation is extended to eight bars in the coda (bars 231–238; Example 5.36), acquiring a three bar crescendo and transitioning smoothly to the grand climax of the movement (bar 239ff.; partly given in Example 5.38), which combines the piano's only protracted passage of simultaneous right- and left-hand brilliant semiquavers with the strings' longest unison passage, all marked *f*. A grandstand finish from coordinated piano and strings thereby demarcates intimacy, and bold and brilliant grandeur.[96] The strings' grandeur is enhanced by Mozart's eventual decision to deploy head-motif-derived material in bars 243–246 as well as in the preceding bars (see Examples 5.37 and 5.38 for original and final versions). Mozart initially envisaged new unison rhythms for the strings in bars 243–246, in a two-bar repeated pattern. While the two-bar repetition is retained in the revision, main theme material so strongly associated with grandeur is now included, also intensifying the pivot to the cadential progression with diminished 7th harmony rather than submediant harmony (as indicated).

Thus, K. 478/i moves from quick-fire stylistic cues in the main theme and early part of the transition to steadier cues in the remainder of the movement, where stylistic lines are more clearly drawn. But the dynamic, dramatic energy of the opening potpourri exerts an influence beyond its immediate confines: subsequent stylistic delineations, often a product of careful transitions, and intensity generated by passages such as the development-section confrontation and the coda, ensure an active presence in the listening experience for the vibrant mixture of string-quartet and concerto qualities.

Events of the first movement are invoked at the opening of the development section of the sonata-rondo finale (bars 170–177; see Example 3.39).

---

[96] For Abert, 'the main theme bursts forth in the strings in all its wildness [bar 239], accompanied by a keyboard figuration . . . designed to add to the general agitation'. See Abert, *W. A. Mozart*, pp. 862–863.

Example 5.36 Mozart, Piano Quartet in G minor, K. 478/i, bars 230–239.

Piano octaves in the minor mode, *f*, answered by an octave anacrusis leap and *p* intimacy, a pattern repeated to outline a i – V – V – i eight-bar progression, bring to mind the beginning of the work; the *f* (piano) to *p* (strings) exchange is also reminiscent of the opening of the first-movement transition. Whether or not the *f* / *p* exchange is conveyed by performers as a confrontation between piano and strings, the simultaneous appearance of the finale's first assertive unison, first minor-mode tonality and boldest *f* / *p* piano–strings alternation produces the biggest effect of the movement so far. Any sense of conflict quickly dissipates when the strings take up the unison figure, and then exchange it with the piano left hand (Example 5.39); the subsequent role switch (bar 192ff.), where the strings take up the *forte* unison and the piano the *piano* answer, also suggests participatory equality. On the whole, though, the development is a piano-dominated section in contrast with the exposition: piano brilliance prevails much of the time; and 'conflicts' involve strings acquiescing to material

Example 5.37 Mozart, Piano Quartet in G minor, K. 478/i, bars 243–246 (original version).

Example 5.38 Mozart, Piano Quartet in G minor, K. 478/i, bars 243–246 (final version).

played by the piano. While a spirit of equanimity pervades the exposition, quartet and concerto cues intermix in the development (as at the beginning of the first movement). Chamber-like qualities sit uncertainly in a piano-dominated section, including dialogue of the main theme's head motif (bars 208–216), which is typical fare for a re-transition: playing with and liquidating first-theme material apparently in preparation for a reprise, the dialogue does not ultimately fulfil its expected function, leading to the piano-dominated re-transition from bar 217 instead. Formal and stylistic signifiers, then, are unsynchronized. And we are reminded, in the solo piano two bars before the reprise (bar 223), of the material to all intents and purposes responsible for this state of affairs. An *sf* accent at the conclusion of a d'' – d-sharp'' – e'' cell in the piano – Mozart's only *sf* in the finale after so many in the first movement – harks back to the effect of E minor and its accompanying unison at the opening of the section.

The events of the development section provide a *raison d'être* for the reprise, namely to re-establish the unequivocally collaborative spirit of the

Example 5.39 Mozart, Piano Quartet in G minor, K. 478/iii, bars 131–182.

exposition. As in the first-movement recapitulations of many of his Viennese piano concertos, Mozart actually reinforces earlier collaboration.[97] He intro- duces new dialogue between the piano and strings in bars 242–246 in preparation for the presentation of the second theme and as a replacement for the piano brilliance from the ten bars preceding the exposition's second theme. A passage from the end of the second theme in the exposition leading back to the sonata-rondo refrain, where the development's disruptive unison figure is first aired in the piano and cello (bars 133[4]–135, Example 5.39), is also replaced; clear re-transitional material is heard instead, linking to the reprise of the main theme (bars 311–321) in a way that the misleadingly 're- transitional' material in the development did not. Finally Mozart revisits in bar 342 the powerful disruptiveness of the d-sharp" cell from the develop- ment, transforming it into an agent of emphatic collaboration: E-flat (enhar- monically D-sharp) is tonicized after a V – ♭VI interrupted cadence and then recast as a German Augmented 6th in the cadential reconfirmation of G, the ensemble acting as one in a coordinated crescendo notated across bars 349 and 350 of the autograph to a coordinated *forte* in bar 351.[98]

Performers will help to convey the position of K. 478 on the piano concerto – string quartet spectrum. Ultimately they will determine how exactly the piano quartet is projected to listeners at specific moments and over extended time spans, accepting (for example) that *piano* and *forte* will not connote the same dynamic level on every occasion, that perception of stylistic capriciousness will depend to some extent on manner of execution, that dialogic intricacies can be conveyed in ways suggestive of string-quartet- like equality or concerto-like drama, that lines between grandeur, brilliance and intimacy can be projected sometimes clearly, sometimes hazily. Good performances and critical interpretations of K. 478 (and other works too) exist in a dynamic relationship where hermeneutic influences can potentially travel in both directions. But for works like this piano quartet, inhabiting a grey area between concerto and string quartet genres, issues at stake in performance are of special ontological significance, affecting how evolving relationships between piano and strings are perceived. In the first move- ment, for example, players have to decide whether to present the beginning of the transition as a confrontation, how to project conflict between piano and strings at the end of the development and how to convey extended crescendi over the dialogued renditions of the intimate appoggiatura figure

---

[97] On this process in the piano concertos, see Keefe, *Mozart's Piano Concertos.*
[98] The Hoffmeister first edition gives an *ff* for the viola and piano parts in bar 351 and a *f* for violin and cello.

in the recapitulation and coda. And their decisions and interpretations will influence how Mozart's stylistic negotiations of string quartet and piano concerto are heard.

Mozart's attention to the nuances of individual sounds and effects, communicated *inter alia* in careful dynamic placements and musical adjustments in the autograph, point to a work for his own use as performer-composer as well as for those who purchased the published parts from Hoffmeister. Like the Viennese piano concertos, K. 478 is designed at least in part to promote Mozart's dual talents: pianistic brilliance and expressivity primarily reflecting performance abilities are complemented by effects for the whole ensemble principally demonstrating compositional acumen. At the join between the sonata-rondo return at the end of the exposition and development section in the finale, the autograph captures in a nutshell the intersection of composition and performance (see Example 5.39 above). For Mozart's 'dal segno' short-hand for the first thirty bars of the sonata-rondo statement brings to life the identity of the dramatic, *f* unison gesture dominant in the first half of the development section.[99] With thirty bars unnotated in the autograph, the unison gesture and the figure in the piano left hand and cello from which it derives (bars 169^4–171 and 133^4–135 respectively) were presumably written down on the autograph in quick succession. In the very bar that Mozart starts notating music again after the 'dal segno', moreover, a D-sharp in the violin initiates the move to E minor. Interpreted as an enharmonic E-flat, it invokes the piano/cello gesture before the refrain written on the autograph immediately before it and prepares for the piano's E-minor unison gesture that pivots around D-sharp immediately after it. Compositional links exposed visually in the autograph imply associations Mozart would have conveyed – and would have wanted his co-players to convey – in performance. His score suggests dramatically evolving relations between the piano and the strings to be realized in performance: cello and piano together derive the *forte* figure before the pause from the preceding E-flat – D appoggiaturas in the cello and viola (bars 132–133); the strings collectively draw inspiration from the new figure's E-flat (D-sharp) for the modulation to E minor; and the piano derives its unison gesture at the beginning of the development section from the piano/cello figure, upping the ante with suggestions of confrontation.

---

[99] 'Dal segno' is a common indication in Mozart's rondo autographs, saving him from rewriting a chunk of repeated material by instructing the replaying of the rondo material up to an appointed place.

We cannot hope to match Mozart's insight as the performer-composer of K. 478, but can draw inspiration from the confluence of string quartet and piano concerto in shaping our critical and performance interpretations. Ultimately, as for the piano concertos, our individual decisions about how to convey specific moments and passages in performance matter less than projecting narratives that situate centre stage sometimes changes and tensions between concerto and string quartet styles and sometimes accommodations of the two. If the piano quartets K. 478 and 493 are generic hybrids for Mozart, then renditions, critical language and critical interpretations should embrace this state of affairs.

*****

The individual works and groups of works discussed in this chapter, all ultimately for publication in the mid-1780s, were affected by different factors when journeying into print: by responses to a concert performance (K. 454) and perhaps to as-yet unidentified ones (K. 478, K. 475); by dedications (K. 457, 'Haydn' quartets); and by informal renditions and thoughts about pieces after submitting autographs for copying and before publication ('Haydn' set, K. 475, K. 457). But there is also a common thread. Whether Mozart made significant adjustments between the autograph and the publication of the first edition ('Haydn' quartets, K. 457 and K. 475) or did not (K. 454, K. 478), he reacted carefully and creatively to performances of his works in fashioning texts for publication. Sometimes, as in the 'Haydn' set, he either reinforced existing features of his music when revisiting it or changed his mind about interpretations; elsewhere, he elaborated ideas at later, prepublication stages (the embellishments of K. 457/ii and the ebb and flow of dynamics in K. 475). We have no reason to suppose that Mozart perceived his later-stage additions and adjustments to autographs and to performance copies as definitive interpretations of the works in question. If Mozart had returned to any of them in the years post publication he would have felt no compunction, surely, about adding further pencil markings to his published texts for performance purposes.[100] He was not chiselling great monuments to his name in fashioning works for publication (even if his works are typically construed in this way), but rather responding to them in the here and now in order to guide interpretations by others. Mozart's live experiences of his works, and contemplation of these experiences, leave their marks on the published texts.

---

[100] As in his annotations to Haydn's string quartet Op. 17 No. 6, described in Eisen, 'Mozart Plays Haydn'.

Mozart's published chamber works from the mid-1780s therefore offer us, as modern players, not only supremely crafted compositions but also models of committed engagement to musical creativity in and through performance. We owe it to these works and their composer to try to mirror in our own interpretations the intensely creative processes that led to their publication, whether we pay special attention to shaping the dynamic discourse of a particular movement or work; to correspondences and/or contradictions between markings in autographs and first editions; to inconsistencies as well as consistencies in dynamics and articulation; to relationships among participants; to the projection of an identity or series of identities for a work. Mozart's engagement with his works in the moment can become the 'liveness' of our own interpretations. As in the piano concertos, Mozart's product and the process that led to the creation of that product provide mutually reinforcing stimuli for our modern renditions.

6 | Operas, Arias, Ensembles, Songs and a Mass
Vocal and Dramatic Music, 1782–1786

The pillars of *Die Entführung* and *Le nozze di Figaro* have dominated biographical and critical discussion of Mozart's vocal and dramatic music from 1782 to 1786. While inevitable and understandable to some extent, given the self-evident quality of these two operas and the weight attached to them by Mozart and posterity, a large quantity of Mozart's music has been implicitly or explicitly marginalized as a result. With the notable exception of the Mass in C minor, K. 427, a work too grand to bypass, relatively little scholarly attention has been paid to a rich and diverse assortment of concert arias and opera inserts, two unfinished operas, the short opera *Der Schauspieldirektor*,[1] a number of songs, and a cantata derived from the C-minor Mass, *Davidde penitente*. The music of the incomplete *L'oca del Cairo* and *Lo sposo deluso*, for example, has rarely been a point of critical focus; when the works are discussed at all, it is usually with reference to weaknesses in their plots and libretti that led Mozart to abandon them.[2] From stylistic and compositional perspectives *L'oca del Cairo* and *Lo sposo deluso*, as well as the concert arias and operatic

---

[1] See Daniel Heartz on the proper designation of *Der Schauspieldirektor* (1786) as a 'Schauspiel' (play), rather than an opera or Singspiel, in *Mozart, Haydn, Early Beethoven*, p. 128. Since it is a drama with music, and was described as an 'operetta' in a review from 1794 (see below), I shall continue to refer to it colloquially as an opera.

[2] See, for example, Braunbehrens, *Mozart in Vienna*, pp. 190–191; Leopold (ed.), *Mozart Handbuch*, pp. 82–83; Steptoe, *The Mozart-Da Ponte Operas*, p. 1; Gutman, *Mozart: a Cultural Biography*, p. 621; Rosselli, *Life of Mozart*, pp. 88–89; Pestelli, *Age of Mozart and Beethoven*, p. 157; Knepler, *Mozart*, pp. 107–108; Rice, *Mozart on the Stage*, pp. 85–87. Jane Everson's article on *L'oca del Cairo* adds much to our understanding of Varesco's source for the story, but continues the orientation towards Varesco's work and its weaknesses rather than Mozart's music; see 'Of Beaks and Geese: Mozart, Varesco and Francesco Cieco', *Music & Letters*, 76 (1995), pp. 369–383. *L'oca del Cairo* and *Lo sposo deluso* receive little or no attention in biographical and critical studies where discussion might have been expected, such as Küster, *Mozart: A Musical Biography*; Till, *Mozart and the Enlightenment*; Landon and Mitchell (eds.), *The Mozart Companion*; Dent, *Mozart's Operas*; Eric Blom, *Mozart* (New York: Collier, 1962). Exceptions to the trend of more or less bypassing the music include Jahn, *Life of Mozart*, vol. 3, pp. 57–59, Abert, *W.A. Mozart*, pp. 913–923, and Goehring, 'The Opere Buffe', in Keefe (ed.), *Cambridge Companion to Mozart*, pp. 131–146, at 136–138. Two studies of *Lo sposo deluso* from 1996, while important to our understanding of the opera, do not include much discussion of Mozart's musical contributions. See Neal Zaslaw, 'Waiting for *Figaro*', in Stanley Sadie (ed.), *Wolfgang Amadè Mozart: Essays on His Life and His Music* (Oxford: Clarendon, 1996),

inserts, can be reasonably interpreted as staging posts on the road to *Figaro*.[3] But once issues concerned with performers and (actual and unrealized) performances are factored fully into the equation, pictures cannot be drawn so clearly: a case in point is Mozart's more frequent engagement from mid-1782 through mid-1786 with singers with whom he had struck up relationships in 1781–1782 and earlier (Lange, Cavalieri and Adamberger) than with those who would come to feature from *Figaro* onwards (Stefano Mandini, Vincenzo Calvesi, Francesco Benucci and Francesco Bussani).

Mozart's well-known letters to Leopold from 1783 on *L'oca del Cairo* underscore a practical-minded philosophy similar to that outlined for *Die Entführung* in 1781–1782, implying continuity of aesthetic and dramatic thought into the middle of the decade: he wanted to control the shape of the plot and details of the libretto, telling Varesco (via Leopold) that he would have to bend repeatedly to Mozart's command; he was sensitive to the resonances of the text, citing the impossibility of setting Celidora's and Lavinia's cavatinas to the same music on account of the differing emotions of the two characters; and he remained highly attentive to the perceived desires, needs and expectations of his projected audience.[4] Specific singers were not named for roles in *L'oca del Cairo*, as they were early in the genesis of *Die Entführung*, nor were instrumental effects mentioned, unsurprisingly on both counts as no commission was issued and Mozart did not proceed beyond his *particella* to orchestrate any of the numbers. But the original catalyst for libretto and composition, the re-establishment of the Italian opera buffa in Vienna, would have enabled Mozart to contemplate a cast. In addition, operatic effects were on Mozart's mind, including onstage fireworks,[5] even if their implications for orchestral writing are unclear. We are therefore justified in evaluating *L'oca del Cairo*, and by extension *Lo sposo deluso*, *Der Schauspieldirektor* and the arias and ensembles from mid 1782 to early 1786, according to criteria established for *Die Entführung* (see Chapter 2), paying particular attention to issues surrounding performers and performances. While lacking explicitly dramatic

pp. 413–435; and Andrew Dell'Antonio, "'Il compositore deluso": the Fragments of *Lo sposo deluso*', in Sadie (ed.), *Mozart: Essays*, pp. 403–412.

[3] See Rushton, *Mozart: Master Musicians*, pp. 187–189; Gutman, *Mozart: a Cultural Biography*, p. 622; Levey, *Life and Death of Mozart*, pp. 184–185; Lieber, *Mozart on the Stage*, pp. 94–95; Landon, *Golden Years*, pp. 139–140.

[4] See MBA, vol. 3, pp. 275, 297–298, 294–295, 268; LMF, p. 853 (21 June 1783), 864–865 (24 December 1783), 861–862 (6 December 1783), 847–848 (7 May 1783). Also, Mozart surely would have welcomed another opportunity to explore the abduction theme in *L'oca del Cairo* (after the success of *Die Entführung*).

[5] MBA, vol. 3, 298; LMF, p. 865 (24 December 1783).

credentials, *Davidde penitente* and *Die Maurerfreude* contain material written for Cavalieri and Adamberger and can be assessed partially according to these same criteria.

With a diverse range of music under consideration and nearly four years of the Viennese decade to accommodate, I shall first proceed chronologically through Mozart's dramatic music, looking at replacement and concert arias and operatic projects carried out while pursuing the formal, full-length-opera commission that would eventually arrive with *Figaro*, and subsequently examining the operatic ensemble inserts, revival of *Idomeneo*, and *Der Schauspieldirektor* that fell during the 1785–1786 season concurrently with *Figaro*. I then turn to the ostensibly non-dramatic vocal music from this four-year period, comprising the Mass in C minor and adaptation as *Davidde penitente*, *Die Maurerfreude* cantata and the songs from 1785–1786 (which have no known associations with a specific singer or singers).

Writing for Lange, Adamberger, and Fischer, 1782–1783

Mozart had several opportunities to write for Lange and Adamberger in 1783. 'Mia speranza adorata', K. 416, owes its origins to Lange's 'big concert' at the Mehlgrube on 11 January and was cleverly incorporated into Mozart's own Burgtheater academy on 23 March as the climactic vocal item towards the end of the programme (see Chapter 3).[6] Then, on 21 June, he reported writing two arias for Lange ('Vorrei spiegarvi, oh Dio' K. 418 and 'No, che non sei capace', K. 419) and one for Adamberger ('Per pietà, non ricercate' K. 420) to be inserted into Pasquale Anfossi's opera *Il curioso indiscreto*.[7] An imbroglio ensued, Mozart complaining that rumours had circulated of an attempt on his part to improve Anfossi's opera; he thus insisted on including a statement with the libretto to explain that the arias were composed for Lange as Anfossi's originals had been written for another singer and did not suit her.[8] Meanwhile, he explained to Leopold, he had also fallen victim to Salieri's 'trick' of persuading Adamberger not to sing 'Per pietà' at the

---

[6] MBA, vol. 3, 249; LMF, p. 836 (8 January 1783). Three sets of orchestral parts for 'Mia speranza' from Mozart's lifetime indicate that two further performances of it took place in the next eight years. See Edge, 'Mozart's Viennese Copyists', pp. 1271–1274.

[7] MBA, vol. 3, p. 275; LMF, p. 852 (21 June 1783).

[8] For Mozart's statement, presented in both Italian and German, see MDL, pp. 192–193 and MDB, p. 217; MBA, vol. 3, p. 276 and LMF, p. 854 (2 July 1783).

opera's performance on account of it displeasing Count Orsini-Rosenberg, the manager of the court theatres.[9]

It is difficult to conceive of Mozart as entirely blameless in this affair, even based on the information he himself provides.[10] Salieri's behaviour, as the influential Kapellmeister at court, was probably motivated by a need for diplomatic mediation rather than by supposed hostility towards his fellow composer.[11] Mozart perhaps exaggerated the 'enemies' (*feinde*) repeatedly referenced in his letter as there is no external evidence to support their existence at this time. If enemies were in fact real rather than imagined, they are as likely to have been motivated by the behaviour of a man 'as touchy as gunpowder'[12] according to Michael Kelly, the first Don Basilio and Don Curzio in *Figaro*, as by jealousy of his extraordinary musical talent. Mozart's statement issued with the libretto about not wanting to damage Anfossi's reputation has a whiff of disingenuousness to it in light of Mozart's report of the success of his numbers and the failure of the rest of the opera.[13] And he shot from the hip at Adamberger after Adamberger had agreed to the omission of 'Per pietà': 'He did not please at all [in the performance], as was the only possible outcome! Now he is sorry, but too late. Because if he asked me today to give him the rondò, I wouldn't hand it over.'[14] As at the beginning of his career in Vienna, then, Mozart's apparently unsubtle behaviour does not harmonize with his refined musical strategies.

Mozart probably had the instrumentation of 'Mia speranza', 'Vorrei spiegarvi' and 'No, che non sei capace' prominent in mind, as well as Lange's vocal qualities, when composing them and envisaging their performance.[15] On sending an earlier Lange aria 'Non so d'onde viene', K. 294, to Leopold in 1778, he explained: 'You cannot imagine what effect the aria makes with

---

[9]   MBA, vol. 3, p. 277; LMF, p. 854 (2 July 1783).

[10] This is a view echoed by John Rice in *Antonio Salieri and Viennese Opera* (Chicago: University of Chicago Press, 1998), pp. 463–464.

[11] Volkmar Braunbehrens, *Maligned Master: The Real Story of Antonio Salieri*, trans. Eveline L. Kanes (New York: Fromm, 1992), p. 117.

[12] MDL, p. 456; MDB, p. 532. Touchiness at this time was further evident in Mozart taking umbrage at Varesco's suggestion that *L'oca del Cairo* might not be a success. See MBA, vol. 3, p. 275; LMF, p. 853 (21 June 1783).

[13] See MBA, vol. 3, p. 276; LMF, pp. 853–854 (2 July 1783). On Mozart's probable disingenuousness, see also Rushton, *Mozart: Master Musicians*, p. 111.

[14] MBA, vol. 3, p. 277; LMF, p. 854 (2 July 1783).

[15] On Lange's qualities, including her 'clarity of vocal tone . . . suspenseful waxing and waning . . . [and] subtle shading', see Schönfeld, 'Yearbook of the Music of Vienna and Prague', p. 306. Lange's vocal qualities are also explained in Gidwitz, 'Vocal Portraits of Four Mozart Sopranos', pp. 42–49. For discussion of 'Mia speranza', 'Vorrei spiegarvi' and 'No, che non sei capace' specifically, including Lange's extended range, developed cantabile and ability to handle coloratura, see Gidwitz, 'Vocal Portraits', pp. 72–75.

instruments. You cannot just look at it [in score]; it really must be sung by a Miss Weber.'[16] A few months earlier, after performing it to great acclaim in Mannheim, Mozart also remarked: 'Here I heard it for the first time with instruments. I wish you also could have heard it, but exactly as it was produced and sung there, with that accuracy in taste, piano and forte. … The orchestra has not stopped praising the aria and talking about it.'[17] As explained in Chapter 2, 'Nehmt meinen Dank' K. 383 (April 1782), probably for Lange, also prioritizes orchestral effects, even if perhaps more for Mozart's benefit than hers in the run-up to the premiere of *Die Entführung*.

From 'Mia speranza adorata', K. 416, it seems Mozart's view at that time was that Lange's voice blended effectively and poignantly with a solo oboe in the same register. As Gandarte (Aloysia) tells lover Zemira 'I won't see you again' and bids farewell forever in the opening recitative, solo oboe lines merge with the voice (see, for instance, Example 6.1). The touching, *empfindsam* qualities of the classical oboe were noted during – and shortly after – Mozart's life, including by Leopold Mozart who commented on the melancholic effect of oboe virtuoso Carlo Besozzi's perfectly executed sustained notes.[18] Moreover, as Johann von Schönfeld and Heinrich Koch respectively explained: the oboe had 'remarkably great similarity' to the voice, possessing a melting quality and gracefulness; and 'The good tone of this instrument, among all wind instruments, draws most close to the treble [Discant] voice.'[19]

'Vorrei spiegarvi, oh Dio!' (K. 418), written a few months after 'Mia speranza adorata', builds on Mozart's association between Lange's voice and the oboe. Here, Clorinda tries to resist the temptation to fall in love with her suitor, the Contino, who has been persuaded by Clorinda's fiancé Marquess Calandrino to test her fidelity.[20] In the Adagio of her two-tempo aria, the text of which is repeated, she talks of the grief and self-restraint

---

[16] MBA, vol. 2, p. 517; LMF, p. 638 (3 December 1778).

[17] MBA, vol. 2, p. 327; LMF, p. 517 (24 March 1778).

[18] MBA, vol. 2, p. 362; LMF, p. 540 (28 May 1778). See also Arnold, *Mozarts Geist* (1803), p. 227 (on oboe solos in *Die Entführung* and *Don Giovanni*); Heinrich Christoph Koch, *Musikalisches Lexikon* (Frankfurt, 1802), col. 1083; Haynes, 'Mozart and the Classical Oboe', p. 58.

[19] Schönfeld, *Jahrbuch der Tonkunst*, pp. 191–192 ('ausserordentlich viel Aehnliches'); Koch, *Musikalisches Lexikon*, col. 1084. ('Der gute Ton dieses Instrumentes nähert sich unter allen Blasinstrumenten der Discantstimme am mehresten'.) See also Johann Georg Sulzer's *Allgemeine Theorie der schönen Künste* (1771–1774); given in Baker and Christensen (eds. and trans.), *Selected Writings of Johann Georg Sulzer and Heinrich Christoph Koch*, p. 97. The ability of the oboe effectively to accompany a female or counter-tenor voice is also noted in Vandenbroeck, *Traité général de tous les instrumens à vent à l'usage des compositeurs*, p. 54.

[20] It is possible that the short score of K. 178 (probably 1783) represents an early version of K. 418. Only the vocal line is in Mozart's hand in the autograph of K. 178; the accompaniment could be by Aloys Fuchs. See NMA, II/7/3, Kritischer Bericht, p. 69.

Example 6.1 Mozart, 'Mia speranza adorata', K. 416, bars 7–11.

that convey unintended cruelty in her interactions with the Count. Mozart's orchestral accompaniment, redolent in this instance of his 'art of dramatic instrumentation' according to Abert,[21] divides into three

---

[21] Abert, *W. A. Mozart*, p. 911.

distinct layers that collectively reinforce support for Clorinda's emotional expression: delicate strings, comprising muted first violins and pizzicato second violins, violas and cellos/basses; warm bassoons and horns (with late-eighteenth-century bassoons now capable of producing a stronger, warmer sound than in earlier eras, partially on account of their thinner walls);[22] and an obbligato oboe that ebbs and flows in sympathy with the vocal melody. The strings are present throughout the section; the horns and bassoons mostly alternate with the oboe after Clorinda's entry, until all are heard together at bar 37 as if collectively trying to rouse Clorinda (or to speak for her) when she mentions falling silent. After dominating the initial orchestral introduction, the oboe intermeshes melodically with the voice, as its *pièce de resistance* colouring the weeping ('piangere') that Clorinda considers fate to have bestowed upon her (bars 27–35, Example 6.2). The oboe and Clorinda are in perfect union in this passage, alternately leading and following: they are cut from the same cloth performing in the same register. At the corresponding moment in the repeat of the text, the musical depiction of the weeping is still more poignant, with a turn to the tonic minor and the aria's vocal peak on e''' (Example 6.3): the registral climax is generated as much by the oboe as by the voice on account of the interweaving of the two parts, Clorinda's e''' immediately following the oboe's a'' – c-natural''' in bar 71. In the Allegro, addressed more to the Count and his need to leave Clorinda and rejoin his lover Emilia than to Clorinda's own emotions, the close inter-meshing of voice and oboe extends to the strings, albeit less colourfully and pictorially. The strings offer phrase links neatly joining vocal con-tributions (bars 82, 92, 108–110), including when Clorinda's intense emotions from the Adagio resurface (108–110).[23] At Clorinda's climactic moment in the Allegro (marked 'più allegro' from bar 124), the strings gently complement her line, rising when she falls and retreating slightly to g-sharp'' when she sings her d''' (see bars 133–136).[24]

Mozart's 'No, che non sei capace' K. 419 for Lange in *Il curioso indiscreto* is a genuine bravura aria, unlike the other two for her.[25] Clorinda reacts

---

[22] See James B. Kopp, *The Bassoon* (New Haven: Yale University Press, 2012), p. 86.

[23] In these bars Clorinda speaks of being 'lost' if the Count stays with her, just as she previously 'weeps' at the cruelty of her fate.

[24] Mozart also tailored K. 418 to Lange's strong portamento singing; see Patricia Levy Gidwitz, '"Ich bin die erste Sängerin": Vocal Profiles of Two Mozart Sopranos', *Early Music*, 19 (1991), pp. 565–579, at 570–571.

[25] In addition to performances of K. 416 and K. 419 during Mozart's lifetime, Lange sang both arias at Constanze's Leipzig Gewandhaus concert on 11 November 1795; see MDL, p. 416 and MDB, p. 478.

Example 6.2 Mozart, 'Vorrei spiegarvi, oh Dio!' K. 418, bars 28–35.

angrily to discovering that the Count had told Marquess Calandrino that she had been unfaithful, explaining to the Count she now abhors him and abhors herself still more for momentarily falling for him. The note of defiance in the text strikes a chord with Konstanze's 'Martern aller Arten' from *Die Entführung*, which is also in C major. To be sure, 'No, che non sei capace' is only half the length of 'Martern', does not build as grand

Example 6.3 Mozart, 'Vorrei spiegarvi, oh Dio!' K. 418, bars 68–72.

a structural edifice and contains less intricate and ostentatious orchestral writing. But there are thematic and gestural parallels between the two arias. The beginning of 'No, che non sei capace' is a kind of composite of gestures from 'Martern', including its one-note *forte* exchanges at 'Nichts, nichts' in bars 77–78, the continuation in bars 79–80 and the melodic outline and octave texture at the first vocal entry in bars 61–62 (see 'No, no', bars 1–2; 'di cortesia, d'onore', bars 9–11, and 'che non sei capace', bars 3–5 in K. 419, Example 6.4). The first nine bars of the 'Allegro assai' of 'No, che non sei capace' (76–84, Example 6.5) also re-work the opening of the 'Allegro assai' from 'Martern' (149ff.): the *forte* orchestra is pitched against the voice, the C-G outline of the former answered by the G-C outline of the latter; and the continuations (bar 80ff. in K. 419 and 154ff. in 'Martern') both feature C pedals in the cellos and basses and accents in the upper strings and wind. Some similarities are to be expected on account of the key, the demonstrations of emotional strength from both characters, and the temporal proximity of the arias. But parallels become more telling once Lange's highly successful association with Konstanze in *Die Entführung* is

Example 6.4 Mozart, 'No, che non sei capace', K. 419, bars 1–12.

factored into the equation. She was the highest paid female singer at the Burgtheater in 1782–1783 and may only have missed the role of Konstanze at the premiere as a result of giving birth in May 1781 and thus being indisposed when singers and roles were settled a couple of

Example 6.5 Mozart, 'No, che non sei capace', K. 419, bars 76–84.

months later.[26] She sang Konstanze in Frankfurt in late 1783, at a benefit performance at the Burgtheater on 25 January 1784 repeated a week later, and on numerous occasions at the Kärntnertortheater and elsewhere in 1785–1789.[27] Thus, it is perhaps no surprise that a replacement aria written expressly to suit Lange's voice bears a resemblance either at Mozart's initiative or at Lange's (or both combined) to one Lange would soon make her own.

Different in orientation to the Lange arias, the two for Adamberger from 1783, 'Per pietà, non ricercate' (K. 420) for *Il curioso indiscreto* and 'Misero! O sogno – Aura, che intorno spiri' (K. 431), also connect vocal and orchestral effects in promoting the solo performer. While Mozart cultivates a special relationship between Lange and the oboe in 'Mia speranza' and 'Vorrei spiegarvi', he primarily exploits Adamberger's interaction with a full cohort of winds in 'Per pietà' and 'Misero!'. The strength and beauty of Adamberger's voice was recognized in the late eighteenth century and even as late as 1798 by Salieri (for the then fifty-five-year-old);[28] thus he was apparently in a position to benefit from singing with a large and colourful complement of winds. In 'Hier soll ich dich denn sehen' from *Die Entführung*, Adamberger is accompanied by the cherished clarinets-bassoons-horns timbre[29] and generally by the wind group as a whole when upper strings are absent; the same wind combination (unaccompanied) leads off the concluding Allegretto of 'Wenn die Freude Tränen fliessen' as well. And in 'Ich baue', the substantial cohort of double flutes, clarinets, bassoons and horns is heard both in isolation and alone with Adamberger. The five-bar Adagio midway through the Allegro assai section of 'Per pietà' is also distinctive for its instrumental and vocal effects (Example 6.6). The slower tempo, the absence of accompaniment for three bars and the three pause markings may have encouraged Adamberger to perform the segment with temporal and expressive freedom.[30] Simultaneously, Mozart nurtures the special effect of a harmonized, swelling chord in the wind

[26] On the first point, see the theatre account books transcribed in Link, *National Court Theatre*, p. 405; on the second, see Rushton, *Mozart*, p. 106.

[27] See MDL, pp. 196, 225, 306, 307; MDB, pp. 221, 256, 348, 350. See also NMD, pp. 110–111. Michael Kelly, the first Don Basilio and Don Curzio in *Le nozze di Figaro*, mistakenly remembered Konstanze being written for Lange, no doubt on account of her later prominence in the role. See MDL, p. 456; MDB, p. 532.

[28] See Bauman, 'Mozart's Belmonte', pp. 559–561.

[29] The aesthetic value of this timbre, associated with the *Harmonie*, is cited in Francoeur, *Diapason général*, p. 35, and discussed in Chapters 1 and 9.

[30] On liberties taken by late-eighteenth-century performers at fermatas, including embellishments and tempo fluctuations, see Brown, *Classical and Romantic Performing Practice*, pp. 421–422, 588–595.

Example 6.6 Mozart, 'Per pietà, non ricercate', K. 420, bars 119–125.

(bars 122–123), again promoting the clarinets-bassoons-horns timbre. Solo wind swells originate in the repeated *p – cresc – p* unison gestures in the Andante of the aria. In the first half of the Allegro assai, wind unisons, wind swells and a moment of freedom for Adamberger occur separately (in imitations, *sfp*s, and two pauses in consecutive bars), with the Adagio then bringing them together: Mozart's compositional skill (harmonious wind sonorities) and Adamberger's strong and beautiful voice thereby had an opportunity to reinforce each other.[31] The Adagio is both a climax to sonorities explored so far and a catalyst for reimagining earlier sounds, including the *sf – p* unisons in winds and tremolo strings at the Primo tempo and the harmonized, chorale-like wind effect. The alternately suave and expansive, and fast and furious final section leaves ambiguous how 'consoled' the Count actually would be by death ('chiamo solo, oh Dio, la morte che mi venga a consolar'), which is perhaps Mozart's point.

Combined compositional and performance effects are also a feature of 'Misero!' K. 431, which was probably written between March 1783

---

[31] Einstein also notes the frequency of dynamic markings in the aria, especially crescendi and sforzandi, considering them redolent of 'an intensification of emotion'. See Einstein, *Mozart: His Character, His Work*, p. 385.

and January 1784 and is adapted from Caterino Mazzolà's libretto *L'isola capricciosa.*[32] In the first half of the aria's Andante sostenuto, the winds principally offer links between vocal statements. But the situation changes at 'Aura, che intorno spiri': a swathe of wind sound envelops the voice's descending sequence and includes a neatly interwoven bassoon in its prized high register (Example 6.7).[33] The most noticeable instrumental and vocal effects of the aria follow after that. Numerous pauses may have encouraged Adamberger to sing flexibly and freely, and in the process to draw attention to advantageous qualities such as fine portamento and beautiful vocal sound. The proliferation of instrumental dynamics from bar 36 onwards invite a greater degree of instrumental nuance than hitherto in the aria. And the *fps* for winds and strings in bars 60–65, meticulously notated on the requisite weak beats in six staves of the autograph, coincide with held notes for Adamberger, an opportunity for him to exploit a known specialty.[34] Like the Adagio in 'Per pietà', this conclusion to the Andante sostenuto, promoting both singer and instrumentalists, is a pivot to a new relationship between voice and orchestra in the remainder of the aria (Allegro assai), the winds being more variedly combined with the voice than earlier, including in imitative dialogue.

Mozart's bass aria 'Così dunque tradisci – Aspri rimorsi atroci', K. 432 (1782–1783) to Metastasio's text from *Temistocle* was almost certainly intended for Johann Ludwig Fischer, the first Osmin in *Die Entführung.*[35] It brings together the explosiveness of 'Solche hergelauf'ne Laffen', including

[32] On a premiere for K. 431 at the Tonkünstler-Societät concert on 22 December 1783, see J. Rigbie Turner's introduction to the autograph facsimile W. A. Mozart, *'Misero! O sogno' – 'Aura, che intorno spiri': Arie für Tenor und Orchester, KV431* (Kassel: Bärenreiter, 1988), n. p. For the December concert advertisement and the probable association of the 'new Rondeaux' listed for Adamberger with K. 431, see MDL, p. 195; MDB, p. 220. In an insightful article on K. 431, however, John Rice has tentatively proposed K. 420 as the work sung by Adamberger on 22 December, referring to features of K. 431 atypical of a rondò. Rice also identified the hitherto unacknowledged adaptation of Mazzolà's text from *L'isola cappriciosa.* See Rice, 'Problems of Genre and Gender in Mozart's Scena "Misero! O sogno, o son desto" K. 431', *Mozart-Jahrbuch 2000*, pp. 73–89.

[33] As Rice explains ('Problems of Genre and Gender', p. 76): 'Aria texts addressed to breezes and zephyrs invited composers to write lavish parts for wind instruments.' On the positive effect of the bassoon's upper register see Béthizy, *Exposition de la théorie et de la pratique de la musique*, p. 306, and *Musikalischer Almanach 1782*, pp. 93–95. The voice and winds are also combined in the Andante con moto of the recitative (bars 8–15).

[34] On held notes as one of Adamberger's specialties, see Bauman, 'Mozart's Belmonte', p. 560. For a facsimile of the autograph see Mozart, *'Misero! O sogno' – 'Aura, che intorno spiri'.*

[35] On the aria being written for Fischer, see Corneilson, *Autobiography of Ludwig Fischer*, p. 13; Rushton, *Mozart*, p. 283; Cliff Eisen, 'Fischer, (Johann Ignaz) Ludwig', in *Cambridge Mozart Encyclopedia*, p. 176; Clive, *Mozart and His Circle*, p. 52; H. C. Robbins Landon (ed.),

Example 6.7 Mozart, 'Misero, o sogno! – Aura, che intorno spiri', K. 431, bars 29–33.

its raging coda, and the obsession of 'O wie will ich triumphieren'; Sebaste's agonized and impulsive reflections on his treacherous behaviour towards the noble Temistocle resonate with Osmin's thirst for revenge over his heroic enemies. The exposed low bass register F – E-natural – E-flat – D in 'Aspri rimorsi atroci', recognized by Mozart and others as one of Fischer's special strengths (see Chapter 2), and the numerous dynamic inflections and accents strategically placed for maximum effect also invoke Osmin's music. When the voice descends into its nether region, perhaps 'glowing' as Mozart said Fischer's did, it is lightly accompanied and always *piano*, but immediately followed by an accent at *fp* or *sf – p* or by a brief *forte* passage: each low note is thereby emphasized in isolation and through its musical surroundings. The lowest of all, the Ds in bars 35 and 38 (Example 6.8), come at the end of the initial statement of the text and shortly before the 'reprise':[36] the first grows from the flute's arpeggiated descent after the *forte* winds have dropped out; the second, following a *crescendo* to *forte* and a return to *piano*, precedes the longest *crescendo* of the aria in the run up

---

The Mozart Compendium (London: Thames & Hudson, 1990), p. 327; Konrad, *Mozart: Catalogue of His Works*, p. 69; Solomon, *Mozart: A Life*, p. 296.

[36] Don Neville identifies K. 432 as a sonata form without development, bar 43 thereby comprising the beginning of the recapitulation. See Neville, 'Metastasio (Trapassi), Pietro', in Eisen and Keefe (eds.), *Cambridge Mozart Encyclopedia*, p. 287.

Example 6.8 Mozart, 'Così dunque tradisci – Aspri rimorso atroci', K. 432, bars 32–39.

to the reprise.[37] Once high notes of e-flat' and f' and big leaps are also factored into the equation, 'Aspri rimorsi atroci' can be seen to play to the kind of vocal flexibility Johann Friedrich Reichardt identified with Fischer in 1792 (see Chapter 2).

L'oca del Cairo and Lo sposo deluso, 1783–1785

Setting aside *Figaro*, begun in mid-1785, three works occupied the lion's share of Mozart's operatic attention in 1782–1786: the unfinished *L'oca del Cairo* (1783–1784) and *Lo sposo deluso* (probably 1784–1785);[38] and *Der Schauspieldirektor* (1786, discussed below). As an extended incomplete work *L'oca del Cairo* offers special insight into Mozart's early-stage thinking about the role of performers in conveying expressive content. Vocal parts and an instrumental bass are apparently complete in most of the numbers for which *particellas* are extant. Other orchestral material, present only from time to time, points to sounds, textures, timbres and effects prioritized by Mozart at the outset, in similar fashion to the Sequence and Offertory movements of the unfinished Requiem (1791).[39]

In *L'oca del Cairo* Mozart carefully plots instrumental and vocal effects for Chichibio's aria no. 3 'Ogni momento', the unnumbered duet 'Ho un pensiero', and the quartet no. 5 'S'oggi, oh Dei'. No. 3, an exit aria for Chichibio who bemoans the lack of fidelity of women in (wrongly) sensing betrayal by his lover Auretta, begins with a ten-bar orchestral introduction (Example 6.9). Timbral intricacies, including trumpets that join the oboes and horns in octaves only for the last four notes of the consequent (bars 3–4), second violins that double the firsts in octaves in bars 6–7 but not elsewhere, and a reduction of the original antecedent-consequent to

---

[37] In the four bars before the reprise, Mozart reimagines events of the last ten bars of the recitative that led to the original statement of the theme at the beginning of the aria and where string tremolos, strictly coordinated rhythms and a crescendo foreshadow the intensity of the ensuing aria.

[38] *Lo sposo deluso* is traditionally dated 1783–1784. But paper types suggest either 1784 or 1784–1785. See Tyson, *Autograph Scores*, p. 240 and 'Proposed New Dates for Many Works and Fragments Written by Mozart from March 1781 to December 1791', in Eisen (ed.), *Mozart Studies*, pp. 213–226, at 219. Neal Zaslaw dates the aria fragments to 1785 on account of Aloysia Lange not featuring on the cast list after her removal from the Italian to the German opera troupe. See Zaslaw, 'Waiting for *Figaro*', p. 415. Andrew Dell'Antonio explains that the listing of 'Signora Fischer' (Storace's married name) on the libretto puts the composition no earlier than May 1784. See 'The Fragments of *Lo sposo deluso*', p. 412.

[39] On the Requiem in this respect, see Keefe, *Mozart's Requiem*, pp. 107–171. For the autograph of *L'oca del Cairo*, see Staatsbibliothek zu Berlin, Mus.ms.autogr. Mozart, W. A. 422.

Example 6.9 Mozart, Aria 'Ogni momento', from *L'oca del Cairo*, K. 422, bars 1–10.

opening and closing gestures at a *piano* dynamic (bars 6–8), presumably explain why Mozart wrote so much for instruments here relative to the rest of the work. With little harmonically, melodically or rhythmically out of the ordinary in an ostensibly brash, hunt-like opening, Mozart signals timbral ebb and flow as a primary focus. Evolving timbres and textures are also a feature of Auretta and Chichibio's 'Ho un pensiero'. Precise attention to performance detail in the orchestral introduction, including numerous *f – p*, *fp*, *p* and *pp* markings in just seven bars (Example 6.10),[40] is followed by a series of introduction-derived annotations in the remainder of the number that are associated with a new timbre each time: trills for two bassoons alone and later two oboes alone (both *piano*); fragments of the main theme for oboes and bassoons together; trills for two oboes and a single bassoon together; the main theme in the horns, partially supported by the bassoons, alongside trills in the oboes and bassoons; the hunting horn alone (*forte*); and the main theme at the end (*forte*), in tutti winds and strings but without bassoons. How Mozart would have completed his orchestration, of course, is unclear. But judging by instrumental annotations across the *particella*, he placed as much emphasis on timbral variety as on '[maintaining] a sense of unity'.[41] The *double entendre* 'Astolf's horn' is the catalyst for the horn's participation in the second half, even if other instrumental writing is seemingly unmotivated by textual imagery. As in *Die Entführung* then,

---

[40] In addition to the autograph itself, see the autograph facsimile of bars 1–8 of 'Ho un pensiero' in NMA, II/5/13/1, p. xv.

[41] See Abert's assessment (*W. A. Mozart*, p. 917) of instrumental annotations promoting unity in this number.

Example 6.10 Mozart, Duet 'Ho un pensiero', from *L'oca del Cairo*, K. 422, bars 1–7.

albeit without the protracted text painting of 'O wie ängstlich', Mozart apparently envisaged instrumental colours and effects opening a channel of communication with his audience. A similar point emerges from the quartet no. 5 for four characters whose unions are thwarted by Don Pippo's marriage plans (Celidora, Lavina, Biondello and Calandrino). After the opening statement, two passages notated for first violins (in addition to cello and bass parts) are closely coordinated with the voices. In bars 39–43 (Example 6.11) the violins interweave with Biondello, beginning with the two gs with which he had ended his previous phrase. Later, the first simultaneous appearance of two voices in the number yields a call and response with violins and an ebb and flow of melodically and rhythmically synchronized and independent voices and violins in the same register (bars 77–86, Example 6.12).[42] Mozart's markings in the quartet also encourage distinctive renditions: violins and cellos/basses are asked to play *sotto voce* at the opening; and the first *pp* of the number, tremolo in the cellos and basses, with a crescendo to *f*, coincides with the first appearance of the four singers as a uniform group at the opening of the Più Allegro.

---

[42] The annotation for first violin in the middle of the duet no. 1 for Auretta and Chichibio 'Così si fa' (see bars 52–59) is somewhat similar to these two passages, the violin being carefully interwoven with the two voices.

Example 6.11 Mozart, 'S'oggi, oh Dei', from *L'oca del Cairo*, K. 422, bars 39–45 (all other staves blank).

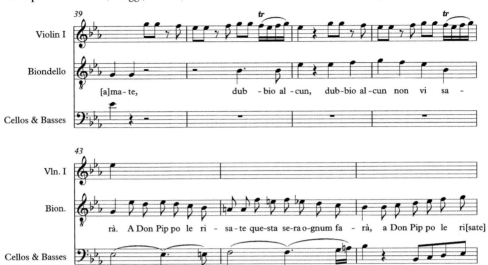

The chain finale of *L'oca del Cairo*, no. 6, foreshadows the famous Act 2 finale of *Figaro* in several respects: tonic and dominant tonalities for the first two sections mirrored in the dominant – tonic tonalities of the concluding sections (B-flat – F; F – B-flat); character entries coinciding with the start of sections and marked by modulations (Auretta and Don Pippo respectively in bar 143 [d] and bar 227 [C]); and a quicker tempo at the end of the ensemble than at the beginning to capture increasingly frenetic activity on stage.[43] Like earlier numbers, the finale continues to foreground instrumental and vocal effects. While the spirits of the lovers are high at the opening, Celidora and Lavina strike a note of uncertainty in the recitative connecting the end of the Allegro to the Adagio by asking what will happen if Don Pippo arrives on the scene and finds them with Biondello and Calandrino. Anxieties are heightened in the Allegro from bar 143 onwards, when Auretta and then Chichibio announce Don Pippo's impending arrival and the consequent danger to Celidora, Lavina, Biondello and Calandrino. Mozart reserves his most substantial instrumental writing since the opening statement of the finale, and most effect-laden music of the entire opera, for the Adagio between the recitative

---

[43] On characteristics of opera buffa finales in late-eighteenth-century Vienna, see Hunter, *Culture of Opera Buffa in Mozart's Vienna*, pp. 210–226. For a brief discussion of the *L'oca del Cairo* finale, see Goehring, 'The opere buffe', pp. 136–138.

Example 6.12 Mozart, 'S'oggi, oh Dei', from *L'oca del Cairo*, K. 422, bars 77–86 (all other staves blank).

and ensuing Allegro (see Example 6.13), the calm before the storm. Decorative elaboration, characteristic of codependent composition and performance (see Chapter 1), appears in the first violin and cellos and basses: neighbour notes quicken twice in bars 130–131 and again in 134–135 as the volume increases from *pp* to *f*; and the scotch-snap arpeggios in bar 137 are elaborated in demisemiquavers two bars later. Numerous dynamics and articulation marks (strokes and slurs), together with *sotto voce* emotion from the voices, point to a desire for especially expressive performance. When Don Pippo does arrive on scene later, the *sotto voce* annotation for the four lovers (bar 235) allows singers to bring the performance of the Adagio to mind at the very moment that implications of Celidora and Lavina's concerned question about Pippo immediately before the Adagio are fully realized. Even incomplete, the Finale's Adagio is reminiscent of the Andantino from the Act 2 quartet of *Die Entführung* (see Chapter 2); in mood and style it foreshadows 'Soave s'il vento' from *Così fan tutte* (1789–1790).

Lo sposo deluso was composed with the singers of Vienna's newly restored Italian opera in mind; on a manuscript of the libretto the seven prospective principals are listed as Francesco Benucci, Nancy Storace (given as Fischer, her married name), Stefano Mandini, Catarina Cavalieri, Francesco Bussani, Pugnetti and Therese Teiber.[44] The one completed number, the trio no. 4 'Che accidenti!' for Eugenia, Don Asdrubale and Bocconio, is of particular interest where issues around performance are concerned. It begins after Don Asdrubale, the lover Eugenia thought dead, reproaches Eugenia for her supposed infidelity. Along with Bocconio, who wants to marry Eugenia himself, the characters ruminate on the tense situation in which they find themselves, commenting on the cruelty of love and the punishment it metes out. As has been noted, the action does not move on significantly during the trio; indeed, for one critic the trio is 'marred by the fact that its opening and concluding situations are identical'.[45] But Mozart creates musical momentum through primarily textural and dynamic intensifications in the second half of the ensemble that coincide with the three voices joining forces to lament their collective suffering. At the opening of the ensemble the orchestra crescendos from *p* to *f* and falls back to *p* (bars 3–5), a swell crystallized in the

---

[44] It is possible that Lorenzo Da Ponte authored the libretto of *Lo sposo deluso*, basing it on a Roman intermezzo. See Alessandra Campana, 'Il libretto de "Lo sposo deluso"', *Mozart-Jahrbuch* (1988–1989), pp. 573–588.

[45] Knepler, *Mozart*, p. 110. See also Rushton, *Mozart*, p. 189; Abert, *W. A. Mozart*, p. 921.

Example 6.13 Mozart, Finale 'Su via putti, presto, presto!' from *L'oca del Cairo*, K. 422, bars 130–142 (all other staves blank).

ensuing *fp*.[46] A number of *fps* in the next forty or so bars can be performed with varying degrees of accented inflection in accordance with late-eighteenth-century practice;[47] for example, those in bar 43 could be relatively pronounced on account of the B-flat minor tonality and the voices singing together for the first time. Irrespective of the rendering of *fps*, the first unambiguous tutti *forte*, heard for a full four beats (bars 54–55), is appreciably different from anything that precedes it: the voices in octaves highlight the cruelty of love, with an *f* marked in every instrumental and vocal part. It is also the first of several moments where the dynamic parameters of the ensemble are broadened, including the longest tutti *f* passage in the ensemble so far (bars 56–60), *sotto voce* indications for the three imitative voices (61–65), and a big *f* – *p* echo (65–67). In the last six bars of the number (Example 6.14) several effects new to the ensemble occur simultaneously, amounting to further dynamic intensification: all voices and instruments are brought down to *pp* (prior to the beginning of Example 6.14); individual instrumental sonorities receive swells (now *sfps*); and the tutti orchestra play *pp* by themselves at the end. Mozart thus asks vocalists and instrumentalists to shape the ensemble in such a way as to intensify the performance of the second half relative to the first half, even in the absence of a concomitant development in the dramatic situation.

We will recall from *Die Entführung* the importance Mozart placed on ending Act 1 'with lots of noise' and bringing his Turkish music into the overture *forte* in the context of 'alternating *pianos* and *fortes*'; dynamic contrasts and other effects are therefore part of Mozart's strategy for engaging his audience. The overture and quartet no. 1 ('Ah, ah, ah, ah') of *Lo sposo deluso*, which are joined together to comprise a single long number sharing thematic material, are also revealing in this respect.[48] Mozart sets the mood for his festive march in the first fifteen bars (fully scored, unlike the rest of the number). But perhaps the most distinctive feature of the overture is Mozart's play with accents and dynamics. After an *sf* – *p* in which the two dynamics are coordinated with the first beat of each bar (16–17), a more unusual *p* – *sf* – *p* effect has the *sf* placed on the fourth quaver of the bar (Example 6.15). *Sforzandi* are then heard on strong and weak beats in the remainder of the exposition and on both in the final bars of the section (Example 6.16) as if to

---

[46] Occurring immediately before the first vocal entry, the *fp* was first notated in a sketch for the ensemble; see NMA, II/5/14, p. 112.

[47] Badura-Skoda and Badura-Skoda, *Interpreting Mozart*, p. 58.

[48] The overture comprises, in effect, an exposition and an Andante that takes the place of a development section. The quartet no. 1 begins with a compressed reprise of the overture's exposition.

Example 6.14 Mozart, 'Che accidenti!' from *Lo sposo deluso*, K. 430, bars 91–94.

Example 6.15 Mozart, Overture from *Lo sposo deluso*, K. 430, bars 26–30 (where only the string parts were written by Mozart).

Example 6.16 Mozart, Overture from *Lo sposo deluso*, K. 430, bars 117–122 (where only the string parts were written by Mozart).

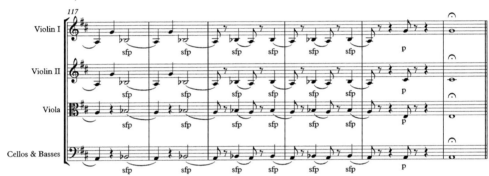

capture in microcosm the eclectic distribution of accents up to this point. Beginning as a thematically compressed recapitulation of overture material, the quartet no. 1 quickly arrives at the gesture in bar 8 to coincide with the indication that the curtain should be opened. Retained for much of the next fifteen bars or so, the gesture heralds the arrival of the voices (see bars 23–28) and subsequently resurfaces in the secondary key area as in the overture (bars 62–67), delineates a moment of thematic and tonal return (bar 85), and takes its place in the concluding Più Allegro (see bars 188–195).

Opera Inserts, 1785–1786

In addition to the arias for Lange and Adamberger in Anfossi's *Il curioso indiscreto* (1783) Mozart wrote opera inserts in 1785–1786: a quartet 'Dite almeno' K. 479 and trio 'Mandina amabile' K. 480 for Francesco Bianchi's opera buffa *La villanella rapita* (5 and 21 November 1785); and a new duet and scena for the Viennese revival of *Idomeneo*, K. 489 and K. 490 (10 March 1786). As in the Lange and Adamberger works, Mozart brings together instrumental effects and the promotion of individual singers, even in ensembles where by his own admission attention often could not be directed towards star performers.[49]

Mozart's work for the Viennese revision of *La villanella rapita* appears not to have created the controversy wrought by his insertion arias for *Il curioso indiscreto* two years earlier; in fact, it was warmly received in the Italian press.[50] Featuring a peasant (Mandina) harassed by a Count in full view of her lover, Pippo, the plot of *La villanella rapita* bears more than a passing resemblance to *Le nozze di Figaro* and other opere buffe staged in Vienna in 1785–1786.[51] In Mozart's trio for Act 1, 'Mandina amabile' K. 480, the Count offers money to a grateful Mandina, who naively accepts it as a princely favour without suspecting lecherous motives, whereupon a confused and suspicious Pippo arrives suddenly on the scene. A notable musical effect coincides with Pippo's entrance (bar 117, Example 6.17), which activates the imbroglio: the full orchestra participate *f* and *sf* to coincide with a change in tempo to Allegro and a shift from the tonic A major to A minor. It resonates with Mozart's description of Osmin's rage, where musical moderation is deemed necessary even in the face of emotional extremes: continuities between the two sections of the trio, including the retention of all instruments from the end of the Andante at the beginning of the Allegro and a move to the tonic minor rather than further afield, coexist with a big musical jolt. The moment gave Mozart at least a little pause for thought, judging by alterations to the autograph: natural signs designating a move to A minor are included on instrumental staves at the opening of bar 117, but are then crossed out and accidentals included when appropriate instead; and a 'col flauti' indication on the oboe stave is smudged out and replaced by material in octaves for two oboes.[52]

The opening of the Allegro follows hot on the heels of a musically intimate relationship in the Andante cultivated between the ingenuous Mandina and

---

[49] See MBA, vol. 3, p. 73; LMF, p. 699 (letter of 27 December 1780).

[50] The *Gazzetta universale* (24 January 1786), no. 7, p. 52 explains that *La villanella rapita* is 'only enriched' ('solo arricchita') by the contributions of the 'celebre Maestro' Mozart. See also *Gazzetta universale* (10 December 1785), no. 99, p. 788, which mentions the 'terzetti e quartetti nuovi dei Maestro Moshard'. Bianchi's opera was first staged in Venice in 1783. It was produced at the Burgtheater in Vienna on 25, 30 November and 7, 16, 30 December 1785 and 16 January, and 6, 17 February 1786; see Link, *National Theatre*, pp. 72–77.

[51] Hunter, *The Culture of Opera Buffa in Mozart's Vienna*, pp. 3–4; Knepler, *Mozart*, p. 114.

[52] For the autograph of 'Mandina amabile', see Staatsbibliothek zu Berlin Mus. ms. autogr. Mozart, W. A. 480.

Example 6.17 Mozart, 'Mandina amabile', K. 480, bars 114–119.

Example 6.18 Mozart, 'Mandina amabile', K. 480, bars 107–113 (voices only).

the Count, sung at the original production by Vincenzo Calvesi, the first Ferrando in *Così fan tutte*. A warm *Harmonie* timbre of two clarinets, two bassoons and two horns, heard unaccompanied at the opening before the entry of the singers, establishes itself as the Andante's dominant wind sonority, supporting the seduction scenario (of which Mandina remains unaware) through flowing imitation and juxtaposition with the voices. Sharing imitative material between themselves as well as with the orchestra, Mandina and the Count become increasingly close during the section, coming together to identify the happiness in their hearts ('che contento in cor mi sento') and – shortly before the end of the Andante – to offer matching lines that include coordinated pauses over two bars (Example 6.18). A strong gesture from Pippo is dramatically and musically necessary, then, as a first stage in dissolving what for him is a worryingly intimate relationship.

The effect at the onset of the Allegro, and developments later in the section, could have been designed specifically to accommodate Stefano Mandini's attributes. When reprising the role of Pippo in Paris in 1789, Mandini, the original Count Almaviva in *Figaro*, was commended not only for his 'very beautiful, unforced, wide ranging bass voice', but also for acting that was 'full of spirit, subtlety, and comic intentions, yet always natural. With a very noble size, figure and deportment he put into his peasant role the stupid awkwardness that suits this character.'[53] Mozart probably would have relied on Mandini demonstrating such qualities in bringing combined confusion, jealousy, inelegance and anxiety to bear on a performance of the trio's allegro, and not just at the beginning of the section. While his arrival initiates the imbroglio, his presence sustains it musically and dramatically. The Allegro

---

[53] *Mercure de France* (27 June 1789), p. 186: 'M. Mandini a une voix de basse très-belle, très-facile, très-étendue, & susceptible de chanter même le Tenore, auquel sa méthode excellente paroit convenir également. Son jeu est plein d'esprit, de finesse, d'intentions comiques, & pourtant toujours naturel. Avec une taille, une figure & un maintien fort nobles, il fait mettre dans son rôle de paysan la gaucherie niaise qui convient a ce caractère.' The critic describes Mozart's trio as 'charming' (*charmant*) (p. 185). For more late-eighteenth-century discussion of Mandini's splendid acting, and strong vocal technique, see Dorothea Link (ed.), *Arias for Stefano Mandini, Mozart's First Count Almaviva* (Middleton, WI: A-R Editions, 2015), pp. xii–xiii, xv, xxi.

integrates Pippo's anxiety-laden predilection for minor keys, modulations, and accents on weak beats with the Count and Mandina's calmer musical dispositions, including the Count's 'sol io lo so' statements suavely accompanied by a full-wind complement of flutes, oboes, clarinets, bassoons and horns (bars 169–175). When all three singers come together, expressing their different points of view, Mozart asks for an emotional rendition from them, writing *sotto voce*. This provides a particular challenge for the singer of Pippo, who must decide how much to blend with – or set himself apart from – his fellow singers, a musical and dramatic negotiation that again would have played to Mandini's strengths as an 'excellent actor' with 'flexible talent'.[54]

Mozart wrote new numbers for an operatic revival of a different kind in spring 1786, a few months after completing 'Dite almeno' and 'Mandina amabile'. On 13 March 1786, his own *Idomeneo* was staged at Prince Auersperg's private theatre in Vienna. The quality of the performers participating in the production was high, which would have pleased a composer who apparently had a special place in his heart for the opera. As the Novellos reported after their fact-finding trip to Austria in 1829 to talk to those who knew Mozart: 'The most happy time of his life was whilst at Munich during which he wrote *Idomeneo* which may account for the affection he entertained towards the work.'[55] Countess Hatzfeld (Elettra) was praised in Cramer's *Magazin der Musik* (1783) for her declamation in recitatives and her *parlante* style in arias.[56] Count Zinzendorf also admired her singing, likening one of her performances at Galitzin's to Nancy Storace (14 October 1783), the Italian Opera's star soprano with whom he was smitten, and marvelling at her Rose in Pierre-Alexandre Monsigny and Michel-Jean Sedaine's *Rose et Colas* (14 March 1784).[57] A reviewer in the Salzburg-based *Pfeffer und Salz* (5 April 1786) found *Idomeneo* too richly orchestrated, but reacted positively to the involvement of the Countess; again, she was mentioned in the same breath as Storace.[58]

---

[54] *Mercure de France* (27 June 1789), p. 186. The opening Allegro of Mozart's Act 1 quartet for *La villanella rapita*, 'Dite almeno' K. 479, shares some musical and dramatic characteristics with the Allegro of 'Mandina amabile': one singer is set against two, elegant writing against angular, accented material (in K. 479, Mandina versus Pippo and her father Biaggio, who sides with Pippo); and all three sing *sotto voce* towards the end, expressing differing perspectives (pain and torment caused by false accusations and by a putatively straying spouse). A character again enters midway through the ensemble (the Count in K. 479); when all four come together at the 'Piu stretto' to step back from their argument, which has escalated dangerously, Mozart asks the collective group to sing *sotto voce* as in the trio.

[55] Rosemary Hughes (ed.), *A Mozart Pilgrimage. Being the Travel Diaries of Vincent and Mary Novello in the Year 1829* (London: Novello, 1955), p. 94.

[56] *Magazin der Musik*, 1 (1783), pp. 387–388.   [57] Link, *National Court Theatre*, pp. 213, 219.

[58] MDL, p. 236; MDB, p. 270 (5 April 1786).

Zinzendorf also praised the Ilia Anna Puffendorf's acting in Johann Andreas Engelbrecht's *Die Nebenbuhler*, Charles Revière Dufresny's *L'esprit de contradiction* and Molière's *Les femmes savantes* in 1784 and 1791.[59]

Prince Auersperg's productions were lavish and employed professional orchestral players.[60] The participation of violin virtuoso Count August Clemens Hatzfeld, perhaps the Countess's brother-in-law,[61] would have brought added benefit to the *Idomeneo* performance. Hatzfeld became a close friend of Mozart when visiting Vienna on secondment from his Eichstätt cathedral appointment in winter and spring 1785–1786. Zinzendorf reported his admirable playing of Scottish airs at Countess Thun's (23 November 1785) and heard him at Countess Rumbeke's as well (10 December 1785).[62] After his premature death in 1787, the *Magazin der Musik* commended his ability to render inseparable genius, talent and artistic feeling.[63] A few years earlier, Friedrich Nicolai recalled 'with genuine pleasure' (*mit wahrem Vergnügen*) Hatzfeld's accompaniment of an aria in Regensburg, drawing attention to his status as a virtuoso.[64] Mozart also exploited Hatzfeld's talents in an operatic context, writing an obbligato violin part for him in 'Non temer, amato bene', K. 490, a new rondò for the tenor Idamante Baron Pollini (1762–1846).[65] While little is known about Pollini's singing, it is clear that he moved to Italy after his stay in Vienna and became a professor at the Milan Conservatory in 1809.[66] At his death, the *Allgemeine musikalische Zeitung* identified him as one of Italy's best pianists, noting both his studies with Mozart and association with K. 490.[67]

As so often, including during the composition of *Idomeneo* in 1780–1781, Mozart made a virtue of a necessity, in this case to reshape Idamante's role for a tenor in Vienna rather than the castrato in Munich

[59] Link, *National Court Theatre*, pp. 219, 221, 374.

[60] Link, *National Court Theatre*, pp. 200, 201.

[61] Mark Everist, '"Madame Dorothea Wendling is 'arcicontentissima'": the Performers of *Idomeneo*', in Julian Rushton, *W. A. Mozart: 'Idomeneo'* (Cambridge: Cambridge University Press, 1993), p. 61.

[62] See the extracts from Zinzendorf's diary (in French), in Link, *National Court Theatre*, pp. 257–258, 259.

[63] Cramer, *Magazin der Musik* (26 July 1787), p. 1383.

[64] Nicolai, *Beschreibung einer Reise*, vol. 2, pp. 350–351.

[65] Peter Clive (*Mozart and His Circle*, p. 69) states that Hatzfeld had returned to Eichstätt by early April 1786; he may have been unavailable, then, for Mozart's Viennese academy on 7 April 1786.

[66] Angermüller, *Mozart, Band 1*, p. 258.

[67] *Allgemeine musikalische Zeitung*, 49 (21 April 1847), col. 268.

(Vincenzo Dal Prato) while utilizing Hatzfeld's instrumental talents.[68] It is possible that a castrato by the name of Viganoni was at one stage slated to sing Idamante but that he arrived in Vienna too late to do so, necessitating the vocal switch.[69] Both tenor and violin soloists are given opportunities to shine and to nurture their individual and collective interaction with the orchestra at the start of the Andante of 'Non temer, amato bene': Idamante is introduced by the eight-bar cantabile theme in the solo violin and also by a clarinets-bassoons-horns phrase link (bar 8) reconstituted as a warm swell at the end of the vocal statement (bars 14–16); and the violin soloist's virtuoso semiquavers guarantee audibility by being placed primarily between vocal phrases. At a subsequent crossroads in the text ('pensa almen, che istante è questo! Non mi posso, oh Dio, spiegar'; 'Think what a moment this is! Oh God, I cannot express myself'), where Idamante contemplates his own fate at the hands of 'barbarous stars' rather than addressing Ilia, Mozart coordinates a series of effects (Example 6.19): the crescendo to *forte* in bars 36–37 (the first in the aria) lends power to the orchestral strings, which unite in an assertive dotted rhythm; the solo violin receives its longest link between vocal phrases in the aria so far and is accompanied for the first time by the wind ensemble alone (bars 39–40); and the text 'Non mi posso, oh Dio' coincides with tied semibreves for the orchestral strings, semiquaver arpeggiated accompaniments for the solo violin and a pizzicato cello and bass line (bars 40–41), all new to this aria. The solo violin and voice, in brilliant mode in the lead back to the main theme and accompanied only by tied horn octaves, have the opportunity to synchronize expressively flexible renditions of imitative and joined material (bars 47–49). Indeed, the passage as a whole, not just the final three bars, would have allowed Pollini and Hatzfeld to display expressive and technical virtuosity and to nurture musical relationships between themselves and with the orchestra. *Forte* interjections from the orchestra in the remainder of the aria, a voice emboldened to perform an *Eingang* at the pause before the Allegro moderato, and brilliant semiquaver passages for

---

[68] On 18 January 1781, Mozart explained to his father that Raaff's last aria would have to be left out of *Idomeneo*, but that a virtue could be made of the omission. See MBA, vol. 3, p. 90; LMF, p. 708.

[69] See Ian Woodfield reporting an announcement in the *Oberdeutsche Staatszeitung* (1786) in *Cabals and Satires: Mozart's Comic Operas in Vienna* (New York: Oxford University Press, forthcoming), Chapter 1, 'Inter-troupe Rivalries: the Reception of *Figaro*'. Mozart notates Idamante's music in K. 489, K. 490 and the revised trio and quartet, in the soprano clef. Rushton tentatively suggests that 'the habit of writing a soprano clef for Idamante was too deeply set to be discarded, at least without conscious effort, or that the original intention for this performance had been to use a castrato or indeed a woman'. See Rushton, *W. A. Mozart: 'Idomeneo'*, p. 46.

Example 6.19 Mozart, 'Non temer, amato bene' K. 490, bars 34–49.

Example 6.19 (cont.)

the solo violin in the Allegro moderato testify to the important role the passage from bars 36–49 plays in shaping the aria as a whole. Just as Mozart 'with a single stroke ... eliminated the weakest number in his Munich score [Arbace's aria no. 10a] and strengthened a main character who was in need of more forceful delineation [in 'Non temer, amato bene']',[70] so he also facilitated a dynamic performance from Pollini, his co-soloist Hatzfeld, and their accompanying orchestra.

In addition to 'Non temer, amato bene' and a duet for Pollini and Puffendorf ('Spiegarvi non poss'io', K. 489) described as 'one of the rare cases in [Mozart's] works of a complete recomposition' with 'everything that was in the original duet plus much more',[71] Mozart rewrote the vocal parts for the Act 2 trio and Act 3 quartet to accommodate Pollini's tenor Idamante rather than Dal Prato's castrato.[72] He also produced a simplified version of the aria 'Fuor del mar' to suit Viennese Idomeneo Giuseppe Antonio Bridi.[73] In the quartet, Mozart almost always gives Pollini the same material as Dal Prato, either an octave below the original or at pitch. At the points where Idamante sings together with lover Ilia and father Idomeneo ('Ah il cor mi si divide!') and with Ilia, Idomeneo and Elettra ('Soffrir più non si può ... Nissun provò'), Mozart places him at the same pitch as the castrato – high in the tenor range, then, rather than in the middle of the castrato range.[74] The increase to tension in performance relative to the original version is palpable in those moments where Mozart requires his tenor to sing quietly and *sotto voce* and thus to maintain particularly close control of his upper register (such as at 'soffrir').[75]

---

[70] See Heartz, *Mozart's Operas*, ed. Bauman, p. 58. Heartz's high opinion of 'Non temer, amato bene' – and mine too – is not shared by all Mozart scholars. See, for example, Stanley Sadie, *Mozart: The Early Years, 1756–1781* (Oxford: Oxford University Press, 2006), pp. 546–547; Abert, *W. A. Mozart*, p. 912; Einstein, *Mozart*, p. 422.

[71] Heartz, *Mozart's Operas*, ed. Bauman, pp. 52–54, 55.

[72] See the NMA edition of *Idomeneo*, where the two versions of the vocal parts of the quartet are both given.

[73] The revisions to 'Fuor del mar' are written on the same type of paper as K. 489, 490 and the alterations to the quartet, thus associating them with the Viennese production in 1786 rather than (as was commonly believed) with Raaff in Munich. See Rushton, *W. A. Mozart: 'Idomeneo'*, pp. 46–47.

[74] Heinrich Koch (*Musikalisches Lexikon*, col. 1504) identifies the standard tenor range as c to g'/a'.

[75] In the Act 2 trio 'Pria di partir' for Munich, the Idamante castrato part is generally higher than in the quartet for Munich. In the first section (Andante), only small modifications are made for the Viennese tenor (for example, bars 39–40); the rest sets the tenor an octave lower than the castrato. In the Allegro con brio, more tenor material is moved up an octave than in the Andante and thus set at the same pitch as the original castrato.

Example 6.20 Mozart, 'Andrò ramingo e solo', from *Idomeneo*, K. 366, bars 59–65 (voices only: Munich and Vienna versions).

Passages in the quartet modifying Ilia, Elettra and Idomeneo's parts as well as Idamante's also shine a light on Pollini's upper register. Instead of having the castrato mid-range at 'maggiore nissun provò' as for Munich, with Elettra subsequently entering mid-range after a three-bar rest, Mozart gives Idamante's part to Ilia for Vienna, allowing both an elevated line for Elettra and a re-entry for Idamante on a high g' and a-flat' after a three-bar rest (see bars 59–65, Example 6.20). In the varied reprise comprising the second half of the quartet, intensity wrought from a high and often quiet tenor rather than a mid-range castrato is further exploited: Idamante's statement with Ilia to Idomeneo is at the original castrato pitch (bars 93ff.) rather than an octave lower as first time around; 'maggiore nissun provò' now has Idamente enter on b-flat' and a' after four bars rest (see bar 135ff.); and imitations on 'pena' for Idamante and Ilia (bars 144–145) include high b-flat' and f' minims for Idamante, rather than mid-range notes for castrato. To be sure, Mozart's register-related modifications for the Viennese Idamante could have been designed to prevent the tenor Idamante from slipping lower than the tenor Idomeneo, and thus to preserve the original registral order of the voices. (The Idamante castrato is almost always lower than the Ilia and Elettra sopranos when two, or all three, sing together.) Equally, the undemanding role for Idamante in the Munich quartet may reflect Mozart's low opinion of Dal Prato, who was specifically identified as the 'stumbling block' (*der Stein des Anstosses*) in a rehearsal of the number.[76] But changes made for Vienna, especially to Idamante's part, provided an opportunity for a slightly more intense and dramatic vocal performance than in Munich, which is not to say the Viennese quartet is 'better' than the original, rather that Mozart responded directly and sensitively – as in the newly composed 'Spiegarvi non poss'io' and 'Non temer, amato bene' – to the changed circumstances of the Viennese production.

Der Schauspieldirektor, 1786

Symbolically and practically for Mozart, *Der Schauspieldirektor* (1786) was an important interface between the worlds of operatic composition and performance. It was first staged on 7 February 1786 alongside Salieri's one-act comic opera *Prima la musica, poi le parole* at an event at the Orangerie, Schönbrunn organized by Joseph II to honour his sister Archduchess Marie Christine and her husband. As explained in the *Protocollum aulicum in Ceremonialibus*, guests rode carriages from town to the palace – a journey of more than an hour – in time for a banquet at 4 p.m. at which Joseph's *Harmoniemusik* was heard; the guests later repaired to a 'brilliantly illuminated' Orangerie for performances of Mozart's then Salieri's works at either end of the temporary theatre, before returning to town at 9 p.m.[77] And on this occasion at least they appear not to have fallen victim to a temperamental river crossing between the town and Schönbrunn that sometimes made an eighteenth-century evening return impossible.[78] For Baron von Reitzenstein, visiting Vienna in 1789–1790, the gardens were the highlight of Schönbrunn, compensating for castle buildings that might have been nice for the average rich man but were 'mediocre' (*mittelmässig*) by imperial standards.[79]

---

[76] For Mozart's comment on Dal Prato in the quartet, see MBA, vol. 3, p. 77; LMF, p. 701 (30 December 1780). For other negative remarks on his singing (and acting), see MBA, vol. 3, pp. 20, 28, 71; LMF, pp. 664, 669, 697–698 (15, 22 November and 27 December 1780).

[77] MDL, p. 231; MDB, pp. 261–262. The estimated journey time is from Reitzenstein, *Reise nach Wien*, p. 94.

[78] Keyßler, *Neueste Reisen*, p. 1234.   [79] Reitzenstein, *Reise nach Wien*, p. 95.

The event of February 1786 brought together those singers with whom Mozart was most closely associated in the first half of his Viennese career (Lange, Cavalieri and Adamberger, in *Schauspieldirektor*) and those with whom he was then collaborating on *Figaro* and for whom he would continue to write in the final years of his life (Benucci, Storace and Mandini, in *Prima la musica*). Like *Prima la musica*, *Der Schauspieldirektor* is a humorous opera about opera: *Prima la musica* comprises preparations for a new opera featuring an intransigent composer and librettist and an arrogant soprano, and included Storace's parody of the well-known castrato Luigi Marchesi, who had sung a few months earlier in Vienna to great acclaim;[80] and *Der Schauspieldirektor*, where two singers vie for the status of prima donna towards the end, pokes fun in the names of its characters at Lange's married status and predilection for lyrical, sentimental arias (Madame Herz) and Cavalieri's unmarried status and penchant for 'silvery' virtuosity (Mademoiselle Silberklang).[81] Understandably, Mozart responds seriously to the task of tailoring his two audition arias, 'Da schlägt die Abschiedsstunde' (Lange) and 'Bester Jüngling' (Cavalieri), to the needs of his singers and continues to exploit their different vocal qualities in the trio 'Ich bin die erste Sängerin'.[82]

Mozart wrote arias for *Der Schauspieldirektor* that to all intents and purposes balance each other.[83] As in Lange's 'Mia speranza' and 'Vorrei spiegarvi', a close relationship is forged between the wind (especially the oboes) and the voice in 'Da schlägt die Abschiedsstunde': phrase links in the Larghetto, with the instruction to play *dolce*, begin on the note on which the singer ends (oboe, bars 17–23, Example 6.21); a simultaneous sustained vocal g″ and oboe g″ are sounded in the Allegro moderato (bars 57–58); and the oboes, bassoons and horns (the oboes by themselves on one occasion) support the vocal semiquaver flourishes with sustained notes (see bars 62–70). At the precise moment that Herz determines her earlier concerns about lover Damon forgetting her forever are unfounded, the orchestra draws attention to her emotional shift by twice distributing *sf, sfp* and *f* surges over two beats in a ripple effect (36–37, 'ach nein', Example 6.22) and then by coming together to reflect her new steadfastness (38–40, 'du kannst gewiss

---

[80] See Braunbehrens, *Maligned Master*, pp. 119–120 and Rice, *Salieri and Viennese Opera*, pp. 376–384. Zinzendorf noted Storace's parody of Marchesi in his diary. See MDL, p. 230; MDB, p. 262.

[81] See Linda Tyler, 'Aria as Drama: A Sketch from Mozart's *Der Schauspieldirektor*', *Cambridge Opera Journal*, 2 (1990), pp. 251–267, at 262.

[82] Tyler, 'Aria as Drama', pp. 262–266.

[83] On contrasts between the writing for Lange and Cavalieri in *Der Schauspieldirektor*, see Gidwitz, 'Vocal Profiles of Two Mozart Sopranos', pp. 573–574.

Example 6.21 Mozart, 'Da schlägt die Abschiedsstunde', from *Der Schauspieldirektor*, K. 486, bars 16–22.

Example 6.22 Mozart, 'Da schlägt die Abschiedsstunde', from *Der Schauspieldirektor*, K. 486, bars 36–41.

nicht treulos sein').[84] In a similar fashion at the end of the aria the orchestra help to depict the 'strong bond' to Damon that Herz says nothing will sever, interweaving imitatively with the voice and presenting two delicate tutti chords after Herz has finished that carry the only *pp* marking in the number.

The vocal stridency and flexibility of 'Bester Jüngling' for Cavalieri replace the instrumental and vocal nuances of 'Da schlägt die Abschiedsstunde' for Lange. Forthright arpeggios bring to mind vocal writing for Cavalieri in 'Martern aller Arten'. The opening of the Allegretto is also a digest of two form-defining antecedent-consequent exchanges in 'Martern': at the beginning of the Allegro Assai (160ff.) with its strong vocal line; and at the secondary theme where orchestral instruments take a lead (93ff.). The augmented 6th – V progression, alongside two pauses (bars 36–37), invokes a near identical gesture in 'Martern' heard immediately before the secondary theme in the solo exposition (see bars 91–92): it also offers an

---

[84] Mozart positions dynamic markings carefully and precisely in this passage in the autograph. See Wolfgang Amadeus Mozart, *Der Schauspieldirektor: The Impresario, K. 486: A Facsimile of the Autograph Manuscript* (London and Oxford: Oxford University Press, 1976).

opportunity for an unnotated vocal flourish. Perhaps Mozart intended mild one-upmanship on Silberklang's part here, as Herz had the same progression at one point in her aria (bars 16–17), but without the fermatas to encourage embellishment.

Ultimately, the similarities between Lange's and Cavalieri's arias are as significant as their differences. Both are two-tempo arias and almost identical in length; the 'Larghetto' and 'Andante' designations for the first sections would have indicated similar speeds in performance too, based on Mozart's standard practice.[85] Also, both are stylistically modest: the vocal-instrumental interactions of no. 1 and stridency of no. 2 are less ostentatious than several of Mozart's earlier arias for Lange and Cavalieri; and neither is as brilliantly virtuosic as previously composed material for them. The hapless impresario, Frank, responds equally positively to Herz and Silberklang; for the plot's dramatic development, then, the musical decks are not to be stacked in favour of one soprano rather than the other in the two arias. Maybe the moderate arias for Herz and Silberklang are an antidote to the immoderate behaviour of the two dramatic characters, Mozart expressing a view about the futility of competition and ego-driven behaviour regularly experienced in the late-eighteenth-century opera world. The *Schlussgesang* no. 4 and trio no. 3 convey the importance of cooperation and artistic integrity.[86] In effect, Mozart also cultivates this message musically in 'Da schlägt die Abschiedsstunde' and 'Bester Jüngling'.

Der Schauspieldirektor, initially quite successful in Vienna with three performances at the Kärntnertortheater on 11, 18 and 25 February 1786 and quick distribution in manuscript copies from Wenzel Sukowaty and Lorenz Lausch,[87] has tended to languish in the critical shadow of *Figaro*, just as *L'oca del Cairo* and *Lo sposo deluso* are routinely regarded only as warm-ups for *Figaro*. A review of a piano reduction of the score of *Der Schauspieldirektor* from Breitkopf & Härtel started the trend in 1794, citing a lack of originality in the ideas and modulations. The finale is admittedly 'pretty' (*hübsch*), we are told, but does not stand comparison with ensembles in Mozart's mighty operas. The reviewer, a self-professed admirer of

---

[85] On Mozart's intended speeds for Larghetto and Andante, see Brown, *Classical and Romantic Performing Practice*, p. 349.

[86] As Monsieur Vogelsang explains when Herz and Silberklang squabble: 'No artist must rebuke another, for this belittles art'. ('Kein Künstler muss den andern tadeln, es setzt die Kunst zu sehr herab'.)

[87] See MDL, pp. 231–232, 233, 235; MDB, pp. 264, 267, 269. Zinzendorf, however, did not enjoy the premiere. See MDL, pp. 229–230; MDB, p. 262.

Mozart's music, ultimately concludes that 'operetta' – his designation for the work – is not a genre for such an 'immortal man' (*unsterblicher Mann*).[88] But, short though it may be in relation to his operatic tomes, *Der Schauspieldirektor* is a performance about performers as much as an opera about opera. For a composer as sensitive as Mozart to the performance of his music, this fact alone ensures it a special place in his Viennese oeuvre.

The Mass in C Minor and *Davidde penitente*, 1782–1785

Crucial facts remain uncertain about the genesis and premiere of the Mass in C minor, K. 427 (1782–1783). First mentioned in a 'half-finished' state by Mozart in a letter to Leopold on 4 January 1783, its composition apparently related both to a promise made to Constanze before they married and a future trip they would undertake together to Salzburg.[89] But the exact nature of the promise is unknown, as is the reason for the work remaining incomplete.[90] Indeed, Mozart's motivations for writing it may have evolved during the extended genesis: '[The] fact that he invested a substantial amount of time and effort in a sacred work that had little practical and especially financial benefit is an indication of the personal significance the project possessed.'[91] It was perhaps first performed at St Peter's in Salzburg on Sunday 26 October 1783, the day before Mozart and Constanze began their return trip to Vienna after a three-month stay in Salzburg. Nannerl's diary records a rehearsal of a Mozart mass on 23 October and a performance three days later, with Constanze in a solo role and the 'whole court music' present (*die ganze hofmusik*), which does not completely rule out a rendition of an earlier Mozart mass instead.[92] Even if K. 427 was performed on 26 October, with Constanze presumably taking the 'Christe' solo and roles in Gloria and Benedictus ensembles and Salzburg-based castrato Ceccarelli the 'Laudamus te', it is not known what

---

[88] *Neue Allgemeine Deutsche Bibliothek*, 11 (1794), pp. 419–421.

[89] MBA, vol. 3, pp. 247–248; LMF, p. 834 (4 January 1783).

[90] For a careful analysis of the portion of Mozart's letter relating to the C-minor Mass, see Ulrich Konrad, 'Mozart the Letter Writer and His Language', trans. William Buchanan, in Keefe (ed.), *Mozart Studies 2*, pp. 1–22, at 13–16.

[91] David Ian Black, 'Mozart and the Practice of Sacred Music, 1781–1791', PhD thesis, Harvard University, 2007, pp. 124–125.

[92] For Nannerl's diary entries, see MBA, vol. 3, p. 290 (not in LMF). Black believes that a performance of K. 427 in Vienna cannot be completely discounted based on evidence offered by the so-called Heilig Kreuz parts (now incomplete). See 'Mozart and the Practice of Sacred Music', pp. 110–119. Cliff Eisen also suggests these parts may date from *after* the putative performance on 26 October 1783, possibly between mid-1784 and mid-1785. See Eisen, 'The Mozarts' Salzburg Copyists', p. 307.

music (if any) stood in for the incomplete Credo and nonexistent Agnus Dei.[93] Constanze's own recollections transmitted in Nissen's biography are sketchy: the mass was said to have been 'finished' in Salzburg in late 1783 and the rehearsal and performance to have taken place on 23 and 25 August.[94] Perhaps Constanze confused the completion of K. 427 with Mozart writing it during the Salzburg sojourn, even if not to the end. Ten-staff Salzburg paper was used for nine leaves of the autograph, situating at least some of Mozart's work between late July and late October 1783.[95]

Viewed in stylistic and liturgical context, the C-minor Mass is also unusual. The *Gottesdienstordnung* ('new order of services', 1783), issued by Joseph II as the last in a series of directives and proclamations about liturgical practice in the first years of his sole rule as emperor, put restrictions on the use of music in church services; Archbishop Colloredo's *Hirtenbrief* (August 1782), to which Mozart refers sarcastically on 25 September 1782, was similarly aimed at simplifying worship practices.[96] While the *Gottesdienstordnung* restrictions were often ignored, appear not unduly to have discouraged Viennese composers from writing sacred music in the remainder of the 1780s, and were less severe than would have been the case had Joseph heeded the advice of his own *Hofkanzlei* and excluded instrumentally accompanied music from services altogether, they created an 'official climate of disapproval' that could hardly be construed as an encouragement to Mozart to write a long and lavish mass.[97] The stylistic archaism of K. 427 is no doubt indebted to Mozart's study of J. S. Bach and Handel with Baron van Swieten in Vienna; it may also evidence a 'continuous if not exactly living tradition of stylistic conservatism in Viennese church music' that includes works by Albrechtsberger and Leopold Hofmann.[98] Operatic characteristics of the work have often been identified.[99] In addition to the style of vocal writing in solo movements such as 'Laudamus te', 'Domine',

---

[93] Only wind parts are extant in the autograph for the Sanctus and Benedictus. See Wolfgang Amadeus Mozart, *Messe c-moll KV427: Faksimile der autographen Partitur* (Kassel: Bärenreiter, 1983).

[94] Nissen, *Biographie W. A. Mozarts*, p. 476 ('Er vollendete die Messe').

[95] See Tyson, *Autograph Scores*, p. 101.   [96] See MBA, vol. 3, p. 231; LMF, p. 822.

[97] See Black, 'Mozart and the Practice of Sacred Music', pp. 53–126 (quote at p. 64).

[98] Black, 'Mozart and the Practice of Sacred Music', pp. 99–102 (quote at p. 101). On the link to Handel, see Silke Leopold, 'Händels Geist in Mozarts Händen: Zum "Qui Tollis" aus der C-Moll Messe KV427', *Mozart-Jahrbuch 1994*, pp. 89–99.

[99] See, for example, Denis Donoghue, 'Approaching Mozart', in James M. Morris (ed.), *On Mozart* (Cambridge: Cambridge University Press, 1994), pp. 32–33; Paul Corneilson, 'The Vocal Music', in Keefe (ed.), *The Cambridge Companion to Mozart*, pp. 126–127; Hildesheimer, *Mozart*, pp. 136–137, 364; Küster, *Musical Biography*, p. 160. Operatic qualities of K. 427 are not parsed positively by Abert: see *W.A. Mozart*, p. 833.

'Quoniam' and the incomplete 'Et incarnatus est', distinctive instrumental effects are integrated into extended movements.[100] While not dramatic *per se*, these effects alongside Mozart's rich instrumentation and ornate vocal writing reinforce the impression that opera and operatic experiences lie close to the musical surface.

Much of the music for the C-minor Mass was performed in Vienna, resurrected as a cantata *Davidde penitente*, K. 469, in concerts organized by the Tonkünstler-Societät on 13 and 15 March 1785. Opinions of the work have not generally been high on account of Mozart setting old music to a new text derided only a decade after his death as 'without coherence and almost without idea'.[101] Minutes of meetings at the Tonkünstler-Societät record Mozart's inability to produce the new Psalm originally planned and the necessary reorganization of the concert programmes: 'Because Herr Mozart has not been able to complete the promised Psalm, he offers instead another Psalm, completely new to Vienna, which, however, is only half as long. Accordingly, another *plan of the Academy* should be established.'[102] As well as *Davidde penitente*, the concerts included a Haydn symphony, arias sung by Mandini, Franziska Dorothea Lebrun and Cavalieri, and concertos from oboist August Ludwig Lebrun and Monsieur Schenker (who perhaps was a harpist). The source for *Davidde penitente*'s text was recently discovered in Saverio Mattei's *Libri poetici della Bibbia* (1766), a translation of the Book of Psalms known in Vienna and already published in ten Italian editions by 1785. It is possible that the Tonkünstler-Societät suggested Mattei's text to Mozart and that Lorenzo Da Ponte – to whom the authorship of the text was traditionally attributed – helped choose and adapt passages to suit music from the C-minor Mass.[103]

---

[100] On instrumental effects in K. 427, see Keefe, *Mozart's Requiem*, pp. 167–169.

[101] *Allgemeine musikalische Zeitung*, 3 (1800–1801), cols. 238–240, at 240. The report on this rendition in Paris reserves still harsher criticism for the performers conducted by Joseph Wölfl. For twentieth-century negativity towards *Davidde penitente* see Einstein, *Mozart: His Character, His Work*, p. 364; Solomon, *Mozart: A Life*, p. 271; Hildesheimer, *Mozart*, pp. 137–138. Abert finds the C-minor Mass uneven and is lukewarm about *Davidde penitente*; see *W. A. Mozart*, pp. 831–835, 835–836.

[102] Quoted in Eisen's translation in NMD, p. 35. At one stage Mozart may have contemplated revising his oratorio *La Betulia liberata* (1771) for this event; see Black, 'Mozart's Association with the Tonkünstler-Societät', pp. 61–65.

[103] See Irene Brandenburg, 'Mozart, *Davide penitente*, and Saverio Mattei', *Mozart Society of America Newsletter*, 15/2 (August 2011), pp. 11–12, 14. For an extended version of the article in German see Brandenburg, 'Neues zum Text von Mozarts *Davide penitente* KV 469', in Lars E. Laubhold and Gerhard Walterskirchen (eds), *Klang-Quellen: Festschrift Ernst Hintermaier zum 65. Geburtstag* (Munich, 2010), pp. 209–229.

Davidde penitente comprises the eight re-set movements of the Kyrie and Gloria of the C-minor Mass, plus two arias newly written for tenor Adamberger and soprano Cavalieri inserted either side of the original 'Qui tollis' (now 'Se vuoi puinscimi'). While different in orientation, 'A te, fra tanti' (no. 6) and 'Tra l'oscure ombre funeste' (no. 8) are well balanced: they are Andante–Allegro, two-tempo arias of similar length.[104] Adamberger's focuses more on the blend of voice and wind instruments than on bravura virtuosity, also drawing on a type of melodic writing witnessed in earlier arias for him by Ignaz Umlauf and Mozart.[105] As in 'Per pietà' for Anfossi's *Il curioso indiscreto*, Mozart primarily uses a full-wind timbre of flute, clarinet, oboe and bassoon (sometimes with horns) to colour Adamberger's voice and to link vocal phrases. Heard first in individual obbligato roles in the orchestral introduction, the four wind instruments come together for the first time in bars 15–16 to introduce the singer (Example 6.23), thereafter playing mostly as a unit.[106] Cavalieri's 'Tra l'oscure ombre funeste', more brilliant than 'A te, fra tanti', also brings to mind several features of earlier arias for her by Mozart: rapid instrumental scales taken up by the voice in the Andante (specifically invoking the ends of the solo exposition and Primo tempo of 'Martern aller Arten'); big leaps between high and low registers; semiquaver pyrotechnics; and pauses in the Allegro where inserted embellishments could have drawn further attention to technical and expressive virtuosity. Just as Mozart wrote comparably weighted roles for the *primo uomo* (Adamberger) and *prima donna* (Cavalieri) in *Die Entführung*[107] and offered equivalent opportunities for the two sopranos to prove their worth in *Der Schauspieldirektor*, so he wrote complementary arias for Cavalieri and Adamberger in *Davidde penitente*.

In addition to accommodating Adamberger and Cavalieri in *Davidde penitente*, Mozart had to integrate his new arias into a structure dictated by the Kyrie and Gloria of the C-minor Mass. Mozart links 'A te, fra tanti' to the chorus 'Se vuoi puinscimi' ('Qui tollis') with two bars of V/g and an *attacca* and 'Tra l'oscure ombre funeste' to the trio 'Tutte, tutte le mie'

---

[104] Mozart marks the beginning of Cavalieri's aria 'Andante' in the autograph, but 'Larghetto' in the *Verzeichnüß*.

[105] On the latter point see Bauman, 'Mozart's Belmonte', p. 562. Bauman also recognizes instrumental richness as characteristic of Mozart's arias for Adamberger (p. 562).

[106] While one or two wind are sometimes absent during passages of wind participation – as in bars 71–72 perhaps to reduce the risk of obscuring the sustained high note (f'), an Adamberger specialty – they soon re-enter.

[107] The demonstrative 'Martern', one among three arias for Cavalieri, is balanced by a less ostentatious four arias for Adamberger.

Example 6.23 Mozart, 'A te, fra tanti', from *Davidde penitente*, K. 469, bars 12–16.

('Quoniam') with a move from C to V/e in the final bars, in preparation for the ensuing E minor. Instrumental writing also helps knit the new arias into the fabric of the work: 'Ah te, fra tanti' takes wind-voice interaction further than 'Lungi le cure ingrate' ('Laudamus te'), increasing the number of participating instruments and expanding their roles, and provides refinement of effect in a solo movement equivalent to the climactic effects of the choral 'Sii pur sempre' and 'Se vuoi puinscimi' ('Gratias' and 'Qui tollis'); and 'Tra l'oscure ombre funeste', beginning with strings and winds together after a protracted process of convergence in 'Se vuoi puinscimi',[108] promotes a *forte* dotted rhythm reminiscent of the most distinctive rhythm from the previous movement. The complementary placement of the two arias, 'A te, fra tanti' after a duet and before a chorus and 'Tra l'oscure ombre funeste' after a chorus and before a trio, underscores symmetrical organization of the last seven numbers (4–10): chorus – ensemble (duet) – aria – chorus – aria – ensemble (trio) – chorus. In spite of the rush to provide a 'Psalm, entirely new to Vienna' for the Tonkünstler-Societät,

---

[108] On this process in the corresponding movement of the C-minor Mass, 'Qui tollis', see Keefe, *Mozart's Requiem*, p. 168.

then, Mozart responded carefully both to performing and compositional considerations in fashioning *Davidde penitente* from the C-minor Mass.

A desire to maximize the impact of the solo performers, including a second soprano as well as Cavalieri, probably explains the interpolated forty-four-bar 'cadenza' towards the end of the concluding 'Chi in Dio' – 'Di tai pericoli' ('Jesu Christe' – 'Cum sancto spiritu'). The new material is distributed evenly among the three performers: they sing almost through-out, each receiving seven or eight bars of quaver melismas, engaging in exchanges of quavers among themselves and presenting the final cadential trill together. The soloistic equality cultivated in 'A te, fra tanti' and 'Tra l'oscure ombre funeste' thereby extends to solo participation in the final movement.

The cantata *Die Maurerfreude*, K. 471 (1785), performed a month after *Davidde penitente*, also includes a solo role for Adamberger. Written to honour Joseph II's ennoblement of Ignaz von Born, master of the Viennese lodge 'Zur wahren Eintracht', the main contributors were all masons: Franz Petran, author of the text; Mozart, the composer; Adamberger, the soloist; and Artaria, publisher of the score to benefit the poor.[109] The communal endeavour dedicated to Born may have encouraged Mozart to promote the collective orchestral group over the individual singer. For the tenor part is relatively simple and at times outshone by the orchestra. At its initial entry, for example, the voice presents a simplified version of the orchestra's opening theme while the orchestra repeats its more ornate version. Decorative semiquaver figures and new phrase links for oboe and clarinet come to prominence in the vocal statement (see Example 6.24). While a long vocal sustained note in bars 32–36 and subsequent fermata (Example 6.24) direct attention to a recognized strength of Adamberger's singing, his held note is as much timbral addition to an orchestral sound (the horn's sounding f) as soloist-centred effect. The orchestra continues to take a lead in the remainder of the work: in the run-up to the reprise of the main theme (bars 65–66); in rhythmically activating the shift from Andante to Presto (bar 134) shortly before the Molto allegro; and in elaborating vocal material in the concluding Molto allegro, where the male chorus joins the solo tenor.

---

[109] MDL, pp. 218–219; MDB, pp. 247–248. In 1785, Artaria published another short cantata by Mozart, in collaboration with Salieri, to celebrate the return to health of the soprano Nancy Storace: 'Per la ricuperata salute di Ophelia', K. 477a. Long considered lost, the cantata was rediscovered at the Czech Museum of Music in Prague in 2016. For the Artaria advertisement on 26 September 1785, see MDL, pp. 222–223; MDB, p. 255.

Example 6.24 Mozart, 'Die Maurerfreude', K. 471, bars 26–36.

Songs, 1785–1786

In contrast to the arias and ensembles discussed above and in spite of generic overlaps with the arias, little is known either about the performers for whom Mozart intended his Viennese songs or about occasions at which they were sung.[110] The Masonic songs can be tentatively linked to specific events: 'Lied zur Gesellenreise', K. 468 (26 March 1785), perhaps to mark Leopold's induction to the rank of journeyman at the 'True Concord' lodge; and 'Zerfliesset heut', geliebte Brüder', K. 483, and 'Ihr unsre neuen Leiter', K. 484, for an initial gathering of 'New Crowned Hope' (the product of two merged lodges) in January 1786. 'Der Zauberer', K. 472, 'Die Zufriedenheit', K. 473, and 'Die betrogene Welt', K. 474, all to texts by Christian Felix Weisse, were entered into Mozart's *Verzeichnüß* on the same day, 7 May 1785, perhaps implying performance together at an as-yet-unidentified event. Several musical connections among K. 472, 473 and 474, alongside Weisse's authorship of the texts, point to performance as an informal set: all include a piano introduction and postlude and are strophic; keys of G minor for K. 472 (with a middle segment in B-flat), B-flat for K. 473 and G major for K. 474 provide tonal coherence; and the same melodic peak (g'') perhaps suggests a specific singer in Mozart's mind.[111]

The ideal of 'blending … singer and keyboardist as one' in the performance of an eighteenth-century Lied, if not the traditional practice of a single individual singing and accompanying simultaneously,[112] can inform our understanding of Mozart's Viennese songs. At the end of his famous 'Das Veilchen' (K. 476), Mozart added two lines to Goethe's poem: 'Das arme Veilchen! es war ein herzigs Veilchen' ('The poor violet! It was a sweet little violet', Example 6.25). It coincides with the moment that singer and keyboardist are explicitly asked to perform freely ('a piacere', bars 61–62) before reuniting in two final 'a tempo' bars that reprise an earlier cadential gesture from bars 12–14. As early as 1790, a reviewer of the first edition of the song from Artaria praised Mozart's textual and musical addition as 'very unexpected and exquisitely beautiful'.[113] The final two bars may indeed represent 'a conscious reflection on what might have been,

---

[110] On blurred distinctions between Mozart's arias and songs, see Corneilson, 'Vocal Music', pp. 128–130; Einstein, *Mozart: His Character, His Work*, pp. 390–396. Dramatic qualities of Mozart's songs are recognized in Abert, *W. A. Mozart*, pp. 909–910 and Blom, *Mozart*, p. 168.

[111] It should be noted that g'' is also the highpoint for three other songs from 1785–86: K. 468, K. 476 and K. 506. Koch identifies the standard range of a high soprano as c' – a'' (or higher) and that of a mezzo soprano as a – e'' or f'', rendering g'' a reasonable upper limit for many voices. K. 484 peaks on g', also identified by Koch as a typical upper limit for the tenor voice. See Koch, *Musikalisches Lexikon*, cols. 433, 1504.

[112] See James Parsons, 'The Eighteenth-Century Lied', in Parsons (ed.), *The Cambridge Companion to the Lied* (Cambridge: Cambridge University Press, 2004), pp. 35–62, at 49.

[113] *Musikalische Real-Zeitung*, 1 (6 January 1790), p. 2 ('sehr überraschend und vorzüglich schön'). In a similar vein, Jahn (*Life of Mozart*, vol. 2, p. 374) remarks that Mozart's ending 'fully reasserts a genuine lyric element'. For the advertisement of the Artaria publication on 5 September 1789, see MDL, p. 308; MDB, p. 351.

Example 6.25 Mozart, 'Das Veichen', K. 476, bars 55–65.

and an appeal to the listener to remember the mood of the opening'.[114] But they also capture in microcosm the bond between singer and pianist throughout the song that is demonstrated in shared and complementary materials and gestures: the grace-note vocal decoration of the piano right hand in bar 10 matched by the piano ornamenting the unadorned voice in bars 36 and 38; the vocal leap of a seventh in bars 18–19 followed by one of an octave in the piano four bars later; and the ebb and flow of voice and piano in the dramatic final verse in which the 'violet' dies, including dotted rhythms that culminate on a diminished seventh before a pause, a vocal ascent to the melodic peak (g''), supported by right-hand arpeggios and a crescendo, and a coordinated semiquaver descent. (See Example 6.25 for the end of the last verse.) Viewed in the context of the song as a whole, then, the piano and voice are surely encouraged to find an imaginative way of blending, rather than contrasting, the arpeggio and falling third performed 'at will' in the declamatory bars 61–62. Thus, Mozart's sensitivity to the nuances of Goethe's text, a musing on lost love

---

[114] Amanda Glauert, 'The Lieder of Carl Philipp Emanuel Bach, Haydn, Mozart, and Beethoven', in Parsons (ed.), *The Cambridge Companion to the Lied*, p. 76.

Example 6.26 Mozart, 'Lied zur Gesellenreise', K. 468, bars 17–24.

symbolized by a crushed violet, is reinforced by the singer and piano performing, in effect, as one.[115]

Other Mozart songs from 1785 to 1786 highlight continuities between performance and composition, even if not always implying that voice and piano speak as one. In 'Lied zur Gesellenweise', K. 468, the piano statement from the opening is subsequently retained alongside a simpler vocal version, the piano thus appearing to engage in decorative variation of the vocal line.[116] It neatly trips around the voice in bars 17–18, the voice returning the favour in bars 21–23 (see Example 6.26), which includes an f' – b-flat' semiquaver elaboration at the end of the phrase duly recast as a b-flat' – f' semiquaver start to the piano postlude. Decoration thus yields further decoration, the piano and voice appearing to treat each other's material as a stimulus to spontaneous creativity. Similar back and forth

---

[115] For an analysis of Mozart's text setting see in particular Glauert, 'Bach, Haydn, Mozart, and Beethoven', pp. 75–76. See also Carl Schachter, in John Arthur and Schachter, 'Mozart's *Das Veilchen*', *Musical Times*, 130 (1989), pp. 149–155. On the interaction of voice and piano in K. 476, Kenneth Whitton draws a tentative historical conclusion: 'Here is perhaps the first *true* example of a musician thinking of voice and accompaniment independently, yet as one.' See Whitton, *Lieder: an Introduction to German Song* (London: Julia McRae Books, 1984), p. 20.

[116] Organ and piano are both listed as accompanimental instruments for K. 468: the former in the autograph and the latter in the *Verzeichnüß*. Since the masonic K. 483 and 484 were played with organ, K. 468 was perhaps performed initially by the organ and later by the piano.

Example 6.27 Mozart, 'Der Zauberer', K. 472, bars 1–10.

characterizes 'Der Zauberer' (K. 472), including, in the first nine bars, quick-fire semiquaver syncopation, a joint homophonic statement, and right-hand c″ – c‴ octaves that decorate the voice's repeated c″s and foreshadow the octave leap at the opening of the next vocal phrase (Example 6.27). But Mozart reserves the most striking decorative act for the final bars (Example 6.28), linking it to demonstrative harmonic and virtuosic effects. The piano's demisemiquavers elaborate the preceding cadential figure in the voice and are launched by both a dramatic leap to a c-sharp‴ and an abrasive, melodically unprepared diminished triad. The piano's postlude is thus simultaneously integrated with and detached from the final vocal cadence. It was common for composers of late-eighteenth-century strophic songs to encourage their performers to introduce *Veränderungen* (variations) into renditions of later verses.[117] Since the end of the first three verses focus on the bewitching man's status as an enchanter (*ein Zaub'rer*) and the final verse on the narrator being saved from the man by her mother, an interpretative *Veränderung* could embrace – through the manipulation of dynamics and articulation to contrasting effect – both the shock of musical and poetic developments in verses 1–3 and the resolution of verse 4.

✳✳✳✳✳

---

[117] See Parsons, 'Eighteenth-Century Lied', pp. 51–53.

Example 6.28 Mozart, 'Der Zauberer', K. 472, bars 14–17.

In a brief, negative appraisal of *Davidde penitente*, Wolfgang Hildesheimer finds 'artistic necessity' and 'practical considerations' fundamentally unreconciled.[118] This well-worn, now largely discredited critical distinction applied to Mozart's oeuvre is dealt a final, decisive blow by issues around performance. In no other sphere of Mozart's musical life are the artistic and the practical so inseparable. And Mozart would have felt this inseparability especially keenly in the potpourri of vocal and dramatic works between *Die Entführung* and *Figaro*, where performance and compositional contexts are so varied and the range of singers accommodated is so diverse.

Accepting mutual dependence of the artistic and the practical necessarily brings to the fore Mozart's interests in the performances of his vocal works from 1782 to 1786. These interests are conveyed in sensitivity to the needs, predilections and expectations of individual singers, to vocal and instrumental effects, and to the impact of dynamics and other markings. Mozart was a leading performer in a 1782–1786 dramatic work perhaps only once, clearly relishing it. In the Pantomime, K. 446, put on at the half-hour interval at the masked ball on Carnival Monday 1783, Mozart played Harlequin of *commedia dell'arte* fame in the only stage role he wrote for himself.[119] He delayed Harlequin's entry until no. 7, '[peeping] out of the cupboard' (according to his own annotation) to impish music in B-flat, no doubt milking the effect for all it was worth. But, as in the piano concertos from 1784 to 1786 (Chapter 4), Mozart's interests extended well beyond his

---

[118] See Hildesheimer, *Mozart*, p. 138.

[119] Describing K. 446 to his father on 12 March 1783, Mozart identified Aloysia Lange, Joseph Lange, himself, Johann Heinrich Merk and Joseph Grassi as the performers and explained that they had 'played really charmingly'. See MBA, vol. 3, p. 259; LMF, p. 842. A few weeks earlier Mozart had asked Leopold to send him his Harlequin costume from Salzburg: MBA, vol. 3, pp. 251–252; LMF, pp. 837 (22 January 1783).

own role. Connections between the music and the written annotations guiding the performers reach their zenith at Pierrot's reaction to Harlequin's death in no. 13, where Mozart is more attentive than at any other stage in the work to dynamic and dramatic fluctuations in the violin.[120] Accents, pizzicati, crescendi and pauses are surely intended to nurture and support lively and expressive acting from Joseph Lange as Pierrot, who 'is afraid of the dead Harlequin'.

As vocal and dramatic works from 1782 to 1786 demonstrate, Mozart understood the act of writing for individual singers to involve more than accommodating them in their vocal lines, the principal focus thus far of the critical literature. He carefully considered how arias for different star performers in the same work should complement each other while exploiting vocal strengths. And he came to associate specific timbres and sonorities with specific voices, such as the oboe with Lange and a full-wind sound with Adamberger, thereby elevating the role of instrumental effects as communicators of expressive content. The audience approbation for which Mozart always strove depended precisely on him creating and nurturing a symbiotic relationship with performers of his vocal and dramatic music, a process requiring all his skills of instrumental as well as vocal manipulation.

---

[120] Only unfinished first-violin parts survive for K. 446, including Mozart's simple written annotations describing the action that takes place.

PART III

The Da Ponte Operas, 1786–1790

L'oca del Cairo and *Lo sposo deluso*, both left incomplete, were Mozart's first attempts to engage with the Italian opera company newly established in Vienna for the 1783–1784 season. According to Lorenzo Da Ponte's *Memoirs*, it was Mozart's idea to set Pierre Beaumarchais' *succès de scandale*, *La folle journée, ou le mariage de Figaro*, which had premiered in Paris in 1784 and was banned in Vienna in early 1785.[1] While Da Ponte is not always a reliable witness, such as when implying that work on *Le nozze di Figaro* was done and dusted in six weeks,[2] and is prone to promote his own participation, his memory perhaps can be trusted on this occasion precisely because he did not claim credit for the choice of subject himself.[3] The decision to set *Figaro* was no doubt influenced by the success in Vienna, from 1783 onwards, of Beaumarchais' *Le barbier de Séville* as *Il barbiere di Siviglia* by Paisiello.[4] Mozart may also have encountered a play about Beaumarchais, Goethe's *Clavigo*, in Salzburg (November 1775).[5] Letters from Leopold Mozart to Nannerl, reporting correspondence no longer extant from Mozart to Leopold and a conversation with the journalist Lorenz Hübner, put Mozart hard at work on *Figaro* by the end of October 1785. Hübner mentioned Mozart's 'new opera' to Leopold shortly before the letter written to Nannerl on 3–5 November 1785.[6] A few days later, having received a twelve-line letter from Mozart, Leopold provided more detail:

---

[1] Arthur Livingston (ed.), *Memoirs of Lorenzo Da Ponte, Mozart's Librettist*, trans. Elisabeth Abbott (New York: Dover, 1967), p. 150. On the banning of Beaumarchais' play, probably more for sexual licentiousness than political reasons, see Beales, *Joseph II: Against the World*, pp. 467–468. See also Ian Woodfield, 'The Trouble with Cherubino', in Keefe (ed.), *Mozart Studies 2*, pp. 168–194.

[2] *Memoirs of Lorenzo Da Ponte*, pp. 149–150; on Da Ponte's muddled memories about *Figaro*, see Edge, 'Mozart's Viennese Copyists', pp. 1419–1424.

[3] John Rice, *Mozart on the Stage* (Cambridge: Cambridge University Press, 2009), pp. 66–67. For an overview of Da Ponte as librettist, see Konrad Küster, 'Lorenzo Da Ponte's Viennese Librettos', in David Wyn Jones (ed.), *Music in Eighteenth-Century Austria* (Cambridge: Cambridge University Press, 1996), pp. 221–231.

[4] See Heartz, *Mozart's Operas*, pp. 108, 140–150; Rushton, *Mozart*, p. 149.

[5] See Toepelmann, 'The Mozart Family and *Empfindsamkeit*', pp. 188, 213, 305. *Clavigo* was also staged at the Burgtheater and Kärntnertortheater in Vienna in January and March 1786 while Mozart was at work on *Figaro*. See Link, *National Court Theatre*, pp. 75, 81.

[6] MBA, vol. 3, p. 439; LMF, p. 893.

He asks for forgiveness [for writing so late], because he is up to his neck making ready the opera *le Nozze di Figaro* . . . I know the piece; it is a very laboured play and the translation from the French certainly will have to be freely altered for an opera, if it is to work as an opera. God grant the action turns out well; of the music, I have no doubt. But it will take him a lot of running around and disputing before he gets the libretto so arranged as to suit his purpose – and he will have put it off, and let time slip by, in accordance with his lovely habit. Now he must get going seriously at once, as he is driven by Count Rosenberg.[7]

Types of paper in the autograph score support the theory that *Figaro* was written in two principal phases, the first until around the end of November 1785 and comprising most of Acts 1 and 2, and the second from March 1786 until the premiere on 1 May. Work on the opera, though, did not stop entirely in between.[8] According to Michael Kelly, who sang Basilio and Don Curzio at the premiere, Mozart won a contest at the emperor's behest to stage *Figaro* at the Burgtheater in advance of new operas by Vincenzo Righini and Salieri.[9] As has been pointed out, back-stage maneuvering 'lends credibility to the hypothesis that *Figaro* may originally have been planned for performance in the season 1785–86, but was subsequently delayed until the beginning of the following season'.[10]

The Italian opera company in Vienna boasted several of Europe's leading singers, Francesco Benucci (Figaro) and Nancy Storace (Susanna) chief among them.[11] According to Giambattista Casti (1782), Benucci, with his 'rich vocal timbre' was a 'most excellent singer: the most graceful buffo known to me, without vulgarity and poor taste, but with elegance and intelligence'. For the *Berlinische musikalische Zeitung* (1793): '*Benucci*, one of the premier buffos in *opera buffa*, combines unaffected, excellent acting with an exceptionally round, beautiful and full bass voice. He is as much a complete singer as a choice actor.'[12] Storace, probably less vocally gifted than Benucci, was a late-eighteenth-century operatic superstar, praised for her captivating characterization, acting and musicianship in *buffa* roles.

---

[7] MBA, vol. 3, pp. 443–444; LMF, p. 893 (11–12 November 1785).

[8] See Edge, 'Mozart's Viennese Copyists', pp. 1436–1437.

[9] Kelly, *Reminiscences*, vol. 1, pp. 253–255.

[10] Edge, 'Mozart's Viennese Copyists', p. 1428. For Rice (*Mozart on the Stage*, p. 30), *Figaro* 'may have been conceived as a Carnival opera, though its premiere had to be delayed until after the festive season'.

[11] The popularity and success of Benucci and Storace can be gauged from the number and variety of roles they took on in the 1770s, early 1780s and beyond: see the lists in Dorothea Link (ed.), *Arias for Francesco Benucci, Mozart's First Figaro and Guglielmo* (Middleton, WI: A-R Editions, 2004), pp. xiv–xvi; and Link (ed.), *Arias for Nancy Storace, Mozart's First Susanna* (Middleton, WI: A-R Editions, 2002), pp. xiv–xvi.

[12] Quotations from Link (ed.), *Arias for Francesco Benucci*, p. viii.

She 'left … the impression, not perhaps of a great singer, but of a highly personable voice embodied in a remarkable and ingratiating stage presence'.[13] Michael Kelly identified Stefano Mandini (Count Almaviva), already encountered as Pippo in Mozart's inserted ensembles for Bianchi's *La villanella rapita* (see Chapter 6 of this volume), and Benucci as 'the two best comic singers in Europe'.[14] Stefano's wife, Maria Mandini, created the role of Marcellina and was described six years later as 'a fascinating singer – her voice nothing, but her grace, expression, soul, all strung to exquisite sensibility'.[15] Luisa Laschi (Countess Almaviva), in her performance in Martín y Soler's *L'arbore di Diana*, was 'grace and wit personified … what painter has ever depicted a mischievous smile more perfectly, what sculptor has portrayed more graceful gestures, what other singer is capable of producing such melting, marvellously smooth singing with such simplicity and genuine emotion?'[16] The other roles at the premiere were taken by Anna Gottlieb (Barbarina), aged just twelve years and two days on 1 May 1786, and the husband and wife Francesco Bussani (Bartolo/Antonio) and Dorothea Bussani (Cherubino), as well as Kelly, a popular buffo tenor admired by the emperor.[17] As was his usual practice, Mozart directed the first three performances of the opera from the keyboard.[18]

Performers and performance issues were inextricably linked to the creation and production of opera buffa in the late eighteenth century.[19] This is captured *inter alia* in the colourful reactions of singers to the music of Martín y Soler's popular *Una cosa rara*, which premiered in Vienna in November 1786 with six of the same principals as for *Figaro* a few

---

[13] On Storace, see Gidwitz, 'Vocal Portraits of Four Mozart Sopranos', pp. 103–205 (quotation at 188). See also Link (ed.), *Arias for Nancy Storace*, pp. vii–xiii. For biographical information on Storace, see Daniel Heartz, 'Nancy Storace, Mozart's Susanna', in Kristine K. Forney and Jeremy L. Smith (eds.), *Sleuthing the Muse: Essays in Honor of William F. Prizer* (New York: Pendragon Press, 2012), pp. 219–233. On trials and tribulations in 1785 in particular, see Dorothea Link, 'Nancy Storace's *annus horribilis*, 1785', *Mozart Society of America Newsletter*, 18/1 (2014), pp. 1, 3–7.

[14] Kelly, *Reminiscences*, vol. 1, p. 194.

[15] Clive, *Mozart and His Circle*, p. 93. For further late-eighteenth-century assessments of Maria Mandini's limitations as a singer, see Link (ed.), *Arias for Stefano Mandini*, pp. ix–x.

[16] Clive, *Mozart and His Circle*, p. 87. Leopold heard Laschi sing in Vienna in mid-February at her own concert, but does not comment on the performance. See his letter to Nannerl in MBA, vol. 3, p. 373; LMF, p. 886 (16 February 1785).

[17] On Emperor Joseph's admiration of Kelly, see Clive, *Mozart and His Circle*, p. 82.

[18] MDL, p. 446; MDB, p. 519.

[19] On the collaborative nature of opera buffa extended to librettists, directors, censors and set designers as well as composers and singers, see Edge, 'Mozart's Viennese Copyists', pp. 69–70, and Hunter, *The Culture of Opera Buffa in Mozart's Vienna*, pp. 4, 16.

months earlier (Benucci, Storace, Laschi, Stefano Mandini, Kelly, Dorothea Bussani).[20] According to Da Ponte:

The moment the parts were distributed, pandemonium broke loose. This one had too much recitative, the other not enough; for one the aria was too low pitched, for the other too high; these did not get into any concerts [ensembles], others had too many; this one was sacrificed to the leading lady, another to the first, second, third and fourth comedian. A general conflagration![21]

For the Italian composer, teacher and impresario Domenico Corri:

[Performers] become not only dictators in ... licentiousness of ornaments, but dictators of the poet and composer, and also of the manager: – the poet, unfortunately, in our modern operas, thus controlled by the singer, is obliged to write, cut, and carve, according to his or her will and pleasure. The composer, likewise, is placed in a similar situation, he must compose a bravura, rondo, pollaca &c.&c. for any situation the singer may select.[22]

A desire to curb the power and influence of singers informed Da Ponte's memorandum to the directors of the Burgtheater on 'Rules most necessary to theater direction', penned at some point before his departure from Vienna in spring 1791: the singer in 'the adjusted arias [altered at the music director's behest] ... must depend absolutely on the maestro, the poet and the director and may not ask the poet to make new changes or to introduce something that pleases him more', must maintain a professional attitude towards rehearsals and performances at all times, not feigning illness, and 'may not arbitrarily omit any piece from the opera ... [demanding] permission from the maestro, and from the poet, who will not concede him the omission without just reasons'.[23] But buffa singers also had positive and productive exchanges with composers. Kelly, for example, recounts negotiations with Mozart over Don Curzio's stuttering in the Act 3 sextet from *Figaro*, 'Riconosci in questo amplesso': Kelly insisted on it, in spite of Mozart's fears about disruption to the music, and was rewarded with audience approbation and the composer's warm acknowledgement that Kelly had been right all along. Kelly also

---

[20] *Una cosa rara* was performed 53 times between its premiere on 17 November 1786 and the end of the theatrical year 1790–1791 in mid April 1791. See Link, *National Court Theatre*, pp. 94–168. On comparisons with *Figaro*, see John Platoff, 'Review-Essay: A New History for Martín's *Una cosa rara*', *Journal of Musicology*, 12 (1994), pp. 85–115.

[21] *Memoirs of Lorenzo Da Ponte*, pp. 167–168.

[22] Translation from Gidwitz, 'Vocal Portraits of Four Mozart Sopranos', p. 3.

[23] As given in Daniel Heartz's translation in *Mozart's Operas*, pp. 104–105.

recalls delight at a spontaneous invitation from Mozart to listen to, and sing through, the Act 3 duet between the Count and Susanna after Mozart had 'just finished' it. And on *Figaro* as a whole, Kelly explained: 'It was allowed that never was an opera stronger cast ... All the original performers had the advantage of the instruction of the composer, who transfused into their minds its inspired meaning.'[24]

Primary sources for *Figaro* point to the impact on Mozart's compositional work of performers and of issues around performance. As is well known, Mozart in the autograph score swapped the music assigned to Susanna and the Countess in the Act 2 trio and Act 2 finale, perhaps first writing these ensembles before knowing for certain who would sing the roles; the higher lines initially for the Countess are later given to Susanna. Storace's vanity and desire for vocal pre-eminence may have motivated the changes.[25] Mozart's own annotations to the original performing score of *Figaro* (Österreichische Nationalbibliothek, OA 295) in Act 2 numbers, the Act 3 letter duet 'Che soave zeffiretto' and Act 4 finale, show him returning to the original conception – with the Countess receiving the higher lines – for the revival of the opera at the Burgtheater in 1789–1791 when the Countess was sung by Cavalieri and Susanna by Ferrarese del Bene.[26] The performing score, and original orchestral parts discovered by Dexter Edge in 1993, strongly suggest cuts made either before the premiere or during the first run of nine performances at the Burgtheater from 1 May to 18 December 1786,[27] although it is unclear whether they were made primarily for performance- or drama-related reasons. The cuts seem to have included Bartolo's aria 'La vendetta' from Act 1, the fifth section of the

---

[24] Kelly, *Reminiscences*, vol. 1, pp. 255–258 (quotations at 255).

[25] Edge, 'Mozart's Viennese Copyists', pp. 1578–1581. The decision not to call Laschi's 'Dove sono' a rondò may have been made for the same reason; see Dexter Edge, 'Musicological Introduction', in Wolfgang Amadeus Mozart, *'Le nozze di Figaro', K. 492: Facsimile of the Autograph Score* (Los Altos, CA: The Packard Humanities Institute, 2007), 3 vols., vol. 3, p. 17. Mozart began a rondò for Storace in Act 4, 'Non tardar amato bene', but did not finish it and ultimately replaced it with 'Deh vieni'. For the musical text of 'Non tardar', see NMA II/5/16, pp. 638–641. On Mozart's fragment, including possible reasons for abandoning it, and Vincenzo Righini's setting of the same text as a rondò, see John Platoff, '"Non tardar amato bene": Completed – but not by Mozart', *Musical Times*, 132 (1991), pp. 557–560.

[26] Edge, 'Mozart's Viennese Copyists', pp. 1569–1571, 1584. Mozart's annotations to the performing score were subsequently cancelled, but when and by whom is unknown. Edge explains (p. 1585): 'These cancellations might well have been made at some later time (in preparation for the revival in 1798, for example).'

[27] The performances in 1786 took place on 1, 3, 8, 24 May, 4 July, 28 August, 22 September, 15 November and 18 December. See MDL, p. 238; MDB, p. 272; Link, *National Court Theatre*, pp. 82–95 (also identifying a performance at the Habsburg's Laxenburg Castle, outside Vienna, on 7 June 1786).

Act 2 finale ('Cognoscete signor Figaro'), and Marcellina's Act 4 aria 'Il capro, e la capretta'. Whether other cuts to recitatives, arias and ensembles in the performing materials were made in 1786 is an open question.[28]

My chapter views intersections between the performance and composition of *Figaro* through the prism of the autograph score. As in the Viennese piano concertos examined in Chapter 4, the autograph of *Figaro* can have captured only a fraction of Mozart's performance-related decisions.[29] And it will not catch Mozart's modifications and refinements made during rehearsals for the premiere or the first run itself in 1786, although these in many cases are difficult to attribute securely to Mozart in the performing score and instrumental parts – rather than to others assuming responsibility – on account of 'very small' handwriting samples.[30] (An absence of vocal parts among the original performing parts also prevents us from determining where any of Mozart's late-stage, post-autograph adjustments could have been coordinated between instruments and voices.) As we shall see, both dynamic and character indications and modifications to the autograph, set in the context of phases of compositional work, point to active collaboration with singers and to orchestral effects maximizing vocal effects, thereby affirming the vibrant impact of performance on the compositional process.

Performing and Composing *Le nozze di Figaro*

In accordance with standard practice, Mozart did not compose *Figaro* chronologically from the first number to the last. As and when numbers were completed in the run-up to the premiere, he probably took them to Wenzel Sukowaty's copy shop at the Burgtheater in order for performance materials to be prepared, often writing at the end of each one which piece in the drama was to follow (such as 'segue scena VI finale' after the Count and Countess' recitative in Act 2, Scene 5).[31] An integrated autograph

[28] See Edge, 'Mozart's Viennese Copyists', pp. 1605–1618, 1628–1651; and Kritischer Bericht, NMA, II/5/16, pp. 14–15. Copyist Lorenz Lausch's advertisement for *Figaro*, listing individual numbers but excluding 'La vendetta', 'Cognoscete signor Figaro' and 'Il capro, e la capretta', also implies that they were cut. See MDL, pp. 242–243; MDB, pp. 276–277.

[29] For a similar point about late eighteenth-century opera primary sources in general, see Hunter, *Culture of Opera Buffa*, p. 18.

[30] On the original orchestral parts and performing score, including discussion of changes to the Act 3 finale and to Susanna's 'Deh vieni' made in 1786 in the hand of copyists and presumably sanctioned by Mozart, see Edge, 'Mozart's Viennese Copyists', pp. 1483–1668. On possible instances of Mozart's hand in the performing materials, see Edge, 'Mozart's Viennese Copyists', pp. 1481, 1512.

[31] See Edge, 'Musicological Introduction', in Mozart, *'Figaro': Facsimile of the Autograph*, vol. 3, pp. 21–22. See also Alan Tyson, 'Some Problems in the Text of *Le nozze di Figaro*: Did Mozart

would have existed, therefore, only 'in retrospect'.[32] As is evident from the autograph's different ink colours, Mozart invariably wrote in two stages, first establishing a *particella* or continuity draft comprising vocal lines, an instrumental bass line and occasional instrumental material, and later completing the remainder of the parts.

We know that Mozart frequently ran through aria *particella*s with his singers,[33] and his autograph of *Figaro* hints at where resulting discussions may have led to revisions. In the Count's Act 3 aria 'Vedrò, mentr'io sospiro', for example, Mozart expanded the vocal exit passage by three bars (to include triplet quavers, an octave leap and a trill): one bar is crossed out and an 'X' symbol directs the copyist to a notated addition on the reverse side of the last page of the aria.[34] (See Examples 7.1a and 7.1b.) It is not impossible, of course, that Mozart made the adjustment as a compositional act independent of his singer. But Mandini is likely to have assessed the aria *particella* and expressed a view, since the addition involves a virtuosic extension for him and the single deleted bar from the *particella* has material only for voice and instrumental bass. The 'wide-ranging' voice identified in Paris in 1789 (see Chapter 6) is accommodated in two types of virtuosity new to the aria in the interpolated segment: triplet quavers (also a prominent feature of an aria written for Mandini two years later in 1788, 'Tutto amabile e galante' from Pietro Alessandro Guglielmi's *La pastorella nobile*, so perhaps a musical element he particularly liked[35]) and a trill. Nancy Storace's involvement in changes to 'Deh vieni' is also plausible.[36] Rejected material at the end of 'Deh vieni' is a *particella*, as it is in the

Have a Hand in Them?' in *Mozart: Studies of the Autograph Scores*, pp. 290–327, at 290–291. At the end of the Countess' aria 'Dove sono' in Act 3, Mozart wrote 'segue l'arietta di Cherubino'; until a late stage in the compositional process Cherubino's 'Se cosi brami' was intended for this juncture (the text appearing in the original printed libretto), although no music for it is extant.

[32] Edge, 'Mozart's Viennese Copyists', p. 1741. See also his remark ('Musicological Introduction', in Mozart, *'Figaro': Facsimile of the Autograph*, vol. 3, p. 21) that 'Mozart's autograph score of *Figaro* probably did not exist as a unified object until around the time of the premiere of the opera, or perhaps even later'.

[33] On this process, focusing on *Cosi fan tutte*, see Ian Woodfield, 'Mozart's Compositional Methods: Writing for His Singers', in Keefe (ed.), *Cambridge Companion to Mozart*, pp. 35–47.

[34] See Mozart, *'Figaro': Facsimile of the Autograph*, vol. 2, pp. 370, 372.

[35] For an edition of 'Tutto amabile' see Link (ed.), *Arias for Stefano Mandini*, pp. 99–106.

[36] The complex compositional process for 'Deh vieni' includes an initial vocal continuity sketch, revisions to the flute and bassoon in the original instrumental parts, and rhythmic adjustments to the string accompaniment that necessitated re-copying the violin performing parts. As Edge remarks, the aria's 'apparently artless simplicity . . . seems to have caused Mozart some difficulty'. See Edge, 'Mozart's Viennese Copyists', pp. 1618–1621 (quotation at 1620). For further discussion, see NMA, II/5/16, Kritischer Bericht, pp. 219–226 and 352–357 (attempting to reconstruct the aria as it may have been heard at the premiere). For the vocal sketch, see NMA, II/5/16, p. 641.

Example 7.1a Mozart, 'Vedrò, mentr'io sospiro', from *Le nozze di Figaro*, original version of the run-up to the vocal exit, with a bar crossed out.

Example 7.1b Mozart, 'Vedrò, mentr'io sospiro', from *Le nozze di Figaro*, late insert at bar 105.

Example 7.2a Mozart, 'Deh vieni', from *Le nozze di Figaro*, bars 62–72 (final version).

Count's aria, suggesting revisions result either (or both) from discussion with Storace, or from Mozart's own recognition that the revised line would better accommodate Storace's voice. (Differences in the ink colour of the rejected *particella* and revised completion, implying the passing of time, also leave open the possibility of composer-singer consultation.) Most musical features of the rejected material resurface in the revision (see Examples 7.2a

Example 7.2b Mozart, 'Deh vieni', from *Le nozze di Figaro*, deleted material between bars 63 and 64.

and 7.2b): ascending semiquaver scales; sustained notes; concluding wind semiquaver imitation; and pauses. But the vocal angularity in rejected segments may have been an issue for Storace: two- and four-bar vocal passages proposed as replacements for material originally in the *particella*

and notated on lower staves in the autograph were then themselves rejected, and a leap in bars 64–65 (the beginning of the revised passage) was replaced by an iteration of the main motto. Judging by other arias written for Storace, she was certainly capable of large leaps from her mid-high range to chest voice, including towards the end of 'Venite inginocchiatevi' as we shall see: examples can be found in Stephen Storace's 'Fra quest'orror—Ma tarde le lagrime' and 'Qual confusion—Potessi di piangere', Salieri's 'D'un dolce amor la face', and Sarti's 'Non dubitar—Là tu vedrai'.[37] But passages such as the four-bar revised and rejected one in 'Deh vieni' are not typical of material written for her. It is also possible that vocal leaps in the segments ultimately rejected in 'Deh vieni' were felt – by performer, composer or both combined – to have stolen the thunder of the f''– f leap towards the end (bars 68–69).[38] In 'Dove sono', Laschi's opinions may have held sway, Mozart adding seven bars to the *particella* (see 73–79). The interpolated passage, expanding a hint of C minor from bar 55 to two bars (74–75), provides a smooth melodic line, including by reprising the material from bar 57. Laschi may have come to desire more 'smooth singing' – for which she was praised – before the arpeggiated ascent to her climactic a'' (bar 85). Another autograph adjustment evened out her vocal line (bars 60–62): the revision retains the same highpoint as the original (g'') but situates it in a more suave, cantabile context.[39]

The accrual of dynamic markings to the autograph often bears witness to the impact of performing considerations on Mozart's compositional process. The three-part aria 'In quegli anni' is a case in point, where Basilio tells a tale of visiting a cottage and receiving an ass' hide (Andante), using it as protection against a storm and a wild beast (Tempo di Menuetto, Allegro). The second and third parts, conveying the intense events, receive *f, p, fp* and *cresc* indications (sometimes in quick succession) at the *particella* stage, fixing in place almost all of the dynamics for these sections of the completed aria. In contrast, only one marking appears in the Andante's *particella* – a *pia:* in the instrumental bass (bar 8). When he orchestrated the aria, as recorded in brown ink, Mozart added a string of quick-fire dynamics *cresc – p – cresc – p – cresc – p – cresc – f – p* shortly before the end of the Andante (Example 7.3). Perhaps after experiencing a rendition of the aria or considering its effect in

---

[37] See editions of these arias in Link, *Arias for Nancy Storace*.

[38] Earlier in 'Deh vieni', in the run up to the cadence in the dominant, C, an arpeggiated vocal line and changed harmonies are the product of a revision (bars 40–41). The harmonies in the strings align with the revised version, rather than the *particella*: we can surmise (from ink colours) that the revision was therefore carried out during the completion phase.

[39] For 'Dove sono', see Mozart, *'Figaro': Facsimile of the Autograph Score*, vol. 2, pp. 402–413.

Example 7.3 Mozart, 'In quegli anni', from *Le nozze di Figaro*, bars 29–33.

performance, he decided to temper the contrast between the first and second to third sections, or to foreshadow the later sections towards the end of the first. At any rate, the situation here – contemplating the performance of the Andante after the *particella* had been written and when completing the aria – is similar to the situation with the first section of Osmin's Act 1 aria in *Die Entführung*, which acquired dynamics in the completion phase of the compositional process after the ensuing rage had already received them in the *particella* (see Chapter 2).

Attention to performing matters when completing a number is also a feature of the ensembles 'Cosa sento', 'Crudel!' and the Allegro molto of the Act 2 finale. In 'Cosa sento' the stage is set for energized orchestral playing as a result of Mozart's work on the completion: *sf* – *p* markings from the *particella* (bars 54 and 81) are preceded and followed by *crescendo* – *p* in the orchestration phase; and a *forte* reached via a *crescendo* in bars 65–66 is initially sustained to the end of the phrase in bar 69 but in the completion drops immediately to *piano* followed by a further crescendo to *forte*. At the end, effects accrue to the completion that are new to the ensemble: a *calando* –

which may designate a slowing of the tempo as well as a decrease in sound[40] – accompanies the final exit of the voices and coincides with a *Harmonie* sonority of two clarinets, two bassoons and two horns; and a *pp* for full ensemble occurs in the final two bars.[41] In the Act 3 duet for Susanna and the Count, 'Crudel!', all dynamics were written at the completion stage, except those ultimately rejected at the end of the number. Dynamic intensification and sensitivity to the voices are combined during the Count's questioning of Susanna in bars 42–54 (Example 7.4), where she mixes up her 'yes'/'no' responses on whether she will come to the garden for their rendezvous or let him down: the Count is asked to sing *dolce* (a rare marking in *Figaro*); his surprised responses are *forte* and the instrumental bass *sf* (with the upper strings *forte*); and Susanna's subsequent (expected) replies on f-sharp" are accompanied *piano* across the board, presumably in order to ensure audibility.[42] At the very end of the *particella* for the Allegro molto section of the Act 2 finale (Example 7.5), where Figaro pretends to have injured his foot in supposedly jumping from the window of the Countess' room, Mozart envisaged nine bars *piano*, instructing Figaro to pretend to be lame ('fingendo d'aversi stropiato il piede'). As shown in brown ink, all instruments (except the bass line) were entered into the score in the completion phase, as were the *forte* at Figaro's expression of confusion, the *p* in the next bar, and the 'colla voce ad libitum' (for viola 'ad libitum colla voce') as Figaro fakes injury. It is as if contemplating or experiencing Benucci's exaggerated behaviour encourages Mozart to instruct orchestral players to enhance onstage activity; the performance comes to life for its composer, then, when envisioned complete and when excellent acting skills exert an influence.[43] Moreover, Benucci's sustained note at the beginning of the ensuing Andante – finishing the description of lameness – activates the wind's distinctive sustained sound-world for the next section of the finale: engagement with Benucci's comic performance apparently affects the orchestration of an extended passage,

---

[40] See Brown, *Classical and Romantic Performing Practice*, p. 62.

[41] One other *pp* appears in 'Cosa sento' (in the *particella* and for strings only), at bar 147.

[42] The extension of the vocal participation from bar 67 (*particella*) to bar 69 (completion) led Mozart to replace the crescendo – *piano* – *forte* from bars 65–67 (*particella*) with a crescendo – *forte* in bars 67–69 (completion).

[43] On Mozart tailoring *Figaro* to Benucci and Storace's esteemed acting skills, focusing on the Act 4 finale, see Alessandra Campana, 'The Performance of Opera Buffa: *Le nozze di Figaro* and the Act IV Finale', in Stefano La Via and Roger Parker (eds.), *Pensieri per un maestro: Studi in onore di Pierluigi Petrobelli* (Turin: EDT, 2002), pp. 125–134. A number of other dynamic additions are made to this sixth section of the Act 2 finale at the completion stage. See, for example, the *forte*, *piano*, and *fortepiano* indications in Mozart, *'Figaro': Facsimile of the Autograph Score*, vol. 1, pp. 286–288.

Example 7.4 Mozart, 'Crudel!' from *Le nozze di Figaro*, bars 42–54.

further demonstrating continuities between Mozart's compositional and performance-based thinking.[44]

---

[44] Sustained notes in various combinations of flutes, oboes, horns and bassoons appear throughout the Andante of the Act 2 finale (bars 605–696).

Example 7.5 Mozart, Act 2 finale from *Le nozze di Figaro*, bars 596–609.

Dynamic markings in the Act 2 aria 'Venite inginocchiatevi', most acquired in the completion, may document a reaction to the nuances of Storace's voice.[45] A case in point is the five settings of the continuation of the

[45] Only the *pia:* at the opening, a *cresc: – for: – pia:* in bars 50–52, and (ultimately rejected) *sfps* in bars 96 and 100 were included in the *particella* of 'Venite inginocchiatevi'. The aria as a whole is

Example 7.6a Mozart, 'Venite inginocchiatevi', from *Le nozze di Figaro*, bars 8–14.

main theme, first heard from the upbeat to bar 11 to bar 14 in unison between voice and violin and an octave above the bassoon, with an *sfp* accent in the cellos/basses on the downbeat of bar 12 (Example 7.6a). The material appears twice in quick succession in the dominant, with partial vocal participation and no accents on the downbeat of the second bar (see bars 37–40, 47–50). The final two statements, one immediately after the other with the voice fully then partially involved, receive *sfp* accents in the *particella*. But the accents were deleted when Mozart came to orchestrate the aria (Example 7.6b); as can be seen in the autograph, the *sfp* in bar 100 is in the dark ink colour of the *particella*, but crossed out in the lighter ink of the completion.[46] The deleted *sfps* coincided with Storace's largest leap (a ninth from e" to d') and lowest note in the number. Given her rich, resonant lower

ideally suited to Storace, the comic performer *par excellence*: '[It] is constructed entirely as a buffa turn, an ensemble piece with stage action and vocal delivery in virtually non-stop nota e parole style' (Gidwitz, 'Vocal Portraits of Four Mozart Sopranos', p. 244).

[46] On account of the heavy crossing out it is more difficult to determine when the *sfp* in bar 96 was deleted, although it appears to have been originally written in the *particella*. The deleted dynamics in bars 96 and 100 are mistakenly identified as *fps* rather than *sfps* in NMA, II/5/16, Kritischer Bericht, p. 140.

Example 7.6b Mozart, 'Venite inginocchiatevi', from *Le nozze di Figaro*, bars 95–102 (including Mozart's deleted dynamics).

register,[47] Mozart presumably wanted to nullify the risk of the strings obscuring her at these moments. The *sfp* in the instrumental bass line in bar 12, from the completion, suggests that an accent was initially conceived for the final iteration of this material at the end of the aria, but ultimately rejected there and (in effect) transferred to the opening iteration, where it would not disturb a demonstrative leap or a note in Storace's chest voice and would take its place among a series of instrumental nuances (including *p*, *mfp* and *sfp* simultaneously in bar 8; see Example 7.6a).

Singers and Effects

As in *Die Entführung* and dramatic works between 1782 and 1786, Mozart maximized the impact of his singers in *Figaro* by deploying instrumental effects in conjunction with accommodating vocal qualities. Benucci's 'Non più andrai' is affectionate satire, '[more] military than anything in the military repertoire itself', and at least partly inspired by a rhythmic pattern in Paisiello's earlier *Figaro* opera, *Il barbiere di Siviglia*.[48] It is also a showstopper, the kind of 'noisy' number Mozart thought would elicit rapturous applause at the end of an act.[49] Michael Kelly recalled a rehearsal of the aria with the full orchestra, sung by Benucci 'with the greatest animation and power of voice':

I was standing close to Mozart, who, *sotto voce*, was repeating, Bravo! Bravo! Bennuci [*sic*]; and when Bennuci came to the fine passage, 'Cherubino, alla vittoria, alla Gloria militar', which he gave out with Stentorian lungs, the effect was electricity itself, for the whole of the performers on the stage, and those in the orchestra, as if actuated by one feeling of delight, vociferated Bravo! Bravo! Maestro. Viva, viva grande Mozart. Those in the orchestra I thought would never have ceased applauding, by beating the bows of their violins against the music desks. The little man acknowledged, by repeated obeisances, his thanks for the distinguished mark of enthusiastic applause bestowed upon him.[50]

The effect deemed so exciting at the end of the aria is a loud, final flourish for Benucci; it projects forwards into the strident orchestral coda bringing down the curtain on Act 1 (Example 7.7). The military wind and brass, Figaro's only

---

[47] See Gidwitz, 'Vocal Portraits of Four Mozart Sopranos', pp. 163–167, and *passim*.

[48] Raymond Monelle, *The Musical Topic: Hunt, Military and Pastoral* (Bloomington: Indiana University Press, 2006), pp. 175–176; Heartz, *Mozart's Operas*, p. 147.

[49] On the final number of the first act of *Die Entführung* in this respect, see MBA, vol. 3, p. 163; LMF, p. 770 (26 September 1781). See also discussion in Chapter 2.

[50] Kelly, *Reminiscences*, vol. 1, p. 256.

Example 7.7 Mozart, 'Non più andrai', from *Le nozze di Figaro*, bars 89–103.

Example 7.7 (cont.)

orchestral accompaniment, is held at a *piano* dynamic, presumably so as not to detract from the singer's exit passage. The concluding *forte* orchestral statement subsequently intensifies the *piano* statement, continuing to promote Figaro's 'glory' after his departure. In fact, the simultaneous winds-brass *piano* and vocal *forte* (implied in Benucci's rendition with 'Stentorian lungs'), and succession of *piano* and *forte* orchestral statements, exploits dynamic interplay witnessed throughout the number, beginning in the very first bar, where a *forte* for strings and bassoons cedes to instrumental *piano*s for the theme. Perhaps Mozart initially envisaged the first appearance of the wind-only march in the second half of the second episode (bar 61ff.) at a *forte* dynamic: an immediately preceding *crescendo* to *forte* marked into the first violin and bass parts at the *particella* stage is not counteracted dynamically by the flute following it in the *particella*. When completing the orchestration, as indicated by the lighter ink, Mozart wrote 'piano assai' for each of the wind parts (flutes, oboes, horns, bassoons).[51] The semiquaver scales to end the second episode (bars 69–76) are dynamically different from the corresponding passage at the end of the first episode: bar-by-bar alternating *forte* and *piano*s with a concluding *crescendo* to *forte* are all in the *particella*,

---

[51] See Mozart, *'Figaro': Facsimile of the Autograph Score*, vol. 1, p. 151.

whereas in the first episode they are *piano* in the *particella* (bars 26–31). When Mozart came to orchestrate the end of the first episode he added a *crescendo, forte, piano* in bars 29–31, bringing it partially into line with the dynamics in the second episode, but without replicating the bar-by-bar *forte – piano* alternation.[52] At the opening of the second episode (bars 43–54) Benucci had opportunities to shine, as at the end of the aria, in spite of orchestral tutti *fortes*: initially the strings drop out to coincide with Benucci's participation; then the voice and orchestra boldly alternate. In sum, 'Non più andrai' promoted both singer and aria by marshaling vocal material and orchestral effects to build to a final climax and roaring conclusion to the act.

In the Act 4 aria 'Aprite un po'', as in 'Non più andrai', orchestral instruments support Benucci's explosiveness, including with a memorable horn fanfare marked *fortissimo* (following *piano* iterations of the same figure) that foreshadows the *forte* burst of Benucci's two-bar exit figure (bars 106–108, Example 7.8).[53] Throughout the aria, including here, the orchestra dynamically reinforce Benucci's e-flat' highpoint.[54] Mozart drew on combined lyrical, *parlando* and patter singing that characterized earlier music for Benucci by Cimarosa and Paisiello, as well as on strident, appeggiated material apparently appropriate for his voice.[55] As in 'Non più andrai', Mozart also enhanced the singer's impact by directing orchestral surges towards a climactic effect at the end.

Mozart paid special attention to wind effects associated with *Figaro's* female singers, mostly at the completion stage but also in the *particella*.[56] In the duettino 'Via, resti servita' with Marcellina, Susanna delivers her insulting *coup de grace* 'Sibilla decrepita, da rider mi fa' ('Decrepit old Sibyl, you make me laugh', bars 36–38) alongside a full-wind contingent of flutes, oboes, horns and bassoons, with strings absent for the only time in the number.[57] When turning quietly to address the Countess in 'Venite

---

[52] See Mozart, *'Figaro': Facsimile of the Autograph Score*, vol. 1, pp. 146–147.

[53] On the association between horns and thoughts of being cuckolded in Salieri's *La fiera di Venezia* (1772), which anticipates 'Aprite un po'', see Rice, *Antonio Salieri and Viennese Opera*, p. 190.

[54] See, for example, the *sf – p* in bar 34 and the *p – cresc – f* in bars 62–66 and 90–94 coinciding with triplet-quaver vocal ascents.

[55] See Link (ed.), *Arias for Francesco Benucci*; and Julian Rushton, 'Theatre Music from Vienna', *Early Music*, 36 (2008), pp. 474–476. Another of Benucci's probable skills acquired during time in Spain, dancing the fandango, was exploited by Mozart in the Act 3 finale. On the famous exclusion and inclusion of the dance in *Figaro*, see Dorothea Link, 'The Fandango Scene in Mozart's *Le nozze di Figaro*', *Journal of the Royal Musical Association*, 133 (2008), pp. 69–92, especially 91–92; reprinted in Keefe (ed.), *Mozart*, pp. 203–226, at 225–226.

[56] For example, at Storace's entry in the first number (the duet 'Cinque') a delicate *mf – p* colouring her vocal line in the oboes, horns and bassoons is notated in the *particella*.

[57] Another statement of this line in bars 64–66, now including Marcellina, is scored in the same way.

Example 7.8 Mozart, 'Aprite un po'', from *Le nozze di Figaro*, bars 102–108.

inginocchiatevi' (the instruction 'piano alla Contessa' was written during
the completion phase), Storace is surrounded by a swathe of sustained,
slow-moving winds to which accrue the aria's only *pp* markings.
Contemplating both Susanna's special relationship with the Countess,
captured in a written instruction, and the complete number in

performance, may have stimulated the refined instrumental effect. In 'Deh
vieni', Mozart decided to include the flute later than the oboe and bassoon,
but before the end of the *particella* phase: the three wind instruments are
not in their normal order in the autograph and the designation '1 flauto' at
the beginning of the score was written later than '1 oboe' and '1 fagotto'.
But a thematic fragment for flute in the rejected ending to the aria
(*particella* only) confirms Mozart's decision to include it before finishing
the *particella*. Perhaps he initially thought to employ the same oboe-
bassoon obbligato combination that graced Laschi and Storace's Act 3
duet, 'Che soave zeffiretto'.[58] Mozart or Storace's views on singer-
orchestra interaction could have provoked the changed ending to the aria
(which is discussed above): the first bars of the revision (64–65), with
coll'arco strings and sustained notes in the three obbligato winds, comprise
a doubly new accompanimental sonority for the aria. The inclusion of
flutes in the B-flat Allegro from the Act 2 finale (section 3), perhaps decided
only at the completion stage, also affects Storace and Laschi's sound
world:[59] one flute offers the first wind contribution to the section, presenting part of the main theme; and two together comprise the only wind
accompaniment to Susanna and the Countess' repeated sniping asides
(until the final iteration in bar 293 by the oboes).

Laschi's 'Porgi amor' and Dorotea Bussani's 'Voi che sapete' also integrate
vocal and instrumental effects. 'Porgi amor', a self-absorbed performance
introducing a character in a song-like environment and appealing directly to
the theatrical audience,[60] renders wind and Countess unambiguous allies, in
the process exemplifying Ignaz Arnold's 'economy of effect'.[61] Once the
Countess has entered, the two-clarinet, two-bassoons, two-horn *Harmonie*
sonority maximizes impact in sparing appearances: it creates a two-bar link
between vocal phrases, supports Laschi's ascent to the modest highpoint of
a-flat" via a *crescendo* to *forte*, reinforces her penultimate E-flat cadence and
provides a *piano* postlude. While 'Porgi amor', late in *Figaro*'s gestation,

[58] On the interweaving voices and obbligato wind in 'Che soave zeffiretto', see Keefe, *Mozart's
Piano Concertos*, pp. 135–136.

[59] When writing the *particella* for the finale Mozart left the middle staves of his autograph free for
wind instruments, but had to adjust the staves on which each of them was notated according to
the number of instruments needed for each section. Switches from one stave to another at the
beginnings of sections were all notated at the completion stage. Where space on his 12-stave
paper was insufficient for all voices and instruments – most notably in the final section of the
finale – Mozart wrote wind parts on extra sheets of paper. See Mozart, *'Figaro': Facsimile of the
Autograph Score*, vol. 2, pp. 595–612.

[60] See Mary Hunter's interpretation of 'Porgi amor' in 'Rousseau, the Countess, and the Female
Domain', in Eisen (ed.), *Mozart Studies 2*, pp. 1–26.

[61] Arnold, 'Oekonomie der Instrumente' in *Mozarts Geist*, pp. 208–231.

probably would have post-dated any putative reaction to Laschi's music from Storace, it still might have raised an eyebrow: Laschi is cocooned by a sonorous wind complement.[62] 'Voi che sapete', a 'sudden invitation [for the audience] to consider a performance as a performance',[63] elicits praise from onstage characters and sympathy from wind instruments not implicated in the diegetic experience. As Abert points out: 'The winds tell the listener what is going on in the heart of the young poet and singer ... the tone colour alone ... sufficient to round out the picture of this infatuated boy's soul.'[64] Wind support and links between vocal phrases are the order of the day, yielding closer voice-instrument relationships later in the number than earlier.[65] At the statement of the main theme in the reprise (Example 7.9) a chromatic link in bar 65 absent from the corresponding moment at the opening of the aria predicts the chromatic continuation by Cherubino in the next bar. Indeed, keenness to support Cherubino instrumentally at this juncture can be inferred from a deletion in the autograph score: when he came to orchestrate the number, Mozart had the flute, oboe, clarinet and bassoon begin their participation in the reprise two bars earlier than in the final version, crossing out the initial material presumably once realizing it did not work with the harmony. The composer-performers Cherubino and Mozart, on stage and off, are eager to impress in compositional and performing domains.[66]

Singing *Sotto Voce*

One recurring effect in Acts 2, 3 and 4 of *Figaro*, supported by instrumental participation, speaks to Mozart's expectations of his singers and to their roles in creating and communicating musical drama. Whether *sotto voce*, literally 'under the voice', denotes a dynamic louder than *p* or between *p* and *pp* with emotion,[67] it requires expressive intensification. And its

---

[62] As mentioned, it is possible that the 'rondò' designation for Laschi's 'Dove sono' was cancelled in order to appease Storace. See Heartz, *Mozart's Operas*, p. 152; Edge, 'Musicological Introduction', in Mozart, *'Figaro': Facsimile of the Autograph Score*, vol. 3, p. 17; and Edge, 'Mozart's Viennese Copyists', pp. 1580–1581.

[63] Hunter, *Culture of Opera Buffa*, p. 46. See also Edward Cone, *The Composer's Voice* (Berkeley, CA: University of California Press, 1974), pp. 30–31.

[64] Abert, *W. A. Mozart*, p. 951.   [65] Keefe, *Mozart's Piano Concertos*, pp. 140–141.

[66] As indicated in the orchestral parts for the premiere, Mozart at one stage envisaged, but then rejected, a 12-bar reprise of 'Voi che sapete' for the Act 4 finale. See Edge, 'Mozart's Viennese Copyists', p. 1598; NMA, II/5/16, Kritischer Bericht, pp. 405–407.

[67] See, respectively, Neumann, *Performance Practices of the Seventeenth and Eighteenth Centuries*, p. 17, and Badura-Skoda and Badura-Skoda, *Interpreting Mozart*, p. 48.

Example 7.9 Mozart, 'Voi che sapete', from *Le nozze di Figaro*, bars 62–67 (including Mozart's deleted wind parts).

appearance has already been noted at important moments in *Die Entführung* (1781–1782), *L'oca del Cairo* (1783) and the ensembles inserted into Bianchi's *La villanella rapita* (1785). Mozart considered it essential for singers and players to follow his expression marks, benefitting both the performer him or herself and (in an operatic context) the drama. In the single extant letter to Aloysia Weber (30 July 1778), he discussed the concert aria 'Ah, lo previdi' K. 272 originally for Josepha Duschek: 'I particularly advise you to pay attention to the expression marks – to think carefully about the meaning and the force of the words – to put yourself with all seriousness into Andromeda's situation and position! – and to imagine yourself to be that very person.'[68] And a few months earlier in Mannheim he explained that the Andante from the piano sonata written for Rosa Cannabich was 'full of expression, and must be accurately played,

[68] MBA, vol. 2, p. 420; LMF, p. 581. Translation from the Italian original in Robert Spaethling, *Mozart's Letters, Mozart's Life*, p. 172. Lange's dynamic and expressive flexibility is warmly praised by Schönfeld in 'Yearbook of the Music of Vienna and Prague', p. 306.

as it stands, with the gusto, forte and piano'.[69] As we shall see, the *sotto voce*s in *Figaro* allow singers proactively to shape the musical drama in the context of expressive intensification. In these instances Mozart did not necessarily try to accommodate the attributes of individual singers, but rather to nurture their fundamentally creative roles in individually and collectively communicating and contributing to the dramatic experience.

Mozart wrote *sotto voce* at the decisive moment in the Act 4 finale when all principal characters, singing together for the first time, emphasize the redemptive power of love, one of the morals of *Figaro*; a large wind contingent is also deployed here at a *pp* dynamic with which they are rarely associated.[70] Two further *sotto voce*s were included earlier in the Act 4 finale to capture Basilio/Don Curzio, Antonio and Bartolo's astonishment: initially at the situation, and the Count's anger, when first entering (bar 351); and later (together with the Count) at the Countess coming on stage and taking off her disguise. If so inclined, then, performers interpreting Mozart's markings can resolve implicit uncertainties associated with the first two *sotto voce*s in the final one.

By the end of the opera, in fact, singers have had several opportunities to construct and communicate narratives from Mozart's *sotto voce* markings, including in the Act 2 finale. At the temporary *rapprochement* between the Count and the Countess/Susanna at the end of the first dramatic 'wave' ('Da questo momento', Example 7.10),[71] Mozart writes *sotto voce* for voices and *pp* for strings into the *particella*. Having from the start envisioned an expressive effect, Mozart adds to it at the completion stage, cushioning the voices with *piano* sustained wind above and below; different dynamics for distinct textural strands, in addition to the *sotto voce*, encourage engaged performance to coincide with a plot development. In the Andante ('Cognoscete', section 5), the Countess, Susanna and Figaro make an appeal, *sotto voce*, to the Count to permit the wedding (bar 449, Example 7.11). Figaro had previously used the same material to try (unconvincingly) to persuade the Count that his face may appear to lie but he himself does not (bar 425). The *sotto voce* request, direct to the Count, emotionally intensifies Figaro's earlier statement of the theme, hinting at

---

[69] MBA, vol. 2, p. 124; LMF, p. 374 (14 November 1777).

[70] The special dynamic effect at this moment is also recognized by Heartz in *Mozart, Haydn, Early Beethoven*, pp. 149–150. As in the Act 2 finale, Act 3 sextet and Act 3 finale, winds are written on additional sheets of paper at this juncture to accommodate the large number of stave required for all of the vocal and instrumental parts.

[71] On the interpretation of the 'dramatic curve' of the Act 2 finale as four 'waves', see Wye Jamison Allanbrook, *Rhythmic Gesture in Mozart: 'Le nozze di Figaro' and 'Don Giovanni'* (Chicago, IL: University of Chicago Press, 1983), pp. 119–135, especially 119–120.

Example 7.10 Mozart, Act 2 finale from *Le nozze di Figaro*, bars 306–311.

a connection performers can make with the effect at the end of the Allegro (section 3, in Example 7.10): a previous moment of reconciliation, the Count and Countess/Susanna agreeing to try to understand each other, is invoked to get the Count to agree to a more significant one in which that understanding will be fully demonstrated. (Initial horn tied notes, *piano*, also act as a reminder of the *p* sustained wind notes in the earlier passage.) In the midst of the musical and dramatic frenzy at the end of the finale, the four characters in the ascendancy (Count, Marcellina, Bartolo, Basilio) sing *sotto voce* of being brought to the scene by a propitious power – first unaccompanied, then with wind support (bar 821ff., Example 7.12). The performers thereby requisition poignantly powerful *sotto voce* effects from earlier in the finale as musical support for demonstrations of dramatic superiority.

In the Act 3 sextet, 'Riconosci in questo amplesso', *sotto voce* markings coincide with revisions to wind orchestration, appearing in an ensemble that communicates the single most significant development in the opera's plot. Mozart wrote the wind parts on sheets of paper separated from the

Example 7.11 Mozart, Act 2 finale from *Le nozze di Figaro*, bars 449–453.

main body of the sextet autograph and, judging by the ink colour, in one compositional phase.[72] He subsequently thinned out wind participation in the 'sua madre / sua padre' and 'Al fiero tormento / Al dolce contento' sections (bars 88–122), apparently quite late in the process of preparing the opera: deleted segments appear in the orchestral parts copied from the autograph and are themselves then deleted in these parts.[73] Once Susanna had been fully apprised of the revelation about Figaro's parentage, her expansive, lyrical line ('Al dolce contento', bars 103ff., Example 7.13) was initially cushioned above and below by the first flute and first bassoon. Storace could have requested the deletion of the instrumental doubling to allow her to soar unhindered above the texture. Equally, Storace's special relationship with flute and bassoon in 'Che soave zeffiretto' and 'Deh vieni' and the *sotto voce* in the voices could explain, respectively, the original scoring and the revision. All of the preceding *sotto voce*s in Act 2 are either

---

[72] For the wind parts of the sextet, see Mozart, *'Figaro': Facsimile of the Autograph*, vol. 2, pp. 587–592.

[73] See Edge, 'Musicological Introduction', in Mozart, *'Figaro': Facsimile of the Autograph*, vol. 3, p. 22.

Example 7.12 Mozart, Act 2 finale from *Le nozze di Figaro*, bars 821–830.

Example 7.13 Mozart, 'Riconosci', from *Le nozze di Figaro*, bars 101–110 (wind and voice parts only, with material for flute and bassoon crossed out).

unaccompanied by winds, or lightly supported by sustained wind notes; none feature melodic doubling of the voices.[74] The deletion therefore aligns the end of the sextet with these earlier passages. And just as the earlier *sotto voces* reinforce important dramatic developments, so the sextet *sotto voce* 'defeats' the *forte* outbursts of the Count/Don Curzio, capturing the definitive failure of the Count's plans to scupper Figaro and Susanna's wedding: the outbursts, heard four times, are eventually subsumed by the *sotto voce*. Thus, continuities between performance and composition – Mozart trying to impress compositionally by actively encouraging engaged, impassioned performance – are again conveyed in autograph materials.

After the Premiere

The fates of the composer and his or her singers were inextricably linked in late-eighteenth-century opera. But for *Figaro* neither could do much to mitigate the effects of a fierce rivalry – shaping the premiere and later performances in 1786 – between the recently re-established Viennese Singspiel and the Italian opera company. The Salzburg journal *Pfeffer und Salz* (5 April) foresaw a rocky ride for *Figaro* on account of a lack of support for 'indigenous artists' in Vienna, Leopold got wind of 'astonishingly powerful cabals' against Mozart shortly before the premiere, and the *Wiener Realzeitung* referred to them on 11 July 1786.[75] In fact, Dittersdorf's *Der Apotheker und der Doktor* and Mozart's *Figaro* went head to head as flagship works for the two camps, Dittersdorf proving especially adept at manipulating the competitive situation to his own side's advantage. Even in Italian journals in 1786, *Figaro* received less attention than *Der Apotheker*. The tide only began to turn towards Italian opera with the premiere of Soler's *Una cosa rara* on 17 November 1786.[76]

In addition to the battle for supremacy with German opera in Vienna, the length of *Figaro* is an important theme in its early history and reception. Da Ponte explained the need to shorten Beaumarchais' play and the

---

[74] The *sotto voce* vocal lines at the beginning of the Allegretto of the Act 3 finale are doubled instrumentally, but are sung by a chorus not by individual soloists.

[75] See MDL, p. 236; MDB, p. 270. Leopold's letter is given in MBA, vol. 3, p. 536; LMF, p. 897 (28 April 1786). For the *Wiener Realzeitung* report, see MDL, p. 244; MDB, p. 278.

[76] For a full account, see Woodfield, *Cabals and Satires*, Chapter 1. After leaving Vienna in 1787, Dittersdorf worked on a satire of *Figaro*; see Woodfield, *Cabals and Satires*, Chapter 3.

still-significant duration of the opera in his preface to the libretto.[77] According to the *Bayreuther Zeitung* on 16 May 1786, just two weeks after the premiere, improvements were deemed necessary by connoisseurs and quickly implemented by Mozart; Dexter Edge's identification of numbers and sections cut during the first run of performances, perhaps capturing an 'improvement' process, documents sensitivity to the opera's length.[78] The same may apply to the imperial decree forbidding encores of arias from the work, the 'early departure . . . before the end of the opera' of the royal attendees at the Prague performance on 14 October 1787 who enjoyed it nonetheless, and the rendition of *Figaro* over two days rather than one at the Teatro della Pergola in Florence in June 1788.[79] The perceived difficulty of *Figaro*, no doubt partially promoted by the German opera faction initially for reasons of self-interest,[80] often focused on the challenges of performance. For Bernard Anselm Weber, a rendition in 1789 'went very well, despite the music of this opera being among the most difficult that we have'.[81] And, implying the advantage of performing *Figaro* several times during the first run, the *Wiener Realzeitung* explained: 'It is correct that the first performance did not go at its best, because the composition is very difficult. But now, after repeated performances, we would be subscribing either to the *cabal* or to *tastelessness* if we wanted to claim that Herr *Mozart's* music is anything but a masterpiece of art.'[82] Neither length nor putative difficulty hindered *Figaro*'s success after the premiere: it was staged frequently in the remainder of the composer's life, including for the first time in Prague (1786); Donaueschingen and Monza (1787); Florence, Graz and Frankfurt (1788); Hannover, Baden, Brunswick and Mainz (1789); Stuttgart, Berlin, Postdam and Mannheim (1790); and Hamburg (1791), in addition to being revived in Vienna between 1789 and 1791.[83] Joseph II's decision to stage a gala performance in Prague on 14 October 1787 to celebrate the marriage of his niece, Maria Theresia, to Prince Anton Clemens of Saxony was a key moment in the opera's reception, probably encouraging productions to be mounted elsewhere.[84] It had already achieved remarkable popularity earlier in 1787 in Prague.

[77] MDL, pp. 239–240; MDB, pp. 273–274.
[78] Woodfield, *Cabals and Satires*, Chapter 1; Edge, 'Mozart's Viennese Copyists', pp. 1605–1618, 1628–1651.
[79] MDL, pp. 241, 244, 265, 278; MDB, pp. 275, 278–279, 300, 317.
[80] See Woodfield, *Cabals and Satires*, Chapter 1.   [81] MDL, p. 303; MDB, p. 345.
[82] MDL, p. 244; MDB, p. 278.
[83] MDL, pp. 261–342; MDB, pp. 298–390. On the Viennese revival of *Figaro*, see Chapter 9 of this volume.
[84] Woodfield, *Cabals and Satires*, Chapter 1.

Witnessing the success himself, Mozart wrote back to his Vienna-based friend Baron Gottfried von Jacquin: 'Here nothing is spoken of but "Figaro". Nothing played, blown, sung or whistled but "Figaro". No opera as watched as – "Figaro" and forever "Figaro". Certainly a great honour for me.'[85] Niemetschek endorsed Mozart's claim: 'The enthusiasm it excited among the public was unprecedented ... [In] short, Figaro's tunes were repeated in the streets and the parks; even the harpist on the alehouse bench had to play "Non più andrai" if he wanted to be heard.'[86]

On 23 February 1787, ten days after returning from Prague, Mozart probably performed the aria 'Ch'io mi scordi di te' K. 505 with Storace at her farewell concert at the Kärntnertortheater.[87] Scored for solo piano, voice and orchestra, it occupies a special place in his output, written for both a star singer and himself ('für Mad[selle] Storace und mich', as recorded in the Thematic Catalogue).[88] Perhaps the insert aria to the same text for the revival of *Idomeneo* in March 1786 (K. 490), for violinist Count August Clemens Hatzfeld as well as voice, gave Mozart the idea of including an instrumental as well as vocal soloist in K. 505; the ebb and flow of two virtuosos also brings to mind Mozart and Regina Strinasacchi in the accompanied sonata in B-flat, K. 454.[89] Mozart's elaborate writing for the piano more than compensates for the absence of vocal bravura (to which Storace was apparently not well suited[90]), including in passages where bravura typically would be anticipated, such as towards the end. Mozart's piano drifts repeatedly above Storace's line, as if to compensate for the 'height' that her voice naturally lacked, and elaborates her music with the

---

[85] MBA, vol. 4, p. 10; LMF, p. 903 (15 January 1787). On the version of *Figaro* Mozart is likely to have encountered in January 1787, based on transmission of materials from Vienna to Prague, see Woodfield, *Le nozze di Figaro*, forthcoming. On changes to the musical text almost certainly not attributable to Mozart, see Alan Tyson, 'The 1786 Prague Version of Mozart's "Le nozze di Figaro"', *Music & Letters*, 69/3 (1988), pp. 321–33.

[86] Niemetschek, *Leben*, p. 26; *Life of Mozart*, p. 35 (translation amended).

[87] 'Ch'io mi scordi di te' was completed on 27 December 1786, shortly before the trip to Prague. Albeit many years later, Thomas Attwood (NMD, p. 39) recalls its performance 'at Storace's Benefit'. Storace left Vienna for London soon after the concert, intending to return in 1788 (although she did not ultimately do so). Leopold entertained Storace, her brother and mother, Attwood, and Michael Kelly, when they passed through Salzburg. See MBA, vol. 4, p. 28; LMF, p. 906 (1 March 1787).

[88] See Mozart, *Eigenhändiges Werkverzeichnis Faksimile*, folio 9v.

[89] For discussion of the Accompanied Sonata K. 454 and the Aria K. 490, see Chapters 5 and 6 respectively. For a brief comparison of K. 490 and K. 505, see Heartz, 'Nancy Storace', pp. 230–232.

[90] See Gidwitz, 'Vocal Portraits of Four Mozart Sopranos', pp. 126, 140–141; Link (ed.), *Arias for Nancy Storace*, p. viii.

semiquavers she would not have wanted.[91] As in both *Figaro* and the piano concertos from 1784 to 1786, the story of Mozart negotiating performing and compositional priorities is partially told through changes to the autograph. Close to the end of the Andante, a six-bar passage is deleted (piano, voice and instrumental bass line only): Mozart had juxtaposed the piano triplet semiquavers and the voice here as a resolution to the immediately preceding confrontation where they were set against each other in alternation.[92] Deciding instead to re-iterate the confrontation one more time and project upward-moving piano triplet semiquavers towards an Augmented 6th – V/E-flat progression and vocal fermata for Storace, Mozart provides an opportunity (should Storace so desire) for embellishments in the fermata effectively to grow out of the piano's semiquavers, reactivating the momentarily abandoned close bond between singer and pianist. At the end of the Allegretto, Mozart expanded the soloists' exit passage from three bars in the original version to eight in the final version (bars 204–211), concomitantly increasing the virtuosity profile of the soloists and their elaborate interweaving. The desire for combined appreciation of soloists and work remained uppermost in Mozart's mind.

As Mozart bade farewell in 'Ch'io mi scordi di te' to a principal vocal collaborator from *Figaro*, he simultaneously celebrated her vocal skills and celebrity, his own as performer-composer, and the continuities and intersections between performance and composition characterizing both his Viennese piano concertos and latest opera. But Mozart may already have had one eye on the operatic future by the time of the aria's presumed performance in late February 1787. He had returned from Prague with discussions of another project in the air (at least) and would soon turn attention to a new group of singers – several encountered among the Prague *Figaro* cast[93] – and a new venue for an operatic premiere.

---

[91] For a similar interpretation of Mozart accommodating Storace's limitations in 'Ch'io mi scordi di te', see Gidwitz, 'Vocal Portraits of Four Mozart Sopranos', p. 178. Gidwitz also discusses parallels between this aria and Stephen Storace's 'Be mine tender passion' written for his sister to sing in London (pp. 183–185).

[92] For the original version see the autograph at the Biblioteka Jagiellońska Kraków, Mus. ms. autogr. W. A. Mozart 505, and NMA, II/5/16, Kritische Berichte, pp. 63–64. On confrontation in the revised version of this passage, see Keefe, *Mozart's Viennese Instrumental Music*, pp. 196–198.

[93] See Woodfield, *Performing Operas for Mozart*, pp. 55–64.

In Prague and Vienna
Don Giovanni, *1787–1788*

Mozart mentioned *Don Giovanni* in his correspondence only once he had arrived in Prague for the rehearsals and premiere in October 1787. Confirming an agreement with Nannerl to inherit 1,000 gulden (a Viennese currency) from their father's estate following Leopold's death on 28 May, Mozart wrote to his brother-in-law Johann Baptist Berchtold von Sonnenburg with practical arrangements for the days ahead (29 September 1787): 'When you send the bill of exchange to me, I ask you please *to address it to Herr Michael Puchberg, at Count Walsegg's house on the Hohe Markt* because he has orders to accept the money as I leave very early on Monday for Prague.'[1] Judging by traveller Johann Kaspar Riesbeck's experience c. 1780, Mozart would have had a pleasant journey: the road from Vienna to Prague was excellent, with regular markers recording location and distance; the land was an attractive colour and the ground good; and Kolin, forty miles or so southeast of Prague, offered an agreeable stopover point.[2]

Mozart almost certainly reached the beautiful capital of a country of 11,000 villages, 244 towns and 1.2 million inhabitants, a city described as the 'fatherland of German music' (*das Vaterland der deutscher Tonkunst*) with 'the most musical people of Germany, or, perhaps, of all Europe', on Thursday 4 October.[3] Once there, he could have enjoyed the nicest view in any big town in Europe, according to Riesbeck on the Charles Bridge, a pretty location (accepting the poor condition of some buildings), and an environment conducive to promoting arts and sciences in general as well as

---

[1] MBA, vol. 4, p. 54 (italics in original); LMF, p. 910.

[2] Riesbeck, *Briefe eines Reisenden Franzosen über Deutschland*, pp. 396–402.

[3] For the quotations, see the unsigned article 'Ueber den Zustand der Musik in Böhmen', *Allgemeine musikalische Zeitung*, 2 (1799–1800), cols. 488–494, 497–507, 513–523, 537–542, at col. 488; and Burney, *The Present State of Music in Germany, The Netherlands, and United Provinces*, vol. 2, p. 3. Mozart's arrival was reported in the *Prager Oberpostamtszeitung* two days later, on 6 October: see MDL, p. 263; MDB, p. 299. On the favourable conditions for Mozart in Prague, see Braunbehrens, *Mozart in Vienna*, pp. 293–302, especially p. 297. The famously well-developed Bohemian musical culture in the eighteenth century, beginning with young children learning instruments at school, is described in Burney, *The Present State of Music*, vol. 2, pp. 3–15, and also noted by the traveller Johann Bernoulli, *Sammlung kurzer Reisebeschreibungen und anderer zur Erweitung der Länder und Menschenkenntniss dienender Nachtrichten* (Berlin, 1783), p. 297 (who provides the listed demographic statistics for Bohemia).

music in particular.[4] In a letter to his Viennese friend Baron Gottfried von Jacquin, written over a ten-day period, Mozart documents the run-up to the premiere of *Don Giovanni*: it was initially delayed from 14 October by the inability of 'local stage personnel' to master the opera quickly and by insufficient preparations prior to his arrival, *Figaro* being given instead to mark the attendance of the Archduchess Maria Theresa, Emperor Joseph II's niece, and her new husband Prince Anton of Saxony; a singer's illness then delayed the first performance by a further five days from its revised date of 24 October.[5] Mozart reported the success of the premiere (29 October), the four performances so far, including the latest for his benefit, and his desire for a production of the opera in Vienna, in a second letter to Jacquin on 4 November.[6]

Without references from Mozart to *Don Giovanni*'s genesis before October 1787, librettist Da Ponte's testimony inevitably assumes significance. In his memoirs, Da Ponte claims credit for choosing *Don Giovanni* for Mozart; with bottles of Tokay to hand and a beautiful sixteen-year-old girl as a muse, he worked on the libretto – 'imagining ... reading the *Inferno*' – concurrently with one for Martín y Soler (*L'arbore di Diana*) and an adaptation of *Tarare* as *Axur, re d'Ormus* for Salieri, nearly completing all three in nine weeks.[7] But he neglected to mention information included in the earlier *Extract from the Life of Lorenzo Da Ponte* (1819) to the effect that Domenico Guardasoni, who had just succeeded Pasquale Bondini as impresario of the Prague Estates Theatre where *Don Giovanni* was to premiere, actually offered Mozart the one-act libretto *Don Giovanni, o sia Il convitato di pietra* by Giovanni Bertati.[8] The latest in a long line of Don Juan stories stretching back at least as far as Tirso de Molina's *El burlador de Sevilla y convidado de piedra* (1630) and Molière's *Dom Juan, ou le Festin de pierre* (1665) and a mainstay of the *commedia dell'arte* tradition, Bertati's libretto was set by Giuseppe Gazzaniga and premiered at the Teatro San Moisè in Venice on 5 February 1787.[9] Used as a model by

---

[4] Riesbeck, *Briefe eines Reisenden Franzosen über Deutschland*, pp. 418–420.

[5] MBA, vol. 4, p. 54–56; LMF, pp. 911–912 (letter of 15–25 October 1787).

[6] MBA, vol. 4, pp. 58–59; LMF, pp. 912–913.

[7] *Memoirs of Lorenzo Da Ponte*, pp. 174–176. For an article taking as its point of departure Da Ponte's reference to Dante's *Inferno*, see Felicity Baker, 'The Figures of Hell in the *Don Giovanni* Libretto', in Link and Nagley (eds.), *Words About Mozart*, pp. 77–106. According to Mozart and Da Ponte's Viennese contemporary Johann Pezzl ('Sketch of Vienna', in *Mozart and Vienna*, p. 165), Tokay from Hungary became popular in Viennese high society when high import duties were placed on wines from countries such as France and Spain.

[8] See Heartz, '*Don Giovanni*: Conception and Creation', in *Mozart's Operas*, p. 158.

[9] On the *Don Juan* legend prior to Mozart, and Mozart and Da Ponte's relationship to it including Da Ponte's adaptation of the Bertati model, see Nino Pirrotta, *Don Giovanni's Progress: A Rake*

Da Ponte, the libretto may have travelled up from Venice with Antonio Baglioni, a singer in Gazzaniga's *Don Giovanni* and the first Don Ottavio in Mozart's opera, when he moved to the Bondini-Guardasoni company in Prague.[10] While Mozart may not have had an opportunity to acquaint himself with Gazzaniga's opera in advance of setting Da Ponte's libretto, his music seems indebted in spirit to the balancing of dark and bright in Salieri's *La grotta di Trofonio* (1785), and in the ballroom scene in particular to Salieri's *La fiera di Venezia* (1772), two operas frequently staged in Vienna in the years before *Don Giovanni* that Mozart would have known.[11] It is not impossible that *Don Giovanni* was intended at one point for a premiere in Vienna, rather than Prague, as a festive performance for the Archduchess and Prince in the Habsburg capital; if mooted as an option, though, it would have been considered only briefly.[12] With an uncertain future for the Prague troupe in January 1787, Guardasoni probably did not offer Mozart a formal contract for a new opera before Mozart left Prague in early February, confirming contractual details at a later date instead.[13]

Irrespective of exactly when Mozart began work on *Don Giovanni*, he clearly had a busy compositional schedule between the two Prague trips in 1787, contending with his father's death as well, and had not finished the opera by the time he arrived in the city on 4 October. In addition to extended works such as the string quintets in C K. 515 and G minor K. 516, the Piano-Duet Sonata K. 521, 'Eine kleine Nachtmusik' K. 525, and the Accompanied Sonata K. 526, all completed between April

---

Goes to the Opera, trans. Harris Saunders (New York: Marsilio, 1994); Abert, *W. A. Mozart*, pp. 1033–1045; Michel Noiray, 'Don Giovanni', in Eisen and Keefe (eds.), *Cambridge Mozart Encyclopedia*, pp. 138–151; Edmund Goehring, 'The Lamentations of Don Juan and Macbeth', *Proceedings of the Modern Language Association*, 120 (2005), pp. 1524–1542; Charles Russell, *The Don Juan Legend Before Mozart* (Ann Arbor, MI: University of Michigan Press, 1993); Edward Forman, 'Don Juan before Da Ponte', in Julian Rushton, *W. A. Mozart: 'Don Giovanni'* (Cambridge: Cambridge University Press, 1982), pp. 27–44. On *Don Giovanni* in popular theatrical traditions, see Thomas Bauman, 'The Three Trials of Don Giovanni', in Peter Oswald and Leonard S. Zegans (eds.), *The Pleasures and Perils of Genius: Mostly Mozart* (Madison, CT: International Universities Press, 1993), pp. 133–144.

[10] Heartz, *Mozart's Operas*, p. 160; Rice, *Mozart on the Stage*, p. 53. Rice points out that the companion piece for Gazzaniga's *Don Giovanni* in Venice, *Il capriccio drammatico*, again featuring Baglioni, concerns goings-on in an opera troupe similar to the one Baglioni was to join in Prague.

[11] On connections between these Salieri operas and *Don Giovanni* see Rice, *Antonio Salieri and Viennese Opera*, pp. 468–474. For Viennese performance dates for *La fiera di Venezia* and *La grotto di Trofonio* from 1785 until early 1787, see Link, *National Court Theatre*, pp. 68–99.

[12] See Ian Woodfield's speculation, following the work of Hans Weidinger, in *The Vienna 'Don Giovanni'* (Woodbridge and Rochester, NY: Boydell Press, 2010), pp. 35, 41; and *Performing Operas for Mozart*, p. 79.

[13] See Heartz, *Mozart's Operas*, p. 160; Woodfield, *Performing Operas for Mozart*, p. 78.

and August, Mozart wrote two concert arias for different bass singers within a few days of each other.

On the evidence of 'Alcandro, lo confesso – Non sò d'onde viene' K. 512 (18/19 March 1787) Ludwig Fischer had lost none of the vocal skill demonstrated as Osmin at the premiere of *Die Entführung* in 1782.[14] Mozart promotes both his glowingly resonant low notes and vocal flexibility (see Chapter 2), especially at the end of the aria's main sections: scales and precipitous leaps appear in the concluding stages of the Andante; an E is sustained for two bars in the run-up to the Tempo primo; and a *tour de force* of scalar ascent through almost two octaves, arpeggios over the same range, and a concluding sustained F, feature in Fischer's final twenty-five bars. In the last two bars, after Fischer's departure (Example 8.1), the flute mimics his vocal flexibility with a two-octave arpeggiated ascent during the aria's only tutti *pp* passage, Mozart as so often at the end of his concert works creating a special orchestral effect to encourage approbation. 'Mentre ti lascio, oh figlia' K. 513 (23 March 1787), for Mozart's friend and amateur singer Jacquin, is a similar length to 'Alcandro lo confesso' but much less vocally challenging. The orchestral writing, including numerous dynamic nuances and elaborate obbligato wind lines, compensates for Jacquin's straightforward part. A flute was not planned at first, being written eventually on the (originally empty) top stave of the autograph manuscript rather than in its usual place in the score.[15] Perhaps Mozart's desire for additional wind colour supported a strategy of instrumental enrichment to balance vocal limitation.[16] As usual, Mozart's antennae in March 1787 were attuned to the needs of different singers and to the ways singer and orchestra could best promote his composition.

Uncertainty about which singer was planned for the lead role in *Don Giovanni* may help to explain why several numbers were written only once Mozart reached Prague. Mozart would have been familiar with many of the Prague troupe from the *Figaro* production he directed in January 1787, although the exact casting on that occasion – aside from the original

---

[14] Fischer put on an academy at the Kärntnertortheater on 21 March 1787, at which 'Alcandro, lo confesso – Non sò d'onde viene' was presumably first performed. See Morrow, *Concert Life in Haydn's Vienna*, p. 267; Link, *National Court Theatre*, p. 101. For an extended analysis of the aria, focussing on form and structure, see Dagmar Schmidt, "' . . . fieri contrasti . . . '": Mozarts Bass-Arie KV 512', in *Mozart Studien*, 10 (2001), pp. 139–180.

[15] For the autograph, see Staatsbibliothek zu Berlin – Preußischer Kulturbesitz, Musikabteilung mit Mendelssohn-Archiv, Mus. ms. autogr. W. A. Mozart 513. See also NMA, II/7/4, Preface, pp. viii, xiv (facsimile of the first page of the autograph).

[16] The Notturni, K. 346, K. 436–439 and K. 549 for two sopranos, bass and three basset-horns were probably written collaboratively with Jacquin c. 1787–1788. See Edge, 'Mozart's Viennese Copyists', pp. 699–708.

Example 8.1 Mozart, 'Alcandro lo confesso', bars 171–179.

Leporello, Felice Ponziani, as Figaro – cannot be confirmed.[17] (He also would have heard them in *Figaro* on 14 October two weeks before the *Don Giovanni* premiere.) Many numbers featuring Don Giovanni in Act 2, including the duets with Leporello 'Eh via buffone' and 'O statua gentilissima', the arias 'Deh vieni alla finestra' and 'Metà di voi', and the Act 2 finale, were written on paper acquired in Prague, leaving open the possibility that the identity of the singer of the title role was fixed only late in the day and that Mozart delayed the composition of some material for him as a result.[18]

Luigi Bassi, the first Don Giovanni and possibly the Count in the earlier Prague *Figaro*, was only eighteen when he joined the Bondini-Guardasoni company in 1784–1785, lured away from his homeland with advice that he would acquire better training outside Italy. After a year spent in secondary roles, as explained in a Bassi obituary, Guardasoni began to assign him primary ones: apparently Bassi had real stage presence, with a soulful glow, expressive eyes, a nicely formed mouth and a noble attitude.[19] But he was still quite inexperienced in 1787; at one stage the more established Gioachino Costa, who sang Don Giovanni with the Prague company in Leipzig in 1788, could have been considered for the lead role.[20]

One or two uncertainties surround other singers cast for the *Don Giovanni* premiere. Giuseppe Lolli's double role as Masetto and the Commendatore may have been a product of 'unforeseen circumstances' in the weeks leading up to the premiere.[21] While Caterina Micelli and Caterina Bondini (wife of impresario Pasquale) probably sang Donna

---

[17] See Woodfield, *Performing Operas for Mozart*, p. 60, including a 'hypothetical reconstruction' of the *Figaro* cast.

[18] On numbers Mozart composed in Prague, based on a study of paper types in the autograph, see Alan Tyson, 'Some Features of the Autograph Score of *Don Giovanni*', *Israel Studies in Musicology*, 5 (1990), pp. 7–26, discussed in Woodfield, *The Vienna 'Don Giovanni'*, p. 17 and Wolfgang Rehm, 'Musicological Introduction' to W. A. Mozart, *'Il dissoluto punito ossia il Don Giovanni': Facsimile of the Autograph Score* (Los Altos, CA: The Packard Humanities Institute, 2009), pp. 13–30, at 27. See also NMA II/5/17, Kritische Berichte, p. 30.

[19] See *Neuer nekrolog der Deutschen, Dritter Jahrgang 1825* (Ilmeneau, 1827), 'LIX. Luigi Bassi', pp. 955–960. The text comprises an obituary by Friedrich Heinse – liberally quoting Bassi's own words – published on 30 November 1825, ten weeks after the singer's death. For more on Bassi, see Till Gerrit Waidelich, '"Don Juan von Mozart, (für mich componirt.)" Luigi Bassi – eine Legende zu Lebzeiten, sein Nekrolog und zeitgenössische *Don Giovanni*-Interpretationen', *Mozart Studien*, 10 (2001), pp. 181–211. For secondhand accounts of Bassi, see Magnus Schneider, 'Laughing with Casanova: Luigi Bassi and the Original Production of *Don Giovanni*', in Libin (ed.), *Mozart in Prague*, pp. 403–419.

[20] Woodfield, *Performing Operas for Mozart*, pp. 106–107.

[21] Woodfield, *Performing Operas for Mozart*, p. 108. Masetto's aria 'Ho capito' was composed late in the opera's genesis, once Mozart had reached Prague, also implying uncertainty about who would sing the role.

Elvira and Zerlina respectively, it is not impossible that the casting was actually the other way around.[22] And it is not known whether Teresa Saporiti's participation as Donna Anna was ever in doubt on account of the death of her sister, Antonia, in September 1787.

At any rate, Mozart established good, lively relationships with his singers, as evidenced in the Act 2 finale composed in Prague. Mention of the 'tasty dish' at the table ('Ah che piatto saporito'), with a further threefold iteration of 'saporito', surely alludes to the attractiveness of his Donna Anna, Saporiti.[23] The three tunes played by the wind band may have been chosen to reflect the onstage Bassi and Ponziani's participation in the three source operas, Martín y Soler's *Una cosa rara*, Giuseppe Sarti's *I due litiganti* and Mozart's own *Figaro*.[24] Leporello's mention of the tune he knows 'too well' as 'Non più andrai' strikes up ('Questa poi la conosco pur troppo') is a humorously self-conscious moment for the singer as well as the composer; Ponziani would have sung the aria many times in the title role at the Prague *Figaro*. According to a famous anecdote related in Nissen's *Biographie* and taken from recollections of Johann Nepomuk Stiepanek, who had witnessed Mozart in action in 1787, Mozart taught Caterina Bondini at a rehearsal to scream with appropriate vigour when accosted by Don Giovanni in the Act 1 finale by grabbing her unexpectedly at the appointed moment and eliciting a scream from her to which he then signalled approval.[25]

Mozart had a similarly positive rapport with the Prague orchestra. Like Saporiti, the harpsichordist Jan Křtitel Kuchař is cited in the Act 2 finale (with text inserted by Mozart rather than Da Ponte): the 'cook' ('Kuchař' in Czech), is complimented for his excellent food for the banquet ('si eccellente è il vostro cuoco'), probably an insinuation of Kuchař 'cooking up' a keyboard reduction of *Figaro* as well as a reference to his name.[26] Mozart also sought Kuchař's reassurance about the likely success of *Don Giovanni* in advance of the premiere.[27] The Prague opera orchestra, described by composer Adalbert Gyrowetz c. 1780 as 'excellent' and by Niemetschek

---

[22] Woodfield, *Performing Operas for Mozart*, p. 103.

[23] Heartz, *Mozart's Operas*, pp. 168–169, citing the work of Tomislav Volek.

[24] See Woodfield, *Performing Operas for Mozart*, p. 74, following Magnus Schneider's interpretation in his PhD thesis, 'The Charmer and the Monument: Mozart's *Don Giovanni* in the Light of its Original Production' (University of Aarhus, 2009). Heartz (*Mozart's Operas*, pp. 169–170) attributes the choice of the Sarti and Soler extracts to meanings in their original context as relevant to Don Giovanni's situation.

[25] Nissen, *Biographie W. A. Mozarts*, pp. 519–520.

[26] Heartz, *Mozart's Operas*, p. 169, again following Volek.

[27] See Franz Niemetschek, *Lebensbeschreibung des K. K. Kapellmeisters Wolfgang Amadeus Mozart* (2nd edition, Prague, 1808), pp. 87–88. (Not in first edition, *Life of Mozart*.)

as 'incomparable ... [they] understood how to convey Mozart's ideas so accurately and diligently',[28] comprised well-grounded musicians. Relinquishing individual idiosyncrasies and predilections in favour of a group performance that emerged as if from a single soul, the *Allgemeine musikalische Zeitung* explained (1800), they were capable of playing Mozart's most difficult compositions at sight.[29] Most famously, they successfully sight-read the overture to *Don Giovanni* at the premiere, Mozart only composing it shortly before 29 October, perhaps even the previous night.[30] According to Niemetschek, Mozart wrote to Jan Joseph Strobach, director of the orchestra, to thank him for the opera orchestra's performance of *Figaro*, '[attributing] to their skilful playing the greater part of the approbation which his music had received in Prague'.[31] And admiration travelled in the other direction too, from orchestra to composer, as Leopold said it must in order to elicit good opera performances.[32]

Above all, Bohemia in general and Prague in particular had become synonymous with expert wind playing, beginning with Count Franz Anton von Sporck's acquisition of horn players from France in the late seventeenth or early eighteenth centuries and subsequent cultivation of wind ensembles.[33] According to the *Prager Oberpostamtszeitung*, performances of *Figaro* in Prague (December 1786) were better than in Vienna on account of masterful wind playing.[34] And Mozart's inclusion of a wind band in the

---

[28] See Zaslaw, *Mozart's Symphonies*, p. 414 (for the Gyrowetz quotation); Niemetschek, *Leben*, p. 26, *Life of Mozart*, p. 35 (translation amended).

[29] See 'Ueber den Zustand der Musik in Böhmen', col. 522. Mozart admired this kind of orchestral discipline and ensemble performance. On the Mannheim orchestra, see MBA, vol. 2, p. 395; LMF, p. 562 (9 July 1778). Rochlitz also reports Mozart saying to the King of Prussia that the ensemble playing of the great Berlin virtuosos in the court orchestra could be improved. See Maynard Solomon, 'The Rochlitz Anecdotes', in Eisen (ed.), *Mozart Studies*, p. 9; reprinted in Simon P. Keefe (ed.), *Mozart* (Aldershot: Ashgate Publishing, 2015), p. 99.

[30] According to Stiepanek's account in Nissen, *Biographie*, p. 520. On slight discrepancies between accounts of the overture's late composition, see William Stafford, *The Mozart Myths: A Critical Reassessment* (Stanford, CA: Stanford University Press, 1991), pp. 106–107.

[31] Niemetschek, *Leben*, p. 28; *Life of Mozart*, p. 37 (translation amended). Although the letter is no longer extant, Niemetschek adds in a footnote that he 'read [it] in the original, and found it very well written'.

[32] MBA, vol. 3, p. 70; LMF, pp. 696–697 (25 December 1780). On the opera orchestra's affection and respect for Mozart, see the review of the first performance in the *Prager Oberpostamtszeitung* (MDL, p. 267; MDB, pp. 303–304); Niemetschek, *Life of Mozart*, p. 35; Stiepanek reported in Nissen, *Biographie W. A. Mozarts*, p. 516.

[33] See 'Ueber den Zustand der Musik in Böhmen', cols. 493, 506; Burney, *The Present State of Music*, vol. 2, p. 14; Christopher Hogwood and Jan Smaczny, 'The Bohemian Lands', in Neal Zaslaw (ed.), *The Classical Era: From the 1740s to the End of the 18th Century* (London: Macmillan, 1989), pp. 188–212.

[34] MDL, p. 246; MDB, p. 281.

Act 2 finale of *Don Giovanni* acknowledged the Bohemian fondness for *Harmoniemusik*. Also, his only composition from the trip to Prague in January to February 1787, six German dances K. 509 (6 February 1787), features an unusually large wind contingent of piccolo, double woodwind, two horns and two trumpets. Laudatory comments on the orchestration of *Don Giovanni*, especially the wind writing, form part of the work's early reception: after a Prague performance directed by Mozart on 2 September 1791, Franz Alexander von Kleist recalls 'a thousand ears' absorbed by 'the quivering of a string, every whisper of a flute'; in an historical overview of eighteenth-century German music, Johann Karl Friedrich Triest (1801) attributes much of the opera's success to Mozart's instrumental writing in it; and in the first musical biography of Mozart, Ignaz Arnold (1803) cites numerous instances of powerful wind effects in *Don Giovanni*, simultaneously countering criticisms of Mozart's operatic orchestration in general.[35] Also showering praise, Niemetschek cites Mozart's wind writing as an initial point of attraction to *Die Entführung* for Prague in the autumn 1782 production, but only implies its beneficial presence in *Don Giovanni* when recognizing Mozart's successful accommodation of Bohemian 'taste'.[36] As we shall see, wind effects offer insight into Mozart's engagement with the performers and performance of *Don Giovanni*.

On 7 December 1787, three weeks after his return to Vienna from Prague, Mozart entered Emperor Joseph II's service by imperial decree as 'chamber musician' (*Kammermusikus*), acquiring an annual salary of 800 gulden.[37] While exact circumstances surrounding the appointment are unclear, it is likely that the success of *Don Giovanni*, the possibility of losing Mozart from Vienna to a mooted move to London, and the death of 'chief [court] composer' (*Hof Compositor*) Gluck on 15 November 1787, freeing up an annual salary of 2,000 gulden and enabling musical posts and responsibilities at court to be restructured, all contributed to the development.[38] As Mozart had hoped while in Prague, *Don Giovanni* was soon staged at the

---

[35] See MDL, p. 381 and MDB, p. 433; Johann Karl Friedrich Triest, 'Remarks on the Development of the Art of Music in Germany', trans. Susan Gillespie (AMZ, 1801) in Sisman (ed.), *Haydn and His World*, pp. 321–394, at 365–366; Arnold, *Mozarts Geist, passim*; and Keefe, 'Orchestrating Don Giovanni's Defeat', in Libin (ed.), *Mozart in Prague*.

[36] Niemetschek, *Leben*, pp. 23, 28–29, 47, *Life of Mozart*, pp. 33, 37–38, 55.

[37] MDL, pp. 269–270; MDB, pp. 305–306.

[38] See Wolff, *Mozart at the Gateway to His Fortune*, Chapter 1, 'Imperial Appointments: Mozart and Salieri', pp. 9–43. For more on Mozart's appointment, situated in the context of comings and goings at the Viennese Hofkapelle in the late eighteenth century, see Dorothea Link, 'Mozart's Appointment to the Viennese Court', in Link and Nagley (eds.), *Words About Mozart*, pp. 153–173; reprinted in Keefe (ed.), *Mozart*, pp. 39–64.

Burgtheater in Vienna, receiving its first performance on 7 May 1788 and fourteen more before the end of the calendar year.[39] He did well out of the opera financially: for the only time between 1782 and 1792 a composer received a fee for a work premiered outside the Habsburg capital (50 ducats).[40]

The singers for the Viennese *Don Giovanni* were different from those in Prague. Two travelled a lot during their careers, were based in Vienna only for the theatrical year 1788–1789, and had not worked with Mozart before: Francesco Albertarelli (Don Giovanni), who performed in Rome in Carnival 1788 in advance of heading to Vienna;[41] and Francesco Morella (Don Ottavio). After *Don Giovanni*, Albertarelli and Morella soon ended up singing together again, in Turin at the Teatro Carignano in spring 1790 for Cimarosa's *Giannina, e Bernardone* and Paisiello's *La molinara* and at La Scala, Milan in the Autumn 1790 season in Pietro Guglielmi's *La pastorella nobile* and Martín y Soler's *Una cosa rara*.[42] Albertarelli subsequently sang at the King's Theatre in London in 1791 and 1792, encountering Haydn during the composer's first sojourn to England, and then in Madrid and Barcelona in 1795 and 1808 respectively.[43] Morella also

---

[39] See the listings in Link, *National Court Theatre*, pp. 125–133. The performances were given on 7, 9, 12, 16, 23, 30 May; 16, 23 June; 5, 11, 21 July; 2 August; 24 October; 3 November; 15 December. Contrary to conventional wisdom, Emperor Joseph II did not attend any of these performances, including the last one, on account of participating at the Turkish front and suffering ill health on his return. See Gutman, *Mozart: A Cultural Biography*, pp. 686–687. But a private performance for the emperor by his chamber musicians, before he left for the front, is a possibility; see Rice, *Mozart on the Stage*, p. 227.

[40] See Dexter Edge, 'Mozart's Fee for *Così fan tutte'*, *Journal of the Royal Musical Association*, 116 (1991), pp. 211–235, at 224, and Rice, *Salieri and Viennese Opera*, p. 460. Solomon (*Mozart: A Life*, p. 426) calculates that Mozart received around 1,275 florins in total from *Don Giovanni*, including commissioning fees and the benefit performance in Prague.

[41] See *Calendrier musical universel. Suite de L'Almanach musical, Tome IX, Annee 1788* (reprint, Geneva: Minkoff, 1972), p. 2740.

[42] See *Almanacco dei Teatri di Torino, per l'anno 1830. Contenante la serie dei Drammi rappresentati nel Regio Teatro dal 1700, e di quelli rappresentati nel Teatro Carignano dal 1765 a tutto il Carnovale del corrente anno* (Turin, 1830), p. 11; and *Serie cronologica delle rappresentazioni drammatico-pantomimche poste sulle scene dei principali teatri di Milano, dall'autunno 1776 sino all'intero autunno 1818* (Milan: Giovanni Silvestri, 1818), p. 41.

[43] See *Music and Dancing: New Songs by the Most Eminent Composers as Performed at the King's Theatre in the Haymarket* (London: Hammond, 1791), pp. ii, 3–7; Johann Wilhelm von Archenholz, *Annalen der Brittischen Geschichte des Jahrs 1792*, vol. 9 (Hamburg, 1794), p. 474; *Que comprehende los meses de Enero, Febrero y Marzo de 1795. Tomo 35* (Madrid, 1795), pp. 112, 400, 408, 554, 572, 592, 596; Giuseppe Farinelli and Giuseppe Foppa, *Un effetto naturale. Farsa fiocosa per musica di un atto solo. Da rapprentarsi nel Teatro della molto illustre Citta di Barcellona, l'anno 1808* (Barcelona: Francesco Generas, 1808). On the encounter with Haydn, see 'Biographische Notizen über Joseph Haydn von Griesinger', *Allgemeine musikalische Zeitung*, 11 (1808–1809), col. 678; also given in G. A. Griesinger and A. C. Dies,

appeared in Barcelona, in 1791.[44] Mozart was familiar with the other principal singers from having created roles and written arias for them: Aloysia Lange (Donna Anna), who now sang with the Italian opera in Vienna following the closure of the German opera; Caterina Cavalieri (Donna Elvira); Francesco Benucci (Leporello); Luisa Laschi-Mombelli (Zerlina); and Francesco Bussani (Masetto and the Commendatore).[45]

Several new numbers and recitatives were written for the first Vienna production: above all, an aria 'Dalla sua pace' (24 April 1788) for Morella in Act 1, following Donna Anna's sudden realization that Don Giovanni was her assailant; a duet 'Per queste tue manine' (28 April 1788) for Benucci and Laschi-Mombelli in Act 2 following the sextet ('Sola, sola in bujo loco'), Zerlina binding Leporello to a chair to punish him for impersonating Don Giovanni; and the *scena* 'In quali eccessi, o numi … Mi tradì quell'alma ingrata' (30 April 1788) for Cavalieri after the new Leporello/Zerlina duet, Elvira desperate at the betrayal by Don Giovanni but continuing to feel pity for him. For a short while, Mozart probably considered placing the duet after rather than before Elvira's *scena*.[46] The new numbers initially seem intended not as replacements for existing material from Prague, as is often stated, but rather as additions to the score: original Viennese orchestral parts exist for both of Don Ottavio's arias 'Dalla sua pace' (Vienna) and 'Il mio tesoro' (Prague) and both the duet 'Per queste tue manine' (Vienna) and Leporello's aria 'Ah pietà' (Prague). Mozart thus appears to have decided independently first to add numbers and then to cut 'Il mio tesoro' and 'Ah pietà'.[47] Since the arias eventually cut do not appear in the printed Viennese libretto, the decision to omit them was probably made before the premiere.[48] The aria 'Mi tradì', written in E-flat, transposed to D, and then promptly restored to E-flat may have undergone tonal changes in order to accommodate its different positions in the sequence of numbers in Act 2: an initial proximity to the graveyard scene (in E-flat) could have provoked the transposition to D, avoiding two numbers close

Haydn: Two Contemporary Portraits, trans. Vernon Gotwals (Madison, WI: University of Wisconsin Press, 1968), p. 26.

[44] See *La statua mattematica. Dramma giocoso per musica da rappresentarsi nel teatro della molto Ille. Città di Barcellona l'anno 1791* (Barcelona: Francesco Genéras, 1791).

[45] On account of her pregnancy, Laschi-Mombelli participated in only seven of the Vienna performances and was replaced by Therese Teyber.

[46] Woodfield, *Vienna 'Don Giovanni'*, pp. 67–81.

[47] See Edge, 'Viennese Copyists', pp. 1801–1803. Pencil foliations in Act 2 of the autograph score also support the idea that the duet and Elvira's *scena* were originally envisaged as additions rather than replacements. See Woodfield, *Vienna 'Don Giovanni'*, p. 64.

[48] Edge, 'Viennese Copyists', p. 1808.

together in the same key, a repositioning of the aria after the new duet then allowing for a return to the original E-flat.[49]

Ultimately, revisions made for Vienna 1788 were not part of a 'single grand plan', but rather responses to separate problems as they arose, capturing the complicated, fraught and pragmatic world of late-eighteenth-century opera – a world influenced by financiers and managers as well as composers, librettists and singers.[50] In some cases, sources do not reveal which material was sung when. The *scena ultima* in the Act 2 finale, conveying the reactions of Donna Elvira, Donna Anna, Don Ottavio, Zerlina, Masetto and Leporello to Don Giovanni's death, is a case in point. While a performance was apparently planned at first, judging by the extant Viennese orchestral parts, its ultimate status is uncertain: a lengthy cut was indicated (in the autograph), taking out the end of the opening sextet, Don Ottavio and Donna Anna's duet and almost all of the trio for Zerlina, Masetto and Leporello; a chord for Elvira, Anna, Zerlina and Ottavio, introduced in response to Don Giovanni's demise and implying consideration of the scene's omission, was subsequently cancelled (perhaps, but not necessarily, by Mozart); and the published libretto did not include the *scena ultima*.[51] The preponderance of evidence tentatively suggests that the *scena ultima* was cut in its entirety at some point in the Vienna 1788 run, but when this may have happened, and whether the scene was ever heard with partial cuts, is not known.[52] Other brief cuts in the original Viennese orchestral parts may have been made by Mozart, including to Leporello's 'Madamina', Zerlina's 'Batti, batti', the Act 2 trio 'Ah taci, ingiusto core' and the Act 2 sextet 'Sola, sola in bujo loco', although firm attributions to the composer are not possible.[53] Masetto's bitter response to the request that he leave Zerlina alone with Don Giovanni, 'Ho capito', may have been cut in Vienna, and for a while at least in Prague too.[54]

As in *Figaro*, autograph materials for *Don Giovanni* will tell only part of the story of intersections between Mozart's composition- and performance-related thoughts and motivations. Since opera was a thoroughly collaborative venture, it is likely that some of the differences between the

[49] Woodfield, *Vienna 'Don Giovanni'*, pp. 71–73. See also Edge, 'Viennese Copyists', p. 1807.

[50] Woodfield, *Vienna 'Don Giovanni'*, p. 63. Both Woodfield's study and Edge's ('Viennese Copyists') ably capture the frenetic operatic world of the 1780s.

[51] Edge, 'Viennese Copyists', pp. 1813–1818. For facsimiles of the Prague and Vienna libretti of 1787 and 1788, see Mozart, *'Don Giovanni': Facsimile of the Autograph Score*, vol. 3, pp. 63–108.

[52] Edge, 'Viennese Copyists', p. 1818; Woodfield, *Vienna 'Don Giovanni'*, pp. 95–110.

[53] See Edge, 'Mozart's Viennese Copyists', pp. 1820–1822; Woodfield, *Vienna 'Don Giovanni'*, p. 85.

[54] Edge, 'Mozart's Viennese Copyists', p. 1819; Woodfield, *Vienna 'Don Giovanni'*, pp. 21–22.

autograph and sources such as the performing score now held at the Prague Conservatory and the Viennese orchestral parts – compiled for the two original productions – would have received his stamp of approval even when his hand is not found.[55] But which specific changes and annotations came with Mozart's authority, rather than being carried out independently by assistants or section leaders during rehearsals either in 1787–1788 or later, is not known.[56] I shall therefore restrict supporting sources for the investigation of relationships between compositional and performance based activities almost entirely to autograph materials, which help to reveal how writing for specific singers and for the Prague opera orchestra shaped the music produced.[57]

Singers and Effects

Working on *Don Giovanni* in Vienna before travelling to Prague for the rehearsals and premiere, Mozart would have been sure of the identities of Leporello, Donna Anna and Don Ottavio at least. The passages of patter for Ponziani in 'Notte e giorno faticar', 'Madamina', 'Ah pietà', and the Act 2 sextet exploit his pristine diction. According to a Berlin critic (1782), he 'combines strength with softness of voice, and has in addition the merit that one can understand every word even in the fastest singing'.[58] Judging by material for Donna Anna, Mozart had confidence in Saporiti's technical and expressive virtuosity: the Adagio 'Protegga' from the Act 1 finale twice soars up to b-flat" via demisemiquavers; 'Sola, sola in bujo loco' includes more brilliantly virtuosic material for her than for any other singer, featuring the longest entry statement with ascents to a-flats" and demisemiquaver turns, and flourishes up to a b-flat" in the Molto allegro; and the rondò 'Non mi dir' incorporates considerable coloratura. Like the Countess in *Figaro*, almost certainly sung by Saporiti at the Prague *Figaro* in January 1787, Donna Anna forms a special bond with the winds.

---

[55] Woodfield, *Vienna 'Don Giovanni'*, p. 17. On the several unambiguous appearances of Mozart's hand in the Prague Conservatory score, see the reproductions in NMA II/5/17, Kritische Berichte, pp. 220–21, and NMA II/5/17, Preface, p. xxvi.

[56] As both Edge and Woodfield point out ('Mozart's Viennese Copyists', p. 1789; *Vienna 'Don Giovanni'*, p. 53), the original Viennese orchestral parts for *Don Giovanni* remained in circulation throughout the nineteenth century, in many cases complicating determinations about when annotations were made.

[57] For a high-quality reproduction of Mozart's autograph, see Mozart, *'Don Giovanni': Facsimile of the Autograph Score*.

[58] As given in Woodfield, *Performing Operas for Mozart*, p. 65.

In 'Protegga', the clarinet's heart beats with Anna's, its semiquavers replaced at one point by triplet semiquavers, intensifying accompanimental material as if in response to both her soaring line and turn figures (Example 8.2). Similarly, in 'Non mi dir', the winds resonate sympathetically: they are marked *dolce* at the beginning of the aria (the strings are also *sotto voce*); they support the voice in every paired wind combination bar one among the flute, clarinets, bassoons and horns in the Larghetto; and, represented by the clarinets and bassoons, they foreshadow the vocal gesture at the pauses before the Allegro moderato (bars 62–63, Example 8.3). Mozart continued to aspire to creative roles for his singers irrespective of when their individual identities were known to him: Bassi attests to Mozart's desire for varied, spontaneous, even quasi-improvised performances of the early part of the Act 2 finale; and, in similar fashion to *Figaro* (Chapter 7), a series of *sotto voce*s in the Act 2 sextet, coinciding with Donna Elvira's appeal for mercy for her 'husband' Don Giovanni (Leporello in disguise) and with the group's shock at capturing Leporello and then reflection on the unfortunate circumstances, encourage singers to contemplate the impact of their performance on the dramatic experience.[59]

Instrumental effects in 'Il mio tesoro', for Baglioni as Don Ottavio, go hand in hand with vocal material. Harshly criticized by one writer in 1794, Baglioni was praised two years earlier in performance with the Guardasoni company for a voice 'rich, pure, and full of expression, so that few theaters can boast of such a tenor. We have not heard his equal in a long time.'[60] Both the muted strings, redolent of tenderness according to Johann Joachim Quantz in the mid-eighteenth century,[61] and a *Harmonie* of clarinets, bassoons and horns provide sonorous support. In the first section, the full-wind timbre is reserved for links between vocal phrases, heard at the same time as the upper strings. At the end of the section, following Baglioni's extended written f' and semiquaver flourish, the wind play

---

[59] For Bassi's account of the Act 2 finale, see Paul Nettl (translated by Arthur Mendel), 'Mozart and the Czechs', *Musical Quarterly*, 27 (1941), pp. 329–342, at 331–332. For David Cairns, the *sotto voce* moment at Leporello's revelation (bar 114), greeted by a modulation from G minor to V/A-flat, is 'imagined as a pitch of intensity exceptional even for Mozart'; see *Mozart's Operas* (London: Allen Lane, 2006), p. 160. For Abert (*W. A. Mozart*, p. 1092): 'The *sotto voce* [when Leporello's true identity become apparent] creates a more truthful and natural impression than any *forte* outcry of theatrical indignation.'

[60] On Baglioni, see Rice, *Mozart on the Stage*, pp. 119–128 (quotation at p. 120) and 'Antonio Baglioni, Mozart's First Don Ottavio and Tito, in Italy and Prague', in Milada Jonášová and Tomislav Volek (eds.), *Böhmische Aspekte des Lebens und des Werkes von W. A. Mozart* (Prague, 2012), pp. 295–321.

[61] See Robin Stowell, *Violin Technique and Performance Practice in the Late Eighteenth and Early Nineteenth Centuries* (Cambridge: Cambridge University Press, 1985), p. 239.

Example 8.2 Mozart, Act 1 finale from *Don Giovanni*, bars 257–263.

together and alone, providing an opportunity for strings to take off wooden mutes in time for a *forte* start to the next section: vocal effect, wind effect, and attention to a practicality of performance are at one. And the run-up to the reprise is similar (Example 8.4): following Baglioni's most protracted

Example 8.3 Mozart, 'Non mi dir', from *Don Giovanni*, bars 61–63.

semiquaver virtuosity in the aria, the strings drop out (and reapply mutes) leaving the *Harmonie* alongside Baglioni two bars to usher in the main theme.

Even if Morella was a less proficient Don Ottavio than Baglioni, as is commonly suggested, the exact reasons for cutting 'Il mio tesoro' from the Viennese production are unknown. 'Dalla sua pace', in any case, appears to have been a good fit. Morella debuted in Vienna a week after the start of the 1788–1789 theatrical year on 31 March, as Count Almaviva in Paisiello's ever-popular *Il barbiere di Siviglia* (1782); he sang the role again on 2 April and 14 April. Mozart therefore would have had at least three opportunities to hear him on stage before completing the new aria on 24 April.[62] The Count's only solo number in *Il barbiere di Siviglia* is the cavatina

---

[62] Zinzendorf records 'le nouvel acteur' Morella replacing Stefano Mandini in Paisiello's opera on 31 March; see Link, *National Court Theatre*, p. 314. For the performance dates of *Il barbiere di Siviglia* in April 1788, including one on the 30th after Mozart had completed 'Dalla sua pace', see Link, *National Court Theatre*, pp. 123–125.

Example 8.4 Mozart, 'Il mio tesoro', from *Don Giovanni*, bars 43–50.

'Saper bramate' in Act 1; Mozart's 'Dalla sua pace' is slightly more demanding, with a range of d – g' rather than f – f' and participation in 68 of 74
rather than 60 of 100 2/4 bars. Nevertheless, both arias locate suave, elegant
vocal material in broad melodic lines. Writing for Morella, then, did not

necessarily begin and end with his limitations: a supposed inability to handle coloratura in 'Il mio tesoro' and in the *scena ultima* duet with Donna Anna is often mooted. It probably involved primarily accommodating positive attributes of his singing.

Cavalieri's participation as Donna Elvira in the Vienna *Don Giovanni*, more than two years after Mozart wrote his last piece for her, may have provided composer and singer with a challenge; her prodigious vocal skills appear to have declined at the end of the 1780s before eventual retirement in 1793.[63] The transposition of 'Mi tradì' down a semitone from E-flat to D is unlikely to represent a concession to diminishing powers as the aria was ultimately transposed back to E-flat.[64] But the quick shift from low to high vocal notes, characteristic of Cavalieri's grand centrepiece in *Die Entführung* 'Martern aller Arten', is less noticeable in 'Mi tradì': e-flat' to a-flat" is traversed over six beats shortly before the vocal exit.[65] Instrumental participation, especially the obbligato flute, clarinet and bassoon, also tells a story. Wind writing in 'Martern aller Arten' cannot be said to compensate for music Cavalieri might have sung, given the overall length and difficulty of the aria. But the frequency of instrumental quaver passages in 'Mi tradì' allows her either to sit out or to cede florid lines to the orchestra – in the context of a mellifluous melody projected throughout – more than would have been necessary in her heyday in the 1770s and early 1780s.[66] Instrumental dynamic nuances also offer Cavalieri expressive support. While *sfps* for the cellos and basses appear in the *particella* of the first fourteen-bar statement, the *p – cresc* in the bassoon and clarinet and *mfps* in bars 8 and 11 were written neither in the *particella* nor in the main notational phase of the completion judging by the faded ink, and may capture reactions to a run through with Cavalieri. For the last statement of the main theme, *mfps* accrue to the cellos and basses in place of the original *sfps* (the main body of instruments is designated 'come prima' and unnotated), avoiding duplication of the orchestra-only *sf* effects

[63] See Gidwitz, 'Vocal Portraits of Four Mozart Sopranos', pp. 253–256; Clive, *Mozart and His Circle*, p. 37.

[64] See Woodfield, *Vienna 'Don Giovanni'*, p. 73. (Gidwitz proposes this theory in 'Vocal Portraits of Four Mozart Sopranos', p. 256.) Edge ('Mozart's Viennese Copyists', p. 1807) also concludes: 'It seems most likely that "Mi tradì" was transposed in order to adjust the sequence of keys.'

[65] In comparison, see the direct leap of a 14th and brisk ascent over more than two octaves in 'Martern aller Arten' (bars 128, 230–232).

[66] Gidwitz explains 'Mi tradì' in a similar way ('Vocal Portraits of Four Mozart Sopranos', p. 256): 'It is written for a flexible voice of great dramatic power that nevertheless must confine itself here to short, unadorned phrases. . . . Music of this sort is what Cavalieri had to offer in 1788, and Mozart made the most of it.'

in the subsequent seven bars. Of course, instrumental dynamic subtleties are a feature of many Mozart arias; and 'Mi tradì' requires a singer of considerable capability, irrespective of any accommodation of Cavalieri's reduced proficiency. But both the consistently flowing obbligato winds and the nuanced orchestral writing would have taken some pressure off Cavalieri, providing instrumental reinforcement for her brilliant and expressive virtuosity. In a similar vein, as we shall see in Chapter 11, Mozart's orchestral effects in the horn concertos K. 495 (1786) and K 447 (probably 1787) were designed to assist the ageing soloist Joseph Leutgeb. In short, 'Mi tradì' fulfilled the interrelated musical-dramatic functions of promoting and supporting the skills of its vocal recipient and augmenting the role of Donna Elvira such that, in Mozart's own words, *opere buffe* have '*two equally good female roles* – one must be *seria*, the other *mezzo carratere* – but *in importance* absolutely equal'.[67]

Although the exact timing of Bassi's confirmation as Don Giovanni is not known, he was presumably *in situ* when the opera's final numbers were written in Prague (October 1787), including the Act 2 arias 'Deh vieni' and 'Metà di voi'. Similar vocal ranges and limited brilliant virtuosity in Don Giovanni's three arias, including 'Fin ch'han dal vino' from Act 1 composed earlier in Vienna, plus comparably swift declamation in 'Fin ch'han dal vino' and 'Metà di voi', imply awareness of Bassi's identity as Don Giovanni during the genesis of Act 1, but offer no conclusive proof.[68]

Above all, the sizzling effect of 'Fin ch'han dal vino' is generated through combined vocal and instrumental energy. Bassi was initially unhappy with the aria, as he told Friedrich Heinse, who later wrote in the singer's obituary:

---

[67] MBA, vol. 3, p. 268; LMF, p. 848 (7 May 1783). Daniel Heartz points out that Mozart's stated aspiration is fully realized not in *Figaro* – his first opera buffa to be completed after this letter was written – as it lacks a true *seria* role, but rather in *Don Giovanni*. See Heartz, 'Goldoni, *Don Giovanni* and the *dramma giocoso*', in *Mozart's Operas*, pp. 195–205, at 200.

[68] The vocal ranges are d – e' ('Deh vieni'), c – e' ('Metà di voi') and d – e-flat ('Fin ch'han dal vino'). Bassi's well-known skills of mimicry, relevant both to Don Giovanni's impersonation of Leporello in Act 2 and to his chameleon-like personality in general, do not necessarily reveal that Bassi's participation was confirmed during the early genesis of the opera: these skills may have become apparent to audiences and critics during his performances as Don Giovanni. On Bassi's mimicry, see Konrad Küster, 'Don Giovannis Canzonetta: Rollenporträt an den Grenzen des Theaters', in Susanne Schaal, Thomas Seedorf and Gerhard Splitt (eds.), *Musikalisches Welttheater: Festschrift Rolf Dammann zum 65. Geburtstag* (Laaber: Laaber Verlag, 1995), pp. 161–175; James Parakilas, 'The Afterlife of *Don Giovanni*: Turning Production History into Criticism', *Journal of Musicology*, 8 (1990), pp. 251–265, at 256; and Elaine Sisman, 'The Marriages of *Don Giovanni*: Persuasion, Impersonation and Personal Responsibility', in Keefe (ed.), *Mozart Studies*, pp. 163–192, at 166.

when Mozart presented him with the Champagne Song, subsequently so much loved, he [Bassi] was so dissatisfied that he asked the composer to write him a bigger aria in the style of that time instead. Mozart told him quite calmly that he would want only to wait for its success on the evening of the first performance, and the success was that the piece was immediately demanded *da capo* by the enthusiastic Prague audience with tumultuous applause.[69]

Mozart's 'presentation' probably comprised an informal rendition at the keyboard with the singer, in line with his standard practice, or an early rehearsal with strings, rather than a full orchestral rehearsal shortly before the premiere by which point there would have been insufficient time for the idea of a replacement aria seriously to be entertained, let alone a different aria written.[70] The composer's advice not to rush to judgement is an exhortation to experience 'Fin ch'han dal vino' in live performance, where its full effect would be unleashed. Mozart considered the impact of the aria's rendition as a complete, performable piece during the orchestration phase of the compositional process. While several dynamics accrued to the *particella*, such as the *crescendo* to *forte* to coincide with Don Giovanni's exit, others including the distinctive *fps* heard first at two-bar intervals, and subsequently at one-bar intervals seven then eleven times in succession (Example 8.5), were notated in the completion phase, as if feeding off and feeding into the aria's inexorable momentum.

Mozart's Don Giovanni in Vienna, Francesco Albertarelli, was apparently an unproblematic replacement for Bassi in 1788: no new aria or ensemble in the opera is associated with him. But Mozart did write

---

[69] *Neuer nekrolog der Deutschen, Dritter Jahrgang*, pp. 959–960. ('. . . als das seitdem so beliebte Champagnerlied ihm von Mozart vorgelegt wurde, mit demselben so unzufrieden war, dass er den Componisten bat, ihm statt dessen eine grössere Arie nach damaligem Zuschnitt zu schreiben. Mozart sagte ihm ganz ruhig, er möchte nur den Erfolg an dem Abend der ersten Aufführung abwarten, und der Erfolg war – dass das Musikstuck von dem enthusiastischen Publikum in Prag, mit stürmischen Beifall sofort *da Capo* gefordert wurde.') Variations on this story were frequently related in the mid nineteenth century. See, for example: E. F. Ellet, 'Mozart's *Don Giovanni*', in *The Ladies' Companion: A Monthly Magazine*, 13 (1840), pp. 276–280, at 276; 'Mozart's *Don Giovanni*', in *The New-York Mirror: A Weekly Journal of Literature and the Fine Arts*, 18 (19 September 1840), pp. 102–103 at 102; 'Mozart's *Don Giovanni*', in *Colhurn's New Monthly Magazine and Humorist*, 2 (1840), pp. 533–541, at 535; '*Don Giovanni*', in *The United States Democratic Review*, 20 (1847), pp. 36–43, at 37; '*Don Giovanni*: An Incident in the Life of Mozart', in *American Art Journal: A Weekly Record of Music, Art and Literature*, 6 (1867), pp. 177–179, at 178.

[70] On the theatre schedule in Prague in late October and early November 1787, identifying possible dress rehearsals on 26 and 27 October, see Woodfield, *Performing Operas for Mozart*, p. 91. On Mozart's standard rehearsal procedures for his operas, see Ian Woodfield, *Mozart's 'Così fan tutte': A Compositional History* (Woodbridge and Rochester, NY: The Boydell Press, 2008), p. 17.

Example 8.5 Mozart, 'Fin ch'an dal vino', from *Don Giovanni*, bars 105–116.

'Un bacio di mano', K. 541 (May 1788), for Albertarelli to insert into Anfossi's *Le gelosie fortunate* staged on eleven occasions at the Burgtheater between 2 June and the end of July.[71] Best known for a theme Mozart would reuse a few weeks later to close the exposition of the first movement of the 'Jupiter' Symphony,[72] this short aria comprises Frenchman Girò's light-hearted advice on love to his friend Pompeo. The vocal range (B – e'), similar to Don Giovanni's solo numbers, also suggests a singer well-suited to Mozart's role. Albertarelli would have had an opportunity, even in his two-minute aria, to demonstrate the stylishness for which eighteenth-century Italian opera-lover Benedetto Frizzi praised him,[73] including in the 'Voi siete

[71] On dates of performances of Anfossi's opera in the year of Albertarelli's residency in Vienna, 1788–1789, see Link, *National Court Theatre in Mozart's Vienna*, pp. 126–128. On *Le gelosie fortunate* as a *pasticcio*, with further contributions from Cimarosa, Sarti, Gazzaniga, Bianchi and others, see Edge, 'Mozart's Viennese Copyists', pp. 1867–1868.

[72] This thematic connection is frequently noted in the secondary literature. See, in particular, Knepler, *Wolfgang Amadé Mozart*, pp. 229–230 (as an example of 'instrumental music semanticized by vocal music'); and Sisman, *'Jupiter' Symphony*, p. 49 (on the connection between the text accompanying the aria theme and the prominence of the theme in the development section of the first movement).

[73] See John Rice, 'Benedetto Frizzi on Singers, Composers and Opera in Late Eighteenth-Century Italy', *Studi musicali*, 23 (1994), pp. 367–393.

un po' tondo' theme reused in the 'Jupiter', and at a pause bar (74) that invited *ad libitum* flourishes.

Writing for the Prague Opera Orchestra

Mozart benefitted from being able to write for a particularly fine orchestra in Prague; it is surely no coincidence, even accepting the high quality of the Burgtheater orchestra in Vienna, that his first opera for Prague was also his most instrumentally rich to date, the orchestra 'itself a player, an extra personage, abetting, questioning, deepening'.[74] In 1796, Johann Ferdinand Ritter von Schönfeld praised individual musicians in every section of the ensemble, which numbered just twenty-seven in total. Since the ensemble had a reputation for retaining a stable roster over long periods, most (perhaps all) musicians would have been *in situ* for the *Don Giovanni* premiere a few years before Schönfeld's descriptions.[75] Among the strings, Praupner plays 'an excellent, pure violin', Wenzl Kral 'a truly tasteful, quite masterful violin', Johann Kutschera 'very pleasantly and full of passion' on the violin, Bernhard Václav Stiastny with a 'very beautiful' tone on the cello, and Johann Eymann 'with perfection' on the double bass; among the woodwind and brass, Leutel plays the flute with 'artful skill', having reached 'a degree of perfection' on the clarinet as well, and Matiegka and Schepka excel on the horn; and the keyboard player Jan (given as Johann) Kuchař has stunning skills both on the organ and the fortepiano.[76] Mozart may have written some numbers with specific instrumentalists in mind, including the obbligato cello in Zerlina's aria 'Batti, batti' for Stiastny (c. 1760 – c. 1835), a long-time principal of the Prague opera orchestra who joined around 1778 and was renowned for his scrupulous ensemble playing.[77] According to Schönfeld, his accompanimental skills in opera

---

[74] Cairns, *Mozart's Operas*, p. 160. On instruments as agents in Mozart's operas, see James Webster, 'The Analysis of Mozart's Arias', in Eisen (ed.), *Mozart Studies*, pp. 101–199, especially 124–130.

[75] Schönfeld, *Jahrbuch der Tonkunst von Wien und Prag*, 'Virtuosen und Dilettanten', pp. 109–138, and 151 (for a list of musicians in the orchestra). On the reputation for stability, see 'Ueber den Zustand der Musik in Böhmen', col. 522.

[76] Schönfeld, *Jahrbuch der Tonkunst von Wien und Prag*, pp. 110 ('seine treffliche reine Violin'), 122 ('eine wahrhaft geschmackvolle, ganz meisterliche Violine'), 124 ('sehr angenehm und emfindungsvoll'), 134 ('sein Ton auf dem Violoncello ist sehr schön'), 124 ('bläst die Flöte mit kunstvoller Fertigkeit, auch auf der Klarinette hat er seinen Grad der Vollkommenheit erreicht'), 126, 131, 123.

[77] On Stiastny, see Margaret Campbell, 'Masters of the Baroque and Classical Eras', in Robin Stowell (ed.), *The Cambridge Companion to the Cello* (Cambridge: Cambridge University Press, 1999), pp. 52–60, at 60. On Stiastny's treatise, the two-volume *Violoncell-Schule*, see

were especially noteworthy, making him an ideal co-participant in Zerlina's aria, especially once the cello's similarities with the human voice are factored into the equation.[78] The dramatic involvement of trombones, with their sepulchral connotations, first in the recitative of the graveyard scene alongside oboes, clarinets and bassoons to interrupt the insouciant Don Giovanni, and later in the Act 2 finale with the full orchestra to mark the arrival of the Commendatore, could also be linked to a premiere in Prague: a distinguished trombonist Gotthard Stolle (1739–1814), the best in Bohemia, trained up a stable of pupils in the late eighteenth century, some of whom would have been available as performers in 1787.[79] Trombones do not appear in the Burgtheater performing score for the Vienna *Don Giovanni* in 1788, nor do extra payments for trombonists in the account book for the theatrical year 1788–1789. Thus, they were almost certainly not deployed in the Vienna production.[80]

Much of *Don Giovanni* would have played well in a country with established and widely respected traditions of wind playing: segments that have no orchestral precedent in *Die Entführung* or *Figaro* for Vienna such as 'Protegga' in the Act 1 finale, where Donna Elvira, Donna Anna and Don Ottavio seek divine protection against Don Giovanni accompanied exclusively by a halo of obbligato wind, and the opera extracts for wind band in the Act 2 finale, were no doubt designed to appeal directly to Bohemian taste. And as I have argued elsewhere, the defeat of Don Giovanni, a manipulator of orchestration who strums a mandolin in 'Deh vieni' and calls for his band's participation in the banquet scene, can be traced through the ebb and flow of powerful and poignant

---

Valerie Walden, *One Hundred Years of Cello Playing: A History of Technique and Performance Practice, 1740–1840* (Cambridge: Cambridge University Press, 1998), *passim*. Stiastny's start date around 1778 is from Grove Music, accessed 18 September 2015. Arnold (*Mozarts Geist*, p. 229) admires the combination of gentle aria and the gentlest orchestral instrument (cello) in 'Batti, batti'.

[78] Schönfeld, *Jahrbuch der Tonkunst in Wien und Prag*, pp. 134, 187.

[79] On Stolle, see Schönfeld, *Jahrbuch der Tonkunst in Wien und Prag*, p. 134; Gerber, *Neues historisch-biographisches Lexikon der Tonkünstler*, vol. 4, p. 288; Gottfried Johann Dlabacz, *Allgemeines historisches Künstler-Lexikon für Böhmen* (Prague, 1815), vol. 3, pp. 215–216. Autographs of the trombone parts in *Don Giovanni*, which were presumably written on separate sheets detached from the main score since there was insufficient room for them on Mozart's twelve-stave paper, are no longer extant. Both the graveyard and banquet scenes featuring trombones were written once Mozart arrived in Prague in October 1787. On Mozart's powerful use of the trombone, in the context of the instrument's sepulchral associations, see Arnold, *Mozarts Geist*, pp. 218–219, 322–323.

[80] See Edge, 'Viennese Copyists', pp. 1825–1828. He speculates that they 'were omitted as a cost-cutting measure' (p. 1828). See also Edge, 'Mozart's Viennese Orchestras', *Early Music*, 20 (1992), pp. 63–88, at 77–78.

instrumental effects (especially for wind) accruing to the music of both Don Giovanni and his pursuers and culminating in the Commendatore's arrival at the banquet in the Act 2 finale to coincide with the biggest, most decisive effect of all.[81]

From time to time Mozart's wind parts responded to already notated effects: as ink colours in the autograph show, he sometimes wrote them down in a discrete block, after the voices and instrumental bass in the *particella* and presumably also after the other completed string parts.[82] A frantic figure passed between Donna Anna and Don Giovanni before the encounter with the Commendatore in the opening scene (Introduzione, bars 101–126) is transformed into Don Giovanni's *sotto voce* response to his combatant's fatal injury, the last in a series of nuanced markings for the singer that include *mezza voce* and *più voce* immediately before the duel (see bars 156–158, 177–180). In an analogous process when notating the wind parts, Mozart created from earlier material an effect identified by Ignaz Arnold (1803) as one of the most powerful and poignant in the opera: the chromatic descent in semibreves for the flute during the duel becomes a solo in shorter note values for the oboe then flutes and bassoons in reaction to the Commendatore's death (bars 167–172, 190–193; see Examples 8.6a and 8.6b).[83]

Elsewhere, the act of notating wind parts in the autograph apparently stimulated thoughts about full orchestral performance of extended sections. In 'Là ci darem la mano', for example, only *forte, pizzicato,* and *piano* markings from the final few bars belong unambiguously to Mozart's

---

[81] See Keefe, 'Orchestrating Don Giovanni's Defeat'. As I explain in the article, Don Giovanni's control of situations is captured by orchestral effects in the famous duet with Zerlina, 'Là ci darem la mano', and the catalogue aria 'Madamina' (Leporello speaking for his master) in Act 1, and the trio 'Ah taci ingiusto core' in Act 2; Donna Elvira, Donna Anna, Don Ottavio, Zerlina, Masetto and the Commendatore hit back with powerful effects of their own in 'Non ti fidar', the Act 1 finale, the Act 2 sextet, the graveyard scene, and the Act 2 finale.

[82] In addition to the duel scene and Act 1 finale discussed below, see Leporello's 'Notte e giorno faticar' and Donna Anna's 'Or sai chi l'onore'. In the orchestration of Donna Anna's aria, Mozart first notated the string parts (in ink that is now a faded brown) and began the wind parts, before running out of ink in bar 26 (Mozart, *'Don Giovanni': Facsimile of the Autograph Score*, p. 194). The e' – f' in the bassoon in bars 25–26 is particularly faint and the note head of the f' crotchet is filled in with a new, sharp and black ink; the crotchets in the oboes on the downbeat of bar 26 are also in the sharp black ink. Since the rest of the wind parts in the aria are in the new ink, it appears Mozart wrote them down as a block (certainly from bar 26 onwards and with the exception of bars 37–40, which were probably written in the *particella*).

[83] Arnold, *Mozarts Geist*, p. 227 (referencing only the solo-wind passage). See also Keefe, 'Orchestrating Don Giovanni's Defeat'. For twentieth-century appreciation of the solo wind at the end of the scene, see Abert, *W. A. Mozart*, p. 1060 and Allanbrook, *Rhythmic Gesture in Mozart*, p. 214.

Example 8.6a Mozart, Introduzione from *Don Giovanni*, bars 167–172.

particella, which comprises the two voices, an instrumental bass line and occasional material for violins. Mozart had perhaps not decided on the exact wind complement for the duet when writing the *particella*, or changed his mind between *particella* and completion, as two staves left blank at the top and bottom of the autograph score and rendered redundant by the

Example 8.6b Mozart, Introduzione from *Don Giovanni*, bars 189–193.

original ten-stave brace could have been used for second oboe and second bassoon parts rather than these parts being doubled up on single staves with their wind partners. When he came to orchestrate the duet, notating all wind material, Mozart also appended the Andante's dynamics, including frequent swells for full orchestra – *p* – *mf* – *p* and on one occasion *p* – *sfp*. These originate with the *p* – *cresc* – *p* wind links between vocal phrases at the beginning (bars 4–5, 12–13; Example 8.7). It is as if contemplating distinctive, warm swells for the opening wind contribution sets a strategy for the entire 2/4 Andante.[84] The quartet 'Non ti fidar' is similar: surges notated throughout in the completion phase originate in wind swells (alongside strings) that coincide with the winds' first participation in the ensemble (bars 6–7, Example 8.8). Again, a distinguishing feature of the sound world of a number may have derived from contemplating wind

---

[84] From the evidence of first- and second-violin orchestral parts for the Vienna production in 1788, it is possible that Mozart decided to extend the swelling motif into the 6/8 'Andiam' section of 'Là ci darem'. As Edge points out ('Mozart's Viennese Copyists', p. 1788): 'A hand strongly resembling Mozart's has added dynamics in red crayon in measures 56 and 57; the word "crescendo" is written under measures 56 and 57, followed by the abbreviation "pia:" at the entry of the voices on the last eighth of measure 57.'

Example 8.7 Mozart, 'Là ci darem', from *Don Giovanni*, bars 1–9.

Example 8.8 Mozart, 'Non ti fidar', from *Don Giovanni*, bars 1–9.

involvement at the opening. A refined wind effect rounds off the quartet as well (Example 8.9). Having notated the strings *pizzicato* for the last two bars at the *particella* stage, and anchored the repeating cadence figure – the 'heartbeat' of the quartet[85] – at *p* in the completion, Mozart reserves the one and only *pp* for his complement of flute, clarinets, bassoons and horns signing off with the cadence figure. And in the Act 1 finale, the wind notation is consistently in a different ink colour from the string and voice parts, indicating inclusion at a discrete stage.[86] Several performance markings for the strings were introduced when the winds were being notated, judging by the wind ink appearing in string parts, such as *mfp*s for the violins and violas in bar 15. In addition, the 'sopra il teatro' (on the stage) instructions both for the individual renditions of the contredanse and minuet and later the simultaneous minuet, contredanse and *Teisch*,[87] plus the boxed-off musical text for the individual renditions of the dances, appear to coincide with the wind notation phase, as revealed by the sandy-coloured ink. In contrast, 'da lontano' (from a distance) at the same points clearly accrued to the original notation of the string parts. Mozart may have intended 'sopra il teatro' as an indication to copyists to generate parts of the boxed musical text for performers to use out of the orchestra pit.[88] But he apparently thought to have musicians on stage – as opposed to just 'from a distance' – only when contemplating the performance as a whole, that is when notating the wind parts in a largely continuous phase of activity across the finale.

Orchestrating the Act 2 finale led Mozart to intensify performance effects already notated in various passages of the *particella*. The swelling ascending-descending semiquaver scales in the first violins to accompany the Commendatore's explanation that he has more important things to do than dine on mortal food with Don Giovanni,[89] were probably not part of Mozart's original conception: he left insufficient room to notate them, extending bar-lines and using unlined spaces at the edge of his paper in order to fit in all of the semiquavers. The *cresc* – *p* surges coinciding with

---

[85] Allanbrook, *Rhythmic Gesture in Mozart*, p. 248.

[86] In parts of the Act 1 finale, Act 2 sextet and Act 2 finale, wind parts were notated on separate sheets of paper, as an insufficient number of staves were available in the main autograph score. But these sheets are no longer extant. Mozart draws attention to their erstwhile existence in annotations to the autograph; see Mozart, *'Don Giovanni': Facsimile of the Autograph*, pp. 268, 281 (Act 1 finale), 365 (sextet).

[87] See Mozart, *'Don Giovanni': Facsimile of the Autograph*, pp. 243, 250, 272.

[88] See Edge, 'Mozart's Viennese Copyists', pp. 1834–1836, on boxed musical text in the autograph fulfilling this function.

[89] Mozart, *'Don Giovanni': Facsimile of the Autograph*, pp. 524–525, 527.

Example 8.9 Mozart, 'Non ti fidar', from *Don Giovanni*, bars 85–88.

the violin scales, and unique to the violins in these passages,[90] are unlikely to have been envisaged, then, at the *particella* stage. Later, when the Commendatore states that Don Giovanni has invited him to dinner so must decide whether to accept the return invitation, repeated *cresc – f – p* (and *fp*) markings are attached to all instruments during the completion phase, including to the bass line previously notated in the *particella*.[91] The Commendatore's request for Don Giovanni's hand as a pledge to the agreement that he dine with him was already envisaged as a big effect at the *particella* stage, through the succession of *f – p – ff – p* dynamics. But the winds and brass notated in the completion up the ante with *pp – sfor – p* (Example 8.10).[92] During the orchestration process for all these passages, then, Mozart intensifies their impact in performance.

Needless to say, the grandest and weightiest effect in *Don Giovanni* coincides with the Commendatore's arrival in the Act 2 finale (Example 8.11). Here, Mozart either copied the first page of the Andante from a pre-existing draft – which would explain the consistent ink colours across the score – or knew that he wanted the *ff* dynamic from the start. In the run-up to the Commendatore's entry at the Andante, Don Giovanni states that he would have to open the door himself, as Leporello will not, enacting a *crescendo* from *p* to *f*; Leporello repeats the phrase to explain that he is going to hide so as to avoid seeing the statue again, now without the *crescendo* and *p*. The last two bars of the Molto allegro and the beginning of the Andante at the Commendatore's entry subsequently stage a dramatic increase in volume from *p* to *f* (full orchestra) to *ff* (full orchestra, including trumpets and timpani, and trombones – at least for the Prague production) that puts Don Giovanni's preceding *crescendo* firmly in the shade. The horror for Don Giovanni and for witnesses to his demise continues when three trombones provide the first wind sound after the opening chords (bars 438, 440), invoking sepulchral associations once again. And the second beats of the Andante's second and fourth bars, sounded only by violas, cellos and basses, still at *ff*, also contribute to the power of the orchestral impact (Example 8.11). The closest equivalent in an otherworldly context in Mozart's Viennese repertory, the lone violin crotchet at the end of the Dies irae from the Requiem four years later, helps to explain the effect created.[93] The frenetic activity of the Dies irae

---

[90] The flutes are unnotated in the autograph in these passages, but instructed to duplicate the first violin lines.

[91] Mozart, *'Don Giovanni': Facsimile of the Autograph*, pp. 528–529.

[92] Mozart, *'Don Giovanni': Facsimile of the Autograph*, p. 531.

[93] See Keefe, *Mozart's Requiem*, p. 133.

Example 8.10 Mozart, Act 2 finale from *Don Giovanni*, bars 516–520.

culminates in the movement's most precipitous drop of two octaves and a single violin d' (played on two strings) propelling itself into a sonic void. It is as if the immense energy generated by the Dies irae cannot dissipate in coordinated fashion, exploding beyond its obvious closing point on the first crotchet of the bar, just as the enormity of the *ff* sound at the Commendatore's arrival cannot be stopped in a uniform way with all instruments finishing at the same time. The end of the Dies irae and the beginning of Don Giovanni's own 'day of judgment' ultimately convey a similar, heightened sense of unsettledness. It is the opera orchestra, then, that signal the protagonist's defeat in advance of his actual banishment to hell, Mozart entrusting communication of the full effect of the loudest, most harrowing sounds in *Don Giovanni* – indeed some of the most harrowing in all opera – to his excellent Prague musicians.

Example 8.11 Mozart, Act 2 finale from *Don Giovanni*, bars 431–440.

After the Prague Premiere

Just five days after the *Don Giovanni* premiere in Prague, Mozart completed an aria 'Bella mia fiamma, addio … Resta, oh cara' K. 528 for
Josepha Duschek, the friend who had hosted him at her home, Bertamka,
for much of the Prague sojourn. Legend has it that she was fed up waiting
for the long-promised aria and locked Mozart in a room until it was
finished.[94] Duschek was a highly respected singer, praised that year for
her strong voice, deep and resonant tone, and general musicality.[95] A few
years later, Schönfeld cited universal admiration for a masterful singer with

[94] NMA II/7/4, Preface, pp. viii–ix.
[95] Wilhelm Vogel, *Beobachten in und über Prag, von einem reisenden Ausländer*, 2 vols. (Prague:
Wilhelm Gerle, 1787), vol. 2, p. 71.

a lovely voice and pleasant, highly expressive delivery (1796), Niemetschek recognized 'an artiste and . . . a cultured woman [who] received acclaim and public esteem' (1798), and the *Allgemeine musikalische Zeitung* identified her as Bohemia's best female singer (1800).[96] Both vocal volume and musicality were not appreciated by all, including Leopold, who wrote to Nannerl (18–22 April 1786): 'How did Madame Duschek sing? I can't help myself! She shrieked and cried an aria by Naumann quite astonishingly with exaggerated expressive force as before but even more annoyingly.'[97] Three weeks earlier, though, Zinzendorf heard her 'sing to perfection' at a concert in Vienna.[98]

'Bella mia fiamma . . . Resta, oh cara' exploits Duschek's resonant chest voice (e', e-flat', d') and bold sound in the kind of bravura aria to which she was particularly well suited.[99] As in his concert and opera arias for Lange, Cavalieri, and Storace, as well as in the expansive *scena* 'Ah, lo previdi!' K. 272 for Duschek herself (written in 1777 when performer and composer first encountered each other in Salzburg), Mozart nurtures a close relationship between Duschek and the accompanying orchestra, especially the wind. In 'Ah, lo previdi!' the pronounced obbligato oboe, interwoven with the voice, becomes a *bona fide* second soloist. And in 'Bella mia fiamma', the first statement of the Andante captures in microcosm Duschek's warm bond with the orchestra (Example 8.12): the strings are copied by the voice, which in turn is imitated by the oboe and bassoon and timbrally enhanced by a contingent of flute, oboes, two bassoons and two horns.

Four months later, Mozart finished a concert aria for Aloysia Lange, who was to sing Donna Anna in the upcoming Vienna *Don Giovanni*, and wrote a short and simple strophic song for amateur bass Friedrich Baumann. 'Ah se in ciel, benigne stelle' K. 538 (4 March 1788) is similar in style and bravura content to Aloysia's 'No, che non sei capace' K. 419 discussed in Chapter 6: coloratura, semiquaver roulades, big leaps, and frequent ascents

---

[96] Schönfeld, *Jahrbuch der Tonkunst in Wien und Prag*, p. 114; Niemetschek, *Leben*, p. 54, *Life of Mozart*, p. 62; 'Ueber den Zustand der Musik in Böhmen', col. 513.

[97] MBA, vol. 3, p. 532 (not in LMF).

[98] Link, *National Court Theatre*, p. 269 ('chanta au perfection'). On Duschek, including further contemporary commentary on her singing and information about the academy in Leipzig on 22 April 1788 at which she performed Mozart's *scena* 'A questo seno . . . Or che il ciel', K. 374, see Woodfield, *Performing Operas for Mozart*, pp. 136–147. See also Paul Corneilson, '"aber nach geendigter Oper mit Vergnügen": Mozart's Arias for Mme Duschek', in Libin (ed.), *Mozart in Prague*, pp. 175–200. Duschek performed arias from *Figaro* and *Don Giovanni* in Leipzig in April 1789, to coincide with Mozart's visit. See MBA, vol. 4, p. 83; LMF, p. 923 (16 April 1789).

[99] On the latter point, see Schönfeld, *Jahrbuch der Tonkunst in Wien und Prag*, p. 114.

Example 8.12 Mozart, 'Bella mia fiamma – Resta, oh cara', K. 528, bars 1–13.

to c''' (on one occasion d''') bear a vocal resemblance to Konstanze's 'Martern aller Arten' from *Die Entführung*, a role with which Aloysia enjoyed considerable success in the late 1780s. Mozart wrote a *particella* for 'Ah se in ciel, benigne stelle' in 1778,[100] but did not include the lengthy orchestral introduction (bars 1–23), the middle ritornello (bars 101–106) or the conclusion after the singer's exit (bars 207–212). Mozart may or may not have envisaged the eventual shape and scope of the aria in 1778, providing the initial *particella* in order for Aloysia to learn her part. In any case, the performable version from 1788 has an orchestra add gravitas – as in 'Martern aller Arten' – in support of vocal grandeur. And for those Viennese unaware either of Aloysia's talents, or of the orchestral riches in Mozart's latest opera, 'Ah se in ciel' would have served as an enticement to experience *Don Giovanni* a few weeks later, assuming Aloysia did actually perform it at the Burgtheater on 4 March, or at a subsequent concert appearance at a Tonkünstler-Societät event at the same venue on 15 March.[101] In contrast, 'Ich möchte wohl der Kaiser sein' K. 539 was a German war song sung by Baumann at a patriotic concert at the Leopoldstadttheater on 7 March early in the Turkish conflict: it covers a vocal range of only one octave (e – e') and contains a large accompanying orchestra and no taxing vocal material. With its politically motivated text capturing 'brief initial [war-time] euphoria', K. 539 was popular for a while in Vienna.[102]

The success, failure or otherwise of the Vienna *Don Giovanni*, which began its run on 7 May 1788 two months after the completion of 'Ah se in ciel' and 'Ich möchte wohl der Kaiser sein', is a matter of debate. Mozart's triumph in Prague is not in doubt, even if Guardasoni's hyperbolic reaction relayed by Da Ponte is in fact apocryphal ('All impresarios, all *virtuosi* should bless [Da Ponte and Mozart's] names. So long as they live we shall never know what theatrical poverty means!').[103] According to critics: 'Connoisseurs and musicians say that Prague has not yet put on its equal ... The extraordinary number of audience members vouches for the public approbation' (*Prager Oberpostamtszeitung* 3 November 1787); 'performed for the first time with public approval ... Mozart conducted in person and was welcomed with joyful cheering by the numerous gathering'

---

[100] Tyson, *Mozart: Studies of the Autograph Scores*, pp. 28–29.

[101] On the possibility of a performance of 'Ah se in ciel' on 4 March, see Landon, *Mozart: the Golden Years*, p. 192; Edge, 'Mozart's Reception in Vienna', p. 87. For Aloysia Lange's participation in the concert on 15 March, see Morrow, *Concert Life in Haydn's Vienna*, p. 272.

[102] On 'Ich möchte wohl der Kaiser sein' (including the quoted phrase) set in historical and critical context, see Beales, *Joseph II: Against the World*, pp. 580–582.

[103] *Memoirs of Lorenzo Da Ponte*, p. 179.

(*Provinzialnachrichten*, 10 November); and 'excellent beyond measure . . . its equal has never before been given in Prague' (*Staats- und gelehrte Zeitung*, 9 November).[104] Writing to Jacquin on 4 November, Mozart identified the 'loudest applause' for the opera and to Nannerl a few weeks after returning from Prague, that news of its great success might have already reached her.[105] Supported by remarks from Count Zinzendorf and Archduchess Elisabeth Wilhelmine, *Don Giovanni*'s putative failure in Vienna is based above all on Da Ponte's account: 'The opera went on the stage and . . . need I recall it? . . . *Don Giovanni* did not please! Everyone, except Mozart, thought that there was something missing. Additions were made; some of the arias were changed; it was offered for a second performance. *Don Giovanni* did not please!'[106] Performing materials for the Vienna production, pointing to alterations during the 1788 run, offer general support for Da Ponte's statement that initial negativity provoked revisions.[107] And if Da Ponte's recollection is accurate in this respect, so might be his statement about *Don Giovanni* eventually finding favour: 'Little by little even Vienna . . . came to enjoy its savor and appreciate its beauties.'[108] At any rate, a respectable tally of fifteen performances in total represents 'far from an abject failure'.[109]

The whiff of failure, the old-fashioned belief that the Prague version is definitive and the Viennese version 'experimental', and the faults found both with the dramatic integrity of the 1788 version and the new numbers themselves, have – in various manifestations through to the present day – ensured a rocky critical ride for the Vienna *Don Giovanni*.[110] In reality, late-eighteenth-century operas were almost always in a state of flux, both under the guidance of composers and librettists carrying out revisions

[104] MDL, p. 267; MDB, pp. 303, 304; and NMD, p. 51.

[105] MBA, vol. 4, pp. 58, 60; LMF, pp. 912, 914 (4 November, 19 December 1787).

[106] *Memoirs of Da Ponte*, p. 180. For Zinzendorf and Wilhelmine's comments, see MDL, pp. 276, 280; MDB, pp. 314, 319.

[107] Edge, 'Mozart's Viennese Copyists', pp. 1861–1862.   [108] *Memoirs of Da Ponte*, p. 180.

[109] Edge, 'Mozart's Viennese Copyists', p. 1749.

[110] On the 'experimental' nature of the Vienna *Don Giovanni*, see in particular Wolfgang Plath and Wolfgang Rehm, NMA II/5/17, Preface, pp. xi–xii. Rehm recently reiterated this view in 'Musicological Introduction', in Mozart, *'Don Giovanni': Facsimile of the Autograph Score*, p. 16. In the early part of the twentieth century a mood of negativity surrounded the Vienna *Don Giovanni*: see, for example, Dent, *Mozart's Operas*, p. 169; Abert, *W. A. Mozart*, pp. 1025–1026; Einstein, *Mozart: His Character, His Work*, p. 456; Blom, 'Don Giovanni', in Biancolli (ed.), *The Mozart Handbook*, p. 240. For recent disapproval, see Heartz, *Mozart, Haydn and Early Beethoven*, pp. 196–197. Rushton is happy 'to grant the accolade of authenticity to the Vienna form of *Don Giovanni*', but agrees with the NMA view about its 'experimental' status, considers it 'certainly not, overall, an improvement, despite the beauties of the two new arias' and advises against 'the common performance convention of combining Prague and Vienna versions' (*W. A. Mozart: 'Don Giovanni'*, pp. 53, 57).

during and after production runs and when transmitted further afield,
defying modernist notions of a final, fixed text. By the time Mozart witnessed
Don Giovanni again in Prague, on 2 September 1791 four days before the
premiere of *La clemenza di Tito*, it had received first performances *inter alia*
in Leipzig in 1788; Frankfurt, Mannheim, Passau, Bonn, Warsaw, Hamburg
and Brno in 1789; Berlin and Augsburg in 1790; and Hanover, Cassel, Bad
Pyrmont and Cologne in 1791.[111] Existing in many different forms, some
promoted by the original Guardasoni troupe including in Leipzig 1788
where 'Mi tradi' was heard outside Vienna probably for the first time, the
opera continued to evolve.[112] And Mozart would no doubt have contributed
to the process of development himself had the situation arisen.[113]

The perception of *Don Giovanni*'s failure in Vienna feeds a traditional
biographical narrative of decline in the final years of Mozart's life and
abandonment by his adopted hometown.[114] Marcia Davenport offers
a classic formulation: '*Don Giovanni* was a plain failure. There was no
applause. ... The last hopes of a brilliant Vienna success, of final and
happy recognition were destroyed in one smashing blow. He knew then
that he was not for this Vienna, and perhaps not for this world.'[115] For
others, such as H. C. Robbins Landon and Michael Levey, the unsuccessful
reception of *Don Giovanni* encapsulated waning appreciation for Mozart
and his music in Vienna.[116] According to Pierre-Petit, again elaborating on
a common theme, the opera failed on account of the snobbish Viennese
turning attention to lesser music instead.[117] But, judging by Mozart's

---

[111] MDL, pp. 299–357; MDB, pp. 341–409 (*passim*). The *Krönungsjournal für Prag* commended
Guardasoni and his company for their excellent performance of *Don Giovanni*
in September 1791. See MDB, pp. 405–406.

[112] On Leipzig 1788 and Warsaw 1789 productions by the Guardasoni troupe, see Woodfield,
Vienna 'Don Giovanni', pp. 115–130 and Woodfield, *Performing Operas for Mozart*,
pp. 114–127. The opera had also begun to circulate in arrangements, including for string
quartet in Vienna (1788) and for eight wind instruments in Speyer (1789). See MDL, pp. 281,
293; MDB, pp. 321, 334.

[113] Woodfield, *Vienna 'Don Giovanni'*, p. 130. According to Stiepanek's account, recorded in
Nissen (*Biographie W. A. Mozarts*, pp. 521–522), Mozart did contribute to the process, sharing
with the Prague company the Viennese additions to *Don Giovanni*.

[114] For a composite 'widely believed narrative of the last years of Mozart's life' see Edge, 'Mozart's
Reception in Vienna, 1787–1791', p. 66.

[115] Davenport, *Mozart*, p. 318.

[116] See Landon, *Mozart's Last Year*, p. 6; Levey, *The Life and Death of Mozart*, p. 216.

[117] Pierre-Petit, *Mozart, ou la musique instantanée* (Paris: Perrin, 1991), pp. 284–285. Less
emotively, Rushton (*Mozart*, p. 159) has suggested that Viennese competition with Martín
y Soler's *L'arbore di Diana* and Salieri's *Axur, re d'Ormus* could account for lesser success in
the Habsburg capital than in Prague, and Edge has speculated ('Mozart's Viennese Copyists',
p. 1862) that high production costs – including onstage musicians, a mandolinist, a chorus,
etc. – 'may have contributed to the relative brevity of ... [*Don Giovanni*'s Vienna] run'.

interactions with his various constituencies, musical enthusiasm and positivity prevailed rather than cynicism and disillusionment. In *Don Giovanni*, both for Prague and Vienna, and (as we shall see) in instrumental and vocal music written during the remaining years of his life, Mozart redoubled efforts to engage practically, proactively, creatively and energetically with listeners and viewers, as well as with performers and purchasers of his music.

The Italian Opera company's theatrical season 1789–1790 at the Burgtheater, when *Le nozze di Figaro* was revived and *Così fan tutte, ossia La scuola degli amanti* premiered, nearly did not take place at all. With attention on the war against the Turks, and an undesirably expensive theatrical operation to underwrite, Emperor Joseph II wanted to close down the company. Da Ponte put together a rescue package, with the backing of fourteen aristocrats, dependent on being granted free access to the Burgtheater. Initially unimpressed, Joseph ultimately agreed to the arrangement. Now installed as impresario as well as librettist, Da Ponte was responsible for recruiting singers and ensuring the books were balanced. He coped with a fiscal crisis in mid-1789, turning finances around by the end of the 1789–1790 season, and did not have it easy in other respects either.[1] His *pasticcio, L'ape musicale,* which premiered on 27 February 1789 towards the end of the previous season and involved a poet discussing arrangements for a new opera with his niece, made an enemy of former close friend Salieri: Da Ponte's preference for the company's new prima donna, Adriana Ferrarese del Bene, with whom he was in love, over Cavalieri, Salieri's supposed *amour,* '[broke] the bonds of a friendship, which should have been of our whole lives'.[2] Louisa Villeneuve, the original Dorabella in *Così,* took umbrage at her omission from the lucrative *L'ape musicale,* and consequently became hostile.[3] And Dorotea Bussani, the first Despina in *Così,* was bluntly described by Da Ponte as 'an Italian *diva* who, though a ridiculous person of little merit, had by dint of facial contortions, clown's tricks, and perhaps by means more theatrical still, built up a great following among cooks, barbers, lackeys, butlers and hostlers'.[4] Francesco Bussani, the original Don Alfonso in *Così* and Dorotea's husband, was also identified as an 'adversary': Bussani had acquired influence in casting decisions at the Italian company, stoking rivalry between the two men.[5]

---

[1] Woodfield, *Cabals and Satires,* Chapters 5 and 6, forthcoming.   [2] Da Ponte, *Memoirs,* p. 186.
[3] Bruce Alan Brown and John Rice, 'Salieri's *Così fan tutte', Cambridge Opera Journal,* 8 (1996), pp. 17–43, at 36–37.
[4] Da Ponte, *Memoirs,* p. 185.   [5] See Woodfield, *Così fan tutte,* pp. 80–81.

Mozart's first assignment of the 1789–1790 season was the revival of *Le nozze di Figaro*. In early August he mentioned making alterations for the imminent opera, which was first staged on 29 August and then another 28 times before completing its run in February 1791.[6] The revival was a notable success. Only Martín y Soler's *L'arbore di Diana* bettered its number of performances across 1789–1790 and 1790–1791 seasons.[7] In addition, the average box-office yield from each performance in 1789–1790 was 218 florins 40 kreutzer, considerably above the average for all operas in the same period and the fourth-highest grossing opera overall.[8] Ferrarese del Bene (Susanna), Cavalieri (Countess), and probably Louise Villeneuve (Cherubino) took the principal female parts; Giovanni Battista Brocchi, another new recruit, sang Figaro, but from time to time handed over to the title role's creator, Benucci.[9] The identity of the Count is unclear: Mandini, Albertarelli and Morella had all left the company by the start of 1789–1790. Girolamo Cruciati, who debuted in Vienna on 28 April 1789, could have sung the Count, but left at the end of the season; Santi Nencini probably took over on his arrival at the Burgtheater in 1790–1791.[10] Zinzendorf, generally ambivalent about Mozart's music, enjoyed both the letter duet, 'Che soave zeffiretto', and the newly composed rondò, 'Al desio' K. 577: 'The duet for the two women and the rondeau for La Ferrarese please, as always.'[11] A revised version of *L'ape musicale* in 1791 included 'Che soave zeffiretto', a sign of its popularity during the revival period.[12] In a little-known review of *Figaro* in the *Pressburger Zeitung* (2 September 1789), Ferrarese, 'Al desio', Mozart and Brocchi were all praised: 'The public were very happy with [*Figaro*]. . . . Madame Ferrarese played the prima donna, and sang with her famous skill and art, and showed it especially in a harmonically artificial Rondeau, where the

---

[6] See MBA, vol. 3, p. 96; LMF, p. 933. For performance dates see Link, *National Court Theatre*, pp. 145–163, and (including receipts for individual performances) Edge, 'Mozart's Reception in Vienna, 1787–1791', in Sadie (ed.), *Essays on His Life and Music*, p. 104.

[7] See Edge 'Mozart's Reception in Vienna, 1787–1791', Table 1, pp. 95–109.

[8] Edge, 'Mozart's Reception in Vienna, 1787–1791', p. 82.

[9] Villeneuve's probable participation is identified by Edge ('Mozart's Viennese Copyists', pp. 1509, 1669–1670), based on an annotation 'La S: Vilneuf' to the original first-desk violin part. On Brocchi, see Woodfield, *Cabals and Satires*, and on Benucci, see Edge, 'Mozart's Viennese Copyists', pp. 1672–1673.

[10] On Cruciati and Nencini, see Edge, 'Mozart's Viennese Copyists', pp. 1671–1672.

[11] Given (in French) in Link, *National Court Theatre*, p. 355 (7 May 1790). ('Le Duo des deux femmes, le rondeau de la ferraresi plait toujours'.) Zinzendorf also referred to the 'charming duet between La Cavalieri and La Ferrarese' ('Charmant Duo entre la Cavalieri et la ferraresi') on 31 August 1789 (*National Court Theatre*, p. 339).

[12] Woodfield, *Cabals and Satires*.

music of Mr. Mozart and the singing of the famous singer vied for supremacy; the same praise was earned by the recently arrived bass Herr Brocehi [*sic*].'[13]

The main revisions for the *Figaro* revival comprise two new arias for Ferrarese, 'Un moto di gioia' K. 579 as well as 'Al desio', and revised versions of 'Dove sono' for Cavalieri and 'Vedrò mentre' for whoever sang the Count. 'Un moto di gioia' and 'Al desio', discussed below, have attracted the wrath of Mozart scholars, no doubt in part because the replaced arias, 'Venite inginocchiatevi' and 'Deh vieni', are held in such high esteem.[14] But, clearly tailored to Ferrarese's vocal qualities, including a strong lower register, pronounced vocal flexibility, and an ability to make big leaps, both arias contribute to a reimagined role for Susanna relative to the original production, more elevated and poetic in 'Un moto di gioia' and 'much more obviously a musical *travestimento*' in imitation of the Countess in 'Al desio', where we are made aware 'that Susanna does not have to remain locked in one particular vocal mold'.[15] While 'Al desio', dated July 1789 in the *Verzeichnüß*, was definitely written before the revival began, 'Un moto di gioia' probably came later. The type of paper on which it was written suggests composition in 1790 rather than 1789, midway through *Figaro*'s run rather than before it started, perhaps in the second half of the year.[16]

'Vedrò mentre' and 'Dove sono' were altered for the revival to accommodate vocal profiles different to those of the original Count and Susanna (Mandini and Storace). Neither revision has survived in autograph form,

---

[13] *Pressburger Zeitung* (2 September 1789), p. 634. ('Das Publikum war damit sehr zufrieden … Madame Ferrarese spielte als Prima Donna, und sang mit ihrer bekanntlichen Geschicklichkeit, und Kunst, zeugte sich besonders in einem künstlich-harmonischen Rondeau, wo die Musik des Herrn Mozart mit dem Gesang der berühmten Sängerinn um die Wette stritten; gleiches Lob verdient der neu angekommene Bassist Herr Brocehi'.)

[14] For criticism in the secondary literature, see discussion in Roger Parker, 'Ersatz Ditties: Adriana Ferrarese's Susanna', in *Remaking the Song: Operatic Revisions from Handel to Berio* (Berkeley, CA: University of California Press, 2006), pp. 42–66, at 55, 60–61. Heartz (*Mozart, Haydn, Early Beethoven*, p. 237) remarks brusquely: '['Un moto di gioia' is] an anodyne little waltz. Mozart did not see fit to enter this piece in his catalogue. … If "Un moto di gioia" could be said to represent the "dumbing down" of Susanna, the other aria ["Al desio"] … could be called the role's "tarting up".' Rushton (*The New Grove Guide to Mozart and His Operas* [Oxford: Oxford University Press, 2007], p. 86) is more circumspect, but still critical: 'Mozart's replacement of "Deh vieni" … by "Al desio" is perhaps a case of his damaging his own work by pandering to a singer's needs, although the new aria is beautiful in its own fashion.'

[15] See Parker's persuasive interpretation in *Remaking the Song*, pp. 52–66 (quotations at pp. 62, 66). On Ferrarese's vocal qualities, see Patricia Gidwitz, 'Mozart's Fiordiligi: Adriana Ferrarese del Bene', *Cambridge Opera Journal*, 8 (1996), pp. 199–214.

[16] See Edge, 'Mozart's Viennese Copyists', pp. 1687–1702.

but 'Dove sono' is transmitted in the original Burgtheater performing score.[17] Since there is no certainty about the identity of the Count, motivations for changing 'Vedrò mentre' are difficult to determine. With frequent high notes in the Allegro assai at g', a fourth above the original, and a higher tessitura in general, it is aimed at an authentic baritone; annotations to the preceding Allegro maestoso, probably in Mozart's hand, take the aria up to written f'.[18] Other changes include the elimination of much of the original note repetition and a short extension to the aria at the end. Adjustments to 'Dove sono' are more substantial and revealing.[19] The final one (Example 9.1), introducing coloratura, an extended g'' for two and a half bars and a semiquaver rising scale not witnessed in the corresponding passage of the original, resonates with other music Mozart wrote for Cavalieri. While virtuosic features accrue to the revision, then, they are more modest than in her earlier Mozart arias and occur in the context of a shortening of the overall length of the original by fifteen bars, perhaps signalling a slight concession to diminished vocal powers, as in 'Mi tradì' from the Vienna *Don Giovanni* (1788).[20] The first cut – eliminating the reprise of the main theme at the end of the Andante – could have been intended 'to make the aria seem less explicitly a rondò, in order that Cavalieri's aria was not seen to compete with Ferrarese's "Al desio"'.[21] But it is unclear why Ferrarese would have worried about the formal type of her rival's aria and not about the additional coloratura its vocal line had now acquired.

Above all, changes to 'Dono sono' for the *Figaro* revival need not be processed as a series of 'concessions ... [effecting] in turn a stylistic departure from the original ... made to the detriment of one of the most affecting solo moments in all of opera', or as a 'weakening ... [of its] finespun filaments'.[22] In angular quaver lines coinciding with Cavalieri's sustained g'' and a' in the second revised passage (Example 9.1), the wind

---

[17] Edge, 'Mozart's Viennese Copyists', pp. 1704–1705.

[18] See Edge, 'Mozart's Viennese Copyists', p. 1719.

[19] The two big adjustments comprise: cutting the Andante's reprise of the main theme (bars 37–51 inclusive) and replacing the initial four and a half bars of the ensuing Allegro with seven and a half bars of new material; and substituting a twelve-and-a-half-bar passage towards the end with ten and a half bars. For a score of the revisions, see NMA, II/5/16, Kritische Berichte, pp. 383–388.

[20] For a similar argument see Gidwitz, 'Vocal Portraits of Four Mozart Sopranos', p. 253; see also Gidwitz, '"Ich bin die erste Sängerinn"', pp. 571–573. On 'Mi tradì', see Chapter 8 in this volume.

[21] Edge, 'Mozart's Viennese Copyists', p. 1711.

[22] See Gidwitz, 'Vocal Portraits of Four Mozart Sopranos', pp. 253, 254; Gutman, *Mozart: a Cultural Biography*, pp. 701–702.

Example 9.1 Mozart, 'Dove sono' from *Le nozze di Figaro* revision (1789), between the original bars 83 and 97.

build on earlier dialogue with the voice, including imitation immediately before the start of the revision. The wind agility too, with large leaps and c'''s in the oboe, may compensate for Cavalieri's diminished suppleness and more limited high notes than in days gone by, analogous to the florid wind quaver lines helping her out in 'Mi tradì' (see Chapter 8). Cavalieri's new passage also extends further the virtuosic quaver material heard earlier in the Allegro. Thus, the revisions to 'Dove sono' catch Mozart re-envisaging his composition for a different performer. Just as experiences and contemplation of performances of the 'Haydn' quartets and string quintets, for example, provoke new interpretations of dynamics and articulation (see Chapters 5 and 10), so a prospective rendition of 'Dove sono' stimulates revisions to the original. The chamber work with altered and interpolated markings, the revised aria, and the replacement aria all exist on a continuum defined by interrelationships between compositional priorities and performance-related activities and concerns.

Once the *Figaro* production had begun, Mozart could turn his attention to *Così fan tutte*. Mozart's success with the revival may have led to a formal commission for the new opera, as is commonly thought. But he had been thinking about writing one at least since spring 1789, mentioning an (ultimately unrealized) arrangement with Guardasoni for Prague.[23] It is not impossible that early ensembles for *Così* had been drafted by then.[24] Da Ponte said nothing about the opera's genesis in his memoirs, only that it held 'third place among the three sisters born of that most celebrated father of harmony'.[25] He also failed to mention that Salieri was originally given his libretto, at that stage titled *La scola degli amanti*. Salieri's start on the project and relinquishment of it, documented in Mary and Vincent Novello's conversations with Constanze in the 1820s, was only verified around twenty-five years ago when his complete and partial settings of the ensembles 'È la fede femine' (*sic*) and 'La mia Dorabella' came to light.[26] Ultimately, Salieri's 'decision to abandon *La scola degli amanti* probably had less to do with the quality of the libretto than with his state of mind in 1788 and 1789 – years marked by artistic indecisiveness, a low level of creative energy, and varying degrees of dependence on earlier music'.[27] The libretto itself, much discussed in the critical literature, draws on a remarkable range of sources and contexts, old and new alike: elaborations of the Ovidian Cephalus and Procris myth from Italian Renaissance drama, including Boccaccio's fourteenth-century *Decameron* and Ludovico Ariosto's sixteenth-century *Orlando furioso*; and, from the eighteenth century, *inter alia* existing libretti by Giovanni Battista Casti, Metastasio and Da Ponte himself, plot symmetries in Metastasio's *opere serie*, the cult of

[23] MBA, vol. 4, p. 80; LMF, p. 920 (10 April 1789).
[24] See Woodfield, *Così fan tutte*, pp. 2–6; and Woodfield, *Performing Operas for Mozart*, p. 130.
[25] Da Ponte, *Memoirs*, p. 185.   [26] See Brown and Rice, 'Salieri's *Così fan tutte*'.
[27] Brown and Rice, 'Salieri's *Così fan tutte*', p. 35.

Mesmer and Mesmerism, and Pierre de Marivaux's plays about the unrealistic ideals of constancy and fidelity.[28] Beaumarchais' defence of the wife of prominent French Mesmer promoter Guillaume Kornman against her husband's allegations of infidelity, coinciding with Beaumarchais and Salieri's residence together in Paris in 1787, perhaps provided a further source of inspiration for Da Ponte's story.[29] And two contemporary adventurers posing as Albanians, Premislas and Stefano Zannowich, could explain Ferrando and Guglielmo's disguise as Albanians in *Così*.[30] One writer memorably characterized *Così* as a 'promiscuous miscegenation' of material from different periods.[31]

Once Mozart had agreed to set *Così* he probably requested a number of changes to the libretto previously in Salieri's possession.[32] The two types of paper in the autograph illuminate compositional chronology especially for Act 1, and confirm Mozart's usual practice of writing most ensembles before most arias: the trios 'La mia Dorabella', 'È la fede delle femmine', 'Una bella serenata', 'Soave sia il vento', 'E voi ridete', the duets 'Ah guarda sorella', 'Al fato', the quintet 'Sento oddio', the sextet 'Alla bella Despinetta', and the arias 'Smanie implacabili' and 'Rivolgete' are all on Alan Tyson's Type I paper and were therefore written first; the quintet 'Di scrivermi' and aria 'Un' aura amorosa' on a combination of Type I and II paper came next; and the arias 'Vorrei dir', 'In uomini', 'Come scoglio', 'Non siate ritrosi', the chorus 'Bella vita militar', the finale and overture exclusively on Type II paper followed later. All but ten of the 238 leaves of

---

[28] On early sources, see Bruce Alan Brown, *W. A. Mozart: 'Così fan tutte'* (Cambridge: Cambridge University Press, 1995), pp. 13–14, 58–70; Edmund J. Goehring, *Three Modes of Perception in Mozart: the Philosophical, Pastoral, and Comic in 'Così fan tutte'* (Cambridge: Cambridge University Press, 2004), p. 106; Steptoe, *Mozart-Da Ponte Operas*, pp. 123–127. For eighteenth-century sources, see Bruce Alan Brown, 'Beaumarchais, Paisiello and the Genesis of *Così fan tutte*', in Sadie (ed.), *Essays*, pp. 312–338; Brown, *Così fan tutte*, pp. 15–18, 70–81; John Rice, 'Musicological Introduction', in W. A. Mozart, *'Così fan tutte ossia La scuola degli amanti'*, *K. 588: Facsimile of the Autograph Score* (Los Altos, CA: Packard Humanities Institute, 2007), vol. 3, p. 11; Goehring, *Three Modes of Perception in Mozart, passim*; Norbert Miller, 'Toying with the Emotions: Da Ponte's and Mozart's School of Lovers', in *'Così': Facsimile of the Autograph Score*, p. 3; Dorothea Link, *'L'arbore di Diana*: a Model for *Così fan tutte*', in Sadie (ed.), *Essays*, pp. 362–373; Till, *Mozart and the Enlightenment*, pp. 229–257; Heartz, 'Three Schools for Lovers, or "Così fan tutte le belle"', in *Mozart's Operas*, pp. 216–227. On the significance of the libretto's settings, see Laurenz Lütteken, 'Negating Opera Through Opera: *Così fan tutte* and the Reverse of the Enlightenment', *Eighteenth-Century Music*, 6 (2009), pp. 229–242, at 231–236.

[29] Pierpaolo Polzonetti, 'Mesmerizing Adultery: *Così fan tutte* and the Kornman Scandal', *Cambridge Opera Journal*, 14 (2002), pp. 263–296.

[30] See Russell T. Bamhart, 'The Two "Albanian Noblemen" in *Così fan tutte*', *Mitteilungen der Internationalen Stiftung Mozarteum*, 46 (1998), pp. 38–41.

[31] Brown, *Così fan tutte*, p. 14.   [32] See Brown and Rice, 'Salieri's *Così fan tutte*', pp. 38–40.

Act 2 are on Type II paper.[33] Philological evidence suggests a two-stage genesis for *Così* as well as a short-lived idea of having the disguised Ferrando and Guglielmo attempt to seduce their own rather than their colleague's partner.[34] Rehearsals were taking place by 31 December 1789 and with a full orchestra by 21 January 1790, five days before the opera's first performance on 26 January.[35] In line with standard practice, a performing score for the Burgtheater (Österreichische Nationalbibliothek, OA 146) was copied from the autograph in the run-up to the premiere and transmits a few cuts almost certainly with Mozart's authority and many others without it.[36] A surviving weekly ledger among the theatre accounts for the week of *Così*'s launch confirms a standard payment of 100 ducats (450 gulden) for writing the opera, rather than the 200 ducats Mozart claimed to expect in a begging letter to Michael Puchberg. Higher commissioning fees were not unprecedented in the 1780s, including 300 ducats for Paisiello (*Il re Teodoro in Venezia*) and 200 for Salieri (*La cifra*, which premiered seven weeks before *Così*, and *La grotta di Trofonio*). But an *ex gratia* payment from Emperor Joseph to raise *Così*'s total to 200 ducats seems unlikely on account of his fatal illness and absence from the opera's rehearsals and performances.[37]

Like Da Ponte's libretto, Mozart's music in *Così* resonates with late-eighteenth-century material. *Così*'s links to Martín y Soler's *L'arbore di Diana* (1787), partially the result of various singers performing in both, produce a 'conversation between [the operas] . . . both amicable and quite specifically inclusive of the audience'.[38] In contrast, the conversation with Casti and Salieri's *La grotta di Trofonio* (1785) seemingly '[tells] a story of

---

[33] See Alan Tyson, 'On the Composition of Mozart's *Così fan tutte*', in *Studies of the Autograph Scores*, pp. 177–221, at p. 182.

[34] On the possible two-stage genesis, see Tyson, *Autograph Scores*, pp. 182–186 and Woodfield, *Così fan tutte*, pp. 20–26. On the crossing and uncrossing of lovers for Ferrando and Guglielmo's seductions of Dorabella and Fiordiligi, see Woodfield, *Così fan tutte*, pp. 99–150.

[35] See Mozart's letters identifying a 'little opera rehearsal' ('eine kleine Oper-Probe') and the full orchestra rehearsal to which Puchberg and Joseph Haydn were invited: MBA, vol. 4, pp. 100, 102; LMF, p. 935 (December 1789; 20 January 1790).

[36] For discussions of this score, see Edge, 'Mozart's Viennese Copyists', pp. 1922–1961 and Woodfield, *Così fan tutte*, pp. 152–161. Woodfield (pp. 178–179) also documents the erstwhile existence of a conducting score by showing that a small segment of it from the Act 2 finale actually appears in the Burgtheater score copied from the autograph. Performing parts associated with the original production do not survive.

[37] See Edge, 'Mozart's Fee for *Così fan tutte*', pp. 211–235. For the letter to Puchberg, see MBA, vol. 4, p. 100; LMF, p. 934 (December 1789).

[38] See Hunter, *Culture of Opera Buffa in Mozart's Vienna*, pp. 250–256 (quotation at p. 256). On parallels between the plots, pastoral elements, treatments of love and eroticism, and uses of magic, disguise and transformation, see also Dorothea Link, '*L'arbore di Diana*: A Model for *Così fan tutte*', pp. 362–373.

unrelieved competitiveness on Mozart's and Da Ponte's parts': plot developments, overall design, dramatic roles, and music in *Così* can be seen to address putative weaknesses in the earlier opera.[39] *Così*'s musical hinterland is informed by Salieri in other ways too: the Act 2 rondò for Ferrarese, 'Per pietà', shows Mozart learning from formal, vocal and instrumental features of the same singer's rondò 'Sola e mesta' in Salieri's *La cifra* (1789); the beautiful canon from the Act 2 finale stands in apparent competition with Salieri's canon from *La cifra*; and the change in the opera's title from *La scola degli amanti* to *Così fan tutte*, almost certainly at Mozart's behest, may represent an attempt to distance the opera from the initial recipient of the libretto, making 'pointed references' to the libretto of *Figaro* instead (specifically Basilio's line 'Così fan tutte le belle' from the Act 1 trio 'Cosa sento').[40] Unsurprisingly, *Così* has musical and dramatic links with *Figaro*, Mozart's previous commission for the Burgtheater and an opera very much on his mind during *Così*'s genesis.[41] In fact, when *Figaro*, *Così* and Paisiello's *Il barbiere di Siviglia* (1782) are considered as an alternative kind of Da Ponte trilogy, 'a renewal of a venerable tradition of plots in which young lovers outwit an old tutor' (*Il barbiere*) followed by an injection of 'strong political overtones into the formula' (*Figaro*) and finally a 'cynicism in love ... pushed to the very limit before the possibility of redemption is revealed' (*Così*), musical, textual and plot-related connections come to light: Don Alfonso's short aria 'Vorrei dir' and the chorus 'Bella vita militar' are modelled on 'L'invidia, oh ciel' (*Il barbiere*) and 'Non più andrai' (*Figaro*) respectively; and 'È la fede femmine' invokes 'Oh che umor' (*Il barbiere*).[42] Other similarities between *Figaro* and *Così* include love and seduction duets in A major and thematic features of the two overtures.[43] As we shall see, the 1786 *Figaro* and the revival together provide a starting point for evaluating relationships between the performance and composition of *Così*.

[39] Hunter, *Culture of Opera Buffa in Mozart's Vienna*, pp. 257–264 (quotation at p. 257).

[40] On these various points see, respectively, Rice, *Salieri and Viennese Opera*, pp. 486–487; Dorothea Link, '"È la fede degli amanti" and the Viennese Operatic Canon', in Keefe (ed.), *Mozart Studies*, pp. 109–136, and Link, 'The Viennese Operatic Canon and Mozart's *Così fan tutte*', *Mitteilungen der Internationalen Stiftung Mozarteum*, 38 (1991), pp. 111–121; Tyson, *Mozart: Studies of the Autograph Scores*, p. 197; Brown and Rice, 'Salieri's *Così fan tutte*', p. 28.

[41] As early as 1803, Arnold (*Mozarts Geist*, pp. 390–391) drew attention to a similar inexhaustible richness of melodic material in *Figaro* and *Così*.

[42] Brown, 'Beaumarchais, Paisiello and the Genesis of *Così*', pp. 313–322 (quoted material at p. 314). See also Brown, *Così fan tutte*, pp. 6–7.

[43] See Heartz, *Mozart's Operas*, pp. 223–225, 234–237.

The principal singers at the *Così* premiere comprised two with whom Mozart had not previously worked before 1789 (Ferrarese and Louisa Villeneuve as Fiordiligi and Dorabella), one who had been in Vienna for several years but had hitherto featured in only two ensembles by Mozart (Vincenzo Calvesi as Ferrando), and three for whom the composer had previously created operatic roles (Francesco Benucci, Francesco Bussani and Dorotea Bussani as Guglielmo, Don Alfonso and Despina). Mozart did not have a high opinion of Ferrarese, whose Viennese debut was in Martín y Soler's *L'arbore di Diana* on 13 October 1788 and who in subsequent months sang in Weigl's *Il pazzo per forza*, Salieri's *Il pastor fido* and Da Ponte's *L'ape musicale*: from Dresden, he remarked that 'the leading female singer Madame Allegranti, by the way, is much better than Madame Ferarese [*sic*] – although that doesn't say much'; and from Vienna, he wrote that the 'little aria ["Un moto di gioia"] that I have done for the Ferraresi [*sic*], ought to please, I think, if indeed she is able to perform it naively which, though, I very much doubt'.[44] Her weaknesses, documented by late-eighteenth-century critics as well as by Mozart, did not obscure genuine qualities, such as the aforementioned dramatic leaps from high to low notes (*cantar di sbalzo*).[45] And her Viennese debut was well received:

Madame Ferrarese was seen, heard and marvelled at for the first time this Monday in *L'arbore di Diana*. . . . She really has as many innate as acquired virtues, which put some in difficulty as to whether it is better to close your eyes just to listen, or to plug up your ears, in order only to watch; really vying with nature and art the whole public rewarded with the loudest applause.[46]

Villeneuve, who travelled to Vienna from Italy and again made her debut in *L'arbore di Diana* (27 June 1789), also elicited praise: 'Her charming appearance, her refined, expressive acting, and her beautiful, stylish singing received the applause they merited'; and 'the public showed inexpressible satisfaction at the prosperity, the truth and the energy with which the young singer showed herself off; her ability in the art of acting, and her

[44] MBA, vol. 4, pp. 83, 97; LMF, pp. 924 (16 April 1789), 933–934 (traditionally dated 19 August 1789, but probably written later; see Edge, 'Mozart's Viennese Copyists', p. 1690). For a list of the operas in which Ferrarese performed at the Burgtheater between 1788 and her departure from Vienna in 1791, see Gidwitz, 'Mozart's Fiordiligi', p. 203.

[45] Gidwitz, 'Mozart's Fiordiligi', pp. 199, 202.

[46] *Oberdeutsche Staatszeitung* (21 October 1788), p. 841. 'Madame Ferrarese hat sich diesen Montag in L'arbore di Diana das erste Mahl sehen, hören, und bewundern lassen. . . . [Wirklich] besitzt sie eben so viele angebohrne, als erworbene Vorzüge, die manche in Verlegenheit setzen, ob es besser sey die Augen zu verschliessen, um bloß zu hören, oder die Ohren zu verstopfen, um nur zu sehen; wirklich wetteiferten Natur, und Kunst dem gesammten Publikum den lautesten Beyfall abzwingen.'

method in singing received the undivided approbation of the numerous listeners.'[47] Mozart wrote three replacement arias for her before the *Così* premiere: 'Alma grande', K. 578, for Cimarosa's *I due baroni* first performed in Rome in 1783 and heard only twice in Vienna (6, 13 September 1789); and 'Chi sà, chi sà, qual sia' K. 582 and 'Vado, ma dove?' K. 583 for Martín y Soler's *Il burbero di buon cuore*, which was revived on 9 November 1789 having premiered in Vienna on 4 January 1786.[48]

The male singers in *Così* were also very experienced by 1789. Calvesi, a high tenor in the *tenore contraltino* tradition and based in Vienna since 1785, possessed a sweet, sonorous voice and had recognized strengths in lyrical and intensely energetic singing rather than coloratura. During his Viennese career thus far and in addition to Bianchi's *La villanella rapita* for which Mozart wrote two ensembles in late 1785 (see Chapter 6), Calvesi participated in premieres of (for example) Stephen Storace's *Gli sposi malcontenti* and *Gli equivoci*, Salieri's *La grotta di Trofonio*, *Axur, re d'Ormus* and *La cifra*, and Martín y Soler's *Una cosa rara* and *L'arbore di Diana*.[49] By *Così*'s premiere, Francesco Bussani had sung operatic roles for over twenty-five years, mostly in Italy. Having married Dorotea Bussani on 23 March 1786, six weeks before her debut as Cherubino in *Figaro* and his creation of Antonio and Bartolo in the same opera, husband and wife performed together in *I due baroni* and *Il Re Teodoro in Venezia* in September 1789 and April 1790, either side of *Così*'s launch.[50] Clashes between the Bussanis and Da Ponte mentioned earlier could have begun with the *Figaro* revival. As the original Cherubino in 1786, which was also

[47] See Clive, *Mozart and His Circle*, p. 161 (Clive's translation); *Pressburger Zeitung*, 1 July 1789), p. 446. ('Das Publikum bezeigte eine unaussprechliche Zufriedenheit über den Wohlstand, die Wahrheit, und den Nachdruck, mit dem sich die jünge Sängerin produziert hat; ihre Fähigkeit in der Schauspielkunst, und ihre Methode im Singen erhielt den ungetheilten Beyfall der zahlreichen Zuhörer.'

[48] On 'Alma grande', 'Chi sà, chi sà' and 'Vado, ma dove?' including important musical-textual issues in 'Alma grande' deriving from the absence of an extant autograph, see Edge, 'Mozart's Viennese Copyists', pp. 1866–1922. For different views of Mozart's possible authorship of an accompanied recitative preceding 'Vado, ma dove?', see Dorothea Link, 'A Newly Discovered Accompanied Recitative to Mozart's "Vado, ma dove", K. 583', *Cambridge Opera Journal*, 12 (2000), pp. 29–50; and Dexter Edge, 'Attributing Mozart (i): Three Accompanied Recitatives', *Cambridge Opera Journal*, 13 (2001), pp. 197–237, especially 217–230.

[49] See Dorothea Link (ed.), *Arias for Vincenzo Calvesi, Mozart's First Ferrando* (Middleton, WI: A-R Editions, 2011), Introduction, pp. ix–xxvii.

[50] For biographical information on the Bussanis, see Rudolph Angermüller, 'Francesco Bussani – Mozarts erster Bartolo, Antonio und Alfonso und Dorothea Bussani – Mozarts erster Cherubino und erste Despina', *Mozart Studien*, 10 (Tutzing: Hans Schneider, 2001), pp. 213–231. Their martial status and co-participation in *Così* as Despina and Don Alfonso may account for some late changes to the libretto; see Woodfield, *Così fan tutte*, pp. 93–95.

her operatic debut, Dorotea could have had a proprietal relationship with the role and therefore not welcomed Villeneuve replacing her.[51]

Benucci, a star of the Viennese firmament, saw his participation change most during *Così*'s genesis. Intended initially for the role of Don Alfonso, Benucci was to receive an aria to the text of 'Donne mie' in Act 1 – for which an abandoned draft survives – similar in character to 'Rivolgete'. Once recast as Guglielmo, the aria 'Rivolgete' was written for him for Act 1, but was then itself replaced by 'Non siate ritrosi' and a new setting of 'Donne mie' (now for Guglielmo) incorporated into Act 2.[52] 'Rivolgete' was rejected late in the opera's genesis, judging by its appearance in the draft libretto.[53] Why Mozart preferred the short and modest 'Non siate ritrosi' to the expansive, instrumentally and vocally virtuosic 'Rivolgete' is a matter of conjecture: the crossing of lovers in the latter's text, Guglielmo directing his attention to Dorabella, may have come to be considered unnecessary at this juncture and the more neutral text of 'Non siate ritrosi' favoured instead; both the tonality of 'Rivolgete', foreshadowing the Act 1 finale's D major, and the overall length of the first act (with this extended aria included), could have given pause for thought; and the aria's high tessitura may have proved challenging for Benucci.[54] Mozart's autograph annotation 'attacca N: 16' (to the trio 'E voi ridete' at the end of 'Rivolgete') would have deprived Benucci of immediate audience approbation in showstopping fashion and thus may not have been well received. At least by his own standards Mozart reworked the aria quite a bit too, suggesting more difficulties than usual with its composition: horn parts are written for all of the Allegro and first six bars of the Allegro molto, but then crossed out; and a fifteen-bar *particella* early in the Allegro molto was rejected. Given the self-evident quality and dramatic import of the music, it is unlikely that any single element by itself provoked Mozart's change of plan: after all, echoes of 'Cherubino alla vittoria' from 'Non più andrai', performed with 'Stentorian lungs' to such memorable effect by Benucci as

---

[51] On Villeneuve's participation as Cherubino in the *Figaro* revival, see Edge, 'Mozart's Viennese Copyists', pp. 1509, 1669–1670. It is possible that Villeneuve was originally intended for the role of Despina and that Dorotea Bussani replaced her. See Woodfield, *Così fan tutte*, pp. 91–98. The Bussanis left Vienna in 1794 having not acquired the recognition they thought was deserved. See Clive, *Mozart and His Circle*, pp. 32–33.

[52] See Woodfield, *Così fan tutte*, pp. 81–91.   [53] Woodfield, *Così fan tutte*, p. 120.

[54] See Woodfield, *Così fan tutte*, pp. 87–88; John Stone, 'Note on "Rivolgete a lui",' in Nicholas John (ed.), *'Così fan tutte': Wolfgang Amadeus Mozart* (London: Calder, 1983), p. 124; Heartz, 'When Mozart Revises: The Case of Guglielmo in *Così fan tutte*' in Sadie (ed.), *Essays*, pp. 355–361; Rushton 'Buffo Roles in Mozart's Vienna', in *Opera Buffa in Mozart's Vienna*, pp. 410, 423–424.

the original Figaro, would no doubt have been warmly welcomed by the same singer. Had Mozart (and Benucci) ultimately wanted to retain 'Rivolgete', then, textual and musical (including tonal) changes could have been made. Rather, a combination of factors, compositional as well as related to performance, probably brought Mozart to a tipping point where replacement became preferable to revision.

In addition to role changes and difficult relationships among several protagonists, egos flared up in the run-up to the *Così* premiere. Inviting Puchberg to the rehearsal on 31 December 1789, Mozart wrote: 'I will tell you about Salieri's cabals, all of which, though, have already fallen through.'[55] Joseph Eybler, an associate of Mozart during the last years of the composer's life, also explained: 'When Mozart wrote the opera *Così fan tutte*, and was not yet finished with the instrumentation, and also time was pressing, he asked me to rehearse the singers, and especially the two female singers Ferarese [*sic*] and Villeneuve; whereupon I had quite enough opportunity to get to know theatre life, with its disorders, cabals, and so on.'[56]

Irrespective of how his singers behaved, Mozart entrusted to them important interpretative decisions potentially affecting the ontology of the drama, as in *Die Entführung, Figaro* and *Don Giovanni*. In the opening duet for the lead women 'Ah guarda sorella', for example, Mozart gives Ferrarese and Villeneuve an opportunity to define Fiordiligi and Dorabella's relationship. The two perform almost entirely apart in the Andante and almost entirely together in the Allegro. The blend between them is clearly paramount in the Allegro and in the bars approaching the pauses that immediately precede it (bars 70–71). While high sustained notes (e" for Dorabella then a" for Fiordiligi; bars 103–127) imply either 'interchangeability'[57] or a kind of one-upmanship, close coordination is paramount in pauses and elaborations and a two-bar Adagio (bars 83–91, Example 9.2): by interrupting the musical flow here, in the context of vocally exposed material, Mozart shines a spotlight on the collaboration of his two female performers. He leaves more to their discretion in the Andante, though. To be sure, vocal material and accompaniments contrast in various ways. But the two singers would have had to decide – as do performers of these roles today – whether

---

[55] MBA, vol. 4, p. 100; LMF, p. 935 (December 1789).

[56] Friedrich Rochlitz, 'Nachschrift zur Recension von Eyblers Requiem', *Allgemeine musikalische Zeitung*, 28 (1826), cols. 337–340 at 338–339. ('Denn als Mozart die Oper *Così fan tutte* schrieb, und mit dem Instrumentiren noch nicht fertig war, gleichwohl die Zeit drängte: so ersuchte er mich, die Gesangproben zu halten und besonders die beyden Sängerinnen, Ferarese und Villeneuve, einzustudiren; wo ich Gelegenheit vollauf fand, das Theaterleben, mit seinen Unruhen, Kabalen u. dgl. m. kennen zu lernen.')

[57] Brown, *Così fan tutte*, p. 29.

Example 9.2 Mozart, 'Ah guarda sorella', from *Così fan tutte*, bars 84–91.

analogous florid embellishments, and individual pause bars carrying opportunities for further embellishments, are to convey similar or differing impressions of the sisters: either they blend beautifully, or are distinct, or compete with each other (see bars 28–65). As is so often the case, Mozart asks interpretative questions and leaves performers to answer them.

Music for the principal male singers also invites performers to enhance the dramatic experience. The sequence of three trios at the opening reaches a climax in the valedictory 'Una bella serenata' – in C major, with trumpets and timpani – where Ferrando and Guglielmo look forward improvidently to the party celebrating winning their bet with Don Alfonso about the faithfulness of Dorabella and Fiordiligi.[58] Judging by 'È la fede femmine' and 'Una bella serenata', the teleological progression of the ensembles is to be boosted by the singers: the impassioned 'con foco' (*fuoco*) statements from Ferrando and Guglielmo in the former set the scene for the brash opening statements of the latter; and the *sotto voce* pronouncements of the women's names at the end of 'È la fede femmine' become alternating *sotto voces* and *fortes* for Ferrando, Guglielmo and Don Alfonso in 'Una bella serenata', supported at one point by *crescendi* and *sforzandi* in strings and

---

[58] For evidence from the autograph of Mozart's concern for dramatic pacing in the first three trios and for developing a 'fast-moving progression of ensembles', see Woodfield, *Così fan tutte*, p. 61.

winds respectively. Right at the start of the opera, then, Mozart encourages Calvesi, Benucci and Francesco Bussani to consider how they will make an impact across two numbers.

Instrumental and vocal features of the aria autographs, like musical evidence from the opening trios and duet, capture ebb and flow between Mozart and his performers. Orchestral participation and instrumental effects in *Così* have long held a special place in critical affections, and occupy much of my attention in the remainder of this chapter, especially as they relate to implications for vocal performance. Ignaz Arnold (1803), who follows Niemetschek in wondering how Mozart's heavenly melodies could have been wasted on such a 'wretched concoction' (*elendes Machwerk*) of a text, admires excellent instrumental accompaniments in the opera as a whole and orchestration in the overture in particular.[59] In 1804, the *Allgemeine musikalische Zeitung* explained: 'One is struck at first by the delicacy with which this opera is scored; how Mozart refrained from all the overburdening [of instrumental accompaniments] for which he has been reproached as well; how appropriately he has attended to the wind instruments.'[60] Nissen (1828) lauded the effective (*zweckmässig*) use of all wind instruments.[61] Later in the nineteenth century, Jahn (1856) warmly commended orchestration in a selection of numbers. Moreover: 'The wind instruments are brought more forward [than in *Figaro* and *Don Giovanni*], in more varied combinations and finer shades of tone-colouring.'[62] And in the twentieth and early twenty-first centuries, critics have lined up to praise wind sonorities and effects in *Così*.[63] But orchestration was not just a matter of polishing 'purely musical' detail in pursuit of 'final [touches] of perfection'.[64] For Mozart's attention would have had to be directed to wind instrumentation in certain numbers from *Così* on account of the principal singers for whom he wrote: two new to him (Ferrarese and Villeneuve), whose successful combinations with wind he still had to determine; one (Benucci) who flourished with big orchestral

[59] Arnold, *Mozarts Geist*, pp. 391–392.

[60] *Allgemeine musikalische Zeitung*, 6 (1803–1804), cols. 422–424, at 423.

[61] Nissen, *Anhang zu Wolfgang Amadeus Mozarts Biographie*, p. 94.

[62] Jahn, *Life of Mozart*, vol. 3, pp. 237–274 (quotation at 274).

[63] See, for example, Abert, *W. A. Mozart*, pp. 1180, 1196, 1300; Saint-Foix, *Mozart, 1777–1791: Le grand voyage, L'épanouissement, Les dernières années*, pp. 642, 646, 649, 650; Landon, *The Golden Years*, p. 179; Steptoe, *Mozart-Da Ponte Operas*, pp. 211–212; Rosselli, *Life of Mozart*, p. 102; Rushton, *New Grove Guide to Mozart and His Operas*, p. 102; Cairns, *Mozart and His Operas*, pp. 180, 189–190; Woodfield, *Così fan tutte*, pp. 60, 74.

[64] For this narrow assessment of the significance of orchestration in *Così fan tutte*, see Woodfield, *Così fan tutte*, pp. 75–77.

effects and therefore could readily bring approbation for composer and performer alike; and another (Calvesi) known to him from years in service in Vienna but not yet in receipt of any of his arias. While the formation of a score's brace at the left-hand side of each page required a decision early in the compositional process about the projected size of an orchestral contingent, Mozart often refined views about wind participation when carrying out the orchestration itself.[65] Indeed, revisions and alterations to wind scoring – many discussed below – reveal it as an issue on Mozart's mind during the opera's genesis.[66] The autographs of *Così* and 'Un moto di gioia' for the *Figaro* revival, moreover, show considerably more changes and refinements than the autographs of the original *Figaro* (1786) and *Don Giovanni*.[67]

Writing for Wind

A comparison between wind instrumentation in *Le nozze di Figaro* and *Così fan tutte* establishes distinctive features of both *Così* and new *Figaro* numbers for the revival (see Table 9.1).

As we can see, the most common wind scoring in *Così* is of a slightly darker hue than the most common for the 1786 *Figaro*: two clarinets, two bassoons and two horns – a traditional six-part *Harmonie* – in contrast to two flutes, two oboes, two bassoons and two horns. Wind instrumentalists available to Mozart at the Burgtheater were probably identical in 1786–1787 and 1789–1790 seasons, so cannot account for the

---

[65] As Woodfield points out (*Così fan tutte*, p. 16), Mozart often orchestrated numbers from *Così* in separate stages for strings and then wind.

[66] For a partial summary of changes, see Woodfield, *Così fan tutte*, p. 64.

[67] In *Figaro* and *Don Giovanni*, as in *Così*, names of wind instruments for individual numbers are often annotated on lines of the original *particella* brace only in the completion phase; whether Mozart changed his mind between *particella* and orchestration cannot be known in these cases. Six numbers in the autograph of the 1786 *Figaro* provide evidence of rethinking: 'Voi che sapete' and 'Hai gia vinta' for which two lines of the autograph are left blank, implying consideration at one stage of larger accompanying wind cohorts than were eventually employed; chorus no. 23, where '2 flauti' and '2 fagotti' are crossed out and replaced by '1 flauto solo' and '1 fagotto solo'; the march in the Act 3 finale, where '2 clarinetti in C' unusually appear on the eleventh stave of the twelve-stave paper; 'In quegl' anni' for which '1 flauto' is notated at the completion stage on the top stave; and 'Deh vieni' which acquires a flute midway through the *particella* (see Chapter 7). Wind instrumentation in one number from *Don Giovanni* is also unambiguously revised: two trumpets and timpani are written in the original brace for Leporello's 'Madamina' but are subsequently crossed out to leave empty the two staves to which they were assigned. For evidence of revisions and refinements to wind instrumentation in *Così* (and 'Un moto di gioia' for the *Figaro* revival), see below.

Table 9.1 Wind instrumentation in the 1786 *Figaro*, the *Figaro* revival and *Così fan tutte*

Instrumentation	*Figaro* (1786)	*Così fan tutte* (1789–1790), and new *Figaro* numbers for 1789–1791 (bold italics)
1fl, 1ob, 1cl, 1bsn, 2hns	1 (No. 11 'Voi che sapete')	
1fl, 1bsn		2 (No. 2 'È la fede delle femmine'; No. 15 'Non siate')
1fl, 1bsn, 2hns		1 (No. 19 'Una donna')
1fl, 1ob, 1bsn	1 (No. 27 'Deh vieni')	1 (No. 12 'In uomini')
1fl, 1ob, 1bsn, 2hns		*1 ('Un moto di gioia', K. 579, for 'Figaro')*
1fl, 2obs, 2cls, 2bsns, 2hns		1 (No. 28 'È amore')
1fl, 2obs, 1bsn, 2hns	1 (No. 21/Chorus)	
1fl, 2cls, 2bsns, 2hns	1 (No. 25 'In quegl'anni')	
2fls, 2obs, 2bsns		2 (No. 31 Act 2 finale, Allegro, bars 205–89; No. 31 Act 2 finale, Allegretto, bars 496–530)
2fls, 2obs, 2bsns, 2hns	12 (No. 1 'Cinque'; No. 2 'Se a caso madama' [alto horns]; No. 5 'Via resti'; No. 12 'Venite'; No. 15 Act 2 finale, Allegro, bars 328–397; No. 15 Act 2 finale, Andante, bars 398–466; No. 15 Act 2 finale, Allegro molto, bars 467–604); No. 18 'Riconosci'; No. 22 Act 3 finale, Andante-Maestoso, bars 132–185; No. 28 Act 4 finale, Con un poco più di moto, bars 51–108; No. 28, Act 4 finale, Allegro assai, bars 335–420; No. 28 Act 4 finale, Andante, bars 421–447)	3 (No. 16 'E voi ridete?'; No. 18 Act 1 finale, Allegro, bars 292–428; No. 31 Act 2 finale, Andante con moto, bars 531–575)
2fls, 2obs, 2cls, 2bsns, 2hns	3 (No. 15 Act 2 finale, bars 167–327; No. 15 Act 2 finale, Andante, bars 605–696; No. 28 Act 4 finale, Andante, bars 275–334)	
2fls, 2obs, 2cls, 2bsns, 2hns, 2trs	4 (Overture; No. 15 Act 2 finale, Allegro assai/Più allegro/ Prestissimo, bars 697–939; No. 22 Act 3 finale, Marcia, bars 1–60; No. 28 Act 4 finale, Allegro assai, bars 448–521)	4 (Overture; No. 18 Act 1 finale, Allegro, bars 485–697; No. 31 Act 2 finale, Maestoso, bars 290–309; No. 31 Act 2 finale, Allegro molto, bars 576–671)
2fls, 2obs, 2bsns, 2trs		2 (No. 8/chorus; No. 18 Act 1 finale, Allegro, bars 62–137)

Table 9.1 (*cont.*)

Instrumentation	Figaro (1786)	Così fan tutte (1789–1790), and new Figaro numbers for 1789–1791 (bold italics)
2fls, 2obs, 2bsns, 2hns, 2trs	4 (No. 4 'La vendetta'; No. 9 'Non più andrai'; No. 17 'Vedrò'; No. 22 Act 3 finale, Allegretto, bars 61–131 & 186–229)	1 (No. 26 'Donne mie')
2fls, 2cls, 2bsns, 2hns	1 (No. 28 Act 4 finale, Larghetto, bars 109–274)	4 (No. 10 'Soave sia il vento'; No. 11 'Smanie'; No. 25 'Per pietà'; No. 31 Act 2 finale, Allegro, bars 310–371)
2fls, 2bsns, 2hns	2 (No. 8/chorus; No. 16 'Crudel')	1 (No. 18 Act 1 finale, Andante, bars 1–61)
2fls, 2bsns, 2trs		1 (No. 22 'La mano')
1ob, 1bsn	1 (No. 20 'Sull'aria')	
2obs, 2cls, 2bsns, 2hns	2 (No. 7 'Cosa sento'; No. 15 Act 1 finale, Molto Andante, bars 126–166)	1 (No. 27 'Tradito')
2obs, 2cls, 2bsns, 2hns, 2trs	1 (No. 15 Act 1 finale, Allegro, bars 1–125)	1 (No. 31 Act 2 finale, Andante, bars 66–172)
2obs, 2cls, 2bsns, 2trs		3 (No. 13 'Alla bella Despinetta'; No. 14 'Come scoglio'; No. 31 Act 2 finale, Allegro, bars 441–465)
2obs, 2bsns, 2hns	4 (No. 3 'Se vuol ballare'; No. 13 'Susanna or via sortite'; No. 19 'Dove sono'; No. 28 Act 4 finale, Andante, bars 1–50)	2 (No. 1 'La mia Dorabella'; No. 29 'Fra gli amplessi')
2obs, 2bsns, 2trs		3 (No. 3 'Una bella serenata'; No. 15a 'Rivolgete', K. 584; No. 31 Act 2 finale, Allegro assai, bars 1–65)
2cls, 1bsn, 2trs		1 (No. 24, 'Ah lo veggio')
2cls, 2bsns		1 (No. 9 'Di scrivermi')
2cls, 2bsns, 2hns	3 (No. 6 'Non sò più'; No. 10 'Porgi amor'; No. 26 'Aprite un po'')	11 (No. 4 'Ah guarda sorella'; No. 6 'Sento oddio'; No. 7 'Al fato'; No. 17 'Un'aura amorosa'; No. 18 Act 1 finale, Allegro, bars 138–291; No. 20 'Prenderò'; No. 21 'Secondate' [with 2fls for concluding chorus]; No. 23 'Il core vi dono'; No. 31 Act 2 finale, Larghetto, bars 173–204; No. 31 Act 2 finale, Andante, bars 372–440; No. 31 Act 2 finale, Andante, bars 466–495)

Table 9.1 (*cont.*)

Instrumentation	Figaro (1786)	Cosi fan tutte (1789–1790), and new Figaro numbers for 1789–1791 (bold italics)
2cls, 2bsns, 2trs		1 (No. 18, Act 1 finale, Andante, bars 429–484)
2basset-horns, 2bsns, 2hns		*1 ('Al desio', K. 577, for 'Figaro') + 1 (revision of 'Aprite un po'' for 'Figaro')?*[68]
No winds	3 (No. 14 'Aprite presto'; No. 23 'L'ho perduta'; No. 24 'Il capro')	2 (No. 5 'Non vorrei'; No. 30 'Tutti accusan')
Wind-only numbers		1 (No. 21 'Secondate')
Unambiguously wind-led numbers		3 (No. 27 'Tradito'; No. 28 'È amore'; *'Al desio', K. 577, for 'Figaro'*)

Notes:

–No. 15a 'Rivolgete' (which Mozart completed) is included for *Così fan tutte*, in spite of having been cut from the opera by December 1789.

–Sections of act finales are included as separate entries.

change.[69] Anton and Johann Stadler, for example, lauded for orchestral as well as solo clarinet and basset-horn playing, and Johann Georg Triebensee, praised for playing the oboe 'with great feeling',[70] would have performed in both seasons. Indeed, almost all the Burgtheater wind instrumentalists were individually identified as exemplary Viennese musicians in 1791.[71] Perhaps Mozart was attracted to the acknowledged harmoniousness of combined clarinets, bassoons and horns in an opera so dominated by tender emotions of love.[72] And he would have benefitted in *Così* from the fact that the Burgtheater orchestra's ways of conveying still and soft expression were particularly remarkable in 1789–1790 (according to Baron von

[68] Edge discovered a second basset-horn part for 'Aprite un po'' – a transposition of the second-clarinet part – among the original performing materials for *Figaro*; the paper type and copyist almost certainly date it to the 1789–1791 revival. See Edge, 'Mozart's Viennese Copyists', pp. 1505, 1507.

[69] The Burgtheater account books, *inter alia* listing instrumentalists, vocalists and their salaries, are no longer extant for the 1789–1790 season. But wind instrumentalists named in the theatre orchestra for 1786–1787 and 1791–1792 (the next available after 1788–1789) are identical. See Link, *National Court Theatre*, pp. 422–423, 438–439.

[70] Schönfeld, 'A Yearbook of Music in Vienna and Prague', pp. 313, 315.

[71] Joseph Marx von Liechtenstein, *Beiträge zur genauern Kenntniss der österreichischen Staaten und Provinzen* (Vienna and Leipzig, 1791), pp. 193–194.

[72] On the harmoniousness of these instruments see Francoeur, *Diapason général de tous les instrumens à vent*, pp. 35, 55 (and Chapter 1 of this volume).

Reitzenstein).[73] The gentle qualities of the three individual instruments may also have appealed to Mozart.[74] Viennese clarinets, especially those manufactured by an associate of Mozart and the Stadlers, Theodor Lotz, were known for their dark sound quality:[75] they participate in twenty-eight numbers from *Così* as opposed to sixteen in *Figaro*. But the presence in 'Al desio' of the clarinet family's still darker basset-horns, 'the most richly toned of all wind instruments' according to the Vienna-based Johann Georg Albrechtsberger in 1790,[76] shows that Mozart's predilection for the clarinet-bassoon-horn sonority in 1789–1790 also extended beyond *Così*.

Four numbers scored exclusively or primarily for wind further distinguish the *Figaro* revival and *Così* from the 1786 *Figaro*. The *Così* duet 'Secondate, aurette amiche', for example, strikes a chord with two wind-orientated segments of *Don Giovanni*: as they do at Don Giovanni's request in the banquet scene from the Act 2 finale, the wind band perform on stage, in effect acting on Ferrando and Guglielmo's command; and, as in 'Protegga' from the Act 1 finale where Donna Anna, Donna Elvira and Don Ottavio request divine protection, Ferrando and Guglielmo implore the wind to blow kisses from their boat to their beloved Fiordiligi and Dorabella on land.[77] Perhaps memories of a positive reception for the passages from *Don Giovanni* acted as a catalyst for Mozart to write 'Secondate' exclusively for wind accompaniment. At any rate, as one critic has noted: 'The sensuous beauty of the whole scene . . . would be enough to

---

[73] Von Reitzenstein, *Reise nach Wien*, p. 256.

[74] On the bassoon in this respect, see Koch, *Musikalisches Lexikon*, col. 549, and Béthizy, *Exposition de la théorie et de la pratique de la musique*, pp. 305–306; and on the horn, see Framery, 'Cor', in *Encyclopédie méthodique*, vol. 1, p. 379, and Schubart, *Ideen zu einer Ästhetik der Tonkunst* (1806), pp. 311–312. For Anton Stadler's tender and gentle playing, see MDL, p. 206; MDB, pp. 232–233. The gentle quality of the clarinet is also exploited in the clarinet quintet, K. 581, completed on 29 September 1789 four months before the *Così* premiere. The fragment K. 581a setting *Così*'s 'Ah lo veggio' theme for clarinet is more likely to have been written after the opera than before, so would not have been considered for inclusion in the clarinet quintet K. 581 as is sometimes suggested. See Tyson, *Autograph Scores*, p. 138. Nevertheless, the sketch offers another point of connection between the clarinet and an opera in which it participates so prominently.

[75] See Eric Hoeprich, *Clarinet* (New Haven and London: Yale University Press, 2008), p. 72.

[76] Albrechtsberger, *Gründliche Anweisung zur Composition* (Leipzig: Breitkopf, 1790), p. 426 ('tonreichste aller Blasinstrumente').

[77] There is no extant autograph of 'Secondate'; the Burgtheater performing score is therefore the primary source for transmitting this number. It was probably added very late in the genesis of the opera (Tyson, *Autograph Scores*, p. 190), having first been conceived in all likelihood as a chorus (Woodfield, *Così fan tutte*, p. 59). Thirteen bars (25–37) – part of the instrumental introduction – appear in the Burgtheater score, but not in other sources. See Edge, 'Mozart's Viennese Copyists', p. 1931.

seduce anyone, let alone two such flighty young ladies as Dorabella and Fiordiligi.'[78]

Thus, wind writing in *Così* and the *Figaro* revival occupies an important place in Mozart's operatic oeuvre to date. As we shall see, wind instrumentation in arias for Calvesi, Benucci, Ferrarese and Villeneuve evolved during the compositional process: refinements to voice-wind timbres were made in many instances possibly in consultation with the singers themselves.[79]

Writing for Singers and Wind

The autograph of 'Al desio', Ferrarese's rondò to replace 'Deh vieni' in Act 4 of *Figaro*, is no longer extant, leaving Mozart's compositional method unknown.[80] The wind, comprising two basset-horns, two bassoons and two horns striking even for a late-eighteenth-century rondò,[81] assume a pre-eminent position among orchestral participants: they frequently appear as a six-instrument unit, often without the strings (especially in the initial Larghetto); they receive virtuosic demisemiquavers, as well as *sf*s and *sfp*s; and they engage in intricate dialogue among themselves and with the voice. Mozart apparently was striving not for consistency with the 1786 *Figaro* – the wind scoring of 'Al desio' has a stronger affinity with *Così* than with the original *Figaro* production (see Table 9.1) – but for vibrant voice-wind timbres that took into account the qualities of an individual singer. Discussion of wind instrumentation between composer and performer is likely to have taken place during the compositional process given the unusual scoring, the pronounced voice-wind interaction, and the aria's status as Mozart's first for Ferrarese.

[78] Heartz, *Mozart, Haydn and Early Beethoven*, p. 250.

[79] On Mozart considering – but not implementing – a larger wind complement than originally envisaged at bar 70 of 'Una donna' for Dorotea Bussani (Despina), see Woodfield, *Così fan tutte*, p. 64. Woodfield (pp. 49–50) also provides autograph-based support for Mozart's development of 'Una donna' 'in the light of views expressed by the singer, desirous perhaps of something rather more substantial than originally planned'.

[80] A sketch of the aria in Mozart's hand has survived; see Janet K. Page and Dexter Edge, 'A Newly Uncovered Sketch for Mozart's "Al desio di chi t'adora" K577', *Musical Times*, 132 (1991), pp. 601–606.

[81] Rice, *Antonio Salieri and Viennese Opera*, p. 482. The rondò often had obbligato wind parts: see Parker, *Remaking the Song*, p. 63, and James Webster, 'Aria as Drama', in Anthony R. DelDonna and Pierpaolo Polzonetti (eds.), *The Cambridge Companion to Eighteenth-Century Opera* (Cambridge: Cambridge University Press, 2009), pp. 24–49, at 30.

The autographs of Ferrarese's arias for *Così*, 'Come scoglio' (Act 1) and 'Per pietà' (Act 2), show the final wind scoring evolving over time, perhaps in consultation with the singer. In 'Come scoglio', for example, clarinets make a late entry into the wind ensemble. Mozart first envisaged using ten of his twelve staves, leaving the top and bottom ones free in the initial brace and assigning two for the two bassoons. Later, crossing out the original '2 fagotti' notation, he wrote '2 fagotti' next to the lower of the two bassoon staves, freeing one up for an additional '2 clarinetti in B' Presumably Mozart made the adjustment here on the first page of the number in order to alert the copyist to the wind instrumentation for the aria as a whole: for the remaining fourteen pages in the autograph, the clarinets are notated on the (originally empty) top line of the paper, with the original brace extended upwards. Ink colours often make it difficult to distinguish *particella* from completion phases of work on 'Come scoglio'.[82] But it is clear that the clarinet notation derives from the completion: on two occasions, tempo markings included in the *particella* ('All:' [allegro] and 'più All:') encroach on the top stave of the paper, indicating that no clarinet material had been written there yet.

In 'Per pietà', too, Mozart either temporarily remained undecided about wind instrumentation or wanted to allow room for manoeuver. Woodfield suggests that the autograph could have been produced from a working draft: the consistency of the ink colour does indeed suggest notation in one phase.[83] Even if this is the case, Mozart kept open the option of adding wind parts, by (unusually) leaving an empty stave in the *middle* of the page rather than at the top or the bottom. The end of the aria – a *tour de force* for winds and voice together – suggests singer-composer consultation before 'Per pietà' was finished: a three-bar exit passage was crossed out and replaced by a more vocally virtuosic seven bars with trills, and an ostentatious scale and arpeggio (see Example 9.3).[84] In the deleted material, Mozart (presumably inadvertently) slipped a stave when notating his flute parts, writing them on the fifth and previously empty sixth staves rather than the fourth and fifth, in continuing wind imitation of ascending

---

[82] See Woodfield, *Così fan tutte*, p. 15, on some of the ink from the 'Come scoglio' *particella* fading rapidly to a light brown.

[83] Woodfield, *Così fan tutte*, p. 74.

[84] Woodfield (*Così fan tutte*, p. 47) considers the revised ending of 'Per pietà' a 'memorable musical improvement'. He also points out (*Così fan tutte*, pp. 19, 42, 55–56) that in several arias in *Così* (including 'Per pietà' and 'Donne mie'), Mozart broke off work shortly before the end in order to gauge the singer's opinion before finishing it off.

Example 9.3 Mozart, 'Per pietà', from *Così fan tutte*, bars 112–121 (including deleted material).

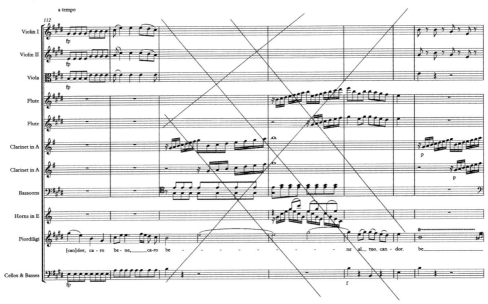

semiquaver scales from clarinets to flutes across a page turn.[85] The blank sixth stave through almost all of 'Per pietà' leaves open the possibility of adding presumably oboes – given the location of the empty stave under the flutes and above the clarinets – if deemed desirable by composer and performer. Once the ending and the wind scoring had been fixed, both perhaps in consultation with Ferrarese or at least after Mozart had experienced her voice, the final bars of the aria could be completed, which by then had no need of a free stave in the middle of the score: for the last page of the aria (comprising the final nine bars), the bottom stave is left vacant rather than the sixth.[86]

Wind instrumentation in 'Un moto di gioia', written to replace 'Venite inginocchiatevi' for the *Figaro* revival, may also have been either or both a subject of discussion between Mozart and Ferrarese and a matter for compositional contemplation. Mozart's initial intention was to include one flute, one oboe and one bassoon; the two horns, written on the top stave of the autograph outside the original brace, came later. The first notation of horn material is in the *particella* at bars 52–53 and 56–57 (Example 9.4): the initial three bar-lines on the horn stave for that page of the autograph are in the black ink of the completion phase (as is the extension of the brace to include the horns), but the two four-quaver figures and the bar-lines in between are in the sandy brown of the *particella*.[87] So, the first genuinely three-way strings-voice-winds dialogue, early in the reprise, coincides with a decision to add two horns into the wind ensemble, an important textural moment perhaps provoking a timbral adjustment ultimately to affect the sound world of the aria once fully orchestrated. Thus, we catch Mozart – midway through the *particella* – reflecting on the best wind scoring to accompany Ferrarese's voice. Edge explains that 'Un moto di gioia' was written part way through the 1789–1791 revival run rather than before it began.[88] In consequence, Mozart's experiences of Ferrarese blending with

---

[85] See '*Così*': *Facsimile of the Autograph*, pp. 453–454. In the revision, Mozart continued to notate the flutes on these same staves for the remainder of the page.

[86] '*Così*': *Facsimile of the Autograph*, p. 455. Mozart (accidentally in all likelihood) notates on only ten staves for one page of 'Per pietà' (see *Così: Facsimile of the Autograph*, p. 442) and has to indicate to the copyist here which staves comprise the flute, clarinet, bassoon and horn parts in the middle of the score. On the next page, annotated wind-instrument names indicate a return to the normal configuration of instruments and staves for this aria, with the sixth stave again remaining free. Woodfield (*Così fan tutte*, p. 74) implies that the variable number of staves used on pages of the 'Per pieta' autograph evidences a copying process on Mozart's part.

[87] '*Figaro*': *Facsimile of the Autograph*, vol. 1, p. 331. (The autograph of 'Un moto di gioia' is given on pp. 327–334 of this volume.)

[88] See Edge, 'Mozart's Viennese Copyists', pp. 1687–1690, which addresses the date of the Mozart letter in which 'Un moto di gioia' is mentioned.

Example 9.4 Mozart, 'Un moto di gioia', from *Le nozze di Figaro*, bars 51–58.

a rich complement of wind instruments in renditions of 'Al desio', 'Come scoglio' and 'Per pietà' at the Burgtheater may have influenced decisions about the wind scoring of this ostensibly light aria.[89]

Villeneuve's blend with the wind is also a focus for attention during the compositional process. In 'È amore un ladroncello', Dorabella's ode to the quixotic nature of love, Mozart probably remained undecided about wind instrumentation during much of the *particella* phase: '1 flauto' and '2 clarinetti in B' were assigned to the fourth and fifth staves of the opening brace in the black ink of the *particella*, but '2 oboe', '2 fagotti' and '2 corni in B alti' were annotated later (in a now faded ink) next to the seventh through tenth staves.[90] The first oboe part in bars 53–56 (see Example 9.5) was written in the dark ink of the *particella*: it matches the ink of the interwoven voice. Since the oboe is at the correct, non-transposing pitch here, written on

---

[89]   Mozart referred to 'Un moto di gioia' as an 'Ariettchen' (little aria). See MBA, vol. 4, p. 97; LMF, p. 933.

[90]   See also Woodfield, *Così fan tutte*, pp. 65–68 for a discussion of the wind instrumentation in this aria.

Example 9.5 Mozart, 'È amore', from *Così fan tutte*, bars 53–57.

the stave below the transposing clarinets, it must have been the intended instrument from the moment of notation, Mozart adding to his wind cohort midway through an aria *particella* for Villeneuve as for Ferrarese in 'Un moto di gioia' and Nancy Storace in 'Deh vieni' as Susanna in the 1786 *Figaro* (see Chapter 7). The crossing out of much of the string bass line from the *particella* and the annotation 'senza basso' also directs attention to the voice-wind timbre in the completion, giving singer and wind unencumbered opportunities to shine together (Example 9.6).[91] With the exception of 'L'alma grande' K. 578, an aria unlikely to have had positive associations for Villeneuve on account of the unambiguous flop of Cimarosa's *I due baroni*, Mozart had not yet included oboes in an aria for her, perhaps explaining initial uncertainty about their involvement in 'È amore'.[92]

---

[91] 'Tacet' markings were later appended in another hand. For both Mozart's markings, and those in the unknown hand, see *'Così': Facsimile of the Autograph*, vol. 2, pp. 500–501, 502–503, 506–507, 510–511.

[92] On the failure of *I due baroni*, see Edge, 'Mozart's Viennese Copyists', pp. 1874–1875.

Example 9.6 Mozart, 'È amore', from *Così fan tutte*, bars 10–15 (including deleted material).

Prominent wind participation is a feature of both 'Chi sà, chi sà', K. 582, and 'Vado', K. 583, scored for the double clarinet-bassoon-horn timbre favoured in *Così*, including in exposed passages for voice and wind alone (as in 'È amore'). In the autograph of 'Vado', the blank ninth and tenth staves of the twelve-stave brace[93] allowed room for a bigger wind and brass complement had it been desired. The wind of 'Smanie implacabili' – double clarinets, bassoons and horns again – are generally less conspicuous than in Mozart's other arias for Villeneuve, but are still promoted timbrally in a four-bar passage alone with the voice at the climax of the piece.

[93] For the autograph of 'Vado', see Staatsbibliothek Berlin, Mus. ms. autogr. W. A. Mozart 583. See also NMA, II/7/3–4, *Kritische Berichte*, p. 123.

The autographs of Mozart's arias for Benucci and Calvesi also document evolving views about wind instrumentation, perhaps in consultation with the singers. If the rejection of 'Rivolgete' created the obvious absence of a showstopping aria for Benucci, the inclusion of 'Donne mie' in Act 2 – written very late in *Così*'s genesis[94] – represented the equally obvious solution. 'Non siate ritrosi', the replacement for 'Rivolgete' in Act 1, and 'Donne mie' could have been written close together, a reasonable hypothesis in light of fundamental changes to the Guglielmo role, including the late rejection of 'Rivolgete'. Paper types at least provide no evidence to the contrary.[95] In spite of significant differences in the length, scale, affect and heft of the finished arias, Mozart notated a ten-stave brace on the first pages of both, leaving the top and bottom staves blank (Examples 9.7 and 9.8): once the light wind scoring of a single flute and bassoon for 'Non siate ritrosi' was confirmed, the seventh, eighth and ninth staves remained unused (as well as the first and twelfth); and when trumpet and timpani parts were added to two passages in 'Donne mie', at the top and bottom of the score respectively, all twelve were employed. Perhaps Mozart kept options open for 'Non siate ritrosi' to exhibit greater instrumental weight than ultimately came to pass, until he had consulted Benucci about the aria in isolation or in combination with 'Donne mie', or until he himself had fully thought through the relationship between Benucci's two arias. The segments for trumpets and timpani add the kind of glitz and glamour to 'Donne mie' that brings to mind Benucci's 'Non più andrai' from *Figaro* (scored for an identical wind complement plus timpani). This is especially noticeable in the first passage for trumpets and timpani in 'Donne mie' (bars 59–71, Example 9.9): the full orchestra is initially set antiphonally against the strident vocal line as in bars 43–53 of 'Non più andrai'. The absence of bar lines in the top and bottom trumpet and timpani staves before their first segment in 'Donne mie' suggests Mozart conceived the full effect only when orchestrating the passage.[96] Thus, Mozart's initial conceptions of Benucci's two arias in *Così* may not have been as far apart as their finished versions, suggesting ongoing thoughts and refinements to the Benucci/Guglielmo role during the compositional process for the two arias, and beyond the point that 'Rivolgete' was rejected from the opera.

[94] See Woodfield, *Così fan tutte*, pp. 54–55.

[95] Tyson (*Autograph Scores*, p. 187) states that 'Non siate ritrosi' must have been written when Act 2 was 'already well under way' as 'Atto I^mo' was written on the first page of the autograph.

[96] Evolving views about wind participation in 'Donne mie' are also demonstrated in small revisions to their parts; see *'Così': Facsimile of the Autograph*, vol. 2, pp. 465–481.

Example 9.7 Mozart, 'Non siate ritrosi', from *Così fan tutte*, bars 1–4 (including blank staves at the top, middle and bottom of the page, as in the autograph).

Example 9.8 Mozart, 'Donne mie', from *Così fan tutte*, bars 1–5 (including, as in the autograph, blank staves at the top and bottom of the page and no indication of trumpet and timpani participation).

Example 9.9 Mozart, 'Donne mie', from *Così fan tutte*, bars 59–71 (with trumpets and timpani on the top and bottom staves of the page, as in the autograph).

Mozart's initial instincts for wind instrumentation in Calvesi's three arias are fairly uniform: double clarinets, bassoons and horns for 'Un' aura amorosa' and 'Tradito, schernito'; and double clarinets, bassoons and trumpets in 'Ah, lo veggio'. The brace at the opening of 'Tradito' does not include the two oboes, which ultimately appear on the clarinet staves at the beginning of the C-major section when the latter are not needed, accompanied by an 'oboe dolce' annotation, and on a single stave when all eight wind play together in the last fifteen bars of the aria (the two clarinets now occupying only one stave in order to accommodate the larger wind complement).[97] In 'Ah, lo veggio', Mozart originally wrote '2 fagotti' between the seventh and eighth staves of the autograph, then crossed it out, wrote '1 fagotti' next to the seventh stave, and left the eighth blank.[98] Ultimately, then, Mozart moves towards exploiting a more diverse range of wind timbres in combination with Calvesi's voice than originally envisaged. Whether cuts sanctioned by Mozart in the court theatre score of 'Un' aura amorosa' can be attributed to easing the strain on the singer, a matter of critical debate,[99] they do not affect wind participation (with the exception of a two-horn sustained note). In fact, the cut bars (50–57, 63–66) are the only substantial passages in the second statement of the aria's text not to feature prominent wind. Whatever Mozart's motivation for slightly shortening 'Un' aura amorosa', he apparently wanted to protect the impact of the wind.[100]

After the Premiere of *Così fan tutte*

Così was staged five times in its first seventeen days on the boards – 26, 28, 30 January; and 7, 11 February – and did very well. Both the box-office receipts for the premiere, suggesting an attendance of around 1,000, and the average receipts of these performances were the highest for any opera at the Burgtheater in the 1789–1790 season.[101] The publication of extracts

---

[97] This last passage coincides with Calvesi's climactic sustained g's, bringing into alignment peaks in vocal writing and size of participating wind cohort.

[98] See '*Così*': *Facsimile of the Autograph*, vol. 2, p. 419.

[99] For differing arguments, see Edge, 'Mozart's Viennese Copyists', p. 1952 (on the need to eliminate Calvesi's high notes); Woodfield, *Così fan tutte*, pp. 43, 158 (on the strain of the Ferrando role on Calvesi); and Link, *Arias for Vincenzo Calvesi*, pp. ix–x (on Calvesi's ability to cope with Mozart's music irrespective of the cuts made).

[100] The cut to 'Ah lo veggio' in the performing score (bars 57–91) is more substantial than those for 'Un' aura amorosa' and consequently affects wind participation.

[101] Edge, 'Mozart's Reception in Vienna, 1787–1791', pp. 81, 110, 112.

from *Così* by Artaria soon after the premiere, including arias, duets, and the march 'Bella vita militar', also testifies to the opera's popularity.[102] But Emperor Joseph II's fatal illness and death prevented further performances in the winter and spring. Handing over to a regency council on 29 January 1790 after a steady deterioration in the previous weeks, he was given the last rites on 13 February and died a week later.[103] The Burgtheater shut up shop on 13 February, remaining closed for the rest of the season, and reopened after Easter on 12 April at the beginning of the theatrical season 1790–1791. Five more performances followed in the summer (6, 12 June; 6 and 16 July; 7 August), traditionally the quietest time of year for theatre attendance, yielding only small average receipts.[104] Joseph's successor, his brother Leopold II, preferred opera seria, ballet and simpler *opere buffe* than Mozart offered; *Così* did not appear on the Viennese stage again until 1794.[105]

An unlucky start for *Così* in Vienna prevented neither quick dissemination further afield nor critical acclaim. In 1791, Domenico Guardasoni's productions in Prague and Leipzig probably involved contact with Mozart over the revised libretto and performance materials.[106] The success of Leipzig performances in 1792 and 1793 can be gauged by pieces from *Così* dominating Leipzig Gewandhaus concerts at that time.[107] The Dresden company, which began a production on 5 October 1791, cut the opera radically to turn it into a star vehicle for the Fiordiligi, Maddalena Allegranti,[108] who Mozart had compared favourably to the original Fiordiligi, Ferrarese, in 1789. The *Journal des Luxus und der Moden* (1790) identified *Così* as 'an excellent work ... That the music is by Mozart says everything, I think'.[109] And the *Musikalische Monatsschrift* (1792) reported that '[after] *Le nozze di Figaro*, an opera ... [taking] precedence over all Mozart's theatrical works, ... [*Così*] is unquestionably the most excellent', in which 'the polyphonic areas ... [have] a force and beauty better felt than described'.[110]

The main problem with *Così* for early audiences – as for later ones – was the text. In the *Annalen des Theaters* (Berlin), it is a 'wretched, southern European product with the powerful, elevated music of a Mozart' and in

---

[102] Brown, *Così fan tutte*, p. 165.   [103] Heartz, *Mozart, Haydn and Early Beethoven*, p. 257.

[104] Edge, 'Mozart's Reception in Vienna, 1787–1791', p. 100.

[105] Brown, *Così fan tutte*, pp. 163–165.   [106] See Woodfield, *Così fan tutte*, pp. 183–188.

[107] Woodfield, *Performing Operas for Mozart*, p. 181.

[108] Woodfield, *Performing Operas for Mozart*, p. 182.   [109] MDL, pp. 318–319; MDB, p. 363.

[110] As given in Gruber, *Mozart and Posterity*, p. 38, and Goehring, *Three Modes of Perception in Mozart*, p. 21.

the diary of Countess Maria Sidonia Chotek it is 'pitiful' (*pitoyable*).[111]
The distinguished German actor and theatre manager Friedrich Schröder
described it in his journal (28 April 1791) as a 'miserable thing, debasing to
all women. It cannot be a success, for no woman in the audience will like it'.
The *Journal des Luxus und der Moden* (1792) also called it 'the silliest
rubbish in the world, and it draws an audience only because of the splendid
music'.[112] Niemetschek and Arnold later issued similar criticisms.[113] Even
Constanze was unimpressed: 'She does not much admire the plot of "Cosi
fan", but agreed with me that such music would carry any piece.'[114]
The idea of the story being based on an incident at a masked ball at the
Redoutensaal, subsequently remembered by the emperor and turned into
an opera at his request, only surfaced in 1837 and is almost certainly
apocryphal.[115] But the quick redistribution of affections in *Così* may not
have been as far divorced from reality as it seemed to some. In Vienna in
1783 it was reported that men 'consider us [women] to be living dolls,
created for their pastime; when they have amused themselves with one doll
for a while they tire of it and seek out another, in which the allurement of
novelty will captivate them for an equally short time'.[116] And in July 1790
halfway around the world in Sydney Bay, with nautical echoes of Ferrando
and Guglielmo's departure from Dorabella and Fiordiligi, a *Così*-like
scenario was playing itself out. A Scot by the name of John Nichol, steward
on the *Lady Julian* ship shepherding female convicts from England to
Australia, had fallen in love with one of his charges, Sarah Whitelam; she
gave birth to their son in Rio de Janeiro, en route to the penal colony.
Nichol was contractually obliged to continue on the ship's journey beyond
Sydney to Canton, so he and Sarah sadly took leave of each other:
'We exchanged faith – she promised to remain true and I promised to

[111] MDL, p. 346, MDB, p. 395; and 'Report of the First Performance of *Così fan tutte*' in
Dexter Edge and David Black (eds.), *Mozart: New Documents*, first published 12 June 2014.
http://dx.doi.org/10.7302/Z20P0WXJ

[112] Both as quoted in Braunbehrens, *Mozart in Vienna*, p. 337. For the Schröder quotation, see
also MDL, p. 346; MDB, p. 394.

[113] Niemetschek, *Leben*, p. 29, *Life of Mozart*, p. 38; Arnold, *Mozarts Geist*, p. 390.

[114] In conversation with Vincent Novello; see Hughes (ed.), *A Mozart Pilgrimage*, p. 94. A similar
remark in Nissen (*Biographie W. A. Mozarts*, p. 544) presumably also carried Constanze's
stamp of approval.

[115] For a report of the story, see in particular Brown and Rice, 'Salieri's *Così fan tutte*', pp. 17–18.
See also Dent, *Mozart's Operas*, p. 189; Einstein, *Mozart: His Character, His Work*,
pp. 458–459; Landon, *The Golden Years*, p. 174.

[116] As given in translation in Lütteken, '*Così fan tutte* and the Reverse of the Enlightenment',
p. 236.

return when her time expired and bring her back to England.' The day after he set sail from Sydney, she married another man.[117]

Following a rough ride for *Così* in the nineteenth century, with entrenched negativity towards the story occasionally catalysing criticism of the music,[118] landmark revivals by Richard Strauss in 1897 and at the first ever Glyndebourne season in 1934 began the process of rehabilitation.[119] *Così*'s rebirth in modern musicology – its rich musical and literary allusions, contexts and relationships providing an ideal subject for study – can also be attributed to our renewed intellectual and aesthetic appreciation of the power and beauty of individual moments in the opera and indeed in Mozart's music in general.[120] There is a historical basis too for this mode of understanding. Perhaps with Arnold's *Mozarts Geist* (1803) in mind, where *Così* is described as a collection of individual beauties rather than a coherent work of art, the *Allgemeine musikalische Zeitung* explained (1804): 'It seems to me that in criticism of Mozart's operas we are too enraptured by the great and excellent totalities and too negligent of the beautiful details, in which resides infinitely more of merit, genius, and

---

[117] See Siân Rees, *The Floating Brothel: the Extraordinary True Story of an 18th-Century Ship and Its Cargo of Female Convicts* (London: Headline Book Publishing, 2001), especially pp. 221–222. See also John Howell (ed.), *The Life and Adventures of John Nichol, Mariner* (Edinburgh, 1822), pp. 108ff. The story did not end well for Nichol. He spent much of the years ahead trying unsuccessfully to travel back to Australia to locate Sarah (who by 1796 had departed for Bombay with her husband and children), apparently without ever finding out that she had married.

[118] See remarks by Edward Holmes (*The Life of Mozart* [1845], ed. Christopher Hogwood [London: Folio Society, 1991], p. 274), as well as Wagner and Hanslick, given in Gernot Gruber, *Mozart and Posterity*, pp. 163, 140. For a substantial *Briefwechsel* about *Così* in the *Berlinische musikalische Zeitung* (1805), probably authored by Johann Friedrich Reichardt and swimming against the critical tide in associating the opera with romantic irony, see Edmund J. Goehring, 'Much Ado About Something; or, *Così fan tutte* in the Romantic Imagination: a Translation of an Early Nineteenth-Century Critique of the Opera', *Eighteenth-Century Music*, 5 (2008), pp. 91–105.

[119] Already in 1936, the Glyndebourne *Così* was considered responsible for 'blowing away all scepticism' about the opera; see '"Don Giovanni" at Glyndebourne', *Musical Times*, 77 no. 6 (1936), p. 553. Although the quality of Mozart's music was rarely doubted in the early to mid-twentieth century, the libretto received mixed reports. For positive evaluations, see Dent, *Mozart's Operas*, p. 190 and Einstein, *Mozart: His Character, His Work*, pp. 459–460; for negative remarks, see Abert, *W. A. Mozart*, p. 805 and Gerald Abraham, 'The Operas', in *The Mozart Companion*, p. 313.

[120] On the latter, including discussion of *Così*, see in particular Scott Burnham, *Mozart's Grace* (Princeton: Princeton University Press, 2013), and Burnham, 'Mozart's *felix culpa: Così fan tutte* and the Irony of Beauty', *Musical Quarterly*, 78 (1994), pp. 77–98; also reprinted in Keefe (ed.), *Mozart*, pp. 227–248. On the power of the moment in *Così* specifically, see Norbert Miller, 'Toying with the Emotions: Da Ponte's and Mozart's School for Lovers', in *'Così': Facsimile of the Autograph*, vol. 3, pp. 9–10.

creative power.'[121] Composer, singers and instrumentalists created *Così's* remarkable moments together. In the quartet 'Di scrivermi', where two clarinets and two bassoons added late at the top and bottom of the autograph provide delicate timbral support for the voices rather than independent lines, Constanze claimed the 'sobs and tears of the performers' could actually be heard and seen.[122] In the quintet 'Sento oddio', which holds 'laughter and sympathy in a beautiful equilibrium' and causes one mid-nineteenth-century fictional character to faint at a 'sublime' moment,[123] Mozart requires performers to contribute actively to realizing a gorgeous climactic effect: when the five come together for the very first time in the opera, a quiet impassioned *sotto voce* is followed by *sf – p* in voices as well as instruments, inflecting to the relative minor to coincide with the collective explanation that human pleasures have been undermined by the impending departure of Ferrando and Guglielmo. And, when required, compositional attractiveness may have been sacrificed to performers' capabilities, including the canon in the Act 2 finale ('E nel tuo, nel mio bicchiero', bars 173–207) that was cut possibly because singers found it too difficult.[124] Mozart pointed out in 1784 that ease and effortlessness in performance came about only through hard work: in response to pianist Georg Friedrich Richter's comment about Mozart making keyboard playing look very easy, he replied that 'I had to work hard in order to be allowed no longer to have to work hard.'[125] Evidence from the autograph of instrumentation and instrumental effects evolving over time bears witness to similar compositional application to achieve fluency in his writing for specific singers. Ultimately, the special poignancy of wind writing reveals as strong a familial bond between *Così* and *Don Giovanni* as between *Così* and *Figaro*: it is *Don Giovanni*'s beautiful daughter as much as *Figaro*'s dark but emollient sibling.

---

[121] *Allgemeine musikalische Zeitung*, 6 (1803–1804), col. 421.

[122] In conversation with Vincent Novello; see Hughes (ed.), *A Mozart Pilgrimage*, p. 94; also in Landon, *1791: Mozart's Last Year*, p. 207.

[123] See Rosen, *Classical Style*, p. 317; and 'The Story of "The Requiem"', in E. Littell (compiler), *Littell's Living Age*, 26 (Boston, 1850), pp. 37–44 at 38. This story is described, and set in the context of legends surrounding the Requiem, in Keefe, *Mozart's Requiem*, pp. 27–28.

[124] On the replacement of the canon from the Act 2 finale with a new thirteen-bar passage, as conveyed in the Burgtheater score OA 146, and including suggestions that singers had problems with it, see Tyson, *Autograph Scores*, pp. 199, 204; Faye Ferguson and Wolfgang Rehm, 'Vorwort', NMA II/5/18/1–2, p. xxviii. See also Edge, 'Mozart's Viennese Copyists', p. 1923; Woodfield, *Così fan tutte*, p. 179.

[125] Mozart reports the conversation to Leopold in MBA, vol. 3, p. 312; LMF, p. 875 (28 April 1784).

Mozart's life in opera would have further twists and turns in 1791, both at a new Viennese venue (for him) and in Prague. Without knowing it, though, he bade farewell to the Burgtheater when the *Figaro* revival finished on 9 February 1791.[126] His relationship with the vibrant, colourful, hectic, frustrating and rewarding operatic world at this most prestigious of theatres, and his extraordinary collaboration with Da Ponte who was himself dismissed by Leopold II in 1791, were now at an end.[127]

---

[126] 'Che soave zeffiretto', now included in a revised *L'ape musicale*, was probably Mozart's final operatic piece to be heard at the Burgtheater during his lifetime, on 9 April 1791. See Woodfield, *Cabals and Satires*.

[127] On Da Ponte's dismissal, see Sheila Hodges, *Lorenzo Da Ponte: The Life and Times of Mozart's Librettist* (London: Granada, 1985), pp. 106–113. For further background, focusing on a pamphlet from 1791 severely critical of Da Ponte, see *Anti-Da Ponte*, trans. and ed. Lisa de Alwis (Malden, MA: Mozart Society of America, 2015).

PART IV

Instrumental Music, 1786–1790

For Publication and Performance
Solo and Chamber Music

Soon after the premiere of *Le nozze di Figaro* at the Burgtheater on 1 May 1786, Mozart wrote a number of solo and chamber works destined for publication within two years, including piano trios and a quartet, a piano duet sonata and variations, and a string quartet.[1] On returning to Vienna in mid-February 1787 from Prague, having witnessed the triumph of *Figaro* and having put on an academy, he embarked on further publication projects, continuing in the years ahead to balance solo and chamber works for publication with operatic duties and concert performances. (See Table 10.1 for a list of the first publications through 1791 of Mozart's solo and chamber works composed between mid-1786 and 1790.) He tried unsuccessfully to distribute as manuscript copies on subscription the string quintets K. 515 in C, K. 516 in G minor and K. 406 in C minor, subsequently bringing them out with Artaria. And he sold his 'Prussian' quartets, K. 575 in D, K. 589 in B-flat and K. 590 in F to Artaria, albeit for a 'pittance';[2] they were published in December 1791, shortly after his death. In 1790, having provided Hoffmeister with a number of works over the previous four years, Mozart negotiated a loan of 2,000 gulden from him through Constanze, guaranteed against works subsequently to be written.[3] As well as the solo and chamber instrumental music examined in this chapter, Mozart wrote and published songs between 1786 and 1789, including 'Lied der Freiheit' K. 506 (Vienna: Wucherer, 1786), 'Die kleine Spinnerin' K. 531 (Vienna: Schrämel, 1787), 'Des kleinen Friedrichs Geburtstag' K. 529 and 'Die Alte' K. 517 (Schrämel, 1788), and 'Das Lied der Trennung' K. 519, 'Abendempfindung' K. 523, 'An Chloe' K. 524

---

[1] The solo piano variations K. 500, completed on 12 September 1786, were published by Artaria in October 1793. The remaining work from the Köchel sequence K. 493–502 immediately after *Le nozze di Figaro*, the Horn Concerto K. 495 (26 June 1786), was published by André in April 1802 and is discussed with other concert works from 1786–1790 in Chapter 11.

[2] MBA, vol. 4, p. 110; LMF, p. 940 (on or before 2 June 1790).

[3] As revealed in letters written to Constanze from Frankfurt and Mannheim: see MBA, vol. 4, pp. 113, 113–114, 117–118, 119; LMF, pp. 942 (28 September 1790), 942–943 (30 September 1790), 945 (8 October 1790), 947 (23 October 1790). No works for Hoffmeister set against the loan ultimately materialized.

Table 10.1 First publications (through 1791) of Mozart's major solo and chamber works composed between mid-1786 and 1790

Work	Date in Mozart's *Verzeichnüß*	First publication
Piano Quartet in E-flat, K. 493	3 June 1786	Artaria, December 1787
Rondo in F, K. 494	10 June 1786	Bossler, April 1787
Piano Trio in G, K. 496	8 July 1786	Hoffmeister, post August 1787
Piano Duet Sonata in F, K. 497	1 August 1786	Artaria, December 1787, as 'Op. 12'
Trio in E-flat, K. 498 ('Kegelstatt')	5 August 1786	Artaria, September 1788 (rescored for violin, viola and piano), as 'Op. 14'
String Quartet in D, K. 499 ('Hoffmeister')	19 August 1786	Hoffmeister, October 1786
Variations for Piano Duet in G, K. 501	4 November 1786	Hoffmeister, post December 1786
Piano Trio in B-flat, K. 502	18 November 1786	Artaria, November 1788, as 'Op. 15'
Rondo in A minor, K. 511	11 March 1787	Hoffmeister, 1787
String Quintet in C, K. 515	19 April 1787	Manuscript copies, early 1788; then Artaria, 1789
String Quintet in G minor, K. 516	16 May 1787	Manuscript copies, early 1788; then Artaria, 1790
String Quintet in C minor, K. 406	[Not in *Verzeichnüß*; arrangement 1787–1788]	Manuscript copies, early 1788; then Artaria, 1792
Piano Duet Sonata in C, K. 521	29 May 1787	Hoffmeister, 1787
Sonata for Piano and Violin in A, K. 526	24 August 1787	Hoffmeister, 1787
Piano Sonata in F, K. 533 (with revised K. 494 as finale)	3 January 1788	Hoffmeister, 1788
Adagio in B minor, K. 540	19 March 1788	Hoffmeister, 1788? (No known extant copy.)
Piano Trio in E, K. 542	22 June 1788	Artaria, November 1788, as 'Op. 15'
Adagio and Fugue in C minor for String Quartet/String Orchestra, K. 546	26 June 1788	Hoffmeister, 1788. (Two-piano fugue K. 426 on which K. 546 is based also published by Hoffmeister in 1788.)
Piano Trio in C, K. 548	14 July 1788	Artaria, November 1788, as 'Op. 15'
Piano Trio in G, K. 564	27 October 1788	Stephen Storace, 1789 (London) Artaria, October 1790
Variations for Piano on a Minuet by Jean-Pierre Duport, K. 573	29 April 1789	Hummel (Amsterdam and Berlin), 1791
String Quartet in D, K. 575	June 1789	Artaria, December 1791, as 'Op. 18'
String Quartet in B-flat, K. 589	May 1790	Artaria, December 1791, as 'Op. 18'
String Quartet in F, K. 590	June 1790	Artaria, December 1791, as 'Op. 18'

(Artaria, 1789).[4] They were originally written for various purposes and performers, including 'Abendempfindung' and 'An Chloe' on the same day in Vienna (24 June 1787), perhaps for a hitherto unknown social occasion, and 'Des kleinen Friedrichs Geburtstag' and 'Das Traumbild' on the same day in Prague (6 November 1787), probably for the Duscheks. But Mozart no doubt had an eye on public dissemination from the start: he only once goes a single semitone below the standard soprano range for a choral singer – c' – g"/a" as designated by Heinrich Koch in 1802 – and never above it; and he writes no vocal material too challenging for competent amateurs.[5]

As earlier in his Viennese decade (see Chapters 1, 3 and 5), Mozart had to think seriously when producing solo and chamber works for publication about the musicians who were to purchase and play them. Clearly he would have hoped and expected successful sales to generate further commissions. Autograph materials continue to offer insight into engagement with pro-spective players. And we can consider on a case-by-case basis Mozart's possible involvement in making changes to a work between submission of an autograph to a publisher and the appearance of that work in print; where such participation occurs, the impact of performance issues on the continuation of Mozart's creative processes can be scrutinized. Artaria allowed a period of up to six months between submission and publication, rendering Mozart's participation in annotating performance copies more likely than for Hoffmeister publications. The very tight turnaround between completion and publication for Hoffmeister can be attributed to the large volume of new material he required for his ambitious monthly series launched in mid-1785. In fact, Mozart's thoroughly marked-up autographs for Hoffmeister, such as the String Quartet K. 499 and the Rondo in A minor K. 511, imply awareness of the unlikelihood of an intervening stage between submission and publication. Conversely, the many Mozart autographs for Artaria publications that contain less performance detail could indicate prior knowledge of an intervening stage.

Biographers have not been reluctant to link interpretations of Mozart's late solo and chamber music to perceptions of his state of mind. The G-minor string quintet gets particular attention in this respect: it relates to the grave state of Leopold's health; to loneliness and strength of mind in

---

[4] Two others, 'Als Luise' K. 520 and 'Das Traumbild' K. 530, were originally circulated as songs by Mozart's Viennese friend Gottfried von Jacquin.

[5] On standard vocal ranges for soprano, alto, tenor and bass voices in the late eighteenth century, see Koch, *Musikalisches Lexikon*, col. 1393. 'Die Alte' K. 517 features a solitary semiquaver b in bar 18. When performed by a male voice an octave below the written pitch, the songs from K. 506 to K. 531 also sit comfortably in the tenor range (c – g' according to Koch).

confronting fate; and to suppressed pain and passion.[6] The Adagio in B minor for piano (K. 540) is also heard as a response to Leopold's death, 'Eine kleine Nachtmusik' as an embodiment of relief after trials and tribulations, and the clarinet quintet as a summing up of the unhappy year of 1789, capturing 'a state of aching despair'.[7] For Abert, the difference between the Rondo in D for piano, K. 485 (1786), and the A-minor rondo for piano, K. 511 (1787) reflects '[Mozart's] own view of the world gradually [becoming] more and more subjective, with the passionate, "demonic" aspect of his character emerging with ever greater prominence'.[8] On occasion, interpretations are demonstrably wrongheaded, including 'Ein musikalischer Spass', K. 522 (1787), as a response to Leopold's death on 28 May 1787: by this date much of the work had already been written.[9]

Attractive though such links often are, they are superseded by Mozart's practical motivation for writing solo and chamber works in mid-1786–1790, namely to make money. Financial problems beset him repeatedly, as evidenced especially in letters to his masonic brother Johann Michael Puchberg begging for loans in 1788, 1789 and 1790.[10] Mozart secured a one-off payment of 1,200 florins (calculated at Viennese currency) from Leopold's estate in autumn 1787, and an annual salary of 800 florins as 'chamber musician' at Joseph II's court from December 1787 onwards, but he soon encountered difficulties; expenses were often high, including medical bills for Constanze, child-related costs, works supplies and clothing, heating and light, and other household outlays, but his cash-flow problems and overall financial situation from 1786 to the end of his life remain a little mysterious.[11] Mozart regarded solo and chamber music, alongside teaching and concertizing, as a helpful resource for digging his

---

[6] See, for example, Henri Ghéon, *In Search of Mozart*, trans. Alexander Pru (London: Sheed & Ward, 1934), pp. 238–239, and Levey, *Life and Death of Mozart*, p. 205; Abert, *W. A. Mozart*, p. 999; Davenport, *Mozart*, p. 280.

[7] Knepler, *Wolfgang Amadé Mozart*, p. 205; Levey, *Life and Death of Mozart*, p. 84; Landon, *Mozart: the Golden Years*, p. 211.

[8] Abert, *W. A. Mozart*, pp. 985–986.

[9] See Tyson's account: 'Notes on the Genesis of Mozart's "Ein musikalischer Spass", K. 522', in *Mozart: Studies of the Autograph Scores*, pp. 234–245. Several accounts linking the work to Leopold's death are mentioned in Melograni, *Mozart: A Biography*, p. 207.

[10] According to Braunbehrens' calculations (*Mozart in Vienna*, p. 321), Puchberg lent Mozart 1,450 florins from 1788 onwards, with roughly two-thirds remaining unpaid at the composer's death.

[11] On the settlement of Leopold's estate following his death on 28 May 1787, see Halliwell, *The Mozart Family*, pp. 545–564. The imperial appointment is discussed in detail in Wolff, *Mozart at the Gateway to His Fortune*, pp. 9–43. For a succinct summary of what is known and unknown about Mozart's financial situation in his final years, see Eisen, 'Mozart, (Johann Chrysostom) Wolfgang Amadeus', in *The Cambridge Mozart Encyclopedia*, p. 317. On Mozart's

way out of holes. He proposed the subscription scheme for his three string quintets as security against one requested loan from Puchberg in June 1788: 'On account of the subscription, you must have no worries; I am now extending the time by several more months. I have hopes of finding more enthusiasts [*Liebhaber*] *abroad* than *here*.'[12] Dedications of piano sonatas and string quartets to Princess Friederike and King Wilhelm of Prussia and later publication of the quartets were also considered potentially useful sources of income.[13]

Mozart was sometimes overly optimistic about income generation from publications, and his commitment to projects may have varied according to contractual arrangements with publishers. He entered into agreements with Artaria to produce the piano trios K. 502 in B-flat, K. 542 in E and K. 548 in C (published together in 1788) and K. 564 in G (published 1790), but may have failed to deliver others that were promised.[14] The relationship with Artaria consequently could have suffered, explaining Mozart's subsequent pursuit of a large advance from Hoffmeister and the planned publication of six easy sonatas with Koželuch.[15] Ultimately, the importance of publishing activities to Mozart is demonstrated by his continued investigation of opportunities for profiting financially from them in spite of considerable challenges.

This chapter examines Mozart's solo and chamber works by genre, paying special attention to information gleaned from primary sources about performance issues. Mozart played – in formal or informal contexts – many of his works from 1786 to 1790 that were destined for publication, including the 'Prussian' quartets, the string trio and quintets and a piano

---

earnings in Vienna see also Solomon, *Mozart: A Life*, pp. 521–528. Mozart's high costs for heating, lights and other household items and services are discussed in Günther G. Bauer, 'Mozarts hohe Licht- und Heizkosten 1781–1792', *Mitteilungen der Gesellschaft für Salzburger Landeskunde* (Salzburg, 2008), pp. 147–186. Bauer's article also contains informative descriptions of Mozart's Viennese residencies. For an argument that Mozart moved to the Alsergrund in the Viennese suburbs in 1788 in order 'to take advantage of the better living conditions in more spacious environs' rather than (as usually suggested) to reduce his expenses, see Michael Lorenz, 'Mozart's Apartment on the Alsergrund', https://homepage.univie.ac.at/michael.lorenz/alsergrund/.

[12] MBA, vol. 4, p. 66; LMF, pp. 915–916 (17 June 1788).

[13] MBA, vol. 4, pp. 93, 106; LMF, pp. 930 (12 July 1789), 938 (beginning of May 1790).

[14] Rupert Ridgewell suggests that Artaria may have expected two further piano trios from Mozart in addition to K. 564 in G, thus explaining the extended delay between completion (27 October 1788) and publication (1790). Another possibility is that Mozart shopped K. 564 around first, before approaching Artaria: in fact, he brought it out with Storace in London in 1789. (Artaria did not use the Storace edition, basing theirs on a different source.) See Ridgewell, 'Mozart's Publishing Plans with Artaria in 1787', pp. 69–70.

[15] Ridgewell, 'Mozart's Publishing Plans with Artaria in 1787', pp. 73–74.

quartet (K. 493 in all likelihood).[16] His appointment to Joseph II's court as composer to the imperial-royal chamber music in December 1787 provided further performing opportunities.[17] Several chamber works perhaps not earmarked for publication at all are examined at the end of the chapter.

Chamber Music for Strings: Quintets, Quartets and a Trio

The string quintets, quartets and trio from 1786 to 1790 collectively represent enterprising attempts to make chamber music pay. The quintets were distributed by subscription to manuscript copies in 1788 (administered by Puchberg), albeit unsuccessfully. After advertising them in the *Wiener Zeitung* on 2 June 1788, Mozart wrote on 25 June 1788: 'Since the number of subscribers is still very low, I find myself forced to postpone the publication of my 3 quintets until 1 January 1789.'[18] Artaria subsequently brought them out one by one in 1789, 1790 and 1792. Having arranged the quintet in C minor, K. 406, from the earlier wind serenade K. 388 in 1787–1788,[19] Mozart then turned to the earlier Fugue for Two Pianos, K. 426 (1783), for the second part of the Adagio and Fugue in C minor K. 546 for string ensemble, publishing it with Hoffmeister in 1788. An earlier single string quartet, K. 499 in D (1786), also came out with Hoffmeister.[20] Following his trip to Northern Germany and possible audience with King Wilhelm II of Prussia in Potsdam, Mozart either received a commission for quartets from the King or decided to write a set for him in the hope that a

---

[16] See MBA, vol. 4, pp. 108, 83 and 105, 10; LMF, pp. 939 (on or before 17 May 1790; the 'Prussian' quartets at Mozart's residence), 923, 937 (16 April 1789 and on or before 8 April 1790; the string trio at a private concert in Dresden and at Count Hadik's in Vienna), 903 (15 January 1787; a piano quartet at Count Thun's in Prague).

[17] On Mozart's turn to chamber music to coincide with his imperial appointment, see Wolff, *Mozart at the Gateway to his Fortune*, especially p. 178. But Wolff's assertion that 'there can be no question that Mozart's deliberate orientation toward chamber-music composition is directly related to the courtly home of his imperial appointment' (p. 178) is too bold. It is unlikely Mozart would have composed chamber music primarily for court performance: his annual salary was guaranteed, irrespective of new works produced. The income generated from publishers of new works would have been a more significant motivating factor.

[18] See MDL, pp. 274, 280; MDB, pp. 312, 319.

[19] Alan Tyson suggests that Mozart began the arrangement of the C-minor wind serenade as the C-minor string quintet in summer 1787, but finished it only in 1788. See Tyson, 'Some Features of the Autograph Score of *Don Giovanni*', *Israel Studies in Musicology*, 5 (1990), p. 10. From his study of inks in the autograph, John Arthur explains that it was 'probably finished in 1788 but begun no earlier than the end of 1787'; Arthur, 'Some Chronological Problems in Mozart', p. 42.

[20] For the first edition, see *Quatuor à deux Violons, alto, et Violoncello, composeé par Mr W. A. Mozart* (Vienna: Hoffmeister [1786]): https://iiif.lib.harvard.edu/manifests/view/drs:14193088 $1i.

dedication would bring in money. As has been pointed out, Mozart's state-ment to Puchberg on 12 July 1789 about 'writing . . . six quartets for the King' does not explicitly identify a commission, even if he wanted Puchberg to infer it.[21] Eventually selling the 'Prussian' quartets K. 575, 589 and 590 to Artaria 'for a pittance, in order to have cash in hand for my difficulties', they were published shortly after Mozart's death without a dedication.[22] A common thread running through the late string chamber works, supported by primary sources, is Mozart's engagement with performance issues. While the quintets, quartets and fugue from K. 546 were intended for publication from the outset, the string trio K. 563 (1788), written for Puchberg, may not have been envisaged primarily for print.

Mozart is known to have reviewed prepublication performance copies of the string quintet in C, K. 515 and probably K. 516 in G minor too. Parts produced by one of Mozart's trusted Viennese copyists, containing annota-tions in Mozart's hand for K. 515 and acquired by the composer Carl Anton Ziegler from Constanze in 1800, recently surfaced among materials donated to the Beethoven-Haus in Bonn. Evidence suggests that the K. 515 parts were copied directly from the autograph and represent a master copy overseen by Mozart; the K. 516 parts were probably produced from a master copy that is no longer extant.[23] Thus, the process surmised for the 'Haydn' quartets and Fantasia and Sonata K. 475 and K. 457 – Mozart's annotations to now-lost performance copies generated from the autograph making their way into the first edition – is documented for the C-major quintet. Running through the parts with fellow musicians could have inspired Mozart to annotate them: Maximilian Stadler attests to often playing the quintets with the composer and Haydn, but whether pre- or post-distribution is not known.[24]

Mozart made additions and adjustments to all instrumental parts for all four movements of K. 515, packing the biggest punch with dynamic inter-polations to the opening Allegro and finale.[25] Those in the last two-thirds of

[21] MBA, vol. 4, p. 93; LMF, p. 930, as explained in Solomon, *Mozart: A Life*, p. 442.

[22] MBA, vol. 4, p. 110; LMF, p. 940. Only K. 575 in the *Verzeichnüß* makes reference to the King. Mozart describes it as 'A Quartet . . . for His Majesty the King of Prussia' ('Eine Quartett . . . für Seine Mayestätt dem König in Preussen'); see Mozart, *Eigenhändiges Werkverzeichnis*, folio 21v.

[23] See Wolfgang Amadeus Mozart, Streichquintette (C-Dur) KV 515 und (g moll) KV 516, Stimmen, Abschrift: Beethoven-Haus Bonn, Sammlung Hanns J. Eller, NE 228, discussed in Ernst Herttrich, 'Eine neue, wichtige Quelle zu Mozarts Streichquintetten KV 515 und 516' in Paul Mai (ed.), *Im Dienst der Quellen zur Musik: Festschrift Gertraut Haberkamp zum 65. Geburtstag* (Tutzing: Hans Schneider, 2002), pp. 435–445.

[24] See Medici and Hughes (eds.), *A Mozart Pilgrimage*, p. 170.

[25] Many small corrections to the parts (especially slurs, phrase markings and staccati) cannot be attributed with certainty to Mozart. See Herttrich, 'Eine neue, wichtige Quelle', p. 441. But additional dynamics contributed by Mozart are evident from an examination of the parts.

the development section of the first movement (bars 168–204, Example 10.1) apparently represent a reappraisal of the section's impact. At *piano* (in the autograph), the protracted minor-mode passage from bars 170–185 has a meditative air, but at *forte* (marked in the performance copy) conveys a more assertive minor-mode mood. Additional *forte*s in the confirmation of V/C (bars 190–192) and for the immediate run-up to the recapitulation, again not in the autograph, bring similar stridency. Mozart's annotation of *fpia*s for the second violin, and first and second violas at the opening of the recapitulation, alongside the cello *fpia* from the autograph, signals a momentarily greater volume for the ensemble than at the opening of the exposition and can perhaps be attributed to intensity wrought by the interpolated dynamics in the development.

Distinctive inflections and surges of sound are already a feature of K. 515 in the autograph: the *f – p* head motif in the Allegro; the *mfp*s and *sf – p*s in the Andante main theme; and *p – cresc – p* and *p – cresc – f – p* markings in the minuet and trio. And they are subsequently developed in Mozart's annotations to the performance copies of both of the outer movements. The juxtaposition of a single instrument *forte* and the others *piano* for the first note of the first movement's main theme is expanded in bars 170–171 of the copy: a *piano* prevails at least in the second violin until the end of bar 171 after three other instruments have entered *forte*. In the finale, all except two of Mozart's dynamics accruing to the performance copy comprise *crescendi* to a brief *forte*, followed by a retreat to *piano*. (No *crescendi* are included in the autograph of the finale in contrast to the autographs of the Allegro and Minuet and Trio.) Mozart's additions to the last movement are mostly for the collective ensemble, but on two occasions are only for the first violin in the context of returns to the rondo theme (bars 36–41, 246–250).

Thus, Mozart's work on the autograph and performance copies of the C-major quintet exists on a continuum (as surmised for the 'Haydn' quartets): dynamic additions to the copies accentuate types of intensity also evident in the autograph. In the copy of the first movement of the G-minor quintet, as in the finale of K. 515, Mozart introduced notated *crescendi* to the secondary theme of the exposition, the development and the primary and secondary themes of the recapitulation:[26] none appear in the autograph. But *crescendi* and other dynamic nuances turn up elsewhere in the

---

[26] Assuming attribution to Mozart of additions to the K. 516 copy, as seems reasonable. See Herttrich, 'Eine neue, wichtige Quelle', p. 443. Other additions to the copy include *forte*s and *piano*s at the ends of the exposition and recapitulation and *mfp*s in the second half of the development.

Example 10.1 Mozart, String Quintet in C, K. 515/i, bars 168–205 (with Mozart's annotations to the performance copy in bold and square brackets under each stave).

Example 10.1 (cont.)

autograph, especially in the Adagio ma non troppo (including *mfp, sfp, sf –
p, fp, f – p*). Being relatively rare in the late eighteenth century, the *con
sordino* instruction would have given the intended amateur subscribers to
the set of quintets in late 1780s Vienna something to ponder.[27] Usually
wooden or metallic, mutes were also more cumbersome to apply and
remove than their modern equivalents. (Johann Joachim Quantz suggests
that effects of tenderness and of madness-despair can be conveyed with
mutes:[28] both, perhaps, are features of K. 516/iii.) Whether, or how, to
differentiate the *sf – p*s in the harmonically audacious transition, domi-
nant-minor theme and lead-back to the recapitulation (bars 13–18, 20–22,
37), and the *mfp*s in the minor theme and the secondary theme's melodic
line (bars 19–31) would have challenged players more in unfamiliar muted
than in familiar unmuted contexts: *con sordino* dynamics, inflections and
accents inevitably had different, less well known timbral qualities to unmuted
ones. Since Mozart sometimes demonstrates 'a preoccupation ... merely with
sound' in the G-minor quintet,[29] he leaves significant interpretational matters
in the hands of his players.

The third string quintet in the subscription set from 1788, K. 406 in C
minor, was Mozart's own arrangement of his wind serenade in C minor, K.
388, from six years earlier.[30] Condensing eight parts for wind into five for

[27] On the rarity of *con sordino* in the late eighteenth century, see Stowell, *Violin Technique and
Performance Practice*, p. 239.

[28] Stowell, *Violin Technique and Performance Practice*, p. 239.

[29] Cliff Eisen, 'Mozart's Chamber Music', in Keefe (ed.), *Cambridge Companion to Mozart*, pp.
105–117, at 112. David Schroeder also draws attention to 'the focus on sound itself' in both K.
515 and 516: see *Experiencing Mozart: A Listener's Companion* (Lanham, MD: Scarecrow Press,
2013), p. 50.

[30] For the autograph manuscripts, see Staatsbibliothek zu Berlin, Preussicher Kulturbesitz,
Musikabteilung mit Mendelssohn-Archiv, Mus. ms. autogr. W. A. Mozart 388 (for K. 388) and
British Library Add MS 31748 (for K. 406). Negativity towards the C-minor quintet from

strings would have made an exact transcription more or less impossible even had it been desired. The octet of wind instruments also offered Mozart a greater range of opportunities for timbral variety and contrast (exploited with aplomb in K. 388; see Chapter 1) than the more homogeneous five-instrument string ensemble. (For example, the fundamental contrast in the serenade of a full-scored minuet followed by a trio just for double reeds would have been difficult to match in a string quintet.) Mozart's motivations for making changes to his serenade in the quintet – such as to articulation and phrasing especially in the last two movements – are not always obvious in spite of the prominent place the string instruments no doubt occupied in his mind when writing it down. For had Mozart had an opportunity to publish the serenade during his lifetime and then either revisited the autograph before handing it over to the publisher or annotated performance copies generated from the autograph, he might have been inclined to make some of the same adjustments. Several small additions to the quintet finale, including a semiquaver arpeggio and three trills in variations 6 and 7 (bars 167, 182, 190, 198; Examples 10.2a and 10.2b), are no more idiomatic to strings than wind and again may represent re-interpretations of the serenade unrelated to issues of rescoring.

But at least three kinds of adjustments to the serenade in the quintet, involving performance markings, sustained notes and tiny cuts, were probably carried out with the new ensemble specifically in mind. With the exception of the *sf*s accruing to the first violin in the recapitulation of K. 406/i (bars 159, 207, 215), there are fewer dynamic differentiations between simultaneously playing instruments in the quintet than in the serenade, and fewer character markings in general; perhaps Mozart expected wind players to foreground the individual timbral and textural qualities of their instruments more than the players of ostensibly homogeneous strings.[31] For example, a *dolce* ('[connoting] a dynamic intensity greater than *piano*'[32]) attached to the secondary theme's oboe melody line in the serenade and set apart from the *piano* in the accompanying instruments, is omitted at the corresponding moment in the quintet. *Dolce*s (for all instruments) in the first-theme section of K. 388/ii are also absent from K. 406/ii, and the character

biographers (for example, Gutman, *Cultural Biography*, p. 666; Hildesheimer, *Mozart*, p. 172; Rosselli, *Life of Mozart*, p. 47; Einstein, *Mozart: His Character, His Work*, pp. 200, 203; Jahn, *W. A. Mozart*, vol. 3, p. 28) on the grounds that Mozart resorted under time constraints to an arrangement rather than composing a new work, is unmerited.

[31] On several occasions in the quintet Mozart changed, or added to, dynamics coordinated between wind participants in the serenade: the *sf*s at K. 388/i, bar 83 become *f*s; and a *crescendo* and *piano* accrue to K. 406/ii, bars 49–50 and 99 respectively, and a *piano* to K. 406/iii, bar 23.

[32] Levin, 'The Devil's in the Details', p. 34.

Example 10.2a Mozart, String Quintet in C minor, K. 406/iv, bars 166–168.

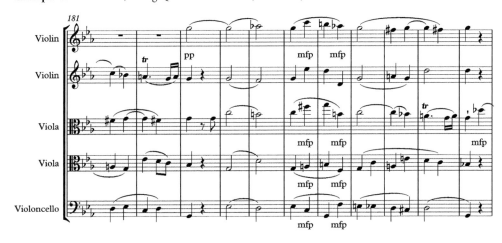

Example 10.2b Mozart, String Quintet in C minor, K. 406/iv, bars 181–191.

indications 'a mezza voce' in the trio of K. 388 changed to *piano*s in the quintet. Syncopated oboe and bassoon melody lines (*piano*) in variation 3 of the K. 388 finale, distinguished from the other parts (*pianissimo*), become a standardized *piano* for the whole string ensemble in K. 406/iv; combined *sfp*s and *fp*s in variation 7 turn into uniform *mfp*s in the quintet (bars 192–199). Sustained notes, which acquired timbral cachet in late-eighteenth-century discourse on wind participation,[33] often appear in the serenade but not the quintet. In K. 406/i they are regularly replaced

[33] See Chapter 1, and Béthizy, *Exposition de la théorie et de la pratique de la musique*, p. 306; Francoeur, *Diapason général*, p. 22; Kollmann, *An Essay on Practical Musical Composition*, p. 18.

by inner-voice, quaver-crotchet-crotchet syncopated writing, including at the big *forte* effect after a one-bar general pause in the development section (bar 108) and when a swathe of sustained notes in the serenade's recapitulation had been played by six of the eight participants (bars 159–164).[34] Distinctive wind timbres are thus transformed into distinctive, energizing rhythms for the strings. And two effects from the serenade were omitted altogether, perhaps too closely associated with wind sounds to be appropriated in the quintet: the *piano* echo from high to low (K. 388/ii, bars 59–60); and the three-crotchet held note before the C-major variation 8 (K. 388/iv, bars 214–215), reduced to a single crotchet in the quintet.[35]

Mozart's arrangement of the two-pianos fugue K. 426 for a string ensemble in K. 546 was a more straightforward task than the arrangement of the wind octet as a string quintet: the four-part texture for K. 426 translates straightforwardly to the four string parts for K. 546 (at least until the final bars when the bottom one divides into 'violoncelli' and 'contrabassi', as marked in the autograph).[36] And it was not the first time he had transcribed a keyboard fugue for four string parts either: in Baron van Swieten's circle in 1782 Mozart produced K. 405 out of five four-part fugues from J. S. Bach's *Well-Tempered Clavier II*.[37] As can be seen in the autograph of K. 546, a copyist wrote out the original fugue on the top four staves of each of the 18 pages; Mozart then wrote the string parts on the sixth through ninth staves, leaving one blank in between. Relative to material provided by the copyist, Mozart added 'staccati' indications, additional strokes, and different (generally longer) slurs, occasionally changed the pitch by an octave to accommodate string instruments, and deleted piano octave figures (for example, bar 30). Towards the end, idiomatic semiquaver alberti figures for the piano become repeated semiquavers for the strings and six bars of crotchets marked 'contrabassi' are

---

[34] Other sustained notes from K. 388/i replaced with syncopated writing in K. 406/i, include bars 10, 28–33, 138. Elsewhere in the movement, sustained notes from the serenade are retained in the quintet, notably in and around the secondary theme.

[35] As a result, the second and fourth movements of the quintet are one bar shorter than those of the serenade. It is a little unclear from the K. 406 autograph whether the pause in the finale at bar 214 belongs to the initial crotchet or the subsequent quaver rest: the first violin, first viola and cello markings are unambiguously located over the quaver rest.

[36] It is not clear whether Mozart intended the Adagio and Fugue to be played one to a part, or by an ensemble with more than one instrument on each part. The *Verzeichnüß* mentions '2 violini, viola, e Basso', but, as stated, 'violoncelli' and 'contrabassi' (plural) are indicated in the autograph towards the end of the fugue. The autograph for the fugue of K. 546 is held in the British Library in London (MS 28966). But the autograph for the Adagio of K. 546 is lost.

[37] For more on K. 405, see Yo Tomita, 'Bach Reception in Pre-Classical Vienna: Baron van Swieten's Circle Edits the "Well-Tempered Clavier" II', *Music & Letters*, 81 (2000), pp. 364–391.

appended to a new stave (see bars 107–116). This exciting, visceral climax to K. 546 outdoes the corresponding passage in K. 426. Perhaps Mozart felt that the profundity of the new preceding Adagio – authoritative *forte* statements alternating with *piano* harmonic purple patches and ethereal imitative passages – necessitated a weightier conclusion to K. 546 than to a self-standing fugue.

Mozart's unsuccessful string-quintet subscription scheme, at a time when quintets by other composers were written and distributed in Vienna,[38] gives pause for thought. The oft-mentioned difficulties of Mozart's Viennese works detected by some late-eighteenth-century critics need to be kept in perspective, as they can be counterbalanced by positive remarks from the same period. And the economic downturn in the late 1780s provoked by the Turkish War also could have contributed to poor sales. But if 'difficulties' are situated in the concerns of performers rather than listeners – and several comments from the 1780s leave open this possibility[39] – Mozart's musical material cannot be ruled out as a contributing factor to the relative lack of commercial appeal. While the C-major and G-minor quintets challenge the technical dexterity of performers no more than Mozart's Viennese quartets or much contemporary Viennese string chamber music, their formal and expressive richness and breadth, producing concomitant interpretative challenges, could have deterred competent amateurs.[40] It is unlikely that the initial purchasers would have had advance knowledge of the content of Mozart's quintets and been put

---

[38] In the years preceding K. 515, 516 and 406, quintets by Albrechtsberger, Pleyel, Boccherini, Sterkel and Piticchio were composed and distributed in Vienna: see Cliff Eisen, 'Mozart and the Viennese String Quintet', in Eisen and Wolf-Dieter Seiffert (eds.), *Mozarts Streichquintette* (Stuttgart: Fritz Steiner, 1994), pp. 127–152, and Eisen (ed.), *Four Viennese String Quintets* (Madison, WI: A-R Editions, 1998), Preface.

[39] See, for example, Cramer and Dittersdorf in 1787–1789. Cramer's rhetorical question about how long the 'too highly seasoned' string quartets by Mozart can be endured may have been addressed to performers as well as listeners (see MDL, pp. 255–256; MDB, p. 290), as might Dittersdorf's remark about 'their overwhelming and unrelenting artfulness', which is 'not to everyone's taste' (NMD, p. 54). Similarly, for Cramer, Mozart orientating his quartets towards 'the difficult and the unusual' (MDL, p. 306; MDB, p. 349) may relate to the experience of performers.

[40] Such richness may likewise explain K. 515's popularity in recent decades as a focus for analytical study. See (for example), Ratner, *Classic Music*, pp. 78–80 and *passim*; V. Kofi Agawu, *Playing with Signs: a Semiotic Interpretation of Classic Music* (Princeton: Princeton University Press, 1991), pp. 80–99; Michael Spitzer, 'A Metaphoric Model of Sonata Form: Two Expositions by Mozart', in Danuta Mirka and Kofi Agawu (eds.), *Communication in Eighteenth-Century Music* (Cambridge: Cambridge University Press, 2008), pp. 189–229, at 200–214; Henry Burnett and Roy Nitzberg, *Composition, Chromaticism and the Developmental Process* (Aldershot: Ashgate, 2007), pp. 217–225; David Damschroeder, *Harmony in Haydn and Mozart* (Cambridge: Cambridge University Press, 2012), pp. 183–204.

off them as a result, of course, but subsequent potential buyers could have learned about the works from the experiences of the first amateurs playing them. As with his first three Viennese piano concertos, K. 413–415, also sold in manuscript copies by subscription (see Chapter 3), Mozart may simply have aimed too high for his intended purchasers and players.

Whether Mozart contributed to the 'Prussian' quartets between submitting the autograph to Artaria and publication is not known.[41] If Mozart did intervene, he did not apparently do so to the same degree as in the 'Haydn' quartets (where dynamics were missing for extended passages of the autograph).[42] At any rate, where performance of the quartets was concerned, Mozart chose above all to accommodate the King of Prussia's well-known prowess as a cellist.[43] Paper types in the autographs show him breaking off K. 589 in B-flat towards the end of the second movement – having completed K. 575 in June 1789 – and returning to finish it in May 1790, as well as to compose K. 590 (June 1790).[44] While the quartets had a protracted genesis and became increasingly distant from the erstwhile dedicatee, their autograph revisions show Mozart retaining interest in prominent cello writing throughout.[45]

---

[41] The Artaria edition of the 'Prussian' quartets has been described as 'mistake-ridden' (*recht Fehlhafte*). See NMA, viii/20/1/3, Kritischer Bericht, p. 35.

[42] Several dynamic markings in the first edition of K. 590/ii but not the dynamically sparse autograph could conceivably have been added by Mozart. On occasion, the nature of differences between the autograph and first edition tentatively suggests Mozart's involvement. In the K. 575 autograph, the bar before the reprise in the second movement has different dynamic markings for the violin 1/violin 2, viola and cello (bar 42): *mf, cresc,* and an uninflected continuation of the prevailing *piano*. The *sf* and *f* for the first and second violin respectively in the edition may not represent Artaria publishing errors but rather Mozart's desire to intensify the dynamic level at this important formal juncture and to individualize participation still more than in the autograph in order to maximize the impact of the four instrumentalists coming together, *piano*, at the beginning of the reprise. Similarly, new dynamics for the second and first violins in bars 121 and 123 of the finale where none are given in the autograph may also derive from Mozart.

[43] Küster (*Musical Biography*, p. 319) also considers it possible that Mozart's cello writing in the 'Prussian' quartets reacted 'to a new ideal of cello sound [produced by Stradivari cellos, one of which the King owned], which was only beginning to gain ground at that period'.

[44] See Alan Tyson's introduction to Wolfgang Amadeus Mozart, *The Late Chamber Works for Strings: Facsimile of the Autograph Manuscripts in the British Library* (London: The British Library, 1987), p. 9.

[45] With a slightly different emphasis, Tyson proposes the 'by no means even' distribution of solo cello passages across the 'Prussian' quartets as evidence that 'not more than two or three weeks after [Mozart] left Potsdam, the royal A-string was still sounding vividly in his inner ear, but after some months in Vienna it could be heard only faintly' (Introduction to Mozart, *The Late Chamber Works for Strings*, p. 9).

The rejection of two passages at the opening of K. 575 catches Mozart contemplating the cello's participation right from the outset (Example 10.3). He originally envisaged the cello carrying the repeat of the main theme in bar 9; in revising, he clarifies through instrument indications above the staves that for six bars the music for viola appears on the cello stave and the cello on the viola stave.[46] Also, Mozart initially conceived a repeat of the octave figure from bars 15–16 in the cello, subsequently deleting the bar (where only a cello part was notated). Whatever the motivation for Mozart's revisions, the net effect is to lend special emphasis to the first genuine 'solo' outing for the cello a few bars later (23ff.): here it imitates the violin's arpeggiated material and duly leads related imitation in the transition (bar 32ff.), standing out from the prevailing *p* with a *dolce* marking. At the confirmation of the secondary key area, Mozart brings back the octave figure, first in the violin *piano* then in the cello *forte* (bars 54–55), 'old' material thus designating a 'monothematic' process.[47] Keeping the cello clear of the octave figure early in the movement, *inter alia* by rejecting the original bar 17, maximizes the figure's impact in the cello, at a *forte* dynamic, in the secondary theme section (bar 55). It is conceivable, then, that Mozart's adjustments early in the movement were designed to accommodate effects envisaged for the cello later on. If the first page of the K. 575 autograph (perhaps) demonstrates Mozart finding his compositional feet where prominent cello writing is concerned (which would be commensurate with the impatience to start work detected by Tyson[48]), the second, third and fourth movements witness an unambiguous flourishing of its role. Even the absence of a *sotto voce* for the cello at the opening of the Andante, where the other three instruments receive it, prepares for cello participation distinguished from first violin, second violin and viola contributions later in the movement (especially bar 21 onwards).

Revisions to the cello part in the autograph of K. 590 in F, may again document thoughts about its role. Mozart initially envisaged either a continuation of the transition in bars 31 and 32 of the first movement (Example 10.4), or more likely a restatement of the main theme in the dominant in place of a new secondary theme: he gave a c' – e' – g' arpeggio in minims (preceded by C – G – e grace notes) before smudging out the g'

---

[46] From the different ink colour for the top three staves and the bottom stave in bars 9–13 it can be determined that Mozart wrote the theme first (on the bottom stave).

[47] The cello also takes a leading role with the octave figure in the development section, including by initiating further *forte* renditions (see bars 94–100).

[48] See Tyson's introduction to Mozart, *The Late Chamber Works for Strings*, p. 9.

Example 10.3 Mozart, String Quartet in D, K. 575/i, bars 1–25 (including switched staves for viola and cello and a deleted bar).

Example 10.4 Mozart, String Quartet in F, K. 590/i, bars 30–34 (including deleted bars).

and the remainder of the cello material in the second bar, considering a continuation to the cello line in the treble clef before crossing out the two bars entirely. Mozart's revision may be designed to delay the main theme's reappearance in the secondary key area until the exposition's codetta (where it is heard in the cello). But the nature of the cello participation also could have been a contributing factor. The ostentatious grace-note flourish Mozart rejected, taking the cello immediately up two octaves from its lowest note (C), is in effect reworked in the broader, more measured arpeggio that provides the finalized bar 31 and acts as an unaccompanied introductory bar to the secondary theme. The movement as a whole is notable for abrupt juxtapositions of brilliance, simplicity and mellifluous melody.[49] Mozart rejected flamboyance here in favour of a simultaneously grand and subtle gesture, thus allowing a new type of cello playing to emerge. (The *pia:* in the second half of bar 31 is probably to be approached via an unnotated diminuendo in the first half following the *for:* on the last beat of bar 30.) Towards the end of the Andante, the cello's elevated status perhaps provoked another revision: soaring to the upper regions of its A string in the development and recapitulation (but not the exposition) the cello is an appropriate recipient of the repeated statement of the closing theme (bars 106–108, Example 10.5), replacing the viola presentation originally desired.[50] Having exploited upper and lower ranges of the cello throughout the movement, Mozart brings them together in an exquisite close: clustered within the interval of a 6th in the third to last bar, the four instruments move apart to embrace a five-octave range (C – c''', Example 10.5).

---

[49] See Keefe, *Mozart's Viennese Instrumental Music*, pp. 110–111.

[50] As can be seen in the musical example, bar 106 of K. 590/ii is originally notated for the viola and then crossed out; the thematic material is subsequently allocated to the cello instead.

Example 10.5 Mozart, String Quartet in F, K. 590/ii, bars 105–122 (including deleted bar).

Before breaking off midway through the second of the 'Prussian' quartets, K. 589, Mozart again turned his attention to the cello, especially in the slow movement. Entrusted with a main theme at the outset high on its A string, featuring *sotto voce* and *mfp* markings and delicate articulation lightly accompanied by the second violin and viola, the cello then offers rich, resonant lower notes in support of the thematic repeat from the first violin. It is as if Mozart wanted the King to have an opportunity to demonstrate in quick succession the different roles of nuanced melodist and warm harmonic reinforcer. He further promotes the cello as melodist in the run-up to the recapitulation, giving it three almost entirely unaccompanied bars with a crescendo and a fall back to *piano*; melodic exposure also goes hand in hand with deep and resonant harmonic support in the final stages of the movement (from the cello's repeat of the secondary theme onwards).

The autograph of the 'Hoffmeister' Quartet K. 499 in D sheds light on Mozart's engagement with publisher and players, rather than with a single intended recipient.[51] As with other works for Hoffmeister's subscription series such as the G-minor piano quartet, K. 478 and the A-minor Rondo K. 511, Mozart included detailed performance markings in the autograph, especially dynamics, probably aware that Hoffmeister's tight turnaround would render unlikely an opportunity for adjustments and additions between submission to the publisher and publication.[52] In the slow movement (Adagio), the brownish ink colour of the majority of dynamic markings is different from the black ink colour elsewhere, probably revealing the addition of dynamics during a pass through the autograph sometime between writing down the musical text and giving the completed work to Hoffmeister. In fact, dynamics play a pivotal role in the expressive discourse of the work, Mozart relying on thoughtful interpretations of the edition to render it meaningful. In the first movement, for example, contrasts between relaxed and urgent passages come alive in a dynamically engaged performance. After a languorous primary theme section all *piano* (bars 1–22), including unhurried exchanges of material and ample cadence-making, a collective *forte* for the ensemble at the beginning of the transition then momentarily individualized dynamics for the cello[53]

[51] For the autograph, see British Library Add MS 37764.

[52] On Hoffmeister's challenging and ultimately unrealistic schedules for the publication of volumes in his series, see Ridgewell, 'Biographical Myth and the Publication of Mozart's Piano Quartets', p. 52. Paper types and ink colours in the autograph suggest that Mozart wrote K. 499 very quickly; see Tyson's introduction to *Mozart: The Late Chamber Works for Strings*, p. 6.

[53] See the *sf* and *f* set against *p*s in the other parts in bars 27 and 31.

lend new energy to the exposition. A lengthy, dynamically uninflected passage coinciding with delays both to the confirmation of the secondary key area and to the secondary theme itself (bars 53–83) is followed by a concluding theme in which rapidly changing dynamics, cello *sfs* offset from the prevailing *forte*, and a *pp* marking new to the movement, again support intense expression (bars 83–98).

The string trio in E-flat, K. 563, stands apart from Mozart's other late string chamber music. He describes it as 'Ein Divertimento ... *di sei pezzi*' (A divertimento ... in six pieces) in the *Verzeichnüß*, not as a trio, even though he identifies string quartets and quintets elsewhere in the same catalogue. Heinrich Christoph Koch (1802) considered divertimenti to be aimed generally at one-to-a-part performance and above all at pleasing the ear ('die Ergötzung des Ohres') rather than expressing specific feelings, a definition that applies to music titled 'divertimento' in the 1780s and 1790s but not earlier.[54] String trios scored for violin, viola and cello lacked the well-developed publication tradition of the accompanied sonata, string quartet and string quintet; after writing the trio for Puchberg, which Mozart documents in a letter to Constanze on 16 April 1789, Mozart might have envisaged its future life primarily in private performances, and in line with the post-1780 Viennese understanding of a divertimento as 'usually not intended for publication'.[55] Two private performances are documented, in fact, in Dresden (1789) and at Count Hadik's residence in Vienna (1790).[56] Irrespective of Mozart's thoughts on dissemination, K. 563 was published by Artaria only after his death, in 1792.

---

[54] Koch, *Musikalisches Lexikon*, cols. 440–441. On the changing meanings and implications of 'divertimento' from 1750 onwards, focusing on Vienna, see James Webster, 'Towards a History of Viennese Chamber Music in the Early Classical Period', *Journal of the American Musicological Society*, 27 (1974), pp. 212–247. See also Webster, 'The Scoring of Mozart's Chamber Music for Strings', in Allan W. Atlas (ed.), *Music in the Classic Period: Essays in Honor of Barry S. Brook* (New York: Pendragon Press, 1985), pp. 259–296; and Webster, 'Joseph Haydn's Early Ensemble Divertimenti', in Cliff Eisen (ed.), *Coll'astuzia, col giudizio: Essays in Honor of Neal Zaslaw* (Ann Arbor: Steglein Publishing, 2009), pp. 111–126. On the generic status of Mozart's string trio, see Laurenz Lütteken, 'Konversation als Spiel: Überlegungen zur Textur von Mozarts Divertimento KV 563', *Mozart-Jahrbuch 2001*, pp. 71–86. See also Veronica Giglberger, '"Man hört *drei* vernünftige Leute sich untereinander unterhalten": Beobachten zur Satztechnik im Divertimento KV 563', *Mozart-Jahrbuch 2001*, pp. 61–70.

[55] For the quotation, see Webster, 'Viennese Chamber Music in the Classical Period', p. 246. For discussion of the string-trio fragment K. Anh. 66 (written some time from late 1789 onwards) as 'a viable counterpart to the earlier completed trio ... [continuing] the path of exploring the manifold challenges of a trio score comprising three homogeneous yet distinct string parts', see Wolff, *Mozart at the Gateway to His Fortune*, pp. 181–184.

[56] MBA, vol. 4, pp. 83, 105; LMF, pp. 923, 937.

While Mozart's 'pieces' depart from the four-movement model, they are certainly no lighter than their string quartet and quintet counterparts, as implied in Koch's definition of divertimento,[57] and evidence the kinds of instrumental effects and expressive and technical virtuosity characteristic of Mozart's publicly orientated Viennese concertos and symphonies. In the latter stages of the Andante, for example, the dynamic effect for the *minore* variation 3 – a *pp* in all instruments sustained from beginning to end – gives way first to a buoyantly virtuosic, *forte* last variation in which violin, viola and cello each receive demisemiquaver passages, and then to new *mfp* inflections coordinated with a statement of the main theme that ends with a return to the *minore*'s *pp* for the final chords.[58] Brilliance in the outer movements is matched by expressive virtuosity in the Adagio, especially in the expansive secondary theme (exposition) and main theme (recapitulation) where violin and cello respectively traverse almost three octaves in the space of four beats. And, as in the Andante, the Adagio ends with a delicate effect, namely the violin's syncopated, arpeggiated ascent to its registral highpoint of the movement, a-flat'''. Rather than 'making purely intimate what had been public [that is divertimento form]' in K. 563,[59] and accepting that private performances would have been envisaged above all, Mozart carefully moved 'intimate' chamber music towards the public realm.

Piano Chamber Music

Autographs and first editions of the piano chamber music, as for the string quartets and quintets, offer insight into performance concerns. It is not known whether Mozart examined performance copies of the piano trios K. 502, 542, 548 and the 'Kegelstatt' trio, K. 498 (all published by Artaria in 1788) and made additions and adjustments that subsequently found their way into the first edition. Given previous history with Artaria, including the 'Haydn' quartets and the Fantasia and Sonata in C minor K. 475 and K. 457, it is possible that differences between these sources – including

---

[57] Mozart's Salzburg divertimenti have varied numbers of movements: K. 113 in E-flat, K. 131 in D and K. 251 in D four, seven and six; those for wind ensemble K. 186, 166, 213, 240, 252, 188, 253, 270 between three and six each; and divertimenti for strings and wind K. 247 in F, K. 287 in B-flat and K. 334 in D seven, six and seven respectively.

[58] In the absence of an extant autograph for K. 563, dynamics cited are those from the first edition. See Mozart, *Gran trio per violino, viola, e basso* (Vienna: Artaria, 1792).

[59] See Rosen, *The Classical Style*, p. 281.

dynamics in K. 542 and K. 498 and phrase markings in the second and third movements of K. 502 – capture Mozart's intervention.[60] It is unlikely that the 'Kegelstatt' was written explicitly for publication, as no real market existed for a trio for piano, clarinet and viola; after an unexplained two-year gap post completion, Artaria published it in a version for violin, viola and piano.[61] In all likelihood K. 498 was first intended for a private performance among Franziska Jacquin (piano), Anton Stadler (clarinet), and Mozart (viola).[62] Two accompanied sonatas, K. 526 in A and K. 547 in F, had different fates. The former, published by Hoffmeister in 1787, embraces the kind of participatory parity Cramer associated with Mozart's first Viennese set in the *Magazin der Musik* (see Chapter 1): brilliant and expressive piano virtuosity in the run-up to the secondary theme of the first movement, for example, acts more as a conduit to the violin's delicately articulated thematic presentation than as a showcase for the piano. K. 547, labelled a 'little sonata for beginners with a violin' ('eine kleine Sonate für Anfänger mit einer Violin')[63] by Mozart himself, was presumably intended for teaching; the Vienna-based Mollo published it only in 1805.

The most noticeable performance issue in K. 502/i, the changing articulation of the main theme and its derivations, is communicated in the autograph (Example 10.6).[64] The primary and secondary themes in the exposition include slurs for the first-to-second and third-to-fourth notes of the head motif – in the piano right and left hands, violin and cello, both in one-bar motifs and as part of more extended thematic statements. After single slurs covering all four notes of the motto in the codetta and at the end of the development section (see bars 69–82, 112–117), Mozart changes approach in the recapitulation (bar 118ff.): single slurs for piano, violin and cello now rule the roost. By asking performers to play the main motto differently at different stages of the movement, Mozart invites them to take it on a journey towards greater breadth in the recapitulation than in the exposition – the strings playing it in a single bow-stroke rather than two, no longer slightly shortening

---

[60] Artaria published K. 502, 542 and 548 in November 1788. See *Tre sonate per il clavicembalo o forte-piano … composte dal Sigr W. A. Mozart* (Vienna: Artaria [1788]): https://iiif.lib.harvard.edu/manifests/view/drs:14786494$1i. As Ridgewell explains ('Mozart's Publishing Plans with Artaria', p. 48): 'It seems likely that Artaria received all three trios from the composer during the summer of 1788, although the possibility that K. 502 was acquired earlier cannot be ruled out.'

[61] Wolfgang Plath and Wolfgang Rehm consider it highly improbable that Mozart oversaw the publication of this particular Artaria edition; see NMA, VIII/22/2, Preface, p. 11.

[62] Colin Lawson, 'A Winning Strike: the Miracle of Mozart's "Kegelstatt"', in Harlow (ed.), *Mozart's Chamber Music with Keyboard*, pp. 123–137, at 124–125.

[63] See Mozart, *Werkverzeichnis*, fol. 17v.

[64] For autograph materials for the piano trios K. 502, 542 and 564, see Kraków, Biblioteka Jagiellonska: Mus. ms. autogr. W. A. Mozart 502.542.564.

Example 10.6 Mozart, Piano Trio in B-flat, K. 502/i, head motif of the main theme.

Main theme: beginning of the exposition

Main theme: beginning of the recapitulation

the second note or slightly accentuating the third as the end or beginning of a slur. Since slurs were seen to convey the character of a musical idea in the late eighteenth century,[65] Mozart's adjustment, which is applied consistently across the recapitulation, helps shape the overall character of the movement. If in fact performance copies of K. 502 were reviewed prior to the publication of the edition, the changed articulation of the motto may have provoked a revision of the *forte*, three-note join to the opening of the secondary development (bars 131–132, Examples 10.7a and 10.7b). The autograph slur in the violin is cancelled and the previously unarticulated cello receives three staccati: in the edition the *forte* coincides with detachment and accentuation as at the corresponding moment of the exposition (bars 16–17), rather than smooth (that is, slurred) continuity. Ultimately, articulation at the phrase-join in the edition contrasts with the now-slurred rendition of the motto, complementing the dynamic contrast put into effect by the two-beat *forte*.[66]

The autograph and Artaria edition of the first movement of the E-major piano trio, K. 542, differ markedly in the latter stages of the development section (Example 10.8). The violin has a *p* in the edition at bar 125, but no dynamic in the autograph, implying continuation of the *f* given in the previous bar as the climax to a crescendo.[67] Thus, the violin is aligned dynamically with the piano in the autograph, but directly opposed to it (and the cello) in the edition. An examination of dynamics elsewhere in the

---

[65] See Brown, *Performing Practice*, p. 145.

[66] Similarly, it is possible that two slurs early in the development section, lengthened in the edition relative to the autograph, also derive from a post-autograph re-contemplation by Mozart. Instead of preserving the autograph slurs in the piano right hand and violin in bars 94 and 97 respectively, new ones are projected over to the fifth quavers of each bar in the edition, lending slightly more emphasis to the sixth, seventh and eighth quavers as a pick-up effect to the onset of the next bar.

[67] The cello in the edition remains at a *forte* dynamic from bar 125 onwards, as in the autograph. Other important changes to the autograph in the edition include the omission of the lower-third C-sharps in the violin immediately before the secondary theme in the exposition of K. 542/i (bars 48–9).

Example 10.7a Mozart, Piano Trio in B-flat, K. 502/i, bars 131–132 (from the autograph).

Example 10.7b Mozart, Piano Trio in B-flat, K. 502/i, bars 131–132 (from the Artaria first edition).

movement offers a potential explanation for the adjustment. In the exposition, for example, *forte* surges are coordinated in the piano, violin and cello: three- and four-crotchet *fortes* culminate in a five-bar *forte* in the first theme; a four-bar *forte* spike is heard at the end of a transition that had been *piano* throughout; and, in the secondary theme, a *forte* coincides with the side-step to natural 6 and a crescendo to *forte* at the subsequent re-establishment of V/V.[68] The twelve-bar *forte* for the piano at the end of the development section is therefore by a considerable margin the longest in the movement. It is a passage of exceptional intensity too, relative to previous events: arpeggiated piano brilliance plunges to G-sharp minor and F-sharp minor (bars 128, 132), landing through sequential extension on E – without significant dominant preparation – for the beginning of the recapitulation

---

[68] The second movement is also characterized by short *forte* surges and, at the end of the B section before the first rondo return, by *sfps* in the piano right hand on the third semiquavers of each beat.

Example 10.8 Mozart, Piano Trio in E, K. 542/i, bars 122–140 (with the *p* from the Artaria edition in bold and square brackets).

(bar 136). The interpretative stakes are high, then, for the violinist in bars 124–135: at *forte* (in the autograph) they appear unambiguously complicit in the dynamic and harmonic intensity that captures a moment of stylistic audacity; at *piano* (in the edition) they are more subjugated by the piano than complicit in its bold move.[69] If piano and violin are at odds dynamically at the end of the development, then the *f* – *p*s at the opening of the recapitulation assume an air of reconciliation, bringing together opposed dynamics from the preceding passage. In short, revisiting the end of the development section at the 'proof' stage could have led Mozart to intensify instrumental interaction in response to harmonic and virtuosic effects.

An unusual primary source for the G-major piano trio, K. 564, autographed violin and cello parts written above and below piano parts in the hand of a copyist (probably Johann Traeg) but also with Mozart's additions and corrections, catches Mozart contemplating performance.[70] The composer seems to have included a large number of the piano's dynamic and articulation markings as annotations to the copyist's piano part in the autograph, rather than in material previously provided to the copyist. For example, the partial piano-only autograph of the first movement has no dynamics and only four slurs (two in bars 95 and for trills in 115 and 116); three are subsequently revised by Mozart in any case in the primary source combining the copyist's and Mozart's hands.[71] Performance markings in the first movement, then, were apparently left almost entirely to a late stage in the compositional process. (We cannot know whether Mozart provided many such markings before bar 95, of course, as the remainder of the piano-only autograph for the first movement is lost.) So, Mozart

---

[69] On the stylistic significance and resonance of this passage, see Keefe, *Mozart's Viennese Instrumental Music*, pp. 181–182.

[70] For this autograph see Kraków, Biblioteka Jagiellonska: Mus. ms. autogr. W.A. Mozart 502.542.564. Edge identifies Traeg as the copyist in 'Mozart's Viennese Copyists', p. 564. Further autograph material (Kraków, Biblioteka Jagiellonska: Mus. ms. autogr. W. A. Mozart 564) comprises a fragmentary piano part: bars 95–117 at the end of the first movement; bars 1–106 in the second; and bars 101–159 in the finale. (For a reproduction see NMA, VIII/22/2, Kritischer Bericht, pp. 86–88.) An edition of K. 564 came out with Stephen Storace in London in 1789 and one from Artaria in 1790, although the latter 'was not a simple pirated re-engraving of Storace, which leaves open the possibility of Mozart's direct involvement in its publication'. See Ridgewell, 'Mozart's Publishing Plans with Artaria', pp. 69–70 (quote on p. 70).

[71] It is unlikely that the copyist worked from the piano-only autograph, as considerable differences exist between the performance markings in the second and third movements of these two sources. Evaluating the unusual source situation, Hartmut Schick speculates that K. 564 originated as an accompanied sonata in 1788. See Schick, 'Originalkomposition oder Bearbeitung? Zur Quellenlage und musikalischen Faktur von Mozarts Klaviertrio KV 564', *Mozart-Jahrbuch 2001*, pp. 273–285.

presumably instructed the copyist to write down the piano part, leaving room for the other parts above and below the piano staves, and then wrote the violin and cello into the score while adding performance markings for the piano as well.

The performance of the first movement of the G-major trio came alive for Mozart when he contemplated the three instruments playing together, rather than at the earlier stage in the compositional process represented by the piano-only autograph: the vitality of an envisioned rendition leaps off the page. *Inter alia*, Mozart now indicates: a secondary theme played *dolce* by the violin and *p* in the piano and cello, giving the violin an opportunity to shine; an energized development section with *fortes* for brilliant semiquavers passed between piano and violin alternating with *piano* passages that carry more nuanced articulation (Example 10.9); and dynamics and articulation in the recapitulation different from corresponding moments in the exposition.[72] Mozart made a number of corrections to the piano part of the rondo finale, probably attributable to copyist errors, including quaver rests in bar 1 and on the upbeat to bar 96.

The autograph score of the five-part rondo middle movement of the B-flat trio, K. 502, sheds light on Mozart's engagement with players of the Artaria edition, including in the deletion of a first draft of the C section and opening of A".[73] Comprising violin and right-hand piano melodic material only, the draft was crossed out and replaced by the revised version; 36 bars supersede the rejected 58. Compositional considerations may have contributed to the dismissal of the original material, of course: two bars of diminished harmony containing (implicit) inflections to either E-flat or C minor are deemed undesirable (rejected bars 20 and 28); and the original end of C, merging into A", complete with a six-bar dominant preparation and an eight-bar piano statement of the main theme repeated by the violin, may have been regarded as *de trop* (Example 10.10). But Mozart's players purchasing the edition were probably also on his mind when revisions were made. For the second half of the rejected material (Example 10.10) contains a much greater quantity of virtuosic elaboration than its shorter revision, including four bars of scalar piano demisemiquavers across two and a half octaves in the run-up to the reprise, and

---

[72] On the last point: bar 78 has no *p* for the piano main theme (see bar 1) and bar 83 no slur in the piano right hand (see bar 6); and bars 94–95 in the piano right hand have different articulation to bars 17–18.

[73] The deletion occurs on pages 6v, 9r and 9v of the autograph, which are grouped together in the manuscript foliation. See NMA, VI/22/2, *Kritischer Bericht*, pp. 49, 57.

Example 10.9 Mozart, Piano Trio in G, K. 564/i, bars 49–61 (where the piano part is in a copyist's hand in the autograph and dynamics for the piano along with all material for violin and cello were written in by Mozart).

heavily elaborated eight-bar statements of the main theme in the piano and violin. Mozart could have concluded that such material unduly taxed the expressive and technical capabilities of his intended purchasers. Equally, the concerto-chamber balance often cited as characteristic

Example 10.10 Mozart, Piano Trio in B-flat, K. 502/ii, second half of rejected passage (section C – A").

of the piano trios[74] might have been upset, in Mozart's view, by excessive technical virtuosity for the solo performer (especially given the brilliant writing in the finale). The final version of the end of C and beginning of A" contains the most protracted elaborations in the movement, but stops considerably short of the material given at the corresponding points of the rejected passage.[75]

The autograph of the 'Kegelstatt' trio, K. 498, also shows piano virtuosity on Mozart's mind.[76] In the last rondo return of the finale, his initial inclination was to proceed straight from the first statement of the theme (clarinet) to the second statement (piano; Example 10.11), as he had at the beginning of the movement. He then decided to add a nine-bar passage between the two (bars 176–184 inclusive, Example 10.12) written on a new sheet of paper, a symbol above the staves at the appointed place in the main body of the autograph and at the beginning of the interpolated bars ensuring accommodation of the new material when the score was copied.[77] The new passage stands out in the finale: it is the most technically brilliant for the piano thus far, with jagged leaps, arpeggios and quick shifts in register; and it contains the only *sf* markings in the whole work (for clarinet and viola as well as piano). As a new effect, then, it draws attention to the piano's solo proficiency. From the piano part, especially in the rondo sections, it

---

[74] See Abert, *W. A. Mozart*, p. 991; Neal Zaslaw and William Cowdery (eds.), *The Compleat Mozart* (New York: Norton, 1990), p. 282. On connections between Mozart's piano trios and concerto and chamber genres, see Keefe, *Mozart's Viennese Instrumental Music*, pp. 168–169, 177–182. A balance between chamber and concerto qualities also characterizes the Artaria edition of the Piano Quartet in E-flat, K. 493 (written 1786, published 1787). (No autograph of K. 493 is extant.) On the combination of these qualities in the first movement and finale in particular, see Simon P. Keefe, 'On Instrumental Sounds, Roles, Genres and Performances: Mozart's Piano Quartets K. 478 and K. 493', in Martin Harlow (ed.), *Mozart's Chamber Music with Keyboard* (Cambridge: Cambridge University Press, 2012), pp. 154–181, at 169–174, 178–179.

[75] Mozart also rejected a first version of the finale of K. 542, perhaps as a result of the considerable technical demands it would have made on an amateur pianist. While no tempo is provided for the 6/8, sixty-five-bar fragment, the profusion of piano semiquavers at a self-evidently brisk tempo is noticeable.

[76] For the autograph, see Paris, Bibliothèque nationale de France, Département de la musique, Malherbe Collection, MS. 222.

[77] It is unclear when Mozart wrote the additional passage, relative to the remainder of the movement. It is possible he got to the end (which coincides with the last system of a page) and then decided to make the addition, realizing he could use 10 recto. Or he may have anticipated requiring the remainder of a sheet (9 recto and 9 verso) to complete the work and added the new nine bars at some stage before completing the movement. The similar ink colour and handwriting of the added passage and the material from bar 185 onwards make it unlikely that Mozart wrote the former significantly later than the latter (such as for publication in the violin, viola and piano version by Artaria in 1788).

Example 10.11 Mozart, Piano Trio in E-flat ('Kegelstatt'), K. 498/iii, bars 168ff. (original version of final reprise).

Example 10.12 Mozart, Piano Trio in E-flat ('Kegelstatt'), K. 498/iii, bars 176–184 (interpolation to the final reprise).

appears Mozart thought carefully about the notation of brilliant virtuosity, perhaps all the more because at least initially he would not have been playing the part himself. The piano's first statement at the beginning of the movement, for example, features mild decoration of the original clarinet statement, including a turn and some additional semiquavers; at the middle return between the C-minor and A-flat episodes, triplet quavers in the piano provide a virtuosic backdrop to the viola's thematic rendition. The added nine bars increase the virtuosic component, and complement the scalar and arpeggiated semiquavers in the remainder of the movement. While the technical brilliance of K. 498/iii does not match a piano concerto, it builds to a climax at the end of the movement, Mozart no doubt recognizing the needs and capabilities of a pupil (Franziska Jacquin) who showed unrivalled diligence and zeal.[78]

The *sf* markings in the passage added to the 'Kegelstatt' finale are typical of attention paid to piano sounds and effects in the work, as is apparent from small revisions to the autograph. The register at which the piano plays imitated material at formal junctures is a focal point: the main mottos at the end of the exposition in the first movement (bar 47) and at the beginning of the trio's reprise (bars 72–73), for example, were originally envisaged an octave higher and lower respectively. Other effects at important moments were also revised: the lead-back to the central reprise in the finale (see bars 103–104) was originally conceived with two crotchet rests on the second and third beats (then only on the second beat), before the final, more resonant version; and the left-hand approach to the A-flat major cadence early in the recapitulation of the first movement (bars 87–88) – coinciding with harmonic departure from the pattern of the exposition – was originally given as quaver – quaver rest – quaver rest for each bar before the dotted crotchets were written. Thus, the refined sounds and textures of the 'Kegelstatt', ably captured by Colin Lawson among others,[79] are glimpsed taking shape in the autograph manuscript.

The Piano Music

There are considerably fewer extant autographs of the solo piano music from the last years of Mozart's life than the string chamber music and

---

[78] See Mozart's comment on Jacquin in MBA, vol. 4, p. 11; LMF, p. 904 (15 Jan 1787).
[79] See Lawson, 'A Winning Strike'.

piano chamber music: the only survivors from the final four solo piano sonatas, for example, are the first movement of K. 570 in B-flat (from bar 65 onwards) and the finale of K. 533 in F (in its earlier form as the rondo, K. 494, not the expanded version for the published sonata). The reasons for composing three of them are not entirely clear: while K. 533 appeared with Hoffmeister in 1788, carrying a dedication to Mozart's new imperial employer Joseph II, K. 545 in C, K. 570 and K. 576 in D were published only posthumously in 1805, 1796 and 1805.[80] A didactic intention presumably lies behind K. 545, Mozart labelling it 'für Anfänger' (for beginners) in his *Verzeichnüß*. But the same does not necessarily apply to the other two sonatas.[81] Autographs of the piano variations K. 500 and K. 573, the gigue K. 574 and the minuet K. 355 are also missing, although they survive for works such as the Rondo in A minor, K. 511, the Adagio in B minor, K. 540, the piano four-hand sonatas K. 497 in F and K. 521 in C and variations K. 501 in G. While the Rondo K. 485 (1786) and variations K. 500 are commonly linked to Hoffmeister's subscription series, the association is unproven as extant copies of the editions have not been located.[82]

Irrespective of the source situation, it is useful to start from the perspective that Mozart's piano works from the late 1780s 'celebrate the absence of separation between a creative act of composition and a creative act of performance'.[83] As earlier in the decade, Mozart promotes improvisatory, fantasia-like qualities where performance and composition intersect. The performer-composer's skills are thereby modelled to listeners, students, and players.

Mozart may have improvised the famous Rondo in A minor, K. 511 (1787) during his trip to Prague in January to February 1787 to witness

---

[80] Christoph Wolff has suggested that Mozart, in a rush to prepare a sonata for the Emperor (K. 533 + 494), encountered problems with the finale, rejected a first attempt (K. Anh. 30) and replaced it with a revised version of K. 494 instead. See Wolff, 'Musikalische "Gedankenfolge" und "Einheit des Stoffes." Zu Mozarts Klaviersonate in F-Dur (K. 533 + 494)', in Hermann Danuser, Helga de la Motte-Haber, Silke Leopold and Norbert Miller (eds.), *Das musikalische Kunstwerk: Geschichte, Ästhetik, Theorie: Festschrift Carl Dahlhaus zum 60. Geburtstag* (Laaber: Laaber-Verlag, 1988), pp. 241–255.

[81] On uncertainties surrounding K. 576, see Irving, *Mozart's Piano Sonatas*, p. 88.

[82] Ridgewell, 'Biographical Myth and the Publication of Mozart's Piano Quartets', pp. 66–7. He suggests a private commission for K. 485 instead, on account of the incomplete words 'Pour Mad: Charlotte de Wü[. . .]' on the autograph. Artaria published K. 485 and K. 500 in 1792 and 1793 respectively.

[83] Irving, *Understanding Mozart's Piano Sonatas*, p. 5. Irving's comment refers only to the piano sonatas, but applies more generally to Mozart's solo piano music.

the success of *Figaro*,[84] or else at his recently discovered Viennese Academy on 28 February 1787 (see Chapter 11) twelve days before entering it into the *Verzeichnüß*. The neat, clean autograph, almost entirely free of corrections, could be a fair copy from another, now-lost source.[85] Embellishments and numerous dynamics written into the main body of the autograph, along with a comparable number of dynamics in the autograph of the Adagio in B minor, K. 540 (1788), could be explained by the extremely fast turn-around of editions in Hoffmeister's subscription series, and Mozart's consequent need thoroughly to mark up the autograph.[86]

K. 511 models the kinds of embellishments Mozart himself would have carried out as performer-composer (even if mediated by his perception of the capabilities of amateur players purchasing the edition) and both K. 511 and K. 540 highlight the creativity required of the player. Embellishments of the main theme of K. 511 become progressively more elaborate as the piece unfolds, culminating in the final rondo section (bar 129ff.). Gestures and passages conveying an improvisatory impression also gather a head of steam. In the middle of the B section, a surprising side-step to D-flat when re-confirmation of the section's F-major tonality is expected, leads to drifting arpeggios and diminished harmonies in the second halves of bars (46–48); similar material towards the end of the same section reinforces the impressionistic mood through a sequence of diminished triads (bar 72). In C and A", harmonization of descending and ascending chromatic lines also draws attention to the wandering performer, invoking a kind of fantasia-like stream of consciousness. Even though brought fairly quickly into line, the player comes across as a creator of effects not merely a reproducer of them. And the same applies to the Adagio K. 540. The six bars comprising the first theme require three types of dynamic contrast and inflection in quick succession, *sf – p, f – p* and *mf – p* (Example 10.13); form-defining *forte* chords appearing on several occasions in the piece also stand out against surrounding *piano* material. The absence of notated dynamic fluctuations in the broad concluding theme of the exposition and recapitulation (bars 15–21, 45–51) and in the coda (52–57) requires a different kind of expressive playing. By following Mozart's markings, and using them to stimulate an interpretation of the piece, the purchaser and

---

[84] Mozart, *Rondo a-Moll KV511: Edition, Faksimile*, ed. Ulrich Leisinger (Vienna: Schott/Universal Edition, 2006), 'Preface'.

[85] See the facsimile of the autograph in Mozart, *Rondo a-Moll KV511*.

[86] The Adagio K. 540 has been widely proposed as an edition in Hoffmeister's series, although no copy is extant. Artaria published it in 1794.

Example 10.13 Mozart, Adagio in B minor, K. 540, bars 1–7.

performer of the (putative) Hoffmeister edition would have gained a practical understanding of the expressive power, flexibility and potential of the late-eighteenth-century fortepiano.

Two sets of piano variations, K. 500 (12 September 1786) and K. 573 (29 April 1789) may also have originated as improvisations, in keeping with Mozart's standard practice in this genre (see Chapter 1). A series of complementary variations in K. 500, including fantasia-like activities towards the end, point to a possible pedagogical function for the piece and to a modelling of spontaneous improvisation as a catalyst for creative activity, in the latter case at least to an extent Mozart considered possible in compiling a musical text for amateurs. The performer needs to demonstrate technical proficiency in various ways in the first nine variations: triplet quavers then semiquavers are transferred from right hand to left in variations 1–4; and brilliantly and expressively virtuosic variations alternate in 5–7, reversing the pattern in 8 and 9. A decorative adagio in 11 is framed by brilliant variations that culminate in *ad libitum* flourishes. Mozart lays a foundation for imaginative interpretation from his players at the ends of variations 10 and 12: after progressively widening the registral range across the former he takes the pianist from the bottom to the top of the fortepiano, encouraging both a rhythmically free rendition of the final bars and one that summarizes preceding events; and following insistent exploration of neighbour-note figures in the latter, he invites recognition of their liquidation as a trill at the end of the variation.

The piano variations K. 573, on a theme by the outstanding cellist Jean-Pierre Duport whose secure finger- and bow-work were 'indescribable' (*unbeschreiblich*) according to Johann Friedrich Reichardt, probably arose opportunistically, representing a clever pitch both to the recipient and the recipient's patron.[87] Before deciding whether to receive Mozart in Potsdam in 1789, the King of Prussia wanted Mozart to meet his director of chamber music and cello teacher, Duport.[88] By setting a minuet from Duport's cello sonata Op. 4, No. 6 – an unusual choice for Mozart variations in the 1780s[89] – Mozart no doubt hoped K. 573 would do double duty, flattering Duport and providing material familiar to the cello-playing king to impress him in the desired audience.[90] Nor is it perhaps coincidental that at least one of Duport's other D-major cello sonatas, dedicated to the Prince de Conty probably in the 1760s, contains a minuet-variations movement.[91] As in the Viennese academy on 23 March 1783, when Mozart played the Gluck variations that would ultimately become K. 455 with Gluck in the audience, piano variations were designed to bond Mozart with influential individuals through renditions as performer-composer.

---

[87] There is uncertainty about whether variations 7–9 are by Mozart. See Konrad, *Catalogue of His Works*, p. 151. (Mozart described K. 573 as '6 Variazionen auf das Klavier allein' in his thematic catalogue; see Mozart, *Werkverzeichnis*, fol. 20v.) For Reichardt's laudatory appraisal of Duport's cello playing, see *Briefe eines aufmerksamen Reisenden die Musik betreffend* (Frankfurt and Leipzig, 1774), vol. 1, pp. 177–178.

[88] Mozart's request for an audience with the King of Prussia, summarized for the king by his cabinet, includes the king's instruction (in a margin) for Duport to handle the matter. See MDL, p. 298; MDB, p. 340. An obituary for Duport reports him having assumed the role of director of chamber music for the king in 1787. See *Allgemeine musikalische Zeitung*, 21 (1819), pp. 108–109.

[89] See Sisman, *Haydn and the Classical Variation*, p. 198.

[90] Deutsch reports Duport's Op. 4, No. 6 as a 'favourite piece of the king's', but provides no supporting evidence. MDL, p. 298; MDB, p. 340. For Braunbehrens (*Mozart in Vienna*, p. 328) 'omniscient legend tells us [Duport's minuet] was the king's favorite piece'.

[91] See Sonata IV in Jean-Pierre Duport, *Six sonates pour le violoncelle ou violon et basse dédiées à son altesse Sérénissime Monseigneur Le Prince de Conty* (Paris, no date). According to the *Allgemeine musikalische Zeitung* obituary, Duport was employed at the court of Prince Conty between 1761 and 1769 before moving to England.

Fantasia-like qualities in the piano variations and the Rondo K. 511 are also found in the late piano sonatas. As discussed in Chapters 1 and 5, Mozart coupled a fantasy-like prelude with a fugue, K. 394, and published a fantasia, K. 475 in C minor, with a sonata. While fantasia features in individual movements of sonatas should come as no surprise then, implications for performance and ontological status need to be considered.

In the slow movements of the piano sonatas K. 533 in F and K. 576 in D, strange harmonic, thematic, gestural and ornamental effects conspire to create a fantasy-like aura. The secondary theme section in K. 533/ii sets the scene (Example 10.14): exposed neighbour-note semiquavers obscure rather than support the left hand (bars 23–27); dreamily improvisatory harmonies coincide with falling arpeggios (diminished – E-flat minor – diminished, bars 28–30); and stop-start triplet semiquavers suggest ruminative contemplation. In the development, increasingly unusual combinations of the head motif and semiquaver triplets lead to a *tour de force* of disorientation, where chromaticism repeatedly obfuscates harmonic direction (Example 10.15).[92] It is as if the performer wanders off of his or her own accord, stumbling ultimately on the V/F that offers a route back to the tonic for the reprise. Even then, the sweeping dominant 7th arpeggiated gesture that ends the development – across more than four octaves from the top to the bottom of the fortepiano – creates a discontinuous rather than continuous join between formal sections (Example 10.15). Indeed, both the progression from the first half of the development to the second (bars 59–60) and the end of the section to the beginning of the recapitulation cultivate the kind of thematic and structural 'haphazardness' witnessed in Mozart's earlier Viennese fantasias. Similar unpredictability characterizes the long, meandering middle section of K. 576/ii, which features a poignant F-sharp-minor theme – a rare key for Mozart – and eight bars of demisemiquaver runs that culminate in a (surprising) return to the same F-sharp-minor theme, not unlike the sequence of events that produces repeated statements of the adagio theme in the D-minor fantasia, K. 397. Whether intending his sonatas primarily for teaching, publication or performance (or a combination thereof), Mozart promoted the role of creative keyboard player by drawing connections with the fantasia and encouraging decisions that would affect how the sequences of musical events are processed and understood by listeners. Neither the first edition of K. 533 nor K. 576 carries any dynamics in the second movement: if this is

---

[92] See Keefe, 'Mozart's Late Piano Sonatas', pp. 73–74 for a description of this process.

Example 10.14 Mozart, Piano Sonata in F, K. 533/ii, bars 23–35.

Example 10.15 Mozart, Piano Sonata in F, K. 533/ii, bars 63–74.

indeed a faithful reflection of Mozart's intentions, he charged players with interpretative responsibility in this area too.[93]

Readying K. 533 for publication with Hoffmeister in 1788 involved Mozart adding a twenty-seven-bar cadenza-like episode to the Rondo

---

[93] Needless to say, Mozart may have planned to wait until the publication process was confirmed, or had begun, before adding dynamics to K. 576 – on the autograph itself, or on a performance copy generated from it. In the end, the sonata was published only in 1805.

K. 494 (bars 143–169, Example 10.16).[94] The interpolated passage enhances the gravitas of the movement, and in a general way, then, may render K. 533/iii a more appropriate successor to K. 533/i and K. 533/ii than the original K. 494 would have been.[95] But a cadenza-like addition, shining a light on the creative skills of the performer, necessitates a more detailed explanation. Incorporating the new material into the published version of the sonata does not mean that Mozart thought exclusively, or even primarily, in abstract compositional terms about it balancing music elsewhere in the work. It could be argued – if timbre is accorded privilege – that the low register featured at the start of the contrapuntal portion of the interpolation is at least as much a preparation for the low ending to the work as the counterpoint itself is a reference back to the events of the first movement. In the absence of cadenza rhetoric at the beginning of the passage, such as a tonic 6/4 and pause, the passage's principal identity emerges only gradually. The repeat of bar 143 in 147 and the extension of the semiquaver figure from 147 into 148 and 149 are early clues. But the definitive sign is the capricious breaking off of the ascending arpeggio in bar 151 on f''' followed by a restart with contrasting material. The ensuing strict imitation, a perceived reference to the counterpoint of the opening Allegro,[96] is actually quite unlike activity in the first movement, in spite of a stretto status to complement bars 49, 133, 176: it is ostentatiously strict and regular, with entries two beats apart moving relentlessly upwards for six bars to reach the exact note (f''') vacated by the right hand immediately before the start of the passage. Bringing the performer's participation into our field of vision highlights a deeper affinity with the first movement. For the strict counterpoint is seamlessly unshackled after reaching its registral apotheosis, drawing attention to a player speeding towards the concluding cadential trill through embellishments and semiquaver runs. A similar progression characterizes parts of the first movement (again in the build up to a cadential trill). The secondary theme section in both the exposition and recapitulation, for example, traces a path from counterpoint (mixed with brilliant virtuosity) to brilliance: imitation early in the section is followed by a four-bar phrase passed from right hand to left that

---

[94] The autograph of the earlier version of the Rondo K. 494 (1786) is preserved, but not the later version comprising the finale of K. 533.

[95] For compositional explanations for the addition of this passage in the published finale see Irving, *Mozart's Piano Sonatas*, p. 85 and *Understanding Mozart's Piano Sonatas*, p. 84. See also Wolff, 'Musikalische "Gedankenfolge" und "Einheit des Stoffes"'.

[96] Irving, *Mozart's Piano Sonatas*, p. 85.

Example 10.16 Mozart, Piano Sonata in F, K. 533/iii, bars 142–171.

merges into quick-fire imitation, and dissolves into right-hand ruminations, triplet-quaver then semiquaver brilliance and finally a cadential
trill, with arpeggiated figuration subsequently ruling the roost until the
end of the section (see bars 66–102; 193–239).[97] Thus, in both the interpolation to the finale and in the first movement, a move from compositional
strictures to free-flowing, apparently imaginative embellishment and brilliance illuminates intersections between composition and performance and
best explains the function and meaning of the finale's interpolated passage in
the context of the published sonata as a whole.

The physical, tactile dimension of performance – two musicians sitting
at the same instrument – distinguishes Mozart's four-hand keyboard
works from those for solo player. In 1777, Charles Burney acknowledged
the pragmatic advantage of four-hand over two-keyboard works for
performance purposes: 'The inconvenience of having two harpsichords
or pianofortes in the same room has prevented the cultivation of this
species of [two-keyboard] music. The playing of duets by two performers
upon one instrument is, however, attended with nearly as many advan-
tages without the inconvenience of crowding a room, and although at first
the near approach of the hands of the different players may seem awkward or embarrassing, a little use and contrivance with respect to the
manner of placing them, and the choice of fingers, will soon remove that
difficulty.'[98] And the popularity of the keyboard duet is reflected in
Mozart writing and quickly publishing with both Artaria and
Hoffmeister three works in 1786–1787: the sonatas K. 497 in F and K.
521 in C; and the Andante with five variations in G, K. 501. He also wrote
98 bars of an Allegro in G major for keyboard duet, K. 357, in 1787–1788,
leaving it unfinished.[99]

Burney's implicit call for considerate behaviour from the two players
finds a parallel in the musical sociability nurtured by Mozart at the outset
of the first of the three completed works, K. 497. With the exception of the
two crotchets in bar 2, a single performer could comfortably play the first
seven bars of the slow introduction (Example 10.17). Self-evidently, the
dynamics in these bars could be rendered more straightforwardly by one

---

[97] Also, in the F-minor episode of K. 494, composed in 1786 before the first and second
movements of K. 533, contrapuntal ruminations give way to a quasi improvisational transition
back to the rondo theme (see bars 116–119).

[98] Quoted in Ernest Lubin, *The Piano Duet: A Guide for Pianists* (New York: Da Capo, 1976),
pp. 9–10.

[99] For K. 357 see NMA, X/30/4, pp. 156–157, and Konrad, *Catalogue of His Works*, pp. 194–195. A
160-bar Andante fragment for keyboard duet was also written in 1791; see NMA, X/30/4,
pp. 202–204, and Konrad, *Catalogue of His Works*, pp. 200–201.

Example 10.17 Mozart, Sonata for Piano Four Hands in F, K. 497, bars 1–7.

player than two, without the discussion, agreement and (at the very least) sensitivity to a partner's performance required from two together.[100] So, Mozart's division of material at the opening makes a statement to the players, requiring them to negotiate all of the dynamic nuances: the manner in which the music is played (by two pianists in close collaboration) is part of its meaning. In this respect, and in spite of probably being written for publication rather than Mozart's own performance,[101] the four-hand sonata is similar to the sonata for two pianos, K. 448 (1781): here the aural and visual element of Auernhammer and Mozart playing together involves passages split between the two of them that could easily have been played by just one (see Chapter 1). Mozart then goes on in K. 497's slow introduction to provide effects enriched by two players at the keyboard, inviting them to exploit the performance situation and its sonic possibilities: for example, the warm modulations of bars 13–24 – principally to C minor, B-flat minor and A-flat major – coincide with simultaneous exposure of the top and bottom of the fortepiano register.

Works for Wind and Strings

Several chamber works from the late 1780s were intended primarily for performances and probably not envisaged as good prospects for publication:

---

[100] Abert identifies the dynamics in the introduction to K. 497/i as 'striking' (*W. A. Mozart*, p. 968), albeit without drawing attention to the four-hand context.

[101] Gutman (*Cultural Biography*, p. 669) suggests a possible link to the Jacquin circle for K. 497 (as for the Four-Hand Sonata K. 521).

the flute quartet, K. 298 (1786 or 1787), 12 duos for two horns, K. 487 (27 July 1786), 'Ein musikalischer Spass', K. 522 (14 June 1787), and the clarinet quintet, K. 581 (29 September 1789) appeared in print more than a decade after Mozart's death.[102] Two performances of K. 581, '[Anton] Stadler's quintet' according to Mozart, are documented soon after completion, at the Tonkünstler-Societät concert on 22 December 1789 and at the Hungarian Count Hadik's Viennese residence probably on 9 April 1790.[103] But none are recorded for the flute quartet, horn duos or 'Musikalischer Spass'. Perhaps intended for private consumption and associated with the Jacquin family, the flute quartet draws on pre-existing themes by Hoffmeister and Paisiello and from French folk music, fuelling the idea of it as a gentle parody of contemporary quartets based on popular airs.[104] Mozart wrote the horn duos while playing skittles; the annotation 'untern Kegelscheiben' appears in his hand on the autograph manuscript.[105] The players and occasion for which they were written are unknown: Joseph Leutgeb and Karl and Johann Türrschmidt are contenders as performers; and a skittles party frequented by highly skilled horn players, who would have been needed for such challenging pieces, is a possibility for the premiere.[106] 'Ein musikalischer Spass' was begun before 1787 and composed over a protracted period: the first movement had been written out in parts by the end of 1786, no doubt with a performance in mind, but the finale was conceived only in the second quarter of 1787 at the earliest.[107] The occasion for which Mozart wrote his famous serenade 'Eine kleine Nachtmusik', K. 525, is unknown. Finished on 10 August 1787 it could have been premiered at an evening event in Vienna in the summer of that year, or even at an event in Prague (to which Mozart was

---

[102] These works were first published by Traeg (flute quartet, 1808), Bureau d'Arts and d'Industrie (horn duos, 1802–1803), André ('Ein musikalischer Spass', 1802) and Artaria (clarinet quintet, 1802). K. 298 may have been the Mozart flute quartet advertised in manuscript copy by Traeg in October 1787 (MDL, p. 265; MDB, pp. 300–301), although Mozart's earlier flute quartets, K. 285 and K. 285a, cannot be ruled out. It is unclear whether Mozart intended 'Ein musikalischer Spass' for one or multiple string players on each part.

[103] See MDL, pp. 315, 321; MDB, pp. 358, 365. For Mozart's reference to 'Stadler's quintet' in the context of the performance at Hadik's, see MBA, vol. 4, p. 105; LMF, p. 937 (on or before 8 April 1790). The *Verzeichnüß* date of 29 September 1789 for the clarinet quintet makes it unlikely that the work was written specifically for the Tonkünstler-Societät concert. See Edge, 'Mozart's Reception in Vienna, 1787–1791', pp. 86–87; and Black, 'Mozart's Association with the Tonkünstler-Societät', pp. 69–70.

[104] This idea originates in Einstein, *Mozart: His Character, His Work*, pp. 262–263.

[105] See the facsimile of the three surviving autograph duos, nos. 1, 3 and 6 in NMA, Preface, viii/21, pp. xxii–xxiv.

[106] NMA, viii/21, Preface, pp. xii.

[107] Tyson, 'Notes on the Genesis of Mozart's "Ein musikalischer Spass", K. 522', in *Mozart: Studies of the Autograph Scores*, pp. 234–245, at 241–245.

soon to travel for the premiere of *Don Giovanni*). It is also uncertain whether an orchestral or a one-to-a-part performance was intended: while the designation 'bassi' for the bass line implies an orchestral rendition, Mozart also wrote 'viola' (singular) rather than 'viole' (plural).[108] Five movements are listed in the *Verzeichnüß*; a minuet and trio between the extant first and second movements has not survived.

Performers of the horn duos K. 487, as well as meeting the demands of semiquaver brilliance and ascents to a high tessitura (with a peak on written g′′′), have to adroitly handle timbral issues, paying close attention to the blend of open and hand-stopped notes. For example, written f-sharp′′ and a′′, problematic notes for the natural horn,[109] feature in the semiquaver approach to the end of the first half of duo no. 1 in the first horn set against (conceivably strident) open-note c′′s and d′′s in the second horn. Timbral practicalities have to be contemplated and managed: downward-resolving appogiaturas in no. 2 first put a tricky f-sharp′′ against a three-quarter-stopped e-flat′′ resolving to d′′ and c′′ open-note crotchets, then an e-flat′′ against an open-note c′′ resolving to half-stopped b′ and a′ crotchets (bars 13, 27); and f-sharp′′ – g and c′′ – b′ quavers in no. 4 (bar 13) situate open notes on different, potentially conflicting beats of the bar. The two players together can convey a kind of timbral virtuosity, including when jointly covering a three-octave range in the space of three beats (no. 3, g′′′ – g, bars 19–20).

Alongside their string counterparts, the natural horn players in 'Ein musikalischer Spass' ('Musical Joke') would have been attentive above all to the kind of participation necessary for conveying a parody of inept composition and performance. As has been pointed out, Mozart would have had to insist on 'unconditional obedience' to his notated text, asking players to resist the temptation to attribute errant notes and dynamics to copying errors.[110] Whether poor composition or poor performance is sent up at a particular moment is often fairly obvious. The uninspired material treated uninspiringly in the first movement, the tonal meandering of the development section of the Adagio and minor rather than major mode at the reprise (with a jolt back to the correct place a few bars later), and the stunted fugal writing in the finale all mimic compositional deficiencies. Equally, the bizarre *dolce* horn in the B section of the minuet, the marauding, self-absorbed violin in the cadenza of the slow movement,

---

[108] Küster, *Mozart: a Musical Biography*, p. 270; for speculation about A Prague performance of 'Eine kleine Nachtmusik', see Rushton, *Mozart*, p. 157.
[109] See Humphries, *The Early Horn*, p. 61.   [110] Küster, *Mozart: A Musical Biography*, p. 263.

and the implosion at the end of the finale, each of the strings playing in a different key, spoof bad performance.

Elsewhere, though, lines between objects of parody are less clearly drawn, in effect subjecting the performer-composer to ridicule.[111] The motley crew of barely coordinated instruments in the minuet and trio – with inelegantly combined rhythms, gratuitous *forte* dynamics, and a bizarre solo violin lead-in to the reprise of the trio – are creatively inept performers not a properly functioning unit. Similarly, the egregious violin cadenza in the Adagio is preceded by a somewhat subtler parody of over elaboration in the early part of the movement: triplet-semiquaver then demisemiquaver embellishments are superfluous for such unpromising material. As in the piano concertos, a change to the autograph may catch Mozart balancing compositional and performance-related considerations. He originally had the end of the first movement (see Example 10.18) comprise the first half of bar 77 followed by the last five bars of the final version realigned in metric position: he crossed out five bars written for the first violin only, thereby revealing that a shorter conclusion analogous to the end of the exposition was initially envisaged.[112] The subsequently incorporated coda, not the least inspired material of the movement, has the performers force a *fortissimo* climax and fall out of sync at the end, when the horn's repeated quavers counter the strings' acceptance that the thematic argument is already over. In a movement characterized more by compositional than performance-related inadequacies, Mozart slightly redresses the balance in his revision by highlighting the ineptitude of the players. Even in the unusual context of a 'musical joke', then, Mozart shines a light on the creative – or in this case creatively impotent – performer and performer-composer.

Unlike 'Ein musikalischer Spass', uncertainties surround the musical text for the Clarinet Quintet in A, K. 581, on account of unavailable sources and the relative rarity of the instrument for which it was written. The work's recipient, Anton Stadler, pioneered the basset clarinet, which extended the range of the standard late-eighteenth-century clarinet down four semitones from e to c. It is generally assumed (albeit unproven) that Mozart's original version of the work included these low notes. By 1800 Stadler had parted company with the

---

[111] In a similar vein, Küster proposes performer improvisation as a subject of parody in K. 522 (*Mozart: A Musical Biography*, p. 269). For the involvement of the listener in K. 522's humourous procedures, see Wheelock, *Haydn's Ingenious Jesting with Art*, pp. 6–10.

[112] For the eliminated bars see NMA vii/18, Kritische Berichte, p. 103.

Example 10.18 Mozart, 'Ein musikalischer Spass', K. 522/i, bars 74–88 (including two violin II parts, as in the autograph).

autograph previously in his possession, either pawning it or having had it stolen while on tour in Germany.[113] Thus, the Artaria and André editions from 1802, both for standard clarinet, were based on a copy or copies of the work, which themselves may have revised Mozart's basset notes to accommodate renditions by the standard clarinet.[114] We need to exercise caution, then, in discussing links between the composition and performance of the work as evidenced in all available editions, old and new alike.

Mozart's exact intentions for the text of the clarinet quintet may be difficult to determine, but he clearly wanted to exploit Stadler's varied skills and gifts, including a rich, full tone, versatility across the range of the instrument, and ability melodically to imitate the human voice.[115] To this end, Mozart explored different types of clarinet writing throughout the work, including long melodic lines in the Larghetto, impish arpeggios in Trio 2, and both protracted figurative brilliance (variation 4) and a fermata primed for embellishment (bar 89) in the finale. Timbral effects to be elicited from Stadler in collaboration with the strings also come to the fore. In the main theme and transition sections of the first movement, for example, the basset clarinet plays with different combinations of strings, culminating in a full-ensemble sonority in the immediate run-up to the secondary theme (bars 36–41, Example 10.19). The full sonority is subsequently developed in the secondary theme section (accepting doubts about the authenticity of performance markings in light of the source situation). After the introduction of a pizzicato cello, a new effect for the movement, the re-entry of the clarinet brings further refinement (Example 10.19): the first *pp* and *dolce* markings coincide with the first appearance of a minor key (E minor), the *dolce* instruction presumably intended to exploit the soft tone Stadler was known to have produced on the basset clarinet. This emollient effect paves the way for a first rendition of the main theme by

---

[113] Constanze is the source of this information. See MBA, vol. 4, p. 356 (31 May 1800). (Not LMF.)

[114] NMA viii/19/2, Kritische Berichte, p. 58.

[115] On Stadler's qualities see Chapter 4 and Pamela L. Poulin, 'Stadler family', in Eisen and Keefe (eds.), *Cambridge Mozart Encyclopedia*, p. 490. According to Colin Lawson (*The Early Clarinet*, p. 86): 'In recognising the strong operatic links with Mozart's clarinet music [including the quintet], the player should choose tempi for slower movements which are vocally conceived and therefore not too pedestrian.' Some of the diverse writing for clarinet in K. 581 also characterizes the ninety-three-bar clarinet quintet fragment, K. Anh. 91 (1789–1791). The fragment, which includes rich melodic lines, a sustained note and versatile semiquavers across the full range of the instrument, may have been written for basset clarinet, and thus for Anton Stadler. For the basset-clarinet possibility, see Tyson, *Autograph Scores*, pp. 341–342 and David Etheridge, *Mozart's Clarinet Concerto: the Clarinetist's View* (Gretna, Louisiana: Pelican, 1998), p. 20. For a facsimile, see NMA, X/30/4, pp. 176–177.

Example 10.19 Mozart, Clarinet Quintet in A, K. 581/i, bars 35–53.

the complete ensemble four bars into the development section and then again at the beginning of the recapitulation; the three-bar sustained g" (sounding e", bars 115–117) preparing for the clarinet's initial note of the reprise would have been another opportunity for Stadler to demonstrate a tone both full and soft.[116] Thus, as in the arias for Valentin Adamberger and Aloysia Lange from 1782–1786 (see Chapter 6), Mozart exploited the clarinettist's skills not only by writing material that evidenced 'the range of idioms' he could produce[117] but also by facilitating his creation of special colours in collaboration with fellow performers.

*****

The clarinet quintet is unusual among Mozart's solo and chamber repertories from 1786 to 1790 in being written for a concert (or concerts) featuring a specific player, rather than primarily for publication and performance by unknown purchasers and players. But intersections and continuities between composition and performance characterized all Mozart's solo and chamber music from this period, irrespective of reasons for writing individual works. While money may have been the ultimate motivation for producing so much solo and chamber music, concerns about money in no way compromised Mozart's intense commitment to complete musical experiences, manifest *inter alia* in the intertwining of compositional and performance-related priorities. At a financial low-point in August 1788, after four loan requests to Puchberg in June and July, Mozart was visited at home by Joachim Daniel Preisler, an actor and orchestral accompanist at the Theatre Royal, Copenhagen temporarily resident in Vienna. Preisler recorded the experience in his journal the following year:

There I had the happiest hour of music that has ever fallen to my lot. This small man and great master twice *extemporized* on a *pedal pianoforte*, so wonderfully! so wonderfully! that I quite lost myself. He intertwined the most difficult passages with the most lovely *themes*. – His wife cut quill-pens for the copyist, a pupil composed, a little boy aged four walked about in the garden and sang recitatives – in short, everything that surrounded this splendid man was *musical!*[118]

The performer-composer in full flow, with material simultaneously readied for dissemination enhancing the musical atmosphere, captures in

---

[116] For Stadler advertising the full sound and soft tone of his basset clarinet, see Albert R. Rice, *The Clarinet in the Classical Period* (New York: Oxford University Press, 2003), p. 72.

[117] Lawson, *Mozart: Clarinet Concerto*, p. 28.

[118] See the German translation from the original Danish in MDL, p. 285; English translation from MDB, p. 325.

microcosm the hectic, fluid and positive nature of Mozart's musical life in late 1780s Vienna, even at a troubled time (as typically parsed by biographers). Mozart had long benefitted from music's palliative effects, including during six of the most difficult months of his life in Paris, ten years earlier, where he had enthusiastically recalled the premiere of the 'Paris' Symphony in a letter written only an hour or two after his mother's death and professed to being 'stuck in music' just a few weeks later.[119] And perhaps the situation in the summer of 1788 was similar: the 'black thoughts' mentioned to Puchberg on 27 June from his new home in Alsergrund, banished only 'by force', coincided with ten days in which he had 'worked more than in two months in my other lodgings'.[120] Performing and composing was Mozart's lifeblood, whether in private or public, for publication or not, whether music written for himself and/or for others. It is to his concert activities in the late 1780s and orchestral works written for them, manifesting similar and different kinds of musical energy, that we shall now turn our attention.

[119] See Keefe, 'Mozart "Stuck in Music" in Paris', pp. 23–54.
[120] MBA, vol. 4, p. 69; LMF, p. 917 (27 June 1788).

11 | Orchestral Music and Concert Activities

Mozart produced considerably fewer orchestral works in the second half of his Viennese decade than the first half, no doubt attributable to his operatic commitments, but continued both to make an impressive number of concert appearances and to have orchestral pieces featured regularly in concerts by others.[1] He probably gave four Viennese concerts in Advent 1786, mentioned by Leopold in a letter to Nannerl.[2] Following his trip to Prague in early January to mid February 1787, at which he put on an academy (19 January), he promptly gave one at the Kärntnertortheater in Vienna on 28 February – contrary to widespread scholarly opinion conditioned by the lack of a poster or an advertisement in the *Wiener Zeitung*. As the *Bayreuther Zeitung* reported a few days later: 'Yesterday Mr Mozzart was permitted to give a musical academy for his benefit and had good receipts.'[3] He probably also played the solo piano part for 'Ch'io mi scordi di te' K. 505 at Nancy Storace's farewell concert on 23 February.[4] His music appeared in quick succession on the programmes of three further Viennese academies at the Kärntnertortheater: pianist Maximiliana Valentina Willmann performed one of his concertos in a concert with her siblings on 7 March 1787; oboist Friedrich Ramm included a symphony on 14 March; and singer Ludwig Fischer accommodated one or possibly two symphonies

---

[1] Listed below are only concerts at which Mozart performed in late 1786–1790 and those in which he can be assumed to have had either direct or indirect involvement. For performances of his symphonies in London in 1787–1789, see NMD, pp. 144–149. For discussion of Josepha Duschek's academy in Leipzig on 22 April 1788, at which she sang Mozart's concert aria 'A questo seno deh vieni . . . Or che il ciel a me ti rende', K. 374, see Chapter 1, and Woodfield, *Performing Operas for Mozart*, pp. 136–147. A performance of a Mozart piano concerto also took place at a benefit concert put on by Count Kolowrat in Prague on 30 March 1787 six weeks or so after Mozart left the city. The soloist, Count Franz Klebersberg, is said to have played nearly as well as Mozart himself. See *Oberdeutsche Staatszeitung*, 8 (3 May 1787), p. 350.

[2] See MBA, vol. 3, p. 618 (8 December 1786). (Not in LMF.) On the 'ill-founded' doubts about these concerts taking place, see Küster, *Musical Biography*, pp. 243–244.

[3] See *Bayreuther Zeitung* (12 March 1787), Anhang, p. 112. Given in Woodfield, *Cabals and Satires*, forthcoming. ('Herr Mozart durfte gestern eine musikalische Academie zu seinen Vortheil geben, und hatte eine gute Einnahme'.)

[4] MDL, p. 251; MDB, p. 285; NMD, p. 39.

on 21 March.[5] In 1788, Mozart probably performed at a Masonic musical academy on 12 January, played at a concert at the Venetian Ambassador's residence on 10 February alongside Stefano Mandini and Anna Morichelli and had one of his symphonies open Mandini's academy five days later.[6] On 26 February and 4 March he conducted C. P. E. Bach's *Die Auferstehung und Himmelfahrt Jesu* at Count Johann Esterházy's, with Aloysia Lange and Valentin Adamberger among the singers and an orchestra of eighty-six, having added flute, trumpet and oboe parts to the aria 'Ich folge dir';[7] he perhaps directed another performance at the Burgtheater on 7 March.[8] It is possible he performed a piano concerto (maybe the newly completed No. 26 in D, K. 537) in the interval as well.[9] He then conducted Handel's *Acis and Galatea* in November at Esterházy's, having re-orchestrated the work at Baron van Swieten's request (K. 566); it was performed again on 30 December at the same location.[10] In 1789 he directed Handel's *Messiah* in his own revised orchestration (K. 572) on 6 March and 7 April, leaving Vienna the very next day for a two-month visit to central and Northern Germany with Prince Lichnowsky.[11] Mozart's reasons for undertaking the tour and unusual back-and-forth trips between Dresden and Leipzig have provided opportunities for racy biographical speculation,[12] but

[5]   See NMD, pp. 48, 49, 50. The programme for the Fischer concert lists a Mozart symphony at the beginning and one at the end; whether the symphony at the end presented the finale to the first one, or was a different work entirely, is unclear.

[6]   David Black, 'Masonic Musical Academy in Vienna: 12 January 1788', in Dexter Edge and Black (eds.), *Mozart: New Documents*, first published 12 June 2014. http://dx.doi.org/10.7302/ Z20P0WXJ; MDB, p. 310; NMD, p. 51. Morrow admits the possibility that Paolo Mandini (tenor) was the singer in question for the academy on 15 February, rather than Stefano Mandini. See *Concert Life in Haydn's Vienna*, p. 438.

[7]   See Konrad, *Mozart: Catalogue of His Works* pp. 162–163, and NMA, X/28/Abt. 3–5, vol. 2, pp. 3–13. Mozart also may have conducted Handel's *Judas Maccabeus* in spring 1788; see *Auszug*, 7 (18 April 1788), as given in Edge and Black (eds.), 'Mozart conducts C.P.E. Bach's *Die Auferstehung* and Handel's *Judas Maccabeus*', *Mozart: New Documents*, http://dx.doi.org/ 10.7302/Z20P0WXJ, first published 23 February 2015.

[8]   MDL, p. 273; MDB, p. 311.   [9]   See Landon, *Mozart: the Golden Years*, p. 192.

[10]   MDL, p. 290; MDB, pp. 330, 331.

[11]   Around 1789–1790 Mozart also added trumpets and timpani parts to the outer movements of Viotti's E-minor violin concerto no. 16 G. 85 (K. 470a), although a performance potentially explaining the larger orchestration has yet to be identified. For more on K. 470a, see Manfred Hermann Schmid, 'Ein Violinkonzert von Viotti als Herausforderung für Mozart und Haydn', in *Mozart-Studien*, 5 (1995), pp. 149–171; and Warwick Lister, *'Amico': The Life of Giovanni Battista Viotti* (New York: Oxford University Press, 2009), p. 170.

[12]   Solomon (*Mozart: A Life*, p. 449) suggests that 'Mozart wanted to leave Vienna in the spring of 1789 to pursue some private agenda', which may have included an affair with the singer Josepha Duschek: 'The opacities, lies, coincidences, evasions, disappearances, and mysteries of the Berlin journey may yield to other explanations – a breakdown, a conflict about returning to Vienna, a momentary impulse to leave Constanze – although these may not be inconsistent

performances at least were numerous: in Dresden, a town with few equals in Germany for cleanliness, care and taste of buildings, and proportionate integration of city and suburbs according to Friedrich Schulz, Mozart gave a private concert with the organist Anton Teyber and nine-year-old cellist Anton Kraft on 13 April, played for the Elector the next day, in a duel with organist Johann Wilhelm Hässler a day later and at 'many noble and private houses' over the duration of his stay; and in Leipzig he gave private performances, an academy at the Gewandhaus on 12 May, and an impromptu rendition on the organ at the Thomaskirche.[13] It is widely believed that he performed at the Prussian court in Berlin in late May, although supporting documentary evidence has yet to emerge.[14] While he was away, at least one of his 'newest symphonies' was played 'really masterfully' (*recht meisterlich*) on the Hoher Markt in Vienna in honour of Vice-Mayor Johann Georg von Augusti's name-day.[15] In 1790, he played his string trio K. 563 and clarinet quintet K. 581 at Count Hadik's residence on 9 April, probably directed performances of his re-orchestrations of Handel's *Alexander's Feast* and *Ode for St. Cecilia's Day* (K. 591, K. 592) in the summer, gave academies at the Great Municipal Playhouse in Frankfurt in conjunction with coronation events for Leopold II and in Mainz (15, 20 October), and performed at the Electoral Palace in Munich at a concert on 4 or 5 November in honour of King Ferdinand IV of Naples and Sicily.[16]

Mozart identified an unfortunate mismatch between the artistic appreciation and financial results of two of the most important concerts from late 1786–1790, the academies in Leipzig and Frankfurt. 'On the applause

---

with a romantic adventure.' For similar speculation, see Piero Melograni, *Wolfgang Amadeus Mozart: A Biography*, trans. Lydia G. Cochrane (Chicago, IL: University of Chicago Press, 2007), pp. 215–219. Much of Solomon's argument is rebuffed in Bruce Alan Brown, 'In Defense of Josepha Duschek (and Mozart): Patronage, Friendship, and Evidence', in Libin (ed.), *Mozart in Prague*, pp. 155–174. Daniel Heartz (*Mozart, Haydn, Early Beethoven*, p. 224) speculates that Lichnowsky, not Mozart, may have been smitten with Duschek.

[13] See MDL, pp. 297–298, 305, 299–300; MDB, pp. 339, 347, 341–342; NMD, pp. 56, 59. Mozart also had his pieces for three basset-horns K. 439b performed by Anton David, Springer and Dworschak at an academy in Leipzig on 14 June, as evidenced by a handwritten concert programme. See Woodfield, *Performing Operas for Mozart*, pp. 150–151, 154. For more on the duel with Hässler and its possible implications for Mozart's academy in Leipzig, see Woodfield, *Performing Operas for Mozart*, pp. 156–159. For Schulz's comment on Dresden, see *Reise eines Liefländers*, vol. 3, p. 15.

[14] See Solomon, *Mozart: A Life*, pp. 442–443; Heartz, *Mozart, Haydn, Early Beethoven*, p. 223.

[15] David Black, 'A Name-Day Concert in Vienna with Mozart's "Newest Symphonies"', in Black and Edge (eds.), *Mozart: New Documents*, first published 12 June 2014. http://dx.doi.org/10.7302/Z20P0WXJ.

[16] MDL, pp. 321, 325, 329, 331, 333; MDB, p. 365, 370, 374, 376, 378. See also MBA, vol. 4, pp. 105, 118, 121; LMF, pp. 937 (on or before 8 April 1790, on the Hadik concert), 946 (15 October 1790, on the Frankfurt academy), 947–948 (before 4 November 1790, on the Munich performance).

and glory side', he wrote to Constanze from Leipzig, 'this was dazzling enough, but all the more meagre in the relevant earnings'.[17] Similarly, Frankfurt was 'marvellous in terms of glory, but a failure in regard to the meagre money.'[18] Others also detected a general disconnect between musical prowess and remuneration. For Franz Kratter (1787): 'But, Artistic Talent, what do you expect of your fatherland, where we fight to hear a few arias negligently sung at a bad academy by the arrogant foreigner Storace, who has a similarly big talent for art and impertinence, and your Mozart, this excellent artist, is not even paid enough for a good academy to be able to cover the expenses for it.'[19] Similarly, Kasimir Kunz's Vienna-based *Allmanach* (1789) remarked on Mozart's imperial appointment from December 1787: 'Herr Wolfgang Mozart has been taken into the actual service of His Majesty the Emperor with a handsome salary. All friends of music will certainly feel most profound pleasure at this promotion, this excellent musician having been underestimated for so long and not valued according to his merits.'[20] Mozart was not helped in Leipzig by the high price of admission to his academy and by a direct clash with a performance of *Figaro*.[21] As one biographer drily observed: 'Mozart discovered that he had entered into rivalry with himself.'[22] Equally, clashes could not be avoided in Frankfurt, a city busy with coronation-related activities and events, where one obstacle or another had presented itself on each day of his stay. On 15 October 1790 specifically a prince was giving 'a big dejeuner' and there was 'a grand manoeuvre of Hessian troops'.[23] Mozart's opportunities for and takings from concerts and other activities in the second half of the decade probably suffered from economic problems associated with the onset of the Turkish War in 1787; few in Vienna were immune to the ensuing heavy taxation, rapid inflation and tough new usury laws.[24] But, finances aside, Mozart the performer remained as popular as ever. In Dresden he was 'heard at the keyboard, so masterfully that he surpassed all who have been heard previously', possessing

---

[17] MBA, vol. 4, p. 86; LMF, p. 925 (16 May 1789). Carl August Grenser, in his *Geschichte der Musik* (1789), confirmed the 'extraordinary approbation' Mozart received. See Woodfield, *Performing Operas for Mozart*, p. 162. Mozart's liberal distribution of free tickets for the event – mentioned in a report for the *Berlin musikalische Zeitung* (1805) given in NMD, p. 59 and in Rochlitz's anecdote (1798) translated in Solomon, 'The Rochlitz Anecdotes', p. 19 – may have enhanced the approbation, but not the receipts.

[18] MBA, vol. 4, p. 118; LMF, p. 946 (15 October 1790).   [19] MDL, pp. 271–272; MDB, p. 309.

[20] MDL, p. 291; MDB, p. 332.

[21] See Braunbehrens, *Mozart in Vienna*, pp. 328–329; Woodfield, *Performing Operas for Mozart*, p. 162.

[22] Gutman, *Mozart*, p. 694.   [23] MBA, vol. 4, p. 118; LMF, p. 946 (15 October 1790).

[24] See Edge, 'Mozart's Reception in Vienna, 1787–1791', pp. 67–68 (footnote 5).

'inexpressible' agility and 'extraordinary skill' in sight-reading; in Leipzig his 'fortepiano playing enchanted private gatherings', his organ playing brought to mind the great J. S. Bach and he 'improvised most magnificently'; and in Frankfurt he played a fantasy in which '*he shone, infinitely making evident all the power of his talent*'.[25] As is rightly recognized, 'Mozart's financial distress needs to be uncoupled from the issue of his popularity in Vienna as a performer and composer.'[26] The old, familiar narrative of Mozart's popularity declining rapidly in his final years, resulting in a dearth of performance opportunities and financial catastrophe, is certainly a myth.[27]

In organizing concerts between the end of 1786 and 1790, the ever-pragmatic Mozart continued to consider new activities and plans, as dictated by circumstances, and to build upon successful, tried-and-tested ones. A trip to England, mooted for early 1787, did not ultimately materialize.[28] At the end of June 1789, a few weeks after returning from the Dresden-Leipzig-Berlin tour, he tried to get another Viennese concert subscription series up and running but attracted the interest only of Baron van Swieten.[29] By May 1790 he envisaged summer subscription concerts at home, which at that stage was Stadt No. 245, 'Zum St. Nikolaus' (now Judenplatz 4), presumably in his own apartment in order to avoid further expenses.[30] For the Leipzig academy, Mozart fused local conventions with established Viennese practices that had served him well.[31] As a nod to the locals he played two full concertos, integrated a skilled virtuoso vocalist (Josepha Duschek) into proceedings, and exploited the popularity of his own operatic music in the city.[32] In line with earlier Viennese academies, he alternated instrumental and vocal items, culminating in a showpiece keyboard improvisation before the final symphony, and – unlike normal

---

[25] NMD, pp. 56, 59; MDL, pp. 304, 330; MDB, pp. 347, 375 (italics as in original).

[26] Edge, 'Mozart's Reception in Vienna, 1787–1791', p. 69.

[27] See Edge, 'Mozart's Reception in Vienna, 1787–1791', which summarizes the composite narrative on p. 66. For recent identification of 'Mozart's declining public appeal' in his final years, see Melograni, *Mozart: a Biography*, p. 214.

[28] See Leopold's letters to Nannerl: MBA, vol. 3, p. 606, vol. 4, pp. 7, 28; LMF, pp. 901, 902, 906 (17 November 1786, 12 January and 1 March 1787).

[29] MBA, vol. 4, p. 92; LMF, p. 930 (12 July 1789).

[30] MBA, vol. 4, p. 106; LMF, p. 938 (beginning of May, 1790). The building comprised a store in the basement taken by a gardener, a shop at ground level, and four residential floors. Mozart's six-room apartment (plus kitchen) occupied an entire floor. He lived there between January 1789 and September 1790. See Lorenz, 'Mozart's Apartment on the Alsergrund': http://homepage.univie.ac.at/michael.lorenz/alsergrund/.

[31] For the Leipzig programme, see MDL, p. 329, MDB, p. 342, and Woodfield, *Performing Operas for Mozart*, p. 161.

[32] Woodfield, *Performing Operas for Mozart*, pp. 149–150, 159.

practice in Leipzig[33] – included only his own works. Given adherence to tradition and the staging of academies of similar scope and duration in Vienna (especially 1783, see Chapter 3) and Frankfurt (1790), we cannot conclude that the programme was 'probably the most ambitious one Mozart ever undertook, [demonstrating] to players and listeners an exceptional degree of innovation at all levels'.[34] Instead it highlighted Mozart's continued sensitivity both to the desires and expectations of his audience and to exhibiting prowess as a performer-composer. The same can also be said of his Frankfurt academy in October 1790. He employed the services of two of the principal court singers from nearby Mainz, Francesco Ceccarelli and Margareta Louise Schick, both known quantities in Frankfurt: Ceccarelli had already given at least one big concert in the city, on 7 November 1788 shortly after taking up his post in Mainz; and Schick sung at the coronation itself on 9 October and regularly in Frankfurt in the summer months each year.[35] Mozart retained the alternation of vocal and instrumental items that promoted the performer-composer first of piano concertos and later – at the apogee of the morning's entertainment – improvisations.[36] One of the attendees, Count Ludwig von Bentheim-Steinfurt, described the performance of the first piano concerto on the programme (possibly K. 459) in a manner similar to the critic writing of Mozart's Augsburg triumph twelve years earlier (see Chapter 4): the work, its rendition and the instrument used by Mozart – a Stein fortepiano again – are all warmly praised.[37] It is difficult to agree, then, with Maynard Solomon's assessment that 'Mozart's flair as an impresario was no longer fully in evidence' by October 1790.[38]

Since Mozart remained firmly committed to a career as performer-composer from late 1786 through 1790, his new orchestral works will be probed in the sections below in similar ways to his earlier Viennese works. The autographs for the piano concertos K. 503 in C and K. 537 in D ('Coronation'), for example, demonstrate continued negotiations between

---

[33] Woodfield, *Performing Operas for Mozart*, p. 160.

[34] Wolff, *Mozart at the Gateway to His Fortune*, p. 67.

[35] On Ceccarelli's performance in Frankfurt in 1788, see *Frankfurter Frag und Anzeigungs Nachrichten*, 41 (28 October 1788), 'Avertissements', n.p. Mozart also worked with Ceccarelli in Salzburg in the late 1770s and in Vienna in 1781. (See Chapter 1.) On Schick, see MDL, pp. 328, 330; MDB, pp. 373, 375.

[36] For the Frankfurt programme, see MDL, p. 329; MDB, p. 374. The final symphony was not ultimately performed, as the concert had already lasted three hours and the audience was hungry for lunch. See MDL, p. 330; MDB, p. 375.

[37] MDL, p. 329; MDB, p. 375. The identification of K. 459 and K. 537 ('Coronation') as the two piano concertos on the programme derives from information in Johann André's edition (1794). See MDL, p. 329; MDB, p. 374.

[38] Solomon, *Mozart: A Life*, pp. 470–471.

performing and compositional profiles. K. 503, perhaps first performed at one of a series of subscription concerts in the Trattner Casino in Advent 1786 and dated 4 December in the *Verzeichnüß*, was almost certainly begun in 1784–1785 alongside the piano concertos K. 459, 466 and 467, remaining a fragment until late 1786: the first six leaves of the autograph comprise a rare type of paper limited to works written between December 1784 and March 1785.[39] If Rochlitz is to be believed – as may be appropriate for Leipzig-based activities, which Rochlitz could have experienced himself or heard about directly from someone who did – Mozart played it at his Leipzig academy in 1789.[40] K. 537 was probably also begun significantly ahead of its *Verzeichnüß* date (24 February 1788), maybe in spring 1787.[41] The first securely dated performance took place at the Dresden court on 14 April 1789,[42] although a rendition in spring 1788 cannot be ruled out, as mentioned above. As we shall see, the incomplete left-hand piano part in the autograph sheds light on Mozart's attitude towards brilliant virtuosity and profile as a solo performer. The horn concertos K. 495 (1786) and K. 447 (probably 1787) are for Joseph Leutgeb, like K. 417, and document attention both to his performing strengths and declining powers.

Uncertainties surround initial renditions of the late symphonies, in particular K. 543 in E-flat, K. 550 in G minor and K. 551 in C ('Jupiter'). The Symphony in D, K. 504 ('Prague'), dated 6 December 1786 in the *Verzeichnüß*, was probably intended first for an Advent subscription concert in Vienna before being taken to Prague for the academy on 19 January 1787, where it was played to great acclaim.[43] According to Niemetschek, Mozart attributed to the skilful playing of the Prague orchestra 'the greater part of the approbation which his music had received' in the city.[44] If Mozart had his trip to Prague in mind when writing the symphony – as is possible, but not certain – he would have known he could rely on a small ensemble of around twenty-seven

---

[39] Tyson, *Autograph Scores*, pp. 151–152.

[40] On the greater veracity of Rochlitz's Leipzig-related anecdotes than his others, see Solomon, 'The Rochlitz Anecdotes', p. 48 and Woodfield, *Performing Operas for Mozart*, p. 153.

[41] See Alan Tyson's introduction to Mozart, *Piano Concerto No. 26 in D major ('Coronation'), K. 537: the Autograph Score* (New York: Dover, 1991), p. viii. For discussion of work carried out in 1787 and 1788, see Irving, *Mozart's Piano Concertos*, pp. 244–246 and NMA, V/15/8, *Kritische Berichte*, pp. 9–10.

[42] See MBA, vol. 4, p. 83; LMF, p. 923 (16 April 1789).

[43] See Zaslaw, *Mozart's Symphonies*, p. 412; Küster, *Musical Biography*, p. 245.

[44] See Niemetschek (*Leben*, p. 28, *Life of Mozart*, p. 37 [translation amended]), who claimed to have read a letter to this effect from Mozart to Joseph Strobach, the director of the orchestra.

instrumentalists independently verified as excellent.[45] Much less is known about performances during Mozart's lifetime of the final three symphonies, dated 26 June, 25 July and 10 August 1788. The romantic notion of Mozart composing out of inner necessity unrelated to the prospect of definite performances is a myth, albeit one that surfaces from time to time even in modern-day scholarship.[46] Orchestral parts for the G-minor Symphony, containing annotations by Mozart himself, indicate a performance of K. 550 soon after completion; the existence of a second version of the work, transmitted through additional clarinet parts and revised oboe parts in the autograph and with its changes pasted over in the annotated parts, also tentatively suggests a planned performance between completing the first version and producing the second.[47] It is now known that the symphony was heard at Baron van Swieten's residence in Vienna, with Mozart in attendance; apparently it was poorly played, resulting in an upset Mozart having to leave the room.[48] A number of reasons for the composition of the three symphonies have been proposed, including subscription concerts planned for late 1788, a possible trip to London, and publication as a three-work opus.[49] Plausible suggestions have been made for performances of the works at the Leipzig and Frankfurt academies in 1789 and 1790 and at Tonkünstler-Societät concerts conducted by Salieri on 16 and 17 April 1791, but remain

---

[45] See Zaslaw, *Mozart's Symphonies*, pp. 412, 414, and John Spitzer, 'Orchestra', in *Cambridge Mozart Encyclopedia*, p. 382. See also Chapter 8 on *Don Giovanni*.

[46] See, for example, Pierre-Petit on Mozart never hearing the works and composing them only for glory, in *Mozart*, p. 286. See also Jane Glover's statement (*Mozart's Women*, p. 161) that 'there was no financial incentive, let alone reward, for writing them. . . . For him the creation of these unquestionable masterpieces was an escape from the personal sorrows and professional anxieties: he entered an untroubled, alternative world . . . where his gifts prospered and soared.'

[47] Cliff Eisen, 'Another Look at the "Corrupt Passage" in Mozart G Minor Symphony, K. 550: Its Sources, "Solution" and Implications for the Composition of the Final Trilogy', *Early Music*, 25/3 (1997), pp. 373–380.

[48] See Milada Jonášová, 'A Performance of the G minor Symphony K. 550 at Baron van Swieten's Rooms in Mozart's Presence', *Newsletter of the Mozart Society of America*, 16/1 (January 2012), pp. 1–4, 17. For more detail, see Jonášová, 'Eine Aufführung der g-moll-Sinfonie KV 550 bei Baron van Swieten im Beisein Mozarts', in Manfred Hermann Schmid (ed.), *Mozart Studien*, 20 (Tutzing: Hans Schneider, 2011), pp. 253–268. K. 539 in E-flat was performed at a memorial concert for Mozart in early 1792 and subsequently described in exalted terms by one of the attendees. See Edge and Black (eds.), 'A Memorial Concert for Mozart in Hamburg on 19 Feb 1792' and 'A Personal Response to the Mozart Memorial Concert in Hamburg and the Symphony in E-flat (K. 543)', in *Mozart: New Documents*, http://dx.doi.org/10.7302/Z20P0WXJ (accessed 23 December 2016).

[49] See Zaslaw, *Mozart's Symphonies*, pp. 421–422. See also David Wyn Jones, 'Why Did Mozart Compose His Last Three Symphonies?' *Music Review*, 51 (1990), pp. 280–289; and Andrew Steptoe, 'Mozart and His Last Three Symphonies: A Myth Laid to Rest?' *Musical Times*, 132 (1991), pp. 550–551.

speculative in the absence of further documentation.[50] And it is not known for certain that the subscription events planned for autumn 1788 took place.[51]

While fewer mysteries surround performances of the re-orchestrated *Acis and Galatea, Messiah, Alexander's Feast* and *Ode for St. Cecilia's Day* than the final three symphonies, critics have tended gently or brusquely to marginalize Mozart's work.[52] The re-orchestrations have been described in the twentieth and early twenty-first centuries as hackwork or 'technical work' for a composer of Mozart's talent, only carried out to assuage a perilous financial position, and characterized implicitly or explicitly as insubstantial; Sitwell commented in the 1930s that it had 'not been accorded an altogether favourable reception by lovers of Handel' and Einstein ignored it altogether in his influential biography a few years later.[53] Abert is also critical of the *Messiah* re-orchestration. Mozart, avoiding the 'most arbitrary excesses' that beset Johann Adam Hiller's *Messiah* re-orchestration from 1786, nonetheless increased the 'stylistic gulf between the original and ... adaptation'.[54] While there were early detractors too, including Johann Friedrich Reichardt,[55] Mozart's re-orchestrations were widely respected and performed at the end of the eighteenth century and in much of the nineteenth.

[50] Wolff (*Mozart at the Gateway to His Fortune*, pp. 67, 208–209) lists the 'Jupiter' Symphony as having been performed at the Leipzig academy on the grounds that a 'C' is annotated in pencil on the playbill. But the annotation is 'of indeterminate date' (Woodfield, *Performing Operas for Mozart*, p. 160), so does not confirm the 'Jupiter' – or for that matter any other C major symphony, such as the 'Linz', K. 425 – as the work in question. Similarly, a judgement that one of the last three symphonies was performed in Frankfurt (Wolff, *Mozart at the Gateway to his Fortune*, p. 48) cannot be made with certainty. On the Tonkünstler-Societät concerts in 1791, see H. C. Robbins Landon, *1791: Mozart's Last Year* (London: HarperCollins, 1990), p. 28 and Zaslaw, *Mozart's Symphonies*, p. 431.

[51] On critical skepticism about the subscription series taking place in 1788, inclining towards the belief that they did, see Braunbehrens, *Mozart in Vienna*, pp. 323–325.

[52] In addition to these four arrangements, it is not impossible that Mozart worked on a recently rediscovered arrangement of Handel's *Judas Maccabeus*. A more likely prospect is that a different musician produced it, perhaps modelling it on Mozart's version of the *Messiah*. See Rachel Cowgill, 'An Unknown Handel Arrangement by Mozart? The Halifax Judas', *Musical Times*, 143 (2002), pp. 19–36.

[53] Pierre-Petit, *Mozart*, p. 286; Davenport, *Mozart*, p. 320; Blom, *Mozart*, pp. 135–1136; Ghéon, *In Search of Mozart*, p. 264; Levey, *Life and Death of Mozart*, p. 225; Cairns, *Mozart and His Operas*, p 171; Sacheverell Sitwell, *Mozart* (London: Peter Davies Limited, 1932), p. 126; Einstein, *Mozart: His Character, His Work*. The payments Mozart received for his work on the Handel arrangements are not known. For a brief, more positive evaluation of the arrangements, suggesting Mozart's 'better understanding of how to utilize the wind and brass instruments' than C. P. E. Bach and Handel, see Beverly Jerold, *The Complexities of Early Instrumentation: Winds and Brass* (Turnhout: Brepols, 2015), pp. 123–132 (quotation at 130).

[54] Abert, *W.A. Mozart*, pp. 1152–1153.

[55] Jahn, *Life of Mozart*, vol. 3, p. 224; Gruber, *Mozart and Posterity*, p. 47.

Revivals took place in the 1790s, *Alexander's Feast* became very popular in Vienna in the ensuing years, partly thanks to the Mozart re-orchestration, and *Messiah* 'standard fare in the nineteenth century' in Mozart's version, which was published by Breitkopf & Härtel in 1803.[56] According to Johann Baptist Cramer (1826), Mozart's *Messiah* 'not only revived that sublime composition on the Continent, but, probably, will tend to prolong its duration for half a century to come'.[57] And for Ignaz Moscheles, writing to Mendelssohn (1836): 'You ask me about my scoring of the Bach Concerto. Well, it seemed to me that one might give it a kind of new varnish, by doing for it what Mozart had done with such perfect taste for the "Messiah".'[58] Niemetschek wrote in his biography from 1798 that Mozart 'was able to enliven Handel's grand ideas with the warmth of his feeling, and through the magic of his instrumental settings to make them enjoyable for our generation'.[59] The letter from van Swieten to Mozart quoted by Niemetschek is perhaps inauthentic, but it still stands as late-eighteenth-century testimony – even if not necessarily from the commissioner of the work – to Mozart successfully treading a fine line: 'Anyone who can clothe Handel so tastefully and solemnly that on the one hand it pleases the fashionable, and on the other hand always shows its sublimity, has felt his value and understood him, has reached the source of his expression and can and surely will draw from it. That is how I view your achievement.'[60]

The Late Symphonies

Few works in Mozart's Viennese oeuvre contain more overt demonstrations of compositional virtuosity than his final four symphonies. Big, ornate slow introductions to two of them act as gateways to the works (K. 504, K. 543); harmonic purple patches surprise, disorientate and amaze

---

[56] Gruber, *Posterity*, p. 33; Nicholas Mathew, *Political Beethoven* (Cambridge: Cambridge University Press, 2013), pp. 105–106; Emily Dolan, *The Orchestral Revolution: Haydn and the Technologies of Timbre* (Cambridge: Cambridge University Press, 2013), p. 198. For nineteenth-century performances of Mozart's Handel arrangements by his Viennese devotee Ignaz von Seyfried, see David Wyn Jones, 'Mozart's Spirit from Seyfried's hands', in Keefe (ed.), *Mozart Studies 2*, pp. 195–228, at 223–224. Otto Jahn in the mid nineteenth century was also largely positive about Mozart's orchestration of the *Messiah*; see *W. A. Mozart*, vol. 3, pp. 223–225.

[57] As given in David Grayson, 'Whose Authenticity? Ornaments by Hummel and Cramer for Mozart's Piano Concertos', in Zaslaw (ed.), *Mozart's Piano Concertos*, p. 380.

[58] As given in Mark Kroll, *Ignaz Moscheles and the Changing World of Musical Europe* (Woodbridge and Rochester, NY: The Boydell Press, 2014), p. 165.

[59] Niemetschek, *Leben*, p. 31, *Life of Mozart*, p. 40 (translation amended).

[60] Niemetschek, *Leben*, p. 31, *Life of Mozart*, p. 41 (translation amended).

(K. 543/ii, K. 550/i, K. 550/iv, K. 551/ii); musical topics interweave intricately and flamboyantly (K. 504/i); dialogue and counterpoint dazzle (K. 504/i, K. 551/iv).[61] The expressive profundity exuded was no doubt partially responsible for early-nineteenth-century praise of Mozart's works: E. T. A Hoffmann (citing K. 543 as an example) experienced Mozart taking us 'deep into the realm of spirits . . . We hear the gentle voices of love and melancholy, the nocturnal spirit-world dissolves into a purple shimmer, and with inexpressible yearning we follow the flying figures kindly beckoning us from the clouds to join their eternal dance of the spheres'.[62]

Performances of the last four symphonies, even when uncertain in time and place during Mozart's lifetime, were central to the conception and production of the works and no mere appendage to demonstrations of compositional skill and strength. As is often pointed out, they would have been technically challenging for late-eighteenth-century orchestras.[63] Challenges go beyond the replication of notes on the page to the proactive interpretations Mozart invited from performers. In other words, compositional virtuosity is complemented by what might be termed virtuosity of effect, namely multi-tiered dynamic, timbral, gestural, harmonic and rhythmic effects that rely on imaginative and engaged renditions from performers in order to be communicated effectively. To be sure, having only one rehearsal before many concerts and using a set of parts rather than a full score (unless Mozart was at the helm) may have worked against an imaginative reading in the late eighteenth century, especially if the

---

[61] On the 'Prague' Symphony, see in particular Elaine Sisman's magisterial analysis of the intertwining formal, rhetorical, contrapuntal, topical and expressive components of the work – especially in the first movement – in 'Genre, Gesture, and Meaning in Mozart's "Prague" Symphony', in Eisen (ed.), *Mozart Studies 2*, pp. 27–84. On the 'Jupiter', see Simon P. Keefe, 'The "Jupiter" Symphony in C, K. 551: New Perspectives on the Dramatic Finale and its Stylistic Significance in Mozart's Orchestral *Oeuvre*', *Acta musicologica*, 75 (2003), pp. 17–43; Keefe, *Mozart's Viennese Instrumental Music*, pp. 137–164 (Chapter 6); and Elaine Sisman, *Mozart: The 'Jupiter' Symphony* (Cambridge: Cambridge University Press, 1993). Harmonic purple patches are discussed in Keefe, *Mozart's Viennese Instrumental Music*, pp. 77–79 and Keefe, 'Harmonies and Effects: Haydn and Mozart in Parallel', in Julian Horton (ed.), *The Cambridge Companion to the Symphony* (Cambridge: Cambridge University Press, 2013), pp. 155–174, at 160–166. Peter Gülke's study of the last three symphonies focuses in particular on connections among them; his idea that they form their own trilogy as a result, in effect belonging together, is a contentious one. *Inter alia* (according to Gülke) the slow introduction to K. 543 and the finale of K. 551 represent an introduction and conclusion to the three-work cycle. See Gülke, '*Triumph der neuen Tonkunst': Mozarts späte Sinfonien und ihr Umfeld* (Kassel, Stuttgart and Metzler: Bärenreiter and Metzler, 1998).

[62] *Allgemeine musikalische Zeitung*, 12 (1809–1810), col. 632 (as given in David Charlton (ed.), *E. T. A. Hoffmann's Musical Writings: 'Kreisleriana', 'The Poet and the Composer', Music Criticism*, trans. Martyn Clarke [Cambridge: Cambridge University Press, 1989], pp. 237–238).

[63] Zaslaw, *Mozart's Symphonies*, pp. 412, 517; Sisman, 'Mozart's "Prague" Symphony', p. 28.

composer himself was not directly involved. But the works as represented by their primary sources carry performance details in ways that would have encouraged choices to be made and interpretations to be crafted, types of activity that may have been beyond many orchestras, but were perhaps within the capabilities of leading ones in (for example) Mannheim, Stuttgart, Vienna and Prague.[64] The late-eighteenth-century concertmaster would have been crucial to the interpretative process, assuming responsibility 'for realizing the composer's expressive intentions either as indicated or according to the (perhaps unwritten) performing conventions of the time, and communicating his interpretation by gesture and example to his orchestra', a role requiring preparation, musicianship and imagination.[65] And the kind of disciplined, concertmaster-led playing admired by Mozart and Leopold, no doubt expected from highly gifted Viennese and Czech musicians, and implied in Baron von Reitzenstein's enthusiastic praise for the 'order' (*Ordnung*) and 'unanimity' (*Uebereinstimmung*) of the Burgtheater orchestra's technical and expressive playing in 1789–1790, would have facilitated effective, creative renditions of orchestral works.[66] For the last two symphonies, revised orchestration (K. 550) and an engagement with the idea of the orchestra as a collective and as a group of individuals (K. 551) also situate performing matters at the heart of Mozart's compositional enterprise.

The contribution of dynamics to musical expression offers examples of virtuosity of effect in the 'Prague' Symphony and in No. 39, K. 543.[67] Their role in the slow introduction of the 'Prague' primarily from the move to D minor at the approximate midpoint onwards (bar 15) has been acknowledged:[68] dynamic surges align with distinctive harmonies in bar-by-bar oscillation of *forte*s and *piano*s (d, VI/d, F7, D6/5, g, diminished). Elsewhere in the introduction dynamics pose interpretative questions. In

---

[64] On the abilities of orchestras to perform the 'finer degrees' and nuances of a score, plus 'the shading of the whole', suggesting that Mannheim and Stuttgart orchestras were able to do so, see Johann Friedrich Reichardt, *Ueber die Pflichten des Ripien-Violinisten* (Berlin and Leipzig, 1776), p. 59; as given in Brown, *Classical and Romantic Performing Practice*, p. 61.

[65] See Robin Stowell, '"Good Execution and Other Necessary Skills": The Role of the Concertmaster in the Late 18th Century', *Early Music*, 16/1 (1988), pp. 21–33, at 24–25.

[66] For Mozart on the Mannheim orchestra, see MBA, vol. 2, p. 395; LMF, p. 562 (9 July 1778). For Leopold Mozart highlighting orchestral discipline, see *Versuch einer gründlichen Violinschule* (Augsburg, 1756); trans. Editha Knocker as *A Treatise on the Fundamental Principles of Violin Playing* (London: Oxford University Press, 1948), p. 224, and on Jommelli in Stuttgart, MBA, vol. 1, p. 76; LMF, p. 23 (11 July 1763). For Reitzenstein's comment, see *Reise nach Wien*, p. 253.

[67] For the autograph of the 'Prague' Symphony, see Biblioteca Jagiellońska Kraków: Mus. ms. autogr. W. A. Mozart 319. 338. 444. 504.

[68] Levey, *Life and Death of Mozart*, p. 203; Volker Scherliess, 'Die Sinfonien', in Leopold (ed.), *Mozart Handbuch*, p. 308; Brown, *The Symphonic Repertoire*, vol. 2, p. 407.

bar 1 (Example 11.1) the *f* to the *p* on beat 3 is followed by an *f* less than two beats later on the upbeat to the next bar. If played as sudden shifts from loud to soft, the brisker move from *p* to *f* than from *f* to *p* prefigures acceleration of a rhythmic kind in bar 2, and the subsequent *p* on bar 3 beat 2 fuels rhythmic deceleration in bars 3 and 4 as well. But if the initial *f* – *p* is performed with a diminuendo, it may be heard as an unstrict metric gesture in effect rendering bars 1 to the second beat of bar 3 'loud' and making the dynamic, rhythmic and textural changes in bar 3 the principal point of contrast. The final bars of the Andante (Example 11.2), a rare *pp* for the entire orchestra combined with the registral high and low points of the movement, again show Mozart signing off a concert piece in distinctive fashion. But whether the effect is to be played in such a way as a suggest a connection to the Andante's two previous *pp*s – in the bars immediately before the exposition and recapitulation second themes (34, 121) – and thus as the final, quietly climactic event of the movement, or whether it is to convey something apparently spontaneous and new, is a matter for performers. For Mozart's written material does not rule in or out either interpretation: like the *pp*s in bars 34 and 121, the *pp* at the end is a tag to the previous bar, prolonging the harmony; but unlike the earlier *pp*s, it supports tonic rather than dominant prolongation and is not part of a written diminuendo from *f* – *p* – *pp*.

Effects in the slow introduction to K. 543 are to be determined by performers, as at the opening of the 'Prague'. For example, the *piano* wind figure in bar 2^{2-3} (Example 11.3) – the first independent of the strings – can be presented either (or both) as a continuation of wind lines from bar 1 in rhythmic diminution, or as an echo of the *forte* rendition of the same rhythm in the timpani. The changed scoring second time around (wind minus horns in bar 4) could conceivably be taken as a cue to interpret the figure differently in relation to surrounding material. And whether the *alla breve* – establishing the minim rather than the crotchet as the principle unit of currency – affects the rendition of these rhythmic figures is another issue for consideration.[69] Decisions entrusted to performers at the opening will affect how subsequent

[69] On the common time slow introduction to the 'Prague' Symphony in comparison to the (quicker) *alla breve* introduction to K. 543, which 'promotes the minim to the role of the key agent of the tempo, that is to say, of the internal (qualitative) organization of the musical flow, as well as the quantitative aspect (speed)', see Jean-Pierre Marty, 'Mozart's Tempo Indications and the Problems of Interpretation', in Todd and Williams (eds.), *Perspectives on Mozart Performance*, pp. 55–73, at pp. 57–58. For further discussion of *alla breve* in the late eighteenth and early nineteenth centuries, see Brown, *Classical and Romantic Performing Practice*, pp. 313–335.

Example 11.1 Mozart, Symphony in D ('Prague'), K. 504/i, bars 1–5.

Example 11.2 Mozart, Symphony in D ('Prague'), K. 504/ii, bars 144–148.

events are perceived: the rhythm in question (usually quaver – semiquaver rest – semiquaver, rather than dotted quaver – semiquaver) becomes the heartbeat of the slow introduction from bar 9 onwards, building to a tutti iteration in bars 19–20 via the *forte* of bar 14 and the wracking dissonance of bar 18. Orchestral instruments come together in conjunction with the rhythmic momentum that is generated. Thus, the accentuation or down-playing of the opening echoes from timpani and winds is no small matter: the interpretation chosen by performers will affect how relationships between the grand opening statements and the passage from bar 9 onwards are understood. In similar fashion, the role played by the wind's solo segment immediately before the reprise – building on their prominent participation in the development section – is left to per-formers (Example 11.4). It must be decided whether to emphasize continuity between the end of the development and the beginning of the recapitulation as suggested by surrounding *piano* indications and

Example 11.3 Mozart, Symphony in E-flat, K. 543/i, bars 1–4.

solo wind participation, or to accentuate discontinuities implicit in the surprising silences (especially the general pause in bar 180), the cursory move back to E-flat, and the flute b-flat" left hanging in bar 183.

The opportunity for an as-yet-unidentified performance of the G-minor Symphony with clarinets – which did not feature in the original scoring – no doubt stimulated the re-orchestration of the work. Since the watermarks of the paper carrying the revised clarinet and oboe parts match in all instances but one those on which the original version of the work was written, the revisions may well have been carried out in late 1788.[70] As we have come to expect from Mozart, the rescoring has practical and aesthetic ramifications. Jahn and Abert mention respectively the gain and loss associated with the new version, namely the 'greater intensity and fullness' of tone colouring

[70] Landon, *1791: Mozart's Last Year*, p. 27.

Example 11.4 Mozart, Symphony in E-flat, K. 543/i, bars 179–186.

and 'the characteristically austere oboe sound'.[71] Irrespective of qualitative judgements, the second version re-shapes the sound world and character of the symphony:[72] while the inclusion of the clarinets is Mozart's *raison d'être* for making changes, the concomitantly altered oboe parts also provided him with an opportunity to re-evaluate timbral and textural effects.

The rescoring of the Andante of K. 550 is a case in point. As a result of ceding thematic material to the clarinets from the opening of the movement until the final bars of the transition, the first and second oboes receive only four notes in total – at the beginning of the transition (bar 20) and a couple of bars later. Marked *forte*, the two oboe chords are new to the

[71] Jahn, *Life of Mozart*, vol. 3, p. 37; Abert, *W. A. Mozart*, p. 1123.

[72] As also noted by Colin Lawson in 'Case Study: Mozart, Symphonies in E Flat Major K543, G Minor K550 and C Major K551', in Lawson and Stowell (eds.), *The Cambridge History of Musical Performance*, pp. 570–571.

second version of the symphony and reinforce material in the strings.[73] Thus, the harmonic and textural climax to the transition – an inflection to G-flat, which subsequently functions as German Augmented 6th in confirming the secondary key area, B-flat (bars 33–35) – is accentuated by a new timbre for the movement, that is the full wind section together after the hitherto near-complete absence of oboes.[74] The next contribution for the oboes also coincides with a purple patch: a combination of iv7 and diminished harmonies (bars 44–46) in the run-up to a I6/4 – V7 – I cadential confirmation. The connection in the exposition between a full-wind cohort, *forte*, and intense harmonic colour is then exploited throughout the first half of the development and in material displaced from the first theme to the secondary development in the recapitulation, where *sf* material heard only in the strings in the exposition now appears in the full wind as well (bar 96).

Given the limited participation of the oboes (always at a *forte* dynamic) in the exposition, their inclusion is worthy of note in the final bar of the section, at *piano* for the first time. Situated in context, the effect at this juncture of the second version of K. 550/ii is very different from the corresponding juncture in the first version: it brings together the three melodically orientated wind instruments in the first version, essentially summing up the timbral prominence of the group thus far, but in the second promotes timbral variety by capturing a new sonority. The special effect at the end of the exposition in version 2 is matched at the end of the movement, which features the only *piano* full-wind sonority of the Andante (following earlier associations with *forte* purple patches).

Mozart's penchant for timbral variety in the revised K. 550 is also a feature of the first and third movements and is captured in a nutshell in the recapitulation of the secondary theme in the Molto allegro. The onset of this presentation comprises a new effect for the second version, even though it mostly reproduces the scoring appearing in the first version. In terms of presenting thematic material, the oboes usurp the clarinets for the first time, pointing to the value Mozart placed on timbral novelty rather than consistency. Omitting the clarinets for the reprise of the secondary theme also

---

[73] The first chord is more timbrally prominent at the corresponding juncture of the recapitulation (bar 86): the reworked end to the first-theme section results in the oboe chord being the only wind contribution for four bars.

[74] At least in the first version of K. 550, Mozart may have come to prefer tied notes for the winds (including the oboes) in bars 29–32 and 100–103 to the demisemiquaver imitative figure. See the discussion of Graz parts for K. 550 for which Mozart himself made small modifications, in Eisen, 'Another Look at the "Corrupt Passage" in Mozart G Minor Symphony, K. 550'.

enables a timbre to reinforce the subsequent harmonic effect, the clarinets being brought back and the oboes left out to coincide with B-flat7 – E-flat inflections (bars 241–244). In the trio, Mozart includes oboes at the expense of clarinets. Since he almost always assigned the oboes' thematic material from the original version to the clarinets in the revision (at least when choosing between instruments), the flute/oboes/bassoons and then flute/oboes/bassoons/horns timbres in the second version of the trio are a fresh effect arising from relative unfamiliarity in local context. This is not a value judgement on the two versions of the work, rather a recognition that in contemplating a performance in a new orchestration Mozart did not feel beholden to his earlier timbral conceptions of the work, seeking out new effects instead that could be exploited in the moment by (probably) familiar orchestral players.

By foregrounding players as a collective *and* as a set of semi-autonomous individuals, Mozart directs attention to orchestral effects and performance in the 'Jupiter' Symphony. The first and last movements, for example, demonstrate how a 'disciplined orchestra was no longer an aggregation of individuals making music in parallel; it was a single social unit, audibly and visibly acting as a group'.[75] The C-minor explosion in the second-theme section of the opening Allegro vivace (bar 81) – marked *forte* after the preceding *piano* – depends for its full effect on all instruments working as a closely coordinated unit. Synchronized subtlety rather than force is then required at the onset of the closing theme of the exposition (bar 101): the mutually reinforcing *piano* in the violins and pizzicato *piano* in violas and basses project uniform delicacy after a high-octane *forte* tutti passage. In the finale too, orchestral instruments function primarily as a single unit, speaking independently of course in the contrapuntal *tour de force*, but mostly with one voice. (In this instance, perhaps the compositional virtuosity on display did indeed preclude much attention on Mozart's part to the genuinely creative contribution performers could make.[76]) An exception is the second half of the development section, where *piano* versions of the main theme in the winds come up against an ascending quaver motto (inverting the descending quaver theme) in the strings, with support from the brass. Mozart depicts a fractured not unified ensemble here, instrumental groups (if not individual instruments) assuming distinct identities that imply conflict.[77] With a wide range of possible renditions of the *pianos*

---

[75] Spitzer and Zaslaw, *The Birth of the Orchestra*, p. 384.

[76] In a similar vein, John Irving argues (*Understanding Mozart's Piano Sonatas*, p. 79) that 'freedom [for performers] is disciplined by counterpoint' in the first movement of the Piano Sonata in D, K. 576.

[77] On confrontation in this passage, see Keefe, *Mozart's Viennese Instrumental Music*, p. 156.

and *fortes*, it is up to performers to decide how much to articulate the different identities and subsequent 'resolutions' conveyed in the strings' *piano* version of the ascending theme (falling into line with the winds) and the brass' *piano* contributions to the imitation directly preceding the recapitulation.

More than the other three movements, the Andante cantabile of the 'Jupiter' emphasizes individual rather than collective instrumental roles. In the transition and development sections, for example, Mozart writes dynamically un-coordinated *sfp, f – p* and *fp* surges across his score (see Example 11.5): how these dynamics are distinguished in performance will affect how relationships between individual and groups of instruments are perceived. Mozart's precise dynamic indications in the autograph give us reason to consider whether decisions processed as apparent oversights by the *Neue Mozart-Ausgabe* and others – such as the omission of *sfp* markings in the flutes and oboes in bar 21, following inclusion at the corresponding moment two bars earlier – are in fact oversights at all: since Mozart embraces diversity rather than uniformity of sound in this passage, assumptions about standardization stand on shaky ground. In the development, which almost entirely comprises the transition material, Mozart brings uniformity and diversity into sharp relief: the colons following his 'cresc' indications for every instrument in the second bar of the section appear at the exact end of the bar in the autograph, indicating dynamic alignment among instruments (in this case wind and first violins) right up to point where the un-coordinated surges begin (bar 47^1).

Dynamic subtleties in the Andante are not confined to passages where varieties of effects were sought. In the final bars, which carry the only *pps* of the movement, Mozart again signs off a Viennese concert piece with a special orchestral effect. Changes to the autograph score capture thematic and dynamic-related thinking operating in tandem (Example 11.6). The final sextuplet semiquavers in the flute and first violin (bar 100) initially matched the pitches of the sextuplets in the first violin one bar earlier; Mozart subsequently raised the pitch. Thus, in revised form, the final two bars are distinguished dynamically and thematically from previous material, ensuring a singular position in the movement as a result.

The Horn Concertos, K. 495 and K. 447

As has been pointed out, Mozart's four Viennese horn concertos – K. 417 (1783) discussed in Chapter 3, K. 495 (1786), K. 447 (probably 1787), and

Example 11.5 Mozart, Symphony in C ('Jupiter'), K. 551/ii, bars 18–24.

Example 11.6 Mozart, Symphony in C ('Jupiter'), K. 551/ii, bars 99–101 (including deleted original notes for violin I and flute in bar 100).

K. 412 (1791, see Chapter 12) – become progressively less taxing over time in order to accommodate their aging soloist.[78] Having scribbled humorously on the autograph of K. 417 about taking pity on his 'donkey, ox and fool' of a horn player, Mozart continued to engage with Joseph Leutgeb (and the orchestra) in the autograph manuscript of K. 495, even though messages conveyed (if any) are not always clear to us. The second movement contains material in red, blue and green ink as well as in black, and the finale in red and black. Franz Giegling proposed a coded system from Mozart with hints for performance, including accentuation of individual lines in the orchestral texture (red), *sotto voce* (green), and echo effects (blue); Konrad Küster, in contrast, detected a loud-to-soft gradation in the different colours, from red to blue to black to green.[79] According to Küster, the latter emerges in purported decrescendi at the end of the second movement, first from bars 77 to 86 and then in the final four horn notes,

---

[78] Humphries, *The Early Horn*, p. 87. As Humphries explains, Leutgeb was fifty-nine in 1791 and apparently retired from playing in 1792.

[79] Franz Giegling, Preface to NMA, V/14/5, pp. xiii–xiv; Küster, *Musical Biography*, p. 231.

Example 11.7 Mozart, Horn Concerto in E-flat, K. 495/ii, bars 85–89.

which are respectively red, blue, black and green.[80] 'One thing is clear, at least', Küster claimed, 'and that is that Mozart did not skip about between inkpots just for fun, but in order to make some musical suggestions.'[81] Yet skipping happily between pots is precisely what Mozart did after the movement, writing four-lined double bars in the horn and bass parts respectively in black, green, red and blue (each one smaller than the next), pause markings in blue, and the word *fine* in black, blue, red and green letters. Such levity does not preclude a more serious meaning for the different colours in the main body of the movement, of course. But the possibility that Mozart was simply amusing himself and Leutgeb, or wanted to give the manuscript a 'festive appearance' perhaps in recognition of Leutgeb's recent marriage, is difficult to deny.[82] Irrespective of whether a decrescendo for the horn was intended across its final four notes, a refined effect is achieved (Example 11.7): the last bar is the only one marked *pp* in the whole movement and one of only two scored for the horn soloist

---

[80] See Küster, *Musical Biography*, p. 231, and the colour facsimile of the final twenty bars of the second movement on the front and back inside covers of his book. For the autograph, see Mozart, *Concertos, Horn, Orchestra, K. 495, E-Flat Major*. Autograph manuscript 1786. The Morgan Library and Museum. Cary 35.

[81] Küster, *Musical Biography*, pp. 231–232.

[82] As suggested by John Humphries in *The Early Horn*, p. 86.

alongside the full ensemble (two oboes, two horns and strings). Mozart
chose a new timbre for the end: a quiet, delicate but full blend of solo and
orchestra.

While brilliant virtuosity is a feature of K. 495, the blend of horn and
orchestra is promoted above all: Leutgeb's acknowledged skill as an expressive player (see Chapter 3) is thereby exploited, without unduly challenging
stamina or flashy technique. In the first movement Mozart introduces his
soloist seven bars before the solo exposition, an octave lower than the oboe
and in thematic response to the first violins. The horn is heard less as a
demonstrative soloist at this juncture and more as a contributor to the new
timbre of an oboe and horn presenting thematic material together. The
positioning of stopped notes relative to open notes in the phrase also
facilitates a consistent tone on the natural horn.[83] Correspondingly at the
end of the solo exposition – reversing the pattern of the original solo horn
passage – Mozart gradually eases the horn out, progressively diminishing
its timbral prominence and blending it with orchestral material. Whereas
up to the secondary theme (bar 75ff.) the strings are kept either below the
soloist's register, or modestly track its melodic line, they move above the
horn from the secondary theme onwards, ascending while the soloist
descends (bars 80–83). The written f-sharp", f', and e-flat" comprising
part of the horn's descent are all stopped notes, potentially leading to a
quieter sound than for the open-note d"s and g" in the two preceding bars.
Also, the two orchestral horns enter on the same note as the solo horn
(written d") shortly before the cadential trill, bringing together the sounds
of soloist and accompanists. And the cadential trill itself is not on written
a'/a" descending to g'/g" (sounding c – b-flat), as might be expected in B-
flat major, but on written f-sharp" (sounding a') – a tricky note for the
natural horn[84] – and set against an orchestral crescendo. The horn gradually retreats as soloist, then, being given plenty of opportunities to blend
expressively with the orchestra in the process.

Mozart is similarly attuned to the implications of timbre and texture at
the soloist's entry and exit points in the development and recapitulation.
The horn is reintroduced at the start of the development (bar 97) by the
most marked textural change of the movement thus far – bare octaves and
fp inflections in the strings. Towards the end of the section, as at a similar
stage of the exposition, the soloist blends with the orchestral horns: its
climactic written g" sustained note subsides through octave leaps (written

---

[83] On this phrase see Humphries, *The Early Horn*, pp. 87–88.
[84] Humphries, *Early Horn*, p. 61.

g' and g) taken up immediately as sustained octaves by the orchestral horns (bars 132–137). Simultaneously, the orchestral horns create a smooth link to the pre-recapitulation ritornello, provide dominant-pedal preparation for the recapitulation, and invoke the previous contribution of the soloist. The immediate run-up to the recapitulation is a concise replay of the run-up to the solo exposition, facilitating the horn's move back to a solo role: entering at the bottom of the texture, it is subsequently tracked by first violins (bar 141), with the oboes one octave higher as at the solo horn's first contribution to the work. Fittingly, on account of its transitions into and out of solo roles, the horn re-surfaces after the cadenza with the material it had first presented before the solo exposition, departing the scene as it had entered it, blended with orchestral instruments. In sum, interaction with the orchestra provided Leutgeb with an opportunity to demonstrate the kind of skilful expressive playing for which he was well known, even if age was perhaps already taking its toll on other aspects of his playing, such as stamina and extended displays of technical brilliance.

If small concessions to Leutgeb are captured in K. 495, more noticeable ones are made in K. 447, which steers clear of the highest notes from the two earlier concertos.[85] The soloist participates considerably less in the first movement of K. 447 than in the corresponding movement of the similarly proportioned K. 417 – in approximately 93 rather than 130 bars. (K. 495/i, longer overall than K. 417/i, has the soloist participate for six fewer bars.) In compensation, the orchestra carefully promotes an aura of brilliant virtuosity around the soloist. At the end of the solo exposition, for example, the strings put into effect rhythmic diminution that propels the music towards the concluding cadential trill (crotchets – quavers – semiquavers in bars 64, 65–66 and 68); at the end of the recapitulation, they introduce triplet quavers subsequently adopted by the soloist to initiate a modestly virtuosic five-bar passage that culminates in the cadential trill. It is as if the orchestra helps Leutgeb along, both stimulating and supporting his virtuosic activity.

Virtuosity of effect from the late symphonies is also a feature of K. 447. In the development section of the opening Allegro the horn launches the most harmonically audacious passage of the movement with a three-quarter-stopped e-flat" (sounding g-flat', bars 95–96, Example 11.8). The thwarted sound of the heavily stopped note, unaccompanied in bar 95, may have encouraged Leutgeb to offer a slightly distant, mysterious introduction to the passage; thereafter, all horn notes are open, facilitating an even

---

[85] Humphries, *Early Horn*, p. 87.

Example 11.8 Mozart, Horn Concerto in E-flat, K. 447/i, bars 95–105.

tone to blend with the orchestra and not distract from the bold harmonic turns.[86] Blended horn and orchestra is also a feature of the ensuing passage: the horn, two clarinets and two bassoons are combined in an extended passage for the first time, creating an aesthetically vaunted sonority (see Chapter 1). Another three-quarter-stopped horn note (d-flat″ sounding f-flat′), employed in a different way, initiates the most harmonically colourful passage in the slow movement, shortly before the reprise (Example 11.9).[87] Here, Mozart's *sfp* and three-quarter-stopping

---

[86] The horn's sounding G-flat, heard enharmonically as F-sharp, forms part of a i6/4 – V7 – I progression in D minor (bars 96–98); the music then moves to E-flat minor via diminished harmony and C minor via V7/c (bars 99–102).

[87] The harmonies in bars 49–53 are as follows: a-flat6/4 (with added f-flat) – diminished – a-flat6 – V/a-flat – a-flat. Attention is also drawn to this moment as 'a most surprising and dramatic use of a stopped note played sforzando-piano' in Horace Fitzpatrick, *The Horn and Horn-Playing and the Austro-Bohemian Tradition from 1680 to 1830* (London: Oxford University Press, 1970), p. 166.

Example 11.9 Mozart, Horn Concerto in E-flat, K. 447/ii, bars 48–54.

probably would have encouraged a rasping sound from Leutgeb, pointing ostentatiously to the start of the purple passage just as the written E-flat in the first-movement development section had flagged the harmonic progression ahead. (Again, the immediate continuation for the horn is a series of open notes in bars 50–52.) Thus, Leutgeb was given ample opportunity in K. 447 to exploit the varied timbral qualities of his playing.

The Piano Concertos, K. 503 and K. 537

While the horn concertos required Mozart to accommodate slightly changed circumstances for their soloist, the piano concertos written between late 1786 and 1790, K. 503 in C and K. 537 in D, did not. In spite of Mozart's drop in appearances as a concerto soloist compared to preceding years, his skills as a pianist did not diminish in any way. Unsurprisingly, Mozart's adjustments to the autographs of K. 503 and 537 are often similar to adjustments in his earlier works in the genre. For example, revisions to the piano part do not always prioritize the showiness of the solo performer, in some cases demonstrating less brilliant virtuosity than their originals: in K. 537/i, left-hand semiquaver scales are changed to crotchets in bars 115 and 117 (solo exposition), an upward semiquaver sweep from left to right hands is compressed and limited to the right hand in bars 156 and 157 (solo exposition), and arpeggiated semiquavers are replaced by arpeggiated triplet quavers in bar 203 (recapitulation).[88] And compositional issues are clearly Mozart's principal concern in some cases: in the recapitulation of K. 537/i he crosses out fourteen bars between bars 305 and 306 apparently to accommodate structural compression, jumping directly from the reprise of bar 94 from the solo exposition to the reprise of bar 122.

But *vis-à-vis* earlier works in the genre, K. 503 and K. 537 also offer modest new perspectives on intersecting performing and compositional activities and priorities. The passage from the solo entry until the return of the main theme in the first movement of K. 503, for example, gave Mozart pause for thought. After five bars of solo-strings dialogue in which the piano elaborates its first triplet-quaver response with semiquavers, Mozart originally wrote ten bars for his own part before the return of the main theme. (No orchestral instruments receive any music here.)

---

[88] Unusually, in bars 156 and 157, it is the later version that Mozart rejects and the original that is retained. As is common for solo-part revisions in the autograph scores, Mozart writes the second version in the two staves above the piano (reserved for the two horns and two bassoons in this movement), but crosses out the revised version in favour of the original.

He subsequently crossed them out, drafted a version expanded to 16 bars on a sketchleaf (Skb1786b), and then incorporated a revision of the sketch in the autograph score, now including material for the orchestra (Example 11.10a).[89] Robert Levin identifies alterations from original to revision, including a deceptive cadence eschewing the repeated tonic arrivals in the first version and varied rhythms and textures: 'The evolution we see here is one from a basic design to a more elaborate execution'.[90] For William Kinderman: 'The solo passage ... seems to *lead into* or even *help bring about* the powerful main theme in the tutti, rather than merely to precede it [as in the original version].'[91] But observations orientated towards compositional priorities, important though they are, do not tell the full story of Mozart's revision. For the final version expands Mozart's profile as solo concerto performer considerably beyond the profile in the original passage, especially once considered in a slightly broader context. The revised passage, in other words, has an impact on more than just the lead back to the main theme. I have explained elsewhere the stylistic significance to Mozart's oeuvre of the thirty bars from the initial solo entry onwards, which balance in a short timespan the characteristically grand, brilliant and intimate qualities of his Viennese piano concertos.[92] Most notably, the piano's figurative semiquavers in bars 118–119, emerging out of the flute's sustained f‴, re-appropriate brilliance as intimacy, setting the scene for the immediate transformation of the grandest of main themes into an object of delicacy (bars 120–123; see Example 11.10b). As a result of the semiquaver virtuosity in the revised build-up to the main theme, bars 118–119 and then 126–127 convey an impression of sublimated brilliance; without the extended build up (as in the original version of the passage) these bars have no immediate context against which the transformation of brilliant virtuosity can be gauged. Mozart presents himself as a soloist with the ability to control musical circumstances through the malleability of the material he performs – not only by elaborating music in the moment as it were (including in unnotated embellishments), but also by changing the implications and meaning of characteristic qualities of his works.

Material absent from, as well as present in the autograph of the 'Coronation' Concerto K. 537 sheds light on performance and composition. For the left-hand piano part is entirely lacking in the Larghetto and

[89] For facsimile reproductions of the sketchleaf, and the original and revised piano openings, see Levin, 'Mozart's Working Methods in the Keyboard Concertos', pp. 389–393.

[90] Levin, 'Mozart's Working Methods in the Keyboard Concertos', p. 394.

[91] Kinderman, *Mozart's Piano Music*, p. 132. (Italics as in the original.)

[92] Keefe, *Mozart's Viennese Instrumental Music*, pp. 59–60.

Example 11.10a Mozart, Piano Concerto in C, K. 503/i, bars 91–113 (final version).

Example 11.10a (cont.)

Example 11.10b Mozart, Piano Concerto in C, K. 503/i, bars 116–126.

also in large chunks of the first and third movements. (The added piano material for the first edition published by André in 1794 shows no sign of having been written by Mozart.[93]) In the solo exposition of the first movement, for example, Mozart wrote the following for the left hand: semiquavers snaking between both hands in the run-up to the secondary theme (bars 108–126); triplets and semiquavers, many of which again move between treble and bass staves, in the approach to a further theme in the secondary-theme section (bars 145–160); material in the ruminative contrapuntal passage towards the end (bars 177–189); and the entire brilliant passage that immediately precedes the cadential trill (bars 190–216). Thus, Mozart wrote material for the piano left hand and in the lower of the two staves assigned to the soloist in the autograph, in large part when the right and left hands are closely intertwined, migrate between staves, or connect contrapuntally.[94]

It is also possible that pianistic brilliance was a priority for Mozart as he wrote down the solo exposition in the autograph. Like the revised piano entry in K. 503/i, the extended passage from the contrapuntal excursion until the cadential trill – fully notated in the left hand and subject to small revisions in both solo and orchestral parts – promotes the virtuoso performer. Much of this passage includes the relative rarity of simultaneous right- and left-hand semiquavers: only three of Mozart's earlier Viennese concertos contain substantial amounts of such material in the final stages of first-movement solo expositions and recapitulations (K. 466, 467 and 503). The sparse orchestral scoring for strings only, the uncommon solo texture, and the reduction in string participation to coincide with moments when only one hand plays semiquavers,[95] identify a desire for specially audible solo brilliance in this passage. In short, Mozart felt it necessary to include the full piano notation for performing purposes rather than leaving it – as he had other left-hand material – to his improvisatory skills or memory. The stylistic experimentation in which Mozart engaged in K. 537 apparently had his own performance profile at its core.[96]

---

[93] Tyson, 'Introduction', *K. 537: the Autograph Score*, p. viii; Irving, *Mozart's Piano Concertos*, p. 243.

[94] The aforementioned bars 177–189 represent a new type of passage in Mozart's piano concertos, perhaps also explaining the complete right- and left-hand piano notation. See Keefe, *Mozart's Viennese Instrumental Music*, pp. 68–70.

[95] See bars 201–204, including string parts originally envisaged for bar 201 that were subsequently crossed out, and bars 212 and 214.

[96] On stylistic experimentation in K. 537 and Mozart's last piano concerto, K. 595 in B-flat, see Keefe, *Mozart's Viennese Instrumental Music*, pp. 64–85 (Chapter 3), and Keefe, 'A Complementary Pair: Stylistic Experimentation in Mozart's Final Piano Concertos, K. 537 in D and K. 595 in B-flat', *Journal of Musicology*, 18/4 (2001), pp. 658–684.

Mozart's Orchestrations of Handel

In late March or early April 1790, Mozart began a short letter to Puchberg: 'Here I send to you, my dearest friend, Handel's life [*Händels Leben*].'[97] No book on Handel was listed among the inventory of Mozart's personal effects at his death,[98] so may only have been lent to him. Van Swieten was surely the source of Mozart's awareness and (temporary) possession of it; he is also mentioned in the letter immediately after the book, as if related to the thought of it. Several books about Handel published before 1790 can be ruled out as possible candidates, either lacking a German translation or covering subject matter more limited than Mozart's reference implies.[99] Charles Burney's *An Account of the Musical Performances in Westminster-Abbey and the Pantheon [1784] in Commemoration of Handel* (London, 1785), translated into German by Johann Joachim Eschenburg as *Nachricht von Georg Friedrich Händels Lebensumständen und zu London im Mai und Jun. 1784 angestellten Gedächtnissener* (Berlin: Nicolai, 1785) is a possible contender, but an unlikely one in focussing on the centennial commemorations preceded by only a short 'Sketch of the Life of G. F. Handel'. The book Mozart mentions, then, is almost certainly John Mainwaring's influential *Memoirs of the Late G. F. Handel* (London: Dodsley, 1760) translated by Johann Mattheson as *Georg Friedrich Händels Lebensbeschreibung nebst einem Verzeichnisse seiner Ausübungswerke und deren Berurtheilung* (Hamburg, 1761) – a principal source for Burney among others.[100]

Needless to say, Mozart's possession of Mainwaring's book does not prove that he read and digested it or that he and van Swieten agreed with the views expressed. But the way that Mozart launches into his letter implies he and Puchberg had discussed it, or had at least talked about Handel, whereupon Mozart had promised to send the book. Since Mozart had carried out two of his four Handel orchestrations at the time of the letter and would complete the others a few months later, Mainwaring's ideas provide useful context for Mozart's work.

---

[97] MBA, vol. 4, p. 104; LMF, p. 936.   [98] See MDL, pp. 509–510; MDB, pp. 601–602.

[99] For example J. Dixwell, *The Life of George-Frederic Handel* (London 1784), which was only twenty-six pages long and not translated into German; and Johann Friedrich Reichardt, *G. F. Händels Jugend* (Berlin, 1785).

[100] Mainwaring's book is assumed by other Mozart scholars (without explanation) to be the one mentioned by Mozart in his letter: see MBA, vol. 6, p. 391; LMF, p. 936; Wolff, *Mozart at the Gateway to his Fortune*, pp. 7–8.

Mainwaring, entirely convinced by Handel's genius, does not shy away from criticizing him.[101] In a similar vein van Swieten venerated Handel but also clearly felt in commissioning the re-orchestrations that improvements (or at least modernizations) could be made by Mozart.[102] Setting national affiliations aside, Mainwaring's final statement in the book could have equated with van Swieten's position in initiating the Handel projects in the late 1780s:

Little indeed are the hopes of ever equalling, much less of excelling so vast a Proficient in his own way: however, as there are so many avenues to excellent still open, so many paths to glory still untrod, it is hoped that the example of this Foreigner will rather prove an incentive, than a discouragement to the industry and genius of our own countrymen.[103]

Where criticism of Handel is concerned, Mainwaring explains that fullness of harmony sometimes comes at the expense of melody, that instrumental parts 'absorb' vocal ones on account of the richness of instrumental writing, that melodies leave something to be desired from time to time, that qualitative unevenness is most apparent in his oratorios, and that musical details often get lost amid grand conceptions.[104]

Mozart's re-orchestrations do not explicitly and directly address the kinds of criticisms raised in the book, and in one case – the richness of instrumental writing – would have added to the problems perceived by Mainwaring from his vantage point in 1760. But additions and alterations do have an impact on the melodic component of numbers and on musical details conveyed in grand contexts. As in Mozart's other Viennese vocal works, alterations and additions are conditioned by the needs of individual singers and the desire for apposite orchestral effects. Examining the first two Handel arrangements, for which early performances are securely documented, sheds light on Mozart's interrelated compositional and performance priorities.

---

[101] On Mainwaring and mid-eighteenth-century aesthetics, see Peter Kivy, 'Mainwaring's *Handel*: Its Relation to English Aesthetics', *Journal of the American Musicological Society*, 17 (1964), pp. 170–178; see also Kivy, *The Possessor and the Possessed: Handel, Mozart, Beethoven and the Idea of Musical Genius* (New Haven: Yale University Press, 2001), pp. 43–49.

[102] Before his death in April 1787 the Vienna-based composer Joseph Starzer had worked at van Swieten's suggestion on arranging Handel's works.

[103] John Mainwaring, *Memoirs of the Late G. F. Handel* (London: Dodsley, 1760), p. 208; Mainwaring, *Georg Friedrich Händels Lebensbeschreibung nebst einem Verzeichnisse seiner Ausübungswerke und deren Berurtheilung*, trans. Johann Mattheson (Hamburg, 1761), p. 155.

[104] Mainwaring, *Memoirs*, pp. 176, 177, 181, 181, 201; *Händels Lebensbeschreibung*, pp. 131, 131–132, 134, 134–135, 149.

In *Acis and Galatea*, Mozart 'modernizes' Handel's orchestration by including a larger complement of wind instruments than Handel and a wider variety of timbral and textural nuances as a result.[105] But Mozart's interpolations and alterations are not concerned solely or even primarily with increasing the size of the wind cohort. In arias for Acis and Damon Mozart introduces new textural strands, concerned both with immediate effects and with the deployment of these effects over time. In No. 12, for example, Handel's two oboes and two violins become flute, bassoon and strings in Mozart's version; the wind participants do not increase in number but are differently distributed by Mozart. Less closely tied to the string parts than the two oboes in Handel's version, the flute and bassoon provide new points of imitation (at the opening and bars 53–56) and short links (bars 115–123). In No. 13, Handel's two oboes become two oboes and two horns and again introduce new imitation (bars 16–19). Mozart both simplifies and embellishes Handel's wind scoring, as is evident in the support for vocal sustained notes: the two oboes playing d" in bars 45–48 of Handel's version are omitted by Mozart; the g" in bars 58–61, with sustained notes again for the two oboes in Handel, is now scored for two oboes and two horns in imitation; and the g" in bars 85–89, supported by oboe semiquavers in Handel, has an oboe and horn in parallel sixths. By introducing varied sonorities and writing at these junctures, Mozart draws attention to the vocal sustained notes themselves, one of Acis-singer Adamberger's known specialties (see Chapters 2 and 6).[106] Adamberger was also accommodated in one of Acis' earlier arias, No. 2, through the extension of Handel's complement of two oboes to two oboes, two clarinets and two bassoons. As in *Die Entführung* and bespoke arias from 1782–1786, Mozart brings a full-wind sonority to music for Adamberger and uses it both to introduce and to accompany him. The new figure from Mozart – wind sustained notes with preceding upbeat – also fills small gaps in Handel's score, including shortly before the Da Capo through the addition of a bassoon (bars 61–64). The same applies to the semi-obbligato bassoon lines added to Damon's aria, No. 4, which produce imitation, links between phrases and other connections

---

[105] The same can be said of Mozart's flute, oboe and trumpet additions to the Allegro A section (bars 1–78) of C. P. E. Bach's tenor aria 'Ich folge dir' from *Die Auferstehung und Himmelfahrt Jesu*. (C. P. E. Bach's original scoring was for strings and trumpet only.) Mozart wrote no wind material for the Andante B section (bars 79–111).

[106] For identification of Valentin Adamberger, Caterina Cavalieri and Tobias Gsur as soloists in the *Acis and Galatea* performance, see MDL, p. 290; MDB, p. 330.

Example 11.11 Handel, 'Every Valley' from *Messiah* (in Mozart's orchestration K. 572), bars 48–51.

between adjacent material that highlight a greater degree of melodic continuity than in Handel's original.

Consonant with Mainwaring's diagnosis of Handel's relative weakness as a melodist, new musical continuity is also a feature of the re-orchestrated *Messiah*. In No. 2, 'Every Valley', Mozart adds two flutes and two bassoons to Handel's strings, often having them participate independently of string lines. After introducing wind imitation of the strings at the singer's first extended melismas (bars 15–18, 21–23), Mozart dovetails bassoon semi-quavers with the voice during a later return to the melismas (Example 11.11). Frilly cadential figures for the two bassoons (bars 60, 68) prefigure Mozart's *coup de grace* for winds in the two bars before the final return of the main theme to coincide with the vocal exit (Example 11.12). While Handel marks rests for his strings in bars 74–75, employing dynamic and textural contrast to accentuate the onset of the last statement of the theme, Mozart has different ideas: his flutes and bassoons, first together then in counterpoint, are a logical outgrowth of prominent wind writing through-out the aria. Where Handel cultivated a momentary lull, then, Mozart added to the musical flow in keeping with the spirit of his re-orchestrated number.

Elsewhere in the *Messiah*, Mozart also paid attention to moment-to-moment musical continuity and accommodating individual singers. No. 6 for soprano 2, 'O thou that tellest good tidings to Zion', to which a flute,

Example 11.12 Handel, 'Every Valley' from *Messiah* (in Mozart's orchestration K. 572), bars 74–77.

two clarinets, two bassoons, two horns and string parts are added, comprises one of Mozart's more radical re-orchestrations, transforming the sound world of the original aria. Used semi-soloistically, the winds introduce numerous points of imitation, increasing the flow of semiquavers compared to Handel's version. In bars 17–20 (Example 11.13), for example, Mozart's flute pre-empts the strings and is also supported by a bassoon. The relationship between the re-orchestration process and the voice of the premiere's second soprano Katharina Altomonte is difficult to gauge as Mozart does not appear to have worked with her on other occasions. But the first soprano, Aloysia Lange with whom he had collaborated since the late 1770s (see Chapters 2 and 6), was much more familiar.[107] The relationships between soprano 1 and the winds blossom

[107] The soloists are documented as Lange, Altomonte, Herr Saal and Adamberger in a handwritten note on the printed text for the 6 March 1789 performance. See MDL, p. 294; MDB, p. 335. Even though Lange is not explicitly identified as the singer of the first soprano part in the note, we are surely right to follow Richard Maunder (*Mozart's Requiem: On Preparing a New Edition* [Oxford: Clarendon Press, 1988], p. 199) in associating her with the primary role. Altomonte's dates are given as c. 1770–1835 in Angermüller, *Mozart*, 2 vols., vol. 1, p. 298; she was nineteen in 1789, then, and performing alongside one of Vienna's leading sopranos. For a positive appraisal of Altomonte as 'one of our foremost amateurs' by Johann Ferdinand Schönfeld in 1796, see Schönfeld, 'A Yearbook of the Music of Vienna and Prague', p. 292.

Example 11.13 Handel, 'O thou that tellest good tidings to Zion' from *Messiah* (in Mozart's orchestration K. 572), bars 16–20.

in No. 24, 'But thou didst not leave his soul in hell', No. 27 'How beautiful are the feet of them that practice the gospel of peace' and No. 33, 'I know that my redeemer liveth'. The sensitivity to wind-voice timbres witnessed in Mozart's arias for Lange earlier in the 1780s is also evident in wind additions made here (albeit not now focussing on the blend between her voice and the oboe): a flute and bassoon are included for the first two, and a flute, bassoon and clarinet for the third. Whereas upper strings perform concurrently with the singer in Handel's original 'How beautiful are the feet', they are almost completely absent from the corresponding passages of Mozart's version and replaced by flute and bassoon separately and together. In 'I know that my redeemer liveth', wind interactions with the voice increase during the aria: they rarely overlap with soprano contributions early on but do so more in the later stages. Even when Mozart does not insert instruments into an aria for Lange, as in No. 14 'He shall feed his flock', he encourages careful responses to her voice by adding orchestral dynamic and expressive markings. Perhaps partially stimulated by Handel's own expressive indication 'Larghetto e piano' at the beginning of the number, as well as by Lange's voice, Mozart instructs the upper strings to play 'con sordini, sempre legato' and (for material repeated throughout) 'f calando p'.[108]

Mozart's modifications to Handel's *Messiah* extend to ensembles and choruses as well as arias. Abert criticized Mozart for confusing compositional and adaptation roles in his work, inadvertently 'imposing his own personality' on *Messiah*.[109] But like Franz Süssmayr completing the Requiem in 1791–1792, Mozart would have had no reason to fret about such things, and every reason to embrace his own emerging voice.[110] Mainwaring's identification of flaws in Handel's works would not have discouraged him either. Divergences between Handel and Mozart are marked in the chorus No. 34, 'Since by man came death', where instrumental effects are very differently conceived. The first and third of the four choral sections specifically address the subject of death: 'Since by man came death'; and 'For as in Adam all die'. (The second section also refers to death, but more indirectly in the context of resurrection: 'by man came also the resurrection of the dead'.) While Handel has these segments hushed and unaccompanied, even omitting the basses, Mozart loads them up with two oboes, two clarinets, three trombones and two bassoons. Trombones had already acquired connotations of death and the otherworldly in *Idomeneo* (1780–1781) and *Don Giovanni* (1787), of course, and would later appear in the Requiem as well; here and elsewhere in the *Messiah* re-orchestration, Mozart's own aesthetic priorities trumped adherence to Handel's. No doubt Mozart also chose violas rather than violins as accompaniment for the duet No. 36, 'O death!' on account of their darker hue.

Needless to say, blatantly overriding Handel's intentions had a practical as well as an aesthetic dimension. As for so many of his newly composed works, Mozart directed attention to specific performing opportunities and to accommodating performers participating on those occasions. Carrying out only re-orchestration of the music of another composer limited Mozart's hand. But, as witnessed in earlier operas and vocal works, instrumental writing could play a productive role in Mozart's creative processes.

*****

---

[108] The viola part is not asked to play 'con sordini', even though it receives a 'sempre legato' indication. We cannot know for sure whether Mozart's 'con sordini' omission is deliberate or an error (as the NMA believes). 'Calando' may designate a slowing of the tempo as well as a decrease in sound; see Brown, *Classical and Romantic Performing Practice*, p. 62.

[109] Abert, *W. A. Mozart*, p. 1153.

[110] On Süssmayr and the Requiem, see Keefe, *Mozart's Requiem*, pp. 172–233 (Chapter 5), and Keefe, '"Die Ochsen am Berge"', pp. 1–65. Mozart's combination of his own sounds and strategies and those of Handel in the four arrangements is discussed briefly in Keefe, *Mozart's Requiem*, pp. 115–116.

With the obvious exception of the final four symphonies – venerated far and wide – Mozart's orchestral music from late 1786–1790 has not received the best twentieth- and twenty-first-century press. The Handel arrangements were marginalized and criticized, as we have seen. The Piano Concerto K. 537 took many a beating.[111] And the horn concertos have rarely elicited detailed study: Abert's and Einstein's short, lukewarm comments sum up the general lack of attention paid to them.[112] Even the Piano Concerto K. 503 has not escaped criticism. Although widely acknowledged as an imposing masterpiece, it has occasionally represented a turning point in Mozart's oeuvre with negative connotations: for Joseph Kerman it is 'strangely cold . . . [and] registers a clear change in mood in the sequence of Mozart concertos', reflecting a disenchantment with the Viennese musical public; for John Rosselli, it perhaps marks the moment when audience and performer-composer tired of each other.[113] In a somewhat similar vein, William Kinderman perceives 'retrenchment in Mozart's completion of this ambitious concerto [in the second/third movements] . . . which involved borrowing a preexisting main theme for the finale' and Arthur Hutchings and Daniel Heartz sense a qualitative drop after the opening Allegro maestoso.[114] Maybe the legend of Mozart's decline as an impresario has influenced critical perceptions of works written during the period, just as his death in 1791 gave critical voice to swansongs.[115]

In truth, Mozart's orchestral music and concert activities from late 1786–1790 demonstrate more continuity than discontinuity with earlier works and practices. Mozart retained the confidence and support of the nobility, remained active and highly esteemed as a performer-composer practitioner, and wrote as carefully and creatively as ever for individual players and singers, including himself.[116] In seeking employment he

[111] On critical condemnation of K. 537, see Keefe, *Mozart's Viennese Instrumental Music*, pp. 64–66.

[112] See Abert, *W.A. Mozart*, p. 899; Einstein, *Mozart: His Character, His Work*, p. 296.

[113] Kerman, 'Mozart's Piano Concertos and Their Audience', in James M. Morris (ed.), *On Mozart* (Cambridge: Cambridge University Press, 1994), pp. 151–168, at 166–167; Rosselli, *Life of Mozart*, p. 49. For critical admiration of K. 503, see Keefe, *Mozart's Viennese Instrumental Music*, pp. 58–59.

[114] Kinderman, *Mozart's Piano Music*, p. 211; Arthur Hutchings, *A Companion to Mozart's Piano Concertos* (8th edition, Oxford: Oxford University Press, 1998), pp. 177–183; Heartz, *Mozart, Haydn, Early Beethoven*, p. 166.

[115] On the latter, see Keefe, *Mozart's Viennese Instrumental Music*, pp. 84–85, and 'A Complementary Pair', pp. 683–684.

[116] On Mozart's support from the nobility (contrary to popular opinion), see Solomon, *Mozart: A Life*, p. 423; Braunbehrens, *Mozart in Vienna*, p. 315; Edge, 'Mozart's Reception in Vienna, 1787–1791'.

continued to realize that combined compositional and performance talents carried a premium: drafting a petition to 'Euere königliche Ho' ('Your Royal Highness'), probably the son of Emperor Leopold II, Archduke Francis, for appointment as second Kapellmeister in Vienna and as musical instructor to the royal family, he modestly extolled his virtues both as *cognescenti* of church music composition and as a piano player.[117] And sounds and effects, evidencing the impact of performance on compositional activity, remained a central consideration: working intermittently on a piece for mechanical organ in Frankfurt in order 'to put a few ducats into the hands of my dear little wife', boredom derived from an inability to write for the organ and only for an instrument '[comprising] little pipes, which sound high pitched and for me too childish'.[118] Mozart may no longer have been the concert-performing meteor of yesteryear in late 1786–1790, but his star as a performer-composer still shone brightly.

---

[117] MBA, vol. 4, p. 107; LMF, pp. 938–939 (early May 1790). Mozart did not send the letter to its intended recipient.

[118] MBA, vol. 4, pp. 115–116; LMF, pp. 943–944 (3 October 1790). The piece to which Mozart refers could have been the nine-bar fragment, K. 593a. See Neal Zaslaw, 'Mechanical Instruments, Music for', in *Cambridge Mozart Encyclopedia*, p. 282.

PART V

Mozart in 1791

12 | New Beginnings, Continuations and Endings
Mozart's Last Year

On 8–9 October 1791, Mozart explained to Constanze, who was recuperating in Baden: 'I would like, as much as possible, to avoid all [financial] *embarrassment*; nothing is more pleasant than when one can live somewhat quietly, thus one must work hard and I like that.'[1] True to his word, the assiduously productive Mozart wrote a remarkable amount of music in eleven-and-a-bit months of 1791, albeit in the context of a hectic, not a quiet, life. By his own standards of compositional activity, 1790 had been a slow year: following the premiere of *Così fan tutte* on 26 January, it yielded among major works only the 'Prussian' quartets K. 589 and 590, and the string quintet K. 593. In contrast, 1791 brought *inter alia* two full-length operas, *Die Zauberflöte* and *La clemenza di Tito*, three concertos in the same calendar year for the first time since 1786, an adagio and rondo for glass harmonica, flute, oboe, viola and cello, a string quintet, concert aria, two cantatas, and an unfinished requiem.[2] The year had considerable financial and emotional challenges for Mozart too, even before his final illness took hold in mid- to late November: requests for financial assistance from Michael Puchberg were made in April and June, and further mysterious transactions with an unidentified individual alluded to in the summer months; costs were incurred for Constanze's health-related stays in Baden in June, July and October and anxieties consequently experienced and processed; and, in November, Mozart lost a lawsuit lodged against him for unknown reasons by Prince Karl Lichnowsky, for the substantial sum of

---

[1] MBA, vol. 4, p. 158; LMF, p. 968. (Italics as in the original.)

[2] Among the concertos, the first and second movements of K. 595 in B-flat may have been composed in 1788; see Tyson, *Autograph Scores*, pp. 153, 156, and, for stylistic implications, Keefe, *Mozart's Viennese Instrumental Music*, pp. 64–85. The second movement of the horn concerto in D, K. 412, was left unfinished and is generally performed in the version completed by Süssmayr (K. 514a). For discussion of the Süssmayr completion and material for the movement left by Mozart, see Christoph Wolff, *Mozart's Requiem: Historical and Analytical Studies, Documents, Score*, trans. Mary Whittall (Berkeley: University of California Press, 1994), pp. 44–51. Sometime from March 1791 onwards Mozart also wrote 160 bars of an incomplete Andante for piano four hands (Fr 1791a) and 72 bars of an incomplete string quintet movement, K. Anh. 87 (K. 515c, Fr 1791c). For facsimiles see NMA, X/30/4, pp. 202–204, 205–207.

1,435 gulden, 32 kreutzer.[3] *Pace* the desire for a peaceful existence, non-musical trials and tribulations actually may have enhanced Mozart's productivity (even though comparable financial problems in 1790 do not appear to have had that effect). One is reminded of a famous cinematic line from *The Third Man* (1949) spoken by villainous Harry Lime at the Prater in Vienna, scene of Mozart's own supposed remarks about having been poisoned and of writing his Requiem for himself:[4] 'In Italy for thirty years under the Borgias they had warfare, terror, murder and bloodshed, but they produced Michelangelo, Leonardo da Vinci and the Renaissance. In Switzerland, they had brotherly love; they had five hundred years of democracy and peace – and what did that produce? The cuckoo clock.'

Mozart is one of few composers in the western tradition to have had two substantial, single-authored new operas premiered within a month of each other (*Tito* and *Die Zauberflöte* on 6 and 30 September respectively).[5] Had circumstances or inclinations been different, Mozart might have written two operas for London in 1791, instead of one each for Prague and Vienna: in a letter dated 26 October 1790, Robert May O'Reilly, manager at the King's Theatre in London, invited him to the city to compose them for

---

[3] For the letters to Puchberg, see MBA, vol. 4, pp. 129, 139–140; LMF, pp. 948, 957 (13 April, 25 June 1791). Mozart expresses anxieties about Constanze's health and wellbeing in several letters from 1791. See, for example, MBA, vol. 4, pp. 133, 134, 137, 143, 143–144; LMF, pp. 950, 951, 954, 958, 959 (late May, 6 June, 12 June, end of June/beginning of July, 2 July 1791). The Lichnowsky case against Mozart was first identified and discussed by Walther Brauneis in '" . . . wegen schuldigen 1435 f 32 xr": Neuer Archivfund zur Finanzmisere Mozarts im November 1791', *Mitteilungen der Internationalen Stiftung Mozarteum*, 39 (1991), pp. 159–163. In the same article, Brauneis suggests that a loan was probably behind enigmatic references to 'N. N.' (*nomen nescio, nomen nominandum*, or *non nominato*, as designated editorially by Nissen) in Mozart's letters to Constanze in summer 1791. See also John Arthur, '"N. N." Revisited: New Light on Mozart's Late Correspondence', in Brandenburg (ed.), *Haydn, Mozart, and Beethoven*, pp. 127–145, at 130–135, who – based on analysis of crossings out in the letters – proposes Baron Raimund Wetzlar von Plankenstern as the named businessman, rather than the more commonly cited Joseph Goldhahn. On Mozart's income in 1791, see Landon, *1791: Mozart's Last Year*, pp. 61–62; on debts at his death, see Braunbehrens, *Mozart in Vienna*, pp. 424–425.

[4] See Niemetschek, *Leben*, p. 34, *Life of Mozart*, p. 43. The Prater is described by Johann Pezzl (1787) as 'a wood inhabited by deer, pheasants and wild boar, and is a favourite place of recreation for the Viennese'. See 'Sketch of Vienna', in *Mozart and Vienna*, p. 158. For an amusing anecdote about Salieri and Michael Kelly's encounter with a boar at the Prater, see Kelly, *Reminiscences*, pp. 199–200. In 1784, Riesbeck (*Briefe*, p. 221) identified the Prater and the Augarten as two of the best public walking places in European cities. For more on the Prater in 1789–1790, extolling its virtues, see Reitzenstein, *Reise nach Wien*, pp. 226–234.

[5] Others to have done so up to the end of the eighteenth century include Niccolò Piccinni, Niccolò Jommelli, Pasquale Anfossi and Domenico Cimarosa. See the work-lists, deriving from the *New Grove Dictionary of Music and Musicians, Revised Edition* (London: Macmillan, 2001), in *Oxford Music Online* (www.oxfordmusiconline.com).

a payment of £300, requiring his presence from late December 1790 onwards.[6]

Die Zauberflöte was written for the Wiednertheater, in the Theater auf der Wien building of the Freihaus complex, which comprised six courtyards, workshops, an apothecary, a mill, a church and around 225 apartments in a relatively poor area of Vienna located off the 'Ring' and close to where the Vienna Staatsoper stands today.[7] The theatre's director Emanuel Schikaneder (1751–1812), an actor, singer, composer and librettist known to the Mozarts since 1780, was employed at the Burgtheater and Kärntnertortheater in 1785–1786 before a move to Regensburg and then a return to Vienna in 1789 after the death of the previous Wiednertheater director, Johann Friedel. Favouring comic operas and fairytale singspiels and aspiring to high-quality performances and frequent new productions, Schikaneder brought two singers with him from Regensburg, Benedikt Schack and Franz Xaver Gerl, hired talented Viennese musicians including the Kapellmeister Johann Baptist Henneberg, 'a clever master of the pianoforte' (1796),[8] and employed teams of house writers (himself, his wife Eleonore, and Franz Ludwig Giesecke) and house composers (Henneberg, Schack, Gerl). At a theatre accommodating more than 500 spectators from high and low income brackets and a full gamut of stagecraft (trap doors, changing backdrops, flying machines, etc.), Schikaneder scored early hits with the collaborative singspiels *Die zween Anton oder Der dumme Gärtner auf dem Gebirge* (1789) and *Der Stein der Weisen* (1790).[9] Mozart probably began work on *Die Zauberflöte* around April 1791 and had finished most of it by July before turning to *Tito*; the Priests' march, Overture and perhaps several other numbers were written shortly before the premiere and after the return from Prague. Ignaz von Seyfried, Mozart's young associate, remembers him 'quickly [getting on] to the instrumentation and catching up with the missing small numbers' after arriving back in Vienna in mid September.[10]

[6] MDL, p. 332; MDB, pp. 377–378. Mozart reply (if any) is no longer extant.

[7] See Egon Komorzynski's description of the Freihaus, given in H. C. Robbins Landon, *The Mozart Essays* (London: Thames & Hudson, 1995), pp. 61–62.

[8] See Schönfeld, 'A Yearbook of the Music of Vienna and Prague', p. 301.

[9] On Mozart, Schikaneder and the Wiednertheater, see David Buch (ed.), *Der Stein der Weisen* (Middleton, WI: A-R Editions, 2007), pp. ix–xviii; Peter Branscombe, *W. A. Mozart: 'Die Zauberflöte'* (Cambridge: Cambridge University Press, 1991), pp. 142–152; Braunbehrens, *Mozart in Vienna*, pp. 372–379. For more on the theatre itself, including (as of 1794) numbers of benches in the *parterre noble*, parterre, and noble gallery, and the number of benches and boxes in the second gallery, see Cole, 'Mozart and Two Theaters', especially pp. 132–138.

[10] MDL, p. 472; MDB, p. 556. For discussion of the opera's chronology, based on paper types in the autograph score, see Karl-Heinz Kohler, 'Zu den Methoden und einigen Ergebnissen der philologischen Analyse am Autograph der "Zauberflöte"', *Mozart-Jahrbuch 1980–83*,

In addition to the opera itself, the *Zauberflöte* circle provided the stimulus for eight variations on 'Ein Weib ist das herrlichste Ding', K. 613, from *Der dumme Gärtner* by Schack and Gerl. It is not hard to imagine the variations originating as an informal improvisation among friends and perhaps capturing creative back and forth between Mozart and Schikaneder.[11] In published form from Artaria in June 1791 the fantasia-like qualities of the final variations – chromatic wanderings in the sixth, tempo changes and free flourishes between pauses in the seventh, an unexpected shunt to the flat submediant B-flat in the eighth – leave the impression of a performer in full-fledged compositional mode.[12]

Tito, a commission from Domenico Guardasoni for the Prague coronation of Joseph II's successor, Leopold II, probably occupied Mozart from early to mid-July until the premiere on 6 September. Mozart and his father crossed paths with Leopold in earlier times: they had audiences in Vienna and Florence (1762, 1770); and they sent him – in his capacity as Grand Duke of Tuscany – *Lucio Silla* (1772) in the hope it would land Mozart a position at court, or at least secure a good recommendation for a post elsewhere. *La clemenza di Tito* thus provided Mozart with a further opportunity to impress Leopold in Leopold's favoured genre of opera seria.[13] Four days before the premiere, which played to a full house buoyed by free

pp. 283–287, and Branscombe, '*Die Zauberflöte*', pp. 80–86. On ink and paper in the autograph, set in chronological and dramaturgical contexts, see Claudia Maurer-Zenck, 'Dramaturgie und Philologie der *Zauberflöte*: Eine Hypothese und vielen Fragen zur Chronologie', *Mozart-Jahrbuch 2001* (Kassel: Bärenreiter, 2003), pp. 383–426. See also Christoph Wolff, 'Musicological Introduction', in Wolfgang Amadeus Mozart, '*Die Zauberflöte*', K. 620: *Facsimile of the Autograph Score* (Los Altos, CA: The Packard Humanities Institute, 2009), 3 vols., vol. 3, pp. 17–32, at 18–21.

[11] Schikaneder improvised (or wrote) further strophes for this aria: 'Mozart's variations then are the musical counterpart to Schikaneder's own improvised strophes, variations on an aria that appears to have achieved a special status.' See David J. Buch, 'On the Context of Mozart's Variations to the Aria, "Ein Weib ist das herrlichste Ding auf der Welt", K. 613', *Mozart-Jahrbuch 1999*, pp. 71–80 (quotation at p. 80).

[12] On K. 613 probably originating as an improvisation and containing fantasia qualities, see Komlós, 'Mozart the fortepianist', pp. 36–39. As she points out: '[In] some old manuscript copies the last three variations are written out continuously, without numberings or double barline' (p. 39), reinforcing improvisatory qualities. For the first edition, *Ariette 'Ein Weib ist das herrlichste Ding' avec variations pour le clavecin ou piano forte par W. A. Mozart* (Vienna: Artaria, 1791), see https://iiif.lib.harvard.edu/manifests/view/drs:17525734$1i.

[13] See John A. Rice, *W. A. Mozart: 'La clemenza di Tito'* (Cambridge: Cambridge University Press, 1991), p. 47. On *Tito* in relation to the opera seria repertory staged at the Regio Teatro di via della Pergola in Florence at the end of the future emperor's period of residency in the city (1780–1790), see Marita P. McClymonds, 'Mozart's "La Clemenza di Tito and Opera Seria in Florence as a Reflection of Leopold II's Musical Taste', *Mozart-Jahrbuch 1984–85* (Kassel: Bärenreiter, 1986), pp. 61–70. Emperor Leopold also would have heard Mozart's music when attending *Der Stein der Weisen* at the Wiednertheater on 3 and 14 February 1791; see Edge and

admission, *Don Giovanni* was staged for the emperor, his royal entourage and another audience packed to the rafters.[14] After a hectic few months readying two operas for the stage, Mozart wrote proudly to Constanze: 'The strangest thing is that on the same evening that my new opera [*Zauberflöte*] was performed for the first time with so much applause, "Tito" was performed in Prague for the last time also with extraordinary applause.'[15]

Mozart's career received an important boost earlier in 1791, away from the world of opera. Reacting in late April to a serious illness for the incumbent Kapellmeister of St Stephen's Cathedral, Leopold Hofmann (1738–1793), and perhaps encouraged by a relaxation in the strictures of the *Gottesdienstordnung* under Leopold II, Mozart successfully petitioned for the post of unpaid adjunct Kapellmeister. According to the City Council decree, Mozart was required 'to assist the said Herr Kapellmeister [Hofmann] in his service free of charge, to stand in for him when he cannot appear himself, and in the case where the real Kapellmeister post becomes vacant, to be satisfied with the salary and with all that the City Council prescribes and deems advisable'.[16] Had he outlived the ailing Hofmann, a reasonable expectation in early 1791, Mozart would have inherited a prestigious, potentially lucrative post. The eye-catching 2,000 florins paid annually to Hofmann was not as generous as often assumed since 1,800 florins of it was intended to cover upkeep for the choirboys, and the post came (as Hofmann discovered) with administrative headaches Mozart would not have relished. But free housing, a fuel allowance and considerable prestige accrued to the post in addition to the salary. It also would have provided Mozart with a venue for promoting his own sacred music and ample time for pursuing interests elsewhere. Mozart's activities as adjunct Kapellmeister in the remaining months of 1791 are difficult to determine; performances at St Stephen's of the 'Coronation' Mass K. 317 and the Mass in C K. 337 are a possibility.[17] It is conceivable too that the thirty-seven-bar

---

Black (eds.), 'The Habsburg Court and Guests attend *Der Stein der Weisen*', in *Mozart: New Documents*. First published 12 June 2014. http://dx.doi.org/10.7302/Z20P0WXJ.

[14] On the *Don Giovanni* performance (2 September 1791), see MDL, p. 353; MDB, pp. 402–403.

[15] MBA, vol. 4, p. 157; LMF, p. 967 (7–8 October 1791). On connections between *Die Zauberflöte* and *Tito*, see Heartz, *Mozart's Operas*, pp. 255–275, and Jessica Waldoff, 'Reading Mozart's Operas "for the sentiment"', in Keefe (ed.), *Mozart Studies*, pp. 74–108, at 107–108.

[16] MDL, p. 346; MDB, p. 395.

[17] For contextual discussion of music at St Stephen's Cathedral in the late eighteenth century and Mozart's appointment, including information given in this paragraph, see Black, 'Mozart and the Practice of Sacred Music, 1781–91', pp. 244–301.

Kyrie fragment K. 323 (K. Anh. 15, Fr. 1790a) was written in connection with duties at the cathedral.[18]

The anonymous request for a Requiem from Franz, Count von Walsegg, resident of Schloss Stuppach near Gloggnitz around fifty miles southwest of Vienna, probably in summer 1791, would have struck Mozart as a coincidence relative to his appointment at St Stephen's and concomitant attention to sacred music.[19] Commissioned in memory of his wife who had died aged 20 on 14 February 1791, Walsegg approached Mozart in all likelihood through his lawyer Dr Johann Sortschan or business manager, Franz Anton Leitgeb. Michael Puchberg, Mozart's fellow mason and beneficiary, lived in a Viennese building owned by Walsegg and may have suggested Mozart for the task.[20] Mozart almost certainly began work only after the premiere of *Die Zauberflöte* on 30 September; in the ensuing weeks the Requiem had to compete for attention with the Masonic cantata K. 623 (dated 15 November in the *Verzeichnüß*), performances of *Die Zauberflöte* at the Wiednertheater, a trip to Baden to fetch Constanze, and fallout from the Lichnowsky lawsuit. But a more decisive interruption lay ahead. In late November Mozart took to his bed and died a few minutes before 1 am on 5 December, perhaps of rheumatic inflammatory fever or of renal failure.[21] At his death, the Introit was in full score, and vocal parts, continuo and some instrumental passages had been written for the Kyrie, Dies irae, Tuba mirum, Rex tremendae, Recordare, Confutatis, Lacrymosa (eight bars only), Domine Jesu and Hostias. Constanze moved quickly to have the work completed, turning first to Joseph Eybler, and then, once Eybler had partially orchestrated the sequence and returned the score, to Süssmayr, who finished it by the end of February 1792.

---

[18] See Black, 'Mozart and the Practice of Sacred Music, 1781–91', p. 190. Konrad (*Catalogue of His Works*, p. 200) dates the fragment at 'probably later' than 1790. Maximilian Stadler completed it in the early nineteenth century, adding sixteen bars after Mozart breaks off.

[19] On the commissioning of the Requiem, see in particular Keefe, *Mozart's Requiem*, pp. 1–2; Wolff, *Mozart's Requiem*, pp. 1–4; and Zaslaw, *Der neue Köchel* (Wiesbaden: Breitkopf & Härtel, forthcoming).

[20] See Walther Brauneis, '"Dies Irae, Dies Illa" – "Tag des Zornes, Tag der Klage": Auftrag, Entstehung and Vollendung von Mozarts "Requiem"', *Jahrbuch des Vereins für Geschichte der Stadt Wien*, 47–48 (1991–1992), pp. 33–48.

[21] Mozart's cause of death has been the subject of exhaustive speculation. For differing perspectives in the last forty years or so, see (for example) Carl Bär, *Mozart: Krankheit, Tod, Begräbnis* (Kassel: Bärenreiter, 1972); Peter J. Davies, *Mozart in Person: His Character and Health* (New York: Greenwood, 1989); Landon, *1791: Mozart's Last Year*, pp. 183–194; Lucien Karhausen, *The Bleeding of Mozart: A Medical Glance on His Life, Illness and Personality* (Dartford: Xlibris Corporation, 2011).

Mozart's accomplishments in 1791 are characterized by new beginnings, continuations of ongoing activities, and endings, often at the same time. The first and last parts of the year offer up good examples. In January, Mozart turned to a familiar medium (*Lieder*), but to a sub-genre with which he had had relatively little experience at least before 1787, namely children's songs.[22] 'Sehnsucht nach dem Frühlinge', 'Der Frühling', and 'Das Kinderspiel', K. 596–598 (dated 14 January in the *Verzeichnüß*) appeared in 'Frühlingslieder', one of Placidus Partsch's two volumes of *Liedersammlung für Kinder und Kinderfreunde*; Mozart's participation was perhaps arranged by the volume's publisher Ignaz Alberti, a Masonic brother at the lodge 'Zur gekrönten Hoffnung'.[23] And the Requiem in October and November took Mozart back to his Salzburg years, as well as to the C-minor mass K. 427 (1782–1783), but now in the as-yet-unexplored context of a mass for the dead.[24]

Even after the achievements of the first eight months or so of 1791, and with two operas in preparation, Mozart kept an eye on career opportunities, and potential new beginnings, away from Vienna. Apparently at Mozart's behest, since information about whereabouts and timeframe for returning from Prague to the capital was presumably passed on for this purpose, Count Rasumovsky wrote to the Russian Field-Marshall, Prince Gregor Potemkim (15 September 1791):

---

[22] Up to the age of around ten, Mozart sang to his father a lullaby apparently of his own composition albeit related to a Dutch folk-song, 'Oragna fiagata fa'. See Nissen, *Biographie W. A. Mozarts*, p. 35. It is also mentioned in correspondence between Mozart and Leopold. See MBA, vol. 2, pp. 273, 286; LMF, pp. 475 (11–12 February 1778), 485 (19 February 1778). On the unlikelihood of the song 'An die Freude' K. 53 being written for the daughter of the doctor in Olmütz who treated Mozart's smallpox in 1768, see Sadie, *Mozart: The Early Years*, p. 158. On 'Des kleinen Friedrichs Geburtstag', K. 529 (1787), 'Die kleine Spinnerin', K. 531 (1787), and 'Lied beim Auszug in das Feld' (1788), as songs for children, see Paul Corneilson, '*Liedersammlung für Kinder und Kinderfreunde*: A Context for Mozart's Songs K. 596–598', *Mozart-Jahrbuch 2011*, pp. 101–117, at 102.

[23] On the *Liedersammlung* and Mozart's involvement in it, see Corneilson, 'A Context for Mozart's Songs K. 596–598'. See also David J. Buch (ed.), *Liedersammlung für Kinder und Kinderfreunde am Clavier (1791)* (Middleton, WI: A-R Editions, 2014), pp. ix–xix. 'Sehnsucht nach dem Frühlinge', the first of thirty in the publication as a whole, draws on the theme from the finale of the B-flat Piano Concerto K. 595 completed a few days earlier.

[24] For a filmic representation of the Requiem invoking in Mozart memories of his early years, see Karl Hartl's *Wen die Götter lieben* (Austria, 1942), discussed in Keefe, *Mozart's Requiem*, pp. 37–38. See also Levey, *The Life and Death of Mozart*, p. 258. For connections between *Die Zauberflöte* and *Tito* and earlier works from Salzburg, see also John A. Rice, 'Leopold II, Mozart, and the Return to a Golden Age', in Thomas Bauman and Marita Petzoldt McClymonds (eds.), *Opera and the Enlightenment* (Cambridge: Cambridge University Press, 1995), pp. 271–296.

It was not up to me, my prince, to send to you the best keyboard player and one of the ablest composers in Germany, named Mozart, who, being somewhat discontent here, might be disposed to undertake this journey. He is in Bohemia now, but will be returning soon. If Your Highness therefore wants to authorize me to engage him, not for a long term, but simply to present himself to you in order to hear him and then to attach him to your service, if you judge appropriate . . .[25]

Perhaps Mozart felt he should capitalize on his reputation as a composer and performer-composer by exploring international pastures new. Given the international esteem in which Mozart was held in 1791, there is no particular reason to doubt Constanze's account of substantial annuities promised from Amsterdam and members of the Hungarian nobility in her petition to the emperor for a pension shortly after her husband's death, even though it was in her interests to emphasize her desperate financial plight and Mozart's unrealizable future earnings.[26] My chapter considers separately Mozart's instrumental music, performance activities and commissions, his operas *Die Zauberflöte* and *La clemenza di Tito*, and his other vocal music from 1791, telling the story of a remarkable year that could so easily have marked a mid-career creative peak, or the onset of 'a new and spectacularly successful stage in his career',[27] rather than a magnificent, tumultuous end.

Instrumental Music: Concerts, Public Performances and Commissions

While the second and third quarters of 1791 were largely taken up with *Die Zauberflöte* and *La clemenza di Tito*, attention was occupied at other times (and occasionally overlapping with operatic work) by a variety of instrumental music, concerts, public performances and commissions. Musical activities in this category collectively represent ongoing obligations and interests as well as opportunistic explorations of new types of composition.

Mozart's principal duty as chamber musician to the emperor was to write dances for the extremely popular balls held during Carnival between 10 pm and 6 am at the Hofburg *Redoutensäle*. He duly supplied sets of minuets, contredanses and German dances in the early months of 1788,

---

[25] MDL, p. 355; MDB, pp. 406–407. Potemkim would have had little chance to act on Rasumovsky's letter (assuming he received it); he died on 16 October 1791 in Bessarabia, now southwest Ukraine.

[26] MDL, pp. 371–372; MDB, pp. 421–422.   [27] Landon, *Mozart: the Golden Years*, p. 216.

1789 and 1791.[28] The Viennese visit in Carnival 1791 of the keen dancer and all-around exhibitionist King Ferdinand of Naples may account for Mozart's special productivity that season.[29] Johann Pezzl (1787) captured the ambience of the balls in general:

When you have pressed through [the] entrance hall and climbed a flight of stairs, all of a sudden you are in the great magical room [the *Grosser Redoutensaal*]. The light from many thousands of wax candles reflected in the great crystal chandeliers and from the pyramid-like candelabras arranged in symmetrical rows dazzles the eye; one's ears are enchanted and captivated by fanfares of trumpets and drums, intermingled with the softer tone of a hundred musical instruments . . .

. . . If only a thousand people attend, it feels too lonely; 1,500 dancers make a nice Redout, and with that number there is still room enough to dance. With 2,000 there is no longer room to dance properly, and in the last few days [of Carnival], when there may be up to 3,000 pleasure seekers, it is a real squeeze. The orchestra plays its minuets and German dances in vain, for there isn't room to take three proper steps; everybody is jammed together, making a great awkward mass of people for whom only a slow wave-like motion is possible.[30]

Mozart shared a love of dance with his Viennese compatriots: according to Nissen, he was so passionate about it he missed neither masked balls in the theatres nor private ones at the homes of friends, and was highly proficient at the minuet in particular.[31] Indeed, 'Mozart's consummate skill as a dancer allowed him, to a degree far greater than Haydn and Beethoven, to compose music that translated the character and movement of the dance into musical motion, thus making his trio music beautiful yet useful for dancing.'[32] A new kind of synergy between performance and composition

---

[28] Most of the dances were subsequently published. See Getraut Haberkamp, *Die Erstdrücke der Werke von Wolfgang Amadeus Mozart* (Tutzing: Hans Schneider, 1986), 2 vols., vol. 1, pp. 420–421.

[29] See Edge, 'Mozart's Reception in Vienna', pp. 88–93. On Ferdinand's dancing at the Carnival balls, see *Bayreuther Zeitung* (21 January 1791), Anhang, p. 61; *Bayreuther Zeitung* (21 February 1791), Anhang, p. 152; *Bayreuther Zeitung* (24 February 1791), p. 164; *Bayreuther Zeitung* (3 March 1791), p. 186; *Bayreuther Zeitung* (10 March 1791), p. 311; *Bayreuther Zeitung* (12 March 1791), p. 317. Mozart's dance compositions for Carnival 1791 include the minuets K. 599, 601, 604, the German dances K. 600, 602, 605, the contredanses K. 603, 607, and the *Ländler* K. 606.

[30] See Pezzl, *Skizze von Wien* (1786–1790), as given in Landon, *Mozart in Vienna*, p. 150. For evidence that 3,000 people attended a ball on 13 February 1791, see *Bayreuther Zeitung* (21 February 1791), Anhang, p. 152.

[31] Nissen, *Biographie W. A. Mozarts*, p. 692.

[32] Eric McKee, *Decorum of the Minuet, Delirium of the Waltz: A Study of Dance-Music Relations in ¾ Time* (Bloomington, IN: Indiana University Press, 2012), p. 62.

is thereby captured in Mozart's Viennese oeuvre. He enjoyed hearing his own music at balls, reporting to Viennese friend Jacquin from Prague: 'I didn't dance and I didn't flirt ... but I watched with great pleasure as all these people danced around so profoundly happy to the music of my *Figaro*, arranged as nothing but contredanses and German Dances.'[33] 'Non più andrai' was subsequently adapted by Mozart himself for the *Redoutensäle* as the first of five contredanses K. 609.[34] And Mozart clearly did not consider the audibility of the music at balls compromised by large numbers of participants. The wide range of effects in his dances comprise quiet and delicate as well as loud and forceful sounds communicated to the 'audience' of participating dancers: the hurdy gurdy is a solo instrument in K. 602/iii, lightly accompanied by bassoons and strings, and again in K. 601/ii with a larger wind complement and uncoordinated *sf* and *mfp* inflections; *pizzicati* appear in K. 571/vi, K. 586/vii, K. 605/ii, K. 609/v and alongside *sotto voce*, *dolce* and *sf* effects in K. 568; and the final, climactic German dance of K. 571, with Turkish-inspired drums and cymbals including in a lengthy coda, ends with a delicate succession of *piano* sonorities (Example 12.1) rather than the more typical *forte* flourish.[35]

Either side of his portfolio of dances for Carnival 1791, Mozart wrote two strings quintets, K. 593 in D (December 1790) and K. 614 in E-flat (12 April 1791). It is not known for whom they were intended. The posthumous Artaria edition of both (1793) states that they were 'composed for a Hungarian connoisseur' (*composto per un amatore Ongarese*) commonly identified as Johann Tost, a distinguished violinist associated with Haydn's string quartets.[36] But there are other potential recipients fitting the epithet too: on 11 December 1791, Constanze reported Mozart as assured 'only a few days before his death of an annual subscription of 1,000 florins from a share of the Hungarian nobility'.[37] Unlike the C-major quintet K. 515 and the 'Haydn' quartets (see Chapters 5 and 10)

---

[33] MBA, vol. 4, p. 10; LMF, p. 903 (15 January 1787).

[34] In spite of traditional dating at March 1791, these dances are now thought to come from 1787–1788. See Tyson, *Mozart: Studies of the Autograph Scores*, pp. 33, 35; Tyson, 'Proposed New Dates', in Eisen (ed.), *Mozart Studies*, p. 225.

[35] K. 605/iii also features a quiet ending to an elaborate, climactic dance, but Mozart's authorship of it is not certain. See 'Appendix One: Worklist', in Eisen and Keefe (eds.), *Cambridge Mozart Encyclopedia*, p. 588; Konrad, *Mozart: Catalogue of His Works*, p. 111.

[36] For the attribution to Tost specifically, see (for example) Landon, *1791: Mozart's Last Year*, pp. 30–31; MDL, p. 372 and MDB, pp. 422–423; Rushton, *Mozart*, p. 208; Gutman, *Mozart: a Cultural Biography*, pp. 716–717. On Tost's association with Haydn's quartets, see Floyd Grave and Margaret Grave, *The String Quartets of Haydn* (New York: Oxford University Press, 2006), pp. 244–247, 264–265.

[37] MDL, p. 372; MDB, p. 421.

Example 12.1 Mozart, Six German Dances K. 571/vi, coda, bars 59–69.

neither performance parts connected to Mozart, nor an edition overseen by him, are available for consultation. But the autograph of the E-flat quintet by itself shows how performing issues had an impact on Mozart's creative process.[38] While the most stylistically striking feature of the first movement is the opposition of *f* (*Sturm und Drang*) and *p* (sensibility) passages in the development section in conjunction with tonal twists and turns,[39] the succession, and juxtaposition, of *f* and *p* dynamics elsewhere in the movement gave Mozart pause for thought, probably as he contemplated effects in performance. For example, he modified the original dynamics at the climax to the exposition and recapitulation, where the first violin has a stratospheric d'''' (in the exposition) and cadential trills (Example 12.2). In both passages he initially envisaged *forte*s in the first violin for the entire climactic ascents – against *piano* in the other instruments – but crossed them out and introduced them a few bars later instead to coordinate *forte* arrivals for all instruments at bars 76 and 202. Also, judging by the lighter ink colour for

[38] For the autograph see the British Library London, Zweig MS 60.
[39] Keefe, *Mozart's Viennese Instrumental Music*, pp. 131–132. See also the analysis of this movement in Ratner, *Classic Music*, pp. 237–245.

Example 12.2 Mozart, String Quintet in E-flat K. 614/i, bars 71–78 (including a crossed out *forte* in bar 72).

the dynamics than the notes at the start of the development section a few bars later, he issued cautionary *p*s as an afterthought, ensuring string players realize the full effect of the *Sturm und Drang forte* shunt to A-flat in bar 90.[40] At the opening of the movement, too, Mozart first wrote *p* for the violas, subsequently changing it to *forte* to introduce *forte – piano* contrast.[41] Thus, a drama of oppositional effects closer to the piano concertos than anywhere else in his Viennese chamber oeuvre[42] was apparently on Mozart's mind

[40] The beginning of the transition in the sonata-rondo finale (bars 23–25) is similar: the *p*s are in a lighter ink than the notes, indicating later inclusion. Since the rondo section before the double bar ended *piano*, the new *p*s are cautionary, guaranteeing an impact for the *forte* / *sf* a few bars later (30–31).

[41] This particular change was probably put into effect before Mozart wrote the corresponding passage at the opening of the recapitulation, where the *forte – piano* was envisaged from the start.

[42] Keefe, *Mozart's Viennese Instrumental Music*, p. 132.

Example 12.3 Mozart, String Quintet in E-flat K. 614/ii, bars 78–84.

during the composition of the movement. A climactic moment in the Andante may also reflect such drama. Wracking dissonances at the beginning of a transition to the 'reprise' in this formally procedurally and generically hybrid movement coincide with uncoordinated dynamics (Example 12.3): three different markings occur simultaneously (*f – p; sf – p; sfp*) after *sf* and *mf* surges had previously promoted homogeneity.[43] As with the 'Haydn' quartets discussed in Chapter 5, this passage invites performers to determine how their internal 'conversation' is communicated:

---

[43] On Mozart in the slow movement of K. 614 manipulating 'not merely markers of genre but markers of form and procedure as well', see Eisen, 'Mozart's Chamber Music', in Keefe (ed.), *Cambridge Companion to Mozart*, pp. 115–117 (at 116). On the transitional passage as an example of Mozart '[conjuring] unheard-of sounds, plaintive and yet pleasantly thrilling, strange and yet exquisite', see Burnham, *Mozart's Grace*, pp. 97–100 (at 100).

Example 12.4 Mozart, Horn Concerto in D K. 412/i, bars 133–135.

in this instance, unusually harsh dissonances and unsynchronized dynamics may encourage cultivation of a kind of dysfunctional exchange.

The three concertos from 1791 were written for an aging horn player (Leutgeb) and two instrumentalists still at the top of their game (Stadler and Mozart himself). Even more than K. 495 and K. 447, the first movement of the horn concerto in E-flat K. 412 accommodates diminished skills attributable to Leutgeb's advancing years. In the earlier concertos the soloist participates in half to two-thirds of the first movement, but in K. 412 – considerably shorter than its predecessors – about 61 of 143 bars. In the development section, the horn is present for just 11 of 47, allowing Leutgeb an extended recovery period. Mozart also smoothes the way for his soloist in the material written: primary and secondary themes comprise mostly open notes, and the main theme of the rondo entirely open notes; the longest consecutive stretch of stopped notes moves slowly in minims (bars 75–76); and the short bursts of semiquavers, including the longest at six successive beats (Example 12.4), usually orientate around written c" – g" with their cluster of open notes c", d", e" and g". As revealed by the autograph score, the movement would have been shorter still had Mozart followed his initial instincts.[44] At bar 85, following the horn's single contribution to the development section, he wrote then crossed out four bars of V7/D harmony in the first violin that were to have led directly to the

---

[44] For the autograph see Biblioteka Jagiellońka Kraków, Mus. ms. autogr. W. A. Mozart 412.

reprise (Example 12.5): he first envisaged a shorter development, then, which included only additional orchestral material in its extended form notated at the end of the first-movement autograph, thus providing further opportunity for Leutgeb to regain his breath before the reprise. Mozart also foresaw more horn participation in the recapitulation than was ultimately realized: a horn scale followed by three fully scored bars including the soloist were deleted at bar 120 (Example 12.6); and a twelve-bar *particella* for horn and first violin leading to the cadential trill was eliminated and replaced by an eight-bar passage, albeit one containing more semiquaver virtuosity for the soloist than the original. In sum, the three substantial changes to the movement recorded in the autograph evidence concern for compositional shape as well as the requirements of the solo performer: Mozart incorporates structural expansion and, for Leutgeb, includes a lengthier break and less participation than first envisaged. While Mozart's running textual commentary above Leutgeb's stave in the incomplete autograph of the rondo is jocular in intent, it probably reveals something about the soon-to-be-retired Leutgeb's limitations: 'Rest a little! . . . rest! . . . ah, the end please! . . . the finish? thank heaven! stop, stop!'; and, when f-sharps" difficult to hand-stop are introduced, 'You beast – what a noise. Ouch! Alas!'[45]

No aged-related concessions were necessary for Anton Stadler. Indeed, Mozart's association with him, stretching back to the early years of the Viennese decade, reached its virtuosic apogee in the Clarinet Concerto, K. 622 (October 1791).[46] Written for a basset clarinet that extended the regular clarinet's range downwards by four semitones (e-flat, d, c-sharp, c), it was probably premiered at Stadler's concert in Prague on 16 October 1791 (at which Mozart was not present).[47] With the autograph no longer extant, a first edition only published ten years after the

---

[45] 'respira un poco! . . . resta! . . . ah termina, ti prego! . . . finisci? grazia al ciel! basta, basta!'; 'à te. bestia oh che stonatura. Ahi! ohimè!' Küster (*Musical Biography*, p. 232) notes a connection between the awkward f-sharp" and Mozart's comment, detecting some insightful musical description in Mozart's textual interpolations. He also questions whether the 'Adagio' above Leutgeb's stave at the opening of the rondo is actually a joke, or an indication of an originally planned slow movement. Since the dark ink colour of 'Adagio' matches that of the 'Allegro' indications for the second violins, viola and bassi, rather than the lighter ink of the 'Rondo', first-violin 'Allegro' and initial instrumental designations written first, my view is that 'Adagio' is, indeed, another joke at Leutgeb's expense.

[46] With black coffee and tobacco to hand, Mozart orchestrated almost all of the finale of the concerto – 'Stadler's rondo' – on Friday 7 October. See MBA, vol. 4, p. 157; LMF, p. 967 (letter of 7–8 October 1791).

[47] Lawson, *Mozart: Clarinet Concerto*, p. 37. As Lawson points out, it was certainly played by Stadler in Riga in 1794.

Example 12.5 Mozart, Horn Concerto in D K. 412/i, original approach to the recapitulation (with four crossed out bars and an indication to the copyist above the horn stave to replace them with twelve bars for orchestra notated at the end of the first-movement autograph).

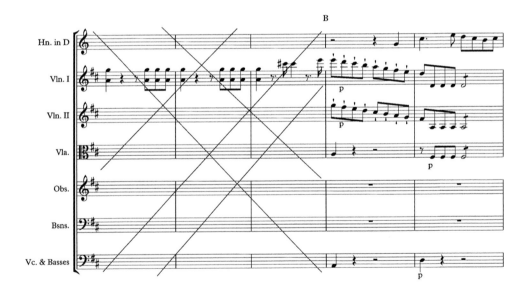

Example 12.6 Mozart, Horn Concerto in D K. 412/i, bars 117ff. (including crossed out material).

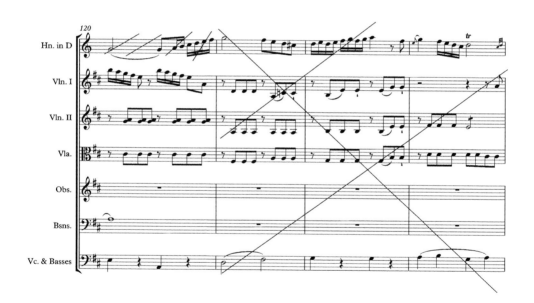

composer's death in a transcription for normal clarinet, and a 'grey area' in the identity of basset clarinets, basset-horns and *clarinettes d'amour* in the late eighteenth century,[48] it is difficult to determine exactly how Mozart

---

[48] On the latter point, see Lawson, *Mozart: Clarinet Concerto*, p. 45.

Example 12.7 Mozart, Basset-horn concerto (fragment), K. 584b (end; all other staves blank).

catered to the needs, predilections and attributes of the star soloist and his new instrument. But the surviving autograph fragment of the first 199 bars of a concerto in G major for basset-horn K. 584b, which provides the full solo line plus some orchestral material of what became the first half of K. 622/i, at least offers traces of Mozart negotiating compositional and performance-related priorities.[49] The ethereal harmonic progression from V/f-sharp to D major via diminished and G7 chords in six bars of the development section (194–199, K. 622/i) is a case in point. By the time he wrote string material on the fragment here, Mozart had reconceived the G-major concerto K. 584b as an A-major concerto (Examples 12.7 and 12.8).[50] Both the K. 584b fragment, and an 1802 reviewer of the first edition of the clarinet concerto who had apparently seen a copy of the original score of the work for basset clarinet, point to the use of low basset notes in

[49] Tyson (*Autograph Scores*, p. 35) dated the fragment – also identified as K. 621b – 'probably a year or two earlier [than K. 622], possibly even as early as 1787'; Konrad (*Mozart: Catalogue of His Works*, p. 196) locates it 'between 1787 and 1790'. But Tyson subsequently changed his mind in favour of 1791, a date also suggested by Lawson and others. See Lawson (including reporting personal correspondence with Tyson) in *Mozart: Clarinet Concerto*, pp. 35, 97. A facsimile of Mozart's autograph fragment K. 584b is given in NMA, V/14/4, pp. 165–176.

[50] For the final twenty bars of K. 584b string material fits with a movement conceived in A major rather than G major, indicating Mozart had changed his mind about the tonality of the work. (The basset-horn material, notated in C, would not have needed adjustment in order to accommodate the tonal modification.) See Ernst Hess, 'Die ursprüngliche Gestalt des Klarinettenkonzerts KV622', *Mozart-Jahrbuch 1967*, pp. 18–30; Lawson, *Mozart: Clarinet Concerto*, pp. 34–35. The change in tonality perhaps coincided with the decision to write for Stadler's basset clarinet – an instrument usually in C, B-flat or A – rather than the basset-horn. See Rice, *From the Clarinet d'Amour to the Contra Bass*, pp. 72, 207.

Example 12.8 Mozart, Clarinet Concerto in A, K. 622/i, bars 194–200 (based on the NMA reconstruction for basset clarinet).

this passage (d and c): the rich, 'other-worldly' quality of this instrument at pitches beyond the reach of the regular clarinet would have reinforced a mystical modulation.[51] Mozart also may have changed his mind about the orchestration and dynamics for this passage, perhaps with projection of the distinctive basset-clarinet notes in mind. Since K. 584b is the only source in Mozart's hand, we cannot know that differences between K. 584b and the first edition of K. 622 via the lost autograph (and any other intervening sources between autograph and first edition) ultimately derive from him. Several closely related discrepancies in the aforementioned passage, though, tentatively suggest Mozart's intervention rather than copying errors, although editorial activity cannot be ruled out. *Forte* crotchet chords in bars 198–199 (first violin and bass line, K. 584b, Example 12.7) become *piano* semibreves and *piano* crotchets (K. 622/i, Example 12.8), perhaps to ensure the audibility of a resonant basset-clarinet c on the downbeat of bar 198. Putting the first-violin crotchets at c-sharp" in bar 195 rather than at c-sharp'" (as in K. 584b) slightly

---

[51] For the review, see *Allgemeine musikalische Zeitung*, 4 (1801–1802), cols. 408–413, as given in William McColl's translation in Lawson, *Mozart: Clarinet Concerto*, pp. 79–83. On the 'other-worldly' quality of basset clarinets and basset-horns, see Lawson, *Mozart: Clarinet Concerto*, p. 58.

darkens the string response to the basset-clarinet es and sets up registral as well as harmonic and timbral contrast with the full-orchestra chords in bar 197 where a d''' appears in the flutes. Again, a distinctive instrumental effect performed by soloist and orchestra is synchronized with a bold modulatory effect. Even evaluated in a general way, avoiding potentially awkward textual issues, the clarinet concerto exploits Stadler's talents: the 'phrases and coloraturas whereby the *skilful* clarinettist can shine' in the first movement, the 'deepest feeling' of the Adagio, and the 'wit and humour' of the finale, recognized in the *Allgemeine musikalische Zeitung* (1802), cater to Stadler's acknowledged versatility; and the aria-like Adagio provides opportunities for the kind of vocal playing praised in a review of Stadler's academy from 1784.[52]

Seven months before writing the clarinet concerto Mozart made probably his last appearance as a soloist at a public concert (4 March 1791), playing the Piano Concerto in B-flat K. 595 at Bohemian clarinettist Josef Beer's academy in the hall of Ignaz Jahn's restaurant on Himmelpfortgasse in Vienna, which had opened three years earlier.[53] A horn player and trumpeter before quickly mastering the clarinet while working in France (c. 1762 to c. 1784), Beer was described by Ernst Ludwig Gerber in 1790 as the greatest clarinet virtuoso of his era, with an inimitable 'floating' (*schwebende*) tone in *decrescendi*.[54] While not approving of Beer's lifestyle, Mozart described him as 'a good clarinettist' during his six-month sojourn in Paris in 1778.[55] Mozart presumably did his old acquaintance – then employed at court in Russia and concertizing around Europe – a favour by performing at his 1791 academy and may have been responsible for enlisting Aloysia Lange's services at the concert as well.[56] Instead of

---

[52] See *Allgemeine musikalische Zeitung* (1802), cols. 409–410 (in McColl's translation in Lawson, *Mozart: Clarinet Concerto*, p. 80); and MDL, p. 206 and MDB pp. 232–233. See also the discussion of the Wind Serenade K. 361 and Clarinet Quintet K. 581 in Chapters 4 and 10.

[53] While the aria 'No, che non sei capace' K. 419 (sung by Aloysia Lange) and a 'grand symphony' by Mozart were performed one month later at the Tonkünstler-Societät concerts (16, 17 April 1791), the nature of Mozart's participation is not known. See MDL, pp. 344–345; MDB, pp. 392–393, and Black, 'Mozart's Association with the Tonkünstler-Societät', pp. 70–71. For information on Jahn's hall, see Morrow, *Concert Life in Haydn's Vienna*, pp. 101–102.

[54] See Gerber, *Historisch-biographisches Lexicon der Tonkünstler*, vol. 1, col. 97, which includes biographical information on Beer.

[55] MBA, vol. 2, p. 399; LMF, p. 566 (9 July 1778).

[56] For a handbill announcing the academy, and citing Beer's employment in Russia, see MDL, p. 339; MDB, pp. 387–388. In his commentary on this document, Deutsch confuses Josef Beer with his younger clarinettist namesake Josef Bähr (1770–1819) who played with Beethoven in the late 1790s. His mistake has been repeated elsewhere too: see, for example, Glover, *Mozart's Women*, p. 171.

composing a new piano concerto from scratch for the occasion, Mozart completed one that had been partially written around 1788, K. 595 in B-flat.[57] As in the most recent piano concertos K. 537 in D (with which initial work on K. 595 is approximately contemporary) and K. 503 in C, Mozart paid special attention to his own virtuosity profile, including in combination with the wind. He may have made small changes to figuration in the autograph to accommodate personal predilections as solo performer: in bars 98, 100 and 259, 261, 263 of the first movement, for example, scalar figures replace angular ones on the first beats of bars in the solo exposition transition and at corresponding points of the recapitulation. And in two form-defining passages, solo virtuosity is subsumed into the orchestral texture in a different way from the grand concertos of 1784 to early 1786: in the run-up to the first-movement recapitulation an oboe floats serenely above the piano's triplet quavers, drifting into the reprise with a limpid beauty rivalled in Mozart's orchestral oboe writing only by Fiordiligi's capitulation to Ferrando in 'Fra gli amplessi' from *Così fan tutte* (bars 97–101); and in the closing stages of the Larghetto, a moment of expressive and (modestly) brilliant virtuosity is enveloped by a cohort of flute, oboes, bassoons and horns, unaccompanied by strings, as a climax to their newly elevated participation in the reprise (Example 12.9). Nurturing appreciation of both performance and compositional abilities was similarly successful in 1791 as during his golden period in the mid-1780s. One critic remarked that, in the rendition of the concerto at Beer's concert, 'everybody admired [Mozart's] art, in composition as well as execution'.[58]

Alongside familiar genres, performers, and musical environments, Mozart's last year brought new instrumental experiences, including writing for glass harmonica and double bass virtuosi and for mechanical instruments that required no live performance as such.[59] The Adagio and Rondo

---

[57] On the composition of parts of the Piano Concerto K. 595 before 1791, see Tyson, *Mozart: Studies of the Autograph Scores*, pp. 153, 156 and Tyson, 'Proposed Dates', in Eisen (ed.), *Mozart Studies*, p. 225. See also Keefe, *Mozart's Viennese Instrumental Music*, pp. 64–85; Irving, *Mozart's Piano Concertos*, pp. 249–250. As Edge points out ('Mozart's Reception in Vienna, 1787–1791', pp. 89–90) it is not impossible that K. 595 was first performed at one of three concerts connected to a visit to Vienna from the King and Queen of Naples in January 1791 closer to the completion date in the *Verzeichnüß*. But no hard evidence is extant.

[58] MDL, p. 339; MDB, p. 387 (*Wiener Zeitung*, 12 March 1791). Mozart's piano concertos also received attention in 1791 with other musicians as soloists. For concerts in Prague and Berlin see MDL, pp. 345, 359; MDB, pp. 393–394, 410–411.

[59] Mozart heard a distinguished harmonica player, Marianne Davies, in his youth, presumably in London. See MBA, vol. 1, p. 438; LMF, p. 198 (letter of 21 September 1771, from Leopold Mozart to his wife, reporting a chance encounter with Davies in Milan and recalling her harmonica playing from an earlier time). On Davies, see Rachel Cowgill, '"Proofs of Genius":

Example 12.9 Mozart, Piano Concerto in B-flat, K. 595/ii, bars 118–121.

for glass harmonica, flute, oboe, viola and cello K. 617 was written for the blind virtuoso Marianne Kirchgessner (1769–1808), who had just begun a grand tour of central and northern Europe ultimately to surpass the length even of Mozart's youthful sojourn.[60] Beginning in Bavaria and Vienna in 1791, she moved on to Moravia, Bohemia, Saxony, Braunschweig, Hannover, Hamburg, Bremen, Holland and Belgium and then crossed the channel to spend three years in England before returning to Germany in early 1796.[61] She gave a concert at the Burgtheater on 10 June 1791, a second at the Kärntnertortheater on 19 August, at which Mozart's quintet was premiered, and a final one at Jahn's Hall on 8 September.[62] The glass harmonica was repeatedly lauded for its sound quality: 'heavenly and pure',

---

Wolfgang Amadeus Mozart and the Construction of Musical Prodigies in Early Georgian London', in McPherson (ed.), *Musical Prodigies*, pp. 511–549, at 519–520.

[60] Mozart almost certainly also wrote the short solo Adagio in C, K. 356, for Kirchgessner in 1791. K. 617 (completed on 23 May 1791) was due to premiere at her academy on Monday 13 June. But the academy was cancelled at short notice and rescheduled for 19 August. See MBA, vol. 4, p. 136; LMF, p. 953 (11 June 1791).

[61] For a biography of Kirchgessner from the year of her death, see Meusel, *Teutsches Künstlexikon*, vol. 1, pp. 461–462.

[62] MDL, p. 351; MDB, p. 400.

with 'soft tones' and 'fantastic chimera'; and 'exquisitely refined . . . when touched with delicacy and skill!'[63] Moreover, 'this instrument . . . exceeds all other musical instruments in melodious sound. The indescribable feelings that it excites attack so violently the nerves of the listeners and even more of the players that tender and sensitive people are unable to endure it for long.'[64] For Karl Leopold Röllig, a harmonica virtuoso who gave a concert in Vienna on 2 April 1791 and a few years earlier wrote a short book on the instrument explaining its 'extraordinary effect' on a variety of people in different settings: 'Only rarely and never for long must it be played, considering that high-pitched passions cannot be subject to long duration. But the harmonica always seeks to express the highest degree of touching passions.'[65] And Dr Franz Anton Mesmer used it at his séances to enhance celestial and ethereal effects.[66] Kirchgessner herself did not disappoint in the emotions conveyed. Explaining in her advertisement for the concert on 19 August that the glass harmonica '[excites] not melancholy and sad, but much happier, gentler and higher feelings',[67] a performance of hers in 1792 elicited a very positive response: 'Mademoiselle Kirchgessner is a true virtuoso on this instrument. She treated it with a delicacy, with a refinement of feeling through which she surpasses the most eager expectations that you just always have from the magic effects of it. Each of her fingers seems animated by a spirit, or at least with each slight touch of the bells magics down a blessed spirit, which, gently swaying on the melodious vibrations, lingers on to teach mortals why music is and will be above the stars.'[68] She described Mozart's work as 'entirely new and extremely

---

[63] *Allgemeine literatur Zeitung*, 115 (15 May 1786), col. 301 ('himmlisch und rein'); Johann Heinrich Moritz Poppe, *Geschichte der Technologie* (Göttingen, 1810), vol. 2, p. 297 ('sanfte Töne'); Karl Leopold Röllig, *Über die Harmonika: Ein Fragment* (Berlin, 1787), p. 17 ('phantastischen Hirngespinstes'); Rev. James Dallaway, *Observations on English Architecture, Military, Ecclesiastical, and Civil* (London, 1806), p. 289.

[64] G. Ph. Funke, *Naturgeschichte und Technologie für Lehrer in Schulen und für Liebhaber dieser Wissenschaften* (Braunschweig, 1806), vol. 3, p. 363: 'Dieses Instrument . . . übertrifft alle andre musikalische Instrumente an Wohlklang. Die unbeschrieblichen Empfindungen, die es erregt, greifen die Nerven der Zuhörenden und noch mehr des Spielers so heftig an, das zärtliche und empfindsame Personen es nicht lange auszuhalten vermögen.'

[65] Röllig, *Über die Harmonika*, pp. 17 ('ausserordentlichen Wirkung'), 24: 'Nur selten und nie lange darf sie gespielt werden. Wenn man bedenkt, daß hochgestimmte Leidenschaften keiner langen Dauer unterworfen sein können. Die harmonika aber stets den höchsten Grad rührender Leidenschaften auszudrücken suchet.' Röllig's playing received a mixed report from Schönfeld in 1796; see 'Yearbook of the Music of Vienna and Prague', p. 311.

[66] Beghin, *The Virtual Haydn*, p. 200.

[67] MDL, p. 351; MDB, p. 400. Leopold Mozart was one musician for whom the harmonica had a melancholic effect. See MBA, vol. 2, p. 362; LMF, p. 540 (28 May 1778).

[68] *Musikalische Korrespondenz der teutschen Filarmonischen Gesellschaft*, 44 (31 October 1792), cols. 352–353, at 353: 'Demoiselle Kirchgessner ist auf diesem Instrumente eine wahre

beautiful'[69] and maintained affection for it for the remainder of her life: in the years before her death in 1808, she performed the 'well-known beautiful quintet' in Berlin (1805) and to a full house at the Redoutensaal in Vienna (1806).[70]

Mozart exploited the distinctive qualities of the glass harmonica in his Adagio and Rondo.[71] Unsurprisingly, given the instrument's special, quiet sound production, Mozart writes extended solo passages for it, often in alternation with the flute, oboe, viola and cello.[72] But he also explores timbres, sonorities and effects over the course of the work that create an impact for the harmonica when heard simultaneously with others. Following the alternation of full ensemble *forte* and harmonica *piano* at the opening, he has it emerge at the top of the ensemble texture mid phrase (bars 7–8); it also floats to the top in its run of chromatic demisemiquavers before the reprise (bars 38–39). The Adagio's second theme, dominated by the harmonica, is greeted by various configurations of accompaniment, including the full ensemble, the flute by itself and the viola and cello. The late addition of dynamics to the flute, oboe, viola and cello in bars 28–31 (Example 12.10) – in a light, faded ink in the autograph distinct from the darker-inked notes – shows sensitivity to the sound of the solo instrument.[73] Given the softness of the harmonica, Mozart initially may not have included *crescendi* swells and an *sf* in the other instruments for fear of overwhelming or overshadowing it even in an alternating exchange; both markings occur here for the only time. New effects appear in the rondo too, including a recurring chorale figure,[74] an outing for the

---

Virtuosin. Sie behandelt es mit einer Delikatesse, mit einer Feinheit des Gefühls, durch die sie die gespantesten Erwartungen übertrift, die man von den Zauberwirkungen desselben nur immer erwartet. Jeder ihrer Finger scheint von einem Geiste belebt, oder wenigstens mit jeder leisen Berührung der Glocken einen seeligen Geist herabzuzaubern, der, auf den melodischen Schwingungen derselben sich sanft wiegend, daher schwebt, die Sterblichen zu belehren, was über den Sternen Musik ist und sein wird.'

[69] See MDL, p. 351, and MDB, p. 400.

[70] *Allgemeine musikalische Zeitung*, 7 (1804–1805), cols. 432–433 ('bekannte schöne Quintett'); *Allgemeine musikalische Zeitung*, 8 (1805–1806), col. 376. Kirchgessner also may have performed the work at one of Salomon's concerts in London on 17 March 1794; see Heartz, *Mozart, Haydn, Early Beethoven*, p. 493.

[71] In Abert's words (*W.A. Mozart*, trans. Spencer, p. 1225), Mozart in K. 617 'is concerned entirely with questions of sonority'.

[72] Kirchgessner acquired a louder instrument in London than she had had in Vienna in 1791. See Meusel, *Teutsches Künstlexikon*, vol. 1, pp. 461–462.

[73] For the autograph of the adagio and rondo, see British Library London, Zweig MS61.

[74] According to Johann Christian Müller in his short treatise on the harmonica, practising chorales is a particularly effective way of learning the instrument. See *Anleitung zum Selbstunterricht auf der Harmonika* (Leipzig, 1788), pp. 10–25.

Example 12.10 Mozart, Adagio and Rondo for glass harmonica, oboe, flute, viola and cello, Adagio, bars 28–31.

harmonica as *bona fide* accompanist, with arpeggiated triplet quavers in the second theme, and a combination of both imitative dialogue and simultaneous countermelody at the end. While Viennese audiences would have been able to hear the glass harmonica in concert on one or two earlier occasions in 1791, Mozart took opportunities to promote to them its special sound in isolation and in combination with others.

Mozart's only double bass obbligato part, for Friedrich Pischelberger (1741–1813) then resident at the Wiednertheater, is found in the aria 'Per questa bella mano', K. 612 (8 March 1791), written for Gerl, the first Sarastro in *Die Zauberflöte*. Pischelberger played in the small private orchestra of Archbishop Patachich in Grosswardein (now Oradea, Romania) under Dittersdorf's direction in the late 1760s.[75] Listed as a member of the Hoftheater orchestra in 1773, Pischelberger does not come up on their rosters in the 1780s, but in 1791 was named by Joseph Marx von Liechtenstein as one of two Vienna-based 'masters' on his instrument.[76] He may also have worked as a freelance copyist in the city.[77] Brilliant

[75] Karl von Dittersdorf, *Lebensbeschreibung* (Leipzig: Breitkopf, 1801), p. 141.

[76] See Johann Heinrich Friedrich Müller, *Genaue Nachrichten von beyden Kaiserl. Königl. Schaubühnen in Wien*, vol. 2 (Vienna: Kurzböck, 1773), p. 127; Link, *National Court Theatre*, pp. 403–448 (for the transcribed theatre account books from 1783 onwards); Liechtenstein, *Beiträge zur genauern Kenntniss*, p. 193.

[77] See Stephen Carey Fischer, 'Haydn's Overtures and their Adaptations as Concert Orchestral Works' (PhD thesis, University of Pennsylvania, 1985), pp. 459–468; as given in Dexter Edge,

virtuosity for the double bass comprises not only demisemiquaver and semi-quaver runs and arpeggios, but also big leaps from high double-stoppings to A and D, the second and third open strings. D major, then, is the obvious choice of key for the aria, enabling rapid switches between the double stops and dominant and tonic notes. Judging by Sarastro's music in *Die Zauberflöte*, F-sharp (and F-natural) were Gerl's lowest notes: the third scale degree deep in the vocal register was therefore ripe for vocal exploitation.[78]

Three pieces for mechanical organs from the last year of Mozart's life occupy a unique place in his Viennese oeuvre. K. 594 in F minor (December 1790), K. 608 in F minor (3 March 1791), and K. 616 in F (4 May 1791) were written for regular public performance, but not actual performers – not Mozart himself, nor musical acquaintances, nor purchasers of his music – and were commissioned by Joseph Nepomuk Franz de Paul, Baron Deym von Stžítéž (pseudonym Müller), a former officer in the Austrian army. Deym's art gallery, displaying curiosities such as wax statues and copies of old sculptures, occupied various Viennese locations between c. 1780 and 1804 and was run by his widow from 1804 until 1819. On the death of an eminent field marshall in the Austrian army, Ernst Gideon, Baron van Laudon (sometimes Loudon), Deym constructed a mausoleum for him, displaying his effigy in a glass coffin. Attendees could not only inspect the effigy, but also listen to 'funeral music' every hour, by different composers according to Deym, although only Mozart's name was mentioned. K. 594 and K. 608, both intense F-minor works, were probably used interchangeably for a while, although the latter came to be preferred.[79]

When first composing for the mechanical organ in Frankfurt in late 1790, possibly the short fragment K. 593a,[80] Mozart found the experience frustrating: 'Because it is one of my most hated types of work, I have

---

'Manuscript Parts as Evidence of Orchestral Size in the Eighteenth-Century Concerto', in Zaslaw (ed.), *Mozart's Piano Concertos*, pp. 437, 452.

[78] For vocal F-sharps in light, exposed scoring, see (for example) bars 55, 109, 116.

[79] For the biographical information, see Neal Zaslaw, 'Mechanical Instruments, Music for', in Eisen and Keefe (eds.), *Cambridge Mozart Encyclopedia*, pp. 281–284; Zaslaw, 'Wolfgang Amadè Mozart's Allegro and Andante ("Fantasy") in F Minor for Mechanical Organ, K. 608', in Jon Newsom and Alfred Mann (eds.), *The Rosaleen Moldenhauer Memorial: Music History from Primary Sources* (Washington: Library of Congress, 2000), pp. 327–340; and Annette Richards, 'Automatic Genius: Mozart and the Mechanical Sublime', *Music & Letters*, 80 (1999), pp. 366–389, especially 384–386 (including a picture of the Deym mausoleum on p. 386). An advertisement for the mausoleum is given in MDL, p. 345; MDB, p. 394. For an analysis of K. 594, see Laurence Dreyfus, 'The Hermeneutics of Lament: a Neglected Paradigm in a Mozartian *Trauermusik*', *Music Analysis*, 10 (1991), pp. 329–343.

[80] Zaslaw, 'Mechanical Instruments', p. 282; Konrad, *Mozart: Catalogue of His Works*, pp. 200–201.

unfortunately not been able to bring it to an end. Every day I write it – but must always break off as it bores me . . . But I still hope to force myself bit by bit. If it were for a large clock and the thing sounded like an organ that would please me. But the work consists of little pipes, which sound high-pitched and for me too childish.'[81] For Mozart the seasoned performer-composer, the absence of live engagement through performance may partially account for a dislike of the type of composition, especially when the sound of the instrument was (to his ears) unpleasant. As always, though, Mozart made the most of a new experience, K. 608 in particular providing 'its own commentary on death and transcendence' through invocation of the sublime.[82] As purely compositional endeavours for Mozart, one at least attracted positive attention ten years later on account of no player being present: 'A glorious flute music, as though inspired by the breath of love, resounds, without it being possible to tell whence the magic notes come. It is an Adagio by the unforgettable Mozart.'[83]

Die Zauberflöte in Vienna

We are aware of neither contractual arrangements between Mozart and the Wiednertheater for *Die Zauberflöte* nor the nature of discussions between composer and librettist about the opera's content.[84] Mozart's association with the Wiednertheater began in 1790 with a collaborative Singspiel, *Der Stein der Weisen* (premiered on 11 September), which is closely related to *Die Zauberflöte* in structure and plot and featured at least seven of the same principal singers.[85] Mozart wrote the wind and most of the string parts for the duet 'Nun liebes Weibchen' between Lubano and Lubanara

---

[81] MBA, vol. 4, pp. 115–16; LMF, pp. 943–944 (3 October 1790).

[82] Richards, 'Mozart and the Mechanical Sublime', p. 389.

[83] As given in Richards, 'Mozart and the Mechanical Sublime', p. 384. She identifies the piece in question as K. 616.

[84] Mozart is known to have received the box-office receipts from the third performance, which may have amounted to around 400 florins. See *Bayreuther Zeitung*, 121 (11 October 1791); given in Edge and Black (eds.), 'Mozart Rewarded with the Receipts from the Third Performance of *Die Zauberflöte*', in *Mozart: New Documents*, first published 16 March 2015, http://dx.doi.org/10.7302/Z20P0WXJ. According to a second- or third-hand account from Ignaz von Seyfried (1840), Mozart was paid 100 ducats by Schikaneder for the opera. See David J. Buch, 'Three Posthumous Reports Concerning Mozart in His Late Viennese Years', *Eighteenth-Century Music*, 2 (2005), pp. 125–129, at 128.

[85] On *Der Stein der Weisen*, and its connections to *Die Zauberflöte*, see in particular Buch (ed.), *Der Stein der Weisen*, pp. ix–xviii. See also David J. Buch, 'Mozart and the Theater auf der Wieden: New Attributions and Perspectives', *Cambridge Opera Journal*, 9 (1997), pp. 295–232; reproduced in Keefe (ed.), *Mozart*, pp. 249–286.

(Schikaneder and Barbara Gerl, his future Papageno and Papagena); based on attributions in a 1790s manuscript of *Der Stein der Weisen* by Kaspar Weiß, a copyist at the Wiednertheater, he was also involved in two segments from the Act-2 finale.[86] In addition to *Der Stein der Weisen* and two more operas from the Wiednertheater, *Oberon* by Paul Wranitzky (1789) and *Der wohltätige Derwisch, oder Die Schellenkappe* attributed to Henneberg, Schack and Gerl (1791), *Die Zauberflöte* drew on other literary sources for libretto and plot: Abbé Jean Terrasson's French novel *Sethos* (Paris, 1731; German translation 1777) on an ancient Egyptian Pharaoh also connected to Mozart's *Thamos, König in Egypten*, K. 345; the essay 'Über die Mysterien der Aegyptier' ('On the Mysteries of the Egyptians', 1784) by the influential intellectual and freemason Ignaz von Born; the medieval romance *Yvain* by Chrétien de Troyes; and the fairytale collection *Dschinnistan oder auserlesene Feen- und Geister-Märchen* (three volumes, 1786–1789).[87]

Mozart's first cast for *Die Zauberflöte* contained colourful characters. In 1781 Mozart described his sister-in-law Josepha Hofer, née Weber (Queen of the Night), as 'a lazy, rough, false person and a sly old dog'.[88] After a performance of Wranitzky's *Oberon*, Friedrich Schröder chastised her (1791) as a 'very unpleasant singer, who does not have the high notes for the role and squeaks them'.[89] But judging by her two arias in *Die*

---

[86] On 'Nun liebes Weibchen', which 'might have been a collaborative effort', see Edge, 'Mozart's Viennese Copyists', pp. 2001–2002, 2014, and David J. Buch, '*Der Stein der Weisen*, Mozart, and Collaborative Singspiels at Emanuel Schikaneder's Theater auf der Wieden', *Mozart-Jahrbuch 2000*, pp. 91–126, at 110–112. For discussion of Kaspar Weiß, see Edge, 'Viennese Copyists', pp. 1998–2067; Buch (ed.), *Der Stein der Weisen*, pp. x–xi.

[87] Sources for *Die Zauberflöte* have been discussed at length in the secondary literature. See, in particular, Branscombe, *W.A. Mozart: 'Die Zauberflöte'*, pp. 1–24; and David J. Buch, *Magic Flutes and Enchanted Forests: The Supernatural in Eighteenth-Century Musical Theater* (Chicago: University of Chicago Press, 2008), especially Chapter 6, 'The Supernatural in the Operas of Mozart', pp. 315–58. On masonic symbolism, extensively covered in Mozart scholarship, see (for example) Katharine Thompson, *The Masonic Thread in Mozart* (London: Lawrence & Wishart, 1977); Paul Nettl, *Mozart and Masonry* (New York: Dorset Press, 1987), pp. 60–101; Jacques Chailly, *The Magic Flute*, trans. Herbert Weinstock (London: Gollancz, 1972); Brigid Brophy, *Mozart the Dramatist* (New York: Da Capo, 1964), pp. 131–202; Landon, *1791: Mozart's Last Year*, pp. 130–142; Knepler, *Wolfgang Amadé Mozart*, pp. 131–147. David J. Buch provides a corrective to masonic-orientated interpretations, situating *Die Zauberflöte* in the fairytale opera tradition instead; see '*Die Zauberflöte*, Masonic Opera, and Other Fairy Tales', *Acta musicologica*, 76 (2004), pp. 193–219. For discussion of *Die Zauberflöte* as 'an allegory of enlightenment', see Waldoff, *Recognition in Mozart's Operas*, pp. 17–43.

[88] MBA, vol. 3, p. 181; LMF, p. 784 (15 December 1781). For more on Hofer, including roles sung for the Schikaneder company and her contract of engagement, see Paul Corneilson, 'Josepha Hofer, First Queen of the Night', in *Mozart-Studien*, forthcoming. For a partial reproduction of the contract, see also Braunbehrens, *Mozart in Vienna*, pp. 376–377.

[89] As given in Stewart Spencer's translation in Abert, *W. A. Mozart*, p. 1267.

Zauberflöte, which ascend to dizzying f"'s, Mozart disagreed.[90] Anna Gottlieb (Pamina) felt a strong association with Mozart for almost her entire life. Singing Barbarina at the premiere of *Le nozze di Figaro* on 1 May 1786 just two days after her twelfth birthday, she created Pamina at seventeen. Gottlieb behaved bizarrely at the Salzburg commemorations of Mozart's death in September 1842, pompously announcing herself as 'die erste Pamina' and expecting royal treatment.[91] An interview with journalist Ludwig August Frankl printed in October 1842 is similarly self-aggrandizing, but also expresses gratitude towards the 'immortal' (*unsterbliche*) Mozart, to whom a laudatory poem was devoted and thanks issued daily for involvement in the *Zauberflöte* premiere.[92] A good singer in her youth, she received high praise for the eponymous role in Florian Gassmann's *La contessina* (in its Singspiel version *Die Gräfinn oder der überlangebrachte Stolz*) on 28 March 1797 at Vienna's Theater in der Leopoldstadt.[93] Franz Xaver Gerl (Sarastro), a stalwart of the Wiednertheater for several years from 1789 and married to Barbara Gerl (Papagena), appears to have had a distinctive low register down to F, which was strategically exploited by Mozart: Gerl's first contribution, in the Allegro maestoso of the Act 1 finale, culminates in an unaccompanied F and another F with just flute and oboes; his last participation in Act 1 has an F-sharp in the final cadential formulation; and his aria 'In diesen heil'gen Hallen' reserves F-sharps for the voice's last five bars.[94]

Benedikt Schack (Tamino), a close friend of Mozart in 1791, was another interesting and talented musician. A composer and wind player as well as vocalist, he elicited admiration from Leopold Mozart: 'He sings *excellently*, has a *beautiful voice, an easy, malleable throat*, and *a fine technique*.'[95] After

---

[90] Another (incomplete) Mozart aria for Josepha Hofer, 'Schon lacht der holde Frühling' K. 580 (17 September 1789) for a German version of Paisiello's *Il barbiere di Siviglia*, also ascends on one occasion to d"' and repeatedly to c"'. Mozart may also have written the (lost) aria 'Ohne Zwang aus eignem Triebe', K. 569, for Hofer; see Corneilson, 'Josepha Hofer'. See also David J. Buch, 'The House Composers of the Theater auf der Wieden in the Time of Mozart (1789–91)', *Israel Studies in Musicology Online*, 5 (2006), pp. 14–19, at 17.

[91] As documented in William Kuhe's *My Musical Recollections* (1896); given in Clive, *Mozart and His Circle*, p. 64. See also Branscombe, *Die Zauberflöte*, p. 150.

[92] See Ludwig August Frankl, 'Die erste Pamina', *Unterhaltungsblatt zur Augsburger Postzeitung*, no. 40 (1 October 1842), n.p.

[93] *Allgemeines europäisches Journal 1797* (Brünn, 1797), vol. 3, p. 225. Gottlieb joined this theatre, Schikaneder's main Viennese competitor, in 1792.

[94] F-natural and F-sharp can be assumed to be Gerl's lowest notes as 'In diesen heil'gen Hallen' is in E major. It would have been reasonable to expect Mozart to take Gerl down to the low tonic note had Gerl been capable of singing it. The Act 1 aria for Eutifronte in *Der Stein der Weisen*, sung by Gerl and attributed to him as composer, also descends to F.

[95] MBA, vol. 3, p. 549. (Not in LMF.) Italics as in original.

walking thirty-six miles from his hometown to Vienna as a seventeen-year-old in 1775, he spent a five-year sojourn in the Imperial capital among other things taking vocal lessons with Joseph von Frieberth, learning how to write effectively for wind instruments, and organizing concerts. Following Kapellmeister duties in Silesia, where he composed a number of wind concertos, Schack joined Schikaneder's company in Regensburg, returning to Vienna with him in 1789.[96] Given Schack's penchant for wind instruments, it is surely no coincidence that a magic flute protects Tamino during the opera.[97] Schack's excellent vocal quality and technique, and his interest in winds, help to explain the suave solo writing and orchestration of the aria 'Dies Bildnis'. The first number in the opera to feature the double clarinet-bassoon-horn scoring favoured in *Così*, 'Dies Bildnis' is also the first seriously to address the subject of love, as Tamino contemplates Pamina's portrait. Mozart initially distinguishes wind from strings both in musical content and performance instructions: *tenuti* in bars 1–2; *fps* against *sfps* in the strings in bar 9; and an unaccompanied *p–cresc–f*, where the *f* coincides with an *mf* in the strings (Example 12.11). But once Tamino identifies the emotion stirred in him as love ('Die Liebe ist's allein'; 'It is love alone'), strings and wind are dynamically aligned, and remain so for the rest of the aria. It is as if the wind material and concomitant dynamics invite wind players first to depict a kind of semidetached beauty independent of the strings, but then unambiguously to support Tamino's personal expression of love by aligning with strings; the character's emotional progression during the aria is reinforced by the winds' progression from quasi-independent agent to integral component of a unified orchestral body.

Mozart's most engaging musical relationship among the *Zauberflöte* cast was with Schikaneder, librettist and director of the Wiednertheater as well as creator of Papageno. 'I am a birdcatcher, you know' ('Der Vogelfänger bin ich ja') Papageno announces in the first line of his opening aria. But he is initially introduced to us as an instrumental performer, twice playing a scale on his panpipes during the orchestral introduction (Example 12.12). The text of the aria concerns Papageno's self-identity as a friendly bird-

---

[96] For a biography of Schack (1758–1826) while still alive, see 'Schack, Benedikt', in Feliz Joseph Lipowsky (ed.), *Baierisches Lexikon* (Munich: Jakob Giel, 1811), pp. 297–302. For more biographical information see the obituary in *Allgemeine musikalische Zeitung*, 29 (1827), cols. 519–521.

[97] It is unlikely that Schack actually played the flute onstage in performances of *Die Zauberflöte*; the flautist was probably Anton Dreyssig. See Theodore Albrecht, 'Anton Dreyssig (c1753/4–1820): Mozart's and Beethoven's *Zauberflötist*', in Link and Nagley (eds.), *Words About Mozart*, pp. 179–192.

Example 12.11 Mozart, 'Dies Bildnis' from *Die Zauberflöte*, bars 25–27.

catcher yearning for a devoted wife. His diegetic rendition on the pipes, 'so spontaneously that it seems almost to issue *through* him from nature',[98] is an organic part of that identity: without an onstage audience to his knowledge (unaware that Tamino is listening) he performs by and for himself not for the self-serving purposes of a Cherubino trying to impress the Countess in 'Voi che sapete', with Susanna strumming the guitar, or a Don Giovanni accompanying himself on the mandolin to put a seduction into effect in 'Deh vieni'. The panpipe scale, moreover, immediately bonds Papageno with the wind, through a call and response with oboes and horns. Mozart knew from the outset that he wanted to include horns in the aria: they appear in the dark ink of the *particella* both as an instrument name in the

---

[98] Rose Rosengard Subotnik, 'Whose *Magic Flute*? Intimations of Reality at the Gates of Enlightenment', *19th Century Music*, 15 (1991), pp. 132–150, at 134. By the end of the article, the pipes assume far grander critical and ontological significance for Subotnik: 'It is this unpretentious, earthy instrument that jars the illusion of a self-contained, harmonious universe in the *Magic Flute*. . . . Papageno's pipes expose Mozart's composition itself, like the symbolical realm of the opera's story, as something other than an autonomous world containing all the keys needed to unlock its own single meaning' (p. 150).

Example 12.12 Mozart, 'Der Vogelfänger' from *Die Zauberflöte*, bars 12–16.

initial brace and in the first thirteen bars of the orchestral introduction. But he may not have made up his mind about the final wind scoring before writing the *particella*: he left four free staves in the middle of his score for further wind parts, but did not append the '2 oboe' and '2 fagotti' designation until orchestrating the number. He also may not have decided initially that the winds were to introduce Papageno's scale, rather than be introduced by it: in the faded ink of the orchestration phase of work the horns' quavers are extended from the dark-inked notes of the *particella*, where a quaver rest was originally given at the end of the bar.

Schikaneder exercised authorial privilege in giving himself the first star turn in *Die Zauberflöte*.[99] The extent to which he had input on the music is not known. Given the overtly collaborative environment of the Wiednertheater, with its frequently multi-authored operas, he could have had more impact than traditional Mozart scholarship might be inclined to

---

[99] Schikaneder is also the only participant in *Die Zauberflöte* with three arias (including the *de facto* aria 'Papagena! Papagena! Papagena!' in the Act 2 finale): the Queen of the Night and Sarastro have two each, and Tamino, Pamina and Monostatos one. Joint with Schack (Tamino) he is involved in more numbers than any other character too – seven (factoring each act finale as a single number). As Julian Rushton points out (*Mozart*, p. 225): 'It is not surprising that Papageno, originally played by the author-actor-manager, sometimes steals the show; and it is not entirely wrong that he should do so, for his own journey to fulfillment is closer to normal human experience than Tamino's.'

allow; it was reported – albeit in 1829, thirty-eight years after the premiere – that Schikaneder sang melodies to Mozart that Mozart subsequently set.[100] A pragmatist to his core, Schikaneder was unafraid to admit writing 'for the pleasure of the public, I don't claim to be a scholar. I am an actor – a director – and I work for my box-office'.[101] Such a straightforwardly articulated position may also lend credence to his statement about having 'diligently thought through' ('fleißig durchdachte') the opera with Mozart.[102] It irritated Schikaneder that Papageno had become by 1795 a two-dimensional character, rather than one with subtler qualities, mood swings and motivations: 'I would wish my Papageno to be played as a whimsical figure, not as a clown, as unfortunately happens on so many stages.'[103] Whether attributed to Mozart or Schikaneder's musical thinking, or to two minds interacting, the panpipes give Papageno depth – as well as *joie de vivre* – that the dramatic creator of the character no doubt relished.

Schikaneder's aria 'Ein Mädchen oder Weibchen' and duet with Barbara Gerl, 'Pa-Pa-Pa', also brim with performativity. In the former, the magic bells 'played' by the singer on stage (actually rendered by a glockenspiel in the orchestra) become increasingly elaborate and virtuosic in the second and third verses;[104] the vocalist thereby presents himself as a productive instrumental improviser, albeit one whose instrument is concealed in a box.[105] On at least one occasion early in *Die Zauberflöte*'s run, moreover, Mozart got caught up in the moment:

I went behind the scenes during Papageno's aria with the glockenspiel, because today I felt a kind of impulse to play it myself. So, having some fun, where Schikaneder first of all has a pause, I played an arpeggio. He was startled – looked

[100] Buch (ed.), *Stein der Weisen*, p. xii. As has been pointed out (Heartz, *Mozart, Haydn, Early Beethoven*, p. 275), Schikaneder's multifaceted participation in *Die Zauberflöte* rarely receives appropriate appreciation: 'Translated into the context of *Le nozze di Figaro* he could be described as: a Beaumarchais for having put together the story; a Da Ponte for turning the story into prose and verse (with help from Mozart); a Count Rosenberg for having the overall direction of the theatrical troupe that produced it; and lastly a Benucci for having been the actor-singer with the largest part.'

[101] Given in Branscombe, *'Die Zauberflöte'*, p. 90.

[102] As given (in German) in NMA II/5/19, Preface, p. xiii.

[103] As given in Hans Joachim Kreutzer, 'The Crowning of Beauty and Wisdom – *The Magic Flute*', in Mozart, *'Die Zauberflöte': Facsimile of the Autograph Score*, vol. 3, pp. 1–16, at p. 7. Kreutzer continues (p. 7): 'A "whimsical" figure (*launig*), in the full sense of the word, is one that is capricious and mercurial, subject to bad moods and even capable of grudging rebellion.'

[104] Mozart provides these embellishments on a separate page in the autograph. See Mozart, *'Die Zauberflöte': Facsimile of the Autograph Score*, vol. 2, p. 319.

[105] For an interpretation of 'the disjunction between sight and sound implicit in the prop itself', which renders Papageno temporarily mute, see Carolyn Abbate, *In Search of Opera* (Princeton: Princeton University Press, 2004), pp. 77–83.

in the wings and saw me – when it came for the second time, I didn't do it – now he stopped and did not want to go on – I guessed his thoughts and again played a chord – then he struck the glockenspiel and said *Shut up* – then everyone laughed. I think that through this fun many [in the audience] learned for the first time that he [Papageno] does not strike the instrument himself.[106]

Reasserting authority as performer-composer by improvising to humorous effect, Mozart did not mind destroying one stage illusion in order to promote spontaneous, good-natured banter with the co-creator of his opera. And such impulsiveness helps us to understand and appreciate musical energy generated by the 'Pa-Pa-Pa' duet as the zippy, vigorous interaction of co-creators as well as a dramatic representation of two earthy, overjoyed lovers uniting: Mozart and Schikaneder, like Papageno and Papagena, bounce off each other instinctively and enthusiastically. If a later anecdote is to be believed, in fact, Schikaneder participated proactively in the creative process for the duet: according to Friedrich Sebastian Mayer, a singer and second husband to Josepha Hofer, Schikaneder did not like an original version of it, suggesting the stuttering at the opening and the gradual assembling of the full names instead.[107]

Mutually reinforcing performing and compositional endeavours for Mozart and Schikaneder are one illustration of how performance assumes a central position in the opera, acquiring dramatic power.[108] *Don Giovanni* and *Così fan tutte*, with their distinctive instrumentation and orchestral effects, were ideal preparation for an opera in which both are woven into the fabric of the drama: the magic flute that shields Tamino; the magic bells (glockenspiel) that entrance Monastatos and his slaves and bring Papagena

---

[106] MBA, vol. 4, p. 160; LMF, pp. 968–969 (letter of 8–9 October 1791).

[107] See MDL, pp. 480–481; MDB, p. 568.

[108] Discussion of the 'power of music' in *Die Zauberflöte*, if not of performance specifically, is a feature of recent secondary literature. Wolff considers it a sub-theme that would have attracted Mozart. See 'Musicological Introduction' in Mozart, *'Die Zauberflöte': Facsimile of the Autograph Score*, vol. 3, pp. 18–19; and Wolff, *Mozart at the Gateway to His Fortune*, pp. 113–116. For further elaboration, see Küster, *Mozart: A Musical Biography*, pp. 365–367; Solomon, *Mozart: A Life*, pp. 509–519 (in a chapter entitled 'The Power of Music'); and Karol Berger, *Bach's Cycle, Mozart's Arrow: An Essay on the Origins of Musical Modernity* (Berkeley, CA: University of California Press, 2007), pp. 280–291. Berger describes Tamino (p. 285) as 'a new Orpheus' who '[uses] the power of music to wrest new life from the clutches of death ... His success is an index of the unique moment of political and cultural optimism between 1789 and 1793.' For Melograni (*Mozart: A Biography*, p. 239), the protective power of music to which attention is drawn in the libretto as Tamino and Pamina move through the final trial of fire, captures 'the profound message of *The Magic Flute*: we will all live better and die better with music to support us than we can without music.'

to Papageno; the panpipe playing, indeed, that represents Papageno.[109] And collective wind timbres are as important as individual instrumental sounds: wind-only threefold chords in Act 2, Scene 1 support Tamino on his uncertain journey and are foreshadowed at the Adagio opening of the overture's development section (with clarinets rather than basset-horns); and a large wind-only group, as well as the magic flute, 'protects' Tamino and Pamina as they walk through fire in the final trial. As one critic has noted: 'It is striking, and for opera by no means customary, that the music ... heard by [*Die Zauberflöte*'s] personages (as opposed to the music heard only by the audience) is entirely instrumental.'[110]

The autograph score of *Die Zauberflöte* evidences attention to instrumental effects as well as to the impact of performing issues on the compositional process. When Hofer (Queen of the Night) ascends to the famous f'''s in 'Der Hölle Rache', for example, she is cushioned by the wind alone (two flutes and one oboe). The string basses originally included in the *particella* are crossed out in the completion phase, Mozart sensitive both to the type and quantity of accompanying sounds in the finished, performable piece (Example 12.13).[111] Near the opening of the aria (bars 14 and 16, Example 12.14), two crescendos marked in the *particella* in the cellos and basses are intensified in the completion once wind instruments have accrued to the score: the first crescendo includes *mfp*s for double flutes, oboes and bassoons, but the second gives *fp*s to the same cohort, plus an *mfp* for the horns. Nothing in the *particella* indicates that the second crescendo is to strengthen the first. Mozart nuances his effect when completing the passage, conscious perhaps of

---

[109] On orchestral involvement in *Die Zauberflöte*, with particular attention to the overture, see Thomas Bauman, 'At the North Gate: Instrumental Music in *Die Zauberflöte*', in Heartz, *Mozart's Operas*, pp. 277–297. For appearances of magic flutes and magic bells in earlier eighteenth-century operas, see Buch, *Magic Flutes, Enchanted Forests*. On magical musical instruments in *Die Zauberflöte* in comparison to those in the contemporary Viennese operas by Wenzel Müller and Joachim Perinet, *Kaspar der Fagottist, oder Der Zauberzither* (1791) and *Pizichi, oder Fortsetzung Kaspars des Fagottisten* (1792), see Nedbal, *Morality and Viennese Opera*, pp. 142–145.

[110] Berger, *Bach's Cycle, Mozart's Arrow*, p. 285. On the significance of timbre in *Die Zauberflöte*, see Subotnik, 'Whose "Magic Flute"?' pp. 145–147, and Buch, *Magic Flutes and Enchanted Forests*, pp. 346–347.

[111] In similar fashion in the second half of the aria, a flute line tracks her descent from d'''s, where there is also evidence (though indecipherable) of modification to the string bass line. See *'Die Zauberflöte': Facsimile of the Autograph Score*, vol. 2, p. 273. The highest notes of the Queen of the Night's Act 1 aria 'O zitt're nicht' are also supported by the upper wind. Based on the precedent in *Così* (Woodfield, *Così fan tutte*, p. 74), an absence of discernible compositional phases in the autograph of 'O zitt're nicht' may indicate Mozart copying from pre-existing material. (See also Corneilson, 'Josepha Hofer', on this aria as a fair copy.) The demanding nature of the vocal writing makes consultation with Josepha Hofer a strong possibility during the compositional process, increasing the likelihood of an erstwhile earlier draft.

Example 12.13 Mozart, 'Der Hölle Rache' from *Die Zauberflöte*, bars 29–43 (including crossed out material).

how wind performers can help accentuate the Queen of the Night's sequential repeat of her descending quaver scale one step higher. The first ten bars of the Act 2 finale (Example 12.15), introducing 'Bald prangt' for the Three Boys, capture in a nutshell enhancement of wind effects during orchestration and once a performance was envisioned: the first clarinet and second bassoon were written on to the *particella*, as indicated by black ink; and all *sotto voce* and *f* – *p* markings (bars 1–5), plus musical material for the other four wind instruments, are in the sandy-coloured ink of the completion.

The autographs of the quintet 'Hm! Hm! Hm!' and the Act 1 finale also catch Mozart negotiating vocal performance and wind impact. In the quintet, vocal and instrumental effects operate in tandem. As when the four lovers sing together and alone for the first time in the Act 2 quartet of

Example 12.14 Mozart, 'Der Hölle Rache' from *Die Zauberflöte*, bars 13–17.

Die Entführung, when all soloists perform simultaneously at the end of *Figaro,* and when the four lovers plus Don Alfonso come together in 'Sento oddio' from *Così,* Mozart asks singers to highlight a moment of vocal unification: they are marked *sotto voce* (or 's: v:') at bar 54. And the *sotto voce* returns later in two similar contexts: at bar 111 when all five characters comment on the value to Tamino of the gift of the magic flute as protection in his quest to rescue Pamina; and at bar 184 when they reflect further on the virtues of silver bells and magic flutes. The most distinctive vocal *sotto voce,* though, comes towards the end of the ensemble (Example 12.16). Mozart had already envisaged a special moment at the *particella* stage (black ink), with a tempo change to Andante and a string pizzicato coinciding with the *sotto voce* (bar 214ff.). But he adds to it during the orchestration (light brown ink) by introducing two clarinets into the quintet for the first time and marking them *dolce pia.* It is unclear when Mozart first foresaw clarinet participation in this ensemble: his

Example 12.15 Mozart, Act 2 finale from *Die Zauberflöte*, bars 1–10 (all other staves blank).

twelve-stave paper accommodates only three staves for wind instruments once the five for the voices, one for the string bass line and three for the upper strings are taken into account, and are occupied by the two oboes, two bassoons and two horns from the start of the number. Had their participation been anticipated during the *particella* – the '2 clarinetti in B' designation to the left of the staves is also in the light brown ink of the completion – Mozart might have been expected to notate them at this initial stage, as the lone carrier of quasi-melodic content for four bars. It seems, then, that he had *sotto voce* effects ringing in his ears when orchestrating the final Andante and decided to add to the effect by

Example 12.16 Mozart, 'Hm! Hm! Hm!' from *Die Zauberflöte*, bars 214–219 (all other staves blank).

including a new instrument, a new clarinet-bassoon timbre and emollient presentation (*dolce pia*).[112] Contemplation of performance and consideration of instrumental impact are thereby aligned.

As in 'Hm! Hm! Hm!', many decisions about instrumentation and performance markings in the opening section of the Act 1 finale (where Tamino interacts with the Three Boys and the Priest on his way to the temple) were probably made after the *particella* had been notated.[113] In several cases, voice-wind timbres apparently affected these decisions. In the *particella* at bars 61–63, Mozart wrote only a single semibreve bar for Schack accompanied by a crescendo – *forte* annotated in the first-violin and string bass lines (see Example 12.17 for the completed score). Orchestrating the passage, he first continued in the same vein, writing the second violin and viola parts and including further crescendos, but subsequently changed all string dynamics to *forte*s at bar 62 (crossing out four crescendo indications). Since the wind (two flutes, two oboes, two bassoons) did not receive crescendos at any stage, only *forte*s, Mozart probably decided to alter the strings' dynamics on reaching the wind orchestration, and/or in conjunction with the squashed interpolation at the orchestration stage of an unaccompanied semibreve bar for Schack (61).[114] Irrespective, semibreves in the completed score are given first to Schack by himself and then to Schack and wind instruments together: initially exposed as a solo note, the vocal g" is then cushioned above and below by wind semibreves, highlighting two qualities of a 'beautiful voice' – as a single and a combined timbre – in successive bars. And later, when Tamino responds to the Priest that he is in search of 'love and virtue' ('Lieb' und Tugend', Example 12.18), Mozart first wrote a flute accompaniment in the *particella* but replaced it at the orchestration stage with two clarinets and two bassoons: a mention of love eventually triggers an invocation of the scoring for Schack's 'Dies Bildnis'.[115] Consideration of the full effect of

---

[112] After their serene opening to the section, the clarinets and bassoons stand out through *sf* – *ps* uncoordinated with the remainder of the ensemble and contribute to the warm full-wind chords at the end.

[113] Instrumentation and performance markings in the light-brown ink of the completion phase include: 'con sordino' and 'bedeckt' for the trumpets and timpani at the opening; tutti cellos and double basses to accompany Tamino's four-bar entry (18–22) following the cellos and bassoons for the Three Boys; *fp* dynamics in the strings (bar 44) and in the strings and winds (bar 108); *mfps*, *fs* and *ps* in the strings (bars 93, 127–136); a *forte* in place of a crescendo – *forte* in winds and strings (bars 62–63); and the two Andante tempo indications (bars 88, 137).

[114] Alternatively, Mozart initially considered uncoordinated dynamics between strings and winds in bar 62 and later decided to coordinate them.

[115] A similar point is made by Erik Smith in 'The Music', in Peter Branscombe, *W. A. Mozart: 'Die Zauberflöte'*, pp. 135–136.

Example 12.17 Mozart, Act 1 finale from *Die Zauberflöte*, bars 59–63 (including deletions and an additional bar [61] squeezed in at the completion stage).

passages in performance, then, leads both to a vocal interpolation and to instrumental and dynamic refinements.

It is an accident of historical circumstances – Constanze's health-related visits to Baden – that Mozart's upbeat, energized reactions to the reception of *Die Zauberflöte* are well preserved. 'What pleases me most is the *silent approval*! You see just how much and always more this opera rises', he explains on 7–8 October 1791.[116] One day later his attention is occupied by 'the usual applause and repetitions [of individual numbers]' and arrangements for Süssmayr, Stoll, Leutgeb and his mother-in-law to attend upcoming performances; he also gleefully relates stories of a crass audience member laughing at everything, including solemn scenes, and of teasing Schikaneder during the performance of 'Ein Mädchen oder Weibchen'.[117]

---

[116] MBA, vol. 4, p. 157; LMF, p. 967.

[117] MBA, vol. 4, pp. 159–160; LMF, pp. 968–969. It has been suggested, based on a study of the letter autograph, that the uncouth audience member was in the box of esteemed singer Valentin Adamberger (Mozart's original Belmonte in *Die Entführung*) and may even have been Adamberger himself; see Arthur, 'New Light on Mozart's Late Correspondence', pp. 143–145.

Example 12.18 Mozart, Act 1 finale from *Die Zauberflöte*, bars 87–90 (including deletion).

And in the last extant letter before his death, Salieri and Cavalieri's reactions are recorded: 'You can't believe how courteous both were – how much they liked not only my music, but the libretto and everything together. They both said it was an *operone* [grand opera] – worthy to be performed at the grandest festival and for the grandest monarch – and they would certainly go to see it often, as they had never seen a more beautiful or pleasant spectacle. He [Salieri] listened and watched with full attention and from the overture to the last chorus there was not a single piece that did not elicit a bravo or bello from him, and they almost could not finish thanking me for this favour.'[118] It is not hard to imagine Mozart having special affection for *Die Zauberflöte*. For its characters are thoroughly absorbed in and by music, like the performer-composer who according to his father had 'a head full of notes', who by his own admission repeatedly lost himself when performing on the keyboard, who wrote passionately about a performance of the 'Paris' Symphony just hours after his mother's death and who less than a month later confessed to being 'stuck in music'.[119]

---

[118] MBA, vol. 4, pp. 161–162; LMF, p. 970 (14 October 1791).

[119] See Keefe, 'Mozart "Stuck in Music" in Paris', pp. 28–35 (including discussion of the letters quoted).

La clemenza di Tito **in Prague**

Guardasoni's contract with the Bohemian Estates for an opera for the Prague coronation of Emperor Leopold II is dated 8 July 1791. It stipulates a payment to him of 6,000 florins, or 6,500 if the famous castrato Luigi Marchesi is engaged, and required employment of a leading castrato and prima donna, inclusion of two new changes of scenery and new costumes as well as lighting and garlands for the theatre, and an urgent trip to Vienna and Italy for recruitment purposes. The libretto was to be one of two proposed by Henrico Conte di Rottenhan (Count of the Castle), or, given the compressed timeframe, a new setting of Metastasio's *Tito*, and the composer a 'celebrated master'.[120] Like *Così fan tutte* in its early incarnation as *La scola degli amanti*, Salieri was the first choice to set *La clemenza di Tito*. But he had to turn Guardasoni down on account of work commitments in Vienna.[121] He later expressed criticism of part of Mozart's setting to Anselm Hüttenbrenner, an associate of Schubert: 'Salieri ... divulged that Mozart had completely misinterpreted the final scene of the first act ... Rome is burning; the whole population is in revolt; the music ought to rage and be tumultuous; but Mozart chose a slow, solemn tempo and rather expressed dread and horror.'[122] Mozart was probably approached formally to compose the opera only in early to mid-July 1791 and had completed it in time for the premiere on 6 September. While *Tito* took Mozart more than the eighteen days suggested by Niemetschek – who wrongly dates the start to the coach trip from Vienna to Prague[123] – its genesis was easily the shortest of any of the Viennese operas and in the rush to the premiere resulted in Mozart having to entrust the *secco* recitatives to an assistant, possibly Süssmayr.[124] The reviser of Metastasio's text, Caterino Mazzolà, temporarily in Vienna on a leave of absence from duties in Dresden, was probably engaged for *Tito* on account of his familiarity to

---

[120] For the entire contract, see NMD, pp. 67–68 and Mozart, *'La clemenza di Tito': Facsimile of the Autograph Score* (Los Altos, CA: The Packard Humanities Institute, 2008), vol. 2, pp. 31–32. For further discussion, see Sergio Durante, 'Musicological Introduction', in *'Tito': Facsimile of the Autograph Score*, vol. 2, pp. 17–34, at 18, and Durante, 'The Chronology of Mozart's *La clemenza di Tito* Reconsidered', *Music & Letters*, 80 (1999), pp. 560–594, at 565–568. On the original stage sets, see Rice, *Mozart on the Stage*, pp. 80–83.

[121] See NMD, pp. 68–69; Landon, *1791: Mozart's Last Year*, pp. 86–87; Durante, 'Musicological Introduction', in *'Tito': Facsimile of the Autograph Score*, vol. 2, p. 18; Durante, 'Chronology of Mozart's *La clemenza di Tito*', pp. 565–568.

[122] As given in Braunbehrens, *Maligned Master*, p. 226.

[123] Niemetschek, *Leben*, p. 32, *Life of Mozart*, p. 41.

[124] See the discussion in Durante, 'Musicological Introduction', in *'Tito': Facsimile of the Autograph Score*, vol. 2, pp. 24–25.

Guardasoni (who produced Mazzolà's *Elisa* and *Il triofo dell'amore sulla magia* in 1788 and 1789 respectively).[125] Based on the historical figure Titus, Roman Emperor in 79–81 AD, adding fictional characters and situations and displaying the influence of the great French classical tradition of Pierre Corneille and Jean Racine, *La clemenza di Tito* was a political allegory with broad eighteenth-century appeal: for the Prague coronation in 1791 Emperor Leopold II was to be recognized in the benevolent, noble Tito.[126]

With one exception, Antonio Baglioni in the title role, the *Tito* singers were unfamiliar to Mozart. Guardasoni hired two experienced and esteemed vocalists from Italy, Domenico Bedini (Sesto) and prima donna Maria Marchetti Fantozzi (Vitellia), deciding against the castrato recently arrived at his own company, Domenico Bruni.[127] Skilled as both an actress and singer and in possession of a strong voice, Marchetti specialized in impassioned heroines; in addition to Vitellia in *Tito* she created two more roles in 1791 alone, in Niccolò Antonio Zingarelli's *La morte di Cesare* and Sebastiano Nasolini's *La morte di Cleopatra*.[128] After *Tito*, she continued her career in Berlin as a leading prima donna, singing (for example) in Vincenzo Righini and Antonio de Filistri's *Il trionfo d'Arianna* (1793), *Athalante und Meleager* (1799) and *La selva incantata* (1803), Righini and Coltellini's *Armida* (1799), and Johann Friedrich Reichardt and de Filistri's *Rosmonda* (1805).[129] Her daughter Josephine (born 1786) sang Sesto,

[125] Durante, 'Musicological Introduction', in *'Tito': Facsimile of the Autograph Scores*, vol. 2, p. 18. On Mazzolà's cuts and modifications to Metastasio's libretto, including the addition of ensembles, see Rice, *'La clemenza di Tito'*, pp. 35–38. See also Sergio Durante, '"La clemenza di Tito" and Other Two-Act Reductions of the Late 18th Century', *Mozart-Jahrbuch 1991*, vol. 2, pp. 733–741.

[126] See Rice, *'La clemenza di Tito'*, pp. 12–26. Other eighteenth-century settings of *Tito* include those by Antonio Caldara (1734), Johann Adolph Hasse (1735; later revised), Georg Christoph Wagenseil (1745), Gluck (1752), Niccolò Jommelli (1753), Pasquale Anfossi (1769), and Giuseppe Sarti (1771). For *Tito* as 'not a conventional hymn to enlightened despotism, as is usually claimed, but a missile lobbed in the aristocratic counter-revolution to absolutism', with the 'princely virtue of clemency ... transmuted into the Christian virtue of forgiveness; sovereign into divine grace', see Till, *Mozart and the Enlightenment*, pp. 258–269 (quotations at pp. 264, 268).

[127] On the last point, see Woodfield, *Performing Operas for Mozart*, p. 169.

[128] On Marchetti qualities as a performer, citing late-eighteenth-century criticism, see Rice, *'La clemenza di Tito'*, pp. 51–52; Durante, 'Musicological Introduction', in *'Tito': Facsimile of the Autograph Score*, vol. 2, p. 26; and Rice, 'Mozart and His Singers: The Case of Maria Marchetti Fantozzi, the First Vitellia', *Opera Quarterly*, 11 (1995), pp. 31–52.

[129] Marchetti is listed as the prima donna in Berlin from December 1793 onwards. See *Indice de'teatrali spettacolo di tutto l'Anno dalla primavera 1793 a tutto il Carnevale 1794* (Milan, 1794), vol. 9, p. 12. See also *Armida: Dramma scritto Dal Signor Coltellini* (Berlin, 1799), pp. 6–7; *Il trionfo d'Arianna: Dramma da Antonio de' Filistri* (Berlin, 1793), n.p.; *Rosmonda,*

naturally as a soprano, in a German version of *Tito* in Munich in 1806.[130] Marchetti and Bedini had performed together in Florence and Genoa in 1785 and 1789 respectively; one of the female singers in Guardasoni's troupe, Margherita Morigi Simoni, had also sung with Bedini in Andreozzi's *Virginia* (1787).[131] Bedini's popularity in Florence from 1780–1786 would have made him familiar to Emperor Leopold, formerly Grand Duke of Tuscany; it is possible, in fact, that Leopold had some involvement in the casting of *Tito*.[132] In February 1791, Bedini was praised for his performance in the title role of Francesco Bianchi's *La morte de Cesare* in Reggio.[133] Indeed, it may have been Bedini's recent success as an onstage Roman leader that led Mozart first to conceive the castrato role for the character of Tito, rather than Sesto: rejected drafts of three numbers from the beginning of the opera all notate Sesto's material in the tenor clef, indicating Sesto as a tenor and thus by implication Tito as a castrato.

Members of Guardasoni's company took the three smaller solo roles in *Tito*. Carolina Perini (Annio) had joined it in Warsaw by autumn 1790 and was gone three years later.[134] Promoted to larger roles post Prague, she is listed as the prima donna for Paisiello's *La nina pazza per amore*, Cimarosa's *Il matrimonio segreto*, Ferdinand Päer's *L'oro fa tutto*, Zingarelli's *La secchia rapita*, and Pietro Guglielmi's *Lo sciocco poeta* in Genoa and Milan in spring, summer and autumn 1793.[135] Antonina Miklaszewicz, or perhaps Anna Antonini (Servilia), also went on to bigger roles after *Tito*, becoming Guardasoni's prima donna in 1793 and singing *inter alia* in *Così*, *Don Giovanni*, *Die Zauberflöte* and *Figaro* in Leipzig in 1793 and 1794.[136] Gaetano Campi (Publio), who married Miklaszewicz soon after the *Tito* premiere, was based in Italy through most of the 1780s, performing in Milan in Sarti's *Fra i due litiganti il terzo gode* (Autumn

---

tragedia lirica scritta da Antonio de'Filistri (Berlin, 1805), p. 14; *Athalante und Meleager: eine Theater-Feyerlichkeit von Antonio de' Filistri* (Berlin, 1799), p. 8; *La selva incantata, dramma di Antonio de' Filistri* (Berlin, 1803), n.p.

[130] See Lipowsky, *Baierisches Lexikon*, p. 198.

[131] Durante, 'Musicological Introduction', p. 25; and Rice, '*La clemenza di Tito*', p. 53; Woodfield, *Performing Operas for Mozart*, p. 171.

[132] Durante, 'Musicological Introduction', p. 26.

[133] See *Gazetta universale*, no. 12 (8 February 1791), p. 95.

[134] Woodfield, *Performing Operas for Mozart*, pp. 168, 169.

[135] See *Indice de' teatrali spettacoli di tutto l'Anno dalla primavera 1793 a tutto il Carnevale 1794* (Milan, 1794), vol. 9, pp. 55, 60; and *Serie cronologica delle rappresentazioni drammatico-pantomimiche poste sulle scene dei principali teatri di Milano, 1776–1818* (Milan, 1818), p. 47.

[136] On the singer's name, see Woodfield, *Performing Operas for Mozart*, pp. 172–173. See also Durante, 'Musicological Introduction', p. 26; Woodfield, *Performing Operas for Mozart*, pp. 224–227.

1785) and Giovanni Valentini's *La statua matematica* and Cimarosa's *Il falegname* (Carnival 1786), and in Turin in *L'impostore punito* (usually attributed to Pietro Guglielmi) and Vincenzo Fabrizi's *I due castellani burlati* (autumn 1786).[137] He was with Guardasoni by the Leipzig residency in summer 1788 and remained at the company until 1800.[138]

In contrast to his other operas from 1781 to 1791, Mozart would have had limited knowledge of, and little opportunity to collaborate closely with his singers for *Tito* when carrying out much of his commission. The limited time between the commission and first performance, the near complete change in the personnel of the Guardasoni company since *Don Giovanni* in 1787, the impresario's contractually obliged recruitment of two leading singers from Italy, and Mozart's late arrival in Prague (28 August, nine days before the premiere) all worked against composer-singer collaboration.[139] Mozart knew Baglioni as Don Ottavio from *Don Giovanni* and may have met Bedini and Marchetti in Vienna as they made their way to Prague from Italy.[140] While the autograph score comprises five different types of paper, Mozart probably mixed three of them as he wrote – contrary to his usual practice – making a precise chronological order of composition difficult to establish.[141] But much work on the opera had clearly been completed by the time of his arrival in Prague: only the overture, No. 4 (march), No. 8 'Ah, se fosse intorno' for Tito, the Act 2 accompanied recitative 'Che orror!' and the end of Vitellia's accompanied recitative before the rondò 'Non più di fiori' were unambiguously written in Prague, notated on a type of paper unavailable to Mozart in Vienna.[142] As noted in discussion of *Così*, blank

---

[137] See *Indice de' spettacoli teatrali di tutto l'anno dalla primavera 1785 a tutto il Carnevale 1786* (Milan, 1786), pp. 180, 5; and *Calendrier musical universel* (Paris, 1788), p. 165.

[138] See Woodfield, *Performing Operas for Mozart*, pp. 114, 214.

[139] For a day-by-day account of coronation-related activities in Prague, from Mozart's arrival on 28 August until 12 September, see Landon, *1791: Mozart's Last Year*, pp. 101–123.

[140] See Durante, 'Chronology of *La clemenza di Tito*', p. 577, on Mozart '[having] to compose quite independently of the singers' and Durante, 'Musicological Introduction', p. 20 on Mozart perhaps meeting Marchetti and Bedini as they travelled through Vienna. For musical evidence that Mozart did not know Marchetti's voice when writing 'Non più di fiori', comparing other material written for her to Mozart's rondò, see Rice, 'Maria Marchetti Fantozzi'.

[141] See Durante, 'Chronology of *La clemenza di Tito*', pp. 579–580. For identification of which numbers are on which paper type, see Tyson, *Autograph Scores*, pp. 52–56.

[142] Tyson, *Autograph Scores*, pp. 52–54. The date of 'Non più di fiori' has long been a matter of scholarly controversy, stemming from its notation on a type of paper not found elsewhere in the *Tito* autograph and an announcement of a 'Rondo by Herr Mozart with basset-horn *obbligato*' performed by Josepha Duschek at her Prague academy on 26 April 1791. (See MDL, p. 345; MDB, p. 393.) The advertisement for Duschek's concert led scholars (beginning with Tomislav Volek in 'Über den Ursprung von Mozarts Oper "La clemenza di Tito"', *Mozart-Jahrbuch 1959*, pp. 274–286) to believe that 'Non più di fiori' was actually written in spring 1791, in spite of this theory leaving unexplained 'how Mozart could have written an aria whose

staves in the middle area of his autographs to be used for wind instruments
may indicate either indecision about wind scoring at the *particella* stage, or
a revised view of it at the completion stage, perhaps after consultation with
singers. For the main three characters in *Tito*, only the protagonist's aria
'Ah se fosse', written in Prague shortly before the premiere, and Sesto's
accompanied recitative 'O Dei, che smania è questa' contain empty staves
in the middle of the score, whereas three of the four arias for the minor solo
characters do, each giving over five staves of the initial ten-stave brace for
wind parts in the *particella*: Annio's 'Torna di Tito' ultimately uses none of
them; and Publio's 'Tardi s'avvede' and Servilia's 'S'alto che lacrime'
eventually employ three and four respectively.[143] Mozart would have had
no direct exposure to Perini, Miklaszewicz and Campi's voices in advance
of reaching Prague; the *particella*s for the arias were probably written in
Vienna and could have benefitted only from secondhand information
about the singers, including anything Guardasoni provided. While we
cannot know exactly when Mozart orchestrated these arias, it is possible
that he waited to do so until he had heard the singers in Prague.

Mozart was on familiar ground writing for Baglioni (Tito), being able to
build on material provided for his original Don Ottavio in *Don Giovanni*.
In addition to tonal, harmonic and coloratura-related correspondences
between 'Il mio tesoro' and 'Se all'impero', Baglioni's showpiece aria in
Tito,[144] the opening four-bar phrase of the Andantino from 'Se all'impero'
resembles the corresponding phrase of Ottavio's 'Or che tutti, o mio Tesoro,
vendicati siam dal cielo' from the *scena ultima* of *Don Giovanni*
(Examples 12.19 and 12.20): similarities include melodic contours –
a descent to the seventh degree via stepwise semiquavers, a re-ascent and a
scale degree 5–4–3 finish – a preponderance of dotted quaver–semiquaver
rhythms, and light string-only accompaniments. As in 'Il mio tesoro', the
wind in Tito's solo numbers support Baglioni's virtuosity and colour his voice:
in the Primo tempo reprise of 'Se all'impero' the longest vocal semiquaver

---

text fits so well into an opera that he had not apparently begun to write' (Rice, '*La clemenza di Tito*', p. 51). The discovery of the same paper type in Publio's surviving partbook for *Tito* (see Durante, 'Chronology of *La clemenza di Tito*', p. 574) indicates that it could have been written in summer 1791 alongside the rest of the opera, as does ink-related evidence (see Arthur, 'Contribution of Ink Studies', pp. 45–52). 'Al desio' K. 577 has been proposed as the rondò performed by Duschek on 26 April 1791 (Marius Flothuis, 'Welche Arien sang Josepha Duschek am 26. April 1791?', *Mitteilungen der Internationalen Stiftung Mozarteum*, 37 (1989), pp. 81–82). In support of this hypothesis, Woodfield explains (*Performing Operas for Mozart*, p. 174) that Duschek sang 'Al desio' at Leipzig on 18 March 1796.

[143] See '*Tito*': *Facsimile of the Autograph Score*, vol. 1, pp. 163–169, 195–199, 267–271.

[144] See Rice, '*La clemenza di Tito*', pp. 56–59.

Example 12.19 Mozart, Act 2 finale from *Don Giovanni*, bars 712–715.

Example 12.20 Mozart, 'Se all'impero' from *La clemenza di Tito*, bars 55–58.

passage (eight bars) is accompanied by solo imitative wind figures and the final vocal exit passage by tutti-wind march figures; in 'Del più sublime', Tito's first aria, the most striking wind contribution is reserved for the four bars that link to the reprise (as in 'Il mio tesoro'), which includes drifting flute and bassoon semibreves and tied minims; and in 'Ah, grazie si rendano' (Tito with chorus), wind groups offer harmonious solo support without upper strings. 'Ah, se fosse intorno', a late addition written in Prague to rebalance the number of solos for individual singers after the inclusion of one for Publio,[145] is a distillation of earlier material for Baglioni: prominent wind *crescendi* to *forte* support vocal virtuosity both at the end of the B section immediately before pauses promoting Baglioni's highest note (g') and offering opportunities for embellishments, and at the final vocal exit; and march-like wind invoke 'Se all'impero'. The large wind group for 'Se all'impero' (double flutes, oboes, bassoons, horns) may explain the one empty stave in the autograph of 'Ah, se fosse intorno': Mozart could have had the scoring of 'Se all'impero' in mind as he began work, only electing subsequently to go with a slightly smaller wind complement than originally envisioned. Baglioni had gained significant experience with the Guardasoni troupe in Prague, Leipzig and Warsaw between the *Don Giovanni* and *Tito* premieres, singing for example in Salieri's *Axur re d'Ormus* (1788, 1789, 1791), Martín's *Una cosa rara* and *L'arbore di Diana* and Salieri's *Il talismano* (1788, 1789), and Paisiello's *Il mondo della luna, Il re Teodoro, La serva padrona, La contadina di spirito, La modista raggiratrice* and *Pirro* (1789–1791).[146] Indeed Mozart may have proactively challenged Baglioni to develop his voice, especially in 'Se l'impero';[147] composer and performer alike would have expected to reap the benefits of vocal progress.

One other important performer at the *Tito* premiere was a known quantity to Mozart and had his talents exploited: the clarinettist Anton Stadler, recipient of obbligato parts for Marchetti's rondò 'Non più di fiori' (basset-horn), where Vitellia expresses guilt at having asked her faithful Sesto to instigate the rebellion against Tito, and Bedini's 'Parto, parto' (basset clarinet), with Sesto pledging love and loyalty to Vitellia. In the larghetto of 'Non più di fiori', Stadler is introduced gradually to the Prague audience as a soloist, carrying the melody with the strings at the outset, quietly accompanying the voice with triplet semiquavers that include the basset-horn's distinctive low notes, and then presenting agile demisemiquaver accompanimental arpeggios in the texturally exposed run-up to the

---

[145] Durante, 'Chronology of *La clemenza di Tito*', pp. 582–583, 589.

[146] See Rice, *Mozart on the Stage*, pp. 131–134, and Rice, 'Antonio Baglioni, Mozart's First Don Ottavio and Tito, in Italy and Prague', in Milada Jonášová and Tomislav Volek (eds.), *Böhmische Aspekte des Lebens und des Werkes von W. A. Mozart* (Prague, 2012), pp. 24–38, at 34–36, for complete lists of productions in which Baglioni participated between 1786 and 1797. For Baglioni's performances with the Guardasoni troupe during its residencies in Leipzig between 1788 and 1794, see Woodfield, *Performing Operas for Mozart*, pp. 222–227.

[147] See Rice, *Mozart on the Stage*, p. 123.

end of the section. Have 'earned' his solo status, Stadler assumes equal billing with Marchetti in the Allegro, ebbing and flowing in dialogue with the singer – often in the melodic lead – and playing semiquaver passages that again expose the low register of the basset-horn and the technical versatility of the performer.[148] The importance of pristine exchange between Stadler and Marchetti emerges in two crossings out in the cellos/basses (Example 12.21). Mozart's first instinct was to have string notes coincide with the beginning of vocal responses in an antecedent-consequent exchange (bars 65, 67). But he quickly decided to delay these notes until the fourth beat, thereby allowing no sound potentially to compromise the immediate succession of basset-horn and voice.[149] The contribution of the basset-horn to the Allegro reaches a timbral as well as a brilliantly virtuosic climax: the four bars of semiquaver figurations (the longest in the aria, bars 168–171) in the approach to the vocal exit are preceded by a passage for basset-horn and voice entirely alone (bars 146–150, Example 12.22). For Stadler, then, 'Non più di fiori' nurtured a type of versatile playing similar to the wind serenade K. 361 at his academy on 23 March 1784 (see Chapter 4). The distinctive properties of the solo instrument, its blend with others, and an ability to 'sing' – a quality admired by Johann Friedrich Schink at the Viennese academy[150] – were all promoted alongside brilliant virtuosity.

Where Stadler was concerned, 'Parto, parto' complemented 'Non più di fiori': for basset clarinet rather than basset-horn, it revealed skills on another instrument from the clarinet family to the Prague audience and provided opportunities to display greater technical virtuosity than Vitellia's rondò. *Particella* and completion phases of activity are not always evident from the aria's autograph. But it is usually clear where the basset clarinet was notated alongside the voice or was part of the original conception and where it accrued to the completion or represented an afterthought to vocal material: since the majority of the basset clarinet writing is in significantly shorter note values than the vocal part, individual bars occupying a large amount of space sufficient for comfortable notation indicate the instrument's presence in Mozart's earliest thoughts, whereas narrowly spaced bars, and cramped notation, suggest later inclusion.

---

[148] As Lawson points out (*Clarinet Concerto*, p. 33), the Allegro's main theme is similar to material written for Stadler in the transition section of the first movement of the clarinet concerto.

[149] Mozart must have decided to delete the third-beat crotchets for cellos and basses soon after writing them: when the same material returns forty or so bars later, there are no such crotchets.

[150] MDL, p. 206; MDB, pp. 232–233.

Example 12.21 Mozart, 'Non più di fiori' from *La clemenza di Tito*, bars 64–68 (including deletions).

Example 12.22 Mozart, 'Non più di fiori' from *La clemenza di Tito*, bars 143–150 (all other staves blank).

Unsurprisingly, given the obbligato instrument's prominent melodic role, there is little of the latter.[151]

In musical content and manner of presentation, Stadler's basset clarinet takes the lead solo role in 'Parto, parto' (factoring in vocal material notated in the autograph score rather than what Bedini actually performed, which cannot be known). In the Adagio it plays demisemiquaver embellishments in the beautiful opening exchange and demisemiquaver arpeggios from high to low registers (bars 13–42); it leads thematically on every occasion in the Allegro (with agile arpeggios even before the voice has been heard at the opening) and twice plays and immediately elaborates *dolce* material; and it receives a greater quantity of triplet-quaver material than the voice in the concluding Allegro assai. No doubt florid, virtuosic writing for Stadler enhanced appreciation of the aria as a whole, to the benefit of its recipient Bedini. Indeed, Stadler conveyed to Mozart in a letter about the final Prague performance of *Tito* on 30 September that 'Bedini sang better than ever'.[152] Embellishments introduced by Bedini also would have rendered vocal material more ornate than on the page: the unelaborated reprise of the Adagio from his rondò 'Deh per questo', a departure from Mozart's standard practice, may indicate a desire on the part of an experienced and esteemed singer to assume control of this aspect of performance.[153] But the impression remains that 'Parto, parto' is as much (if not more) a vehicle for Stadler as for Bedini, especially as Stadler's predilections and considerable skills were so well known to Mozart, while time to consult and collaborate with Bedini would have been limited. Asked to perform on two euphonious members of the clarinet family in varied, complementary ways provided an ideal platform for a gifted instrumentalist, a fact not lost on players and audience alike at the Estates Theatre: '"Oh, Bohemian miracle!" he [Stadler] writes – "bravo" shouted from the parterre and even the orchestra. "But I *did my very best*", he writes.'[154]

Mozart was naturally delighted with the reception of *Tito* at its last Prague performance. In addition to Bedini's singing and Stadler's playing, 'The little duet in A major from the two girls ["Ah, perdona"] was repeated; and – had they not spared Marchetti – they would also gladly have had the rondò ["Non più di fiori"] repeated.'[155] But, all in all, the premiere itself met with a mixed response. Zinzendorf described *Tito* as 'the most boring

---

[151] Cramped basset clarinet material is evident in bars 36, 54–55, 137–144; see *'Tito': Facsimile of the Autograph Score*, vol. 1, pp. 93, 95, 105–106.

[152] MBA, vol. 4, p. 157; LMF, p. 967 (7–8 October 1791).

[153] See Rice, *'La clemenza di Tito'*, p. 93, and Rice, *Mozart on the Stage*, p. 155.

[154] MBA, vol. 4, p. 157; LMF, p. 967 (7–8 October 1791).   [155] MBA, vol. 4, p. 157; LMF, p. 966.

spectacle', although both he and the Emperor were very impressed with Marchetti; Empress Maria Luisa found it 'not much and the music very bad so that almost all of us fell asleep'; and the Berlin *Musikalisches Wochenblatt* reported that it 'did not please'.[156] The *Krönungsjournal für Prag* also sounded an equivocal note: 'The composition is by the famous Mozart, and does him honour, though he did not have much time for it and was also the victim of an illness, during which he had to complete the last part of the same.'[157] There were extenuating circumstances, irrespective of whether Mozart's illness affected his work schedule: *Tito* had to compete with numerous other festive activities associated with the coronation on 6 September, which may already have exhausted some audience members by the time of the Emperor's arrival at the Estates Theatre (around 7:30 pm); and, given the tight timeframe, it was probably under-rehearsed.[158] But others enjoyed the premiere. For Kleist: 'In the evening a very beautiful opera, *La clemenza di Tito*, was given free. The music is by Mozart, and fully worthy of its master; he especially pleases here in the Andantes, where his melodies are so beautiful as to lure the angels down from above.'[159] Niemetschek, whose soft spot for *Tito* would have derived at least partially from its connection to Prague, took stock a few years later:

Every part, even the smallest instrumental part, bears this stamp [of simplicity and nobility], and coalesces into the most beautiful unified whole. . . . The last scene or the finale of the first Act is certainly the most perfect of Mozart's work; expression, character, feeling all compete with one another to bring forth the greatest effect. The singing, instrumentation, variety of tone and echo of distant choruses produced at each performance an emotion and illusion seldom apparent at operas.[160]

---

[156] See, respectively, MDL, p. 355, MDB, pp. 404–405; NMD, p. 109 (Empress Maria Luisa); MDL, p. 380, MDB, p. 432. Küster (*Mozart: A Musical Biography*, p. 355) over-confidently speculates that Zinzendorf's criticism 'can hardly refer to that part of the evening's entertainment for which Mozart himself was responsible' and must allude to the *secco* recitatives.

[157] MDB, p. 405 (not MDL; translation from MDB). Niemetschek (*Leben*, p. 34, *Life of Mozart*, p. 43) also attests to Mozart's illness in Prague.

[158] See Niemetschek, *Leben*, p. 74, *Life of Mozart*, p. 82; Durante, 'Musicological Introduction', in '*Tito': Facsimile of the Autograph Score*, vol. 2, p. 26. On the Emperor's arrival at the theatre at about 7:30 pm, see MDL, p. 355; MDB, pp. 404–405. If under-rehearsed at the premiere on 6 September, it would be expected to be better performed by 30 September, perhaps explaining the apparently improved reception (as reported to Mozart by Stadler) at the end of the initial run.

[159] MDL, p. 381; MDB, p. 433.

[160] Niemetschek, *Leben*, p. 73, *Life of Mozart*, pp. 81–82 (translation amended). The quintet at the end of Act 1 was also admired by Rochlitz (1798) for '[displaying] so unmistakably and with such hair-raising intensity Mozart's Shakespearian, omnipotent power for the grand, the magnificent, the terrifying, the monstrous, the staggering, scarcely matched by the celebrated

Even in the most challenging of circumstances, then, extremely pressed for time for reasons beyond his control, ill, and with few opportunities to work with the singers creating his leading roles, Mozart was still able to produce an opera in which mutually reinforcing performing and compositional activities create a complete dramatic experience.[161]

The Requiem and Other Vocal Works

Stimuli for non-operatic vocal music in 1791 came from Vienna and further afield. Mozart completed his 'Ave, verum corpus' K. 618 on 17 or 18 June 1791 in Baden during a visit with his wife and while working on *Die Zauberflöte*. It may have been written for – and first performed by – the choirmaster Anton Stoll at the Baden Pfarrkirche on Corpus Christi, 23 June 1791, as is usually assumed. But, in the absence of corroborating evidence, a Viennese venue cannot be ruled out for the premiere, perhaps St Stephen's or the Piaristenkirche, even on Corpus Christi itself once Mozart was back in the capital.[162] It is difficult to determine, then, whether the modest vocal material ultimately represents either (or both) a concession to the abilities of a provincial choir, or a stylistic move towards compressed and direct vocal writing.[163]

Mozart's self-described 'kleine deutsche Kantate' for voice and piano, 'Die ihr des unermeßlichen Weltalls Schöpfer ehrt', K. 619, was written a few weeks after 'Ave, verum corpus'.[164] It was requested by the Regensburg-based writer Franz Heinrich Ziegenhagen as a setting of his own utopian, pantheistic, masonic-inspired text extolling the virtues of

Finale of the first act of his *Don Giovanni*'. See Solomon, 'The Rochlitz Anecdotes', p. 33; reprinted in Keefe (ed.), *Mozart*, p. 123.

[161] On the reception of *Tito* for the thirty years after the premiere, see Emanuele Senici, *La Clemenza di Tito: I premi trent'anni (1791–1821)* (Amsterdam and Cremona: Brepols, 1997). See also Senici, '"Adapted to the Modern Stage": *La clemenza di Tito* in London', *Cambridge Opera Journal*, 7 (1995), pp. 1–22. Woodfield discusses Guardasoni's second run of performances in 1794; see *Performing Operas for Mozart*, pp. 200–203. For general discussion of *Tito* reception through to the present day, including its popularity in the first quarter of the nineteenth century and subsequent decline, the romantic critical tradition that stretches well into the twentieth century, modern stagings, and critical re-evaluations in the last fifty years see Rice, '*La clemenza di Tito*', pp. 104–159.

[162] See Black, 'Mozart and the Practice of Sacred Music', pp. 334–336.

[163] Black, 'Mozart and the Practice of Sacred Music', p. 337; on the stylistic point see Wolff, *Mozart's Requiem*, pp. 33–36. The modest vocal and instrumental forces at the Pfarrkirche under the direction of Anton Stoll are described in Black, 'Mozart and the Practice of Sacred Music', pp. 306–307.

[164] For Mozart's reference to a 'kleine deutsche Kantate' see *Werkverzeichniß: Faksimile*, fol. 27v.

love and fraternity as instigators of peace. Ziegenhagen wanted to include Mozart's work in his *magnum opus, Lehre vom richtigen Verhältnisse zu den Schöpfungswerken, und die durch öffentliche Einfürung deselben allein zu bewürkende algemeine Menschenbeglükkung* [*sic*] (Hamburg, 1792) alongside illustrations by the Polish-German artist Daniel Chodowiecki. Apparently of the view that attaching Mozart (and Chodowiecki) to the volume would enhance sales, Ziegenhagen listed him on the title page: 'mit 8 Kupfert [engravings] von D. Chodowiescki, und einer Musik von W. A. Mozart'. Mozart's considerable reputation in 1791, even outside musical circles, is thereby endorsed. The text, printed at the end of the volume followed by Mozart's musical setting, is introduced by Ziegenhagen as a 'song to sing in meeting houses with the accompaniment of instrumental music'.[165]

While the 'Ave, verum corpus' and 'kleine deutsche Kantate' temporarily interrupted Mozart's operatic work, the cantata 'Laut verkünde unsre Freude', K. 623, came after *Die Zauberflöte* and *Tito* were off his desk and the Requiem had moved on to it. Written for the formal opening of a temple at Mozart's masonic lodge 'Neu gekrönten Hoffnung' to a text by Schikaneder, 'Laut verkünde unsre Freude' was first performed under the composer's direction on 17 November 1791. It is not known who else was involved in the premiere. But neither tenor nor bass solo roles are especially challenging, featuring modest vocal ranges (e – a'; c – e') and no coloratura or particularly large leaps.

Mozart's delight at the success of the cantata's premiere and temporary respite from the illness that would prove fatal less than three weeks later is reported by Niemetschek and Mary and Vincent Novello, drawing on information obtained in both cases from Constanze: 'The good performance and the great applause with which it was received gave his spirit new energy'; and 'The great success ... cheered his spirits for a time'.[166] It cannot be known whether Constanze, Niemetschek and the Novellos accurately report Mozart's state of health at the time of the cantata performance or construct a biographical narrative about the ebb and flow of his illness in the final months not entirely rooted in fact. The recuperative powers of performance are conveyed in Mozart's own letters nonetheless, especially on his travels in 1777–1779: playing the piano at the Duchesse de Chabot's house in Paris, in concert in Strasbourg and with Count von Sickingen in Mannheim cured

---

[165] *Lehre vom richtigen Verhältnisse zu den Schöpfungswerken*, p. 632 ('Ein Lied in den Versammlungshäusern unter Begleitung von Instrumentalmusik zu singen').

[166] Niemetschek, *Leben*, pp. 34–35, *Life of Mozart*, p. 44 (translation amended); Medici and Hughes (eds.), *A Mozart Pilgrimage*, p. 128. See also Nissen, *Biographie W. A. Mozarts*, pp. 563–564.

headaches, warmed him up and banished lethargic sentiments; and writing energetically about the premiere of the 'Paris' Symphony K. 297 at the *Concert Spirituel* may have helped him cope with his mother's death just hours earlier.[167]

Accounts of Mozart's renditions of parts of the Requiem, in the throes of his final illness, suggest altogether more stressful experiences. The Novellos ascertained from Constanze (1829) that 'on one occasion he himself with Süssmayr and Madame Mozart tried over part of the Requiem together, but some of the passages so excited him that he could not refrain from tears, and was unable to proceed'.[168] According to Mozart's sister-in-law, Sophie Haibel (1825), who was present at Mozart's death: 'His last [movement] was a desire to express with his mouth the drum passages in the Requiem, which I can still hear.'[169] And a posthumous tribute to Schack (1827), relaying information from Schack himself, famously reports a rehearsal hours before Mozart's death:

As soon as he had completed a number, he had it sung straight away, and played the instrumentation for it on his piano. Even on the eve of his death he had the score of the Requiem brought to his bed, and himself sang (it was two o'clock in the afternoon) the alto part; Schack, the family friend, sang the soprano part, as he had always been in the habit of doing previously, Hofer, Mozart's brother-in-law, the tenor, Gerle, later bassist at the Mannheim Theatre, the bass. They were at the first bars of the Lacrimosa when Mozart began to cry bitterly, put the score aside, and eleven hours later passed away, at one o'clock in the morning (of 5 December 1791, as is well known).[170]

Without reporting Mozart's emotions, Süssmayr also explained dispassionately in a letter to the publisher Gottfried Christoph Härtel (1800) 'that during Mozart's lifetime I . . . often played through and sung with him the movements already composed'.[171]

---

[167] See Keefe, 'Mozart "Stuck in Music" in Paris (1778)', pp. 23–35.

[168] *A Mozart Pilgrimage*, p. 128. Mozart claimed that he had to stop singing bits of *Die Zauberflöte* as it made him overly emotional in Constanze's absence. See MBA, vol. 4, p. 150; LMF, p. 964 (7 July 1791). The coming together of a performance and a poignant situation to induce an emotional response from Mozart and others was also witnessed in Mannheim in December 1777 when Rosa Cannabich played the piano sonata Mozart had written for her in the wake of confirmation that no position would be available to him at court in Mannheim and that he would have to leave the town as a result. See MBA, vol. 2, p. 178; LMF, p. 414 (10 December 1777).

[169] MBA, vol. 4, p. 464; LMF, p. 977 (7 April 1825).

[170] *Allgemeine musikalische Zeitung*, 29 (1827), col. 521. Also given in MDL, p. 460; MDB, pp. 536–537.

[171] My translation, as given in Keefe, *Mozart's Requiem*, p. 175. For the German text of Süssmayr's letter, see Joseph Eibl, 'Süssmayrs "Requiem"-Brief vom 8. Februar 1800', *Mitteilungen der*

The accuracy of the Schack and Haibel accounts would have been difficult enough to verify in the late 1820s, thirty-five years or so after the events described, with Süssmayr, Schack, Gerl and Hofer all dead and Constanze increasingly distant from Requiem-related discussion.[172] But verification is impossible almost 200 years later. Irrespective of whether true, partially true or false, statements from the key protagonists reflect a desire to represent Mozart engaging intently with his final work both compositionally *and* as a quasi performer.

It is not known how much Mozart was told at the point of commission about Walsegg's plans for the projected premiere of the Requiem.[173] Anton Herzog participated in the eventual first performance mounted by Walsegg on 14 December 1793, explaining: 'Since it was not possible to find all the necessary performers in the neighbourhood of Stuppach, it was decided that the first performance should take place in Wiener-Neustadt. The performers were chosen so as to give the solos and the most important parts to the best, wherever they came from: thus the solo parts were taken by the male soprano Ferenz of Neustadt, the contralto Kernbeiss of Schottwien, the tenor Klein of Neustadt and the bass Thurner of Gloggnitz. The rehearsal took place on the evening of 12 December 1793 in the choir of the Cistercian abbey and parish church at Wiener-Neustadt, and on 14 December at 10 o'clock, Mass for the Dead was celebrated at the same church, at which the famous Requiem was performed for the first time, for its intended purpose. Count Walsegg himself directed the whole performance.'[174] The fact that a rendition in Wiener-Neustadt would have had greater visibility than one in Stuppach, but still taken place fairly close to home, may also have entered Walsegg's calculations. An ex-bishopric of

Internationalen Stiftung Mozarteum, 24 (1976), pp. 21–23, and Keefe, *Mozart's Requiem*, pp. 249–250.

[172] As Deutsch explains (MDL, p. 460; MDB, p. 537) there are inaccuracies in Schack's recollections of Mozart in 1791, including about his trip to Prague (remembered as Frankfurt). Constanze had seemingly lost the desire to engage in discussion of Requiem-related issues by the 1820s, perhaps weary from earlier disputes about the work with the commissioner Walsegg. She consequently left friend and associate Maximilian Stadler to fight Mozart's corner in the so-called 'Requiem-Streit'. On the 'Requiem-Streit', see Keefe, *Mozart's Requiem*, pp. 49–57. Nissen's request for Sophie Haibel's account of Mozart's last days when researching his biography may point to the sketchiness of Constanze's memory of her husband's demise (which would be unsurprising in the circumstances).

[173] On performances of the Requiem in Vienna that predate Walsegg's in Wiener-Neustadt, see Keefe, *Mozart's Requiem*, p. 3.

[174] For Herzog's full document, see Josef Heinz Eibl (ed.), *Mozart: Die Dokumente seines Lebens, Addenda und Corrigenda* (Kassel: Bärenreiter, 1978), pp. 101–107; MDB, pp. 551–555, at 553 (translation from MDB). Gloggnitz is located within a mile of Stuppach and Schottwien within five miles; both are identified as Walsegg's estates (MDB, p. 551).

around 4,000 inhabitants, occupying an important position in the Austrian guild system,[175] Wiener-Neustadt's profile had been boosted in 1793: a Viennese plan was hatched to save valuable firewood for the construction of a canal to provide better transport links to the capital; and the church of the former Carmelite nunnery was turned into the town's first theatre at a cost of 6,874 florins.[176] But high-quality professional musicians would not necessarily have been available to Walsegg, judging by a performance on 15 October 1796 of the Süssmayr-Rautenstrauch patriotic cantata 'Der Retter in Gefahr' in the Wiener-Neustadt theatre shortly after the Viennese premiere and in honour of the late Empress Maria Theresia.[177] Twenty performers came from Vienna for the cantata concert; the amateur-musician contingent of clergymen, doctors, counsellors and professors in the seventy-strong orchestra would therefore have comprised a healthy majority.[178]

Needless to say, the somewhat *ad hoc* Wiener-Neustadt performance in 1793 may not have been Walsegg's intention when commissioning the Requiem in 1791. But, assuming Walsegg from the start envisaged a first performance at a provincial venue close to home, the limited musical resources available in Wiener-Neustadt and Stuppach areas render unlikely a specific request for the unusual combination of basset-horns, bassoons, trombones, trumpets and timpani that Mozart supplied, since orchestral participants presumably would have had to be sourced locally (following the model for soloists and choir) and uncommon instrumentation therefore would have complicated practical arrangements. In addition, after a second performance in nearby Semmering on 14 February 1794, the anniversary of Anna Walsegg's death, Walsegg turned away from the fully orchestrated version of the work: 'From this

[175] See Josef Ehmer, 'Rural Guilds and Urban-Rural Guild Relations in Early Modern Central Europe', in Jan Lucassen, Tine De Moor and Jan Luiten zan Zanden (eds.), *The Return of the Guilds* (Cambridge: Cambridge University Press, 2009), pp. 143–158, at 150.

[176] Ferdinand Carl Böheim, *Chronik von Wiener-Neustadt* (Vienna, 1830), vol. 2, pp. 175–176, 174. Böheim explains that prior to the construction of the theatre, performances had taken place in Gasthäuser.

[177] For publication of the text of the cantata, see *Eine Kantate von Rautenstrauch in Musik gesetzt von F. X. Süßmayer* (Vienna, 1796). For more on this work, see Jones, *Music in Vienna*, pp. 124–125.

[178] For these numbers, and references to the professions of the amateur performers, see *Chronik von Wiener-Neustadt*, vol. 2, p. 178. A clarinet obbligato part was written for Anton Stadler for the cantata; he could have been one of the musicians who travelled to Wiener-Neustadt for the performance. While Rautenstrauch attended (*Chronik*, p. 180), Süssmayr's participation is not mentioned. For more on Stadler's clarinet obbligato in 'Der Retter in Gefahr', see Martin Harlow, 'The Clarinet in Works of Franz Xaver Süssmayr (1766–1803): Anton Stadler and the Mozartian Example', *Acta mozartiana*, 57 (2010), pp. 147–165, at 153–157.

time on the Count made no further use of it, except to arrange it for string quintet, of which version I [Herzog] had a score for several years.'[179] Given his predilection for commissioning and playing chamber music,[180] Walsegg may always have envisaged the Requiem taking a place in his chamber repertory as well as being performed by full orchestra in his wife's memory.

In short, it is likely that Mozart's distinctive instrumentation for the Requiem was as much – or more – for his own benefit as for Walsegg's, even though specific scoring requests from the commissioner clearly cannot be ruled out. Mozart may have contemplated using the work at St Stephen's Cathedral (although he did not live long enough to turn thoughts into reality), perhaps with the Stadler brothers taking the basset-horn parts. Many orchestral effects – even in a Mozart score remaining a *particella* for the Kyrie, Sequence and Offertory – evidence concern for precise and pristine execution that will create an impact in performance: the jagged, explosive *forte* violin line appearing out of the blue in the autograph to open the 'Quam olim Abrahae' fugue in the Domine Jesu that has been heard to '[undermine] faith and [confront] fear';[181] the precipitous two-octave leap in the final bar of the Dies irae to an unaccompanied d' played on two strings of the first violin simultaneously, capturing the piece's wrath, terror and energy in a single concluding note; the obbligato trombone heard ominously by itself to initiate the process of judgement then interwoven with the bass soloist at the opening of the Tuba mirum so seamlessly as to promote an instrumental-vocal union as close as in, for example, the letter duet from *Le nozze di Figaro*; the delicate, consoling *sotto voce*s towards the end of the Tuba mirum to coincide with abstract textual description giving way to personal reaction; the *piano*s in the latter stages of the Rex tremendae expressing subjugation in voices and instruments alike, with the first violin left to capture the submissive mood in a final D-minor arpeggio without singers; and in the Lacrymosa the crescendo to *forte* at mention of the 'homo reus' ('guilty man') to be judged where the autograph breaking off leaves us to ponder biographical as well as musical reasons for Mozart ending his contribution to the Sequence at such a remarkable textual juncture.[182] It would be Süssmayr's responsibility to

---

[179] MDB, p. 554 (translation as given in MDB).   [180] MDB, pp. 551–552.

[181] Cliff Eisen, 'Mozart's Leap in the Dark', in Simon P. Keefe (ed.), *Mozart Studies* (Cambridge: Cambridge University Press, 2006), pp. 1–24, at 21.

[182] For more discussion along these lines, including the aforementioned passages, see Keefe, *Mozart's Requiem*, 'Mozart's Work on the Requiem: Sounds and Strategies', pp. 107–171 (Chapter 4).

turn the Requiem into a performable work after Mozart's death.[183] But enough exists in Mozart's hand for us tentatively to recognize incipient attention to impassioned, engaged performance as a complement to the informal, emotion-inducing renditions reportedly involving the composer himself.

After Mozart's Death

It seems appropriate that someone as absorbed in music as Mozart, who had playing and composition on his mind even when visiting his ailing wife for forty-eight hours in Baden and 'frequently in the midst of company would become abstracted and lost in musical composition', should be remembered by a family member and a close friend singing bits of one of his works in the hours before his death and by others as '[expiring] when the pen dropped from his hand'.[184] Initially, the Masonic cantata 'Laut verkünde unsre Freude' acquired special status as Mozart's last completed work and last public appearance as performer-composer: 'We can justly call [it] his swan-song, worked on with his usual skill, and the first performance of which he himself directed two days before his last illness among a circle of his best friends.'[185] An obituary in the *Bayreuther-Zeitung* (13 December 1791) also remarked: 'Music has suffered an irreparable loss. . . . He died too early for his family and for art, to which he would have presented still more monuments to his abilities. His last work was the composition of a cantata which he had supplied the local Freemasons, of which he was a member . . . said to be a masterpiece of noble simplicity.'[186] But the cantata would soon cede its place as swan song to

---

[183] On Süssmayr's achievements in building on Mozart's incomplete score and developing his own vision for the work, see Keefe, '"Die Ochsen am Berge"' and *Mozart's Requiem*, pp. 172–233. For different perspectives on the value (or otherwise) of Süssmayr's contribution, including from modern-day completers, see Robert D. Levin, Richard Maunder, Duncan Druce, David Black, Christoph Wolff and Simon P. Keefe, 'Colloquy: Finishing Mozart's Requiem', *Journal of the American Musicological Society*, 61 (2008), pp. 583–608.

[184] Expressing great desire to see Constanze on 8 June, Mozart nonetheless wished he could bring his piano with him. See MBA, vol. 4, p. 135; LMF, p. 952 (7 June 1791). For the first quotation, from Mary Novello recording a conversation with Aloysia Lange in Vienna, see *A Mozart Pilgrimage*, p. 151. For the second quotation, from Mary Novello in the company of Maximilian Stadler at the Rauhensteingasse where Mozart died, see *A Mozart Pilgrimage*, pp. 152–153. Vincent Novello (p. 129) also writes of trying 'to persuade Eybler to have a facsimile engraved of the last Page [of the Requiem] which Mozart wrote before the pen dropped from his weak hand'.

[185] MDL, pp. 385–386; MDB, p. 440.

[186] *Bayreuther Zeitung* (13 December 1791), p. 1089. 'Die Tonkunst hat einen unersetzlichen Verlust erlitten . . . Er starb zu früh für seine Familie und die Kunst, welcher er noch manches

the Requiem and surrounding legend, which proved too enticing for later commentators to resist. While the Requiem legend did untold good for Mozart's reputation, it could not be expected – given biographical circumstances – to put Mozart's own performing activities centre stage.[187]

The meteoric rise in Mozart's posthumous reputation across Europe in the last decade of the eighteenth century and first decade of the nineteenth was naturally connected to audiences' appreciation of his works more than his performances.[188] His keyboard expertise was recalled in the aftermath of his death: a testimonial for Emanuel Aloys Förster from Augustinus Erasmus Donath around 7 December set the incomparable playing of 'the late, great master Mozart' as a yardstick; Förster himself admitted on 8 December that 'on the one hand he is not quite so perfect in keyboard playing and composition as the late Mozart was, on the other hand the complete certainty that no-one is found to equal Mozart in this area, speaks for him'; and the *Bayreuther Zeitung* identified him as 'the greatest master of the keyboard'.[189] And memories of Mozart's playing lived on until the mid nineteenth century, whereupon, in the fullness of time, all of those who had witnessed him firsthand had themselves died. Needless to say, in the absence of an unperishable musical artefact in a pre-recording age, it is to be expected that the impact of a successful performer will not last as long as the impact of a comparably successful composer.[190]

Denkmal seiner Fähigkeiten geschenkt haben würde. Seine letzte Arbeit war die Composition einer Cantate, welche er den hiesigen Freymaurern, deren Mitglied er war, bey Anlass der Einweihung ihres neuen Tempels geliefert hatte, und die ein Meisterstuck von edler Einfalt seyn soll'.

[187] On the legend of the Requiem in the nineteenth and twentieth centuries, see Keefe, *Mozart's Requiem*, pp. 11–43.

[188] This can be gleaned from important early critical writings whose authors seem not to have encountered Mozart as a performer. Ignaz Arnold in *Mozarts Geist* (1803), for example, talks little about Mozart's performing skills and a lot about his composition-related achievements. Ernst Ludwig Gerber, slightly dubious about Mozart's significance as a composer, draws attention to Mozart's status as one of the great keyboard players of his generation in *Historisch-biographisches Lexicon der Tonkünstler* (1790–1792), cols. 977–979. But the huge, thirteenfold increase in the length of the Mozart article in Gerber's *Neues historisch-biographisches Lexicon der Tonkünstler* (4 volumes, Leipzig, 1812–1814) accommodates Mozart's compositional rather than performance-related achievements. On Mozart's evolving reputation in the last decade of the eighteenth century and first decade of the nineteenth, witnessed through revisions to Gerber's lexicon and Niemetschek's biography, see Simon P. Keefe, 'Across the Divide: Currents of Musical Thought in Europe, c. 1790–1810', in Keefe (ed.), *Cambridge History of Eighteenth-Century Music*, pp. 663–687.

[189] See MDL, pp. 369–370, MDB, pp. 419–420; and *Bayreuther Zeitung* (13 December 1791), p. 1089.

[190] Exceptions include late-eighteenth-century performers who, by virtue of their teaching or other dissemination of performance skills, intentionally or unintentionally established a school of playing that flourished after their death. Giovanni Battista Viotti, Pierre Rode, and

And the resulting biographical conclusion, as for John Sainsbury (1824) that 'Mozart was one of the first pianists in Europe . . . But his most brilliant and solid glory is founded upon his talents as a composer', naturally follows suit.[191] Nevertheless, when the creation of so much music is intrinsically connected to Mozart's status – and the status of those for whom he wrote – as star performers, such discrepancy in the kind of fame and repute enjoyed by him as a multi-talented musician can distort the lens through which his music is viewed. By returning to autograph scores, early published editions, and performance copies, and bringing other performing contexts and concerns to the fore we begin to recapture – or at least to rethink – some of the negotiations encountered and decisions taken by Mozart as performer-composer, as well as the seamless fluidity of the composition-performance dynamic. Explanations that bring together process and product, richly intertwined for Mozart in performing and compositional activities, return us to the straightforward but special fact that works from Mozart's Viennese decade were invariably designed to promote talents, accommodate desires and satisfy predilections – for himself and others – in both domains and in the interests of enhancing the appreciation of various audiences. That the end results from Mozart are remarkable is rarely doubted – the 'beautiful products of his spirit', according to one obituary, 'left to console us'.[192] That the *process* is also remarkable, fundamentally linked to the meaning, ontological status and very existence of the works, and capturing a musician completely immersed in the practicalities and implications of performing them, must also be appropriately recognized, appreciated and understood in a biographical context.

Pierre M. Baillot of the virtuoso French violin school are cases in point, although Viotti's compositions have also now received attention: see Massimiliano Sala (ed.), *Giovanni Battista Viotti: A Composer Between Two Revolutions* (Bologna: Ut Orpheus Edizioni, 2006).

[191] John Sainsbury, *A Dictionary of Music from the Earliest to the Present Times* (London, 1824), 2 vols., vol. 2, p. 194.

[192] MDL, p. 377; MDB, p. 428.

Appendix
Mozart's Decade in Vienna, 1781–1791: A Chronology

Mozart's principal activities and works during his decade in Vienna, 1781–1791, are recorded chronologically below. It is a selective not comprehensive list, focussing on completion dates of works and on important personal and professional events. For the most part, advertisements and reviews of publications and concerts and non-Viennese performances of Mozart's works beyond his direct control are not included. Dates for works from February 1784 onwards are almost always given in Mozart's thematic catalogue, the 'Verzeichnüß aller meiner Werke', and designated with a '(V)'. Where specific dates for works or activities are unknown, entries are made at the beginning of a year, or month of a year, as appropriate.

Most works and professional activities and events listed below are discussed in the main text of this book. The principal sources used in compiling the chronology are as follows: MDL, MDB and NMD; MBA and LMF; Wolfgang Amadeus Mozart, *Eigenhändiges Werkverzeichnis: Faksimile* (British Library Stefan Zweig MS 63) (Kassel: Bärenreiter, 1991); Ulrich Konrad, *Mozart: Catalogue of His Works* (Kassel: Bärenreiter, 2006); Cliff Eisen and Simon P. Keefe (eds.), *The Cambridge Mozart Encyclopedia* (Cambridge: Cambridge University Press, 2006); Mary Sue Morrow, *Concert Life in Haydn's Vienna: Aspects of a Developing Musical and Social Institution* (Stuyvesant, NY: Pendragon Press, 1989) and Dexter Edge, 'Review Article: Mary Sue Morrow, *Concert Life in Haydn's Vienna*', *Haydn Yearbook*, 17 (1992), pp. 108–166; Dorothea Link, *The National Court Theatre in Mozart's Vienna: Sources and Documents, 1783–1792* (Oxford: Clarendon Press, 1998); Ian Woodfield, *Performing Operas for Mozart: Impresarios, Singers and Troupes* (Cambridge: Cambridge University Press, 2012); and Dexter Edge and David Black (eds.), *Mozart: New Documents*, http://dx.doi.org/10.7302/Z20P0WXJ.

1781

March

16   Mozart arrives in Vienna from Munich, where he had supervised the premiere of *Idomeneo* (29 January 1781), to join Archbishop Colloredo, his staff and musicians. He participates in a concert

17   Archbishop Colloredo's musicians play at Count Galitzin's residence

24   Archbishop Colloredo's musicians play at Councillor Johann Gottlieb von Braun's residence

April

Recitative and aria, 'A questo seno deh vieni ... Or che il cielo a me ti rende', K. 374 composed before 8 April 1781

2   Rondo for violin and orchestra in C, K. 373 (for Antonio Brunetti)

3   Improvises on the keyboard and has one of his symphonies performed at a concert of the Tonkünstler-Societät at the Kärntnertortheater

7   Writes K. 379 quickly on 7 April, notating the violin part but leaving the piano part incomplete for performance the next day

8   Concert at the Colloredo residence in Vienna, at which Mozart performs K. 373, with Antonio Brunetti as soloist; the Accompanied Sonata K. 379 in G (again with Brunetti); and probably the Aria K. 374 with Francesco Ceccarelli as soloist

27   Concert for Archbishop Colloredo by the Salzburg musicians (including Mozart, whose participation included an improvisation at the keyboard)

May

1/2   Moves into the house of Caecilia Weber (mother of his future wife, Constanze), the 'Auge Gottes'

10   Resigns from Archbishop Colloredo's service in a letter given to Count Arco, Colloredo's chief steward, after an acrimonious encounter with Colloredo the previous day

June

8   Formally dismissed from Colloredo's service by Count Arco

July

Spends some of the month at Court Vice-Chancellor Count Cobenzl's summer residence in Reisenberg, around twenty miles south of Vienna

30 Begins work on *Die Entführung aus dem Serail*, K. 384, after receiving the libretto from Gottlieb Stephanie

August

Moves at the end of August to a room on the Graben in the middle of Vienna

October

Wind serenade in E-flat, K. 375 (version for two clarinets, two horns, two bassoons)

15 Performance of wind serenade K. 375 on St Theresa's Day
31 Visits Baroness Waldstätten at Leopoldstadt and witnesses a performance of his wind serenade K. 375

November

Publication of six accompanied sonatas by Artaria, including K. 376 in F, K. 377 in F, K. 379 in G and K. 380 in E-flat composed earlier in 1781 after the move to Vienna

16 Meets, and plays for, Duke Friedrich Eugen of Württemberg
23 Sonata for two pianos in D, K. 448, performed at a private concert with pupil Josepha Auernhammer at Auernhammer's residence in Vienna. Mozart's friends and benefactors Countess Thun, Baron van Swieten and Baron Wetzlar von Plankenstern were in the audience

December

15 Expresses to his father for the first time his love for – and desire to marry – Constanze Weber
24 Keyboard contest between Mozart and Muzio Clementi at court, in front of Emperor Joseph II and the Russian Grand Duke and his consort, the Princess of Württemberg

1782

Rondo for piano and orchestra in D, K. 382, as a new finale for Piano Concerto K. 175 (early 1782)

Fantasia in D minor, K. 397, possibly 1782

Suite for piano, K. 399, probably 1782 (Sarabande incomplete)

Five fugues by J. S. Bach, arranged for strings, K. 405, probably 1782

Horn quintet in E-flat, K. 407, late 1782 (for Joseph Leutgeb)

Three marches for orchestra, K. 408, probably 1782 (no. 3 possibly 1783)

Recitative and aria, 'Così dunque tradisci ... Aspri rimorso atroci', K. 432, 1782–1783 (almost certainly for Ludwig Fischer)

March

Variations for piano on 'Salve tu, Domine', K. 398, from Giovanni Paisiello's opera *I filosofi immaginarii* (probably March 1783, or later)

3   Mozart gives his first public academy in Vienna, including numbers from *Idomeneo*, the Piano Concerto K. 175 + 382, and a keyboard improvisation

April

Prelude (fantasy) and fugue in C, K. 394, probably April

10   Aria, 'Nehmt meinen Dank, ihr holden Gönner', K. 383 (probably for Aloysia Lange)

May

7   Plays on the piano for Countess Thun *Die Entführung aus dem Serail*, Act 2

26   Participates in the first of Philipp Jakob Martin's Sunday concerts at the Augarten in Vienna, performing a symphony and the Two-Piano Concerto K. 365 with Auernhammer

30   Completion of *Die Entführung aus dem Serail*, K. 384. Act 3 is played for Countess Thun

June

3   Rehearsals for *Die Entführung aus dem Serail* begin at the Burgtheater

July

Wind serenade in E-flat, K. 375 (revised version for two oboes, two clarinets, two horns, two bassoons) probably late July
  Wind serenade in C minor, K. 388, probably July
  Symphony no. 35 in D ('Haffner'); publication by Artaria in 1785

16   Premiere of *Die Entführung aus dem Serail* at the Burgtheater in Vienna. Subsequent performances took place in 1782 on 19, 26, 30 July; 3, 6, 20, 27 August; 6, 20 September; 8 October; 10 December. It was then staged on at least a further twenty-six occasions at the Burgtheater and Kärntnertortheater between 1783 and 1788
20   Travels with Count Zichy to Laxenburg Palace to meet Prince Kaunitz
23   Moves from the Graben to 'Red Sabre' on the Hohe Brücke

August

4   Marries Constanze Mozart (*née* Weber) at St Stephen's Cathedral in Vienna. Baroness Waldstätten hosts a celebratory dinner for them afterwards
8   Dines with Gluck, after Gluck attends *Die Entführung* two days earlier
18   A concert for this day organized by Martin at the Neumarkt advertises inclusion of a wind arrangement of *Die Entführung aus dem Serail*

October

19   Rondo in A major for piano and orchestra, K. 386

November

3   Plays at Josepha Auernhammer's concert at the Kärntnertortheater

December

Moves to a different residence on the Hohe Brücke, the 'Little Herberstein House', with Baron Wetzlar von Plankenstern as his landlord

14   Plays at Countess Thun's; Count Zinzendorf was present
31   String quartet in G, K. 387

1783

Piano concertos no. 11 in F, K. 413; no. 12 in A, K. 414; no. 13 in C, K. 415
winter 1782–1783; distribution in manuscript copy through subscription
in 1783 and published by Artaria in 1785
    L'oca del Cairo, K. 422 (incomplete), composed in Vienna and Salzburg
in late 1783
    Duos for violin and viola, K. 423 in G, K. 424 in B-flat, composed in
Salzburg, July–October 1783.
    Mass in C minor, K. 427 (incomplete), composed in Vienna and
Salzburg, 1782–1783
    Recitative and aria, 'Misero! O sogno . . . Aura, che intorno spiri', K. 431
(for Johann Valentin Adamberger)
    Piano sonatas K. 330 in C, K. 331 in A, K. 332 in F, K. 333 in B-flat
probably late 1783 (although K. 332 may have been written a little earlier);
first three published by Artaria in August 1784 and K. 333 by Torricella in
August 1784

January

4   Plays at Councillor Anton Spielmann's residence
8   Recitative and aria 'Mia speranza adorata . . . Ah, non sai qual pena
    sia', K. 416 for Aloysia Lange, performed by Lange at the Mehlgrube
    three days later
15   Advertises – in the *Wiener Zeitung* – subscription to manuscript
    copies of the three piano concertos, K. 413, K. 414 and K. 415

February

Revision of 'Haffner' Symphony, K. 385 (February–March), to include two
flutes and two clarinets
    Moves to lodgings on the Kohlmarkt in the centre of Vienna

March

3   Performs music for a Carnival pantomime, K. 446, at the Hofburg
11   Performs the Piano Concerto K. 175 + 382 at Aloysia Lange's
    academy; Lange sings 'Alcandro, lo confesso', K. 294. Gluck is in
    attendance

12   Plays at Count Esterházy's residence

23   Puts on an academy at the Burgtheater, listing all pieces on the programme in a letter of 29 March 1783. Emperor Joseph II is in attendance

30   Plays the Piano Concerto K. 415 at Therese Teyber's academy and improvises at the keyboard. Emperor Joseph II is again in attendance

April

24   Moves to the Judenplatz in central Vienna

May

27   Horn concerto in E-flat, K. 417 (for Joseph Leutgeb)

June

Aria, 'No, che non sei capace' for Pasquale Anfossi's opera, *Il curioso indiscreto*, K. 419 (for Aloysia Lange)
   String quartet in D minor, K. 421, probably June
   String quartet in E-flat, K. 428, probably June–July

17   Constanze gives birth to the Mozarts' first child, Raimund Leopold. He dies on 19 August in Vienna while Mozart and Constanze are visiting Salzburg

20   Aria, 'Vorrei spiegarvi, oh Dio!' for Pasquale Anfossi's opera, *Il curioso indiscreto*, K. 418 (for Aloysia Lange)

21   Aria, 'Per pietà, non ricercate', for Pasquale Anfossi's opera, *Il curioso indiscreto*, K. 420 (for Johann Valentin Adamberger). Christoph Friedrich Bretzner, author of *Belmont und Constanze*, criticizes Gottlieb Stephanie's adaptation of it as *Die Entführung aus dem Serail*, having objected to Mozart's 'misuse' of it in 1782

30   The libretto to Anfossi's *Il curioso indiscreto* is published, including a 'Notice' about Mozart writing two arias for Aloysia Lange

July

28   Mozart and Constanze arrive in Salzburg for a three-month visit with Mozart's father and sister, Leopold and Nannerl

October

26   A Mozart mass (perhaps the incomplete K. 427) is performed at St Peter's in Salzburg, following a rehearsal three days earlier

27   Mozart and Constanze leave Salzburg

29   Mozart and Constanze arrive in Linz, where they remain for a month as guests of Count Thun

November

4   Premiere of Symphony No. 36 in C ('Linz') at an academy in Linz, following rapid composition in the preceding days

30   Mozart and Constanze arrive back in Vienna on or around this day

December

22   Performs a piano concerto and provides a vocal rondò for Johann Valentin Adamberger at a Tonkünstler-Societät concert (Burgtheater)

29   Fugue in C minor for two pianos, K. 426 (arranged for strings to form part of K. 546 published by Hoffmeister in 1788)

1784

Lo sposo deluso, K. 430, probably 1784, or 1784–1785

January

Moves to the Trattnerhof, on the Graben, a building owned by the printer Johann Thomas von Trattner

25   Conducts a performance of *Die Entführung aus dem Serail* for Aloysia Lange's benefit at the Kärntnertortheater, with Lange in the role of Konstanze. (Repeated on 1 February.)

February

9   Piano concerto No. 14 in E-flat, K. 449 (V)

26   Plays at Prince Galitzin's residence

March

1   Plays at Count Esterházy's residence (also on 5, 8, 12, 15, 19, 22, 26, 29 March)

4   Plays at Prince Galitzin's residence (also on 11, 18, 25 March)

15   Piano concerto No. 15 in B-flat, K. 450 (V)

17   First subscription concert at the Trattnerhof

20   Performs at pianist Georg Friedrich Richter's subscription concert at the Trattnerhof; also plays at Count Zichy's residence. Sends to his father a list of the contributors to his own Trattnerhof concerts

22   Piano concerto No. 16 in D, K. 451 (V)

23   Clarinet virtuoso Anton Stadler's academy at the Burgtheater includes a performance of the wind serenade in B-flat, K. 361

24   Second subscription concert at the Trattnerhof

27   Performs at pianist Georg Friedrich Richter's subscription concert at the Trattnerhof

30   Quintet for piano, oboe, clarinet, horn and bassoon in E-flat, K. 452 (V)

31   Third subscription concert at the Trattnerhof

April

1   Gives an academy at the Burgtheater with a programme that includes the premiere of the quintet K. 452, at least two symphonies and a piano concerto

3   Performs at pianist Georg Friedrich Richter's subscription concert at the Trattnerhof

9   Plays at Count Leopold Pálffy's residence

10   Plays at Prince Kaunitz's residence

12   Piano concerto No. 17 in G, K. 453 (V)

21   Sonata for piano and violin in B-flat, K. 454 (V)

29   Plays K. 454 with Italian violinist Regina Strinasacchi at her academy at the Kärntnertortheater. (K. 454 is published by Torricella in August 1784.)

May

8   Plays at Therese von Trattner's private concert. Trattner, one of Mozart's students, was also the wife of his landlord.

June

13   Sonata for two pianos in D, K. 448, is performed with pupil Barbara Ployer at a private concert at the Ployer residence in Döbling, near Vienna. Mozart takes Giovanni Paisiello with him

August

23   Nannerl Mozart marries Johann Baptist von Berchtold in St Gilgen; Mozart sends congratulations to her five days earlier
25   Ten variations for piano on Gluck's 'Unser dummer Pöbel meint' in G, K. 455 (V)

September

21   Karl Thomas, the second child of Mozart and Constanze, is born. He died on 31 October 1858, aged 74
29   Moves to Schulerstrasse (now Domgasse), close to St Stephen's Cathedral in the centre of Vienna
30   Piano concerto No. 18 in B-flat, K. 456 (V)

October

14   Piano sonata in C minor, K. 457 (V); publication by Artaria (with the C-minor Fantasia K. 475) in December 1785
31   Hosts a concert at his house, including performances by his pupils

November

9   String quartet in B-flat, K. 458 (V)

December

5   Formally proposed for membership in the masonic lodge 'Beneficence' ('Zur Wohlthätigkeit') with his acceptance confirmed nine days later
11   Piano concerto No. 19 in F, K. 459 (V)

1785

January

10   String quartet in A, K. 464 (V)

14   String quartet in C, K. 465 ('Dissonance') (V)

15   Plays probably the first three 'Haydn' quartets, K. 387, K. 421 and K. 428, to their dedicatee Joseph Haydn

February

10   Piano concerto in D minor, K. 466 (V)

11   First subscription concert at the Mehlgrube; Leopold arrives in Vienna for a ten-week visit with Mozart and Constanze. Mozart applies for membership of the Tonkünstler-Societät, but the application is held in abeyance in the absence of his birth certificate

12   Plays the last three 'Haydn' quartets, K. 458, K. 464 and K. 465, to their dedicatee

13   Plays a piano concerto at Luisa Laschi's academy at the Burgtheater; Emperor Joseph II attends

15   Plays the Piano Concerto K. 466 at Elisabeth Distler's academy at the Burgtheater

18   Second subscription concert at the Mehlgrube

21   Plays at Count Zichy's residence, alongside the oboist Lebrun and his wife

25   Third subscription concert at the Mehlgrube

March

4   Fourth subscription concert at the Mehlgrube

6   Aria 'A te, fra tanti affanni' for cantata *Davidde penitente*, K. 469 (V)

9   Piano concerto No. 21 in C, K. 467 (V)

10   Gives an academy at the Burgtheater, including on the programme the Piano Concerto K. 467 and a keyboard improvisation

11   Aria 'Tra l'oscure ombre funeste' for cantata *Davidde penitente*, K. 469 (V); fifth subscription concert at the Mehlgrube

13   *Davidde penitente* is performed at a Tonkünstler-Societät concert

15   *Davidde penitente* is performed at a second Tonkünstler-Societät concert

18   Sixth subscription concert at the Mehlgrube

26   Masonic song 'Lied zur Gesellenreise', K. 468 (V)

April

20   Masonic cantata, *Die Maurerfreude*, K. 471 (V); publication by Artaria in August 1785

24   K. 471 is premiered at an event at 'New Crowned Hope' in honour of the distinguished master of the 'Concord' lodge, Ignaz von Born. Mozart and his father are in attendance

25   Leopold Mozart leaves Vienna, arriving back in Salzburg in mid May, after stays in Linz and Munich

May

1   Archbishop Colloredo formally rebukes Leopold Mozart for over-staying his six-week leave of absence from Salzburg, threatening to cease payment to him if he is not back *in situ* by mid May

7   Songs: 'Der Zauberer', K. 472; 'Die Zufriedenheit', K. 473; 'Die betrogene Welt', K. 474 (V)

20   Fantasy in C minor, K. 475 (V); publication by Artaria (with the C-minor Sonata K. 457) in December 1785

June

8   Song, 'Das Veilchen', K. 476 (V); publication by Artaria in 1789

July

Masonic Funeral Music in C minor, K. 477 (V)

September

Publication of the 'Haydn' quartets (K. 387, K. 421, K. 428, K. 458, K. 464, K. 465) by Artaria, including Mozart's dedication to Haydn written in Italian and dated 1 September 1785

October

15 An invitation to hear Anton Stadler and Mozart perform on 20 October 1785 is issued to Viennese lodges by the 'Three Eagles' and 'Palmtree' lodges. Mozart is to improvise at the keyboard

16 Piano quartet in G minor, K. 478 (given as 'month of July [1785]' in the *Verzeichnüß*); publication by Hoffmeister, November/December 1785

November

5 Quartet 'Dite almeno, in che mancai', K. 479, for Francesco Bianchi's opera *La villanella rapita* (V)

17 The Masonic Funeral Music (*Mauerische Trauermusik*), K. 477, is performed at the 'Crowned Hope' lodge to honour distinguished, recently deceased masons Georg August, Duke of Mecklenburg-Strelitz and Count Franz Esterházy von Galántha

21 Trio 'Mandina amabile', K. 480, for Francesco Bianchi's opera *La villanella rapita* (V)

25 Bianchi's *La villanella* rapita is staged at the Burgtheater, including Mozart's ensembles K. 479 and K. 480. (Also performed on 30 November, 7, 16, 30 December 1785 and 16 January, 6, 17 February 1786.) Aloysia Lange returns from serious illness to sing Konstanze in *Die Entführung* at the Kärntnertortheater

December

12 Sonata for piano and violin in E-flat, K. 481 (V); publication by Hoffmeister in January 1786

15 Plays a piano concerto, improvises at the keyboard and has *Die Maurerfreude* cantata performed at a 'New Crowned Hope' concert

16 Piano concerto No. 22 in E-flat, K. 482 (V)

23 Performs a piano concerto, possibly K. 482, as an entr'acte to Dittersdorf's oratorio *Esther* at a Tonkünstler-Societät concert

1786

January

14 Two masonic songs (with chorus), K. 483 and K. 484, are performed at the 'New Crowned Hope' lodge

February

3   *Der Schauspieldirektor*, K. 486 (V)

7   *Der Schauspieldirektor* premieres at the Orangerie, Schönbrunn in Vienna, alongside Salieri's *Prima la musica, poi le parole*, with subsequent performances at the Kärntnertortheater on 11, 18, 25 February

March

2   Piano concerto No. 23 in A, K. 488 (V)

10   Duet 'Spiegarti non poss'io', K. 489, and scena and rondò 'Non più . . . Non temer, amato bene', K. 490 for the revival of *Idomeneo* (V)

13   *Idomeneo* revived at Prince Auersperg's private theatre in Vienna

24   Piano concerto No. 24 in C minor, K. 491 (V)

April

7   Gives an academy at the Burgtheater, probably playing the Piano Concerto K. 491

29   *Le nozze di Figaro*, K. 492 (V)

May

1   Premiere of *Le nozze di Figaro* at the Burgtheater in Vienna. It is subsequently staged at the Burgtheater on 3, 8, 24 May, 4 July, 28 August, 22 September, 15 November and 18 December 1786 and at the Habsburg's Laxenburg Castle outside Vienna on 7 June 1786

June

3   Piano quartet in E-flat, K. 493 (V); publication by Artaria in December 1787

10   Rondo for piano in F, K. 494 (V); publication by Bossler in April 1787

26   Horn concerto in E-flat, K. 495 (V)

July

8   Piano trio in G, K. 496 (V); publication by Hoffmeister, post August 1787

27   Duos for two horns, K. 487

August

1   Sonata for piano four hands in F, K. 497 (V); publication by Artaria, December 1787

5   Trio for piano, clarinet and viola in E-flat, K. 498 ('Kegelstatt') (V); publication by Artaria, in a version for violin, viola and piano, in September 1788

19   String quartet in D, K. 499 ('Hoffmeister') (V); published by Hoffmeister, October 1786

September

12   Twelve variations for piano in B-flat, K. 500 (V)

October

18   Johann Thomas Leopold, the third child of Mozart and Constanze, is born. He died less than one month later, on 15 November 1786

November

4   Five variations for piano four hands, K. 501 (V); published by Hoffmeister, post December 1786

18   Piano trio in B-flat, K. 502 (V); published by Artaria, November 1788

December

Probably gave four Viennese concerts in Advent, which may have included a performance of the Piano Concerto K. 503 and the 'Prague' symphony, K. 504

4   Piano Concerto No. 25 in C, K. 503 (V)

6   Symphony No. 38 in D, K. 504 ('Prague') (V)

12   The *Prager Oberpostamtszeitung* reports a 'rumour' that Mozart will travel to Prague to witness first hand the remarkable success of *Le nozze di Figaro*, which had already been performed 'several times' in the city

27   Scena and rondò 'Ch'io mi scordi di te ... Non temer, amato bene', K. 505 (V) (for soprano Nancy Storace and Mozart on the piano)

1787

Horn concerto in E-flat, K. 447 (for Joseph Leutgeb; probably 1787)

January

11   Arrives in Prague with Constanze, having departed Vienna on 8 January

12   Plays one of the piano quartets (K. 478 or K. 493) at Count Thun's in Prague

13   Visits the Clementium in Prague and attends a performance of Paisiello's *Le gare generose*

17   Attends a performance of *Le nozze di Figaro* at the Nostitz Theater (Estates Theatre) in Prague

19   Gives an academy at the Nostitz Theater, including on the programme the 'Prague' Symphony, K. 504 and keyboard improvisations

22   Conducts a performance of *Le nozze di Figaro*

30   Mozart's friend, the virtuoso Count August von Hatzfeld for whom the obbligato violin part in the *Idomeneo* aria 'Non temer amato bene' K. 490 was written, dies in Düsseldorf, aged 32

February

6   Six German dances for orchestra, K. 509 (V)

8   Leaves Prague to return to Vienna

23   Probably performs 'Ch'io mi scordi di te', K. 505, with Nancy Storace at her farewell concert at the Kärntnertortheater in Vienna

27   Leopold Mozart shows Nancy Storace, Michael Kelly and Thomas Attwood around Salzburg as they pass through the town on route to London

28   Gives an academy at the Kärntnertortheater

March

Sixteen-year-old Beethoven travels to Vienna (March–May) and may have played for Mozart

7   Maximiliana Valentina Willmann performs a Mozart piano concerto at her academy at the Kärntnertortheater

11   Rondo in A minor for piano, K. 511 (V); published by Hoffmeister, 1787

14   Friedrich Ramm includes a Mozart symphony at his academy at the Kärntnertortheater

18   Recitative and aria 'Alcandro lo confesso . . . Non so, d'onde viene', K. 512 (V) (for Ludwig Fischer)

21   Ludwig Fischer includes one or possibly two Mozart symphonies on his academy programme and sings a new Mozart aria

23   Aria 'Mentre ti lascio, oh figlia', K. 513 (V) (for Gottfried von Jacquin)

April

4   Writes to his father, Leopold, for the last time, aware of Leopold's serious illness

19   String quintet in C, K. 515 (V); distributed in manuscript copy alongside string quintets K. 516 and K. 406 in early 1788, then published by Artaria in 1789

24   Moves to the Viennese Landstrasse suburb

May

16   String quintet in G minor, K. 516 (V); distributed in manuscript copy alongside string quintets K. 515 and K. 406 in early 1788, then published by Artaria in 1790

18   Song, 'Die Alte', K. 517 (V); published by Schrämel in 1788

20   Song, 'Die Verschweigung', K. 518 (V)

23   Song, 'Das Lied der Trennung', K. 519 (V); published by Artaria in 1789

26   Song, 'Als Luise', K. 520 (V)

28   Leopold Mozart dies in Salzburg, aged 67

29   Sonata for piano four hands in C, K. 521 (V); published by Hoffmeister in 1787

June

14   Sextet in F, 'Ein musikalischer Spass', K. 522 (V)

24   Songs, 'Abendempfindung an Laura', K. 523; 'An Chloe', K. 524 (V) (both published by Artaria in 1789)

July

13   The score of *Figaro* requested by Haydn arrives at Esterháza

August

10   Serenade in G for strings, 'Eine kleine Nachtmusik', K. 525 (V)

24   Sonata. for piano and violin in A, K. 526 (V); published by Hoffmeister in 1787

September

25   Leopold Mozart's possessions are auctioned at his home in Salzburg (and for the following four days), Mozart having come to a prior agreement with his sister and brother-in-law to receive 1,000 gulden at Viennese currency from his father's estate

October

4   Arrives in Prague with Constanze for the rehearsals and premiere of *Don Giovanni*, K. 527. Da Ponte arrives in Prague four days later, staying only for one week

14   *Le nozze di Figaro* is given in Prague under Mozart's direction to celebrate the marriage of Maria Theresia, Emperor Joseph II's niece, to Prince Anton Clemens of Saxony

25   Giacomo Casanova visits Prague and may have attended the premiere of *Don Giovanni*

28   *Don Giovanni*, K. 527 (V)

29   Premiere of *Don Giovanni* at the Nostitz Theater in Prague; repeat performances follow in the next few days (31 October, 2 November, 3 November)

November

3   Recitative and aria, 'Bella mia fiamma, addio . . . Resto, oh cara', K. 528 (V) (for Josepha Duschek, Mozart's host at Betramka for much of his stay in Prague)

6   Songs, 'Des kleinen Friedrichs Geburtstag', K. 529 and 'Das Traumbild', K. 530 (V); published by Schrämel in 1788

11   Song, 'Die kleine Spinnerin', K. 531 (V); published by Schrämel in 1787

13   Leaves Prague to return to Vienna

15   Christoph Willibald Gluck, 'chief [court] composer' (*Hof Compositor*) at Emperor Joseph II's court, dies in Vienna, aged 73

December

Early in the month Mozart moves back to the centre of Vienna, residing on Schultergasse, at 'Unter den Tuchlauben'

6   A Mozart mass is performed at the Church of St. Nicolas (Malá Strana) in Prague

7   Enters Emperor Joseph II's service as 'chamber musician' (*Kammermusikus*), with a salary of 800 gulden per annum

15   The German Opera company in Vienna is closed down

27   Theresia, the fourth child of Mozart and Constanze, is born. She died on 29 June 1788

1788

String quintet in C minor, K. 406 (arrangement of wind serenade, K. 388); distributed in manuscript copy alongside string quintets K. 515 and K. 516 in early 1788, then published by Artaria in 1792

January

3   Allegro and Andante for piano in F (V); published with expanded version of the rondo K. 494 as the Piano Sonata K. 533 by Hoffmeister in 1788

12   Mozart probably performs at a Masonic academy

14   Contredanse for orchestra 'Das Donnerwetter', K. 534 (V)

23   Contredanse for orchestra 'La Bataille', K. 535 (V)

27   Six German dances for orchestra, K. 536 (V)

February

4   The performances of German Singspiel at the Kärntnertortheater come to an end and the theatre is closed until 1791. The last opera staged is *Die Entführung aus dem Serail*

10   Plays at the Venetian Ambassador's residence in Vienna, alongside Stefano Mandini and Anna Morichelli

15   Stefano (or Paolo?) Mandini open a Viennese academy with a Mozart symphony

24   Piano concerto No. 26 in D, K. 537 ('Coronation') (V)

26   Conducts C. P. E. Bach's *Die Auferstehung und Himmelfahrt Jesu* at Count Johann Esterházy's residence, after adding wind parts to the aria 'Ich folge dir', does so again on 4 March and perhaps also conducts the work at the Burgtheater on 7 March

March

4   Aria, 'Ah se in ciel, benigne Stelle', K. 538 (V) (for Aloysia Lange)

5   Song with orchestra, 'Ich möchte wohl der Kaiser sein', K. 539 (V)

7   Friedrich Baumann sings K. 539 at a patriotic concert at the Leopoldstadttheater

19   Adagio for piano in B minor, K. 540 (V); published by Hoffmeister in 1788?

April

22   Singer Josepha Duschek gives an academy in Leipzig at which she performs Mozart's Recitative and Aria K. 374

24   Aria, 'Dalla sua pace', K. 540a, for the Vienna premiere of *Don Giovanni* (V) (for Francesco Morella)

28   Duet, 'Per queste tue manine', K. 540b, for the Vienna premiere of *Don Giovanni* (V) (for Francesco Benucci and Luisa Laschi-Mombelli)

30   Recitative and aria, 'In quali eccessi . . . Mi tradì quell'alma ingrata', K. 540c, for the Vienna premiere of *Don Giovanni* (V) (for Caterina Cavalieri)

May

Aria, 'Un bacio di mano', K. 541 for Pasquale Anfossi's *Le gelosie fortunate* (V) (for Francesco Albertarelli)

7   *Don Giovanni* receives its Viennese premiere at the Burgtheater and fourteen further performances before the end of 1788

June

2   Francesco Albertarelli sings 'Un bacio di mano', K. 541 at the Burgtheater as an aria inserted into Anfossi's *Le gelosie fortunate*. (Eleven further performances of the opera take place in the next two months.)

17 Moves to a house 'Zu den 3 Sternen' on Währingerstrasse in the Alsergrund suburb

22 Piano trio in E, K. 542 (V); publication by Artaria, November 1788

26 Symphony No. 39 in E-flat, K. 543; Piano sonata in C, K. 545; Adagio in C minor for strings (published by Hoffmeister in 1788 together with an arrangement for strings of the fugue for two pianos, K. 426, as K. 546) (V)

July

10 Sonata for piano and violin in F, K. 547 (V)

14 Piano trio in C, K. 548 (V); publication by Artaria in November 1788

16 Canzonetta for two sopranos and bass, 'Più non si trovano', K. 549 (V)

25 Symphony No. 40 in G minor, K. 550 (V)

August

10 Symphony No. 41 in C, K. 551 ('Jupiter') (V)

11 Song, 'Beim Auszug in das Feld', K. 552 (V)

24 The Danish actor Joachim Daniel Preisler visits Mozart at home and has 'the happiest hour of music that has ever fallen to my lot . . .. [E]verything that surrounded this splendid man was *musical!*'

September

2   Eight four-voice canons, K. 553–558, K. 560, K. 561; two three-voice canons, K. 559, K. 562 (V)

27 Divertimento for string trio in E-flat, K. 563 (V)

October

27 Piano trio in G, K. 564 (V); published by Stephen Storace in London in 1789 and by Artaria in October 1790

November

Arrangement of Handel, *Acis and Galatea*, K. 566 (V); Mozart conducts it at Esterházy's

December

6   Six German dances for orchestra, K. 567 (V)
24   Twelve minuets for orchestra, K. 568 (V)
30   Conducts his arrangement of Handel's *Acis and Galatea* at Esterházy's

1789

Early in 1789, Mozart moves back to the centre of Vienna, to the house 'Mother of God' on the Judenplatz

February

Piano sonata in B-flat, K. 570 (V)

21   Six German dances for orchestra, K. 571 (V)
27   *L'ape musicale*, a *pasticcio* by Lorenzo Da Ponte, premieres at the Burgtheater and includes a parody of the duet 'Là ci darem' from *Don Giovanni*. It receives a further seven performances in the next two weeks

March

Arrangement of Handel's *Messiah*, K. 572, for Baron van Swieten (V)

6   Conducts his arrangement of Handel's *Messiah* at Count Esterházy's

April

7   Conducts his arrangement of Handel's *Messiah* at Count Esterházy's
8   Sets off on a two-month trip to central and Northern Germany with Prince Lichnowsky
13   Gives a private concert in Dresden with organist Anton Teyber and cellist Anton Kraft

14 Plays for the Elector in Dresden, including the 'Coronation' piano concerto, K. 537

15 Contests a musical duel with organist Johann Wilhelm Hässler in Dresden and attends a performance of Cimarosa's *Le trame deluse* in the evening

22 After travelling from Dresden to Leipzig, Mozart improvises on the organ at the Thomaskirche in Leipzig, with the Cantor Johann Friedrich Doles and organist Karl Friedrich Görner present

23 Around this day, one of Mozart symphonies is performed at the Hoher Markt in Vienna in honour of Vice-Mayor Johann Georg von Augusti's name-day

25 Arrives in Potsdam probably on this day and petitions to play for the King of Prussia

29 Variations for piano, K. 573, on a minuet by Jean-Pierre Duport (V); published by Hummel in Amsterdam and Berlin in 1791

May

Probably performs at the Prussian court in Berlin in late May

8 Arrives in Leipzig

12 Gives an academy at the Gewandhaus in Leipzig, including two symphonies, two concertos, two arias sung by Josepha Duschek and an improvisation

17 Gigue in G for piano, K. 574 (V)

19 Arrives in Berlin

28 Leaves Berlin, reaching Vienna on 4 June after a stopover in Prague (31 May–2 June)

June

String quartet in D, K. 575 (V); published by Artaria with quartets K. 589 and K. 590 in December 1791

July

Piano sonata in D, K. 576 (V)

Rondò, 'Al desio', di chi t'adora', K. 577, for the upcoming revival of *Le nozze di Figaro* (V)

August

Aria, 'Alma grande e nobil core', K. 578, for Domenico Cimarosa's opera *I due Baroni* (V)

    Visits Constanze, who is suffering from a foot problem, in Baden in mid-August (possibly 15–18)

19   Rehearsals for the revival of *Le nozze di Figaro* begin

29   *Le nozze di Figaro* is revived at the Burgtheater and staged a further twenty-eight times in the next seventeen months

September

17   Aria, 'Schon lacht der holde Frühling', K. 580, for a German-language version of Giovanni Paisiello's opera *Il Barbiere di Siviglia* (V)

29   Clarinet quintet in A, K. 581 (V) (for Anton Stadler)

October

Arias, 'Chi sà, chi sà, qual sia', K. 582, and 'Vado, ma dove?', K. 583 for Vicente Martín y Soler's opera *Il Burbero di buon cuore* (V)

November

16   Anna Maria, Mozart and Constanze's fifth child, is born, but dies the same day

December

Aria, 'Rivolgete a lui lo sguardo', K. 584, for *Così fan tutte* (but unused in the first production) (V)

    Twelve minuets for orchestra, K. 585 (V)

    Twelve German dances for orchestra, K. 586 (V)

    Contredanse for orchestra, 'Der Sieg von Helden Coburg', K. 587 (V)

22   Clarinet quintet, K. 581, is performed at a Tonkünstler-Societät concert at the Burgtheater

31   Rehearsals for *Così fan tutte* had begun by this date

1790

January

Così fan tutte, K. 588 (V)

21 First orchestral rehearsal for *Così fan tutte* takes place
26 Premiere of *Così fan tutte* at the Burgtheater in Vienna, with subsequent performances on 28, 30 January; 7, 11 February; 6, 12 June; 6, 16 July; 7 August 1790
29 The critically ill Emperor Joseph II hands over to a regency council

February

20 Emperor Joseph II dies, aged 48, and is succeeded by his brother, Leopold II

April

9 Clarinet quintet K. 581 and the string trio K. 563 are performed at Count Hadik's Viennese residence

May

String quartet in B-flat, K. 589 (V); published by Artaria with quartets K. 575 and K. 590 in December 1791

June

String quartet in F, K. 590 (V); published by Artaria with quartets K. 575 and K. 589 in December 1791

Stays with Constanze in Baden, probably for a protracted period

13 A Mozart mass is performed at the Baden Pfarrkirche, where Mozart's friend Anton Stoll was choirmaster

July

Arrangement of Handel's *Ode for St. Cecilia's Day*, K. 592, and *Alexander's Feast*, K. 591 (V); probably conducts performances in summer 1790

September

11   The Singspiel *Der Stein der Weisen* premieres at the Wiednertheater; Mozart wrote wind and (most) string parts for the duet 'Nun liebes Weibchen' and was perhaps involved in two segments of the Act 2 finale as well

23   Sets off for Frankfurt with the singer (and his brother-in-law) Franz de Paula Hofer, to attend the coronation festivities for Leopold II

30   Constanze moves (with son Karl Thomas) to Rauhensteingasse no. 970 – Mozart's final residence – in central Vienna while Mozart is in Frankfurt

October

9   Leopold II is crowned in Frankfurt

15   Gives an academy at the Great Municipal Playhouse in Frankfurt, including two piano concertos, a symphony, arias sung by Margareta Louise Schick and Ceccarelli, and a keyboard improvisation

20   Gives an academy at the electoral palace in Mainz

23   Reaching Mannheim, Mozart attends a rehearsal of *Le nozze di Figaro* and then the first performance the following day

November

4/5 Plays in honour of King Ferdinand IV of Naples and Sicily at the Electoral Palace in Munich, having travelled there via Augsburg

10   Arrives back in Vienna on or around this day

December

String quintet in D, K. 593 (V)
   Adagio and Allegro in F minor for mechanical organ in clock, K. 594 (V)

14   Attends a farewell dinner for Haydn in Vienna, before Haydn's departure for London

1791

January

5   Piano concerto No. 27 in B-flat, K. 595 (V)

14   Songs: 'Sehnsucht nach dem Frühlinge', K. 596; 'Im Frühlingsanfang', K. 597; 'Das Kinderspiel', K. 598 (V) (published in spring 1791 in 'Frühlingslieder', one of Placidus Partsch's two volumes of *Liedersammlung für Kinder und Kinderfreunde*)

23   Six minuets for orchestra, K. 599 (V)

29   Six German dances for orchestra, K. 600 (V)

February

4   Leopold II, plus Neapolitan royal guests King Ferdinand IV of Naples and his wife who are visiting Vienna, attend a performance of *Der Stein der Weisen* at the Wiednertheater. (Leopold II goes again on 13 February.)

5   Four minuets for orchestra, K. 601; four German dances for orchestra, K. 602; two contredanses for orchestra, K. 603 (V)

9   The revival of *Le nozze di Figaro* at the Burgtheater, which had begun on 29 August 1789, comes to an end. King Ferdinand IV of Naples and his wife attend this performance along with members of the imperial court

12   Two minuets for orchestra, K. 604; two German dances for orchestra, K. 605 (V)

14   The wife of Count von Walsegg, resident of Schloss Stuppach in Niederösterreich, dies aged 20, leading eventually to the commission for a requiem from Mozart

28   Contredanse for orchestra, K. 607; six Ländler dances for two violins and bass (wind parts lost), K. 606 (V)

March

Variations for piano on the song 'Ein Weib ist das herrlichste Ding', K. 613 (written between 8 March and 12 April 1791) (V)

3   Allegro and Andante (Fantasy) in F minor for mechanical organ in clock, K. 608 (V)

4   Performs the Piano Concerto K. 595 at an academy given by Bohemian clarinetist Josef Beer at Jahn's Hall in Vienna

6   Contredanse for orchestra, K. 610; German dance for orchestra, K. 611 (V)

8   Aria, 'Per questa bella mano', K. 612 (V)

23   A revised version of Da Ponte's *pasticcio L'ape musicale* is staged at the Burgtheater, now including the duet 'Che soave zeffiretto' from *Le nozze di Figaro*. It is repeated a further five times up to 9 April 1791

24   'Funeral Musique' is played on the hour every hour from this day onwards (possibly until late July) at Müller's Viennese Mausoleum in honour of Austrian Field-Marshall Ernst Gideon, Baron van Laudon. The Adagio and Allegro K. 594 and Allegro and Andante K. 608 were probably both heard in this context.

April

12   String quintet in E-flat, K. 614 (V)

16   Tonkünstler-Societät concert at the Burgtheater, conducted by Antonio Salieri, includes a Mozart symphony and a Mozart aria sung by Aloysia Lange. (Repeated on 17 April 1791.)

26   Josepha Duschek gives an academy in Prague at which she performs two Mozart arias. The pianist Jan Vitásek also plays a Mozart piano concerto at the concert

May

4   Andante in F for mechanical organ, K. 616 (V)

7   In a City Council decree, Mozart is confirmed as the unpaid adjunct Kapellmeister at St. Stephen's Cathedral in Vienna and the named successor to Leopold Hofmann as Kapellmeister. (Mozart predeceased Hofmann, who died in 1793.)

23   Adagio and Rondo in C for glass harmonica, flute, oboe, viola and cello, K. 617 (V) (for blind harmonica virtuoso Marianne Kirchgessner)

June

8   Visits Constanze, who is taking the waters in Baden, and stays for three days, returning to Vienna on 11 June

15   Travels to Baden again, remaining there for about a week

18   Motet, 'Ave, verum corpus', K. 618 (V), probably first performed five days later on Corpus Christi, either in Baden or in Vienna

26   Partakes in the Corpus Christi procession in the Vienna suburb of Josefstadt

July

German cantata for voice and piano, 'Die ihr des unermesslichen Weltalls Schöpfer ehrt', K. 619 (V)

Die Zauberflöte, K. 620 (V)

8   Impresario Domenico Guardasoni is issued a contract by the Bohemian Estates for an opera (which became Mozart's *La clemenza di Tito*) to be staged during the Prague coronation of Emperor Leopold II

9   Travels to Baden again, returning to Vienna on 11 July. Constanze and son Karl go back to Vienna a few days later

10   Missa brevis, K. 275, is performed in the Baden Pfarrkirche

26   Franz Xaver Wolfgang, Mozart and Constanze's sixth child is born. He died in Carlsbad on 29 July 1844, aged 53

August

19   The Adagio and Rondo, K. 617, is premiered by Kirchgessner at her academy at the Kärntnertortheater

28   Arrives in Prague in preparation for the premiere of *La clemenza di Tito*

September

2   Directs a performance of *Don Giovanni* in Prague

5   *La clemenza di Tito*, K. 621 (V)

6   Premiere of *La clemenza di Tito* at the Nostitz Theater in Prague as part of the city's coronation festivities for Emperor Leopold II. Further performances were given until 30 September

15   Leaves Prague around this day to return to Vienna

28   Priests' March and Overture to *Die Zauberflöte*, K. 620 (V)

30   Premiere of *Die Zauberflöte*, K. 620 at the Wiednertheater in Vienna. By 6 November 1791 it had probably received twenty-four performances

October

Clarinet concerto in A, K. 622 (V)
   Works on the Requiem, K. 626, probably until taking to his bed with his final illness in late November.

7   Constanze travels to Baden again to recuperate, returning to Vienna on 15 October

8   Improvises Papageno's glockenspiel to humorous effect at an early performance of *Die Zauberflöte*

13   Takes Antonio Salieri and Caterina Cavalieri to see *Die Zauberflöte*

16   Anton Stadler probably premieres the clarinet concerto K. 622 at his academy in Prague

November

Loses a lawsuit lodged against him by Prince Karl Lichnowsky, who is awarded 1,435 gulden, 32 kreutzer

15   Masonic cantata, 'Laut verkünde unsre Freude', K. 623 (V)

17   Conducts first performance of K. 623 at the masonic lodge 'New Crowned Hope' and takes to his bed a few days later

28   Drs Thomas Franz Closset and Matthias Sallaba meet to discuss Mozart's illness

December

4   In the evening, Dr Closset is called to attend to Mozart

5   Dies just before 1 am, aged 35, at home on Rauhensteingasse

6   Mozart's body is blessed in the afternoon at St Stephen's Cathedral and taken to St Marx's cemetery for burial. His death is recorded as resulting from 'severe military fever'

Select Bibliography

Autographs, Facsimiles and First Editions

[K. 284, K. 333, K. 454] Mozart, *Trois sonates pour le clavecin ou pianoforte. La troisième est accomp. d'un Violon oblg: composées par Mr W. A. Mozart*. Vienna: Torricella, 1784.

[K. 296, K. 376, K. 377, K. 378, K. 379, K. 380] Mozart, *Six sonates pour le clavecin, ou pianoforte avec l'accompagement d'un violon*. Vienna: Artaria, 1781.

[K. 330] Biblioteka Jagiellońska Kraków Mus. ms. autogr. W. A. Mozart 330.

[K. 330, K. 331, K. 332] *Trois sonates pour le clavecin ou pianoforte composée par W. A. Mozart* (Vienna: Artaria, 1784): https://iiif.lib.harvard.edu/manifests /view/drs:14495231$1i.

[K. 331] Biblioteca Mozartiana der Internationalen Stiftung Mozarteum Salzburg, Signatur: KV 300i.

[K. 332] Scheide Music Library, Princeton, New Jersey, MS 134.

[K. 333] Staatsbibliothek zu Berlin, Mus. ms. autogr. W. A. Mozart 333.

[K. 361] *Gran Partita, K. 361 by Wolfgang Amadeus Mozart: A Facsimile of the Holograph in the Whittall Foundation Collection*. Washington, DC: The Library of Congress, 1976.

[K. 373] *Rondo pour le violon avec accompagnement de grand orchestra composé par Mozart*. Offenbach: Johann André, 1800.

[K. 374] Staatsbibliothek zu Berlin, Mus. ms. autogr. W. A. Mozart 374.

[K. 375] Staatsbibliothek zu Berlin, Mus. ms. autogr. W. A. Mozart 375.

[K. 376] Mozart, *Sonatas, Violin, Piano, K. 376, F Major*. The Morgan Library and Museum. Cary 28.

[K. 377] British Library, London, Zweig MS 53.

[K. 379] Library of Congress, Washington, ML30.8b.M8 K.379.

[K. 382, K. 413, K. 414, K. 415] Biblioteka Jagiellońska, Kraków, Mus. ms. autogr. W. A. Mozart 382.413.414.415.

[K. 384] Mozart, 'Die Entführung aus dem Serail', K. 384: *Facsimile of the Autograph Score*. 2 vols. Los Altos, CA: The Packard Humanities Institute, 2008.

[K. 385] Mozart, *Symphony no. 35 in D, K. 385. 'Haffner' Symphony. Facsimile of the Original Manuscript owned by the Orchestral Association, New York*, ed. Sydney Beck. New York: Oxford University Press, 1968.

[K. 387, K. 421, K. 428, K. 458, K. 464, K. 465] Mozart, *The Six 'Haydn' Quartets: Facsimile of the Autograph Manuscripts in the British Library, Add. MS 37763.* London: The British Library, 1985.

[K. 387, K. 421, K. 428, K. 458, K. 464, K. 465] *Sei Quartetti per due violini, viola, e violoncello composti e dedicati al Signor Giuseppe Haydn... dal suo amico W.A Mozart.* Vienna: Artaria, 1785.

[K. 388] Staatsbibliothek zu Berlin, Mus. ms. autogr. W. A. Mozart 388.

[K. 406] British Library Add MS 31748.

[K. 412] Biblioteka Jagiellońska Kraków, Mus. ms. autogr. W. A. Mozart 412.

[K. 417, K. 447, K. 487, K. 495] *Das Horn bei Mozart: Facsimile Collection,* ed. Hans Pizka. Munich: Schöttner, 1980.

[K. 422] Staatsbibliothek zu Berlin, Mus. ms. autogr. W. A. Mozart 422.

[K. 423, K. 424] Mozart, *Zwei Duos für Violone und Viola: Faksimile der autographen Partitur von 1783 und Stimmen-Ausgabe nach dem Urtext, und Berücksichtigung der Varianten des Artaria-Erstdrucks von 1792,* ed. Ulrich Drüner. Winterthur, Switzerland: Amadeus Verlag, 1980.

[K. 427] Mozart, *Messe c-moll KV427: Faksimile der autographen Partitur.* Kassel: Bärenreiter, 1983.

[K. 431] Mozart, *'Misero! O sogno' – 'Aura, che intorno spiri': Arie für Tenor und Orchester, KV431.* Kassel: Bärenreiter, 1988.

[K. 449] Biblioteka Jagiellońska Kraków, Mus. ms. autogr. W. A. Mozart 449.

[K. 450] Herzogin Anna Amalia Bibliothek, Weimar: Mus V: 125.

[K. 451] Biblioteka Jagiellońska Kraków, Mus. ms. autogr. W. A. Mozart 451.

[K. 452] Mozart, *Quintette pour piano, hautbois, clarinette, cor et basson, K. 452: manuscript autographe 1784,* ed. Michel Giboureau. Courlay: Editions J. M. Fuzeau, 1999.

[K. 453] Biblioteka Jagiellońska Kraków, Mus. ms. autogr. W. A. Mozart 453.

[K. 454] *Sonat för cembalo och violin av W. A. Mozart Köchel nr 454.* Stockholm: Stiftelsen Musikkulturens Främjande, 1982.

[K. 456] Staatsbibliothek zu Berlin, Mus. ms. autogr. W. A. Mozart KV 456.

[K. 457, K. 475] Mozart, *Fantasie und Sonate C-moll: Die Originalhandschrift an Mozarts Clavier Interaktiv zum Klingen gebracht.* Salzburg: Internationale Stiftung Mozarteum, 2006.

[K. 457, K. 475] Mozart, *Fantaisie et sonate pour le forte-piano composées pour Madame Therese de Trattnern.* Vienna: Artaria, 1785.

[K. 459] Mozart, *Klavierkonzert in F-Dur, KV459: Faksimile der autographen Partitur.* Kassel: Bärenreiter, 1988.

[K. 466] Gesellschaft der Musikfreude Wien: VII 3405.

[K. 467] Mozart, *Piano Concerto No. 21 in C major, K. 467: The Autograph Score* (New York: Dover, 1985).

[K. 476] John Arthur and Carl Schachter, 'Mozart's Das Veilchen'. *Musical Times,* 130 (1989), pp. 149–155, 163–164.

[K. 477] Staatsbibliothek zu Berlin, Mus. ms. autogr. W. A. Mozart 477.

[K. 478] Mozart, *Quartett in g für Klavier, Violine, Viola und Violoncello KV 478. Faksimile nach dem Autograph im Museum der Chopin-Gesellschaft Warschau mit einer Einführung von Faye Ferguson.* Salzburg: Internationale Stiftung Mozarteum, 1991.

[K. 478] *Quatuor pour le clavecin ou forte piano, violon, tallie et basses composé par Mr Wolfg. Amad. Mozart* (Vienna: Hoffmeister, 1785]): https://iiif.lib .harvard.edu/manifests/view/drs:14728776$3i.

[K. 480] Staatsbibliothek zu Berlin, Mus. ms. autogr. W. A. Mozart 480.

[K. 482] Staatsbibliothek zu Berlin, Mus. ms. autogr. W. A. Mozart 482.

[K. 486] Mozart, *Der Schauspieldirektor: The Impresario, K. 486: A Facsimile of the Autograph Manuscript.* London and Oxford: Oxford University Press, 1976.

[K. 488] Mozart, *Klavierkonzert A-dur, KV 488: Faksimile nach dem Autograph Ms. 226 im Besitz der Musikabteilung der Bibliothèque nationale de France, Paris.* Munich: Henle, 2005.

[K. 491] Mozart, *Klavierkonzert C-moll, KV 491: Bärenreiter Facsimile.* Kassel: Bärenreiter, 2014.

[K. 492] Mozart, *'Le nozze di Figaro', K. 492: Facsimile of the Autograph Score.* 3 vols. Los Altos, CA: The Packard Humanities Institute, 2007.

[K. 495] Mozart, *Concertos, horn, orchestra, K. 495, E-flat major.* Autograph manuscript The Morgan Library and Museum. Cary 35.

[K. 498] Paris, Bibliothèque nationale de France, Département de la musique, Malherbe Collection, MS. 222.

[K. 499, K. 575, K. 589, K. 590, K. 614] Mozart, *The Late Chamber Works for Strings: Facsimile of the Autograph Manuscripts in the British Library.* London: The British Library, 1987.

[K. 499] *Quatuor à deux Violons, alto, et Violoncello, composeé par Mr W. A. Mozart* (Vienna: Hoffmeister, 1786): https://iiif.lib.harvard.edu/man ifests/view/drs:14193088$1i.

[K. 502, K. 542, K. 564] Kraków, Biblioteka Jagiellońska, Mus. ms. autogr. W. A. Mozart 502.542.564.

[K. 502, K. 542, K. 548] *Tre sonate per il clavicembalo o forte-piano . . . composte dal Sigr W. A. Mozart* (Vienna: Artaria, 1788): https://iiif.lib.harvard.edu/man ifests/view/drs:14786494$1i.

[K. 503] Staatsbibliothek zu Berlin, Mus. ms. autogr. W. A. Mozart 503.

[K. 504] Biblioteka Jagiellońska Kraków, Mus. ms. autogr. W. A. Mozart 319.338. 444.504.

[K. 505] Biblioteka Jagiellońska Kraków, Mus. ms. autogr. W. A. Mozart 505.

[K. 511] Mozart, *Rondo a-Moll KV511: Edition, Faksimile,* ed. Ulrich Leisinger. Vienna: Schott/Universal Edition, 2006.

[K. 513] Staatsbibliothek zu Berlin, Mus. ms. autogr. W. A. Mozart 513.

[K. 515] Autograph score, Library of Congress, Washington DC, ML30.8b. M8 K. 515 Case.

[K. 515, K. 516] Mozart, Streichquintette (C-Dur) KV 515 und (g moll) KV 516, Stimmen, Abschrift: Beethoven-Haus Bonn, Sammlung Hanns J. Eller, NE 228.

[K. 527] Mozart, *'Il dissoluto punito ossia il Don Giovanni': Facsimile of the Autograph Score*. 3 vols. Los Altos, CA: The Packard Humanities Institute, 2009.

[K. 527] W. A. Mozart, *Don Giovanni*; 1 C 276/1–4, Prague Conservatory, Czech Republic.

[K. 533 + K. 494] Mozart, *Sonate pour le fortepiano, ou clavecin*. Vienna: Hoffmeister, 1788.

[K. 537] Mozart, *Piano Concerto No. 26 in D major ('Coronation'), K. 537: The Autograph Score*. New York: Dover, 1991.

[K. 546 (fugue only)] British Library, London, MS 28966.

[K. 551] Mozart, *Symphonie C (Jupiter): Facsimile Reproduction of the Original Manuscript*. Vienna: Wien Philharmonischer Verlag, 1923.

[K. 563] Mozart, *Gran trio per violino, viola, e basso*. Vienna: Artaria, 1792.

[K. 575, K. 589, K. 590] Mozart, *Tre quartetti per due violini, viola e basso*. Vienna: Artaria, 1791.

[K. 583] Staatsbibliothek zu Berlin, Mus. ms. autogr. W. A. Mozart 583.

[K. 588] Mozart, *'Così fan tutte ossia La scuola degli amanti', K. 588: Facsimile of the Autograph Score*. 3 vols. Los Altos, CA: Packard Humanities Institute, 2007.

[K. 595] Mozart, *Klavierkonzert in B-dur, KV595: Faksimile der autographen Partitur*. Kassel: Bärenreiter, 1989.

[K. 613] *Ariette 'Ein Weib ist das herrlichste Ding' avec Variations pour le clavecin ou piano forte par W. A. Mozart*. Vienna: Artaria, 1791: https://iiif.lib.harvard.edu/manifests/view/drs:17525734$1i.

[K. 617] British Library London, Zweig MS61.

[K. 620] Mozart, *'Die Zauberflöte', K. 620: Facsimile of the Autograph Score*. 3 vols. Los Altos, CA: The Packard Humanities Institute, 2009.

[K. 621] Mozart, *'La clemenza di Tito': Facsimile of the Autograph Score*. 2 vols. Los Altos, CA: The Packard Humanities Institute, 2008.

[K. 626] Mozart, *Requiem, KV 626: vollständige Faksimile-Ausgabe im Originalformat der Originalhandschrift in zwei Teilen nach Mus. Hs. 17.561 der Musiksammlung der Österreichischen Nationalbibliothek*, ed. Günter Brosche. Kassel: Bärenreiter, 1990.

Books, Articles, Book Chapters and Modern Editions

Abbate, Carolyn. *In Search of Opera*. Princeton: Princeton University Press, 2004.

Abert, Hermann. *W. A. Mozart* (1919–1921). Trans. Stewart Spencer, ed. Cliff Eisen. New Haven, CT: Yale University Press, 2007.

Agawu, V. Kofi. *Playing with Signs: A Semiotic Interpretation of Classic Music.* Princeton: Princeton University Press, 1991.

Albrecht, Theodore. 'Anton Dreyssig (c. 1753/4–1820): Mozart's and Beethoven's *Zauberflötist*'. In Dorothea Link and Judith Nagley (eds.), *Words About Mozart: Essays in Honour of Stanley Sadie.* Woodbridge and Rochester, NY: The Boydell Press, 2005, pp. 179–192.

'The Soloists in "Martern aller Arten", Mozart's Sinfonia Concertante Movement for Flute, Oboe, Violin, Violoncello, and One-Eyed Soprano'. *Mozart Society of America Newsletter*, 17/1 (January 2013), pp. 6–11.

Albrechtsberger, Johann Georg. *Gründliche Anweisung zur Composition.* Leipzig: Breitkopf, 1790.

Allanbrook, Wye Jamison. *Rhythmic Gesture in Mozart: 'Le nozze di Figaro' and 'Don Giovanni'.* Chicago, IL: University of Chicago Press, 1983.

'"To Serve the Private Pleasure": Expression and Form in the String Quartets'. In Stanley Sadie (ed.), *Wolfgang Amadè Mozart: Essays on His Life and His Music.* Oxford: Clarendon Press, 1996, pp. 132–160.

Alwis, Lisa de (trans. and ed.). *Anti-Da Ponte.* Malden, MA: Mozart Society of America, 2015.

Anderson, Emily (trans. and ed.). *The Letters of Mozart and his Family.* 3rd edn, London: Macmillan, 1985.

Angermüller, Rudolph. 'Francesco Bussani – Mozarts erster Bartolo, Antonio und Alfonso und Dorothea Bussani – Mozarts erster Cherubino und erste Despina'. *Mozart Studien*, 10 (Tutzing: Hans Schneider, 2001), pp. 213–231.

Mozart, 1485 bis 2003. Band 1: 1485/86 – 1809. Tutzing: Hans Schneider, 2004.

Arnold, Ignaz. *Joseph Haydn: seine kurze Biographie und ästhetische Darstellung seiner Werke: Bildungsbuch für junge Tonkünstler.* Erfurt, 1810.

Mozarts Geist: seine kurze Biographie und ästetische Darstellung seiner Werke. Erfurt: Henningschen Buchhandlung, 1803.

Arthur, John. '"N.N." Revisited: New Light on Mozart's Late Correspondence'. In Sieghard Brandenburg (ed.), *Haydn, Mozart, and Beethoven: Studies in the Music of the Classical Period. Essays in Honour of Alan Tyson.* Oxford: Clarendon Press, 1998, pp. 127–145.

'Some Chronological Problems in Mozart: The Contribution of Ink Studies'. In Stanley Sadie (ed.), *Wolfgang Amadè Mozart: Essays on His Life and His Music.* Oxford: Clarendon Press, 1996, pp. 35–52.

Arthur, John., and Carl Schachter. 'Mozart's Das Veilchen'. *Musical Times*, 130 (1989), pp. 149–155.

Autexier, Philippe A. 'Wann würde die Maurerische Trauermusik uraufgeführt?' *Mozart-Jahrbuch* 1984–85, pp. 6–8.

Badura-Skoda, Eva. 'On Improvised Embellishments and Cadenzas in Mozart's Piano Concertos'. In Neal Zaslaw (ed.), *Mozart's Piano Concertos: Text, Context, Interpretation.* Ann Arbor, MI: University of Michigan Press, 1996, pp. 365–371.

Badura-Skoda, Eva, and Paul Badura-Skoda. *Interpreting Mozart: The Performance of His Piano Pieces and Other Compositions*. 2nd edition, New York and London: Routledge, 2008.

Baker, Felicity. 'The Figures of Hell in the *Don Giovanni* Libretto'. In Dorothea Link and Judith Nagley (eds.), *Words About Mozart: Essays in Honour of Stanley Sadie*. Woodbridge and Rochester, NY: The Boydell Press, 2005, pp. 77–106.

Baker, Nancy Kovaleff, and Thomas Christensen (eds.). *Aesthetics and the Art of Musical Composition in the German Enlightenment: Selected Writings of Johann Georg Sulzer and Heinrich Christoph Koch*. Cambridge: Cambridge University Press, 1995.

Bamhart, Russell T. 'The Two "Albanian Noblemen" in *Così fan tutte*'. *Mitteilungen der Internationalen Stiftung Mozarteum*, 46 (1998), pp. 38–41.

Bär, Carl. *Mozart: Krankheit, Tod, Begräbnis*. Kassel: Bärenreiter, 1972.

Barak, Helmut. 'Valentin Adamberger: Mozarts Belmonte und Freund'. In Ingrid Fuchs (ed.), *Internationaler Musikwissenschaftlicher Kongress zum Mozartjahr 1991, Baden-Wien*. Tutzing: Hans Schneider, 1993, pp. 463–474.

Bauer, Günther G. 'Mozarts hohe Licht- und Heizkosten 1781–1792'. *Mitteilungen der Gesellschaft für Salzburger Landeskunde*. Salzburg: Gesellschaft für Salzburger Landeskunde, 2008, pp. 147–186.

Bauer, Wilhelm A., Otto Erich Deutsch, and Joseph Heinz Eibl (eds.). *Mozart: Briefe und Aufzeichnungen, Gesamtausgabe*. 8 vols. Kassel: Bärenreiter, 1962–2005.

Bauman, Thomas. 'At the North Gate: Instrumental Music in *Die Zauberflöte*'. In Daniel Heartz, *Mozart's Operas*, ed. Bauman. Berkeley: University of California Press, 1990, pp. 277–297.

'Coming of Age in Vienna: *Die Entführung aus dem Serail*'. In Daniel Heartz, *Mozart's Operas*, ed. Bauman. Berkeley: University of California Press, 1990, pp. 64–87.

'Mozart Belmonte'. *Early Music*, 19 (1991), pp. 556–563.

'The Three Trials of Don Giovanni'. In Peter Oswald and Leonard S. Zegans (eds.), *The Pleasures and Perils of Genius: Mostly Mozart*. Madison, CT: International Universities Press, 1993, pp. 133–144.

W. A. Mozart: 'Die Entführung aus dem Serail'. Cambridge: Cambridge University Press, 1987.

Bayly, Anselm. *Practical Treatise on Singing and Playing with Just Expression and Real Elegance*. London, 1771.

Beales, Derek. *Joseph II: Against the World, 1780–1790*. Cambridge: Cambridge University Press, 2009.

Joseph II: In the Shadow of Maria Theresa, 1741–1780. Cambridge: Cambridge University Press, 1987.

Beghin, Tom. '"Delivery, Delivery, Delivery!" Crowning the Rhetorical Process of Haydn's Keyboard Sonatas'. In Beghin and Sander M. Goldberg (eds.), *Haydn and the Performance of Rhetoric.* Chicago, IL: University of Chicago Press, 2007, pp. 131–171.

The Virtual Haydn: Paradox of a Twenty-First Century Keyboardist. Chicago: University of Chicago Press, 2015.

Beicken, Suzanne J. (ed. and trans.). *Treatise on Vocal Performance and Ornamentation by Johann Adam Hiller* (1780). Cambridge: Cambridge University Press, 2001.

Berger, Karol. *Bach's Cycle, Mozart's Arrow: An Essay on the Origins of Musical Modernity.* Berkeley, CA: University of California Press, 2007.

Bernoulli, Johann. *Sammlung kurzer Reisebeschreibungen und anderer zur Erweitung der Länder und Menschenkenntniss dienender Nachtrichten.* Berlin, 1783.

Béthizy, Jean-Laurent de. *Exposition de la théorie et de la pratique de la musique.* Paris, 1764.

Black, David Ian. 'Mozart and the Practice of Sacred Music, 1781–1791'. PhD thesis, Harvard University, 2007.

'Mozart's Association with the Tonkünstler-Societät'. In Simon P. Keefe (ed.), *Mozart Studies* 2. Cambridge: Cambridge University Press, 2015, pp. 55–75.

Blom, Eric. *Mozart.* New York: Collier, 1962.

Böheim, Ferdinand Carl. *Chronik von Wiener-Neustadt.* Vienna, 1830.

Bonds, Mark Evan. 'Listening to Listeners'. In Danuta Mirka and V. Kofi Agawu (eds.), *Communication in Eighteenth-Century Music.* Cambridge: Cambridge University Press, 2008, pp. 34–52.

'Replacing Haydn: Mozart's "Pleyel" Quartets'. *Music & Letters*, 88/2 (2007), pp. 201–225.

'The Sincerest Form of Flattery? Mozart's "Haydn" Quartets and the Question of Influence'. *Studi musicali*, 22 (1993), pp. 365–409.

Wordless Rhetoric: Musical Form and the Metaphor of the Oration. Cambridge, MA: Harvard University Press, 1991.

Brandenburg, Irene. 'Mozart, *Davide penitente*, and Saverio Mattei'. *Mozart Society of America Newsletter*, 15/2 (August 2011), pp. 11–12, 14.

'Neues zum Text von Mozarts *Davide penitente* KV 469'. In Lars E. Laubhold and Gerhard Walterskirchen (eds), *Klang-Quellen: Festschrift Ernst Hintermaier zum 65. Geburtstag.* Munich: Strube-Verlag, 2010, pp. 209–229.

Branscombe, Peter. *W. A. Mozart: 'Die Zauberflöte'.* Cambridge: Cambridge University Press, 1991.

Braunbehrens, Volkmar. *Maligned Master: The Real Story of Antonio Salieri.* Trans. Eveline L. Kanes. New York: Fromm, 1992.

Mozart in Vienna, 1781–1791. Trans. Timothy Bell. New York: Grove Weidenfeld, 1989.

Brauneis, Walther. '"Dies Irae, Dies Illa" – "Tag des Zornes, Tag der Klage": Auftrag, Entstehung and Vollendung von Mozarts "Requiem"'. *Jahrbuch des Vereins für Geschichte der Stadt Wien*, 47–48 (1991–1992), pp. 33–48.

'". . . wegen schuldigen 1435 f 32 xr": Neuer Archivfund zur Finanzmisere Mozarts im November 1791'. *Mitteilungen der Internationalen Stiftung Mozarteum*, 39 (1991), pp. 159–163.

Breene, Samuel. 'Mozart's Violin Sonatas and the Gestures of Embodiment: The Subjectivities of Performance Practice'. PhD thesis, Duke University, 2007.

Brophy, Brigid. *Mozart the Dramatist*. New York: Da Capo, 1964.

Brown, A. Peter. *The Symphonic Repertoire, Volume II. The First Golden Age of the Viennese Symphony: Haydn, Mozart, Beethoven, and Schubert*. Indianapolis, IN: Indiana University Press, 2002.

Brown, Bruce Alan. 'Beaumarchais, Paisiello and the Genesis of *Così fan tutte*'. In Stanley Sadie (ed.), *Wolfgang Amadè Mozart: Essays on His Life and His Music*. Oxford: Clarendon Press, 1996, pp. 312–338.

'In Defense of Josepha Duschek (and Mozart): Patronage, Friendship, and Evidence'. In Kathryn Libin (ed.), *Mozart in Prague: Essays on Performance, Patronage, Sources, and Reception*. Prague: Czech Academy of Sciences, 2016, pp. 155–174.

'Gluck's *Rencontre Imprévue* and Its Revisions'. *Journal of the American Musicological Society*, 36 (1983), pp. 498–518.

W. A. Mozart: 'Così fan tutte'. Cambridge: Cambridge University Press, 1995.

Brown, Bruce Alan, and John Rice. 'Salieri's *Così fan tutte*'. *Cambridge Opera Journal*, 8 (1996), pp. 17–43.

Brown, Clive. *Classical and Romantic Performing Practice, 1750–1900*. Oxford and New York: Oxford University Press, 1999.

Buch, David J. (ed.). *Der Stein der Weisen*. Middleton, WI: A-R Editions, 2007.

'*Der Stein der Weisen*, Mozart, and Collaborative Singspiels at Emanuel Schikaneder's Theater auf der Wieden'. *Mozart-Jahrbuch* 2000, pp. 91–126.

'*Die Zauberflöte*, Masonic Opera, and Other Fairy Tales'. *Acta musicologica*, 76 (2004), pp. 193–219.

(ed.). *Liedersammlung für Kinder und Kinderfreunde am Clavier (1791)*. Middleton, WI: A-R Editions, 2014.

Magic Flutes and Enchanted Forests: The Supernatural in Eighteenth-Century Musical Theater. Chicago: University of Chicago Press, 2008.

'Mozart and the Theater auf der Wieden: New Attributions and Perspectives'. *Cambridge Opera Journal*, 9 (1997), pp. 295–232. Reprinted in Simon P. Keefe (ed.), *Mozart*. Aldershot: Ashgate Publishing, pp. 249–286.

'On the Context of Mozart's Variations to the Aria, "Ein Weib ist das herrlichste Ding auf der Welt", K. 613'. *Mozart-Jahrbuch* 1999, pp. 71–80.

'The House Composers of the Theater auf der Wieden in the Time of Mozart (1789–91)'. *Israel Studies in Musicology Online*, 5 (2006), pp. 14–19.

'Three Posthumous Reports Concerning Mozart in His Late Viennese Years'. *Eighteenth-Century Music*, 2 (2005), pp. 125–129.

Burney, Charles. *The Present State of Music in Germany, the Netherlands and United Provinces* (1775). New York: Broude, 1969.

Burnham, Scott. 'Mozart's *felix culpa: Così fan tutte* and the Irony of Beauty'. *Musical Quarterly*, 78 (1994), pp. 77–98. Reprinted in Simon P. Keefe (ed.), *Mozart*. Aldershot: Ashgate Publishing, pp. 227–248.

    Mozart's Grace. Princeton: Princeton University Press, 2013.

Butt, John. *Playing with History: The Historical Approach to Musical Performance*. Cambridge: Cambridge University Press, 2002.

Cairns, David. *Mozart's Operas*. London: Allen Lane, 2006.

Campana, Alessandra. 'Il libretto de "Lo sposo deluso"'. *Mozart-Jahrbuch* 1988– 1989, pp. 573–588.

    'The Performance of Opera Buffa: *Le nozze di Figaro* and the Act IV Finale'. In Stefano La Via and Roger Parker (eds.), *Pensieri per un maestro: Studi in onore di Pierluigi Petrobelli*. Turin: EDT, 2002, pp. 125–134.

Carew, Derek. *The Mechanical Muse: The Piano, Pianism and Piano Music, c. 1760–1850*. Aldershot: Ashgate Publishing, 2007.

Chailly, Jacques. *The Magic Flute*. Trans. Herbert Weinstock. London: Gollancz, 1972.

Charlton, David (ed.). *E.T.A. Hoffmann's Musical Writings: 'Kreisleriana', 'The Poet and the Composer', Music Criticism*. Trans. Martyn Clarke. Cambridge: Cambridge University Press, 1989.

Clive, Peter. *Mozart and His Circle: A Biographical Dictionary*. New Haven, CT: Yale University Press, 1993.

Cole, Malcolm S. 'Mozart and Two Theaters in Josephinian Vienna'. In Mark A. Radice (ed.), *Opera in Context: Essays on Historical Staging from the Late Renaissance to the Time of Puccini*. Portland, OR: Amadeus Press, 1998, pp. 111–145.

Cone, Edward. *The Composer's Voice*. Berkeley, CA: University of California Press, 1974.

Cook, Nicholas. *Beyond the Score: Music as Performance*. Oxford and New York: Oxford University Press, 2013.

Cooper, Anthony Ashley, 3rd Earl of Shaftesbury. *Characteristics of Men, Manners, Opinions, Times*. 3 vols. London, 1711. Reprint, Hildesheim: Georg Olms, 1978.

Corneilson, Paul. '"aber nach geendigter Oper mit Vergnügen": Mozart's Arias for Mme Duschek'. In Kathryn Libin (ed.), *Mozart in Prague: Essays on Performance, Patronage, Sources, and Reception*. Prague: Czech Academy of Sciences, 2016, pp. 175–200.

    'Josepha Hofer, First Queen of the Night'. In *Mozart-Studien*, forthcoming.

    '*Liedersammlung für Kinder und Kinderfreunde*: A Context for Mozart's Songs K. 596–598'. *Mozart-Jahrbuch* 2011, pp. 101–117.

    (ed. and trans.). *The Autobiography of Ludwig Fischer: Mozart's First Osmin*. Malden, MA: Mozart Society of America, 2011.

    'The Mannheim Years of Ludwig Fischer (1745–1825)'. In Ludwig Finscher, Baerbel Pelker and Ruediger Thomsen-Fuerst (eds.), *Mannheim: Ein*

'Paradies der Tonkünstler'? Kongressbericht Mannheim 1999. Frankfurt: Peter Lang, 2002, pp. 375–386.

'The Vocal Music'. In Simon P. Keefe (ed.), *The Cambridge Companion to Mozart*. Cambridge: Cambridge University Press, 2003, pp. 118–130.

'Vogler's Method of Singing'. *Journal of Musicology*, 16 (1998), pp. 91–109.

Cowgill, Rachel. '"Proofs of Genius": Wolfgang Amadeus Mozart and the Construction of Musical Prodigies in Early Georgian London'. In Gary MacPherson (ed.), *Musical Prodigies: Interpretations from Psychology, Music Education, Musicology and Ethnomusicology*. New York: Oxford University Press, 2016, pp. 511–549.

'An Unknown Handel Arrangement by Mozart? The Halifax Judas'. *Musical Times*, 143 (2002), pp. 19–36.

Cremeri, Anton. *Sympathien mit Joseph den II.* Linz, 1784.

Dallaway, Rev. James. *Observations on English Architecture, Military, Ecclesiastical, and Civil*. London, 1806.

Damschroeder, David. *Harmony in Haydn and Mozart*. Cambridge: Cambridge University Press, 2012.

Davies, Peter J. *Mozart in Person: His Character and Health*. New York: Greenwood, 1989.

Dell'Antonio, Andrew. '"Il compositore deluso": The Fragments of *Lo sposo deluso*'. In Stanley Sadie (ed.), *Wolfgang Amadè Mozart: Essays on His Life and His Music*. Oxford: Clarendon Press, 1996, pp. 403–412.

Dent, Edward. *Mozart's Operas: A Critical Study* (2nd edition, 1947). Oxford: Clarendon Press, 1991.

Derr, Ellwood. 'Some Thoughts on the Design of Mozart's Opus 4, the "Subscription Concertos" (K. 414, 413, and 415)'. In Neal Zaslaw (ed.), *Mozart's Piano Concertos: Text, Context, Interpretation*. Ann Arbor: University of Michigan Press, 1996, pp. 187–210.

Deutsch, Otto Erich. *Mozart: Die Dokumente seines Leben*. Kassel: Bärenreiter, 1961. Trans. Eric Blom, Peter Branscombe and Jeremy Noble as *Mozart: A Documentary Biography*. 3rd edition, London: Simon & Schuster, 1990.

Dittersdorf, Karl Ditters von. *Lebensbeschreibung. Seinem Sohne in die Feder diktirt*, ed. Carl Spazier. Leipzig, 1801. Trans. A. D. Coleridge as *The Autobiography of Karl von Dittersdorf*. London: Richard Bentley and Son, 1896.

Dlabacz, Johann. *Allgemeines historisches Künstler-Lexikon für Böhmen*. Prague, 1815.

Dolan, Emily. *The Orchestral Revolution: Haydn and the Technologies of Timbre*. Cambridge: Cambridge University Press, 2013.

Donoghue, Denis. 'Approaching Mozart'. In James M. Morris (ed.), *On Mozart*. Cambridge: Cambridge University Press, 1994, pp. 15–35.

Dreyfus, Laurence. 'The Hermeneutics of Lament: A Neglected Paradigm in a Mozartian Trauermusik'. *Music Analysis*, 10 (1991), pp. 329–343.

Duport, Jean-Pierre. *Six sonates pour le violoncelle ou violon et basse dédiées à son altesse Sérénissime Monseigneur Le Prince de Conty*. Paris, c. 1761–1769?

Durante, Sergio. '"La clemenza di Tito" and Other Two-Act Reductions of the Late 18th Century'. *Mozart-Jahrbuch* 1991, vol. 2, pp. 733–741.

'Mozart and the Idea of "Vera" Opera: A Study of *La clemenza di Tito*'. PhD thesis, Harvard University, 1993.

'The Chronology of Mozart's *La clemenza di Tito* Reconsidered'. *Music & Letters*, 80 (1999), pp. 560–594.

Edge, Dexter. 'Attributing Mozart (i): Three Accompanied Recitatives'. *Cambridge Opera Journal*, 13 (2001), pp. 197–237.

'Manuscript Parts as Evidence of Orchestral Size in the Eighteenth-Century Concerto'. In Neal Zaslaw (ed.), *Mozart's Piano Concertos: Text, Context, Interpretation*. Ann Arbor, MI: University of Michigan Press, 1996, pp. 427–460.

'Mozart's Fee for *Così fan tutte*'. *Journal of the Royal Musical Association*, 116 (1991), pp. 211–235.

'Mozart's Reception in Vienna, 1787–1791'. In Stanley Sadie (ed.), *Wolfgang Amadè Mozart: Essays on His Life and His Music*. Oxford: Clarendon Press, 1996, pp. 66–117.

'Mozart's Viennese Copyists'. PhD thesis, University of Southern California, 2001.

'Mozart's Viennese Orchestras'. *Early Music*, 20 (1992), pp. 63–88.

'Musicological Introduction', in Wolfgang Amadeus Mozart, *'Le nozze di Figaro', K. 492: Facsimile of the Autograph Score*. 3 vols. Los Altos, CA: The Packard Humanities Institute, 2007, vol. 3, pp. 13–24.

'Recent Discoveries in Viennese Copies of Mozart's Concertos'. In Neal Zaslaw (ed.), *Mozart's Piano Concertos: Text, Context, Interpretation*. Ann Arbor: University of Michigan Press, 1996, pp. 51–65.

'Review Article: Mary Sue Morrow, *Concert Life in Haydn's Vienna: Aspects of a Developing Musical and Social Institution*'. *Haydn Yearbook*, 17 (1992), pp. 108–166.

Edge, Dexter, and David Black (eds.). *Mozart: New Documents*, http://dx.doi.org/10.7302/Z20P0WXJ.

Eibl, Joseph (ed.). *Mozart: Die Dokumente seines Lebens, Addenda und Corrigenda*. Kassel: Bärenreiter, 1978.

'Süssmayrs "Requiem"-Brief vom 8. Februar 1800'. *Mitteilungen der Internationalen Stiftung Mozarteum*, 24 (1976), pp. 21–23.

Einstein, Alfred. *Mozart: His Character, His Work*. Trans. Nathan Broder and Arthur Mendel. London: Cassell, 1945.

Eisen, Cliff. 'Another Look at the "Corrupt Passage" in Mozart G Minor Symphony, K. 550: Its Sources, "Solution" and Implications for the Composition of the Final Trilogy'. *Early Music*, 25/3 (1997), pp. 373–380.

(ed.). *Four Viennese String Quintets*. Madison, WI: A-R Editions, 1998.

(ed.). *Mozart: A Life in Letters*. Trans. Stewart Spencer. London: Penguin, 2006.

'Mozart and Salzburg'. In Simon P. Keefe (ed.), *The Cambridge Companion to Mozart*. Cambridge: Cambridge University Press, 2005, pp. 7–21.

'Mozart and the Viennese String Quintet'. In Eisen and Wolf-Dieter Seiffert (eds.), *Mozarts Streichquintette*. Stuttgart: Fritz Steiner, 1994, pp. 127–152.

'Mozart Plays Haydn'. *Mozart-Jahrbuch 2006*, pp. 409–421.

'Mozart's Chamber Music'. In Simon P. Keefe (ed.), *The Cambridge Companion to Mozart*. Cambridge: Cambridge University Press, 2003, pp. 105–117.

'Mozart's Leap in the Dark'. In Simon P. Keefe (ed.), *Mozart Studies*. Cambridge: Cambridge University Press, 2006, pp. 1–24.

'New Light on Mozart's "Linz" Symphony'. *Journal of the Royal Musical Association*, 113 (1988), pp. 81–96.

(ed.). *New Mozart Documents: A Supplement to O. E. Deutsch's Documentary Biography*. London and Palo Alto, CA: Stanford University Press, 1991.

'The Mozarts' Salzburg Copyists: Aspects of Attribution, Chronology, Text, Style and Performance Practice'. In Eisen (ed.), *Mozart Studies*. Oxford: Oxford University Press, 1991, pp. 253–307.

'The Primacy of Performance: Text, Act and Continuo in Mozart's Piano Concertos'. In Dorothea Link and Judith Nagley (eds.), *Words About Mozart: Essays in Honour of Stanley Sadie*. Woodbridge: Boydell & Brewer, 2005, pp. 107–119.

'The Rise (and Fall) of the Concerto Virtuoso in the Late Eighteenth and Nineteenth Centuries'. In Simon P. Keefe (ed.), *The Cambridge Companion to the Concerto*. Cambridge: Cambridge University Press, 2005, pp. 177–191.

'The Scoring of the Orchestral Bass Part in Mozart's Salzburg Keyboard Concertos: The Evidence of the Authentic Copies'. In Neal Zaslaw (ed.), *Mozart's Piano Concertos: Text, Context, Interpretation*. Ann Arbor: University of Michigan Press, 1996, pp. 411–425.

Eisen, Cliff, and Simon P. Keefe (eds.). *The Cambridge Mozart Encyclopedia*. Cambridge: Cambridge University Press, 2006.

Eisen, Cliff, and Christopher Wintle. 'Mozart's C minor Fantasy, K. 475: An Editorial "Problem" and Its Analytical Consequences'. *Journal of the Royal Musical Association*, 124 (1999), pp. 26–52.

Everist, Mark. '"Madame Dorothea Wendling Is 'arcicontentissima'": The Performers of *Idomeneo*'. In Julian Rushton, *W. A. Mozart: 'Idomeneo'*. Cambridge: Cambridge University Press, 1993, pp. 48–61.

Everson, Jane. 'Of Beaks and Geese: Mozart, Varesco and Francesco Cieco'. *Music & Letters*, 76 (1995), pp. 369–383.

Feldman, Martha. 'Staging the Virtuoso: Ritornello Procedure in Mozart, from Aria to Concerto'. In Neal Zaslaw (ed.), *Mozart's Piano Concertos: Text, Context, Interpretation*. Ann Arbor: University of Michigan Press, 1996, pp. 149–186.

Finscher, Ludwig. 'Aspects of Mozart's Compositional Process in the Quartet Autographs: I. The Early Quartets, II. The Genesis of K. 387'.

In Christoph Wolff (ed.), *The String Quartets of Haydn, Mozart and Beethoven: Studies of the Autograph Scores*. Cambridge, MA: Harvard University Press, 1980, pp. 121–153.

Flothuis, Marius. 'A Close Reading of the Autographs of Mozart's Ten Late Quartets'. In Christoph Wolff (ed.), *The String Quartets of Haydn, Mozart and Beethoven: Studies of the Autograph Scores*. Cambridge, MA: Harvard University Press, 1980, pp. 154–173.

  Mozart's Piano Concertos. Amsterdam: Rodolpi, 2001.

  'Welche Arien sang Josepha Duschek am 26. April 1791?'. *Mitteilungen der Internationalen Stiftung Mozarteum*, 37 (1989), pp. 81–82.

Framery, Nicolas-Étienne, and Pierre-Louis Ginguené (eds.). *Encyclopédie méthodique: musique*. Paris, 1791; reprint New York: Da Capo, 1971, 2 vols.

Francoeur, Louis Joseph. *Diapason général de tous les instrumens à vent avec des observations sur chacun d'eux*. Paris, 1772.

Frankl, Ludwig August. 'Die erste Pamina'. *Unterhaltungsblatt zur Augsburger Postzeitung*, no. 40 (1 October 1842), n.p.

Funke, G. Ph. *Naturgeschichte und Technologie für Lehrer in Schulen und für Liebhaber dieser Wissenschaften*. Braunschweig, 1806.

Gallarati, Paolo. 'Mozart and Eighteenth-Century Comedy'. In Mary Hunter and James Webster (eds.), *Opera Buffa in Mozart's Vienna*. Cambridge: Cambridge University Press, 1997, pp. 98–111.

Georgiou, Christina. 'The Historical Editing of Mozart's Keyboard Sonatas: History, Context and Practice'. PhD thesis, City University London, 2011.

Gerber, Ernst Ludwig. *Historisch-biographisches Lexicon der Tonkünstler*. 2 vols. Leipzig, 1790–1792.

  Neues historisch-biographisches Lexicon der Tonkünstler. 4 vols. Leipzig, 1812–1814.

Ghéon, Henri. *In Search of Mozart*. Trans. Alexander Pru. London: Sheed & Ward, 1934.

Gidwitz, Patricia. 'Mozart's Fiordiligi: Adriana Ferrarese del Bene'. *Cambridge Opera Journal*, 8 (1996), pp. 199–214.

  '"Ich bin die erste Sängerin": Vocal Profiles of Two Mozart Sopranos'. *Early Music*, 19 (1991), pp. 565–579.

  'Vocal Portraits of Four Mozart Sopranos'. PhD thesis, University of California at Berkeley, 1991.

Giglberger, Veronica. '"Man hört drei vernünftige Leute sich untereinander unterhalten": Beobachten zur Satztechnik im Divertimento KV 563'. *Mozart-Jahrbuch* 2001, pp. 61–70.

Girdlestone, Cuthbert. *Mozart and His Piano Concertos*. London: Cassell, 1948; reprint New York: Dover, 1964.

Glauert, Amanda. 'The Lieder of Carl Philipp Emanuel Bach, Haydn, Mozart, and Beethoven'. In James Parsons (ed.), *The Cambridge Companion to the Lied*. Cambridge: Cambridge University Press, 2004, pp. 63–83.

Glover, Jane. *Mozart's Women: His Family, His Friends, His Music*. London: Macmillan, 2006.

Goehr, Lydia. *The Imaginary Museum of Musical Works*. Oxford: Clarendon Press, 1992.

Goehring, Edmund J. 'Much Ado About Something; or, *Così fan tutte* in the Romantic Imagination: A Translation of an Early Nineteenth-Century Critique of the Opera'. *Eighteenth-Century Music*, 5 (2008), pp. 91–105.

'The Lamentations of Don Juan and Macbeth'. *Proceedings of the Modern Language Association*, 120 (2005), pp. 1524–1542.

'The Opere Buffe'. In Simon P. Keefe (ed.), *The Cambridge Companion to Mozart*. Cambridge: Cambridge University Press, 2003, pp. 131–146.

Three Modes of Perception in Mozart: The Philosophical, Pastoral, and Comic in 'Così fan tutte'. Cambridge: Cambridge University Press, 2004.

Gooley, Dana. *The Virtuoso Liszt*. Cambridge: Cambridge University Press, 2004.

Grave, Floyd, and Margaret Grave. *The String Quartets of Haydn*. New York: Oxford University Press, 2006.

Grayson, David. 'Whose Authenticity? Ornaments by Hummel and Cramer for Mozart's Piano Concertos'. In Neal Zaslaw (ed.), *Mozart's Piano Concertos: Text, Context, Interpretation*. Ann Arbor: University of Michigan Press, 1996, pp. 373–391.

Gruber, Gernot. *Mozart and Posterity*. Trans. R. S. Furness. London: Quartet Books, 1991.

Gülke, Peter. *'Triumph der neuen Tonkunst': Mozarts späte Sinfonien und ihr Umfeld*. Kassel, Stuttgart and Metzler: Bärenreiter and Metzler, 1998.

Gutman, Robert. *Mozart: A Cultural Biography*. New York: Harcourt Brace, 1999.

Haberkamp, Getraut. *Die Erstdrücke der Werke von Wolfgang Amadeus Mozart*. 2 vols. Tutzing: Hans Schneider, 1986.

Halliwell, Ruth. *The Mozart Family: Four Lives in a Social Context*. Oxford: Clarendon, 1998.

Harlow, Martin. 'Action, Reaction and Interaction, and the Play of Style and Genre in Mozart's Piano and Wind Quintet, K. 452'. In Harlow (ed.), *Mozart's Chamber Music with Keyboard*. Cambridge: Cambridge University Press, 2012, pp. 198–219.

'The Clarinet in Works of Franz Xaver Süssmayr (1766–1803): Anton Stadler and the Mozartian Example'. *Acta mozartiana*, 57 (2010), pp. 147–165.

Haynes, Bruce. 'Mozart and the Classical Oboe'. *Early Music*, 20 (1992), pp. 43–63.

The End of Early Music: A Period Performer's History of Music for the Twenty-First Century. New York: Oxford University Press, 2007.

Head, Matthew. *Orientalism, Masquerade and Mozart's Turkish Music*. London: Royal Musical Association, 2000.

Heartz, Daniel. *Haydn, Mozart and the Viennese School, 1740–1780*. New York: Norton, 1995.

Mozart, Haydn and Early Beethoven, 1781–1802. New York: Norton, 2009.

Mozart's Operas, ed. Thomas Bauman. Berkeley: University of California Press, 1990.

'Nancy Storace, Mozart's Susanna'. In Kristine K. Forney and Jeremy L. Smith (eds.), *Sleuthing the Muse: Essays in Honor of William F. Prizer*. New York: Pendragon Press, 2012, pp. 219–233.

'When Mozart Revises: The Case of Guglielmo in *Così fan tutte*'. In Stanley Sadie (ed.), *Wolfgang Amadè Mozart: Essays on His Life and His Music*. Oxford: Clarendon Press, 1996, pp. 355–361.

Hellyer, Roger. 'Mozart's "Gran partita" and the Summer of 1781'. *Eighteenth-Century Music*, 8 (2011), pp. 93–104.

'The Transcriptions for *Harmonie* of *Die Entführung aus dem Serail*'. *Proceedings of the Royal Musical Association*, 102 (1975–1976), pp. 53–66.

Herttrich, Ernst. 'Eine neue, wichtige Quelle zu Mozarts Streichquintetten KV 515 und 516'. In Paul Mai (ed.), *Im Dienst der Quellen zur Musik: Festschrift Gertraut Haberkamp zum 65. Geburtstag*. Tutzing: Hans Schneider, 2002, pp. 435–445.

Hess, Ernst. 'Die ursprüngliche Gestalt des Klarinettenkonzerts KV622'. *Mozart-Jahrbuch* 1967, pp. 18–30.

Hildesheimer, Wolfgang. *Mozart*. Trans. Marion Faber. New York: Vintage, 1983.

Hodges, Sheila. *Lorenzo Da Ponte: The Life and Times of Mozart's Librettist*. London: Granada, 1985.

Hoeprich, Eric. *Clarinet*. New Haven and London: Yale University Press, 2008.

Hogwood, Christopher, and Jan Smaczny. 'The Bohemian Lands'. In Neal Zaslaw (ed.), *The Classical Era: From the 1740s to the End of the 18th Century*. London: Macmillan, 1989, pp. 188–212.

Holmes, Edward. *The Life of Mozart* (1845), ed. Christopher Hogwood. London: Folio Society, 1991.

Hortschansky, Klaus. 'Autographe Stimmen zu Mozarts Klavierkonzerten KV 175 im Archiv André zu Offenbach'. *Mozart-Jahrbuch* 1989–1990, pp. 37–54.

Howell, John (ed.). *The Life and Adventures of John Nichol, Mariner*. Edinburgh, 1822.

Hughes, Rosemary, and Nerina Medici (eds.). *A Mozart Pilgrimage. Being the Travel Diaries of Vincent and Mary Novello in the Year 1829*. London: Novello, 1955.

Humphries, John. *The Early Horn: A Practical Guide*. Cambridge: Cambridge University Press, 2000.

Hunter, Mary. 'Haydn's London Piano Trios and His Salomon String Quartets: Private vs. Public?' In Elaine Sisman (ed.), *Haydn and His World*. Princeton: Princeton University Press, 1997, pp. 103–130.

'Haydn's String Quartet Fingerings: Communications to Performer and Audience'. In Hunter and Richard Will (eds.), *Engaging Haydn: Culture, Context, and Criticism*. Cambridge: Cambridge University Press, 2012, pp. 281–301.

Mozart's Operas: A Companion. New York: Oxford University Press, 2008.

'Rousseau, the Countess, and the Female Domain'. In Cliff Eisen (ed.), *Mozart Studies 2*. Oxford: Clarendon Press, 1996, pp. 1–26.

The Culture of Opera Buffa in Mozart's Vienna: A Poetics of Entertainment. Princeton: Princeton University Press, 1999.

'"To Play as if from the Soul of the Composer": The Idea of the Performer in Early Romantic Aesthetics'. *Journal of the American Musicological Society*, 58/ 2 (2005), pp. 357–398.

Hunter, Mary, and James Webster (eds.). *Opera Buffa in Mozart's Vienna*. Cambridge: Cambridge University Press, 1997.

Hutchings, Arthur. *A Companion to Mozart's Piano Concertos*. London: Oxford University Press, 1948; 8th edition, Oxford: Oxford University Press, 1998.

Ingrao, Charles W. *The Habsburg Monarchy 1618–1815*. 2nd edition, Cambridge: Cambridge University Press, 2000.

Irving, John. *Mozart's Piano Concertos*. Aldershot: Ashgate, 2003.

Mozart's Piano Sonatas: Contexts, Sources, Style. Cambridge: Cambridge University Press, 1997.

Understanding Mozart's Piano Sonatas. Aldershot: Ashgate Publishing, 2010.

Ivanovitch, Roman. 'Variation in the Display Episodes of Mozart's Piano Concertos'. *Journal of Music Theory*, 52 (2008), pp. 181–218.

Jahn, Otto. *Life of Mozart* (1856). Trans. Pauline D. Townsend. 3 vols. London: Novello, Ewer & Co., 1891.

Jamason, Corey. 'The Performer and the Composer'. In Colin Lawson and Robin Stowell (eds.), *The Cambridge History of Musical Performance*. Cambridge: Cambridge University Press, 2012, pp. 105–134.

Jerold, Beverly. *The Complexities of Early Instrumentation: Winds and Brass*. Turnhout: Brepols, 2015.

John, Nicholas (ed.). *'Così fan tutte': Wolfgang Amadeus Mozart*. London: Calder, 1983.

Jonášová, Milada. 'A Performance of the G minor Symphony K. 550 at Baron van Swieten's Rooms in Mozart's Presence'. *Newsletter of the Mozart Society of America*, 16/1 (January 2012), pp. 1–4, 17.

'Eine Aufführung der g-moll-Sinfonie KV 550 bei Baron van Swieten im Beisein Mozarts'. In *Mozart Studien*, 20 (Tutzing: Hans Schneider, 2011), pp. 253–268.

Joncus, Berta. '"Ich bin eine Engländerin, zur Freyheit geboren": Blonde and the Enlightened Female in Mozart's *Die Entführung aus dem Serail*'. *Opera Quarterly*, 26 (2010), pp. 552–587.

Jones, David Wyn. 'Mozart's Spirit from Seyfried's Hands'. In Simon P. Keefe (ed.), *Mozart Studies 2*. Cambridge: Cambridge University Press, 2015, pp. 195–228.

Music in Vienna: 1700, 1800, 1900. Woodbridge and Rochester, NY: The Boydell Press, 2016.

'Why Did Mozart Compose His Last Three Symphonies?' *Music Review*, 51 (1990), pp. 280–289.

Karhausen, Lucien. *The Bleeding of Mozart: A Medical Glance on His Life, Illness and Personality*. Dartford: Xlibris Corporation, 2011.

Keefe, Simon P. 'A Complementary Pair: Stylistic Experimentation in Mozart's Final Piano Concertos, K. 537 in D and K. 595 in B-Flat'. *Journal of Musicology*, 18/4 (2001), pp. 658–684.

'Across the Divide: Currents of Musical Thought in Europe, c. 1790–1810'. In Keefe (ed.), *Cambridge History of Eighteenth-Century Music*. Cambridge: Cambridge University Press, 2009, pp. 663–687.

'"Die Ochsen am Berge": Franz Xaver Süssmayr and the Orchestration of Mozart's Requiem, K. 626'. *Journal of the American Musicological Society*, 60 (2008), pp. 1–65.

'"Die trefflich gewählte Instrumente": Orchestrating Don Giovanni's Defeat'. In Kathryn Libin (ed.), *Mozart in Prague: Essays on Performance, Patronage, Sources, and Reception*. Prague: Czech Academy of Sciences, 2016, pp. 343–369.

'"Greatest Effects with the Least Effort": Strategies of Wind Writing in Mozart's Piano Concertos'. In Keefe (ed.), *Mozart Studies*. Cambridge: Cambridge University Press, 2006, pp. 25–46.

'Harmonies and Effects: Haydn and Mozart in Parallel'. In Julian Horton (ed.), *The Cambridge Companion to the Symphony*. Cambridge: Cambridge University Press, 2013, pp. 155–174.

'Mozart "Stuck in Music" in Paris (1778): Towards a New Biographical Paradigm'. In Simon P. Keefe (ed.), *Mozart Studies 2*. Cambridge: Cambridge University Press, 2015, pp. 23–54.

'Mozart the Child Performer-Composer: New Musical-Biographical Perspectives on the Early Years to 1766'. In Gary MacPherson (ed.), *Musical Prodigies: Interpretations from Psychology, Music Education, Musicology and Ethnomusicology*. New York: Oxford University Press, 2016, pp. 550–575.

Mozart's Piano Concertos: Dramatic Dialogue in the Age of Enlightenment. Woodbridge and Rochester, NY: The Boydell Press, 2001.

Mozart's Requiem: Reception, Work, Completion. Cambridge: Cambridge University Press, 2012.

Mozart's Viennese Instrumental Music: A Study of Stylistic Re-Invention. Woodbridge and Rochester, NY: Boydell Press, 2007.

'On Instrumental Sounds, Roles, Genres and Performances: Mozart's Piano Quartets K. 478 and K. 493'. In Martin Harlow (ed.), *Mozart's Chamber Music with Keyboard*. Cambridge: Cambridge University Press, 2012, pp. 154–181.

'The Aesthetics of Wind Writing in Mozart's "Paris" Symphony in D, K. 297'. *Mozart-Jahrbuch 2006*, pp. 329–344.

'The Concertos in Aesthetic and Stylistic Context'. In Keefe (ed.), *The Cambridge Companion to Mozart*. Cambridge: Cambridge University Press, 2003, pp. 78–91.

Kelly, Michael. *Reminiscences of Michael Kelly, of the King's Theatre, and Theatre Royal Drury Lane* (1826). 2 vols. Cambridge: Cambridge University Press, 2011.

Kerman, Joseph. *Concerto Conversations*. Harvard, MA: Harvard University Press, 1999.

  'Mozart's Piano Concertos and Their Audience'. In James M. Morris (ed.), *On Mozart*. Cambridge: Cambridge University Press, 1994, pp. 151–168.

Keyßler, Johann Georg. *Neueste Reisen durch Deutschland, Böhmen, Ungarn, die Schweiz, Italien und Lothringen*. Hannover, 1751.

Kinderman, William. *Mozart's Piano Music*. New York: Oxford University Press, 2006.

Kivy, Peter. 'Mainwaring's *Handel*: Its Relation to English Aesthetics'. *Journal of the American Musicological Society*, 17 (1964), pp. 170–178.

  The Possessor and the Possessed: Handel, Mozart, Beethoven and the Idea of Musical Genius. New Haven: Yale University Press, 2001.

Klorman, Edward. *Mozart's Music of Friends: Social Interplay in the Chamber Works*. Cambridge: Cambridge University Press, 2016.

Knepler, Georg. *Wolfgang Amadé Mozart*. Trans. J. Bradford Robinson. Cambridge: Cambridge University Press, 1994.

Koch, Henrich Christoph. *Musikalisches Lexikon*. Frankfurt, 1802.

Kohler, Karl-Heinz. 'Zu den Methoden und einigen Ergebnissen der philologischen Analyse am Autograph der "Zauberflöte"'. *Mozart-Jahrbuch* 1980–1983, pp. 283–287.

Kollmann, Augustus Frederick Christopher. *An Essay on Practical Musical Composition*. London, 1799.

Komlós, Katalin. '"Ich praeludirte und spielte Variazionen": Mozart the Fortepianist'. In R. Larry Todd and Peter Williams (eds.), *Perspectives on Mozart Performance*. Cambridge: Cambridge University Press, 1991, pp. 27–54.

Konrad, Ulrich. 'Compositional Method'. In Cliff Eisen and Simon P. Keefe (eds.), *The Cambridge Mozart Encyclopedia*. Trans. Ruth Halliwell. Cambridge: Cambridge University Press, 2006, pp. 100–108.

  '"Mithin liess ich meinen gedanken freyen Lauf": Erste Ueberlegungen und Thesen zu den "Fassungen" von W. A. Mozarts *Die Entführung aus dem Serail* KV384'. In Werner Breig (ed.), *Opernkomposition als Prozess*. Kassel: Bärenreiter, 1996, pp. 47–64.

  Mozart: A Catalogue of His Works. Trans. J. Bradford Robinson. Kassel: Bärenreiter, 2006.

  'Mozart the Letter Writer and His Language'. Trans. William Buchanan. In Simon P. Keefe (ed.), *Mozart Studies 2*. Cambridge: Cambridge University Press, 2015, pp. 1–22.

  Mozarts Schaffensweise: Studien zu den Werkautographen, Skizzen und Entwürfen. Göttingen: Vandenhoeck & Ruprecht, 1992.

'Musicological Introduction'. In W. A. Mozart, *'Die Entführung aus dem Serail', K. 384: Facsimile of the Autograph Score*. Trans. J. Bradford Robinson. Los Altos, CA: The Packard Humanities Institute, 2008, 2 vols., vol. 2, pp. 12–19.

Kopp, James B. *The Bassoon*. New Haven: Yale University Press, 2012.

Kramer, Lawrence. *Interpreting Music*. Berkeley, CA: University of California Press, 2011.

Krug, William Traugott. *Allgemeines Handwörterbuch der philosophischen Wissenschaften, nebst ihrer Literatur und Geschichte*. Leipzig: Brockhaus, 1827.

Küster, Konrad. 'Don Giovannis Canzonetta: Rollenporträt an den Grenzen des Theaters'. In Susanne Schaal, Thomas Seedorf and Gerhard Splitt (eds.), *Musikalisches Welttheater: Festschrift Rolf Dammann zum 65. Geburtstag*. Laaber: Laaber Verlag, 1995, pp. 161–175.

'Lorenzo Da Ponte's Viennese Librettos'. In David Wyn Jones (ed.), *Music in Eighteenth-Century Austria*. Cambridge: Cambridge University Press, 1996, pp. 221–231.

Mozart: A Musical Biography. Translated by Mary Whittall. Oxford: Clarendon Press, 1996.

Lacépède, Bernard Germain, Comte de. *La poëtique de la musique*. 2 vols. Paris, 1785.

Landon, H. C. Robbins. *1791: Mozart's Last Year*. London: HarperCollins, 1990.

Haydn, Chronicle and Works: Volume 2, Haydn at Eszterháza, 1766–1790. London: Thames & Hudson, 1978.

Haydn, Chronicle and Works: Volume 5, Haydn: The Late Years, 1801–1809. London: Thames & Hudson, 1977.

Mozart and Vienna. New York: Schirmer, 1991.

Mozart: The Golden Years, 1781–1791. London: Thames & Hudson, 1989.

(ed.). *The Mozart Compendium*. London: Thames & Hudson, 1990.

The Mozart Essays. London: Thames & Hudson, 1995.

Landon, H. C. Robbins, and Donald Mitchell (eds.). *The Mozart Companion*. New York: Norton, 1956.

Lawson, Colin. 'A Winning Strike: The Miracle of Mozart's "Kegelstatt"'. In Martin Harlow (ed.), *Mozart's Chamber Music with Keyboard*. Cambridge: Cambridge University Press, 2012, pp. 123–137.

'Case Study: Mozart, Symphonies in E flat major K543, G minor K550 and C major K551'. In Lawson and Robin Stowell (eds.), *The Cambridge History of Musical Performance*. Cambridge: Cambridge University Press, 2012, pp. 552–573.

Mozart: Clarinet Concerto. Cambridge: Cambridge University Press, 1996.

The Early Clarinet: A Practical Guide. Cambridge: Cambridge University Press, 2000.

Leeson, Daniel N. 'A Revisit: Mozart's Serenade for Thirteen Instruments, K. 361 (370a), the "Gran Partitta"'. *Mozart-Jahrbuch* 1997, pp. 181–223.

Leeson, Daniel N., and David Whitwell. 'Concerning Mozart's Serenade in B-flat for Thirteen Instruments, K. 361 (370a)'. *Mozart-Jahrbuch* 1976–1977, pp. 97–130.

Le Guin, Elisabeth. *Boccherini's Body: An Essay in Carnal Musicology*. Berkeley, CA: University of California Press, 2006.

Leopold, Silke. 'Händels Geist in Mozarts Händen: Zum "Qui Tollis" aus der C-Moll Messe KV427'. *Mozart-Jahrbuch* 1994, pp. 89–99.

(ed.). *Mozart Handbuch*. Kassel: Bärenreiter, 2005.

Levey, Michael. *The Life and Death of Mozart*. London: Penguin, 1971.

Levin, Robert D. 'Improvisation and Embellishment in Mozart's Piano Concertos'. *Musical Newsletter* 5/2 (1975), pp. 3–14.

'Improvising Mozart'. In Gabriel Solis and Bruno Nettl (eds.), *Musical Improvisation: Art, Education, and Society*. Urbana and Chicago: University of Illinois Press, 2009, pp. 143–149.

'Instrumental Ornamentation, Improvisation and Cadenzas'. In Howard Mayer Brown and Stanley Sadie (eds.), *Performance Practice After 1600*. London: Macmillan, 1990, pp. 267–291.

'Mozart's Working Methods in the Keyboard Concertos'. In Sean Gallagher and Thomas Forrest Kelly (eds.), *The Century of Bach and Mozart: Perspectives on Historiography, Composition, Theory and Performance in Honor of Christoph Wolff*. Cambridge, MA: Harvard University Press, 2008, pp. 379–406.

'Speaking Mozart's Lingo: Robert Levin on Mozart and Improvisation'. In Bernard Sherman (ed.), *Inside Early Music: Conversations with Performers*. Oxford: Oxford University Press, 1997, pp. 315–338.

'The Devil's in the Details: Neglected Aspects of Mozart's Piano Concertos'. In Neal Zaslaw (ed.), *Mozart's Piano Concertos: Text, Context, Interpretation*. Ann Arbor, MI: University of Michigan Press, 1996, pp. 29–50.

Levin, Robert D., Richard Maunder, Duncan Druce, David Black, Christoph Wolff, and Simon P. Keefe. 'Colloquy: Finishing Mozart's Requiem. On "'Die Ochsen am Berge': Franz Xaver Süssmayr and the Orchestration of Mozart's Requiem, K. 626" by Simon P. Keefe, Spring 2008'. *Journal of the American Musicological Society*, 61 (2008), pp. 583–608.

Levy, Janet M. 'Texture as a Sign in Classic and Early Romantic Music'. *Journal of the American Musicological Society*, 35 (1982), pp. 482–531.

Liebner, Janos. *Mozart on the Stage*. London: Calder & Boyars, 1972.

Liechtenstein, Joseph Marx von. *Beiträge zur genauern Kenntniss der österreichischen Staaten und Provinzen*. Vienna and Leipzig, 1791.

Link, Dorothea. 'A Newly Discovered Accompanied Recitative to Mozart's "Vado, ma dove", K. 583'. *Cambridge Opera Journal*, 12 (2000), pp. 29–50.

(ed.). *Arias for Francesco Benucci, Mozart's First Figaro and Guglielmo*. Middleton, WI: A-R Editions, 2004, pp. xiv–xvi.

(ed.). *Arias for Nancy Storace, Mozart's First Susanna*. Middleton, WI: A-R Editions, 2002.

(ed.). *Arias for Stefano Mandini, Mozart's First Count Almaviva*. Middleton, WI: A-R Editions, 2015.

(ed.). *Arias for Vincenzo Calvesi, Mozart's First Ferrando*. Middleton, WI: A-R Editions, 2011.

'"È la fede degli amanti" and the Viennese Operatic Canon'. In Simon P. Keefe (ed.), *Mozart Studies*. Cambridge: Cambridge University Press, 2006, pp. 109–136.

'*L'arbore di Diana*: A Model for *Così fan tutte*'. In Stanley Sadie (ed.), *Wolfgang Amadè Mozart: Essays on His Life and His Music*. Oxford: Clarendon Press, 1996, pp. 362–373.

'Mozart's Appointment to the Viennese Court'. In Link and Judith Nagley (eds.), *Words About Mozart: Essays in Honour of Stanley Sadie*. Woodbridge and Rochester, NY: The Boydell Press, 2005, pp. 153–173. Reprinted in Simon P. Keefe (ed.), *Mozart*. Aldershot: Ashgate Publishing, 2015, pp. 39–64.

'Mozart in Vienna'. In Simon P. Keefe (ed.), *The Cambridge Companion to Mozart*. Cambridge: Cambridge University Press, 2003, pp. 22–34.

'Nancy Storace's *annus horribilis*, 1785'. *Mozart Society of America Newsletter*, 18/1 (2014), pp. 1, 3–7.

'The Fandango Scene in Mozart's *Le nozze di Figaro*'. *Journal of the Royal Musical Association*, 133 (2008), pp. 69–92. Reprinted in Simon P. Keefe, *Mozart*. Aldershot: Ashgate Publishing, 2015, pp. 203–226.

The National Court Theatre in Mozart's Vienna: Sources and Documents 1783–1792. Oxford: Clarendon Press, 1998.

Lipowsky, Felix Joseph (ed.). *Baierisches Lexikon*. Munich: Jakob Giel, 1811.

Lister, Warwick. *'Amico': The Life of Giovanni Battista Viotti*. New York: Oxford University Press, 2009.

Livingston, Arthur (ed.). *Memoirs of Lorenzo Da Ponte, Mozart's Librettist*. Trans. Elisabeth Abbott. New York: Dover, 1967.

Lockwood, Lewis. 'Performance and Authenticity'. *Early Music*, 19 (1991), pp. 501–508.

Lorenz, Michael. 'Mozart's Apartment on the Alsergrund'. https://homepage.univie .ac.at/michael.lorenz/alsergrund/.

'New and Old Documents Concerning Mozart's Pupils Barbara Ployer and Josepha Auernhammer'. *Eighteenth-Century Music*, 3/2 (2006), pp. 311–322.

Lowe, Melanie. *Pleasure and Meaning in the Classical Symphony*. Indianapolis: Indiana University Press, 2007.

Lubin, Ernest. *The Piano Duet: A Guide for Pianists*. New York: Da Capo, 1976.

Lütteken, Laurenz. 'Konversation als Spiel: Überlegungen zur Textur von Mozarts Divertimento KV 563'. *Mozart-Jahrbuch* 2001, pp. 71–86.

'Negating Opera Through Opera: *Così fan tutte* and the Reverse of the Enlightenment'. *Eighteenth-Century Music*, 6 (2009), pp. 229–242.

Mainwaring, John. *Memoirs of the Late G. F. Handel*. London: Dodsley, 1760. Translated by Johann Mattheson as *Georg Friedrich Händels*

Lebensbeschreibung nebst einem Verzeichnisse seiner Ausübungswerke und deren Berurtheilung. Hamburg, 1761.

Marty, Jean-Pierre. 'Mozart's Tempo Indications and the Problems of Interpretation'. In R. Larry Todd and Peter Williams (eds.), *Perspectives on Mozart Performance.* Cambridge: Cambridge University Press, 1991, pp. 55–73.

Massin, Jean, and Brigitte Massin. *Wolfgang Amadeus Mozart.* Paris: Fayard, 1959.

Mathew, Nicholas. *Political Beethoven.* Cambridge: Cambridge University Press, 2013.

Maunder, Richard. *Mozart's Requiem: On Preparing a New Edition.* Oxford: Clarendon Press, 1988.

The Scoring of Early Classical Concertos, 1750–1780. Woodbridge and Rochester, NY: The Boydell Press, 2014.

Maurer-Zenck, Claudia. 'Dramaturgie und Philologie der *Zauberflöte*: Eine Hypothese und vielen Fragen zur Chronologie'. *Mozart-Jahrbuch* 2001, pp. 383–426.

Maus, Fred. 'Musical Performance as Analytical Communication'. In Salim Kemal and Ivan Gaskell (eds.), *Performance and Authenticity in the Arts.* Cambridge: Cambridge University Press, 1999, pp. 129–153.

McClymonds, Marita P. 'Mozart's "La Clemenza di Tito" and Opera Seria in Florence as a Reflection of Leopold II's Musical Taste'. *Mozart-Jahrbuch* 1984–1985, pp. 61–70.

McKee, Eric. *Decorum of the Minuet, Delirium of the Waltz: A Study of Dance-Music Relations in 3/4 Time.* Bloomington, IN: Indiana University Press, 2012.

Melamed, Daniel R. 'Evidence on the Genesis of *Die Entführung aus dem Serail* from Mozart's Autograph Score'. *Mozart-Jahrbuch* 2003–2004, pp. 25–42.

Melograni, Piero. *Wolfgang Amadeus Mozart: A Biography.* Trans. Lydia G. Cochrane. Chicago, IL: University of Chicago Press, 2007.

Meusel, Johann Georg. *Teutsches Künstlerlexikon oder Verzeichniss der jetztlebenden teutschen Künstler.* Lemgo, 1809.

Mikusi, Balázs. '"Possible, Probable or Certain Errors in the First Edition"? Evaluation of a Newly Found Autograph Fragment of the Sonata in A major, K. 331'. *Mozart-Jahrbuch* 2014, pp. 335–346.

Mirka, Danuta, and V. Kofi Agawu (eds.). *Communication in Eighteenth-Century Music.* Cambridge: Cambridge University Press, 2008.

Monelle, Raymond. *The Musical Topic: Hunt, Military and Pastoral.* Bloomington: Indiana University Press, 2006.

Moore, Julia. 'Mozart in the Market Place'. *Journal of the Royal Musical Association*, 114 (1989), pp. 18–42. Reprinted in Simon P. Keefe (ed.), *Mozart.* Aldershot: Ashgate, 2015, pp. 65–89.

Morrow, Mary Sue. *Concert Life in Haydn's Vienna: Aspects of a Developing Social Institution.* Stuyvesant, NY: Pendragon Press, 1989.

'Vienna'. In Cliff Eisen and Simon P. Keefe (eds.), *The Cambridge Mozart Encyclopedia*. Cambridge: Cambridge University Press, 2006, pp. 517–526.

Mozart, Leopold. *Versuch einer gründlichen Violinschule*. Augsburg, 1756. Trans. Editha Knocker as *A Treatise on the Fundamental Principles of Violin Playing*. London: Oxford University Press, 1948.

Mozart, Wolfgang Amadeus. *Konzert für Klavier und Orchester ('Jeunehomme') Es-dur KV 271*, ed. Cliff Eisen and Robert D. Levin. Wiesbaden: Breitkopf, 2001.

Neuer Ausgabe sämtlicher Werke. [NMA] Kassel: Bärenreiter, 1955–2007. Available at Digital Mozart Edition: http://dme.mozarteum.at.

Symphonie D-dur (Prager) KV504, ed. Cliff Eisen. Wiesbaden: Breitkopf, 2002.

Symphony in C major, No. 36, K. 425 'Linz', ed. Cliff Eisen. London: Edition Peters, 1992.

Violin Sonatas, K301–306, ed. Cliff Eisen. London: Peters, 2003.

Müller, Johann Christian. *Anleitung zum Selbstunterricht auf der Harmonika*. Leipzig, 1788.

Müller, Johann Heinrich Friedrich. *Genaue Nachrichten von beyden Kaiserl. Königl. Schaubühnen in Wien*, vol. 2. Vienna: Kurzböck, 1773.

Nedbal, Martin. *Morality and Viennese Opera in the Age of Mozart and Beethoven*. London: Routledge, 2017.

Nettl, Paul. *Mozart and Masonry*. New York: Dorset Press, 1987.

'Mozart and the Czechs' (trans. Arthur Mendel). *Musical Quarterly*, 27 (1941), pp. 329–342.

Neue Mozart-Ausgabe. See Mozart, Wolfgang Amadeus.

Neumann, Frederick. *Ornamentation and Improvisation in Mozart*. Princeton, NJ: Princeton University Press, 1986.

Performance Practices of the Seventeenth and Eighteenth Centuries. New York: Schirmer, 1993.

Nicolai, Friedrich. *Beschreibung einer Reise durch Deutschland und die Schweiz im Jahre 1781*. Berlin, 1783.

Niemetschek, Franz. *Leben des K. K. Kapellmeisters Wolfgang Gottlieb Mozart* (1798), ed. E. Rychnovsky. Munich: Bibliothek zeitgenössischer Literatur, 1987. Trans. Helen Mautner as *Life of Mozart*. London: Hyman, 1956. 2nd edition: *Lebensbeschreibung des K. K. Kapellmeisters Wolfgang Amadeus Mozart*. Prague, 1808.

Nissen, Georg Nikolaus. *Biographie W. A. Mozarts* (1828). Hildesheim: Georg Olms, 1991.

Otter, F. J., and G. J. Schinn. *Biographie Skizze von J. M. Haydn*. Salzburg, 1808.

Oulibicheff, Alexandre. *Nouvelle Biographie de Mozart*. 3 vols. Moscow: Auguste Semen, 1843.

Page, Janet K., and Dexter Edge. 'A Newly Uncovered Sketch for Mozart's "Al desio di chi t'adora" K577'. *Musical Times*, 132 (1991), pp. 601–606.

Parakilas, James. 'The Afterlife of *Don Giovanni*: Turning Production History into Criticism'. *Journal of Musicology*, 8 (1990), pp. 251–265.

Parker, Roger. 'Ersatz Ditties: Adriana Ferrarese's Susanna'. In *Remaking the Song: Operatic Revisions from Handel to Berio*. Berkeley, CA: University of California Press, 2006, pp. 42–66.

Parsons, James. 'The Eighteenth-Century Lied'. In Parsons (ed.), *The Cambridge Companion to the Lied*. Cambridge: Cambridge University Press, 2004, pp. 35–62.

Pezzl, Johann. 'Sketch of Vienna' (1786–1790). In H. C. Robbins Landon, *Mozart and Vienna*. New York: Schirmer, 1991, pp. 54–191.

Pierre-Petit. *Mozart, ou la musique instantanée*. Paris: Perrin, 1991.

Pirrotta, Nino. *Don Giovanni's Progress: A Rake Goes to the Opera*. Trans. Harris Saunders. New York: Marsilio, 1994.

Plantinga, Leon. *Clementi: His Music and Life*. London: Oxford University Press, 1977.

Platoff, John. '"Non tardar amato bene": Completed – But Not by Mozart'. *Musical Times*, 132 (1991), pp. 557–560.

'Review-Essay: A New History for Martín's *Una cosa rara*'. *Journal of Musicology*, 12 (1994), pp. 85–115.

Polzonetti, Pierpaolo. *Italian Opera in the Age of the American Revolution*. Cambridge: Cambridge University Press, 2011.

'Mesmerizing Adultery: *Così fan tutte* and the Kornman Scandal'. *Cambridge Opera Journal*, 14 (2002), pp. 263–296.

Poppe, Johann Heinrich Moritz. *Geschichte der Technologie*. Göttingen, 1810.

Poulin, Pamela. 'A Little-Known Letter of Anton Stadler'. *Music & Letters*, 69 (1988), pp. 49–56.

'A View of Eighteenth-Century Musical Life and Training: Anton Stadler's Music Plan', *Music & Letters*, 71 (1990), pp. 215–224.

Ratner, Leonard. *Classic Music: Expression, Form, and Style*. New York: Schirmer, 1980.

Rees, Siân. *The Floating Brothel: The Extraordinary True Story of an 18th-Century Ship and Its Cargo of Female Convicts*. London: Headline Book Publishing, 2001.

Reichardt, Johann Friedrich. *Briefe eines aufmerksamer Reisenden die Musik betreffend*. Frankfurt and Leipzig, 1774.

Reitzenstein, Baron Carl Philipp Caspar von. *Reise nach Wien*. Hof, 1795.

Rice, Albert R. *From Clarinet d'Amour to the Contra Bass: A History of Large Size Clarinets, 1740–1800*. New York: Oxford University Press, 2009.

The Baroque Clarinet. Oxford: Oxford University Press, 1992.

The Clarinet in the Classical Period. New York: Oxford University Press, 2003.

Rice, John. 'Antonio Baglioni, Mozart's First Don Ottavio and Tito, in Italy and Prague'. In Milada Jonášová, and Tomislav Volek (eds.), *Böhmische Aspekte des Lebens und des Werkes von W. A. Mozart*. Prague: Czech Academy of Sciences, 2012, pp. 24–38.

Antonio Salieri and Viennese Opera. Chicago: University of Chicago Press, 1998.

'Benedetto Frizzi on Singers, Composers and Opera in Late Eighteenth-Century Italy'. *Studi musicali*, 23 (1994), pp. 367–393.

'Leopold II, Mozart, and the Return to a Golden Age'. In Thomas Bauman and Marita Petzoldt McClymonds (eds.), *Opera and the Enlightenment*. Cambridge: Cambridge University Press, 1995, pp. 271–296.

'Mozart and His Singers: The Case of Maria Marchetti Fantozzi, the First Vitellia'. *Opera Quarterly*, 11 (1995), pp. 31–52.

Mozart on the Stage. Cambridge: Cambridge University Press, 2009.

Music in the Eighteenth Century. New York: Norton, 2013.

'Problems of Genre and Gender in Mozart's Scena "Misero! O sogno, o son desto" K. 431'. *Mozart-Jahrbuch* 2000, pp. 73–89.

'Vienna under Joseph II and Leopold II'. In Neal Zaslaw (ed.), *The Classical Era: From the 1740s to the End of the 18th Century*. London: Macmillan, 1989, pp. 126–165.

W. A. Mozart: 'La clemenza di Tito'. Cambridge: Cambridge University Press, 1991.

Richards, Annette. 'Automatic Genius: Mozart and the Mechanical Sublime'. *Music & Letters*, 80 (1999), pp. 366–389.

Ridgewell, Rupert. 'Biographical Myth and the Publication of Mozart's Piano Quartets'. *Journal of the Royal Musical Association*, 135 (2010), pp. 41–114.

'Mozart's Publishing Plans with Artaria in 1787: New Archival Evidence'. *Music & Letters*, 83 (2002), pp. 30–74.

Riesbeck, Johann Kaspar. *Briefe eines Reisenden Franzosen über Deutschland an seine Bruden zu Paris*. 2nd edition, Zurich, 1784.

Riggs, Robert. 'Authenticity and Subjectivity in Mozart Performance: Türk on Character and Interpretation'. *College Music Symposium*, 36 (1996), pp. 33–58.

'Mozart's Sonata for Piano and Violin, K. 379: Perspectives on the "One-Hour" Sonata'. *Mozart-Jahrbuch* 1991, pp. 708–715.

Rochlitz, Friedrich. *Für Freunde der Tonkunst*. Leipzig: Carl Knobloch, 1825.

'Nachschrift zur Recension von Eyblers Requiem', *Allgemeine musikalische Zeitung*, 28 (1826), cols. 337–340.

Roesner, Valentin. *Essai d'instruction à l'usage de ceux qui composent pour la clarinette et cor*. Paris, 1764.

Rohrer, Joseph. *Bemerkungen auf einer Reise von der Türkischen Gränze über die Bukowina durch Ost und Westgalizien Schlesien und Mähren nach Wien*. Vienna, 1804.

Röllig, Karl Leopold. *Über die Harmonika: Ein Fragment*. Berlin, 1787.

Rosen, Charles. *The Classical Style: Haydn, Mozart, Beethoven*. London: Faber, 1971.

Rosen, David. '"Unexpectedness" and "Inevitability" in Mozart's Piano Concertos'. In Neal Zaslaw (ed.), *Mozart's Piano Concertos: Text, Context, Interpretation*. Ann Arbor: University of Michigan Press, 1996, pp. 261–284.

Rosselli, John. *The Life of Mozart*. Cambridge: Cambridge University Press, 1998.

Rowland, David. *Early Keyboard Instruments: A Practical Guide*. Cambridge: Cambridge University Press, 2001.

Rushton, Julian. 'Buffo Roles in Mozart's Vienna: Tessitura and Tonality as Signs of Characterization'. In Mary Hunter and James Webster (eds.), *Opera Buffa in Mozart's Vienna*. Cambridge: Cambridge University Press, 1997, pp. 406–425.

Mozart: Master Musicians. New York: Oxford University Press, 2006.

'Play or Compulsion? Variation in Recapitulations in Mozart's Music for Wind Instruments'. In Simon P. Keefe (ed.), *Mozart Studies*. Cambridge: Cambridge University Press, 2006, pp. 47–73.

'Theatre Music from Vienna'. *Early Music*, 36 (2008), pp. 474–476.

The New Grove Guide to Mozart and His Operas. Oxford: Oxford University Press, 2007.

W. A. Mozart: 'Don Giovanni'. Cambridge: Cambridge University Press, 1982.

W. A. Mozart: 'Idomeneo'. Cambridge: Cambridge University Press, 1993.

Russell, Charles. *The Don Juan Legend Before Mozart*. Ann Arbor: University of Michigan Press, 1993.

Sadie, Stanley. *Mozart: The Early Years, 1756–1781*. Oxford: Oxford University Press, 2006.

(ed.). *New Grove Dictionary of Music and Musicians, Revised Edition*. London: Macmillan, 2001. *Oxford Music Online*: www.oxfordmusiconline.com.

Saint-Foix, Georges de, and Théodore de Wyzewa. *W.-A. Mozart: sa vie musicale et son oeuvre*. Paris: Desclée de Brouwer, 1912–1946.

Sala, Massimiliano (ed.). *Giovanni Battista Viotti: A Composer Between Two Revolutions*. Bologna: Ut Orpheus Edizioni, 2006.

Schick, Harmut. 'Originalkomposition oder Bearbeitung? Zur Quellenlage und musikalischen Faktur von Mozarts Klaviertrio KV 564'. *Mozart-Jahrbuch* 2001, pp. 273–285.

Schilling, Gustav (ed.). *Encyclopädie der gesammten musikalischen Wissenschaften, oder Universal-Lexicon der Tonkunst*. Leipzig, 1825.

Schlichtegroll, Friedrich. *Johannes Chrysostomus Wolfgang Gottlieb Mozart* (1793), ed. Erich Hermann Müller von Asow. Leipzig, 1942.

Schmid, Manfred Hermann. 'Ein Violinkonzert von Viotti als Herausforderung für Mozart und Haydn'. *Mozart-Studien*, 5 (1995), pp. 149–171.

'Variation oder Rondo? Zu Mozarts Wiener Finale KV 382 des Klavierkonzerts KV 175'. *Mozart Studien*, 2 (1992), pp. 59–80.

Schmidt, Dagmar. '"... *fieri contrasti* ...": Mozarts Bass-Arie KV 512'. *Mozart Studien*, 10 (2001), pp. 139–180.

Schneider, Magnus. 'Laughing with Casanova: Luigi Bassi and the Original Production of *Don Giovanni*'. In Kathryn Libin (ed.), *Mozart in Prague: Essays on Performance, Patronage, Sources, and Reception*. Prague: Czech Academy of Sciences, 2016, pp. 403–419.

Schönfeld, Johann von. *Jahrbuch der Tonkunst von Wien und Prag*. Vienna, 1796. Partial translation by Kathrine Talbot as 'A Yearbook of the Music of Vienna and Prague, 1796'. In Elaine Sisman (ed.), *Haydn and His World*. Princeton: Princeton University Press, 1997, pp. 289–320.

Schroeder, David P. *Experiencing Mozart: A Listener's Companion*. Lanham, MD: Scarecrow Press, 2013.

Schubart, Christian Friedrich Daniel. *Ideen zu einer Aesthetik der Tonkunst*. Vienna, 1806; reprint Hildesheim: Georg Olms, 1969.

Schuler, Heinz. 'Mozarts *Maurerische Trauermusik* KV 477/479a: Eine Dokumentation'. *Mitteilungen der Internationalen Stiftung Mozarteum*, 40 (1992), pp. 46–70.

Schulz, Friedrich. *Reise eines Liefländers von Riga nach Warschau*. Berlin, 1796.

Schumann, Christiane. *Mozart und seine Sänger: Am Beispiel der 'Entführung aus dem Serail'*. Frankfurt: Peter Lang, 2005.

Seiffert, Wolf-Dieter. 'Mozart's "Haydn" Quartets: An Evaluation of the Autographs and First Edition, with Particular Attention to mm. 125–42 of the Finale of K. 387'. In Cliff Eisen (ed.), *Mozart Studies 2*. Oxford: Clarendon, 1997, pp. 175–200.

Senici, Emanuele. '"Adapted to the Modern Stage": *La clemenza di Tito* in London'. *Cambridge Opera Journal*, 7 (1995), pp. 1–22.

   La clemenza di Tito: I premi trent'anni (1791–1821). Amsterdam and Cremona: Brepols, 1997.

Sisman, Elaine. 'Genre, Gesture, and Meaning in Mozart's "Prague" Symphony'. In Cliff Eisen (ed.), *Mozart Studies 2*. Oxford: Clarendon Press, 1997, pp. 27–84.

   Haydn and the Classical Variation. Cambridge, MA: Harvard University Press, 1993.

   Mozart: The 'Jupiter' Symphony. Cambridge: Cambridge University Press, 1993.

   'Observations on the First Phase of Mozart's "Haydn" Quartets'. In Dorothea Link and Judith Nagley (eds.), *Words About Mozart: Essays in Honour of Stanley Sadie*. Woodbridge and Rochester, NY: The Boydell Press, 2005, pp. 33–58.

   'The Marriages of *Don Giovanni*: Persuasion, Impersonation and Personal Responsibility'. In Simon P. Keefe (ed.), *Mozart Studies*. Cambridge: Cambridge University Press, 2006, pp. 163–192.

Sitwell, Sacheverell. *Mozart*. London: Peter Davies Limited, 1932.

Smallman, Basil. *The Piano Quartet and Quintet: Style, Structure, and Scoring*. Oxford: Clarendon, 1994.

Solomon, Maynard. *Mozart: A Life*. New York: HarperCollins, 1995.

   'The Rochlitz Anecdotes'. In Cliff Eisen (ed.), *Mozart Studies*. Oxford: Clarendon Press, 1991, pp. 1–59. Reprinted in Simon P. Keefe (ed.), *Mozart*. Aldershot: Ashgate Publishing, 2015, pp. 91–149.

Spaethling, Robert (ed. and trans.). *Mozart's Letters, Mozart's Life*. London: Faber, 2000.

Spitzer, John, and Neal Zaslaw. *The Birth of the Orchestra: History of an Institution, 1650–1815.* New York: Oxford University Press, 2004.

Stafford, William. *The Mozart Myths: A Critical Reassessment.* Stanford: Stanford University Press, 1991.

Steblin, Rita. 'A Problem Solved: The Identity of Georg Friedrich Richter, Virtuoso "Claviermeister" from Holland, Mozart's Friend and Partner in the Trattnerhof Subscription Concerts of 1784'. *Mozart Society of America Newsletter*, 13/2 (2009), pp. 5–9.

Steptoe, Andrew. 'Mozart and His Last Three Symphonies: A Myth Laid to Rest?' *Musical Times*, 132 (1991), pp. 550–551.

   The Mozart- Da Ponte Operas: The Cultural and Musical Background to 'Le nozze di Figaro', 'Don Giovanni', and 'Così fan tutte'. Oxford: Clarendon Press, 1990.

Stock, Jonathan P. J. 'Orchestration as Structural Determinant: Mozart's Deployment of Woodwind Timbre in the Slow Movement of the C Minor Piano Concerto K. 491'. *Music & Letters*, 78 (1997), pp. 210–219.

Stowell, Robin. '"Good Execution and Other Necessary Skills": The Role of the Concertmaster in the Late 18th Century'. *Early Music*, 16/1 (1988), pp. 21–33.

   Violin Technique and Performance Practice in the Late Eighteenth and Early Nineteenth Centuries. Cambridge: Cambridge University Press, 1985.

Subotnik, Rose Rosengard. 'Whose *Magic Flute*? Intimations of Reality at the Gates of Enlightenment'. *19th Century Music*, 15 (1991), pp. 132–150.

Sulzer, Johann Georg (ed.). *Allgemeine Theorie der schöne Künste.* 4 vols. Leipzig, 1771–1774.

Taruskin, Richard. *Text and Act: Essays on Music and Performance.* New York: Oxford University Press, 1995.

Thompson, Katharine. *The Masonic Thread in Mozart.* London: Lawrence & Wishart, 1977.

Till, Nicholas. *Mozart and the Enlightenment: Truth, Virtue and Beauty in Mozart's Operas.* London: Faber, 1992.

Tomita, Yo. 'Bach Reception in Pre-Classical Vienna: Baron van Swieten's Circle Edits the "Well-Tempered Clavier" II'. *Music & Letters*, 81 (2000), pp. 364–391.

Töpelmann, Viktor Yün-Liang. 'The Mozart Family and Empfindsamkeit: Enlightenment and Sensibility in Salzburg 1750–1790'. PhD thesis, King's College London, 2016.

Triest, Johann Karl Friedrich. 'Remarks on the Development of the Art of Music in Germany in the Eighteenth Century'. Trans. Susan Gillespie. In Elaine Sisman (ed.), *Haydn and His World.* Princeton: Princeton University Press, 1997, pp. 321–394.

Tromlitz, Johann Georg. *The Virtuoso Flute Player* (1791). Trans. and ed. Ardal Powell. Cambridge: Cambridge University Press, 1991.

Türk, Daniel Gottlob. *School of Clavier Playing* (1789). Trans. Raymond H. Haagh. Lincoln: University of Nebraska Press, 1982.

Tyler, Linda. 'Aria as Drama: A Sketch from Mozart's *Der Schauspieldirektor*'. *Cambridge Opera Journal*, 2 (1990), pp. 251–267.

Tyson, Alan. *Mozart: Studies of the Autograph Score*. Harvard, MA: Harvard University Press, 1987.

'Proposed New Dates for Many Works and Fragments Written by Mozart from March 1781 to December 1791'. In Cliff Eisen (ed.), *Mozart Studies*. Oxford: Clarendon Press, 1991, pp. 213–226.

'Some Features of the Autograph Score of *Don Giovanni*'. *Israel Studies in Musicology*, 5 (1990), pp. 5–26.

'The 1786 Prague Version of Mozart's "Le nozze di Figaro"'. *Music & Letters*, 69/3 (1988), pp. 321–333.

Vandenbroek, Othon-Joseph. *Traité général de tous les instrumens à vent à l'usage des compositeurs*. Paris: Boyer, 1793.

Volek, Tomislav. 'Über den Ursprung von Mozarts Oper "La clemenza di Tito"'. *Mozart-Jahrbuch* 1959, pp. 274–286.

Waidelich, Till Gerrit. '"Don Juan von Mozart, (für mich componirt.)" Luigi Bassi – eine Legende zu Lebzeiten, sein Nekrolog und zeitgenössiche *Don Giovanni*-Interpretationen'. *Mozart Studien*, 10 (2001), pp. 181–211.

Walch, Johann Georg. *Philosophisches Lexikon*. Leipzig, 1775; reprint, Hildesheim, 1968, 2 vols.

Waldoff, Jessica. 'Reading Mozart's Operas "for the sentiment"'. In Simon P. Keefe (ed.), *Mozart Studies*. Cambridge: Cambridge University Press, 2006, pp. 74–108.

Recognition in Mozart's Operas. New York: Oxford University Press, 2006.

Walls, Peter. 'Opus 1, take 2: Mozart's Mannheim and Paris Sonatas for Keyboard and Violin'. In Martin Harlow (ed.), *Mozart's Chamber Music with Keyboard*. Cambridge: Cambridge University Press, 2012, pp. 45–68.

Wangermann, Ernst. *The Austrian Achievement 1700–1800*. London: Thames and Hudson, 1973.

Webster, James. 'Aria as Drama'. In Anthony R. DelDonna and Pierpaolo Polzonetti (eds.), *The Cambridge Companion to Eighteenth-Century Opera*. Cambridge: Cambridge University Press, 2009, pp. 24–49.

Haydn's 'Farewell' Symphony and the Idea of Classical Style: Through-Composition and Cyclic Integration in His Instrumental Music. Cambridge: Cambridge University Press, 1991.

'Joseph Haydn's Early Ensemble Divertimenti'. In Cliff Eisen (ed.), *Coll'astuzia, col giudizio: Essays in Honor of Neal Zaslaw*. Ann Arbor: Steglein Publishing, 2009, pp. 111–126.

'The Analysis of Mozart's Arias'. In Cliff Eisen (ed.), *Mozart Studies*. Oxford: Clarendon Press, 1991, pp. 101–199.

'The Rhetoric of Improvisation in Haydn's Keyboard Music'. In Tom Beghin and Sander M. Goldberg (eds.), *Haydn and the Performance of Rhetoric*. Chicago: University of Chicago Press, 2007, pp. 172–212.

'The Scoring of Mozart's Chamber Music for Strings'. In Allan W. Atlas (ed.), *Music in the Classic Period: Essays in Honor of Barry S. Brook*. New York: Pendragon Press, 1985, pp. 259–296.

'Towards a History of Viennese Chamber Music in the Early Classical Period'. *Journal of the American Musicological Society*, 27 (1974), pp. 212–247.

Wheelock, Gretchen. *Haydn's Ingenious Jesting with Art: Contexts of Musical Wit and Humor*. New York: Schirmer, 1992.

Whitton, Kenneth. *Lieder: An Introduction to German Song*. London: Julia McRae Books, 1984.

Wolf, Eugene K. 'The Rediscovered Autograph of Mozart's Fantasy and Sonata in C Minor, K. 475/457'. *The Journal of Musicology*, 10/1 (1992), pp. 3–47.

Wolff, Christoph. 'Creative Exuberance vs. Critical Choice: Thoughts on Mozart's Quartet Fragments'. In Wolff (ed.), *The String Quartets of Haydn, Mozart, and Beethoven: Studies of the Autograph Manuscripts*. Cambridge, MA: Harvard University Press, 1980, pp. 191–210.

Mozart at the Gateway to His Fortune: Serving the Emperor, 1788–1791. New York: Norton, 2012.

Mozart's Requiem: Historical and Analytical Studies, Documents, Score. Trans. Mary Whittall. Berkeley: University of California Press, 1994.

'Musikalische "Gedankenfolge" und "Einheit des Stoffes." Zu Mozarts Klaviersonate in F-Dur (K. 533 + 494)'. In Hermann Danuser, Helga de la Motte-Haber, Silke Leopold and Norbert Miller (eds.), *Das musikalische Kunstwerk: Geschichte, Ästhetik, Theorie: Festschrift Carl Dahlhaus zum 60. Geburtstag*. Laaber: Laaber-Verlag, 1988, pp. 241–255.

'The Many Faces of Authenticity: Problems of a Critical Edition of Mozart's Piano Concertos'. In Neal Zaslaw (ed.), *Mozart's Piano Concertos: Text, Context, Interpretation*. Ann Arbor: University of Michigan Press, 1996, pp. 19–28.

'Two Köchel Numbers, One Work'. In Melania Bucciarelli and Berta Joncus (eds.), *Music as Social and Cultural Practice: Essays in Honour of Reinhard Strohm*. Woodbridge and Rochester, NY: Boydell Press, 2007, pp. 81–99.

Woodfield, Ian. *Cabals and Satires: Mozart's Comic Operas in Vienna*. Oxford and New York: Oxford University Press, forthcoming 2018.

'Così fan tutte': A Compositional History. Woodbridge and Rochester, NY: The Boydell Press, 2008.

'Mozart's Compositional Methods: Writing for His Singers'. In Simon P. Keefe (ed.), *The Cambridge Companion to Mozart*. Cambridge: Cambridge University Press, 2003, pp. 35–47.

Performing Operas for Mozart: Impresarios, Singers and Troupes. Cambridge: Cambridge University Press, 2012.

'The Trouble with Cherubino . . .'. In Simon P. Keefe (ed.), *Mozart Studies 2*. Cambridge: Cambridge University Press, 2015, pp. 168–194.

The Vienna 'Don Giovanni'. Woodbridge and Rochester, NY: Boydell Press, 2010.

Zaslaw, Neal. 'Contexts for Mozart's Piano Concertos'. In Zaslaw (ed.), *Mozart's Piano Concertos: Text, Context, Interpretation*. Ann Arbor: University of Michigan Press, 1996, pp. 7–16.

(ed.). *Der neue Köchel*. Wiesbaden: Breitkopf & Härtel, forthcoming.

(ed.). *Mozart's Piano Concertos: Text, Context, Interpretation*. Ann Arbor: University of Michigan Press, 1996.

Mozart's Symphonies: Context, Performance Practice, Reception. Oxford: Clarendon, 1989.

'Waiting for *Figaro*'. In Stanley Sadie (ed.), *Wolfgang Amadè Mozart: Essays on His Life and His Music*. Oxford: Clarendon, 1996, pp. 413–435.

'Wolfgang Amadè Mozart's Allegro and Andante ("Fantasy") in F Minor for Mechanical Organ, K. 608'. In Jon Newsom and Alfred Mann (eds.), *The Rosaleen Moldenhauer Memorial: Music History from Primary Sources*. Washington: Library of Congress, 2000, pp. 327–340.

Zaslaw, Neal, and William Cowdery (eds.). *The Compleat Mozart*. New York: Norton, 1990.

Ziegenhagen, Franz Heinrich. *Lehre vom richtigen Verhältnisse zu den Schöpfungswerken, und die durch öffentliche Einfürung deselben allein zu bewürkende algemeine Menschenbeglükkung* [sic]. Hamburg, 1792.

Zohn, Steven. 'The Overture-Suite, Concerto Grosso, Ripieno Concerto and *Harmoniemusik* in the Eighteenth Century'. In Simon P. Keefe (ed.), *The Cambridge History of Eighteenth-Century Music*. Cambridge: Cambridge University Press, 2009, pp. 556–582.

Index of Mozart's works by Köchel number

Index of Mozart's works by genre

General Index